The Life of

Johannes Brahms.

Second edition.
Two volumes in one book

Florence May

Travis & Emery

The Life of
Johannes Brahms.

Second edition, revised by the author,
with Additional Material and Illustrations.

First published, London, circa 1948.

Republished Travis & Emery 2009.

Published by
Travis & Emery Music Bookshop
17 Cecil Court, London, WC2N 4EZ, United Kingdom.
(+44) 20 7240 2129
neworders@travis-and-emery.com

Hardback: 978-1-84955-034-5 Paperback: 978-1-84955-035-2

Florence May (1845-1923), English pianist and author.

She studied with Clara Schumann and later under Brahms, which made her well positioned to write about them both.

Her biographies are well researched and also provide an insight to music of her time.

This edition was written in the 1910s but not published till 1948.

More details available from
- Stanley Sadie: The New Grove Dictionary of Music and Musicians.

© Travis & Emery 2009.

THE LIFE OF JOHANNES BRAHMS

VOLUME I

THE LIFE

OF

JOHANNES BRAHMS

BY
FLORENCE MAY

Second Edition revised by the Author, with
Additional Matter and Illustrations, and an
Introduction by Ralph Hill

IN TWO VOLUMES. VOL. I

WILLIAM REEVES
BOOKSELLER LIMITED

83 CHARING CROSS ROAD,
— LONDON, W.C.2. —

TO
THE MANY KIND FRIENDS
WHOSE SYMPATHY
HAS HELPED ME DURING THE WRITING OF THESE VOLUMES,
THEY ARE GRATEFULLY DEDICATED

Printed by The New Temple Press, London, S.W.16, Great Britain.

PREFACE TO THE SECOND EDITION.

THE task of preparing a second edition of my Life of Brahms, a German version of which was published in 1911, has been the more welcome to me since it has given me the opportunity of correcting a few trifling inaccuracies which found their way into the original version, as well as to determine certain doubtful points by the aid of the valuable additions to the previously existing Brahms literature that have appeared in recent years.

The publication especially of Brahms' correspondence with Joachim and Grimm, brought to light new details respecting the origin and growth of some of Brahms' early works, whilst the conclusion of Litzmann's "Clara Schumann," the second volume of which appeared in 1905—almost simultaneously with my Brahms biography—and the third volume in 1906 supplied incontrovertible chronological data as to the events with which it deals to which all future works dealing with the same matters must in future be referred.

The appearance of this monumental work not only affords opportunity, but makes it absolutely incumbent on Brahms' biographers to enter more in detail on the subject of the friendship between the composer and Clara Schumann than seemed to me appropriate in the first instance in my own case.

I have also introduced into the book some additional

scenes or incidents which throw new light on the master's individuality and have in a few cases partially revised and enlarged my remarks on the works.

I have to add the following names to the list of friends who have helped me with information and sympathy:

>Herr Senator Brandt.
>Mrs. Brodsky.
>Herr F. Burg.
>Herr Dr. Georg Fischer.
>Herr Oskar Fux.
>Frau Dr. Nina Grieg.
>W. H. Hadow, Esq.
>Herr Geheimrath Dr. Oskar von Hase.
>Herr Kapellmeister Friedrich Hegar.
>George Henschel, Esq.
>Herr J. Marbach.
>Lady Thompson.
>Frau Professor Ellen Vetter.

PREFACE TO THE FIRST EDITION.

THE biographical materials from which I have written the following Life of Brahms have, excepting in the few instances indicated in footnotes, been gathered by me, at first hand, chiefly in the course of several continental journeys, the first of which was undertaken in the summer of 1902. Dates of concerts throughout the volumes have been authenticated by reference to original programmes or contemporary journals.

My aim in giving some account of Brahms' compositions has not been a technical one. So far as I have exceeded purely biographical limits my object has been to assist the general music-lover in his enjoyment of the noble achievements of a beautiful life.

Preface to the First Edition. vii

I feel it impossible to ignore numerous requests made to me to include in my book some particulars of my own acquaintance with Brahms—begun when I was a young student of the pianoforte. I have not wished, however, to interrupt the main narrative of the Life by the introduction of slight personal details, and therefore place together in an introductory chapter some of my recollections and impressions, published a few years ago in the *Musical Magazine*. These were verified by reference to letters to my mother in which I recorded events as they occurred. Written before the commencement of the Biography, they are in no way essential to its completeness, which will not suffer should they remain unread.

I am indebted for valuable assistance and sympathy to:

    H.R.H. Alexander Friedrich, Landgraf of Hesse.
    Herr Carl Bade.
    Fräulein Berninger.
    Mrs. Jellings Blow (b. Finke).
    Fräulein Theodore Blume.
    Frau Professor Böie.
    Herr Professor Dr. Heinrich Bulthaupt.
    Herr Professor Julius Buths.
    The late Gerard F. Cobb, Esq.
    Frederic R. Comee, Esq.
    Herr Hugo Conrat.
    Fräulein Ilse Conrat.
    Fräulein Johanna Cossel.
    Frau Elise Denninghoff-Giesemann.
    Herr Geheimrath Dr. Hermann Deiters.
    Herr Hofcapellmeister Albert Dietrich.
    Herr k. k. Hofclavierfabrikant Friedrich Ehrbar.
    Herr Geheimrath Dr. Engelmann.
    Herr Professor Julius Epstein.
    Fräulein Anna Ettlinger.
    Frau Dr. Maria Fellinger.
    Herr Professor Dr. Josef Gänsbacher.
    Otto Goldschmidt, Esq., Hon. R.A.M., Member of Swedish A.M., etc.
    Herr Carl Graf.
    Dr. Josef Ritter Griez von Ronse.

Preface to the First Edition.

Fräulein Marie Grimm.
Frau Grüber.
Herr Professor Robert Hausmann.
Fräulein Heyden.
Herr Professor Walter Hübbe.
Herr Dr. Gustav Jansen.
Frau Dr. Marie Janssen.
Frau Dr. Louise Langhans-Japha.
Herr Professor Dr. Joseph Joachim.
Mrs. Johann Kruse.
Herr Carl Lüstner.
J. A. Fuller Maitland, Esq., F.S.A.
Herr Dr. Eusebius Mandyczewski, Archivar to the Gesellschaft der Musikfreunde.
Carl Freiherr von Meysenbug.
Hermann Freiherr von Meysenbug.
Herr Richard Mühlfeld, Hofkammermusiker.
Herr Professor Dr. Ernst Naumann.
Herr Professor Dr. Carl Neumann.
Herr Christian Otterer.
Fräulein Henriette Reinthaler.
Herr Capellmeister Dr. Rottenberg.
Herr Kammermusiker Julius Schmidt.
Herr Fritz Schnack.
Herr Professor Dr. Bernhard Scholz.
Herr Heinrich Schröder.
Fräulein Marie Schumann.
Frau Simons (b. Kyllmann).
Herr Professor Josef Sittard.
Herr Dr. Julius Spengel.
Mrs. Edward Speyer.
Sir Charles Villiers Stanford, Mus.Doc.
Mrs. Edward Stone.
Frau Celestine Truxa.
Herr Superintendent Vogelsang.
Herr Dr. Josef Victor Widmann.

And others who prefer that their names should not be expressly mentioned.

F. M.

South Kensington,
September, 1905.

CONTENTS.

VOLUME I.

PERSONAL RECOLLECTIONS 1

CHAPTER I.
1760-1845.

The Brahms family—Johann Jakob Brahms; his youth and marriage—Birth and childhood of Johannes—The Alster Pavilion—Otto F. W. Cossel—Johannes gives a private subscription concert 47

CHAPTER II.
1845-1848.

Edward Marxsen—Johannes' first instruction in theory—Herr Adolph Giesemann — Winsen-an-der-Luhe — Lischen — Choral Society of school-teachers—"A.B.C." Part-song by Johannes—The Amtsvogt Blume—First public appearance—First visit to the opera 65

CHAPTER III.
1848-1853.

Johannes' first public concert—Years of struggle—Hamburg Lokals—Louise Japha—Edward Reményi—Sonata in F sharp minor—First concert-tour as Reményi's accompanist—Concerts at Winsen, Celle, Lüneburg and Hildesheim—Musical parties in 1853 — Leipzig and Weimar -- Robert Schumann — Joseph Joachim 85

CHAPTER IV.
1853.

Brahms and Reményi visit Joachim in Hanover—Concert at Court—Visit to Liszt—Joachim and Brahms in Göttingen—Wasielewski, Reinecke and Hiller—First meeting with Schumann—Albert Dietrich 108

CONTENTS.

CHAPTER V.
1853.

Schumann's article "New Paths"—Johannes in Hanover—Sonatas in C major and F minor—Visit to Leipzig—First publications—Julius Otto Grimm—Return to Hamburg via Hanover—Lost Violin Sonata—Songs—Marxsen's influence as a teacher ... 131

CHAPTER VI.
1854-1855.

Brahms at Hanover—Hans von Bülow—Robert and Clara Schumann in Hanover—Schumann's illness—Brahms in Düsseldorf—Variations on Schumann's theme in F sharp minor—B major Trio—First public performance in New York—First attempt at symphony 159

CHAPTER VII.
1855-1856.

Lower Rhine Festival—Madame Jenny Lind-Goldschmidt—Edward Hanslick—Brahms as a concert-player—Retirement and study—Frau Schumann in Vienna and London—Julius Stockhausen—Schumann's death 188

CHAPTER VIII.
1856-1858.

Brahms and Joachim in Düsseldorf—Grimm in Göttingen—Brahms' visit to Detmold—Carl von Meysenbug—Court Concertmeister Bargheer—Joachim and Liszt—Brahms returns to Detmold—Summer at Göttingen—Pianoforte Concerto in D minor and Orchestral Serenade in D major tried privately in Hanover 215

CHAPTER IX.
1859.

First public performances of the Pianoforte Concerto in Hanover, Leipzig and Hamburg—Brahms, Joachim and Stockhausen appear together in Hamburg—First public performance of the Serenade in D major—Ladies' Choir—Fräulein Friedchen Wagner—Compositions for women's chorus 242

CONTENTS.

CHAPTER X.
1859-1861.

Third Season at Detmold—"Ave Maria" and "Begräbnissgesang" performed in Hamburg and Göttingen—Second Serenade first performed in Hamburg—Lower Rhine Festival—Summer at Bonn—Music at Herr Kyllmann's—Variations on an original theme first performed in Leipzig by Frau Schumann—"Marienlieder"—First public performance of the Sextet in B flat in Hanover 262

CHAPTER XI.
1861-1862.

Concert season in Hamburg—Frau Denninghoff-Giesemann—Brahms at Hamm—Herr Völckers and his daughters—Dietrich's visit to Brahms—Music at the Halliers' and Wagners'—First public performance of the G minor Quartet—Brahms at Oldenburg—Second Serenade performed in New York—First and second Pianoforte Quartets—"Magelone Romances"—First public performances of the Handel Variations and Fugue in Hamburg and Leipzig by Frau Schumann—Brahms' departure for Vienna 282

APPENDIX No. I.
THE MAGELONE ROMANCES—PIERRE DE PROVENCE 306

APPENDIX No. II.
RULES OF THE HAMBURG LADIES' CHOIR 321

VOLUME II.
CHAPTER XII.
1862-1864.

Vienna — Musical societies — Leading musicians — The Prater — Brahms' appearance at a Hellmesberger Quartet concert—Brahms' first concert in Vienna—Conductorship of the Hamburg Philharmonic—First Serenade at Gesellschaft concert—Brahms' second concert—Richard Wagner—Second Serenade at Vienna Philharmonic concert—Return to Hamburg—Brahms elected conductor of the Vienna Singakademie—Return to Vienna—Singakademie Concerts under Brahms 325

CHAPTER XIII.
1864-1867.

Frau Schumann in Baden-Baden—Circle of friends there—Hermann Levi—Madame Pauline Viardot-Garcia—The Landgräfin of Hesse and the Pianoforte Quintet—Death of Frau Brahms—Concert-journey—The Horn Trio—Frau Caroline Schnack—Last visit to Detmold—First Sonata for Pianoforte and Violoncello—The German Requiem—Brahms at Zürich—Billroth—Brahms and Joachim on a concert-tour in Switzerland—Hans von Bülow—Reinthaler 353

CHAPTER XIV.
1867-1868.

Brahms' holiday journey with his father and Gänsbacher—Austrian concert-tour with Joachim—The German Requiem—Performance of the first three choruses in Vienna—Tour with Stockhausen in North Germany and Denmark—Performance of the German Requiem in Bremen Cathedral—First performance of Pianoforte Quintet 390

CHAPTER XV.
1868-1869.

Max Bruch's E flat minor Symphony—Brahms at Bonn—Friendship with Hermann Deiters—The added number of the German Requiem—Frau Schumann and Brahms—Brahms settles finally in Vienna—Song publications of 1868—Brahms and Stockhausen give concerts in Vienna and Budapest 412

CHAPTER XVI.
1869-1872.

Brahms and Opera—Professor Heinrich Bulthaupt—The Liebeslieder—First performance—The Rhapsody (Goethe's "Harzreise") performed privately at Carlsruhe—First public performance at Jena—Geheimrath Gille—The "Song of Triumph"—Performance of first chorus at Bremen—Bernhard Scholz—The "Song of Destiny"—First performance—Death of Johann Jakob Brahms—First performance of completed "Triumphlied" at Carlsruhe—Summary of Brahms' work as a composer since 1862 435

CONTENTS. xiii.

CHAPTER XVII.
1872-1876.

Publication of the "Triumphlied" with a dedication to the German Emperor William I—Brahms conducts the "Gesellschaft concerts"—Schumann Festival at Bonn—Professor and Frau Engelmann — String Quartets — First performances — Anselm Feuerbach in Vienna—Variations for Orchestra—First performances—"Triumphlied" at Cologne, Basle and Zürich—Resignation of appointment as "artistic director" to the Gesellschaft—Third Pianoforte Quartet 465

CHAPTER XVIII.
1876-1878.

Tour in Holland—Third String Quartet—C minor Symphony—First performances—Varying impressions created by the work in Vienna and Leipzig—Brahms and Widmann at Mannheim—Second Symphony—Vienna and Leipzig differ as to its merits
500

CHAPTER XIX.
1878-1881.

Hamburg Philharmonic Jubilee Festival—Violin Concerto; first performance by Joachim—Pianoforte Pieces, Op. 76—Sonata for Pianoforte and Violin—First performances—Brahms at Crefeld—Rhapsodies for Pianoforte—Heuberger's studies with Brahms—Second Schumann Festival at Bonn—The two Overtures—Breslau honorary degree 530

CHAPTER XX.
1881-1885.

Second Pianoforte Concerto—First visit to the ducal castle of Meiningen—"Nänie"—Frau Henriette Feuerbach—Hans von Bülow in Leipzig—Brahms' friends in Vienna—Dr. and Frau Fellinger—Pianoforte Trio in C major—First String Quintet—The "Parzenlied"—Third Symphony 557

CONTENTS.

CHAPTER XXI.
1885-1888.

Vienna Tonkünstlerverein—Fourth Symphony—Hugo Wolf—Brahms at Thun—Three new works of chamber music—First performances of the second Violoncello Sonata by Brahms and Hausmann—Frau Celestine Truxa—Double Concerto—Marxsen's death—Eugen d'Albert—The Gipsy Songs—Conrat's translations from the Hungarian—Brahms and Jenner—The "Zum Rothen Igel"—Ehrbar's asparagus luncheons—Third Sonata for Pianoforte and Violin 580

CHAPTER XXII.
1889-1895.

Hamburg honorary citizenship—Christmas at Dr. Fellinger's—Second String Quintet—Mühlfeld—Clarinet Quintet and Trio—Last journey to Italy—Sixtieth birthday—Pianoforte Pieces—Billroth's death—Brahms' collection of German Folk-songs—Life at Ischl—Clarinet Sonatas—Frau Schumann, Brahms and Joachim together for the last time 614

CHAPTER XXIII.
1895-1897.

The Meiningen Festival—Visit to Frau Schumann—Festival at Zürich—Brahms in Berlin—The "Four Serious Songs"—Geheimrath Engelmann's visit to Ischl—Frau Schumann's death—Brahms' illness—He goes to Carlsbad—The Joachim Quartet in Vienna—Brahms' last Christmas—Brahms and Joachim together for the last time—The Vienna Philharmonic concert of March 7—Last visits to old friends—Brahms' death
648

CHRONOLOGICAL CATALOGUE OF THE PUBLISHED WORKS 677
WORKS WITHOUT OPUS NUMBER 683
CLASSIFIED CATALOGUE OF WORKS 684
WORKS EDITED BY BRAHMS 687
INDEX 688

LIST OF ILLUSTRATIONS.

VOLUME I.

Brahms at Ischl	Frontispiece
	Facing page
No. 60 Speckstrasse, Hamburg	48
Brahms at the age of twenty	96
Reproduction of Brahms' first letter to Breitkopf and Härtel, dated November 8, 1853	128
Reproduction of original manuscript of the first page of Brahms' Trio for Piano, Violin and Violoncello, Op. 8	176
Brahms and Joachim, 1885	240
Silhouette by Dr. Böhler	288

VOLUME II.

Brahms at the age of thirty	Frontispiece
Brahms and Stockhausen, 1868	384
Brahms' dwelling, 4 Carlsgasse, Vienna	432
Brahms at the age of forty	480
Mürz Zuschlag, in the Styrian Alps, where Brahms completed his Fourth Symphony in the summer of 1885	560
Brahms' residence near Thun	592
Brahms' residence at Ischl	624
Brahms at Dr. Fellinger's, 1896	640

THE LIFE OF JOHANNES BRAHMS

PERSONAL RECOLLECTIONS

BADEN-BADEN.

IT was to the kindness of Frau Schumann that I owed my introduction to Brahms, which took place the very day of my arrival on my first visit to Germany. I had had lessons from the great pianist during her visit to London early in the year 1871, and on her departure from England she allowed my father to arrange that I should follow her, as soon as I could possibly get ready, to her home in Lichtenthal, a suburb of Baden-Baden, in order to continue my studies under her guidance.

I can vividly recall the bright morning in the beginning of May on which I arrived at Baden-Baden, rather home-sick and dreadfully tired, for owing to a railway breakdown *en route* my journey had occupied fourteen hours longer than it ought to have done, and my father's arrangements for my comfort had been completely upset. It was too early to go at once to Frau Schumann's house, and I remember to have dreamily watched, whilst waiting at the station, a passing procession of young girl communicants in their white wreaths and veils, as I tried to realise that I was, for the first time in my life, far away from home and from England. When the morning was sufficiently advanced, I took an open Droschke, and driving under the great trees of the Lichtenthaler Allée to the door of Frau Schumann's house, I obtained the address of the lodgings that had been taken for me in the village. Without alighting, I proceeded at once to my rooms, where I was almost immediately joined by Frau Schumann herself, who came round, as soon as she had finished breakfast, to bid me welcome.

My delight at seeing the great artist again, combined with her irresistible charm and kindness, at once made me feel less strange in my new surroundings, and I joyfully accepted the invitation she gave me at the close of a few minutes' visit, to go to her house the same afternoon at four o'clock and take coffee with her in her family circle.

On presenting myself at the appointed hour, I was at once shown into a pleasant balcony at the back of the house, overlooking garden and river. In it was seated Frau Schumann with her daughters, and with a gentleman whom she presently introduced to me as Herr Brahms. The name awakened in my mind no special feeling of interest, nor did I look at its owner with any particular curiosity. Brahms' name was at that time almost unknown in England, and I had heard of him only through his arrangement of two books of Hungarian dances for four hands on the pianoforte. As, however, from that day onwards I was accustomed, during a period of months, to meet him almost daily, it may be convenient to say at once a few words about his appearance and manner as they seemed to me after I had had time to become familiar with them.

Brahms, then, when I first knew him, was in the very prime of life, being thirty-eight years of age. Below middle height, his figure was somewhat square and solidly built, though without any of the tendency to corpulency which developed itself at a later period. He was of the blonde type of German, with fair, straight hair, which he wore rather long and brushed back from the temples. His face was clean-shaven. His most striking physical characteristic was the grand head with its magnificent intellectual forehead, but the blue eyes were also remarkable from their expression of intense mental concentration. This was accentuated by a constant habit he had of thrusting the rather thick under-lip over the upper, and keeping it compressed there, reminding one of the mouth in some of the portraits of Beethoven. His nose was finely formed. Feet and hands were small, the fingers without "cushions."

"I have none," he said one day, when I was speaking to him about pianists' hands; and he spread out his fingers, at my request, to show me the tips. "Frau Schumann has them, and Rubinstein also; Rubinstein's are immense."

His dress, though plain, was always perfectly neat in those days. He usually wore a short, loose, black alpaca coat, chosen, no doubt, with regard to his ideas of comfort. He was near-sighted, and made frequent use of a double eyeglass that he wore hanging on a thin black cord round his neck. When walking out, it was his custom to go bareheaded, and to carry his soft felt hat in his hand, swinging the arm energetically to and fro. The disengaged hand he often held behind him.

In Brahms' demeanour there was a mixture of sociability and reserve which gave me the impression of his being a kindly-natured man, but one whom it would be difficult really to know. Though always pleasant and friendly, yet there was a something about him—perhaps it may have been his extraordinary dislike to speaking about himself—which suggested that his life had not been free from disappointment, and that he had reckoned with the latter and taken his course. His manner was absolutely simple and unaffected. To his own compositions he alluded only on the very rarest occasions, nor could he be induced to play them before even a small party. His great satisfaction and pleasure were evidently found in the society of Frau Schumann, for whom he displayed the most devoted admiration, an admiration that seemed to combine the affection and reverence of an elder son with the sympathetic camaderie of a colleague in art. He had established himself for the spring and summer months at Lichtenthal, in order to be near her, and was always a welcome guest at her house, coming and going as he liked. I met him there continually at the hour of afternoon coffee, as on the day of my arrival; and very often, when the coffee-cups were done with, it was my good fortune to listen to the two great artists playing duets; Brahms, the favoured, being always allowed to retain the beloved cigar or cigarette between his lips during the performance, and taking his turn in playing the treble part.

It was Frau Schumann's kind habit to invite me to her mid-day dinner on Sundays, and frequently to supper during the week. Brahms was rarely absent, and was sometimes accompanied by one or two of his friends. The talk on these occasions was more or less general, but naturally my chief interest was in listening to Frau Schumann and Brahms, who used to discuss all sorts of topics with great animation. Brahms' interest in politics was keen, and although he had been settled in Vienna for some years, and had become much attached to that city and to his friends and surroundings there, yet it was evident that he remained an ardent German patriot.

He was a great walker, and had a passionate love of nature. It was his habit during the spring and summer to rise at four or five o'clock, and, after making himself a cup of coffee, to go into the woods to enjoy the delicious freshness of early morning and to listen to the singing of the birds. In adverse weather he could still find something to admire and enjoy.

"I never feel it dull," he said one day, in answer to some remark about the depressing effect of the long-continued rain, "my view is so fine. Even when it rains, I have only another kind of beauty."

He was considerate for others, even in trifles. I remember that one evening, before we had quitted the supper-table, someone produced a copy of "Kladderadatsch," and, pointing out to Brahms a set of sarcastic verses dedicated to John Bull, begged him to read them aloud for the entertainment of the assembled party. Brahms, after glancing down the column, playfully declined to do as he was asked, indicating, with a wave of the hand, his English *vis-à-vis* as his reason for objecting; and it was not until I had laughingly and repeatedly expressed my earnest wish to hear whatever might be in store for me as Mr. Bull's representative, that he at length, and still reluctantly, complied with the request.

Frau Schumann often spoke to me of his extraordinary genius and acquirements both as composer and executant, as well as of his general intellectual qualities, and especially of his knowledge and love of books. She wished me to hear him play, but said it was no easy matter to do so, as he was extremely dependent on his mood, and not only disliked to be pressed to perform, but was unable to do justice either to himself or his composer when not in the right humour. The first time, indeed, that I heard him, at a small afternoon gathering at Frau Schumann's house, I was utterly disappointed. After a good deal of pressing, he crossed over to the piano and gave the first movement of the G major Fantasia-Sonata and the first movement of the A minor Sonata, Op. 42, both of Schubert, but his playing was ineffective. It appeared to me to be forced and self-conscious, and he himself seemed to remain, as it were, outside the music. I missed the living throb and impulse of feeling by which I had been accustomed to be carried away when listening to Frau Schumann, and he left one of his audience, at all events, cold and unmoved. When I told this to Frau Schumann afterwards, she answered that I had not yet really heard him; that he had not wished to play, but had yielded to over-persuasion, and that I must wait for a better opportunity of judging before forming an opinion.

The opportunity came the very next evening, when the same friends were assembled and Brahms played again. The next day I wrote home as follows:

" . . . . Then Brahms played. It was an entirely different thing from the day before. Two pieces were by some composer whose name I can't remember, and then he played a wild piece by Scarlatti as I never heard anyone play before.

He really did give it as though he were inspired; it was so mad and wild and so beautiful. Afterwards he did a little thing of Gluck's. I hope I shall hear him often if he plays as he did last night. The Scarlatti was like nothing I ever heard before, and I never thought the piano capable of it."

Such were the general impressions I formed of Brahms during the first seven or eight weeks of my stay at Lichtenthal. To say the truth, I thought but little about him at the time, my whole attention being absorbed in my studies and in the charm of my new experiences of life. To me he seemed a very unaffected, kind-hearted, rather shy man, who appeared quietly happy and content when under the influence of Frau Schumann's society. As yet I had had scant opportunity of testing my own capacity for appreciating his musical genius, and next to none of individual personal intercourse with him. Frequently, when my landlady's servant came to attend me to my lodgings after an evening spent at Frau Schumann's house, and Brahms and I took our leave at the same moment, he would say, "I am coming, too," and, our ways lying partly in the same direction, would walk the short distance by my side; but these occasions did not add much to my knowledge of him. He would make a few casual remarks, often playful, always kindly, on any topics of the hour, but did not touch on musical subjects. One evening, however, I asked him if he intended to visit England. "I think not," he immediately replied, as though his mind were definitely made up on this point. I ventured to pursue the subject, telling him he ought to come, in order to make his compositions known. "It is for that they are printed," he said rather decidedly, and with these words he certainly gave me some real insight into his character. The composer of a long series of works which included such masterpieces as the second serenade, the two string sextets, the first and second pianoforte quartets, the inspired German Requiem, and a host of others already before the world (but of which I then knew nothing), could, of course, do no otherwise than allow his compositions to rest quietly on their merits; and doubtless the intense pride which is equally inherent with intense modesty in the higher order of genius had its share in causing Brahms' reticence about all things concerning himself.

From his determination not to visit England I do not believe he ever seriously wavered. Only on one occasion—a few years before his death—did I ever hear him speak doubtfully on the subject, and then I felt sure that he was only playing with the idea of coming. Of when or why he formed his resolution I cannot speak with absolute certainty; it had become fixed before I made his acquaintance. His want of familiarity with our language may have had something to do with it; he could read English a little, but I never heard him attempt to speak it. He had a horror of being lionized and of involving himself in an entanglement of engagements; perhaps, also, he was possessed with an exaggerated notion of the inflexibility of English social laws, especially as to the wearing of dress-clothes and the restrictions with regard to smoking. Before and behind all such superficial considerations, however, I suspect that early in his career the idea had taken root in him, right or wrong as it may have been, that to visit England would not further his artistic development. Brahms had certainly formed the clearest conception not only of his purpose in life, but of the means by which he felt he could best pursue and achieve it, and from first to last he inflexibly adhered to the conclusions he had come to on these points. If his aim was to give the most complete possible expression in his musical creations to the very best that was in him, his method, while it satisfied an inner craving of his being, was yet, as I believe, deliberately adopted; and it was to lay himself open to every kind of influence which could healthily foster the ideal side of his nature, and more or less completely to eschew all others. It would be ridiculous, at the present time, to touch upon the completeness of his technical musical equipment, to dilate on his easy grasp of all the resources of counterpoint, on his mastery of form, of harmonic and rhythmic combinations, and the like. These things are matter of course. But Brahms knew that not alone his intellect, but his mind and spirit and fancy, must be constantly nurtured if they were to bring forth the highest of which they were capable, and he so arranged his life that they should be fed ever and always by poetry and literature and art, by solitary musing, by participation in so much of life as seemed to him to be real and true, and, above all and in the highest degree, by the companionship of Nature.

"How can I most quickly improve?" I asked him one day later on. "You must walk constantly in the forest," he answered; and he meant what he said to be taken literally. It was his own favourite prescription that he advised for my application. For such a man, with a name practically unknown in England, life in London, and especially during a concert season, would have been not only uncongenial, but impossible. It would only have been a hindrance to him for the time being. It was not his business to push his works before either conductors or the public, and, after early successes and failures in this direction, he had almost entirely given up planning for the future of his compositions, and had yielded himself wholly to his destiny, which was to create.

In adopting this attitude, there was nothing whatever of outward posing. He simply did faithfully what he found lying before him to do, and did not look beyond.

Life at Lichtenthal passed quickly onwards, and the time approached when Frau Schumann would pay her annual visit to Switzerland. At the close of one of my lessons she said to me:

"I have been thinking that perhaps you might like to have some lessons from Herr Brahms whilst I am away. It would be a very great advantage for you in every way, and he would be able to help you immensely with your technique. He has made a special study of it, and can do anything he likes with his fingers on the piano. He does not usually give lessons, but if you like I will ask him, and I think he would do it as a favour to me."

I must here explain that my visit to Germany had been undertaken with the special object of correcting certain deficiencies in my mechanism which Frau Schumann had pointed out, she having advised me to study for a year with this aim particularly in view.

It need hardly be said that I now eagerly accepted her proffered kindness, and it was decided that she should sound Herr Brahms on the question of his willingness to give me lessons. If he should show himself favourable to the project, the arrangement was to be considered as decided, subject only to the approval of my father, who was on the point of starting from London to join me at Lichtenthal. The next morning Frau Schumann informed me that Brahms had consented to the plan, and a few days later, on my receiving my father's ready assent to my request, all preliminaries were settled, and it was arranged that I should have two lessons every week from Brahms.

"You must ask him to play to you," Frau Schumann said; "and if he will do it, it will give you a real opportunity to hear him. And now, now you will begin to know Brahms."

Brahms as Teacher of the Pianoforte.

Brahms united in himself each and every quality that might be supposed to exist in an absolutely ideal teacher of the pianoforte, without having a single modifying drawback. I do not wish to rhapsodise; he would have been the first to object to this. Such lessons could only have come from such a man. I have never to this day got over the wonder of his giving them, or the wonder and the joy of its having fallen to my lot to receive them.

He was strict and absolute; he was gentle and patient and encouraging; he was not only clear, he was light itself;

he knew exhaustively, and could teach, and did teach, by the shortest possible methods, every detail of technical study; he was unwearied in his efforts to make his pupil grasp the full musical meaning of whatever work might be in hand; he was even punctual.

I cannot hope in what I may say to convey more than a faint impression of what his lessons were to me. From the very first hour of coming under his immediate musical influence I felt that it was a power which would continue to act upon and develop within me to the end of life. Perhaps, however, I may succeed in helping lovers of his music to add to their conception of his character and his gifts, by writing of him as he was in a capacity in which, so far as I know, he has not hitherto been described. Such personal details as I may introduce will be given with the object of illustrating that side of Brahms' character which I once knew so well; of exhibiting him as the all-capable, single-hearted, encouraging, inspired and inspiring teacher and friend.

Remembering what Frau Schumann had said of his ability to assist me with my technique, I told him, before beginning my first lesson, of my mechanical difficulties, and asked him to help me. He answered, "Yes, that must come first," and, after hearing me play through a study from Clementi's "Gradus ad Parnassum," he immediately set to work to loosen and equalise my fingers. Beginning that very day, he gradually put me through an entire course of technical training, showing me how I should best work, for the attainment of my end, at scales, arpeggi, trills, double notes, and octaves.

He not only showed me how to practise: he made me, at first, practise to him during a good part of my lessons, whilst he sat watching my fingers; telling me what was wrong in my way of moving them, indicating, by a movement of his own hand, a better position for mine, absorbing himself entirely, for the time being, in the object of helping me.

He did not believe in the utility for me of the daily practice of the ordinary five-finger exercises, preferring to form exercises from any piece or study upon which I might be engaged. He had a great habit of turning a difficult passage round and making me practise it, not as written, but with other accents and in various figures, with the result that when I again tried it as it stood the difficulties had always considerably diminished, and often entirely disappeared. "How must I practise this?" I would ask him, with confidence, which was never disappointed, that some short-cut would be found for me by which my way would be effectually smoothed.

His method of loosening the wrist was, I should say, original. I have, at all events, never seen it or heard of it excepting from him, but it loosened my wrist in a fortnight, and with comparatively little labour on my part.

How he laughed one day, when I triumphantly showed him that one of my knuckles, which were then rather stiff and prominent, had quite gone in, and said to him: "You have done that!"

It may seem incredible, but it is none the less true, that after a very few weeks of work with him the appearance of my hands had completely changed. My father says, writing to my mother:

"Her hand has an entirely different conformation from what it used to have; it has lost all its angular appearance, and it really is the case, as she says, that her knuckles are disappearing. I have given up all idea of inducing her to go anywhere with me; she will allow nothing to interfere with her practising. She is enthusiastic in her admiration of Brahms, and says his patience is wonderful. He keeps her strictly to finger-work."

He was never irritable, never indifferent, but always helped, stimulated, and encouraged. One day, when I lamented to him the deficiencies of my former mechanical training and my present resultant finger difficulty, "It will come all right," he said; "it does not come in a week nor in four weeks."

Perceiving at once the extraordinary value of my technical studies with him, I was desirous of not being hampered by feeling obliged, at first, to get up many pieces to play through. That, he said, was quite right; I must practise a great deal in little bits for a time. Here is an extract from one of my letters. I copy it exactly as it stands, without altering the careless wording of a girl's letter hastily penned for home perusal in an interval between practice times:

"My lessons with Brahms are too delightful; not only the lessons themselves, but he makes me feel I must practise all day and all night. I have begun to eat a great deal for the mere purpose of being able to practise! He is so patient, and takes such pains, and I ask all sorts of questions, and the lessons are too delightful. I can't understand his giving lessons, and yet he is never angry at any sort of foolishness, only says, 'Ah! that is so difficult.' As for an hour's lesson, that is nothing. He systematically arranges for an hour and a half. I absolutely revel in my lessons. He makes the saraband sound on the piano just as on a violin. Then he never expects too much, and does not give much to learn, but is always satisfied with little if one is really trying."

He was extremely particular about my fingering, making me rely on all my fingers as equally as possible. One day whilst watching my hands as I played him a study from the "Gradus," he objected to some of my fingering, and asked me to change it. I immediately did so, but said, knowing there was no danger of his being offended by the remark, that I had used the one marked by Clementi. Brahms, not having had his eyes on the book at the moment, had not perceived this to be the case. He at once said I must, of course, not change it, and would not allow me to adopt his own, as I begged him, saying: "No, no; he knew."

I had with me at Lichtenthal my own copies of Bach, which I had brought from England, but the edition was unfingered, and Brahms desired me to get copies with Czerny's fingering, and always to use it. The other indications in the edition I was not to adopt.

A good part of each lesson was generally devoted to Bach, to the "Well-tempered Clavier," or the English Suites; and as my mechanism improved Brahms gradually increased the amount and scope of my work, and gave more and more time to the spirit of the music I studied. His phrasing, as he taught it me, was, it need hardly be said, of the broadest, whilst he was rigorous in exacting attention to the smallest details. These he sometimes treated as a delicate embroidery that filled up and decorated the broad outline of the phrase, with the large sweep of which nothing was ever allowed to interfere. Light and shade, also, were so managed as to help to bring out its continuity. Be it, however, most emphatically declared that he never theorised on these points; he merely tried his utmost to make me understand and play my pieces as he himself understood and felt them.

He would make me repeat over and over again, ten or twelve times if necessary, part of a movement of Bach, till he had satisfied himself that I was beginning to realise his wish for particular effects of tone or phrasing or feeling. When I could not immediately do what he wanted, he would merely say, "But it is so difficult," or "It will come," tell me to do it again till he found that his effect was on its way into being, and then leave me to complete it. On the two or three days that intervened between my lessons, I would, after practising at the pianoforte, sometimes take my music into the forest to try to think myself more completely into his mind, and if, when he next came, I had partially succeeded, he took delight in showing his satisfaction. His face would light up all over, and he would be unstinting in his praise. "Very good, quite right; Frau Schumann would be very surprised to hear you play like that," or, "That will make a great effect with Frau Schumann."

In spite of his extraordinary conscientiousness about detail, Brahms was entirely free from pedantry and from the tendency to worry or fidget his pupil. His great pleasure was to commend, and if I played anything to him for the first time, in the way he liked, nothing would induce him to suggest, with one word, any change at all. "That is quite right; there is nothing to say about it," he would say; and though I have felt disappointed not to get any remark from him, and have entreated him to make some suggestions, he would remain firm. "No, it must be like that; we will go on," and there was an end of the matter.

One morning my father, coming into the room at the close of my lesson, asked Brahms: "Has she been a good girl to-day?" "Sehr fein,"* answered he, and suddenly turning to me added imperatively: "Tell your father that." I was equal to the occasion, however, and promptly translated: "Herr Brahms says he is not very satisfied to-day, papa." My father's face fell a little. Brahms looked straight before him, displeased and impassive. "I have told him," said I. "No, you have not told him." "But you don't know that; you don't understand English." "I understand enough to know that"—stonily. "Herr Brahms says I have done pretty well," I reassured my father; then to Brahms: "Now I have." "Yes, now," he admitted, with relenting countenance.

Another day, in the middle of my lesson, the door of my sitting-room opened, and my landlady begged to speak to me. "No, Frau Falk," I said; "I am engaged and can see no one; you must please go away." "One moment, gnädiges Fräulein," she said, and persisted, to my displeasure, in coming in. I then perceived she had with her a pretty little girl of about five years old, who held some beautiful yellow roses in her hand. Frau Falk led the child straight up to the piano and made her little speech. The small maiden was the daughter of the gentleman living in the neighbouring villa, and, being with her father in his

---

* An expression of commendation peculiarly German.

beautiful rose-garden, had begged him to let her carry some of his roses to the Fräulein to whose playing they had been listening. The little one, seeing I was not alone, became suddenly shy as she handed me the lovely flowers, and, turning away her face, looked downwards with very red cheeks as she stood quietly at Brahms' knee. But this was not the kind of interruption to displease him. "Na," he said, coaxing her, "you must look at the Fräulein, and let her thank you. Look at her; she wants to thank you." Between us we reassured the little one, who held up her face to me to be kissed, and sedately allowed Frau Falk to lead her away.

Soon after beginning my work with Brahms, I asked him at the end of my lesson if he would play to me, telling him I did so by Frau Schumann's desire. There was an instant's hesitation; then he sat down to the piano. Just as he was about to begin, he turned his head round, and said almost shyly: "You must learn by the faults also." That was the beginning. From that day it became his regular habit to play to me for about half an hour at the close of the hour's lesson, which he never shortened. Oftenest he chose Bach for his performance. He would play by heart one or two of the preludes and fugues from the "Well-tempered Clavier," then take up the music and continue from book as the humour took him. When he reached the end of a composition, I would say little or nothing beyond "Some more," for fear of stopping him, and he would turn over the leaves to find another favourite. I do not remember his ever making a remark to me either between-whiles or after he had finished playing, beyond, perhaps, telling me to get him another book. Once, and once only, he resisted. I had made my usual request at the end of the lesson, when he quaintly and unexpectedly replied: "Not every time; it is silly. Frau Schumann would say it is silly to play every time." "It is so disappointing," I wished to say, but was uncertain of the right German word. He, as was his wont on similar occasions, made me show it him in the dictionary.

There was some little argument between us, and he returned to the piano and took his place there. It was of no use, however. He could not play that day, and almost seemed to take pleasure in doing as badly as possible. Every time he was conspicuously faulty he turned round to me with a sardonic smile, as though he would say: "There! you have got what you wanted; how do you like it?" "Very unkind," I murmured, and he soon rose. "I will *not* play next time," he angrily declared as he took leave. "I will *never* ask you again," I rejoined. A shrug of the shoulders was his only answer, and, with the usual "good-day," he left the room.

After two days came my next lesson. It passed off delightfully, as usual, and at the close Brahms departed, without a word about his playing being said on either side; but I was left with a feeling of something having been very much wanting. In the middle of the following lesson, giving way to a sudden impulse which I could not have explained, but which, perhaps, arose from the fear of renewed disappointment, I abruptly ceased playing in the middle of my piece, saying, "I cannot play any more to-day." Brahms glanced at me with rather an inquiring expression, and asked, "Why?" "I don't know; I cannot," I replied. There was an instant of dead silence, during which I did not look round. Then Brahms spoke. "I will play to you," he said quietly, "in order that you may have something." We immediately changed places, and he never refused me again.

My father, writing to my mother, says:

"Brahms is recognised in Germany as the greatest musician living. It is said to be most difficult to get him to play; however, after every lesson he plays piece after piece. He is a delightful man—so simple, so kind and quiet. He lives in a beautiful situation among the hills, and cares only for seclusion, and time to devote himself to composition. He was pleased the other day by F.'s asking him about a passage in Goethe that she could not comprehend, and went into it in a way which delighted her. With all his genius he is thoroughly practical. Punctual to a minute in his lessons, and of extreme delicacy."

It was my happiness to hear, amongst other things, his readings of many of the forty-eight preludes and fugues, and his playing of them, and especially of the preludes, impressed me with such force and vividness that I can hear it in memory still. His interpretation of Bach was always unconventional and quite unfettered by traditional theory, and he certainly did not share the opinion, which has had many distinguished adherents, that Bach's music should be performed in a simply flowing style. In the movements of the suites he liked variety of tone and touch, as well as a certain elasticity of *tempo*. His playing of many of the preludes and some of the fugues was a revelation of exquisite poems, and he performed them, not only with graduated shadings, but with marked contrasts of tone effect. Each note of Bach's passages and figures contributed, in the hands of Brahms, to form melody which was instinct with feeling of some kind or other. It might be deep pathos, or light-hearted playfulness and jollity; impulsive energy, or soft and tender grace; but sentiment (as distinct from sentimentality) was always there; monotony never. "Quite tender and quite soft," was his frequent admonition to me, whilst in another place he would require the utmost impetuosity.

He loved Bach's suspensions. "It is here that it must sound," he would say, pointing to the tied note, and insisting, whilst not allowing me to force the preparation, that the latter should be so struck as to give the fullest possible effect to the dissonance. "How am I to make this sound?" I asked him of a few bars of subject lying for the third, fourth, and fifth fingers of the left hand, which he wished brought out clearly, but in a very soft tone. "You must think particularly of the fingers with which you play it, and by and by it will come out," he answered.

The same kind of remarks may be applied to his conception of Mozart. He taught me that the music of this great master should not be performed with mere grace and lightness, but that these effects should be contrasted with the expression of sustained feeling and with the use of the deep legato touch. Part of one of my lessons was devoted to the Sonata in F major—

Brahms let me play nearly a page of the first movement without making any remark. Then he stopped me. "But you are playing without expression," said he, and imitated me, playing the same portion, in the same style, on the upper part of the piano, touching the keys neatly, lightly, and unmeaningly. By the time he left off we were both smiling at the absurd performance.

"Now," he said, "with expression," and he repeated the first few bars of the subject, giving to each note its place as an essential portion of a fine melody. We spent a long time over the movement that day, and it was not until the next lesson, after I had had two, or perhaps three, days to think myself into his conception, that I was able to play it broadly enough to satisfy him. At the close of the first of these two Mozart lessons I said to him: "All that you have told me to-day is quite new to me." "It is all there," he replied, pointing to the book.

Brahms, in fact, recognised no such thing as what is sometimes called "neat playing" of the compositions either of Bach, Scarlatti, or Mozart. Neatness and equality of finger were imperatively demanded by him, and in their utmost nicety and perfection, but as a preparation, not as an end. Varying and sensitive expression was to him as the breath of life, necessary to the true interpretation of any work of genius, and he did not hesitate to avail himself of such resources of the modern pianoforte as he felt helped to impart it; no matter in what particular century his composer may have lived, or what may have been the peculiar excellencies and limitations of the instruments of his day.

Whatever the music I might be studying, however, he would never allow any kind of "expression made easy." He particularly disliked chords to be spread unless marked so by the composer for the sake of a special effect. "No apége," he used invariably to say if I unconsciously gave way to the habit, or yielded to the temptation of softening a chord by its means. He made very much of the well-known effect of two notes slurred together, whether in a loud or soft tone, and I know from his insistence to me on this point that the mark has a special significance in his music.

Aware of his reluctance to perform his compositions, I let some weeks pass before I asked him to play me something of his own. When I at length ventured to do so, he objected: "Not mine; something by another composer." But I had resolved to carry my point. "No, no," I insisted; "a composition played by the composer himself is what I wish to hear," and my importunity gained the day. He gave me a splendid performance of a splendid theme with variations, which, as I found out some months afterwards, was from the now familiar string Sextet in B flat. It was the first time I had heard anything of Brahms' composition with the exception of one or two songs, and it raised in me a tumult of delight. Probably I said to him little beyond thanks, but the power of the music and the performance must have worked itself in me to some manifest effect, for on my taking my seat directly after the lesson at the *table d'hôte* of the Hôtel Bär, the village inn where my father and I used to dine, a lady of our acquaintance exclaimed: "What is the matter with you to-day that you look so excited?" I remember answering her: "Brahms has just played me something quite magnificent—something of his own—and it keeps going in my head."

Since then I have heard the movement times innumerable in England and on the Continent, performed by various combinations of artists, but I never listen to it without being carried back in thought to the gardener's house on the slope of the Cäcilienberg where, in my blue-papered, carpetless little room, Brahms sat at the piano and played it to me. The scent of flowers was borne in through the open lattice-windows, of which the green outside sun-shutters were closed on one side of the room to keep out the blazing August sun, and open on another to views of the beautiful scenery.

The merits of our respective views had been the subject of some friendly argument soon after my arrival at Lichtenthal. Brahms had declared that no prospect from any windows in the village could possibly be as fine as his, whilst I was equally sure that mine must be quite unrivalled. Two of my windows looked right across the valley of the Oos as far as the plain of Strassburg, and showed, in fine weather, the distant peaks of the Vosges glimmering in the sunlight. Two others commanded a prospect of the pine-covered ranges of Black Forest hills. The first time Brahms came to my rooms, in order to give me a lesson, the variety and loveliness of my view drew from him an exclamation of delight. "But yours is really grander and sterner, is it not?" I magnanimously asked. "This is more suitable for a girl," he prettily replied.

On the next occasion after the day when he had performed his own work, I reminded Brahms that he had promised he would allow my father, who was anxious to hear him play to better advantage than from the room overhead, to share with me this great pleasure some time. "But he is not here," he said, and taking this as a token of assent, I quickly called my father, who was writing letters above, to come down. When we were all three seated, I told Brahms I wished to have the piece he had played to me two or three days before, but he said he would not play anything of his own—"something else." "No," I said, "something of

yours, and the same; my father wishes to hear the same."
"Ah, I forget what it was; I have composed a great many things. I will play something else." "But no, no, no!" I urged. "I know what it was. I must have the same. Play the first two or three chords." "Well, then, I think it was this," said he, giving way; and he repeated the movement from beginning to end, carrying us both completely away.

Brahms' playing at this period of his life was, indeed, stimulating to an extraordinary degree, and so *apart* as to be quite unforgettable. It was not the playing of a virtuoso, though he had a large amount of virtuosity (to put it moderately) at his command. He never aimed at mere effect, but seemed to plunge into the innermost meaning of whatever music he happened to be interpreting, exhibiting all its details and expressing its very depths. Not being in regular practice, he would sometimes strike wrong notes—and there was already a hardness, arising from the same cause, in his playing of chords; but he was fully aware of his failings, and warned me not to imitate them.

He was acutely, though silently, sensitive to the susceptibility or non-susceptibility of his audience. As I have already mentioned, but few words passed between him and myself during the momentary intervals between his playing of one piece and another, but he would now and then suddenly turn his head round towards where I sat and give me a swift, searching glance, as though to satisfy himself that I understood and followed him. Once only he refused to go on. It was soon after his performance before my father. I had begged for another of his compositions, and he had begun to play one. I was sitting rather behind him, listening intently and trying to follow, but I knew I did not understand. Very soon he turned to give his usual scrutinising look, and immediately ceased playing, saying: "No, really I can't play that." I did not attempt to make him think I had entered into the meaning of the music, but only entreated him to begin it again and give me one more chance, as it was difficult to follow. Nothing would induce him, however, to play another note of it, and he went on to something by another composer, much to my disappointment and mortification.

Brahms disliked to hear anything said which could possibly be interpreted as depreciation of either of the great masters. Once, when two or three people were present, a remark was made on the growing indifference of the younger musicians to Mendelssohn, and particularly on the neglect with which his once popular "Songs without Words" had for some time been treated. "If it is the case, it is a great pity," observed Brahms, "for they are quite full of beauty."

He especially loved Schubert, and I have heard him declare that the longest works of this composer, with all their repetitions, were never too long for him.

He greatly admired my copy, which was of the original edition and in good preservation, of Clementi's "Gradus," and asked me to lend it him for a day or two to compare with his own. I did not at that time attach much value to original editions; and, fancying he merely wished to prevent me from overworking, against which he often cautioned me, I said I could not spare it. "You won't lend it me!" he exclaimed, very much astonished indeed. I answered that if he did take it away it would make no difference, as I could practise as well without it. Finding, however, that he really wished to examine the copy, I said it was too hot for him to carry so large a book in the middle of the day, and that I would send it in the evening. "I am not so weak!" he replied, but consented to the proposal. He sent it back after a few days, strongly scented with the odour of his tobacco, which it retained through many a long year, and which rather enhanced its value to me.

Rather curiously, he liked the scent of eau-de-Cologne. My father brought me a case from Cöln, and if, on my lesson day, I had an open bottle near at hand, and offered some to Brahms, he would place his hands together, palm upwards, for me to pour into, and dipping his head, would rub the scent over his forehead, protesting as he did so, "But it really does not become a man." Seeing that he liked it, I used it sometimes to wash the keys of the piano when he was coming, but I do not think he ever found me out.

He delighted in the music of Strauss' band, which was engaged to play daily at Baden-Baden through some weeks of the season. It was then conducted by the great Johann Strauss, Brahms' particular friend, and he used to walk over every evening to hear it. "Are you so engrossed?" said a voice behind me one evening as I was standing in the Lichtenthal village street with a friend, looking at the performances of a dancing bear. On turning round I found Brahms, hat in hand, smiling with amusement at our preoccupation, himself on his way, as usual at that hour, to listen to the delicious music of the Vienna waltz-king.

Brahms disliked mere compliment, but he had a warm appreciation of the genuine expression of friendly feeling towards himself, and did not try to hide the pleasure it gave him. His countenance would change, and he would answer in a simple, modest way that was almost touching. One day when I told him how I valued his teaching, and felt it was something for my whole life, "You ought to tell Frau Schumann," replied the composer of the German Requiem, as though he were asking me to give a good report of him. On my assuring him that I had already done so by letter, he added hastily: "You will make Frau Schumann angry with me. But not too much"; and he added, "never praise too highly; always keep within bounds."

Shortly before Frau Schumann's return I said to him that I hoped he would not lose all interest in my music at the termination of my lessons with him, and that I should like, if it were possible, to make some additional arrangement by which it might be maintained. He did not give me any definite reply at the moment one way or the other, but on my saying the same thing to him another day he replied:

"It is very nice and very kind of you, but I don't think it can be done. You must, however, play to me very often. Everything you learn with Frau Schumann you must play to me."

About this time, however, my father, who was about to start on his homeward journey, persuaded me to go away with him for a week's holiday before his departure for England, and on my return to Lichtenthal Frau Schumann arranged that I should continue my studies under Brahms for the remainder of my stay, saying I had become more his pupil than hers. There were, indeed, but few more lessons to look forward to. Autumn had set in, and everyone was thinking of departure. Brahms had to go sometimes to Carlsruhe, where he was occupied with rehearsals, but he punctually kept his remaining appointments with me. His concluding lessons were as magnificent as the earlier ones, and when I went back to England my ground was clear. I do not mean to assert that my hand was already completely developed from a pianist's point of view, or my technique as yet fully in my possession. These things were physically impossible; but Brahms had shown me the path which led straight to my goal, and had himself brought me a considerable distance on my way. A cast of one of my hands taken on my return to England, when compared with one that had been done shortly before I left, could not have been recognised as being from the same person.

Those were, indeed, golden days, when Brahms sat by my side, and taught me; memorable to me no less for their revelation of an exquisite nature than for the musical advantages they brought. I have often been told that there was another side to his character, and that he could, even at that time, be bitter and rough and satirical. I dare say he was not faultless, but I do not think that he can at any period of his life have been bitter in the sense of being soured. He no doubt had a strong feeling about the indifference and downright antagonism against which his works long had to struggle; but if it had ever been a feeling even of disappointment, I am sure this had mellowed, before I knew him, into a firm though silent belief in the future of his compositions, and had only served to intensify, if possible, his determination to put into them of his very best.

Rough he may have been sometimes, and in later years I had occasional opportunity of perceiving that he was not always gentle, though he was never otherwise with me. His roughness was, in certain instances, no doubt caused by his resolution in protecting his time from celebrity-hunters, and even from friends. It may have been partly traceable, also, to the circumstances of his youth, when he must often have been placed amid surroundings where rough-and-ready frankness of speech was more cultivated than conventional polish of manner. It is, however, certain that during the latter part of his life he sometimes availed himself of the privilege of the *enfant gâté* to yield to the caprice of the moment, and that he now and again said things which could not but wound the feelings of others. This was to be regretted, and it hardly excused him that his pungent words came from the lips only, and not from the heart. I am, however, quite certain that many of his acerbities were assumed to cover his naturally acute sensibility of temperament, of which he stood a little in dread, and which he liked to conceal even from himself. He was a firm believer, for himself and for others, in the salutary process of bracing both mental and physical energies.

A year or two before Brahms' death I revisited Lichtenthal, staying a night at the Hôtel Bär, where I used to dine in the old days. I looked up old acquaintances, and amongst them the former mistress of the dear old inn, whom I found retired and living in a charming villa close by, her brother being still the proprietor of the hotel. She, of course, had known Brahms well, and during the hour or two that I spent with her we talked chiefly about him. She repeated the verdict given by everyone really acquainted with him: "So simple and natural, so kind and cheerful, able to take pleasure in trifles. He was such a simple-hearted man." A tease, certainly, but his teasing was never unkind, never more than mere raillery. He would often bring a friend to dine at the Bär in the old days, and she always had the cloth laid for him in a private room or in the back part of the garden, so that he should not be worried by the visitors. "He never minded what he did. He would sometimes drop in, if he were passing, to say good-morning to us, and if we were very busy he would make a joke of sitting down and amusing himself by helping us cut up the vegetables for dinner. Only he could not bear to go into formal society, or to have to wear his dress-clothes. I have not seen him now for several years. The last time was in September, 1889, when he paid a flying visit to the Bär. He was very angry to find that three pine-trees had been cut down near the house where he used to lodge, thinking the poetry of the view had been impaired, and he said he would never stay in the place again. What a warm heart he had! He liked to know all the country people of the neighbourhood, and took a pride in feeling that every man, woman, and child whom he met in his early morning walks interchanged greetings with him. I begged for his autograph the last time he was here. You would like to see what he wrote"; and my old friend sent for the album in which the master had written:

"Johannes Brahms.   ("J. B.
 eines schönen Tages   one fine day
 im schönen Baden   in beautiful Baden
 im lieben Bären."   at the dear Bear.")

BERLIN.

Years were destined to elapse before my next meeting with Brahms. After my return to England I worked unremittingly on the lines he had indicated, and found that by the observation and practice of his principles I was guided straight onwards in the path of progress. His teaching had been of such a kind that its development did not cease with the actual lessons. As the weeks and months went by I found myself growing continually into a clearer perception of the aims and results it had had in view. It caused me no surprise to find, on becoming acquainted with his pianoforte compositions, that I must postpone for a time the delightful task of getting them up. Brahms himself had prepared me for this. He had always been extremely careful, when selecting music for me to work at, to choose what would develop my technical powers without straining my hands, and when I had wished to study something of his had answered that his compositions were unfit for me for the present, as they required too much physical strength and grasp. He fancied, indeed, at that time that nearly all of them were beyond a woman's strength. When I asked why it was that he composed only such enormously difficult things for the pianoforte, he said they came to him naturally, and he could not compose otherwise ("Ich kann nicht anders").

In the winter of 1881-82 I found myself in Berlin. It is difficult to describe the feelings with which I one day read the announcement that von Bülow, in the course of a *tournée* with the Meiningen Orchestra, of which he was conductor, would shortly visit the city to give a three days' series of concerts in the hall of the Singakademie; that Brahms' compositions would figure conspicuously in the programmes; that Brahms himself would be present, and that he would probably take part in one or more of the performances. The life at Lichtenthal had come to seem to me a sort of far-away fairy-tale impossible of any sort of renewal, and I could hardly realise that I should soon see Brahms again. Finding, however, from subsequent announcements, that the concerts were really to take place, I lost no time in securing a subscription ticket for the series.

Feeling sure that every moment of Brahms' short stay in Berlin would be occupied, I decided that my only chance of getting a word or two with him would be to gain admission to one of the rehearsals, and to watch for a favourable moment in which to make myself known to him. As ill luck would have it, I was claimed on the first day by engagements that could not be postponed. I was, however, the less inconsolable since Brahms was to take an active part only in the second and third concerts. Their respective programmes included a new pianoforte concerto still in MS. (No. 2 in B flat), to be played by the composer, with von Bülow as conductor; and the first pianoforte concerto, with Bülow as pianist and Brahms at the conductor's desk.

Betaking myself to the Singakademie in good time for the rehearsal on the second morning of the series, I explained, to the friendly custodian at the entrance-door, my claims to admission. He allowed me to enter the hall and to take my place amongst the small audience of persons privileged to attend.

The members of the orchestra were already assembled, and after some moments of waiting von Bülow came in with several gentlemen. Lusty applause broke forth from platform and stalls, and a small stir of greetings took place. But where was Brahms? I could perceive him nowhere at first, and it was only as the rehearsal proceeded, and he took his place on the platform, that I felt certain he was really present. I had prepared myself to find him looking changed and older, but not beyond recognition. It is, however, no exaggeration to say that as I gazed at him, knowing him to be Brahms, I was utterly unable to recognise the man I had known ten years previously. There, indeed, was the great head with the hair brushed back as of old, though less tidily than in former days; but his figure had become much heavier, and both mouth and chin were hidden by a thick moustache and shaggy, grizzled beard that had completely transformed his appearance. When I first knew him at the time of his early middle age, one might fancy that his countenance and expression had retained more than a trace of his youthful period of *Sturm und Drang*, but this had now quite vanished. I felt, with a shock, that my foreboding that I should never see my old friend again had been realised, though in a way different from that anticipated by me.

Brahms received an ovation when he had finished his performance of the new concerto, and as he was retiring from the platform Bülow, unable to restrain his excitement, darted forward and gave him a kiss. It seemed to take him rather aback, but he submitted passively.

At length the rehearsal came to an end, and Brahms was immediately surrounded by friends eager to offer their congratulations and to receive a word of greeting from him. "Now or never," I thought, and taking my courage in my hand, I managed to get near, though a little behind him. "I, also, should like to say a word of thanks to you, Herr Brahms," I said. Brahms turned his head. "Are you here in Berlin, then?" he rejoined instantly, answering as he might have done if we had met the previous week. Someone else pressed forward to claim his attention as I was replying, and I fell behind again. I did not like to wait for a second opportunity, feeling there was no chance of his being free, so I straightway departed and went back to my lodgings.

Thinking things over on my road, I came to the conclusion that Brahms had not recognised me, but that when my words caught his ear he had uttered the first casual reply that rose to his lips, and which might be appropriate to any acquaintance whom he did not at the moment remember. However exceptional his memory for faces might be, it appeared to me incredible that, after the lapse of so many years, he should have known me without the hesitation of a second at a moment when his attention was preoccupied by the concert business of the day and by the claims of his Berlin friends.

It was in this frame of mind that I took my seat in the evening to hear the concert. Having got over the first excitement of seeing Brahms again, and knowing what I had to expect in regard to his personal appearance, I was able to listen to the music in a more composed mood than had been possible to me in the morning. My pleasure in the performance of the concerto was, of course, in some measure impaired by the circumstance that the long, intricate work was quite new. I think, however, that I should have enjoyed it more if Brahms had conducted and Bülow performed the solo. I did not think Brahms' playing what it had been. His touch in *forte* passages had become hard, and though he might, perhaps, be said to have mastered the difficulties of his part, he had not sufficiently surmounted them to execute them with ease. It could not, in fact, have been otherwise. No composer having attained to the height of Brahms' greatness could have kept his technical command of the pianoforte unimpaired; life is too short for this. I knew, however, that I had listened to a magnificent work of immense proportions, and longed for opportunity to hear it again that I might assimilate it.

There was a scene of tumultuous enthusiasm at the close of the work. The public applauded wildly, and shouted itself hoarse; the band joined in with its fanfare of trumpet and drum; Brahms and von Bülow were recalled again and again separately and together; and in the moment of the great composer's triumph I saw the earlier Brahms once more standing before me, for, whilst his eyes shone and his face beamed with pleasure, I recognised in his bearing and expression the old familiar look of almost diffident, shy modesty which had been one of his characteristics in former days.

I did not, of course, seek for a further opportunity of speaking to Brahms on the evening of which I am writing, but I laid my plans for the next morning, and at the proper hour again made my way to the Singakademie and successfully begged for admission to the rehearsal.

During the first part Brahms sat as one of the audience

in the front row of stalls, and in a convenient break between the pieces I sent my English visiting-card to him, having written on it a few lines recalling myself to his remembrance. He read it and looked round. "I know that already," he said coldly, but rising and coming towards me. "I saw you yesterday." "But you did not know who I was?" I returned, still sceptical. "Yes, I knew." "It seemed to me quite impossible you could have recognised me!" I ejaculated. "Oh yes, yes—*oh* yes!" said Brahms in quite a different tone, and for a couple of seconds I forgot to look up or say anything.

"Are you taking notes?" he asked by way of recalling me to myself, touching my pencil. But the rehearsal had to proceed, and Brahms presently took his place on the platform with Bülow for the performance of the Concerto in D minor. When the rehearsal was over, I did not leave the hall so quickly as on the previous day, but waited in the hope of getting another word with Brahms, and was rewarded by having a good many.

In the evening, as he faced the audience, before the commencement of the concerto, catching sight of me in the third row of stalls, he was at the pains to bestow upon me a kind bow and smile of recognition. He glanced slightly at me again once or twice during the evening, and I knew, though his appearance still seemed a little strange to me, that Brahms was in the world after all.

The execution of the D minor Concerto was one of those rare performances that remain in the memory as unforgettable events. Brahms, when conducting, indulged in no antics, and was sparing of his gestures, often keeping his left hand in his pocket, or letting it hang quietly at his side; but he cast the spell of his genius over orchestra and pianist alike. The performance was remarkable for its power and grandeur, but not chiefly so, for these qualities were to be expected. It was made supremely memorable by the subtle imagination that touched and modified even the rather hard intellectuality of von Bülow's usual style. Good performances of Brahms' orchestral works may not seldom be heard, and great ones occasionally; but the particular quality of his poetic fancy, by which, when conducting an orchestra, he made the music sound from time to time as though it were floating in some rarefied atmosphere, vibrating now with fairy-like beauty and grace, now with ethereal mystery, was, I should say, peculiar to himself, and is hardly to be reproduced or imitated.

As soon as Brahms had finished his share in the evening's programme I quitted the hall, for I was thoroughly exhausted by the excitement of the past two days, and felt I could bear nothing more. Early the next morning he left Berlin to fulfil engagements in another town.

Vienna.

During the next four years much of my time was passed in Berlin. I delighted in the concerts and general musical atmosphere of the German capital, and did not allow my plans to be disturbed by a vague invitation to visit Vienna which Brahms had given me in the course of our short interview in the hall of the Singakademie. I felt that however kind and friendly his recollection of me might have remained, yet I could not hope to derive direct musical benefit from one absorbed in the intense thought and brooding to which the life of a really great composer must be largely devoted.

It was not until December, 1888, that I paid my first visit to Vienna. I arrived there towards the end of the month, armed with letters of introduction which met with a kind response and obtained for me immediate admission into those English and Austrian circles to members of which they were addressed. I waited for a week before letting Brahms know of my arrival, as I wished not only to be settled before calling on him, but also to be in such a position in regard to my acquaintance as would make it impossible for him to suspect that I could want anything whatever of him beyond the delight and honour of seeing him again, and of recalling myself to his remembrance.

Meanwhile I gathered, from all I heard, that his dislike of anything approaching to general society had steadily grown upon him. Some, even, of his old friends spoke of the increasing rarity of his visits. A lady at whose house he had been intimate for many years told me it had once been his custom to announce himself for the evening from time to time at a few hours' notice, with the proviso that he should find her and her husband alone in their family circle, or at most with one or two chosen friends. On these occasions he had been used to play to them one after another of his newest compositions. This habit, however, he had almost entirely given up.

I heard but one opinion, both from friends and outsiders, as to his essentially high character and sterling qualities of nature; but his manners were described with unanimity, by those not within his immediate circle, as difficult, sarcastic, and arrogant. I was, indeed, so repeatedly assured that I should do no good by trying to see him that I almost began to fear I should find he had become rude and impossible, if not hopelessly inaccessible. To all that was said to me on the subject I answered merely that I had once known him well, and had never found him otherwise than kind and simple, but that I had prepared myself to find him changed and rough in his behaviour to me.

At length, on a dark afternoon of one of the closing days of the year, I made my way to the Wieden, the quarter of Vienna inhabited by Brahms, and, turning in at the doorway of No. 4, Carlsgasse, I ascended the worn stone staircase as far as the third *étage*. Here I pulled the shining brass handle of the old-fashioned door-bell, and the feeling of doubt which had possessed me changed to one of positive alarm as I listened to the prolonged peal I had awakened. I thought it must sound to Brahms like the announcement of a most daring and determined intruder, and that it would inevitably prove the death-knell of any chance of my admission.

The door was soon opened by a friendly maid-servant, who told me, indeed, that the Herr Doctor was not at home, but satisfied me that I was not being put off with a mere phrase by adding that she thought he would probably be back by six o'clock, and that she advised me to return about that hour if I particularly wished to see him, as he was to start on a journey early the next morning. I thanked the girl, said I would follow her suggestion, and, without leaving my name, returned to my rooms to wait for the evening.

The second visit was again unsuccessful, but on trying a third time, at seven o'clock, I found that Brahms had returned. "Please to walk in," said the landlady, who this time opened the door. But this unexpected facility of access to the master was even more embarrassing than would have been the conflict of argument I had anticipated. "Please take my card," said I, "to the Herr Doctor, and ask if he will see me." "Oh, it is not necessary," she said; but took it in, returning immediately and asking me to enter. As I advanced, the formidable and overbearing Brahms hastened to meet me. "Why did you not leave your address? I should have come to find you out," he said, giving me his hand. And returning with me to the sitting-room, he bade me take a seat on the sofa, whilst he placed himself on a chair opposite.

He did not try to hide that he was pleased to see his old pupil. He evidently wished me to understand that our acquaintanceship was to be taken up from the exact point at which it had been last left, and reminded me, when I alluded to his lessons at Baden-Baden, that he had seen me since those early days. "Oh, for a moment at the rehearsals at Berlin," I answered. "But since then," he insisted. "Only at the concert," said I, rather surprised. "Yes, at the concert," he agreed, "and you sat downstairs, I remember."

I told him I had lately been getting up the same B flat Concerto which he had played at the time, and had performed it in London before a private audience. He was interested in hearing the particulars of the occasion, and when I said, laughingly, that the fatigue entailed by the practice of its enormous difficulties had given me all sorts of aches and pains, and made it necessary for me to go into the country for change of air after the performance was over, he replied in the same vein: "But that is very dangerous; one must not compose such things. It is too dangerous!"

He informed me rather slyly, "I am the most unamiable of all the musicians here," as though he would like to know if I had heard of his reputation for cross-grained perversity, and was frankly gratified when I answered: "That I will never believe, Herr Brahms—never!" He was to be absent at the longest for ten days only, and when I took leave of him it was with the pleasant consciousness that he would be glad to find me still in Vienna on his return.

In appearance, Brahms had again greatly altered since our meeting in Berlin. Though not fifty-six, he looked an old man. His hair was nearly white, and he had grown very stout. I had a good opportunity of observing him, myself unnoticed, soon after his return from his journey. The first public performance in Vienna was given of his newly-published Gipsy Songs, at the concert of a resident singer, one of his friends. Brahms had not been announced to take part in the performance, but when the evening came, he walked quietly on to the platform as the singers were arranging themselves in their places and took his seat at the pianoforte as accompanist. Of course his appearance was the signal for an outburst of enthusiastic welcome from the crowded audience, some hopes, but no certainty, having been entertained that he would show himself.

As I sat in my corner and watched, I was aware that both his general aspect and his expression had undergone another and a curious change during the last years. He now wore the happy, sunshiny look of one who had realised his purpose, and was content with his share in life; of one to whom the complete measure of success had come, and not too late to be valued. If in Baden-Baden he had made upon me the impression of a man awaiting full recognition, who had already waited long for it; if in Berlin, the impression of one who, having attained a glorious pinnacle of fame, whilst still in the plenitude of his powers, was untiringly pressing onward towards higher summits of fulfilment—I had the feeling, when I looked at him in Vienna, that the second phase, too, was more or less belonging to the past, and that he had entered upon a period of reward, and perhaps of less strenuous exertion.

One of the very few opportunities I ever had of seeing Brahms avail himself of a great man's licence to follow his whims regardless of convention, and, perhaps, of due respect to others, was afforded me at a meeting of the Vienna Tonkünstlerverein, the musicians' club, of which he was honorary president. It was one of the special social evenings of the society, when the members supped together. Brahms was late in coming, and when he arrived supper was proceeding. He allowed himself to be conducted to the place, at the top of a long table, which had been reserved for him as president, but did not sit down. Leisurely scanning the assembled company, he picked out the position he preferred, which happened to be at the side near the bottom. A slight space was certainly there, but not enough for a seat. "There," he said, pointing to it, and he sauntered down the room, apparently quite unconcerned at the disturbance and inconvenience which he caused, a bench having to be moved and several people being obliged to shift their places to make room for him. When once in occupation of the seat he fancied, he contributed his share to the cordiality of the evening, and was in no hurry to leave.

Another occasion was very similar. He was again dissatisfied with a place that had been assigned him at a supper-party. This time it was at a private house, and, as he could not have declined the seat without making himself unbearably rude, he submitted, with a kind of half-protest, to occupy it. During the greater part of the entertainment, however, he was not only in a wayward mood, but in a thoroughly bad temper, which he could not control. There was, when all is said, certainly no ill-natured intention in what he did on either occasion, but at the worst a mere childish petulance and over-excitability under slight disappointment.

I discovered, though Brahms had no fixed hour, that the right time to call upon him was about eleven o'clock. Always an early riser, he had then completed his morning's work, and if at home, as was generally the case, was ready to receive a visitor. He was sometimes to be found seated at the piano with an open volume (often Bach) on the music-stand, which was placed on the closed top lid of the instrument, playing softly, or silently studying the work in front of him. I have never felt that I was disturbing him when I called. It is true that I only went occasionally, and when provided with a legitimate excuse. Still, I do not altogether understand how he acquired such a reputation for incivility. He was, in his own way, of a sociable disposition.

One day when I was with him, some terrible pianoforte strumming was going on in the flat above him. I commented on the strange constitution of people who could deliberately plant themselves in his immediate neighbourhood—for he had occupied the same rooms for years—and then worry him with such noise. He said there was sometimes bad singing and violin-playing, both of which he found harder to bear than the piano, but added: "They have their rights, and I know how to help myself"; and he held out his hands in keyboard position, to indicate that when too much disturbed to do anything else, he shut out the sounds and employed his time by playing.

Brahms generally went out at about a quarter to twelve

at latest, and would arrive before one o'clock at his favourite restaurant, Zum Rothen Igel. After his early dinner he walked, finding his way to a café in another part of the town, where he would read the papers over a cup of black coffee. After this was his best time for paying visits, and about six o'clock he often returned to his rooms to write letters or do other work. Later on he would go out again to fulfil his evening engagements. Sometimes it happened that he did not go home, after leaving in the morning, until after supper. These details I learnt incidentally in the course of my stay in Vienna.

Brahms made a great point of being polite to ladies on the question of smoking, and was very particular in asking permission before lighting his cigar. Of course, if I found him alone, he never smoked. One day, however, when I had been with him only a very few minutes, the door-bell rang, and two gentlemen appeared, one a friend of Brahms, the other a youth whom he had brought to introduce to the master. Brahms wished me to remain, and I therefore kept my seat. Very soon he produced his box of cigars, according to Continental custom, and handed it to his visitors, saying, however: "But I do it unwillingly, as a lady is present." The elder of the two gentlemen put his cigar into his breast-pocket, the younger lighted his and vigorously puffed away alone, from sheer confusion, I think, at finding himself in the presence of the master. Brahms returned to his seat without taking one. "But won't you smoke, Herr Brahms?" I said, after a few seconds. "If you allow it," he answered, making as much as possible of the few words, and taking a cigar.

Though Brahms was not, during the latter part of his life, a frequenter of concert-rooms, he nearly always attended the concerts of the Philharmonic Society and of the Gesellschaft der Musikfreunde in Vienna, sitting usually, in the "artists' box" in the gallery. In the intervals between the pieces he would lean forward, both arms on the front, with his opera-glasses to his eyes, spying out his acquaintances in different parts of the hall.

When I called to say good-bye to him at the close of my first visit to Vienna, I happened to mention that I had made a small collection of works written for the keyed instruments of the seventeenth and eighteenth centuries, and had picked up one or two rather valuable first editions. He was greatly interested, and saying, "We have done the same thing," took down from the bookcase one or two of his own old music-books to show me. I especially remember an original edition of Scarlatti's Sonatas, in first-rate preservation, but without the title-page, of which he was particularly fond and proud. He asked if I would bring one or two of mine to show him on my next visit, and I told him that I happened to have one with me—an original Rameau—and that if he had not got a copy I would send it him at once.

"No," he answered; "it is too late now—you are going away to-morrow—but next year when you come again." "But I mean," I rejoined, "that I will give it you." Brahms did not immediately answer, and I added: "Would you rather not? If so, I will not do it." "No, I would *not* 'rather not,' but you must not immediately give your things away," he replied. "Then I will do it," I declared, delighted that I possessed something he would like to have, and to accept from me. Later in the day I sent him the book, with a few lines telling him how much pleasure it would give me if I might leave it with him as a remembrance. Early the next morning I left Vienna. I was not to arrive in London for another week, having engagements *en route*, and this Brahms knew. On the evening of my return home, as soon as my mother's first greetings were over, she said: "There is a letter for you from Brahms; it arrived this morning." "From Brahms! How do you know?" I answered. "From his having written his name on the outside," she returned, handing me the precious missive.

On the outside of the envelope, above the adhesive, he

had written "J. Brahms, Vienna, Austria," and, opening the envelope, I read as follows:

"Very esteemed and dear Fräulein,

"It was too late the other evening for me to be able to do as I wished, and come and express my thanks to you in person.

"Let me, therefore, send them very heartily after you, for your so kind and valuable gift.

"It was indeed much too kind of you to part with the pretty treasure in order to give me pleasure, and it shall still be at your disposal next year!

"In the hope of seeing you here again next year, and of being able to repeat my hearty thanks,

"Yours very sincerely,

"J. Brahms."*

On my first visit to Brahms in the following winter, he led the way to his bookcase and showed me the Rameau, saying: "I shall die in ten years, and you will get it back again." I told him that should I outlive him I should prefer not to have it back, but to let it go with his collection, and thus the matter remained.

The success of my first visit to Vienna induced me to pay several subsequent ones, the last of which took place rather more than a year before Brahms' death. A minute account

---

* "Sehr geehrtes und liebes Fräulein,

" Es war neulich zu spät am Abend geworden als dass ich, wie ich wünschte, Sie selbst noch hätte aufsuchen u. Ihnen meinen Dank aussprechen können.

"So lassen Sie mich denn nachträglich diesen sehr herzlichen sagen für Ihr so freundliches u. werthvolles Geschenk.

"Es war in der That gar zu liebenswürdig von Ihnen sich mir zu gefallen von dem hübschen Schatze zu trennen u. es soll Ihnen im nächsten Jahre auch noch zur Verfügung stehen!

"In der Hoffnung Sie aber im nächsten Jahre wieder hier zu sehen u. Ihnen meinen herzlichen Dank wiederholen zu können,

"Ihr sehr ergebener,

"J. Brahms."

of each would be wearisome, and I will only allude, therefore, to the opportunity that I had, in the course of two separate winters, of hearing the concerts of the Joachim Quartet in Vienna, and of seeing Brahms as one of the audience. On one of these enchanting evenings the Clarinet Quintet was given, with Mühlfeld as clarinettist. Brahms had his seat downstairs, at the end of the room reserved for resident and other musicians, and separated from the general audience by the performers' platform. My place was only two or three away from his, and so situated that I could see him all the time the work was being played. His face wore an unconscious smile, and his expression was one of absorbed felicity from beginning to end of the performance. When the last movement was finished, he was not to be persuaded to come forward and take his part in acknowledging the deafening clamour of applause, but, as it were, disclaimed all right in it himself by vigorously applauding the executants. At the last moment, however, as the noise was beginning to subside, up he got, and stepping on to the platform, in his loose, short, shabby morning-coat, made his bow to the audience. Another item in the programme was the Clarinet Trio, played by himself, Mühlfeld, and Hausmann. Joachim, sitting on the right-hand side of the piano, turned over for him. I changed my seat during the performance of this work, taking the place that Brahms had vacated, which was close to the piano and gave me a full view of the keyboard. In spite of my several experiences of the master's tenacious memory for small things, I confess that I felt a thrill of surprise at the end of the first movement, and again at the end of the second, when he turned his head suddenly round and glanced straight at me in the very same quick, searching way to which I had been accustomed in the old Lichtenthal days, as though to satisfy himself as to whether or not I had understood.

Ischl.

I spent several weeks at Ischl during the summers of 1894 and 1895, and was much interested in observing the life of my old friend in surroundings that were new to me. His habits, during these closing years of his life, were in all essential respects the same as when I had first known him in Baden-Baden. Rising soon after four o'clock, his days were passed in the same simple, natural routine of walking, studying and composing, in the enjoyment of the society of his friends and of the cordial relations which he maintained with the people of the country, between whom and himself a perfect understanding existed.

His love of children has often been recorded. I have seen him sitting reading on the bench of the little garden of his lodgings, apparently quite undisturbed by his landlady's boys, who romped round and about him, jumping on and off the bench, playing hide-and-seek behind his back, and the like. Now and then he would interrupt his studies to caress a couple of kittens that were taking part in the frolics.

"I know this man," said a droll, tiny boy of five or six, in a funny red suit, who, taking a stroll along the promenade one afternoon with some companions, came upon Brahms sitting under the trees before Walter's coffee-house, the centre of a large group of musicians and friends. The great composer was quite ready to acknowledge the acquaintanceship, and called his small friend to his table to receive a spoonful of half-melted sugar from his coffee-cup.

"My Katie knows Brahms," said a village dressmaker to me, alluding to her pretty little fair-haired daughter of eight. "We have met him out walking very early in the morning, but Katie was frightened the other day and cried because he ran round her and pretended he wanted her piece of bread."

"The Herr Doctor has already seen him," a young peasant mother observed to me as she showed me her three-months-old son, "and says he is a strapping boy."

One morning when I called on Brahms to say good-bye, I found him in the midst of preparations for his own departure. An open portmanteau, in process of being packed, was in the sitting-room, and there was a litter of small things about. Brahms invited me to take a seat on the sofa. A book which he had been reading lay open, face downwards. I ventured, with an apologetic glance at him, to take it up and look at it. This he did not at all mind. He had been amusing himself with an essay on Bismarck. After we had chatted a little while, as I rose to say farewell, my eye was caught by a table on which were a number of cheap German playthings—small boxes of puzzles, toy knives and forks, etc., evidently destined for parting or returning gifts to quite poor children.

"What is this?" I involuntarily exclaimed, taking up, before I knew what I was doing, a toy fork of most ungainly make, broad, squat, and almost without handle. An inquisitiveness, however, which seemed to hint at the soft side of Brahms' nature could not be allowed. "What does that matter to you?" he cried. Then, instantly, as though afraid he had been rough, he added: "It is for small things —fruit, fish, or the like." Only I, having seen the clumsy toy, can quite appreciate the comicality of the answer, which of course simply meant: "No allusion, if you please." Brahms, however, had saved appearances, and without being hard on me, had drawn a thin veil over his kind intentions to his little friends. I held the fork another instant, and then replaced it on the table, saying with gravity: "I thought it was a plaything, Herr Brahms."

A young lady, an inhabitant of Ischl, who taught singing, and gave an annual concert there, and who, during the season, presided over a milliner's business on the Promenade, was a great ally of Brahms', and never omitted to stand outside the door of her atelier as the hour approached for him to pass to his café, in order to get a greeting from him. The little ceremony was duly honoured by the great composer, who was always ready with, at the least, his genial "Good-day."

Fräulein L. talked of him to me in just the same way as all others did who were content to be natural and unostentatious in their manner towards him. He was so good-natured and bright, she remarked, and though he loved to tease, his teasing was so kindly. He made a point of calling on her formally once every season. Taking advantage of this ceremony, she one day placed before him a cabinet photograph of himself, and asked if he could do her the honour of writing his name underneath.

"Yes, I can do that," he answered in his cheerful tone, "I learned that at school. But why do you keep this ugly old face? Why not have a handsome, curly-haired one? Ah, what have we here?"—catching sight of a little saucer containing cigar-ash. "*You smoke!*"

Fräulein L. laughingly assured him that neither she nor her assistant had been guilty of the cigar. "So much the worse!" he retorted. "Who was it? Is he dark or fair?"

By such genial intercourse and harmless banter, Brahms endeared himself to all the towns-people with whom he came in contact, and his preference for Ischl was a source of pride and gratification to them. His sociability had in it no suggestion of patronage; it was that of a friend with friends, and was valued accordingly.

A few words spoken to me by his landlady at Ischl are not without their value, coming, as they do, from one who had the opportunity of knowing him in small things. The occasion was as follows. My lodging was opposite to Brahms' on the other side of the valley, but on a much higher mountain slope. I could see his house from my balcony and windows, but was too far away to have the least apprehension that he could be disturbed by hearing anything of my piano. Someone suggesting to me, however, that, with the wind in a certain direction, the sound might possibly reach his windows, I went across one afternoon, when I knew he would be out, to interview his landlady on the subject. She assured me nothing had ever been heard, and added: "You can play quite without fear, gnädiges Fräulein, nothing is heard here—the water makes too much noise. And even if a tone were to be heard now and then —it could not be more—the master is not so particular: it would not disturb him. He is not capricious: no one can say that of him."

That Brahms had his little prejudices and limitations, however, cannot be denied, and these grew more pronounced as he advanced in years and became less pliable. The mere circumstance of his having inflexibly adhered to the particular method of life adopted by him as a young man, by which he shut himself away as much as possible from whatever was at all distasteful to him in ordinary social intercourse, contributed, as time went on, to increase his sensitiveness and make him impatient of contradiction. He became rather too prone to suspect people to whom he did not take a fancy, of conceit and affectation; and, without knowing it, he acquired a habit, which sometimes made conversation with him difficult, of dissenting forcibly from trifling remarks made more with the object of saying something than for the sake of asserting a principle. He had his own particular code of polite manners, and was rigorous in expecting others to adhere to it, yet he was apt, in his latter years, to be intolerant of those whose ideas of what was due to the amenities of life were more extended than his own, or somewhat differed from them.

What, however, were his prepossessions, his little sarcasms, and occasional roughnesses, but as the tiniest flecks on the sun? We may well be thankful, we musicians and music-lovers of this generation, to have passed some part of our lives with Brahms in our midst—Brahms the composer and Brahms the man. As his music may be searched through and through in vain for a single bar that is not noble and pure, so also in his mind dwelt no thought which was otherwise than good and true. We may even be glad that he was not perfect, but human, the dear, great tender-hearted master, whose lofty message, vibrating with the pulsations of the nature he so loved, was of such rare beauty and consolation.

The few lines with which I conclude these slight personal reminiscences were the last I ever received from Brahms. They were written on his card and sent, enclosed in an envelope, when I was at Ischl. I had been expecting him to come to see me, and he had not appeared.

"ESTEEMED FRÄULEIN,

"Prevented by many things, I venture to ask if it is not possible for you to call on

"Yours most sincerely,

"JOHANNES BRAHMS."*

---

* "GEEHRTES FRÄULEIN,

"Mannichfach abgehalten, erlaube ich mir die Anfrage ob es Ihnen nicht möglich ist vorzusprechen bei

"Ihrem ergebensten,

"JOHANNES BRAHMS."

CHAPTER I

1760-1845

The Brahms family—Johann Jakob Brahms: his youth and marriage—Birth and childhood of Johannes—The Alster Pavilion—Otto F. W. Cossel—Johannes' private subscription concert.

JOHANNES BRAHMS came of a race belonging to Lower Saxony. This is sufficiently indicated by the family name, which appears in extant church records variously as Brahms, Brams, and Brahmst. The word Bram belongs to the old Platt-Deutsch, the near kin to the Anglo-Saxon and English languages. It is still the common name in some of the Baltic districts of Germany, the Hanoverian provinces, and, with a modified vowel, in England, for the straight-growing *Planta genista*, the yellow-flowering broom, and is preserved in its original form in the English word "bramble."

The letter *s* at the end of the name has the same meaning in German as in English, and just as "Brooks" is a contraction of the words "son of Brook," so "Brahms" signifies, literally, "son of Bram," or "Broom."

Peter Brahms, the great-grandfather of the composer, and the first of his family of whom there is authentic record, was a child of the people. He trekked across the mouth of the Elbe from Hanover into Holstein, and settled down to ply his trade of joiner at Brunsbüttel, a hamlet or small township situated in the fertile fen-country which lies along the shore of the North Sea between the mouths of the Elbe and the Eider. This district is remembered as the land of the Ditmarsh Peasants, who were distinguished, some centuries ago, by their fierce and obstinate struggles for the maintenance of their independence, but who finally settled down about the year 1560 under the dominion of the Princes of Holstein. They are said to have been pre-eminent amongst neighbouring peoples, not only in courage, but in a simple untaught genius for the arts of poetry and music. They loved to turn their various adventures into verse, which they afterwards sang to the most expressive and appropriate melodies of their own invention, and their war-songs and ballads, though now forgotten, were long a cherished possession of their children's children. The little country has in recent times proved not unworthy of its former reputation. Niebuhr the traveller, and his son, the celebrated historian, both belonged to Meldorf. Claus Groth, the Low-German poet, was a native of Heide, where his grandfather and father were millers living on their own land in patriarchal fashion. Groth has drawn, notably in his volume "Quickborn," pathetically naïve pictures of his beloved Ditmarsh; of its homely scenery, its changing cloud-effects, its sudden bursts of storm, its simple, hard-working, honourable peasant life; and it is a striking circumstance that he should have been in a position to describe, as old family friends and neighbours, living amongst the memories of his childhood, the great-grandfather, grandfather, father, and uncle of Johannes Brahms.*

Old Peter the trekker was respected as a thoroughly well-mannered, orderly citizen. He was short and robust, and lived to a ripe old age. He passed the closing years of his life at Heide, where he spent most of his time sitting on a bench in front of his house, smoking a long pipe, and was wont to startle the dreamy Claus Groth, as he passed by every morning on his way to school, with a loud, jocular greeting.

Johann his son, who was tall and handsome, with straight,

---

* "Brahms Erinnerungen," in *Die Gegenwart*, No. 45.

No. 60 Speckstrasse, Hamburg.

yellow hair and fair complexion, combined the callings of innkeeper and retail dealer first at Wöhrden and afterwards at Heide. He married Christiana Asmus, a daughter of the country, and who knows what strain of latent poetic instinct, inherited from some old minstrel and patriot ancestor, may have been transmitted, through her veins, into the sturdy Brahms family? There is some presumption in favour of such a conjecture.

Two sons were born of her marriage with Johann, each of whom had a marked individuality. Peter Hinrich, the eldest, married at the age of twenty, and settled down as his father's assistant and future successor. Groth has described his adventure in the fields one memorable Sunday afternoon. Accompanied by his little son, he carried a huge kite, taller than himself, with a correspondingly long, thick string, which he successfully started. A strong north-west wind carried it along, and, to the delight of a crowd of small spectators, he tied to it a little cart of his own manufacture, in which he placed his boy. The cart began to move, drawn by the kite, slowly at first, then more quickly. Faster and higher flew the monster, quicker and quicker rolled the wheels, the child in the carriage, the father by its side. Then a scream, a crash! The terrified Claus knew no more till next day, when he heard that the little carriage had been dragged over a wall and upset, that the child had fallen out unhurt, and the kite been found on a high post a mile or two distant.

This Peter Hinrich added to the vocations of his father that of pawnbroker, and gradually acquired a large business as a dealer in antiquities. In the end, however, his delight in his possessions gained decided predominance over his business instincts. Becoming partially crippled in old age, he would sit in a large armchair for which there was barely space, surrounded by his beloved pots and pitchers, weapons and armour, and point out desired objects to would-be purchasers with a long stick. Often, however, he could not persuade himself to part with his curiosities, and would send his customers away empty-handed, satisfied with the mere pleasure of showing the treasures with which he packed his house quite full. His children and grandchildren remained and spread in the Ditmarsh, where some of them prosper to this day.

Johann Jakob, the second son of Johann and Christiana, destined to become the father of our composer, was his brother's junior by fourteen years, and was born on June 1, 1806. From his early boyhood he seems to have had no doubt as to his choice of a vocation. He could by no means be persuaded to settle down to the routine of school-work, to be followed in due course by the humdrum existence of a small country innkeeper or tradesman, such as had sufficed for his father and grandfather, and was contentedly accepted by his elder brother. He was upright, good-natured, and possessed of a certain vein of drollery, which made him throughout life a favourite with his associates; he was born, also, with a quietly stubborn will. He had an overmastering love of music—music of the kind he was accustomed to hear at neighbours' weddings, at harvest merry-makings, in the dancing-rooms of village inns. A musician he was resolved to be, and a musician, in spite of the determined opposition of parents and family, he became.

There existed, not far from his home, a representative of the old "Stadt Pfeifereien," establishments descended directly from the musicians' guilds of the Middle Ages, whose traditions lingered on in the rural districts of Germany for some time after the original institutions had become extinct. The "Stadt Pfeiferei" was recognised as the official musical establishment of its neighbourhood, and was presided over by the town-musician, who retained certain ancient privileges. He held a monopoly for providing the music for all open-air festivities in the villages, hamlets, and small townships within his district, and formed his band or bands from apprenticed pupils, who paid a trifling sum of money, often helped with their manual labour in the work of his house and the cultivation of his garden or farm, and, in return, lived with him as part of his family and received musical instruction from himself and his assistants. At the termination of their apprenticeship he provided his scholars with indentures of character and efficiency, according to desert, and dismissed them to follow their fortunes. Country lads with ambition, who desired to see something of the world, or to attain a better position than that of a peasant or journeyman, would persuade their parents to place them in one of these establishments. They were expected to acquire a practical knowledge of several instruments, so as to be able to take part upon either as occasion might demand, and the bands thus formed were available for all local functions. Johann Jakob would readily have applied himself to learn, from the nearest town-musician, all that that official was able to teach him, but his father could not be brought to consent to his exchanging the solid prospects of a settled life in the Ditmarsh for the visionary future of an itinerant performer. The boy's inclination was, however, unconquerable, and he settled the matter in his own fashion. He ran away from home several times and made his own bargain with his musical hero. Twice he was recalled and forgiven, and after the third escapade was allowed to have his own way, and bound over to serve his time in the usual manner. "I cannot give such proofs of my devotion to music," wrote his son Johannes to Claus Groth many years afterwards. Five years of apprenticeship were spent, the last three at the more distant town of Wesselbüren, in the study of the violin, viola, 'cello, flute, and horn, and, in the beginning of the year 1826, the quandam musical apprentice obtained his indentures, which testified to his faithfulness, desire to learn, industry, and obedience,* and quitted the old home country to try his luck at Hamburg.

It is not easy to imagine the feelings of this youth of nineteen or twenty on his arrival, fresh from the simple life

---

* Printed verbally in Max Kalbeck's "Johannes Brahms," p. 4.

of the Ditmarsh peasants, in the great commercial fortress city, still the old Hamburg of the day, with its harbour and shipping and busy river scenes; its walls and city gates, locked at sunset; its water-ways and bridges; its churches and exchange; its tall gabled houses; its dim tortuous alleys. Refined ease and sordid revelry were well represented there; the one might be contemplated on the pleasant, shady Jungfernstieg, the fashionable promenade where rich merchants and fine ladies and gay officers sat and sipped punch or coffee, wine or lemonade, served to them by the nimble waiters of the Alster Pavilion, the high-class refreshment house on the lake hard by; the other, in the so-called Hamburger Berg, the sailors' quarter, abounding in booths and shows, small public houses, and noisy dancing saloons, in which scenes of low-life gaiety were regularly enacted. Johann Jakob Brahms was destined to appear, in the course of his career as a musician, in both localities. He made his debut in the latter.

Thrown entirely on his own resources, with a mere pittance in his pocket for immediate needs, he had to pick up a bare existence, as best he could, in the courtyards and dancing-saloons of the Hamburg Wapping. He seems to have preserved his easy imperturbability of temper throughout his early struggles, and to have kept his eyes open for any chance opportunity that might occur. Helped by his natural gift for making himself a favourite, he managed, by-and-by, to get appointed as one of the hornists of the Bürger-Militair, the body of citizen-soldiers, or town-guard, in which, with a few exceptions, every burgher or inhabitant between the ages of twenty and forty-five was bound to serve. Each battalion of the force had its own band, and each band its own uniform, the musicians of the Jäger corps, to which Johann Jakob was attached, wearing a green coat with white embroidered collar, headgear decorated with a white pompon, and a short weapon called a Hirschfänger. This was a distinct rise in the fortunes of the wanderer. He won for himself a recognised place in the world, obscure though it might be, when he acquired the right to wear a uniform of the city of Hamburg, and in due time he enrolled himself as one of its burghers. The document of his citizenship has been preserved, and will be mentioned again near the close of our narrative.* It cannot be said that his further advancement was rapid. His partiality for the music he knew of is suggestive rather of a struggling instinct than an actual talent. His professional acquirements were slender, and of general education he had none; but he was not without shrewdness, was upright and diligent, and he made gradual progress. He and his colleagues used to form themselves into small brass bands, and to play wherever they saw opportunity, sometimes getting trifling engagements in dancing-rooms, sometimes dependent on the goodwill of a chance audience in a beer-garden or small house of entertainment. He did not earn much, but was no longer entirely dependent on the very meanest exercise of his industry, and may be said to have obtained a footing on the lowest rung of fortune's ladder.

On June 9, 1830, a few days after completing his twenty-fourth year, Jakob committed himself to the second great adventure of his life. He married, choosing for his wife Johanna Henrika Christiana Nissen, who was forty-one years of age and in very humble circumstances. She was small and plain, and limped badly; was sickly in health, and somewhat complaining; of a very affectionate if rather oversensitive disposition, and had a sweet expression in her light-blue eyes that testified to the goodness of her heart. She was an exquisite needlewoman, possessed many good housewifely virtues which she exercised as far as her very limited opportunities allowed, and is said to have been endowed with great refinement of feeling and superior natural parts. One of her husband's colleagues has described her as having faded, later on, into a "little withered mother who busied herself unobtrusively with her own affairs, and was not known outside her dwelling."

---

* Vol. II, Chap. XXII.

The strangely-matched couple began their life together on the smallest possible scale, and in February of the following year a daughter was born to them, who was christened Elisabeth Wilhelmine Louise. The young father's material resources seem to have remained much as they were, but before this time his dogged perseverance had added yet another instrument to the list of those he had already practised. He contrived to learn the double-bass, and as his friends increased, and he became more known, he began to get occasional engagements as double-bass substitute in the orchestras of small theatres. Meanwhile he did not neglect his other instruments, but performed on either as occasion presented itself.

On May 7, 1833, the angel of life again visited the poor little home, and Johanna Henrika Christiana presented her husband with a son, who was baptised on the 26th of the same month at St. Michael's Church, Hamburg. The child, being emphatically the "son of Johann," was called by the single name Johannes, after his father, mother, and paternal grandfather, and the grandfather was one of the sponsors.

The house in which Johannes Brahms was born was in Speck Lane, subsequently known as 60 Speckstrasse, and formed part of the Gänge-Viertel, the "Lane-quarter" of the old Hamburg. Want of space within the city walls had led to the construction of rows of houses along a number of lanes adjacent to one another, which had once been public thoroughfares through gardens. A neighbourhood of very dark and narrow streets was thus formed, for the houses were tall and gabled, and arranged to hold several families. They were generally built of brick, loam, and wood, and were thrown up with the object of packing as many human beings as possible into a given area. The Lane-quarter exists no longer, but many of the old houses remain, and some are well kept and picturesque to the eye of the passer-by. Not so 60 Speckstrasse. This house does not form part of the main street, but stands in a small dismal court behind, which is entered through a close passage, and was formerly called Schlüter's Court. It would be impossible for the most imaginative person, on arriving at this spot, to indulge in any of the picturesque fancies supposed to be appropriate to a poet's birthplace; the house and its surroundings testify only to the commonplace reality of a bare and repulsive poverty. A steep wooden staircase in the centre, leads right and left, directly from the court, to the various stories of the building. Each of its habitations is planned exactly as every other, excepting that those near the top are contracted by the sloping roof. Jakob and Johanna lived in the first-floor dwelling to the left on facing the house. On entering it, it is difficult to repress a shiver of bewilderment and dismay. The staircase door opens on to a diminutive space, half kitchen, half lobby, where some cooking may be done and a child's bed made up, and which has a second door leading to the living-room. This communicates with the sleeping-closet, which has its own window, but is so tiny it can scarcely be called a room. There is nothing else, neither corner nor cupboard. Where Jakob kept his instruments and how he managed to practise are mysteries which the ordinary mind cannot satisfactorily penetrate, but it is probable that his easy-going temperament helped him over these and other difficulties, and that he was fairly content with his lot. If Johanna took life a little more hardly, it is certain that husband and wife resembled each other in their affection for the children, and that the strong tie of love which bound the renowned composer of after-years to father and mother alike, had its earliest beginning in the fondness and pride which attended his cradle in the obscure abode in Schlüter's Court.

The family moved several times during the infancy of Johannes, and their various homes are partly to be traced in back numbers of the Hamburg address-book, which may be consulted in the library of the Johanneum. These early changes, however, have but little interest for the reader, and it will suffice to record that when the hero of our narrative was four or five years old, and the proud senior by two years of a little brother Friederich, known as Fritz, they moved into quarters less confined than those they had yet occupied at 38 Ulricus-strasse. Here the anxious wife and mother was able to add a trifle to Jakob's scanty earnings, by engaging on her own account in a tiny business for the sale of needles, cotton, tapes, etc., which had been carried on for many years previously at No. 91 of the same street by the "sisters Nissen," and by taking as boarder an acquaintance of her husband's, who, though not a musician, remained a life-long family friend. The intimacy descended to the next generation, and his son, Herr Carl Bade, has many a droll anecdote to relate of Jakob, whom he remembers with affectionate regard.

From such particulars as can be gathered, it is evident that the childhood of "Hannes" gave early promise of the striking characteristics of his maturity, and that some of the most powerful sentiments of his after-life are to be traced to influences acting on him from his birth. Indications of his possession of the musical faculty were apparent at a very tender age. He received his first actual instruction from his father, but his sensitive organisation, aided by the music of one sort and another that he was constantly hearing, seems almost to have anticipated this earliest teaching. In his clinging affection for his parents the child was father to the man, and one of his constant petitions was to be allowed to "help." It is easy to imagine the little tasks he learned to perform for the mother whom he worshipped, and the feeling of pride with which he watched his tall father on the exercise-days of the Jäger corps may have had something to do with his partiality for his beloved lead soldiers, the favourite toys which he kept locked in his writing-table long after he was grown up. He was sent, when quite a young child, to a little private school on the Dammthorwall, close to his parents' house, where the teaching was probably neither better nor worse than that usual in the very small day-schools of the period. Until he was nearly eight his musical education was carried on at home, and did not include the study of the piano. It seems to have been taken for granted that he would, in due course, follow his father's calling, which was gradually ripening into that of a reliable performer in the humbler orchestras of the city. It is hardly surprising that Jakob, who knew nothing about genius, and was not troubled by notions about art for its own sake, should have looked forward contentedly to the career of an orchestral player for his boy. He himself, after more than twelve laborious years, was only struggling into a position of acceptance by musicians of this class. That Johannes should begin life by taking his place amongst them as a fiddler or 'cellist, who might work his way to some distinction, must necessarily have appeared to him a sufficiently ambitious object, the attainment of which would enable his son to support himself and help the family. The orchestral players of the Hamburg of that time carried on their work under peculiar circumstances. They were bound together in a kind of musical trade union, the Hamburger Musikverein, founded in 1831, which protected them from competition, no member being allowed to play in any band that included an outsider. They met constantly at their "Börse," or club, through which most of their engagements were made. It was open every morning for a couple of hours for the transaction of business, and there was a Lokal in the same building available for a chat over a glass of beer and a smoke. The establishment was for some time presided over by a man named Rose, whose son became well-known in Great Britain as Carl Rosa, the proprietor of an English opera company. Johann Jakob Brahms was one of the original members of the Musikverein, and his copy of the rules, still in existence, bears, underneath his signature, the date May 1, 1831. The system of working by deputy was extensively practised in the arrangements of the union. If a member engaged for a certain performance happened to get a more lucrative offer for the same day and hour, he would give notice to the "Börse" to furnish a substitute for the first appointment. The substitute might repeat the process in his turn, and it sometimes happened that a single engagement passed through several hands in succession before the date of its fulfilment. Under these conditions music was very much a mere business, but, on the other hand, orchestral players were expected to be fairly good all-round musicians, capable of performing passably on several instruments, and able to fill a gap at short notice. Many of these men, who made the musical atmosphere with which Johannes Brahms was familiar in his childhood, lived in the Lane-quarter, partly because it was cheap, partly in order to be near their "Börse," which was situated in the Kohlhöfen. They were, as a rule, shrewd, hard-working, honourable members of their profession, happy in their calling and in their mutual friendly intercourse, and striving to bring up their children to improved circumstances. Those among them who were not able to obtain better employment were glad to acquire experience, and to earn something, by playing in dancing-saloons and Lokals of various degrees of repute, hoping for a rise of fortune in days to come.

Proofs of continual advancement in Jakob's career are to be found in the fact that, from about the year 1837 onwards, his services were requisitioned from time to time as substitute in the small band which played from six till eleven, every evening throughout the year, in a room of the Alster Pavilion, and especially in the circumstance that he by and by became one of its regular members, succeeding to the duties of double-bass player. The orchestra was composed of two violins, viola, two flutes, and double-bass, and performed "evening entertainment-music," consisting of overtures, airs, operatic selections, and pot-pourris. The public, which was a good one, was served with light refreshments outside, or crowded into the house to listen, according to inclination and the season, and the musicians were paid by contributions collected during intervals between the pieces. Count Woronzow from St. Petersburg, who was present with his son in the audience one fine summer evening, was so delighted with the music, and so gratified at hearing the Russian national air played *con amore* in his honour, that he not only put a gold piece on the plate, but wanted to carry off the six performers to Russia, guaranteeing that they would make their fortunes there, and would not take a refusal till they had had a week or two to consider the matter.

There lived at this time at No. 7, Steindamm, a young pianist of Hamburg, Otto Friedrich Willibald Cossel, who was well known to the set of men belonging to the musicians' union, and in great and just repute with them as a teacher of his instrument. He was a pupil of the eminent teacher and theorist, Marxsen of Altona, and had cherished dreams of fame as a pianoforte virtuoso. Adverse circumstances, delicate health, and want of self-confidence, may have been the causes of his failure to realise his aspirations; but whether or not this be the case, he has left behind him the reputation of having been a good player, an excellent instructor, and a thoroughly high-minded man. He was devoted to his art, and had a large number of pupils; but they were chiefly recruited from the classes who could not afford to pay much, and it was not in Cossel's nature to be difficult on the question of remuneration. He was fain to content himself with the consciousness of hard work well done as a great part of his reward.

To Cossel came, one day in the winter of 1840-1, Jakob Brahms with the little seven-year-old Hannes, a pale, delicate-looking child with fair complexion, blue eyes, and a mane of flaxen hair falling to his shoulders. He was as neat and trim as a new pin—a little "patenter Junge"—and wore over his home-knitted socks pretty wooden shoes such as are seen to this day in the shops of Hamburg, an effective protection against the wet climate of the city. Too pale and serious to be called pretty, there was a something most attractive in his appearance, and when his face lighted up on hearing the conclusion of his father's business Cossel's heart was won.

"I wish my son to become your pupil, Herr Cossel," said Jakob, speaking in his native Low-German tongue. "He wants so much to learn the piano. When he can play as well as you do, it will be enough!"

The short interview brought about important results to Hannes, whilst for Cossel it insured the future enduring respect of the musical world. He soon perceived that in his new scholar he had no ordinary pupil, and his affection went out more and more to the docile, eager, easily-taught child. He got into the habit of keeping the little fellow after his lesson that he might practise on his piano, and be spared some of the fatigue entailed by constant walks between home, school, and the somewhat distantly-situated Steindamm. Hannes, on his part, grew passionately fond of his teacher, and the special relation in which he stood to him was soon recognised and accepted by Cossel's other pupils. The two were brought still closer together at the end of about a year, for Jakob and his wife, on the impending marriage of their boarder, moved again into smaller quarters close by—at No. 29, Dammthorwall—whilst Cossel took over their rooms in Ulricus-strasse. Well for Hannes that an admirable method of instruction enabled him to get through the necessary drudgery of acquiring a good position of the hand and free movement of the fingers at a very early age, and that he was prepared by wise guidance easily to encounter successive steps of his master's system, which included the practice of the best masters of études— Czerny, Cramer, Clementi—of the great classical masters, and of pieces of the bravura school in fashion at the time.

In the course of the year 1843 Cossel added to the many proofs he had already given of his affection for his pupil, an admirable instance of generosity and sacrifice of personal considerations. It became evident to him that, notwithstanding—or perhaps in consequence of—the rapid progress made by Hannes, influence was being brought to bear on Jakob to induce him to transfer the boy to the care of some other teacher, and he at once determined that in spite of the keen pangs of disappointment any change would cause him, his darling should, if possible, be placed under Marxsen. Various causes may have led him to this resolution— anxiety to protect the boy from the chance of being thrown too early on the world as a regular bread-winner, to the detriment of the quiet course of his development; unselfish desire that he should grow up with the prestige of association with a man of established musical authority; above all, a profound sense of his own responsibility in regard to the genius of which he found himself guardian, and of the duty incumbent on him to submit its possibilities to the direction of the widest experience and best skill attainable.

La Mara* has related, on Marxsen's authority, the steps taken for the fulfilment of the plan, and their immediate issue. Cossel brought the ten-year-old Johannes to Altona, with the request that his master would examine the boy, and, if satisfied of his possession of the necessary gifts, undertake his further musical instruction. Marxsen, however, did not prove ready to accept this charge. After hearing Johannes play "very capitally" some studies from Cramer's first book, he pronounced him in the best hands, saying nothing could be more desirable for the present than that he should remain, as heretofore, under Cossel's guidance.

The friends of the family, however, continued to press Jakob, pointing out that Cossel had been too retiring in his own case, prophesying that the history of his career would be repeated in that of Johannes if some change were not made, and insisting that the teacher was too cautious and pedantic in his methods with the boy, who now required to be brought forward. The upshot of these things was that, a few months after the interview with Marxsen, a private subscription concert was arranged "for the benefit of the further musical education" of Johannes, which took place in the assembly-room of the Zum Alten Raben, a

---

* "Musikalische Studien Köpfe," vol. iii.

first-class refreshment-house, long since pulled down, that stood in its own pleasure-garden near the Dammthor. The programme included a Mozart quartet for pianoforte and strings, Beethoven's quintet for pianoforte and wind, and some pianoforte solos, amongst them a bravura piece by Herz, the execution of which, by the youthful concert-giver, seems to have caused immense sensation in the circle of his admiring friends. Hannes, who was the only pianist of the occasion, was assisted in the quintet by Jakob and three of his friends, and in the quartet by Birgfeld and Christian Otterer, two well-known musicians of Hamburg, and Louis Goltermann of the same city, afterwards professor at Prague (not to be confounded with the 'cellist-composer, C. E. Goltermann, native of Hanover). The concert was a great success both from an artistic and a financial point of view, and as its result Jakob himself visited Marxsen to prefer, in his own name and that of Cossel, a second request that the distinguished musician would accept Johannes as a pupil. This time Marxsen consented, saying he would receive him once a week provided that the lessons from Cossel were continued without interruption side by side with his own. The mandate was carried into effect, and the arrangement worked smoothly for a time without let or hindrance; but the successful concert had brought danger as well as advantage in its train. An impresario, who had obtained admission on the occasion to the "Old Raven," conceived the idea of taking Johannes on a tour and exhibiting him as a prodigy, and presently made proposals to this effect to Jakob, who, not unnaturally, was transported to the seventh heaven by the dazzling prospects which the wily stranger presented to his imagination. The first step to be taken, for which he prepared, probably, with some perturbation of mind, was to break the news to Cossel.

"Well, Cossel," he said, finding the young musician at home, "we are going to make a pile of money."

"What?" shouted Cossel.

"We are going to make a pile of money. A man has been who wants to travel with the boy."

Poor Cossel! all his worst fears seemed about to be realised; his heart leapt to his mouth.

"Then you are a word-breaker!" he thundered.

It was now Jakob's turn to look aghast, for Cossel, as described by all who knew him personally, was no stickler for ceremony, and could show his wrath right royally when he felt he had righteous cause for indignation. "You are a word-breaker!" he cried, and adopting a sudden idea, went on: "You said to me, 'You shall keep the boy till he knows as much as you do.' He can only learn that from Marxsen!"

A heated argument followed, which ended in a compromise. The affair was to be allowed to stand over for a time, and, in fact, several succeeding months passed as quietly as heretofore. But the impresario renewed his proposal, and the struggle recommenced. Cossel perceived the only means of securing a permanent victory for the benefit of Hannes, and he determined to use it, cost him what it might. It lay in his own complete self-renunciation. He went again to Altona, and besought Marxsen to take entire charge of the boy's musical career, only to be once more refused. Marxsen did not yet feel convinced that the great progress made by Johannes during the past year had been due to other qualities than those of assiduous industry and eager wish to learn. Cossel, however, was not to be beaten. He returned to the attack, actually declaring to his bewildered master that the boy made such rapid strides he felt he could teach him nothing more. The kind Marxsen at length gave way, and consented to take the musical education of Johannes into his own hands henceforth, and to teach him without remuneration, saying he did so the more willingly since the parents were not able to pay for the training they wished to secure for their child, and because he had become fond of the little pupil for his own sake.

"How could you let yourself be put off from such business?" said Aunt Detmering after the impresario had been finally dismissed. She had been partner with Johanna in the little shop of the "sisters Nissen," and had married into somewhat better circumstances than Jakob's wife. "I can't interfere in it," answered Johanna simply, for her boy's good was more precious to her than silver and gold, in spite of her hard, struggling existence. "Min soote Hannes!" she would say, throwing her arms round him, when he came up sometimes to give her a kiss.

Thus was the rich, budding faculty of Johannes guided to the safe shelter of Marxsen's fostering care, and it is not too much to say that Cossel, by his noble action, secured the future of the genius the significance of which he was the first to recognise. It would be idle to speculate about the unrealities of a non-existent might-have-been, and to contemplate a fancied picture of Brahms' career based upon circumstances and events other than those actual to his childhood. It is, however, certain that no mere natural musical endowment, however splendid, can attain to its perfect growth without having been put in the right way, and those who have entered into the heritage of Brahms' songs and symphonies, his choral works and chamber music, may well cherish Cossel's name in grateful remembrance. Although he will not again occupy a prominent place in our account of Brahms' life, his private relations with his pupil did not cease. His piano and his sympathy were still at the service of Hannes, who was grateful for one and the other, and who, remembering his early teacher and friend to the end of his life with admiring affection, strove, as opportunity served in later years, to obtain for him the more widely-known professional position to which his qualities so justly entitled him. Cossel died in 1865 at the age of fifty-two.

CHAPTER II.

1845-1848.

Edward Marxsen—Johannes' first instruction in theory—Herr Adolph Giesemann—Winsen-an-der-Luhe—Lischen—Choral society of school-teachers—"ABC" Part-song by Johannes—The Amtsvogt Blume—First public appearance—First visit to the opera.

EDWARD MARXSEN was born on July 23, 1806, at Nienstädten, a village close to Altona, where his father combined the callings of schoolmaster and organist. His musical talent showed itself in early childhood, and was cultivated by his father to such good purpose that, whilst still a lad, he became competent to take the organist's duty from time to time when a substitute was needed. He was not, however, destined for the musical profession, and was on the verge of manhood when he was at length allowed to follow his unconquerable desire to apply himself with all his energies to the serious study of art. At eighteen he became the pupil of Johann Heinrich Clasing, a musician well qualified to bring up his students in the traditions of the classical school in which he had himself been trained.* His warm interest was soon aroused by the enthusiasm and

---

* Clasing was a pupil of C. F. G. Schwenke, who succeeded C. P. Emanuel Bach as cantor and music-director of St. Catharine's Church, Hamburg. On the death of Emanuel Bach in 1788, a portion of his library came into Schwenke's possession, including the score, in Sebastian Bach's own handwriting, of the great B minor Mass.

unremitting application of his new pupil. Marxsen allowed nothing to interfere with the regularity of his lessons, and walked the two miles separating Nienstädten from Hamburg and back again, on dark winter evenings, by the light of his hand-lantern, no matter how stormy the weather. He continued to live at home, studying, teaching, and helping more and more frequently with the organ, till he reached the age of twenty-four, when his father's death left him free from ties. He soon resolved to go to Vienna, with the especial purpose of perfecting his theoretical knowledge under Ignaz von Seyfried, a prolific composer now chiefly remembered as editor of the theoretical works of his master, the renowned Albrechtsberger. Seyfried received the newcomer cordially, and, probably finding Marxsen's musicianship to be but little inferior to his own, treated him, during his lengthened sojourn at Vienna, more as a friend than a pupil. He did not give him formal instruction, but admitted him to frequent musical intercourse, which was chiefly devoted to the discussion of artistic questions and to the free interchange of opinion, and which brought to the younger musician, amongst other benefits, the special gain of an exceptional insight into the principles underlying Beethoven's development of form. Seyfried's society was interesting and stimulating. He had had pianoforte lessons, as a child, from Mozart, and had been on terms of personal acquaintance with Haydn and with Beethoven, who was his hero. He was of a kind disposition, moreover, and the many opportunities he was able to offer for forming friendships, for hearing music, and for living in musical society, were placed unreservedly at the disposal of his protégé. Marxsen at the same time pursued his study of the pianoforte under Carl Maria von Bocklet, a pianist and musician of eminence, and a very successful teacher, who had enjoyed the favour of Beethoven and been the close intimate of Schubert. Bocklet was one of the earliest to appreciate the genius of the younger master, and, with his colleagues Schuppanzigh and Linke, gave the first performances, early in 1828, of Schubert's two pianoforte trios, written a few months previously.

Marxsen returned to Altona, after an absence of between two and three years, with the matured confidence of the travelled musician who has associated with the authorities of his art, his previous enthusiasm for the works of the great Vienna masters and for the then known instrumental works of the mighty Sebastian Bach fanned into ardent worship. That his mind was sufficiently powerful to rise entirely above the musical artificiality and bad taste of his time cannot be said. To us, who belong to a generation that has been educated on the purist principles first made widely acceptable by Mendelssohn's influence and since popularised by the genius of a few famous executants, with Clara Schumann, Rubinstein, and Joachim at their head, it is difficult to realise the revolution that has taken place in the general condition of musical art since the days when Marxsen, three years Mendelssohn's senior, was young. Many things were then accepted and admired in Vienna, in Berlin, in Leipzig, in London, which would now be regarded as impossible atrocities. Marxsen was capable of setting the Kreutzer Sonata for full orchestra, but this is hardly so surprising as that the Leipzig authorities should have produced the arrangement at one of the Gewandhaus concerts, or that Schumann should have mentioned it indulgently, on whatever grounds, in the *Neue Zeitschrift für Musik*.

Marxsen came for the first time before the public of Hamburg on November 19, 1833, at the age of twenty-seven, in a concert of his own compositions. Such a programme was a novelty in the northern city, and excited attention. The occasion was successful, and established the reputation of the concert-giver as a sound and earnestly striving musician, and from this time his position as a teacher and theorist continuously rose. He was a man of catholic tastes and liberal culture, and his influence over his pupils was not merely that of the instructor of a given subject, but was touched with the power of the philosopher who has a wide outlook on life. The central aims of his theoretical teaching were to guide his pupils to a mastery of the principles illustrated in the works of the great composers, and to encourage each student to develop his own creative individuality on the firm basis thus afforded. He produced a very large number of works, which include examples of the most complex as well as of the simpler forms of composition, and many of them were brought to a hearing. That few show the attempt to appeal to a higher tribunal than the musical taste of the day may, perhaps, be a sign that Marxsen was conscious of not being endowed with original creative power, and did not try to go beyond his natural limitations. He had a genial, encouraging manner which invited his pupils' confidence, and his lively interest in all questions concerning literature, philosophy and art, gave constant impulse to the minds of the really gifted amongst them, which was not the least of the benefits they derived from association with him.

We shall not be far wrong if we fix the age of Johannes, at the time he became entirely Marxsen's pupil, as about twelve; and from this date his time, always well employed, must have been very fully occupied. He had to go to Altona for his pianoforte lessons (the question of his learning composition had not yet arisen), to practise at Cossel's or at the business house of some pianoforte firm—for there were too many interruptions at home—and to go regularly to school. Not to the one on the Dammthorwall mentioned above. He now attended F. C. Hoffmann's school in ABC-strasse, an establishment several grades higher than that of which he had formerly been a pupil, and one of good repute in its degree. Hoffmann was a conscientious as well as a humane man, and won the liking and respect of his scholars. He gave them sound elementary instruction, and even had them taught French and English. Brahms retained some knowledge of both languages, as the present writer can testify from her personal acquaintance with him, begun when he had entered middle age. He could read English to some extent, though he could not speak it, and was able to help himself out, when necessary, with a phrase or two of French, though his accent was hopeless. He preserved a pleasant remembrance of Hoffmann in after-life, recommended his school on one or two suitable occasions, and sent him a present on the celebration of his jubilee in the middle of the seventies.

Marxsen's interest and pleasure in Johannes' progress increased every week as he became more convinced of his exceptional capacity. "One day I gave him a composition of Weber's," he says,* "going carefully through it with him. At the following lesson he played it to me so blamelessly and so exactly as I wished that I praised him. 'I have also practised it in another way,' he said, and played me the right-hand part with the left hand." (No doubt Weber's *moto perpetuum*, published by Brahms, without opus number, as a left-hand study.)

Part of Marxsen's discipline was to accustom Johannes to transpose long pieces at sight, a practice he had probably learnt from Seyfried, who relates as a *tour de force* of Albrechtsberger that on some public occasion, when he had to play on a low-pitched organ, he transposed an entire Mass from G to G sharp at sight, and without error. Brahms, it may be parenthetically remarked, continued to find diversion in this pastime, and would play fugues of Bach and other works for his own edification in various transposed keys when at the height of his mastership.

The boy had, almost from infancy, shown signs of the tendency to creative activity. Widmann† speaks of a conversation held with Brahms within the last decade of his life, during which the master, recalling early memories, described the bliss experienced by him as a very young child on making the discovery, unaided, that a melody could

---

* La Mara, "Studien Köpfe."
† "Brahms in Erinnerung."

be represented on paper by placing large round dots in higher or lower positions on lines. "I made a system for myself before I knew of the existence of such a thing." When a few years older, he was fond of writing the separate parts of concerted works one under the other—of copying them into score, in fact. Nor was he to be kept from trying his hand at original composition. Louise Japha, an eminent pianist of Hamburg, whose more intimate acquaintance the reader will make later on, speaks of having heard him play a sonata of his own when he was about eleven, at Schroeder's pianoforte house, where she one day found him practising. Cossel, responsible for his advance in playing, is said to have been anxious at his spending too much of his time in these childish attempts; but the instinct was unconquerable, and Marxsen no doubt discovered this when he had Johannes constantly with him. After a time he began to teach him theory. Referring to the commencement of the new study, he writes to La Mara:

"I was captivated by his keen and penetrating intellect, and though his first attempts produced nothing of consequence, I perceived in them a mind in which, as I was convinced, an exceptional and deeply original talent lay dormant. I therefore spared myself neither pains nor trouble to awaken and cultivate it, in order to prepare a future priest of art, who should proclaim in a new idiom through his works, its high, true, and lasting principles."

At what age precisely Johannes began to earn regular money by playing in the dancing-rooms and Lokals of Hamburg cannot now be ascertained. It is possible that he occasionally performed on the violin from early childhood, in cases of emergency, as substitute for his father or one of his father's colleagues, though the conjecture is not borne out by reliable record. There is no doubt, however, that loosely repeated anecdotes have given rise to considerable false impression on the point. The notion at one time prevalent, that Jakob made systematic use of his boy from a tender age, employing his gifts for the family benefit, was warmly repudiated by those who had the best means of knowing the circumstances. "With the best will," declared Christian Otterer, who, about twelve years Johannes' senior, retained until at the age of eighty, a bright and unclouded remembrance of old days, "I cannot recollect that Johannes played, as a young child, in Lokals. I was daily with his father at the time, and must have known if it had been the case. Jakob was a quiet and respectable man, and kept Hannes closely to his studies, and as much as possible withdrawn from notice."

"It cannot be true," said Mrs. Cossel repeatedly, referring to such tales; "my husband never mentioned such a thing to me when speaking of Johannes' childhood; and even if it had been proposed, I am sure he would never have allowed it." Two authentic sources of information, however, establish the fact that from the age of about thirteen the boy regularly fulfilled engagements of the kind. The earnings derived from them were eagerly contributed to the general family fund.

A glimpse of him at this period is furnished by Christian Miller,* then a young musical student, who has related that he used to play for a small payment on Sunday afternoons during the summer of 1846, at a restaurant in Bergedorf, near Hamburg. Miller heard him there, and, fascinated by his performance, begged to be allowed to play duets with him. After this the two lads met frequently until Miller left Hamburg to become a pupil of the Leipzig Conservatoire. The companionship would seem to have been tolerated rather than actively desired by Johannes, who rarely spoke when out walking with Miller, but was accustomed to march along, hat in hand, humming!

There was a band of six members which had, during the late eighteen-thirties, delighted the fashionable loungers of the Jungfernstieg, patrons of the Alster Pavilion. Its activity had been continuous up to the year 1842, when the

---

* Steiner's "Johannes Brahms." Neujahr'sblatt der Allg. Musikgesellschaft in Zürich, 1898.

disastrous fire which broke out in Hamburg during the night of May 4-5, and was not extinguished till the morning of the 8th, destroying the churches of St. Nicholas and St. Peter, St. Gertrude's Chapel, the Guildhall, the old Exchange, the Bank, and over 1,200 dwelling-houses and warehouses, had interrupted the pleasant labours of the musicians. The Alster Pavilion had miraculously been left untouched by the flames, whilst the Alster Halle, a similar establishment close by, had been razed to the ground; and the demolition of the row of shops and houses on the Jungfernstieg had changed the agreeable promenade into a scene of ruin. Little could be thought of in the city for a time save how to meet and repair the ravages inflicted by the calamity, which had stricken the grave citizens of Hamburg with dismay, and made an impression of mixed bewilderment and awe upon the sensitive soul of our little Hannes that was never completely effaced. Gradually, however, public edifices and private houses were rebuilt, Hamburg was restored and beautified, and long before the year 1847, at which our story has arrived, the little orchestra had again become used to assemble, though with a somewhat changed personnel, in the familiar room of the Pavilion, to discourse in lively strains before the ever-shifting guests of the establishment. Jakob retained his position as bass player, and, from his long association with the house, had come to be regarded as an important support to its artistic attractions.

Amongst the most faithful patrons of the Pavilion concerts of this period was a certain Herr Adolph Giesemann, owner of a paper-mill and a small farm in the not very distant country townlet of Winsen-an-der-Luhe. He was in the habit of paying frequent business visits to Hamburg, and, being very fond of music, a performer on the guitar, and the possessor of a good voice, liked nothing better than to spend a leisure hour on the Jungfernstieg listening to a movement of Haydn or Mozart. A familiar acquaintance had grown up between him and Brahms. Giesemann willingly listened to Jakob's eager talk about the achievements of Johannes and the promise of his younger brother Fritz. He had a little daughter of his own at home in Winsen, and hoped she might some day be able to take her part in the private musical doings there—at any rate, learn to play the piano well enough to accompany his guitar. One evening in spring Jakob approached him with a request. His Hannes had found constant employment during the past winter in playing the piano until well into the night in the dancing-rooms of various Hamburg Lokals, and the something under two shillings earned by each engagement had amounted to a valuable addition to the scanty family means. But the late hours had told sadly upon his health. Now the work had ceased for a time, and the little toiler could be spared from home. Would Giesemann give him a few weeks' holiday at Winsen? The boy's musical services would be at his command in return. He could accompany him, play to him, and give pianoforte lessons to the little Lischen, a year younger than himself.

Giesemann's kind heart was instantly touched. He had no need to think twice about his own reply, and could answer for that of his wife. Johannes was to be made ready to accompany him back to Winsen after his next visit to Hamburg, which would take place very soon.

And so, in the bright springing month of May, when the buds were bursting and the birds singing, and the gray skies of Hamburg beginning to show a little blue, our dear Hannes took his departure from his big, busy native city to taste for the first time the delights of a free country life, with a kind little sister as companion. He never for a moment felt like a visitor on his arrival, but forgot his constitutional shyness, becoming a child of the house to be petted and brought back to health by fresh air and good food and Frau Giesemann's motherly care. Lischen was at school all the morning, but this was quite a good thing. Hannes had his tasks to attend to also, and could not afford to lose time, for Jakob had made such arrangements as were at his limited command to ensure that his boy's general progress should not suffer by the holiday.

Fresh air, however, was all-important, so Johannes had come provided with a small dumb keyboard for the mechanical exercise of his fingers, and every day after breakfast, after he had got through such practice as had to be done in the house, Frau Giesemann used to turn him into the fields with a bag slung over his shoulder, containing his books and lunch, the clavier under his arm, the notebook, without which he never stirred anywhere, peeping from his pocket, and orders not to show himself again till dinnertime. He had already been enjoying himself out of doors long before this hour. He used to rise at four o'clock, and begin his day by bathing in the river. Joined not long afterwards by Lischen, the two would spend a couple of delightful hours rambling about, discovering birds' nests and picking flowers.

Johannes was quite a simple child in spite of his fourteen years and hard experience, and revelled in the happy days passed amidst sunshine, wild blossoms, and fragrant air. He was very pale and thin, and had little strength on his arrival, but soon gained flesh and colour, to which the glass of fresh milk put by for him every day no doubt contributed. The animals about the place—the cows and pigs, the big dog, the doe—gave him great delight, and he was charmed when the crane spread its wings and flew high overhead as he and Lischen approached it, clapping their hands. He liked to join in the games with which the children of Winsen amused themselves by the river-side on cool summer evenings, but could not be persuaded to take part in the boys' rough sport, and would only play with the girls. The lads, of course, despised him for this, telling him he was no better than a girl himself; but he did not seem to mind, and continued quietly to follow his inclination. One evening, however, soon after his arrival, before he had picked up much strength, as he was returning with several children from wading in the river, Lischen well on in front, one or two rough boys set on him, emptied his pockets, and robbed him of all his possessions, even of the precious pocket-book. He could not help crying at this, but Lischen, seeing him standing on the bank rubbing his knuckles into his eyes, soon found out what was the matter, and, dashing back into the water, forced the molesters to restore everything to her.

To the pocket-book Johannes confided his inspirations on every subject. Sometimes it was a melody, sometimes a line or two of verse, that occurred to him. Then, whether he were walking, or climbing trees, or practising, or doing his lessons, out came the book that the idea might be fixed on the spot.

It was not long before his musical talents awakened the admiration of the neighbourhood. There was a pleasantly situated Lokal at Hoopte, a village about two miles from Winsen, which contained a large apartment suitable for dancing and music. This and one or two adjoining rooms were annually taken by the Giesemann circle for the Sunday afternoons of the summer season, and after morning church and mid-day dinner as many of the subscribers as felt inclined would meet there to pass a few sociable hours. Johannes soon became the central figure of these occasions. It was found that he could play, not only the most inspiriting music for the dancers, but a variety of solos also, including some lovely waltzes to which it was delightful to listen quietly; and on being asked, one day, to conduct the men's choral society that was to contribute to the afternoon's programme, he showed himself so astonishingly competent for the rôle he consented to assume, and inspired such confidence and sympathy, as he stood before his forces in short jacket and large white turn-down collar, his fair girlish face, with its regular features and shock of long, light hair, adding to the impression made by his childlike manner, that he was unanimously elected conductor of the society for so long as he should remain at Winsen; a period which was, as now decided, to be prolonged until he should be recalled to the recommencement of his autumn duties.

The men's choral society of Winsen consisted of about twelve members, the majority of whom were school-teachers of the neighbouring villages. The teachers Backhaus of Winsen, Albers of Handorf, Schröder of Hoopte, belonged to it; other prominent members were the goldsmith Meyer and the big master-baker Rieckmann, who had a splendid bass voice. The practices were held on Saturdays from six to eight o'clock, generally in Rector Köhler's schoolroom, because it contained a piano, but when this was not available, in the billiard-room of the Deutsches Haus, Winsen's best Lokal. The singers used to stand round the billiard-table, and Johannes would take his place at the top. Lischen was privileged to attend all meetings of the society during the period that her friend officiated as its conductor.

The boy found a most valuable ally in teacher Schröder, who had great talent and love for music, had worked hard at thorough-bass and counterpoint, and had been a composer since his fourteenth year. When Johannes came upon a knotty point in his theoretical studies that required discussion, he would walk over to Hoopte and consult Schröder, who was always ready with sympathy and counsel. He had not returned late one evening from an expedition of the kind, and Giesemann, becoming uneasy, was about to start in search of his young guest, when up drove the carriage-superintendent from Pattenzen, a few miles away. "Here is your Johannes," he cried as the boy jumped from the gig; "he went out by the wrong gate this morning and missed his way. I found him asleep by the side of a ditch some distance out on the Lüneburger Heath, the clavier by his side and the notebook fallen from his pocket; lucky they had not all rolled in together!"

The theoretical exercises and the little compositions for voices on which Marxsen encouraged his pupil to try his hand were regularly carried to Altona, for, with Marxsen's concurrence and the advice of the schoolmaster Hoffmann, it had been arranged that Johannes should go every week by steamboat to Hamburg and remain there two nights, which allowed him a clear day for his music-lessons and for general private instruction. Now and then Lischen was invited to accompany him, and to share sister Elise's tiny chamber in the Brahms' little dwelling on the Dammthorwall. The journeys were easily managed, for "Uncle" Adolph Giesemann's brother, manager of the restaurant at the Winsen railway-station, was also contractor for the refreshment department of the steamboat service to and from Hamburg, and nothing could be simpler than for one or both of the children to go and return as his friends. Frau Giesemann used to see that they started with a liberal supply of "belegtes Brödchen," a crusty roll cut through, buttered, and put together again, with slices of cold meat, sausage, cheese, or what not, between the two halves. Their friend the restaurateur provided each of them, at the proper time, with a large mug of thin coffee, and Lischen and Hannes, sitting together in the bottom of the boat, thoroughly enjoyed these picnic dinners.

Johannes always began the day after his arrival at Hamburg by exercising his fingers on the upright piano that stood against the parlour wall, on the music-desk of which a book invariably stood open, into which he poked his head —for he was very near-sighted—reading as he worked. Lischen saw little of him afterwards, for his time was occupied by his various lessons, but she did not mind this. She soon became very fond of his dear, kind old mother, and liked to watch her at her duties, sometimes able to help her by fetching water from the pump at the bottom of the steps outside the house, a task which Johanna's lameness prevented her from performing herself. Lischen much admired the portrait of Frau Brahms that hung above the piano, and thought, as she looked at the youthful figure arrayed in a pink dress made Empire fashion, with flowing skirt, short waist, and low neck, the hair dressed with little curls in front and a high comb behind, that Hannes' mother must have been very pretty in her youth. The parlour was rather bare, containing little beyond the piano, table, chairs, a few shelves filled with books, and one or two small prints; but Lischen did not think this mattered, as everything was so neat and clean. She felt sorry, however, that it was so dark, and that its one small window had no other prospect than a close, dreary courtyard—for Johanna still had her little shop in front—and proposed to Hannes that they should bring some scarlet-runners from Winsen, which could be planted in the courtyard and trained up sticks. There would soon be something bright in front of the parlour window. Johannes greatly approved of the plan, which worked well up to the planting of the beans and the placing of some immensely high sticks in readiness for the training. After this stage it disappointed expectations, as the plants failed to do their part and firmly abstained from growing.

It would have been impossible for Johannes to pass with entire enjoyment through the months of his visit to Winsen if he had been without the means of gratifying a taste hardly less strong in him than his passion for music. From the very early age at which he was first able to read, he had been devoted to books, and, whilst showing the child's natural preference for the romantic and wonderful, had displayed strange discrimination in the choice of his favourite tales. He had always contrived by some means or other to provide himself with reading material, preferring books for his little birthday and Christmas gifts, buying them from time to time from pedlars' wheelbarrows with his collection of halfpennies, or begging the loan of a volume from a friend. Brahms' exceptional knowledge of the Bible grew from the time when, as a young child, he was accustomed to eat his dinner with the book lying open beside his plate, absorbed in the Old Testament stories which were then his prime favourites, misty speculations forming in his brain which laid the foundation of his future attitude towards many of life's problems. He had not been long at Winsen before he had exhausted the mental nourishment afforded by Uncle Giesemann's collection of volumes. Fortunately, another resource was at hand. There was a lending library in the neighbourhood belonging to a certain Frau Löwenherz, a Jewess, who had a son called Aaron. With Aaron the two children made friends, and of him, in the absence of sufficient funds to pay the full price of a constant supply of literature, they sought counsel. He proved an able adviser, and, whilst promising to obtain for them access to the coveted books, showed that he was not wanting in the capacity of turning opportunity to profit on his own account. He promised that he would, on his private responsibility, bring one volume at a time for the perusal of Hannes and Lischen, to be put back when done with and replaced by another; the price demanded and agreed to for this secret service being one groschen (about a penny) for each supply.

By this expedient Hannes and Lischen—the latter having probably been the active partner in striking the bargain, for Johannes had few spare pennies—found themselves provided with as many books as they could desire. Their best time for reading was when they sat together by the riverbank, or fished in the pond during the afternoon. Forgetting their rods, they used to pore silently over the open book supported between them, devouring one tale after another of knights and tournaments, outlaws and bandits. Aaron received very particular instruction as to the kind of selections he was to make, and took pains to suit the taste of his patrons. He appeared one afternoon with a volume containing the history of "The Beautiful Magelone and the Knight Peter with the Silver Keys." That was a red-letter day in the history of the young subscribers to the lending library which neither Hannes nor Lischen ever forgot. The romance made an indelible impression on both of them. As for bandits, what better could Johannes desire than a work bearing the stimulating title of "The Robbers," which Aaron offered another day, insisting with justifiable pride on the success of his researches? The book was written by one Schiller, and proved so satisfactory that Hannes begged Aaron to be on the look-out for other volumes bearing this name on the title-page.

It might be expected that the young conductor of the Winsen Choral Society and the pupil of the distinguished musician of Altona would turn his studies to account by writing something for the use of his choir, and so it was. Johannes composed an "ABC" four-part song for his school-teachers, consisting of thirty-two bars in two-four time, preceded by three bars of introduction and followed by a kind of signature. The introduction and first three of the four eight-bar phrases had for their text the letters of the alphabet arranged, first in order, and then in syllables of two letters as in a first spelling lesson; the fourth phrase was set to a few words introduced at random. The composition closed with the words "Winsen, eighteen hundred seven and forty," sung in full chorus, *lento* and *fortissimo*, on the reiterated tonic chord. The little composition, tuneful and spirited, showing a feeling for independent part-writing, and conceived in a vein of boyish fun that was fully appreciated by the teachers, was soon succeeded by a second, "The Postilion's Morning Song," composed to the well-known words "Vivat! und in's Horn ich stosse." The young musician was also requested by a deputation from the school-children of Winsen to assist them in the performance of a serenade with which they were desirous of greeting their Rector Köhler on his birthday. He accordingly looked out one suitable to the occasion, arranged it in two parts, practised the boys and girls until they were perfect with it, and conducted the performance outside the Rector's house on the eve of the birthday celebration. He was very strict and serious when engaged in these professional duties, beat time with great verve, and insisted on careful observance of the *pianos* and *fortes*, as well as on the proper graduation of the *rallentandos*. The singing of the Ständchen was declared brilliantly successful by the quite considerable audience that assembled near the Rector's house to enjoy it.

Rumours of the increased musical acitivity of Winsen could not fail to reach the ears of the Amtsvogt, Herr Blume, an official of good social standing residing there, whose duties, as administrator of some of the rural districts of northern Hanover, brought him into touch with the life of such parts of the country as were included in his circuit. Herr Blume was not far short of seventy when Johannes paid his first visit to the Giesemanns, but his interest in music and love for Beethoven's art were as strong as ever, and Johannes, before leaving Winsen, was invited to his house, and pressed to use his piano for practice. The boy delighted the Amtsvogt by playing with him some four-hand pianoforte arrangements of Beethoven's works, and won the heart of Frau Blume, in spite of his shy, awkward manner, by his simple, childlike nature. If, as was hoped, he should be able to repeat his visit to Uncle Giesemann next year, he was to come often to the Blumes' house, and use the piano as long as he liked. Great regret was felt throughout the circle of Winsen friends at the news of the young musician's impending departure, but the arrival of autumn brought with it the necessity for the resumption of duties in Hamburg, and nothing remained save to hope for a renewal of the pleasures his long visit had brought to many beside himself.

Johannes returned to his home in such a satisfactory condition of health and spirits that he was able, with Marxsen's approval, to take a decided step forward in his career. He played in the Apollo Concert-room on November 20, at a benefit concert given by Birgfeld, already known to our readers as the violinist of the subscription concert at the "Old Raven," performing Thalberg's Fantasia on airs from "Norma." Marxsen's affection for his pupil and appreciation of his gifts are clearly to be read in the summary of concerts which appeared a week later in the *Freischütz*, a widely-read Hamburg paper to which he was one of the chief contributors:

"Birgfeld's concert is said to have been interesting and

enjoyable as regards both the vocal and instrumental portions of the programme. A very special impression was made by the performance of one of Thalberg's fantasias by a little virtuoso called J. Brahms, who not only showed great facility, precision, clearness, power, and certainty, but occasioned general surprise and obtained unanimous applause by the intelligence of his interpretation."

On the 27th of the same month, Johannes appeared in the small room of Tonhalle at a concert of the pianist, Frau Meyer-David, whom he assisted in the performance of a duet for two pianofortes, also by Thalberg, whose fame was at this time at its height. Marxsen's influence is again apparent in the special mention of Johannes in the *Freischütz* review, though it is evident, from the mis-spelling of the name, that he was not the writer of the notice:

"The duet performed by the concert-giver and the young pianist Bruns, who lately appeared for the first time in public with such marked success, gave satisfaction, and was played with laudable unity and facility."

With the exception of a mere record of the same performance in the *Hamburger Nachrichten*, no further mention of Johannes is to be found in the newspapers of the winter 1847-48. It was passed by the young musician in much the same routine of severe study by day and fatiguing labour by night as the previous one had witnessed. He was, however, spared in the spring for another visit to the Giesemanns' house, to which he returned as to a second home. The members of the choral society were delighted to welcome their conductor, who, in the course of the season, added to their répertoire by arranging two folk-songs for use at the practices. These must be accepted as the earliest recorded illustrations of the partiality for national songs and melodies which remained one of the great composer's most characteristic traits, and which culminated, less than three years before his death, in the publication, in seven books, of his well-known collection of German Volkslieder.

Johannes was frequently at the Blumes' this year, and

often played duets with the Amtsvogt. Lischen's pianoforte lessons were not resumed, as they had not been attended by any great result. It was difficult to confine her to the house to practise on bright summer afternoons, when she longed to be enjoying herself out of doors. She never entirely forgot what Johannes had taught her on his first visit, however, and continued to be very fond of music. It was hoped that by and by it might be possible to have her voice thoroughly trained. Johannes felt sure it would develop into a fine one.

Meanwhile she succeeded in procuring for her companion the greatest pleasure he had as yet experienced. He wanted very much to hear an opera, and Lischen thought she would like it, too, so one day, when they were going together to Hamburg, she persuaded her father to stand treat for two places in the gallery. It was to be a great night. Formes, then of Vienna, had been secured for a few weeks by the managers of the Stadt Theater (the opera-house of Hamburg), and was making a great sensation. Lischen and Hannes were to hear him in "The Marriage of Figaro," the title-rôle of which was one of his great parts. They started early from the house on the Dammthorwall, supplied by Frau Brahms with some buttered rolls, and waited for two hours in the street before the door opened, which was part of the pleasure. They got capital places, and enjoyed sitting in the gallery before the performance, looking at the house and seeing people come in. But when the music began Johannes was almost beside himself with excitement, and Lischen has never to this day forgotten his joy. "Lischen, Lischen, listen to the music! there never was anything like it!" Uncle Adolph was made so happy when he heard all about the evening and perceived the delight he had given, that he said the visit to the opera must be repeated, and accordingly the pair of friends went a little later on, to hear Kreutzer's "Das Nachtlager von Granada," which both of them enjoyed very, very much.

Johannes was not able to stay so long at Winsen this

year as last, and still greater sadness was felt as the day drew near on which his visit would terminate, as it was the last of the kind he would pay. It was his confirmation year. He was past fifteen now, his general school education was finished, and he was to take his position in the world as a musician who had his way to make and would be expected to contribute regularly to the support of his family and the education of his brother Fritz, destined for a pianist and teacher. He copied out the four-part songs, dedicated to the Winsen Choral Society, beautifully, as a parting present to Lischen, putting headings to each in splendid calligraphy, and adding her name with a special inscription. Lischen treasured the manuscripts long after she had become a wife and mother, in memory of a happy episode of her youth.

There was a solemn farewell ceremony at the last meeting of the choral society, which took place at the Deutsches Haus. After the conclusion of the practice, the conductor addressed his singers in a poem written by himself for the occasion, which began with the line: "Lebt wohl, lebt wohl, ihr Freunde schlicht und bieder" (Farewell, farewell, ye friends, upright and simple). An instant's sorrowful silence followed; then there was a tremendous stamping and clapping and shouting, and the big master-baker Rieckmann, calling out, "Here, young one!" hoisted Johannes over his shoulder pickaback, and marched several times round the table, followed by Lischen and the other members of the society, singing a last chorus.

It was a concluding scene of Johannes' childhood, which had been unusually protracted, in spite of its drawbacks; but, as everybody said, he was to come often again to Winsen, and whenever he should be able to take a short relaxation from the serious duties of life awaiting him, he would know where to find a number of friends ready to greet his arrival amongst them with heartiest welcome.

CHAPTER III.

1848-1853.

Johannes' first public concert—Years of struggle—Hamburg Lokals —Louise Japha—Edward Reményi—Sonata in F sharp minor— First concert-tour as Reményi's accompanist—Concerts at Winsen, Celle, Lüneburg, and Hildesheim—Musical parties in 1853 —Leipzig and Weimar—Robert Schumann—Joseph Joachim.

IT was on September 21, 1848, that Johannes made his fresh start in life by giving a concert of his own, thus presenting himself to his circle as a musician who was now to stand on an independent footing. It took place in the familiar room of the "Old Raven," "Herr Honnef's Hall," with the assistance of Marxsen's friends, Madame and Fräulein Cornet, and some instrumentalists of Hamburg. The price of tickets was one mark (about a shilling), and the programme, as printed in the *Hamburger Nachrichten* of the 20th, was as follows:

FIRST PART.

1. Adagio and rondo from Rosenhain's Concerto in A major for Piano, performed by the concert-giver.
2. Duet from Mozart's "Figaro," sung by Mad. and Fräul. Cornet.
3. Variations for Violin, by Artôt, performed by Herr Risch.
4. "Das Schwabenmädchen," Lied, sung by Mad. Cornet.
5. Fantasia on Themes from Rossini's "Tell," for Piano, by Döhler, performed by the concert-giver.

SECOND PART.
6. Introduction and Variations for Clarinet, by Herzog, performed by Herr Glade.
7. Aria from Mozart's "Figaro," sung by Frl. Cornet.
8. Fantasia for Violoncello, composed and performed by Herr d'Arien.
9. *(a)* "Der Tanz" } Lieder, sung by Mad. Cornet.
   (b) "Der Fischer auf dem Meer"
10. *(a)* Fugue by Sebastian Bach.
    (b) Serenade for left hand only, by E. Marxsen.
    (c) Étude by Herz, performed by the concert-giver.

Unattractive as it now seems, this selection of pieces was no doubt made with a view to the taste of the day, and the inclusion of a single Bach fugue was probably a rather daring concession to that of the concert-giver and his teacher. The two vocal numbers from "Figaro" may be accepted as echoes of the boy's delight on the evening of his recent first visit to the opera. No record remains of the result of the concert, but its success may fairly be inferred from the fact that it was followed, in the spring of 1849, by a second, for which the price of the tickets was increased to two marks. This was announced twice in the *Nachrichten* as follows:

"The undersigned will have the honour of giving a musical soirée on April 14 in the concert-room of the Jenisch'schen Haus (Katharine Street, 17), for which he ventures herewith to issue his invitation. Several of the first resident artists have kindly promised their assistance to the programme, which will be published in this journal.

"J. BRAHMS, Pianist."

The programme was appended to the third and last advertisement of April 10:

FIRST PART.

1. Grand Sonata in C major, Op. 53, by Beethoven. (The concert-giver.)
2. Romance from Donizetti's "Liebestrank." (Th. Wachtel.)

3. Schubert's "Ave Maria," performed on the Horn by Herr Börs.
4. "O geh' nicht fort," Lied, by E. Marxsen, sung by Frl. Cornet.
5. Fantasia for Piano on a favourite Waltz, composed and performed by the concert-giver.

SECOND PART.

6. Concerto for Violin, by Fr. Mollenhauer, performed by Herr Ed. Mollenhauer.
7. Songs. Me. Cornet.
8. Fantasia on Themes from "Don Juan," by Thalberg, performed by the concert-giver.
9. Duet, sung by Me. and Frl. Cornet.
10. Variations for Flute, by Fräsch, performed by Herr Koppelhöfer.
11. Air Italien, by C. Meyer, performed by the concert-giver.

The performance of Beethoven's "Waldstein" sonata, Op. 53, was regarded long after the close of the eighteen-forties, as a great technical feat, and, taken together with the execution of the "Don Juan" fantasia, would represent something near the height of the pianistic virtuosity of the time, whilst with the Fantasia on a favourite waltz the concert-giver made his first public entrée as a composer. This work must be identified with the variations on a favourite waltz mentioned by La Mara, as having been played at his concert by the young Brahms, of which one variation took the form of a "very good canon." Marxsen's notice of the concert in the *Freischütz* of April 17 was the only one that appeared:

"In the concert given by J. Brahms, the youthful virtuoso gave most satisfactory proofs of advancement in his artistic career. His performance of Beethoven's sonata showed that he is already able to devote himself successfully to the study of the classics, and redounded in every respect to his honour. The example of his own composition also indicated unusual talent."

Although the report adds that the room was so full as to oblige many listeners to be content with seats in the anteroom, it is probable that the young musician found concert-giving more vexatious and expensive than useful or profitable. Though he appeared from time to time at the benefit-concerts of other artists, and repeated his own fantasia at one given on December 5 by Rudolph Lohfeldt, his third soirée in Hamburg, given under conditions of which he could not at this time have dared to dream, did not take place till after the lapse of another decade. The four or five years immediately succeeding his formal entry into life were, perhaps, the darkest of Brahms' career. Money had to be earned, and the young Bach-Mozart-Beethoven enthusiast earned it by giving wretchedly-paid lessons to pupils who lacked both talent and wish to learn, and by his night drudgery amid the sordid surroundings of the Hamburg dancing-saloons.

It was an amelioration in his life and a step forward in his career, when he was engaged by the publisher, August Cranz, as one of several contributors to a series of popular arrangements of light music, published under the name "G. W. Marks." We have read in Widmann's pages of the spirit in which the great composer, a few years before his death, recalled these passages of his struggling youth:

"He could not, he said, wish that it had been less rough and austere. He had certainly earned his first money by arranging marches and dances for garden orchestras, or orchestral music for the piano, but it gave him pleasure even now, when he came across one of these anonymously circulating pieces, to think that he had devoted faithful labour and all the knowledge at his command, to such hireling's work. He did not even regard as useless experience that he had often had to accompany wretched singers or to play dance music in Lokals, whilst he was longing for the quiet morning hours during which he should be able to write down his own thoughts. 'The prettiest songs came to me as I blacked my boots before daybreak.'"

And if the master could so speak and think of his early trials, must not we, who are, perhaps, the richer through them, treasure the remembrance of the nights of uncongenial toil through which he passed to become, even on the threshold of life, its conqueror and true possessor? The iron entered his soul, however, and the impression derived from his night work remained with him till death. He was accustomed to read steadily through the hours of his slavery. Placing a volume of history, poetry, or romance on the music-desk before him, his thoughts were away in a world of imagination, whilst his fingers were mechanically busy with the tinkling keys. He did not lift his eyes to the scene before him after his first entrance, though there were times when he felt it with shuddering dismay. It is, however, right to repeat that, as we have hinted in a previous chapter, this kind of industry was a more or less recognised means by which struggling musicians of the class to which Jakob Brahms belonged, were enabled to help their needy circumstances, and it would not be difficult to name more than one executant afterwards well known who fulfilled similar engagements in youth. The position of Johannes was not in itself exceptional, though the contemplation of it is now startling from its contrast with his tender nature, his sensitive genius, and the great place which he ultimately won.

An engagement of which Kalbeck speaks, to act as accompanist behind the scenes and on the stage of the Stadt Theater, may have been less irksome to the young musician than his other hack work, and it is possible to believe that the experience drawn from it may have been of some appreciable value to him in after-life, even though his artistic development did not result in dramatic composition. Evidence is not wanting, however, to show that he kept his thoughts steadily fixed upon the higher practical possibilities of his profession, and that, though his position continued very obscure, it did not remain at a standstill. His terms to pupils increased to about a shilling a lesson, and occasionally he was able to get more. Every now and then he obtained a small concert-engagement, or officiated at a private party, and on one occasion he appeared with Otto Goldschmidt, the then leading pianist of Hamburg, who was about four years his senior, in a performance of Thalberg's duet for two pianofortes on airs from "Norma."

Conditions at home remained unfavourable for practice, and Johannes now worked regularly at the establishment of Messrs. Baumgarten and Heinz, where an instrument was always at his service. Here, one day, he met Fräulein Louise Japha, who remembered the circumstance, already recorded in these pages, of having heard him play five or six years previously as a child of eleven. A talk ensued, a sympathetic note was struck, and a comradeship quickly grew up between the two young musicians. Louise, born in 1826, and therefore some seven years the senior of Johannes, was possessed of high musical endowment. At the time of which we write, she was the pupil of Fritz Wahrendorf for pianoforte, and of William Grund for theory and composition. She achieved eminence later on, becoming well known in Germany and a great favourite with the public of Paris. Her competent sympathy was a valuable addition to young Brahms' pleasures in life, in the days when he knew little of congenial artistic companionship. They met constantly to play duets and compare notes as to their compositions, for Louise was a song-writer of ability. Johannes used to discuss with her both his favourite authors and his manuscripts. One day it was a long exercise in double counterpoint that he brought to show her, another day a pianoforte solo. On a third occasion he produced a pianoforte duet in several movements, which he begged her to try with him, and, acknowledging its authorship at the close of the performance, asked her opinion of the work. This proving generally favourable, the composer, going more into detail, took exception to one of his themes, which he feared was rather "ordinary," but when Louise was half inclined to agree with him, he cried angrily: "Why did you not say so yourself? Why was I obliged to ask you?"

He was always composing, and as time went on, was ably guided by Marxsen to the practice of the large musical forms, over which he soon acquired conspicuous mastery, showing extraordinary facility in applying to them the skill he had gradually attained in free contrapuntal writing, whilst allowing to his fancy the stimulus of the classical-romantic literature that appealed with special force to his imagination. "It came into my head after reading so-and-so," he would say. The whole of his small amount of spare cash was devoted to the purchase of second-hand volumes from the stalls to be found in the Jews' quarter of Hamburg, and what he bought he read. Sophocles and Cicero, Dante and Tasso, Klopstock and Lessing, Goethe and Schiller, Eichendorff, Chamisso, Pope, Young, and many other poets, were represented in the library collected by him between the ages of sixteen and twenty-one.* His favourite romances were those of Jean Paul and E. T. A. Hoffmann, whose influence over his mind is easily recognisable in the published compositions of his first period. No other work on which he might be engaged, however, prevented him from the composition of many songs. He threw one off after another. "I generally read a poem through very slowly," he said to Louise, "and then, as a rule, the melody is there."

Fräulein Japha was before her time in conceiving an enthusiasm for Schumann's art, and tried hard to win over Johannes to an appreciation of its beauties, but he was too entirely under the influence of Marxsen, who, in training him as a composer, rightly proceeded on strictly orthodox lines, to become a present convert. He, on his part, made efforts to induce Louise to change her teachers and put herself under his master. She had quite other views, however. Schumann and his wife paid a visit to Hamburg in 1850, appearing several times in public, and Louise resolved that if it could be made possible, she would enter on a fresh course of study of composition and the piano under the two

---
* Cf. Kalbeck, p. 186.

great artists respectively. She only waited for a convenient opportunity to carry out her plan. Johannes approached Schumann in another fashion, by sending a packet of manuscripts to his hotel and begging for his opinion. It is no wonder that the master, who was besieged on all sides during his fortnight's stay, found no time to look at them, and returned the parcel unopened.

It must not be supposed that the young Brahms was always so companionable as we have shown him when in the society of his chosen friends. He had his moods. Christian Miller's early experiences of his persistent taciturnity had not been exceptional. He spent a few evenings at the Japhas' house, but Louise's family, her sister Minna only excepted, by no means took a fancy to her favourite. One evening, when he was about eighteen, a gentleman of the Japha circle, who had been interested in hearing him play the scherzo now known as Op. 4, the earliest written of his published instrumental works, accompanied him on the way home, and made repeated but quite hopeless efforts after sociability. Not one word would Johannes say. Perhaps he felt subsequent secret prickings of conscience, for he made confession to Louise, though not in any apparently repentant spirit. "One is not always inclined to talk," he said; "often one would rather not, and then it is best to be silent. You understand that, don't you?" "No, you were very naughty," she told him, but forgave him nevertheless. She could overlook his occasional whims. She perceived his genius, admired his candid nature, and felt her heart warm to him when he talked to her of the old mother to whom he was devoted, and of Marxsen, whom he revered with all the enthusiastic loyalty of his true heart. Soon after his walk with the Japhas' friend he had a chance opportunity of playing his scherzo to Henry Litolff, who bestowed high praise on the composition.

Meanwhile the friends at Winsen faithfully remembered their young musician. Uncle Adolph and friend Schröder seldom missed going to see him when occasion brought either of them to Hamburg, and Lischen came over to be introduced to Madame Cornet and Marxsen. Johannes persevered in his desire that her voice should be trained for the musical profession, and wished her to obtain a good opinion on the subject. The verdict of the authorities proved, however, unfavourable to the project.

Of the general invitation to visit the Giesemanns Brahms gladly availed himself, staying sometimes for a few days, sometimes in the summer for a week or two, as his occupations allowed. He was never again able to undertake the choral society, but there was always a great deal of music at the Amtsvogt's house when he was at Winsen, as well as at the Giesemanns' and Schröders'. Town-musician Koch was a good violinist, and but too happy to have the chance of playing the duet sonatas of Haydn, Mozart, and Beethoven with such a colleague, and every now and again compositions were looked out in which Uncle Giesemann could take part with his guitar. Pretty Sophie Koch, the younger of the town-musician's two daughters, took great interest in these artistic doings, and it was rumoured, as time went on, that her fondness for music was not untinged by a personal element connected with the Giesemanns' popular guest. If this were so, Johannes himself was probably the last person to become observant of it. He was wholly absorbed in his profession, and several quite independent informants have concurred in describing him to the author as being, at this time of his life, something less than indifferent to the society of ladies, and especially of young ones. For his early playmate, Lischen, his affection continued unchanged, and with her he remained on the old terms of frank and cordial friendship.

It happened as a natural consequence of the political revolution which took place early in the year 1848 in Germany and Austria, that, during the year or two following its speedy termination, there was an influx into Hamburg and its neighbourhood of refugees on their way to America. Conspicuous among them were a number of Hungarians of various sorts and degrees, who found such sympathetic welcome in the rich, free merchant-city that they were in no hurry to leave it. Some of them remained there for many months on one pretext or another, and amongst these was the violinist, Edward Reményi, a German-Hungarian Jew whose real name was Hoffmann.

Reményi, born in 1830, had been during three years of his boyhood a pupil of the Vienna Conservatoire, studying under Joseph Böhm, now remembered as the teacher of Joachim. He had real artistic endowment, and played the works of the classical masters well, if somewhat extravagantly; but something more than talent was displayed in his rendering of the airs and dances of his native country, which he gave with a fire and abandon that excited his hearers to wild enthusiasm. Eccentric and boastful, he knew how to profit to the utmost by his successes in Hamburg, where he created a furore. Johannes, engaged one evening to act as accompanist at the house of a rich merchant, made his personal acquaintance, and Reményi, quickly perceiving the advantage he derived from having such a coadjutor, made overtures of friendship in his swaggering, patronising way, which were not repulsed by the young pianist. Brahms had, in fact, been fascinated by Reményi's spirited rendering of his national Friskas and Czardas; he was willing that the chance acquaintance should be improved into an alliance, and, on his next visit to the Giesemanns' house, was accompanied by his new friend.

The violinist had connections of his own in the neighbourhood. Begas, a Hungarian magnate, had settled down into a large villa at Dehensen, on the Lüneburg Heath, that had been placed at his disposal for as long a time as he should find it possible to elude or cajole the police authorities, and kept open house for his compatriots and their friends. To his circle Brahms was introduced, and much visiting ensued between Dehensen and Winsen, for one or two musicians staying with Begas were pleased to come and make music with Reményi and Johannes, and to partake of the Giesemanns' hospitality. It was a feather in Brahms' cap, in the eyes of many of his friends, that he had been able to capture for Winsen such a celebrity as Reményi, though they were not all quite of one mind. Lischen, for example, did not care for him at all, but much preferred the tall, handsome fiddler Janovitch, with his flashing black eyes and his velvet jacket, who wrote a splendid characteristic waltz expressly that he might dedicate it to her. The jolly party broke up suddenly at last, running off to take speedy ship for America, for they had heard that the police were on their heels. Johannes, who happened to be at Winsen when this crisis occurred, accompanied them as far as Hamburg, where he remained to pursue his ordinary avocations. Meanwhile the Friskas and Czardas continued to revolve in his brain.

Time went on, the Hungarians were no longer vividly regretted, and somewhere about the autumn of 1852, Brahms was left more lonely than ever by the departure of Louise Japha, who found opportunity to carry out her cherished wish to stay at Düsseldorf, where the Schumanns had now been settled for about two years. Her sister Minna was to accompany her, to carry on the cultivation of her own special gift under Professor Sohn, of the Düsseldorf Academy of Art. The thought of losing his friend caused Johannes great sorrow. "Do not go," he entreated; "you are the only person here that takes any interest in me!" His prospects do not seem to have been improving at this time, and his best encouragement must have been derived from his own sense of his artistic progress. This was advancing by enormous strides, the exact measure of which is furnished by the manuscript of the Sonata in F sharp minor at one time in the possession of Hofcapellmeister Albert Dietrich. It bears the signature "Kreisler jun.," a pseudonym adopted by Brahms out of love for the capellmeister Johannes Kreisler, hero of one of Hoffmann's tales, and the date November, 1852.

This work, which, though published later on as Op. 2,

was written earlier than the companion sonata known as Op. 1, is, in many of its fundamental characteristics, immediately prophetic of the future master. In it the mastery of form and skill in contrapuntal writing, the facility in the art of thematic development, the strikingly contrasted imaginative qualities—here subtly poetic, there large and powerful—bring us face to face with the artist nature which united in itself high purpose, resolute will, sure capacity, sensitive romanticism, boundless daring. The fancy, however, has not yet crystallised; the young musician has still to pass out of the stage of mental ferment natural to his age before he will be able to mould his thoughts into the concentrated shape which alone can convince the world. The sonata, not perhaps destined ever to become widely familiar, must always remain a treasure to the sympathetic student of Brahms' art, not only by reason of the beauties in which it abounds, but also because it is absolutely representative of its composer as he was at nineteen. We may read his favourite authors in some of its movements without the need of an interpreter, and we know, from his own communication to Dietrich, that the melody of the second movement was inspired by the words of the German folksong, "Mir ist leide, Das der Winter Beide, Wald und auch die Haide, hat gemachet kahl."

It would be difficult, and is fortunately unnecessary, to trace the exact steps of Reményi's career after his flight from Germany. For the purpose of our narrative the facts suffice that he reappeared in Hamburg at the close of 1852, giving a concert in the Hôtel de l'Europe, which does not seem to have created any great sensation, and that he found himself in the same city in the spring of 1853. Brahms, depressed by the hopeless monotony of his daily grind, was no doubt glad enough to see him, and, as his slack time was at hand, it was proposed, perhaps by Reményi, perhaps by Uncle Giesemann, possibly by Johannes himself, that the two musicians should give a concert to their friends in Winsen, who would, no doubt, hail the prospect of such an

BRAHMS AT THE AGE OF TWENTY.

event, and assist it to the utmost of their power. Communications were opened, and the proposal was not only entertained, but developed, as such ideas are apt to do. If at Winsen, why not also at Lüneburg and Celle? Amtsvogt Blume had influence in both towns, which he would be only too happy to exert. In the end, the project expanded into the plan of a concert-tour. Johannes and Reményi would give performances in the three localities named, and from Celle it would be no distance to go on to Hanover, where the twenty-one-year-old Joachim, already a European celebrity, had a post at Court. Reményi had known him for a short time when they had both been boys at the Vienna Conservatoire; they would go and see him. He was bound to welcome his compatriot and former fellow-pupil. Who could tell what might happen?

The two artists left Hamburg for Winsen on April 19. No doubt Brahms felt some heart-stirrings as he set out on this his first quest of adventure and probably not the least ardent of his anticipations was that of making the personal acquaintance of the celebrated violinist whose first appearance in Hamburg at the Philharmonic concert of March 11, 1848, with Beethoven's Concerto, remained vividly in his remembrance as one of the few great musical events of his own life. Before starting, he exacted a promise from his mother that she would write to him regularly once a week—not a mere greeting, but a real letter of several pages. It was a serious undertaking for Johanna, who was not practised in penmanship, but she gave her word to Hannes, and found means to keep it. The travellers took but little luggage with them. Such as Johannes carried was made the heavier by his packet of manuscripts, which contained his pianoforte sonata-movements and scherzo, a sonata for pianoforte and violin, a pianoforte trio, a string quartet, a number of songs, and possibly other works. One programme was to suffice for the concert *tournée*, and this the two artists had in their heads.

The exact date of the Winsen concert is forgotten, apparently beyond chance of recall, but the event may be fixed with certainty as having taken place in the last week of April. In the meanwhile both musicians were the guests of the Giesemanns, and spent the greater part of their mornings practising together, beginning before breakfast. They gave a great deal of time to the Hungarian melodies, and it would seem as though Johannes had been preparing a pianoforte accompaniment; for they repeated the periods over and over again, Reményi becoming very irritable during the process. The season was a warm one; they worked energetically in their shirt-sleeves, and the violinist more than once made his colleague shout by bringing the violin bow suddenly down on his shoulder to emphasise the capricious *tempo* he required. One morning Johannes, very angry, jumped up from the piano, and declared he would no longer bear with Reményi; but the concert came off nevertheless, and turned out a brilliant success. It took place in the large room of the Rusteberg club-house; the entrance fee was about eightpence, and the profits to be divided came to rather over nine pounds. Beethoven's C minor Sonata for pianoforte and violin headed the programme, and was followed by violin solos; Vieuxtemps' Concerto in E major, Ernst's "Elégie," and several Hungarian melodies, all accompanied by Brahms, who, it must be remembered, was but the junior partner in the enterprise. Only one thing was to be regretted. Schröder had been ill, and could not come to Winsen for the concert. He managed, however, to attend a repetition of the programme, which the two artists gave the next day in his schoolroom at Hoopte, expressly in order that he might get some amount of pleasure out of the great doings of the neighbourhood.

The next concert took place on May 2 at Celle. It had been arranged with the assistance of Dr. Köhler, a well-known inhabitant of the town, probably a relation of the Rector of Winsen, and a friend of Amtsvogt Blume, who, besides seeing through the business arrangements, had neglected no opportunity of arousing general interest in the event. The single public announcement appeared in the *Celler'scher Anzeiger* of Saturday, April 30:

"Next Monday evening at seven o'clock the concert of the Herren Reményi and Brahms will take place in the Wierss'-schen room. The subscription price is 12 g.gr.* Tickets may also be obtained of Herr Wierss jun. at Herr Duncker's hotel, and on the evening at the room for 16 g.gr."

At Celle there was a sensation. The two artists, going, on the morning of May 2, to try their pieces in the concert-room, were dismayed to find that the only pianoforte of which it boasted was in such an advanced state of old age as to be unusable for their purpose. Classical concerts were rare events in Celle, and it had occurred to no one to doubt the excellence of the instrument; a piano was a piano. It was arranged that every effort should be made, during the few hours that remained, to procure a better one, and a better one was actually discovered and sent in just as the hour had arrived for the concert to begin. But a fresh difficulty arose. The second instrument proved to be nearly a semitone below pitch, and Reményi refused to make so considerable a change in the tuning of his violin. What was to be done? The practised and intrepid Johannes made short work of the difficulty. If Reményi would tune his fiddle slightly up, so as to bring it to a true semitone above the piano, he himself would transpose his part of the Beethoven sonata a semitone higher than written, and play it in C sharp minor instead of C minor. No sooner said than done. The young musician performed the feat without turning a hair, though his colleague allowed him no quarter, and the performance was applauded to the echo. Reményi behaved well on this occasion. Addressing the audience, he related the circumstances in which he and his companion had found themselves placed, and said that all approval belonged by right to Brahms, whose musicianship had saved the situation. History does not relate whether

---

* Two Guter Gröschen were of about the value of 2½d.

the young hero transposed his parts throughout the evening, or whether the old instrument was sufficiently serviceable for the accompaniments of the violin solos, and the question does not appear to have suggested itself until the present time, when it cannot be solved. Johannes himself seems to have thought but little of his achievement. Writing presently to let Marxsen know how he was getting on, he mentioned the incident, not as worthy of comment, but as one amongst others.

The day after these events Reményi and Brahms retraced their steps as far as Lüneburg, where they were welcomed by Herr Calculator Blume, son of the Amtsvogt. At his hospitable house they were presented to the musical circle of the town, so far as it included members of the sterner sex. At the earnest persuasion of Brahms, no ladies were invited to the party arranged by Frau Blume in the interests of the forthcoming concert. "It is so much nicer without them," he said, and was so serious about the matter that his hostess regretfully gave way to him. He played part of the C major Sonata, on the composition of which he had lately been engaged, on this private occasion, making but little impression with it. Perhaps the double consciousness, which cannot but have been secretly present with him, of his great artistic superiority to Reményi, and of the quite secondary place to which he found himself relegated whenever they appeared together, may have increased the awkward shyness which placed him at such a disadvantage by the side of his colleague. He was incapable of making any effort to assert himself in general society, and attracted little notice from ordinary strangers who had no particular reason for observing him closely. However, everyone behaved very kindly to him throughout the journey. He was certainly a good pianist, and accompanied Reményi delightfully.

The concert was advertised in the *Lüneburger Anzeiger* of May 7, the twentieth birthday anniversary of our Johannes:

"The undersigned propose to give a concert on Monday evening, the 9th inst., at 7.30, in Herr Balcke's Hall, and have the honour to invite the attendance of the music-loving public. Amongst other things, the concert-givers will perform Beethoven's Sonata for Pianoforte and Violin in C minor, Op. 30, and Vieuxtemps' grand Violin Concerto in E major.

"Tickets to be had," etc. "EDWARD REMÉNYI.
JOHANNES BRAHMS."

Again a great success was scored, and the next day a second concert "by general desire" was announced, with the same programme and special mention of the "Hungarian Melodies," for Wednesday, May 11. It brought the visit to Lüneburg to a brilliant conclusion, and the performances were again repeated on the 12th at a second concert in Celle, advertised in the Celle journal of the 11th.

With the account of these five soirées, exact record of the public concerts of the journey is exhausted. Neither advertisement nor local recollection of any other can be traced, though Heuberger speaks, on the authority of Brahms' personal recollection, of two given at Hildesheim.* The first was very sparsely attended, and the artists, after supping at a restaurant where they seem to have made merry with some companions, paraded the streets with a queue of followers until they arrived underneath the windows of a lady of position who had been their principal patron. Reményi greeted her with some violin solos, the assembled party followed suit with a chorus, and the ingenious advertisement proved so successful that a second concert-venture on the following evening drew a crowded audience. The circumstances thus related point to the conclusion that the first concert at Hildesheim was hastily arranged, and the explanation may be that some unexpected introduction caused the musicians to visit the town. This would fit in with the fact that there is no reference in any Hildesheim journal of the date to Brahms and Reményi, and with the

---

* Heuberger, "Musikalische Skizzen."

absence of all knowledge, on the part of several persons still living who have personal associations with the journey, of any other concerts than those in Winsen, Lüneburg, and Celle, and of one other of a different kind in Hanover, to which we shall return.

It is necessary for the understanding of what is to follow that we should here part company, for a time, with the travellers. Before introducing Johannes to the great musical world which he is to enter before long, we must glance at the party questions by which it was agitated in the early eighteen-fifties, and which had hitherto been unknown or unheeded by our young musician in the inexperience of his secluded life.

The musical world of Leipzig, the city raised by the leadership of Mendelssohn to be the recognised capital of classical art, had become split after the death of the master in November, 1847, into two factions, both without an active head. The Schumannites, whilst receiving no encouragement from the great composer whose art they championed, decried Mendelssohn as a pedant and a phrasemaker, who, having nothing particular to say, had covered his lack of meaning by facility of workmanship. The Mendelssohnians, on the other hand, declared Schumann to be wanting in mastery of form, and perceived in his works a tendency to subordinate the objective, to the subjective, side of musical art. The division soon spread beyond Leipzig throughout Germany, and, in the course of years, to England, with the result that Mendelssohn, once a popular idol, was rarely represented in a concert programme.

Meanwhile Franz Liszt, perhaps the greatest pianoforte executant of all times, and one of the most magnetic personalities of his own, had exchanged his brilliant career of virtuoso for the position of conductor of the orchestra of the Weimar court theatre, with the avowed noble purpose of bringing to a hearing such works of genius as had little chance of being performed elsewhere. He declared himself the advocate of the "New-German" school, and, making active propaganda for the creeds of Hector Berlioz and Richard Wagner, succeeded in attracting to his standard some of the most talented of the younger generation of artists, amongst whom Joseph Joachim, Joachim Raff, and the gifted and generous Hans von Bülow, were some of the first converts. There were, therefore, three different schools of serious musical thought in the year 1853, each of which boasted numerous and distinguished adherents.

The purists of Leipzig held sacred the memory of Mendelssohn, clung to the methods as well as the forms of classical tradition, and declined to recognise as legitimate art anything that savoured of progress.

The Schumannites believed it possible to give musical expression to the world-spirit of the time by expanding their methods within the old forms—i.e., by free use of chromatic harmonies, varied cadences, mixed rhythms, and so forth.

The Weimarites, rejoicing in the potent leadership of Liszt, declared they would no longer be hampered either by old methods or old forms, which they regarded as worn out and perishing of inanition.

The party disputes as to the respective merits of Mendelssohn and Schumann, were as nothing beside the violent controversies which raged for years around the theories professed by the founders of the so-called "music of the future." For some time the battle was fought chiefly between the "academics" of Leipzig and the "revolutionists" of Weimar. The classical-romantic art of Schumann had points of contact with that of each of the extremists. Animated by new impulse and instinct with modern thought, it was by no means coupled by the leaders of the new party with that of Mendelssohn, but was accepted by them for some years with more than toleration, and some of the master's works, such as the overtures "Genoveva" and "Manfred," were performed at Weimar under Liszt's direction. Schumann himself, however, whilst warmly appreciating the great qualities of Wagner's musicianship, was well aware that any relationship between his own works and that of the new school was merely superficial. He was second to none in his reverence for the forms of the great masters, upon which he based his compositions, and, though it may possibly be the case that the originality of his idiom did not attract the entire sympathy of Mendelssohn, he clung to the memory of this departed friend as that of a beloved comrade-in-arms.

Schumann, who had long since retired from his labours as editor of the *Neue Zeitschrift für Musik*, of which he was the founder, lived quietly at Düsseldorf, where he had, in 1850, succeeded Ferdinand Hiller as municipal conductor. The success achieved by him there, during the first season of his activity as director of the orchestral subscription concerts and the choral society, was only transient. His reserved nature, and the progress of the malady that threatened him, unfitted him for the position, and he was subject to the constant annoyance that resulted from differences with his committee. To this was added the serious disappointment of knowing that the periodical to which he had devoted untiring energy during some of the best years of his life, had become, under the editorship of Franz Brendel, the organ of the New-German party, from whose principles he felt increasing alienation. These vexations probably augmented his nervous condition, and his habitual silence and reserve increased. His chief pleasure was found in the absorbing work of composition, and in his generous sympathy with a group of young musicians who regarded themselves as his disciples. Perhaps feeling that the best part of his own career was already behind him, he lived in the constant hope that someone would appear of creative genius sufficiently decisive to indicate him as the worthy successor to the prophet's mantle of classical art.

Many of our readers are aware that Joseph Joachim was born on June 28, 1831, at Kittsee, a village near Presburg in Hungary; that at the age of twelve he had learnt all that the distinguished violinist, Böhm, of the Vienna Conservatoire, master of many famous pupils, could teach him; and that he lived at Leipzig, well known at the Conservatoire, though not its pupil, for the next six years, happy during the first four of them in the affection of Mendelssohn, to whom he was passionately attached, and who lost no opportunity of furthering his protégé's genius and of laying the foundation of his future career.

It was not until after Mendelssohn's death that either of the party questions to which we have referred became acute, and Joseph grew up an unquestioning believer in the principles of musical tradition, which he reverenced with something of religious fervour. The loss of Mendelssohn left him, at the age of sixteen, lonely and disconsolate, in spite of his being himself already a distinguished personality and a universal favourite. The peculiar place in his life which the master had occupied could not again be filled, and for more than two years he was unable to regard anyone as even the partial successor to his best affections. It happened, however, that two events of the year 1850, awakened in his heart something of the personal enthusiasm which had made his early happiness. A few weeks spent by the Schumanns at Leipzig in the month of March, convinced him of his sympathy with the composer and his art; and a visit which he paid to Weimar in August, on the occasion of the first performance of Wagner's "Lohengrin," stirred him so strongly that by the end of the year he had resigned his position in Leipzig and taken up his residence in Weimar as concertmeister in Liszt's orchestra.*

Here he lived for two years, and it seemed for a time as though he would become one of the most enthusiastic of the band of young musicians, amongst whom were Bülow, Raff, Cornelius, and the violoncellist, Cossmann, who proclaimed themselves disciples of the new school. His genius and his already eminent position as an artist made him by

---

* The concertmeister is the leader—i.e., leading violin of the orchestra. The capellmeister is the conductor of the orchestra.

far the most important member of the group, and he was treated by Liszt almost on equal terms, as a younger colleague. In the constant companionship of this fascinating master, Joachim felt some renewal of the satisfaction in life which he had experienced when with Mendelssohn at Leipzig; but his early convictions and affections were too deeply rooted to be effaced by newer impressions, and his allegiance to the school of the future was not permanent. Liszt's aspirations, as the composer of sounding orchestral works which Joachim ought to have admired, but could not, gradually caused the young concertmeister to feel his position a false one, and he was glad to accept a post offered him, at the close of 1852, as court concertmeister and assistant capellmeister at Hanover. By this step he regained his independence without hurting the feelings of his Weimar friends. His absence of warmth on the subject of the Symphonic Poems had, indeed, been observed by Liszt, but Joachim had naturally refrained from expressing himself about them in detail, and Liszt could not guess that his young companion had conceived a positive aversion to his compositions. Joachim remained for some years yet on terms of affectionate intimacy with Liszt, Bülow, and the others, and was, indeed, so lonely and depressed during the first few months of his residence in Hanover, that he was impelled to express his state of mind by the composition of an overture to "Hamlet." Sending the manuscript to Liszt in the middle of March, he wrote:

"I have been very much alone. The contrast between the atmosphere which is constantly resounding, through your influence, with new tones, and an air which is completely tone-still, is too barbarous. Wherever I have looked there has been no one to share my aims—no one; instead of the phalanx of like-minded friends at Weimar . . . I took up 'Hamlet' . . . I am certain that you, my ever-indulgent master, will look through the score, and will advise me as though I were sitting near you, dumb as ever, but listening eagerly to your musical wisdom."*

---

* Moser's "Life of Joachim."

The Festival of the Lower Rhine, held in the year 1853 at Düsseldorf (May 15-17), was a particularly brilliant function. The names of Robert and Clara Schumann, Ferdinand Hiller as chief conductor, Joseph Joachim, the English artist Clara Novello, and others of high distinction, roused lively expectations which were perhaps exceeded by the performances. Schumann's D minor Symphony, Pianoforte Concerto played by his wife, and Overture and final chorus on the "Rheinweinlied," all given under his own direction, were received with enthusiasm; and the first appearance on the Rhine of the young concertmeister from Hanover, with Beethoven's then little-known Violin Concerto, resulted in a triumph that defies description. "He opened a veritable world of enchantment." "He was the hero of the festival." "We will not attempt to describe his success; there was French frenzy, Italian fanaticism, in a German audience," say the critics of the day.

For our readers, the peculiar interest of the occasion lies in the fact that Joachim, increasingly attracted by Schumann's art and individuality, took advantage of his few days' stay in Düsseldorf to draw closer his relations with the master, and it may be said that his future attitude was finally determined at this time. He saw in Schumann the living representative of the music that he loved, and to him and his became bound henceforth by ties that death itself was but partially able to sever.

CHAPTER IV.

1853.

Brahms and Reményi visit Joachim in Hanover—Concert at Court—
Visit to Liszt—Joachim and Brahms in Göttingen—Wasielewski,
Reinecke, and Hiller—First meeting with Schumann—Albert
Dietrich.

LEAVING Düsseldorf on May 18, the day following the close
of the festival, Joachim proceeded on a week's visit to
Weimar, and, returning thence to spend a day or two at
home in Hanover before settling for the summer at Göttingen, where he proposed to attend University lectures, was
surprised by a call from Reményi and Brahms.* His first
attention was naturally devoted to his old school-fellow, but
by and by he turned to the stranger, and an account of the
interview may be given in his own words:

"The dissimilar companions—the tender, idealistic
Johannes and the self-satisfied, fantastic virtuoso—called on
me. Never in the course of my artist's life have I been more
completely overwhelmed with delighted surprise, than when
the rather shy-mannered, blonde companion of my countryman played me his sonata movements, of quite undreamt-of
originality and power, looking noble and inspired the while.

---

* The accounts of some authors place the visit in Göttingen. They
must be regarded as, in this respect, mistaken. Joachim was positive, when consulted by the author on the point. "The whole scene
lives clearly in my memory," he said; "it occurred in my rooms in
Princes Street, Hanover."

His song, 'O, versenk dein Leid,' sounded to me like a revelation, and his playing, so tender, so imaginative, so free and so fiery, held me spell-bound. No wonder that I not only foresaw, but actually foretold, a speedy end to the concert-journey with Reményi. Brahms parted from him soon afterwards, and, encouraged before long by an enthusiastic recognition, marched proudly onwards in his own path of endeavour after the highest development."*

Reményi had not been mistaken in building hopes for the success of the concert-journey upon the chance of an interview with Joachim, who proved the medium through which both he and his companion were guided to the respective spheres for which each was peculiarly fitted. The great violinist was at this, his first interview with Brahms, so deeply penetrated by the certainty of his genius, so impressed by its daring, and so profoundly touched by the evident sincerity and childlike freshness of his nature, that he took the newcomer then and there to his heart, and made his cause his own. The conviction to which he had been stirred is reflected in a few lines written by him at the end of May or beginning of June, shortly after his arrival in Göttingen, whither he was immediately followed by the two concert-givers:

"MY DEAR JOHANNES,

"The piano has not arrived; it is afraid of the wet weather! Your sonata need not fear this, however. No doubt it struggles bravely like all your things against the waters of triviality! How would it be if we were to meet at Wehner's (a musician of Göttingen) from ten to twelve with violin, music, and (last but not least) friend Reményi, to bring the composition to life, i.e., to play it? . . . . "†

Joachim's enthusiasm did not exhaust itself in mere professions of goodwill. He was prompt to use his influence in high quarters on behalf of his new friend, and exerted it

---

* Festival address at Meiningen, October 7, 1899.
† Brahms-Joachim Briefwechsel, No. 1.
N.B.—The letter refers to the sonata for pianoforte and violin mentioned on p. 97 of this volume.

to such good purpose as to procure for the travellers an immediate engagement to appear before King George and the royal circle of Hanover:

"There is in Brahms' playing," he wrote to the Countess Bernstorff, a lady of great musical accomplishment attached to the Hanoverian court, "that concentrated fire, what I may call that fatalistic energy and precision of rhythm, which prophesy the artist and his compositions already contain much that is significant, such as I have not hitherto met with in a youth of his age."[*]

To Heinrich Ehrlich, court pianist at Hanover, who was present on the important occasion of Brahms' first performance before a royal audience, and has recorded that his debut was made with the E flat minor Scherzo. Joachim wrote:

"Brahms has a quite exceptional talent for composition and a nature that could have been developed in its integrity only in the strictest retirement—pure as the diamond, tender as snow."

On Brahms' departure for Hanover, he was warmly pressed by the generous young concertmeister to return to Göttingen if his relations with Reményi should come to the early termination which Joachim anticipated for them.

From Hanover, Reményi and Brahms travelled to Weimar, where Joachim had ensured them a welcome by writing to Liszt on their behalf. Of the first meeting between the world-famous musician, who lived in a style of ostentatious luxury in a house on the Altenburg belonging to the Princess Caroline von Sayn-Wittgenstein, and the obscure young composer from the Lane-quarter of Hamburg, we have, fortunately, the account of an eye-witness, William Mason, of New York, who was at the time resident in Weimar as a pupil of Liszt, and one of the ardent young champions of the new school.

"One evening early in June," says Mason,[†] "Liszt sent

---

[*] Ehrlich's "Dreissig Jahre Künstlerleben."
[†] "Memoirs of a Musical Life."

us word to come up the next morning to the Altenburg, as he expected a visit from a young man who was said to have great talent as a composer, and whose name was Johannes Brahms. He was to come accompanied by Edward Reményi.

"The next morning, on going to the Altenburg with Klindworth, we found Brahms and Reményi already in the reception-room with Raff and Pruckner. After greeting the new-comers, of whom Reményi was known to us by reputation, I strolled over to a table on which were lying some manuscripts of music. They were several of Brahms' unpublished compositions, and I began turning over the leaves of the uppermost of the pile. It was the pianoforte solo, Op. 4, Scherzo in E flat minor. . . . Finally Liszt came down, and after some general conversation he turned to Brahms, and said: 'We are interested to hear some of your compositions whenever you are ready and feel inclined to play them.'

"Brahms, however, who was in a highly nervous state, declared that it was quite impossible for him to play, and as the entreaties of Liszt and Reményi failed to induce him to approach the piano, Liszt went over to the table, saying, 'Well, I shall have to play'; and taking the first piece at hand from the heap of manuscripts, he performed the scherzo at sight in such a marvellous way, carrying on, at the same time, a running accompaniment of audible criticism of the music, that Brahms was surprised and delighted. Raff found reminiscences, in the opening bars, of Chopin's Scherzo in B flat minor, whereupon Brahms answered that he had neither seen nor heard any of this composer's works. Liszt then played a part of Brahms' Sonata in C major, Op. 1.

"A little later, someone asked Liszt to play his own sonata, a work which was quite recent at that time, and of which he was very fond. Without hesitation he sat down and began playing. As he progressed, he came to a very expressive part, which he always imbued with extreme pathos, and in which he looked for the especial interest and sympathy of his listeners. Glancing at Brahms, he found that the latter was dozing in his chair. Liszt continued playing to the end of the sonata, and then rose and left the room. I was in such a position that Brahms was hidden from my view, but I was aware that something unusual had taken place, and I think it was Reményi who told me what had occurred. It is very strange that among the various accounts of this first Liszt-Brahms interview—and there are several—there is not one which gives an accurate description of what took place on the occasion; indeed, they are all far out of the way. The events as here related are perfectly clear in my own mind; but not wishing to trust implicitly to my memory, I wrote to my friend Klindworth, the only living witness of the incident except myself, as I suppose, and requested him to give me an account of it as he remembered it. He corroborated my description in every particular, except that he made no specific reference to the drowsiness of Brahms, and except also that, according to my recollection, Brahms left Weimar on the afternoon of the day on which the meeting took place; Klindworth writes that it was on the morning of the next day—a discrepancy of very little moment."

It is to be observed, in the first place, with reference to this interesting account, that Brahms' panic was probably caused by his finding that he was expected to play before not only Liszt himself, but a party of his pupils, the most unnerving kind of audience with which he could possibly have been confronted; and in the second, that Reményi, in saying his companion had fallen asleep, unquestionably merely intended to convey the meaning that he had not taken prudent advantage of his opportunity to ingratiate himself with the great man. The very different methods employed by the violinist for the advancement of his own ambition are illustrated by a letter written by him to Liszt soon after this first interview which throws an illuminating sidelight upon the scene and its immediate sequel. It is clear that Reményi at once took steps for the purpose of ingratiating himself with the leader of Weimar and his rising young musicians by acquainting himself with, at all events, the names of Liszt's compositions, and announcing himself a convert to the New-German music. He remained associated with the party for a considerable time, and Liszt recognised his gifts whilst ridiculing his extravagances. The letter referred to opens with a kind of preamble:

"This scribbler ventures to address the great man, after having heard the sonata, the scherzo, the rhapsodies, the Dante fantasia, etc. One must have courage to dare to write to such a man. Let us see, let us try, nevertheless. We shall see whether I have the talent to continue. Now to work!

"TISZTELT LISZT UR!

"Admirable compatriot!

"I am here on the Altenburg, the place where I have had the happiness (read effrontery) of being received by Liszt, and where I have the happiness of finding myself again!

"Conceive the immense joy you have given me by forwarding the letter addressed to me from Hungary. Every bad thing is of some use; when I reflect that this bit of a Hungarian letter has procured me the sublime lines of Liszt —Ah! yes, I have read this letter four or five times—no! devoured it, but not altogether; some fragments fortunately remain for me to point to proudly in the future (when I shall have become a great man??!!): do you see, gentlemen? I am a happy mortal. I possess the writing—no, *a personal letter from Liszt*. You may be assured that that is *everything* for me—it will be my talisman! If you by chance ask what I am doing, really I cannot tell you—of what interest can it be to you if I scrape on the violin or compose some new mazourek fantastiques? That is zero for you. . . .

"As for my political confession, it is already sent—Raff has edited it!

"Now, I think this letter is much too long. I shall finish it by telling you quite simply, but very sincerely, that the good God has you in His holy keeping, and that He ever directs your genius for the honour and glory of the human race in general, and particularly (but particularly) of your dear country.

"Adieu, great compatriot!

"I subscribe myself,
"E. REMÉNYI,
"*Citizen of the Altenburg, ci-devant of Hungary.*

"P.S.—Brahms has left for Göttingen."*

---

* From La Mara's "Briefe hervorragender Zeitgenossen an Franz Liszt."

And no wonder! one feels inclined to exclaim, on reading the postscript, the first of three appended to the epistle. Johannes must have felt that his power of endurance was being strained to its utmost limit by daily association with such a comrade, and determined to break it, helped, very likely, to his resolution by the recollection of the very different personality of that other violinist, the young king of fiddlers, who had invited him to Göttingen. The story frequently related, that Brahms and Reményi, or one of them, stayed on for several weeks as Liszt's guests at the Altenburg, is contradicted by all contemporary testimony, negative as well as positive evidence. It is established by one of Joachim's few dated letters, that he wrote to Weimar on Brahms' behalf on June 15; and by a letter of Liszt's of June 29 to the Princess Caroline von Sayn-Wittgenstein that the Weimar master had, at the latter date, left the Altenburg for the summer. Moreover Liszt writes in a letter to Joachim of June 23:

" . . . . Reményi and Brahms are staying in the rooms formerly occupied by Bülow. I am obliged to you for having introduced them to me and am glad to believe that they will become creditable artists."*

The morning at the Altenburg can, indeed, have left little behind it in the mind of our musician beyond a feeling of mortification, and Mason expressly states that the impression it produced on the young men present was that it had not been a success. It is likely that Klindworth was substantially correct as to the exact date of Brahms' departure from Weimar. Perhaps hoping to appear to better advantage in a *tête-à-tête* interview, he seems to have called a second time on Liszt, who presented him with a leather cigarette-case in which was placed an autograph inscription in remembrance of their meeting.†

---

* "Briefe von und an Joseph Joachim," edited by Johannes Joachim and Andreas Moser. Vol. I.

† According to a personal communication to the author by Frau Dr. Langhans-Japha, to whom Brahms showed the case.

Towards the close of June, then Joachim, at work one day in his rooms at Göttingen, had hardly time to call out, "Come in" in answer to a knock at the door, before the door opened and in walked Brahms. This was the beginning of the intimate acquaintance between the two youthful musicians, which ripened into the historic friendship that endured until the death of Brahms forty-four years later. What a discovery was each to the other! Alike in no respect, perhaps, save in earnest devotion to art, and a profound feeling of obligation in her service, the dissimilarity of their dispositions was such as to make them mutually interesting and to cement the growing bond between them. To Joachim the worship of art, adored goddess though she might be, could never be all in all; it could never appease the craving for human sympathy which, since Mendelssohn's death, he had at times felt to be almost intolerable. Johannes, haunted by a vision of the delight of intimate sympathy, was not convinced of its being either possible or indispensable, and knew that he could, if necessary, live his life without it. To Joachim, possessed of strong likings and antipathies, and firm to convictions involving a principle, it was not difficult, in a conflict of mere inclinations, to yield. In Johannes, with all his childlike sweetness of nature, there dwelt an ineradicable combative instinct. To Joachim life had been one continued triumph; he had never known even the taste of failure. A personality from childhood, he had conquered his world once and for all with scarcely an effort. Hannes had passed his days in obscurity, and had seen and known only struggle. And now, to Joachim, who had never had to plan for his own advancement, what a fresh joy it was to think and hope and suggest for the future of Johannes, and to Johannes, who had known little of the satisfaction of intelligent appreciation from colleagues of his own standing, what an astonishing experience was this enthusiastic and authoritative approval from such a comrade! The companions, engrossed in the first place by their compositions—

for Joachim was engaged upon two overtures, and Johannes busy with sonatas and songs—found plenty of time for other occupations. They studied and made music together, and walked and talked and dined together, and compared opinions and argued and agreed together. No doubt Johannes heard much about the Leipzig of Bach and Mendelssohn, and he found to his surprise that Joachim, the unparalleled interpreter of Bach and Beethoven, shared Louise Japha's opinion of Schumann's music. He certainly touched Joachim's heart by his loving talk of Hamburg, rich in proud traditions, and not without art memories of its own, associated with the great names of Klopstock and Lessing, of Telemann and Keiser, of Handel and Mattheson and Emanuel Bach. The fêted violinist, familiar since his ninth year with one or other centre of musical learning, brilliant pupil of the conservatoire of Vienna, beloved favourite of that of Leipzig, listened, moreover, with no little interest to all that Johannes chose to relate of his solitary studies with his Marxsen. The happy young Hamburger felt that he could tell Joseph anything. He spoke to him of his struggles, his kind friends at Winsen, his acquaintance with Louise Japha, the difficulties of his journey with Reményi. Joachim was so much interested in the Winsen episodes that he could not refrain from writing to Uncle Giesemann to tell him that his young musician would be a great man some day.

In one thing only Johannes would not bear his friend company. He declined to attend the university lectures of Ritter and Waiz, voting lectures a bore, and preferring to take his mental food, as usual, from books. He was very ready, however, to join the jovial fellowship that met at the Saxsen, the students' club-restaurant frequented by Joachim and his friends. He entered with great zest into all the fun of the social evenings, and on the night when he and Joachim were called upon, as the youngest of the party, to perform the "Fox-ride," he sat astraddle on his little chair, and galloped round the table with the court concertmeister from Hanover as though he were bent on keeping his terms with the most serious-minded student of them all. The happy holiday was crowned by a concert given by the two "students," which attracted an overflowing audience and provided Brahms with welcome funds for the prosecution of his immediate plans. He wished to make a walking excursion along the Rhine before the summer should have passed away, and left Göttingen about the middle of August, armed with several of his friend's visiting-cards with which to introduce himself to musical houses on his route. The acquaintance which Joachim desired to secure for him above all others was that of Schumann, but Johannes, probably sore from his recent experiences of an interview with a leader surrounded by his followers, was uncertain if he should stay at Düsseldorf. The separation between himself and Joachim was to be a short one only. They were to meet in October at Hanover, where Johannes was to pass the winter in his friend's society.

We have to picture our traveller as passing, during the next two or three weeks, from point to point along the beautiful Rhine valley in a frame of mind rendered almost ecstatic by the combined influences of his daily surroundings, his recent experiences, and his well-grounded hopes for the future. We meet him again early in September in the house of J. W. von Wasielewski, who at this period filled a post as music-director at Bonn, and who has given an interesting account of Brahms' arrival in that city.

"Towards the end of the summer," he says,* "I was surprised by a visit from an attractive-looking, fair-haired youth, who delivered to me one of Joachim's visiting-cards, on the reverse side of which was his own humorously-written signature.† It was Johannes Brahms. Coming in the direction from Mainz, he had travelled on foot through the Rhine valley, and presented himself to me staff in hand and knap-

---

* "Aus siebzig Jahren."
† "Joh. Kreisler, jun."

sack on his back. His fresh, natural, unconstrained manner impressed me sympathetically, so that I not only bade him welcome, but invited him to stay a day or two with me, to which he then and there consented. After the first hours of our intercourse, I naturally felt a desire to learn to know my guest from the musical side. He at once favoured me with a performance of one of his then unpublished early works, a pianoforte sonata, the quality of which immediately revealed to me his great talent for composition. I also heard him in other things. I particularly remember his characteristic execution of the Rakóczy March, which he was fond of playing and gave with great effect."

Asked by Wasielewski whether he intended to visit Schumann, Johannes replied that he had come to no decision on the point, giving as the reason for his uncertainty, the failure of his effort to approach the master on his visit to Hamburg in 1850, and no persuasion of his new friend availed to bring him to a resolution. He did not quit the neighbourhood of Bonn immediately. Acting, no doubt, on Wasielewski's advice, he retraced his steps a little in order to present himself at a great house in the vicinity—that of Commerzienrath Deichmann, a gentleman widely known, not only from his wealth and hospitality, but also by the warm interest taken by himself and his family in matters connected with literature and art. Distinguished visitors of many varieties of social rank, from royal personages downwards, were entertained by Frau Deichmann at her residence at Mehlem, opposite Königswinter. Celebrities on a visit to the Rhine country were generally to be met in her drawing-rooms in the course of their stay, many of the artists resident in the neighbourhood belonged to her intimate circle, and young musicians of promise were received by her with especial kindness. Needless to say that the arrival of Brahms as Joachim's intimate was hailed by her with lively satisfaction, and the familiar friends of the house, amongst whom were Franz Wüllner, the 'cellist Reimers, Wasielewski himself, and other young musicians, hurried to Mehlem on receiving her hasty summons, prepared to extend to the new-comer's performances as much approbation or criticism as the event might justify.

"I found," said Wüllner, in a memorial speech delivered after Brahms' death in the conservatoire of Cologne, "a slender youth with long fair hair and a veritable St. John's head, from whose eyes shone energy and spirit. He played us the just-finished C major Sonata, the earlier completed F sharp minor Sonata, the E flat minor Scherzo, and several songs—amongst them the now familiar 'O versenk dein Leid.' We young musicians were immediately delighted and carried away by his compositions."

As might have been expected, Brahms was not allowed to leave Mehlem immediately. He was persuaded to remain on as the Deichmanns' guest, to improve his acquaintance with their friends, and to further explore the Rhine and its beauties from their house, and it was during this visit that he found the opportunity, eagerly desired by him since his stay at Göttingen, to begin the real study of Schumann's compositions, till now but little known to him. What must have been his wonder and his joy as he found himself brought face to face in many of their pages with his favourite authors, Jean Paul and E. T. A. Hoffmann, and perceived in them as in a mirror the dreamings of his own soul! His surprise was probably but little less on making the discovery that Schumann's tone-poems, with all their fresh originality of method and their fascinating romance, were no mere erratic imaginings, but were firmly rooted in the great traditions of classical art. It is, perhaps, impossible to realise in its strength the revulsion of feeling that must have attended this first real spiritual meeting of "Kreisler jun." with the composer of the "Kreisleriana"; but it is safe to say that it settled him in the determination to pay the visit to Schumann which Joachim had planned and that it had its share in producing the temper of mind manifest in a letter written by Johannes in the third week of September, whilst he was on a few days' excursion with the boys of the Deichmann family, to the Amtsvogt Blume of Winsen:

"DEAR HERR AMTSVOGT,

"Permit me to offer most heartfelt wishes for your own and for Frau Blume's happiness on the joyful festival which you celebrate this month. The great esteem and love which I have for you may excuse me for troubling you from so great a distance, and perhaps at the wrong time, with these lines; I only know that you celebrate your golden wedding in the middle of this month. May God long preserve you in health, that I may often again, as hitherto, spend many happy hours at your house. In case you still feel some interest in my fate, you may, perhaps, be pleased to hear that I have passed a heavenly summer, such as I have never before known. After spending some gloriously inspiring weeks with Joachim at Göttingen, I have now been rambling about for five weeks according to heart's desire on the divine Rhine. I hope to be able to pass this winter at Hanover in order to be near Joachim, who is equally noble as man and artist. Begging you to remember me most warmly to your wife and daughter, I would also request you to express my heartiest greeting to your son with his wife and children, to dear Uncle Giesemann, and to all acquaintances. With best greeting, Your JOH. BRAHMS.

"IN THE LAHNTHAL, *Sept.*, 1853."[*]

Johannes' thoughts were engaged at this time on the Pianoforte Sonata in F minor, Op. 5, that was finally completed early in November. Who that has really tasted of the enchantment of that wonderful composition, great in spite of its immaturity, can doubt, on reading these lines, that the shining Rhine with its wooded heights, that Rolandseck and Nonnenwerth and the Drachenfels, and the deep blue sky and gorgeous starry nights, had their part, with the romance and wonder and gratitude and delight dwelling

---

[*] This letter and another to Amtsvogt Blume, which follows in Chapter VI, were first published in the *Lüneburger Anzeiger,* March 29, 1901.

in his young heart, in the making of the work—not, perhaps, in the sense of supplying the composer with a programme for his inspiration; but as the sunbeam caught by the plant—as mingling with his nature and becoming a portion of the very elemental force that blossomed into the flower of his imagination?

Yet another important halt was made by Brahms at Cologne, where two more interesting names were added to the long list of acquaintances already formed by him during the short five months of his absence from home. He delivered a letter from the university music-director of Göttingen, Arnold Wehner, and a greeting from Wasielewski, to Carl Reinecke at the time professor of pianoforte and counterpoint in the conservatoire of the Rhenish capital, and Reinecke, after hearing some of his compositions, conducted him to Ferdinand Hiller's house, and subsequently accompanied him to the railway-station at Deutz. Here he took train for Düsseldorf,* full, no doubt, of fluttering expectation at the thought that he was about to seek an interview with the great master of his day; sole successor, since the death of Mendelssohn, to the mighty giants in whose traditions he had been steeped since early childhood by Cossel and Marxsen. And as we accompany the young musician in imagination on this last stage of his Rhine journey, we may fittingly pay the tribute of passing remembrance to these two men. To their talents and attainments and character he owed it that he was able to approach the supreme hour of entrance upon the manhood of his artistic life, shortly to dawn for him, with the certainty of equipment and devotion of purpose that had already stamped upon his genius the unmistakable pledge of mastership.

Joachim had neglected no opportunity that had presented itself since Brahms' departure from Göttingen for furthering the interests of his new friend. A few days visit to the Schumanns at the end of August had enabled him to enlarge

---

* "Gedenkblätter an berühmte Musiker," by Carl Reinecke.

to his heart's content to very sympathetic listeners on the extraordinary gifts of the young musician with whom he had formed so sudden an intimacy; and thus it came to pass that whilst Johannes was still engrossed with the pleasures of his Rhine journey, a welcome to the Schumanns' house had been secured for him by the most potent influence that could have been exerted there on his behalf. His first call on the master recorded in Schumann's diary under date September 30 in the words "Hr. Brahms from Hamburg," seems to have been merely preliminary, but in an entry of the following day we read: "Visit from Brahms, a genius." To October 1, therefore, must be referred the incidents related by Dr. Julius Schübring—whose account is supported by the negative evidence of Schumann's memoranda of the first week in October, taken together with certain details of his later correspondence—of the first artistic interview between the two composers. Schumann desired the young Brahms to play something of his own composition. Scarcely was the first movement of the C major Sonata concluded when the master rose and left the room, and, returning with his wife, desired to hear it again. And as Johannes had played it three months previously to the amazement and delight of Joseph Joachim, so he now played it to the amazement and delight of Robert and Clara Schumann; and when he had finished one movement these two great artists bade him play another, and at the end of that, another, and still desired more, so that when, at length, the performance was at an end their hearts had gone out to him in affection, whilst in his the first link had already been forged of that chain of love by which he soon became bound to the one and the other till the end of both their lives.

Johannes lost no time in finding out his old friends Louise and Minna Japha. What wonderful adventures he had to relate to them, more than could be got through in one or even two interviews! There was the tour with Reményi, the performance at Court—how far away these things seemed!—then the visit to Weimar, the student-life at Göttingen, the journey along the Rhine. He had made the acquaintance of many young musicians, who had one and all welcomed his coming amongst them; he had been introduced to Hiller, become Joachim's closest friend, and now had, he thought, won Schumann's approval. "He patted me on the shoulder," Johannes told Louise, "and said, 'We understand each other.' What did he mean?" Schumann's meaning was made very obvious to Joachim, who received the following note from the master in answer to the introduction and messages of greeting he had sent him by Brahms: "This is he that should come."

To this verdict, delivered but a few days after Brahms' arrival in Düsseldorf, Schumann had been led by the hearing of a number of compositions great and small. The strength of the impression derived by the master from the performance of October 1 is well illustrated by the fact that Johannes was invited to play to him again the next afternoon; and, by the end of a week, Schumann had made acquaintance with as many of his young colleague's completed works as Brahms considered worthy of presentation to him. These included the pianoforte Sonata in F sharp minor, now known as Op. 2; the pianoforte scherzo, Op. 4; a sonata for violin and pianoforte, a trio-fantasia for strings, a string-quartet, and a number of songs; not to mention the arrangements of Hungarian melodies. Of the trio-fantasia Frau Schumann speaks particularly in a memorandum of October 4:

"Brahms played us a fantasia for pianoforte, violin and violoncello and his fine scherzo in E flat minor. Brahms' scherzo is another remarkable, youthfully mild piece, but full of imagination and glorious ideas. Here and there the sound of the instruments was not quite suited to their character, but these are but trifles in comparison with his rich imagination and mind."*

Louise Japha was present on this occasion and preserved a vivid recollection of it. "What shall I play?" asked

---

* Litzmann II, p. 282.

Johannes, crossing the room to her side when Schumann, after the performance of the trio, again summoned him to the piano. She suggested the scherzo: "Schumann has heard your two sonatas; choose something short this time. Play the scherzo, Schumann has not heard that." She eventually got a scolding for her pains, however. Johannes, nervous and excited, persuaded himself that his performance of the piece was a failure. "Why did you give me that advice?" he asked, returning to his faithful ally; "Liszt did not care for the scherzo and now Schumann does not like it."

We may now turn to the delightful account given by Albert Dietrich,* one of Schumann's favourite disciples, who lived at Düsseldorf in daily intercourse with the great composer, of his first acquaintance with the new-comer:

"Soon after Brahms' arrival in September, Schumann came up to me before the commencement of one of the choral society practices with mysterious air and pleased smile. 'Someone is come,' said he, 'of whom we shall one day hear all sorts of wonderful things; his name is Johannes Brahms.' And he presented to me the interesting and unusual-looking young musician, who, seeming hardly more than a boy in his short gray summer coat, with his high voice and long fair hair, made a most agreeable impression. Especially fine were his energetic, characteristic mouth, and the earnest, deep gaze in which his gifted nature was clearly revealed."†

Here was another companion of the right sort for Brahms. He and Albert met daily from this time forward during his four weeks stay at Düsseldorf, breakfasting together at an open-air restaurant in the Hofgarten, and sharing each other's confidences and pleasures. Albert's recognition of the powers of his new friend was no less thorough than

---

* "Erinnerungen an Johannes Brahms."

† Examination of the entries in Frau Schumann's diary (Litzmann) shows that the scene at the choral society must have taken place either on September 30, the date of Brahms' arrival in Düsseldorf, or October 1.

Joachim's had been, and he sent enthusiastic reports of him to Kirchner, Naumann, and other young musicians of the Schumann set. Himself a *persona grata* in the various artistic circles of Düsseldorf, he was able to open to Johannes a new and inexhaustible source of interest. He introduced him to Schirmer, Lessing, Sohn, and other of the leading painters, at whose houses the young musician heard much talk about the sister arts which bore due fruit in a mind whose first need was, in Joachim's words, "the harmonious cultivation of its various powers and the loving assimilation of all sorts of knowledge." A charming young society was quite ready to welcome a new playfellow—and such a playfellow—into its midst, and Johannes was invited by Albert's friends to many parties and excursions. He managed to waive the objection to ladies' society which he had once found insuperable, and discovered that a festivity from which they were not rigorously excluded was not therefore a necessarily tiresome affair! Music in general and his music in particular, was much in demand at frequent evening gatherings, and his hearers knew not whether they were more delighted by his interpretations of the great masters or of his own compositions.

"Everyone was filled with astonishment," says Dietrich, "and the young people, especially, were dominated by the impression of his characteristic, powerful, and, when necessary, extraordinarily tender playing. He used to receive the enthusiastic praise accorded to his performances in a modest, deprecatory manner.

"His constitution was thoroughly sound; the most strenuous mental exertion scarcely fatigued him, but then he could go soundly to sleep at any hour of the day he pleased. With companions of his own standing he was lively, sometimes arrogant, dry, and full of pranks. When he came to see me, he used to rush up the stairs, thump on the door with both fists, and burst in without waiting for an answer. . . . Brahms never spoke of the works with which he was busy, or of his plans for future compositions, but he told me one day that he often recalled folk-songs when at work, and that then his melodies suggested themselves spontaneously."

At the Schumanns' house Brahms learned chess and table-turning. He was soon made free of the master's library, and borrowed from it many a book to lend to the Japhas, who had to submit to a term of quarantine during Minna's recovery from an attack of measles. Johannes refused, for his own part, to acquiesce in the decree, and paid long daily visits to the sisters as soon as they were able to receive him. He often sat at Louise's side reading with her from an open volume placed between them, as he had once been used to do with Lischen in the Winsen fields. One day he brought some volumes of Hoffmann, to re-read his favourite tales from Schumann's own copy. He carried the old memories and friends, and the simple home with its dear affections, faithfully in his heart throughout his excitements and successes, and throughout the weeks and months of his absence Johanna kept her promise to her boy. "Look," said Hannes one day, pulling a letter out of his pocket, and holding it open before Louise and Minna as he told them of the stipulation he had made, "I get one like this every week; my old mother keeps her promise. Some of it is copied from the newspapers; what is she to do when she has no more news? she cannot write a philosophical treatise, but she always sends me three whole pages."*

The passionate admiration quickly conceived by Brahms for the character and genius of Schumann, which was intensified by the recollection of his past misconception of the great composer's art, was returned in appropriate measure. Schumann became every day fonder of his young friend, and inclination united with conviction to strengthen the strong first impression he had received as to the extraordinary nature of his gifts. "Princeps" is written in one of Schumann's pocket-books against the name Johannes Brahms, added, in the master's handwriting, to a list of his favourite young musicians. It has sometimes been sug-

---

* At this period envelopes were not in universal use. The large "letter-paper" was folded and sealed, and addressed on the blank fourth page.

gested that the secret of the immediate fascination exercised over him by Brahms' compositions lay in his perception of their dissimilarity from his own. This, however, is only part of the truth. Though it be the case that Schumann's influence is not traceable either in the melody, harmony, or structure of Brahms' first published movements, it is equally the fact that the "delicate youth with dreamy expression, who, without a tinge of affectation, spoke naturally in poetic phrases; who signed his manuscripts 'Joh. Kreisler jun.'; who exactly answered Joachim's description, 'pure as the diamond, tender as snow'";[*] had elements in his many-sided nature of near kin to the characteristic spirit of Schumann's genius, which were by no means without influence on the individuality of his works, and especially the works of his first period. Schumann, astonished beyond measure by the mastery and originality of Brahms' technical attainment, was, in regard to his ideal qualities, certainly penetrated as much by the romance as by the independence, by the tenderness as by the power, by the subjective, as by the objective side, of his art, and the elder musician loved the younger as much because of the affinity as of the difference between them. Both contrasting sides of Brahms' nature are strikingly manifest in the very beautiful drawing of him which was executed for Schumann at this time by the painter de Laurens, a representation of which we are enabled by the kindness of Frau Professor Böie, to whom the original belonged, to place before the reader as one of our illustrations.

Schumann had not been forgetful of the overtures to closer intimacy made to him by Joachim in the spring of the year, and composed two concert-pieces for violin and orchestra about this time, during the writing of which the famous young violinist and his performances at the Düsseldorf festival were constantly present to his mind. In

---

[*] Ehrlich, "Dreissig Jahre Künstlerleben."

a letter to Hanover concerning these and other matters, written by him on October 8, the following passages occur: *

"I think if I were younger I could make some polymetres about the young eagle who has so suddenly and unexpectedly flown down from the Alps to Düsseldorf. Or one might compare him to a splendid stream which, like Niagara, is at its finest when precipitating itself from the heights as a roaring waterfall, met on the shore by the fluttering of butterflies and by nightingales' voices. . . .

"The young eagle seems to be content in the Lowlands; he has found an old guardian who is accustomed to watch such young flights, and who knows how to calm the wild wing-flapping without detriment to the soaring power."†

On the same day he wrote to Dr. Härtel, head of the great Leipzig publishing firm:

"A young man has just presented himself here who has most deeply impressed us with his wonderful music. He will, I am convinced, make the greatest sensation in the musical world. I will take an opportunity of writing more in detail about him."‡

Five days later, writing again on business to Joachim, who was to take part on the 27th, in the first Düsseldorf subscription concert of the season, he adds:

"I have begun to put together my thoughts about the young eagle. I should wish to help him on his first flight through the world, but fear I have grown too fond of him to be able to describe the light and dark colours of his wings quite clearly. When I have finished the paper, I should like to show it to his comrade [Joachim], who knows him even better than I do."

A postscript is subjoined: "I have finished the essay and enclose it. Please return it as soon as possible."

---

* "Robert Schumann's Briefe." Neue Folge. Edited by Gustav Jansen.

† The movements of the F minor Sonata were no doubt submitted to Schumann's criticism during the process of their composition.

‡ See, for this and other letters of Schumann, Dr. Jansen's collection referred to above.

Euer Wohlgeboren

erlaube ich mir hiermit einige meiner Compositionen zu übersenden, mit der Bitte dieselben durchzusehen, und mir dann gütigst sagen zu wollen, ob ich meiner Hoffnung erfüllt sehen kann, dieselben durch Ihren Verlag zu veröffentlichen.

Es ist nicht eigne Kühnheit, sondern mehr der Wunsch künstlerischer Freunde, denen ich meine Manuscripte mittheilte, welcher mich zu dem Schritte führt, mit denselben vor die Öffentlichkeit zu treten.

Damit mögen Sie, hochgeehrter Herr, diese

REPRODUCTION OF BRAHMS' FIRST LETTER TO BREITKOPF & HÄRTEL, DATED THE 8TH NOVEMBER, 1853.

Wollen entschuldigen, falls Ihnen der
Inhalt nicht willkommen ist.

In verehrungsvoller Ergebenheit

Hannover d. 1ᵗᵉⁿ Nov 1853   Johs Brahms.
Tapenstieg Nᵒ 4 (vor dem Aegidienthor.)

A second letter to Dr. Härtel enters into some of the promised detail:

"You will see before long, in the *Neue Zeitschrift für Musik*, an article signed with my name on young Johannes Brahms from Hamburg, which will give you further information about him. I will then write to you more fully about the compositions he intends to publish. They are pianoforte pieces and sonatas, a sonata for violin and piano, a trio, a quartet, and a number of songs—all full of genius. He is also an exceptional pianist."

On the 14th of the month the Schumanns were pleasantly surprised by another visit from Joachim. The popular young concertmeister had been spending his time pleasantly enough during the progress of the events just related. After taking part in a festival at Carlsruhe, where he met his Weimar friends Liszt, Pruckner, Cornelius, Bülow, and the others, in full force, he had gone on to Basel with Liszt and some of the younger members of the party to be introduced to Wagner and pass a couple of days in his society, and was now returning to the duties of his post in Hanover. A day remained to be spent with his friends in Düsseldorf, part of which was, of course, devoted to the delights of music-making, and the short reunion was followed by a result of some permanent interest to the musical world. As Joachim was to come back to take part in the Düsseldorf subscription concert of the 27th, Schumann proposed to Dietrich and Brahms that a surprise should be prepared for his return in the shape of a sonata for pianoforte and violin to be written by the three of them jointly. Thereupon Albert undertook the first movement, Johannes the scherzo, and the master himself the intermezzo and finale. The work was duly completed within the ten days available for its composition; and its presentation, postponed until the more serious business of the concert should have been disposed of, took place on October 28 in the presence of the group of interested musicians and of Frau von Arnim (the Bettina Brentano of Goethe and Beethoven fame) and her daughter Gisela, a young lady much admired by Joachim. At an appointed moment Gisela, charmingly attired in rustic costume, stepped forward and handed a large basket of flowers to the hero of the occasion. Hidden beneath blossoms and foliage was the manuscript sonata of welcome, on the title-page of which Schumann had written:

"F. A. E.*

"In expectation of the arrival of their honoured and beloved friend,

"JOSEPH JOACHIM,

"This sonata was written by Robert Schumann, Johannes Brahms, Albert Dietrich."

The sonata was performed at an evening party at the Schumann's house, which followed the presentation, and Joachim was required to guess the authorship of the several movements, a problem he had no difficulty in solving correctly. The work remained in manuscript in his possession until the autumn of 1906, when he sanctioned the publication of the scherzo—the movement contributed by Brahms—by the German Brahms Society.†

The concert of the following day was the last given in Düsseldorf under the direction of Schumann, who was about to start with his wife on a concert tour in Holland. He was at this time seriously contemplating a permanent removal to Vienna, whence he had received overtures that were attractive to himself and Frau Schumann. Whether he would have made up his mind to the step cannot be determined. The decision was, as we know, taken out of his hands by one of the tragedies of fate.

---

* "Frei aber einsam" (free but lonely), Joachim's favourite device at this time.

† The complete sonata was published in 1938, and the first performance in England was broadcast on July 30 of that year.—R. H.

CHAPTER V.

1853.

Schumann's article "New Paths"—Johannes in Hanover—Sonatas in C major and F minor—Visit to Leipzig—First publications—Julius Otto Grimm—Return to Hamburg viâ Hanover—Lost Violin Sonata—Songs—Marxsen's influence as a teacher.

SCHUMANN'S article appeared on October 28 in the *Neue Zeitschrift für Musik*. Brahms seems to have read it for the first time, however, in Hanover, whither, in pursuance of the plans formed in the summer with Joachim, he followed his friend on the evening of November 2. Its contents were so unexpected, and their influence on Brahms' career was so far-reaching, that, though it may already be familiar to many readers, it seems right to quote it *in extenso*.

"NEW PATHS.

"Years have passed—almost as many in number as those dedicated by me to the previous editorship of this journal, namely, ten—since I appeared on this scene so rich to me in remembrances. Often, in spite of arduous productive activity, I have felt tempted; many new and considerable talents have appeared, a fresh musical energy has seemed to announce itself through many of the earnest artists of the present time,* even though their works are, for the most part,

---

* "I have here in my mind Joseph Joachim, Ernst Naumann, Ludwig Norman, Woldemar Bargiel, Theodor Kirchner, Julius Schäffer, Albert Dietrich, not forgetting the earnest-minded E. F. Wilsing. As trusty heralds in the right path, Niels W. Gade, C. F. Mangold, Robert Franz, and St. Heller, should also be named here."

known to a limited circle only. I have thought, watching the path of these chosen ones with the greatest sympathy, that after such a preparation someone must and would suddenly appear, destined to give ideal presentment to the highest expression of the time, who would bring us his mastership, not in process of development, but would spring forth like Minerva fully armed from the head of Jove. And he is come, a young blood by whose cradle graces and heroes kept watch. He is called Johannes Brahms, came from Hamburg, where he has worked in obscure tranquillity, trained in the most difficult laws of art, by an excellent and enthusiastic teacher, and was lately introduced to me by an honoured, well-known master.* He bore all the outward signs that proclaim to us, 'This is one of the elect.' Sitting at the piano, he proceeded to reveal to us wondrous regions. We were drawn into circles of ever deeper enchantment. His playing, too, was full of genius, and transformed the piano into an orchestra of wailing and jubilant voices. There were sonatas, more veiled symphonies—songs, whose poetry one would understand without knowing the words, though all are pervaded by a deep song-melody—single pianoforte pieces, partly demoniacal, of the most graceful form—then sonatas for violin and piano—quartets for strings—and every one so different from the rest that each seemed to flow from a separate source. And then it was as though he, like a tumultuous stream, united all into a waterfall, bearing a peaceful rainbow over the rushing waves, met on the shore by butterflies' fluttering, and accompanied by nightingales' voices.

"If he will sink his magic staff in the region where the capacity of masses in chorus and orchestra can lend him its powers, still more wonderful glimpses into the mysteries of the spirit-world will be before us. May the highest genius strengthen him for this, of which there is the prospect, since another genius, that of modesty, also dwells within him. His companions greet him on his first course through the world, where, perhaps, wounds may await him, but laurels and palms also; we bid him welcome as a strong champion.

"There is in all times a secret union of kindred spirits. Bind closer the circle, ye who belong to it, that the truth of art may shine ever clearer, spreading joy and blessing through the world. "R. S."

---
* Joachim.

Such was the proclamation by which Schumann, carried away by the impulsive generosity of his nature, designed to facilitate the entrance into the jealous musical world of the composer of twenty, whose gifts had not been tested by the publication of a single composition, whose name was hardly known to rumour.

"It is doubtful," says Mason, "if, up to that time, any article had made such a sensation through musical Germany. I remember how utterly the Liszt circle in Weimar were astounded at it. It was at first, no doubt, an obstacle in Brahms' way, but, as it resulted in stirring up great rivalry between two opposing parties, it eventually contributed much to his final success."

In sober truth, Brahms' worst enemy could scarcely have weighted him with a heavier mantle of immediate difficulty. It made his name an easy subject of ridicule to those who would in any case have been inclined to regard a new-comer with incredulity; it drew upon him the sceptical attention of others who might have been prepared to receive him with indifference or indulgence; it was calculated to awaken extravagant expectations in the minds of some whom it disposed to be his friends.

The musical world generally, adopted an attitude of hostile expectancy, and this was shared especially by the "Murls,"* as the young satellites of Liszt styled themselves. Their "Padisha," Liszt himself, could afford to be more or less indifferent, though he was not unobservant. "Avez-vous lu l'article de Schumann dans le dernier numéro de Brendel?" he says, writing on November 1 to Bülow, who replies on the 5th, alluding to supposed Brahms resemblances: "Mozart-Brahms ou Schumann-Brahms ne trouble point du tout la tranquillité de mon sommeil. Il y a une quinzaine d'années que Schumann a parlé en des termes tout-à-fait analogues du génie de W. Sterndale Bennett. Joachim, du reste, connait Brahms, de même l'ingermanique Reményi."

---

* Anti-philistines.

What Brahms' own feelings were on reading the paper cannot be difficult of conjecture. Joy and bewilderment, gratitude and dismay, must have struggled within him for mastery. The steady sense of proportion which was one of his lifelong characteristics, the consciousness of the almost crushing weight of artistic responsibility thus thrust upon him at the outset of his career, must have conflicted severely with his natural loyalty and his delight at having won from Schumann such an overflowing measure of approval. To a man of weaker moral fibre, the temptation to overmuch exaltation or undue depression might have proved more than perilous. Brahms, however, was made of stuff that enabled him to face the situation, to accept it, and finally to triumph over it, and the means which he used are the only means that can enable even genius to win the kind of victory that he obtained. They were unswerving loyalty and single-hearted devotion to an exalted purpose.

The matter of the selection of works to be submitted for the approval of the publishers was much discussed both before and after the departure of Joachim and Johannes from Düsseldorf, with the result that Schumann wrote on November 3, to Dr. Härtel, and proposed for publication; as Op. 1, String Quartet; 2, Set of six Songs; 3, Pianoforte Scherzo; 4, Second set of six Songs; 5, Pianoforte Sonata in C major. He hoped, he said, to arrive at an understanding by which, whilst the young composer would derive an immediate pecuniary advantage, the publishers would not run too much risk, and he suggested that if the sale of the works should, after five years, have realized expectations, Brahms should then receive further proportionate remuneration. He proposed as first payments; ten Louis-d'ors (about £9 10s.) each, for the quartet and sonata, eight Louis-d'ors (about £7 12s.) for the scherzo, six (£5 14s.) for each of the two sets of songs—in all about £38. Should these proposals meet Dr. Härtel's views, he would put Brahms into direct communication with him in order that the works might be submitted for his consideration.

"He is an intimate of Joachim's in Hanover, where he proposes to spend the winter. Joachim has written an extremely fine overture to Hamlet, and an equally original and effective concerto for violin and orchestra, which I can recommend to you with the warmest sympathy."*

Schumann's kindness did not stop here. He sent a sympathetic note to Jakob Brahms at home in Hamburg, tidings of which, and of the rejoicing family circle, just established in a new dwelling at No. 7 Lilienstrasse, were forwarded by the father to the young musician at Hanover. Dr. Härtel did not delay in sending word that he would be glad to see the manuscripts, for on November 9, Schumann wrote him a letter of thanks for his favourable reply, and added:

"I will write to-day to Brahms, and beg him to go as soon as possible to Leipzig to introduce his compositions to you himself. His playing belongs essentially to his music. I do not remember to have heard such original tone effects before."

Dr. Härtel's note was forwarded to Hanover by Schumann in a letter to Joachim with the words: "Give the enclosed to Johannes. He must go to Leipzig; persuade him to do this, or they will get a wrong idea of his works; he must play them himself. This seems to me very important." After relating the arrangements pending with the publisher, he adds: "Once again, pray urge him to go to Leipzig for a week"; and concludes: "Now good-bye, dear friend. Write again before our Dutch journey, and tell Johannes, the lazy-bones, to do the same."

Johannes had, in fact, not written to Schumann since leaving Düsseldorf, and he still waited, letting nearly three weeks go by before thanking the master for his article in the *Neue Zeitschrift*. Perhaps this fact may be regarded as confirmation of the surmise that he had not read Schumann's prophetic announcement with feelings of unmixed satisfaction, but if it be so, he allowed no other

---

* "Robert Schumann's Briefe." Neue Folge. Edited by Gustav Jansen.

sign to appear of such a possibility. He very anxiously reconsidered his choice of works for publication, however, and before receiving Härtel's letter to Schumann, had forwarded to Leipzig a somewhat different selection from that decided on at Düsseldorf, withholding from it the string quartet. Having settled this matter as far as he could to his satisfaction, and brought himself to consent to Joachim's persuasions that he should go to Leipzig for a week, his attitude to Schumann remained one of unmixed gratitude and affection, as may be read in the following letter :*

"HONOURED MASTER,

"You have made me so immensely happy that I cannot attempt to thank you in words. God grant that my works may soon prove to you how much your affection and kindness have encouraged and stimulated me. The public praise you have bestowed on me will have fastened general expectation so exceptionally upon my performances that I do not know how I shall be able to do some measure of justice to it. Above all it obliges me to take the greatest care in the selection of what is to be published. I do not propose to include either of my trios, and think of choosing as Op. 1 and 2 the Sonatas in C and F sharp minor, as Op. 3 Songs, and as Op. 4 the Scherzo in E flat minor. You will think it natural that I should try with all my might to disgrace you as little as possible.

"I put off writing to you so long because I had sent the four things I have mentioned to Breitkopf and Härtel, and wished to wait for the answer, to be able to tell you the result of your recommendation. Your last letter to Joachim, however, informs us of this, and so I have only to write to you that I shall go, as you advise, within the next few days (probably to-morrow) to Leipzig.

"Further I wish to tell you that I have copied out my F minor Sonata, and made considerable alterations in the finale. I have also improved the violin sonata. I should like also to thank you a thousand times for the dear portrait

---

* The letters in this and the following chapters from Brahms to Schumann were first published by La Mara in the *Neue Freie Presse* of May 7, 1897.

of yourself that you have sent me, as well as for the letter
you have written to my father. By it you have made a pair
of good people happy, and for life Your

"BRAHMS.

"HANOVER, 16 *Nov.*, 1853."

The reader may have noted that the work chosen by
Brahms with which to introduce himself, not only to
Joachim, but to the Deichmann circle, to Wasielewski, and
to Schumann himself, was the C major Sonata now known
as Op. 1; and the natural inference to be drawn, that he
considered it his best as it was his latest achievement, is
confirmed by his reply to Louise Japha when she asked him,
later on, why he had numbered his scherzo, a much earlier
work, as Op. 4. "When one first shows one's self," he
said, "it is to the head and not the heels that one wishes to
draw attention."

That the composer was not mistaken, if we may thus take
his own estimate of his published works by implication, may
be safely affirmed. Sharing the fundamental characteristics,
technical as well as temperamental, of the earlier written
work of the same form—unity of plan, wealth of resource,
impetuous vigour, dreamy romance, a breath that is repeatedly suggestive of the folk-lore in which the composer loved
to steep his imagination—the Sonata in C gives evidence
that the process of crystallization had already begun which
was to distinguish Brahms' development towards maturity,
which, indeed, did not stop at maturity, but may be traced
continuously down to the close of his career. This process
is to be observed, as regards the work in question, in the
themes of the principal movements, which are not only more
pregnant in themselves, but are presented in more concentrated form than those of the Sonata in F sharp minor.
That the first theme of the opening movement bears traces
of the composer's study of Beethoven's Sonata in B flat,
Op. 106, is of no great consequence. The question of
musical reminiscence is so frequently misunderstood that
it may be well to devote a few words to it on the threshold

of our narrative of Brahms' career as a composer, which will take but little account of such occasional examples as may easily be found in his works—in the opening bars of the scherzo of Op. 5, the second subject of the first allegro of Op. 73, and so forth. No one would affirm that reminiscences are in themselves desirable, but they are almost inevitable, and the important question is, not whether this or that rhythmical figure, this or that passing melodic progression, may be found anticipated in some earlier work, but whether it has been so used the second time as to have become an integral part of a composition with a distinct individuality of its own. The parentage of Brahms' sonata Op. 1, as, indeed, of every work published by him, is loudly proclaimed by each one of its pages. The opinion entertained by our composer, when in his maturity, of the self-satisfied reminiscence-hunter, is well illustrated by his reply to a conceited acquaintance who was courageous enough, on an occasion late in the seventies, to draw his attention to a transient resemblance in one of his great works to a passage of Mendelssohn. "Some booby has already been telling me something of the kind" (So was hab'ich schon von einem Rindvieh gehört), he answered. "Such things are always discovered by the donkeys," he said one day to a friend.

That the C major Sonata has been heard more frequently than that numbered as Op. 2, and is still occasionally to be found in a concert-programme, may be accepted both as evidence and result of its advance upon the Sonata in F sharp minor. The step from the C major to the F minor Op. 5, is, however, more remarkable. In this work we find not only that the "wild wing-flapping" of which Schumann wrote has been calmed by the faithful guardian with strange increase of certainty and endurance to the soaring power, but that the composer's advancing recognition of the value of restraint has also strengthened the exceptional skill in the treatment of form manifest in his earlier compositions. In the quality of its ideas, the sonata is consistently romantic. It has, indeed, but few rivals amongst works of musical art in its successful presentation of pure romanticism within the limits of classic form, and hence it possesses a peculiar interest, apart from that of its intrinsic beauty; as being illustrative no less of the young Brahms' participation in the spirit of his own time than of his reverence for the achievements of past generations.

In spite of its defects of immaturity and of the difficulties it presents both to listener and performer, the Sonata in F minor, which was a favourite with von Bülow, has grown very gradually into some measure of general acceptance, and it seems not impossible that it may some day be heard frequently in the concert room. Brahms played it in practically finished shape to Schumann and his wife when he called to take leave of them before his departure for Hanover on November 2. It is the only one of his extant works which was submitted to Schumann's criticism before final completion. In consequence of a mischance presently to be related, the violin sonata referred to in the letter quoted above and played at Göttingen by Brahms and Reményi, was never published.*

Amongst the young Schumannites who had been roused by Joachim's and Dietrich's accounts of Brahms to an extreme expectation, which had not been lessened by the appearance of Schumann's essay, was one Heinrich von Sahr, a musician from choice rather than necessity, who lived at Leipzig in the intimacy of the notabilities of its artistic circle. He had written in October to Dietrich:

---

* Schumann's memorandum of October 12: "Industrious. Music at home in the afternoon. F minor Sonata. Brahms played particularly well"—refers to his own Sonata in F minor.

This is made clear by Frau Clara's entry of the same date: "We had music at home in the afternoon. First I played Robert's F minor sonata, then Brahms' scherzo, then Robert's trio with Becker and Bockmühl"; which evidently means that Clara played her husband's two works and Brahms his own scherzo.

Compare Litzmann, pp. 280 and 283.

"Send me your real opinion of Brahms. I am dreadfully anxious to know him. . . . What is he like personally? Ah, write! do please write soon and tell me what you think of him. Is he still in Düsseldorf? What is his music like? What has he composed?"

Von Sahr was the first person in Leipzig to make Brahms' acquaintance. Carrying him off to his rooms the morning after his arrival, he insisted that Johannes should stay on as his guest, and constituted himself the guide of his new friend's immediate movements. He took him to call on his publisher, Dr. Härtel; on Julius Rietz, the conductor, and David, the celebrated concertmeister, of the Gewandhaus concerts; on Moscheles and Wenzel, Schumann's particular friends; Friedrich and Marie Wieck, Frau Schumann's father and sister; Julius Otto Grimm, a young musician whose room was on the same staircase as his own and who soon came to be numbered among Johannes' special friends; and introduced him, generally speaking, to the entire Leipzig circle. So rapid were the events of the next few days, that Johannes, who arrived in Leipzig on the evening of Thursday, November 17, was able to announce to Joachim the following Sunday that he had performed his C major Sonata and E flat minor Scherzo at Dr. Härtel's one day, played his violin sonata with David another; had been pressed to take part in a Gewandhaus chamber music concert, and invited by a second publisher, Senff, to send him any compositions he cared to dispose of.

"He is perfect," exclaims von Sahr in a letter to Albert Dietrich; "the days since he has been here are amongst the most delightful in my recollection. He answers so exactly to my idea of an artist. And as a man!—But enough, you know him better than I do. . . . Unfortunately, he can only stay till Friday. He has, however, promised, and I think he will keep his promise, to come again soon."

Important considerations had determined Johannes to return to Hanover for a few days at the end of his first week in Leipzig. He was anxious, in the first place, to make himself quite certain, by means of a personal consultation with Joseph, as to the propriety of certain dedications that he desired to place on the title pages of his compositions. He wished, also, to have his friend's opinion on the details of some further desirable alterations in the F minor Sonata which he proposed sending, together with a book of songs, to Senff. As it proved that the revision could not be completed immediately, it was agreed between the two young musicians that the violin sonata should be despatched for publication in the meantime. This work was, however, declined by Senff on the ground that it was against his rule to publish compositions for violin and that he preferred to wait for the sonata for pianoforte solo.

A letter written by Johannes early in December to inform Schumann of his arrangements gives lively expression to the satisfaction felt by him at the extraordinary turn in his affairs. The style of the address is in allusion to the brilliant success achieved by the master and his wife during their concert journey in Holland.

"MYNHEER DOMINE,

"Forgive him, whom you have made so boundlessly glad and happy, for the jesting address. I have only the best and most satisfactory news to relate.

"To your warm recommendation I owe my reception in Leipzig, friendly beyond all expectation, and especially beyond all desert. Härtels declared themselves ready, with great pleasure, to print my first attempts. They are these: Op. 1, Sonata in C major; Op. 2, Sonata in F sharp minor; Op. 3, Songs; Op. 4, Scherzo in E flat minor.

"I delivered to Herr Senff for publication: Op. 5, Sonata in A minor for Violin and Pianoforte; Op. 6, six Songs.

"May I venture to place Frau Schumann's name upon the title-page of my second work? I scarcely dare to do so, and yet I should like so much to offer you a little token of my respect and gratitude.

"I shall probably receive copies of my first things before Christmas. With what feelings shall I then see my parents again after nearly a year's absence. I cannot describe what is in my heart when I think of it.

"May you never regret what you have done for me, may I become really worthy of you. Your

"JOH. BRAHMS."

The opening of December found the musical circles of Leipzig in a condition of unusual flutter and excitement. Berlioz had arrived from Paris; Liszt, supported by a body of his "Murls" from Weimar, on an occasion that was of considerable importance to the New-German party. Berlioz had, for the second time, been invited to conduct a selection of his works within the precincts of the classical Gewandhaus, and the second part of the subscription concert of December 1, was to be devoted to the following compositions: "The Flight into Egypt," "Harold in Italy," "The Young Shepherd of Brittany," the fairy Scherzo from "Romeo and Juliet," selections from "Faust," and the overture to the "Carnaval Romain." Brahms returned in time to be present with his friends on the occasion; which was made lively by the demonstrations and counter-demonstrations of two conflicting parties in the audience, but seems to have resulted as satisfactorily for the Weimarites as they could reasonably have expected. Brahms and his messiahship were discussed, and none too gently handled, at a supper-party at which Berlioz, Liszt, Gouvy, and others of their set, met after the concert, but the hostile attitude adopted towards the young musician was not enduring. The personal animus which Schumann's essay had aroused against him was generally disarmed, as he became known in Leipzig, by the attraction of his unassuming manner—the more speedily, perhaps, because it was felt that his modesty rested upon an underlying feeling of confidence in himself and his purpose. He at once showed his indifference to party jealousies, and ran some risk of offending his companions, by calling on Liszt, who, with Berlioz, Raff, Laub, Reményi, and others, was staying at the Hôtel de Bavière, and it will presently be shown that Liszt, who promptly returned the visit, reconsidered his position to the young musician towards whom public attention had been so suddenly and strikingly directed.

Johannes presented himself on the Sunday (December 4) following the Gewandhaus concert at two houses always open to visitors on the first day of the week, into both of which we are enabled to penetrate by means of detailed accounts written immediately after the occurrences they describe. One is contained in a volume by Helene von Vesque;* the other in an "open letter" written by Arnold Schloenbach to the editor Brendel, for publication in the *Neue Zeitschrift für Musik* of December 9, 1853.

Hedwig, younger daughter of the wealthy house of Salamon, was not only possessed of literary and artistic talents, but of a magnetic personality which enabled her to form many distinguished friendships. She was long intimate with the families of Mendelssohn, Schumann, Schleinitz, Hauptmann, and other leaders of musical Leipzig, knew Joachim as a boy, and was for some time looked upon by her circle as the probable future wife of the Danish composer, Niels Gade. At the time of which we write she had nearly completed her thirty-second year, but her marriage with the composer Franz von Holstein did not take place until nearly two years later. The extracts from her diaries and letters contained in Helene von Vesque's book include several of interest to musical readers. Of young Brahms she says:

"Yesterday Herr von Sahr brought me a young man who held in his hand a letter from Joachim. He sat down opposite me, this young hero of the day, this young messiah of Schumann's, fair, delicate-looking, who, at twenty, has clearly-cut features free from all passion. Purity, innocence, naturalness, power, and depth—this indicates his being. One is so inclined to think him ridiculous and to judge him harshly on account of Schumann's prophecy; but all is forgotten; one only loves and admires him. In the evening

---

* "Eine Glückliche. Hedwig von Holstein in ihren Briefen und Tagebuchblättern."

he came to a small party at Elizabeth's [Hedwig's sister, Frau von Seebach]. . . . He placed himself at a little table near me, and spoke so brightly and continuously that his friends at the other table could not be surprised enough, for he is generally extremely quiet and dreamy. We had plenty of points in common: Joachim, the Wehners, our mutual favourite poets, Jean Paul and Eichendorf, and his, Hoffmann and Schiller. . . . He vehemently urged me to read 'Kabale und Liebe' and the 'Serapionsbrüder,' but above all Hoffmann's musical novels, of which he spoke with real enthusiasm. 'I spend all my money on books; books are my greatest pleasure. I have read as much as I possibly could since I was quite little, and have made my way without guidance from the worst to the best. I devoured innumerable romances of chivalry as a child until the "Robbers" fell into my hands. I did not know that it had been written by a great poet. I asked for something more by the same Schiller, however, and so made gradual progress.' He speaks in the same fresh way of music, and when I said to him, 'You will not care so much about music when you have a post as music-director or professor,' he answered smiling, but quite decidedly: 'Yes; I shall not take a post.'

"And with all this independent strength, a thin boy's voice that has not yet changed! and a child's countenance that any girl might kiss without blushing. And the purity and firmness of his whole being, which guarantee that the spoiled world will not be able to overcome this man; for, as he has been able to bear his elevation from obscurity to the perilous position of an idol without losing any of his modesty, or even his naïveté, so God who created such a beautiful nature will continue to help him!"

Schloenbach's "open letter" is written in too inflated a style to deserve a lengthy quotation, but one or two extracts may be welcome as describing our composer's first semi-public appearance in Leipzig. Franz Brendel's "at home" on the particular Sunday in question was a more than usually brilliant function. "Composers, teachers, virtuosi, lyric and dramatic poets, romancists, booksellers, critics and journalists—even preachers—clever, artistic women, charming girls," were gathered in the editor's reception-rooms, and one artist after another performed for the edification of the distinguished audience. A harp solo executed by Jeanette Paul, and rewarded by a double handshake from Berlioz; one on the pianoforte by Krause; a number of vocal contributions by the great tenor Götze—songs by Schumann and Wagner, and, in association with the accomplished amateur and Wagner enthusiast, Frau Lily Steche, the famous "Lohengrin" duet—formed the earlier part of the impromptu programme.

"The last performance of all was of special interest. Following maturity came immaturity, but immaturity of rare endowment and rich promise; immaturity already considerably defined, because possessed of individual power and true originality. We listened now to the young Brahms from Hamburg, referred to the other day in Schumann's article in your journal. The article had, as you know, awakened mistrust in numerous circles (perhaps in many cases only from fear). At all events it had created a very difficult situation for the young man, for its justification required the fulfilment of great demands; and when the slender, fair youth appeared, so deficient in presence, so shy, so modest, his voice still in transitional falsetto, few could have suspected the genius that had already created so rich a world in this young nature. Berlioz had, however, already discovered in his profile a striking likeness to Schiller, and conjectured his possession of a kindred virgin soul, and when the young genius unfolded his wings, when, with extraordinary facility, with inward and outward energy, he presented his scherzo, flashing, rushing, sparkling; when, afterwards, his andante swelled towards us in intimate, mournful tones, we all felt: Yes, here is a true genius, and Schumann was right; and when Berlioz, deeply moved, embraced the young man and pressed him to his heart, then, dear friend, I felt myself affected by such a sacred tremour of enthusiasm as I have seldom experienced. . . . If you should smile now and then whilst reading my letter, remember that it is the poet who has spoken, and that it was yourself who invited him to do so.

"LEIPZIG,"
  December 5, 1853.

It must not be forgotten, in connection with these effusive lines, that the party circumstances of the time and the excitement caused by Schumann's article made Brahms' appearance amongst the guests of Brendel, who had identified himself with the New-Germans, an event of importance, to be regretted by the younger and more excitable of the Leipzigers, and welcomed by the Weimarites. It no doubt contributed to the satisfaction expressed by Liszt, in a letter to Bülow, on his return to Weimar after a second appearance of Berlioz in Leipzig, and the sympathetic tone of this communication clearly shows that the motive of policy which dictated it was supported by a more personal feeling of approbation. He says on December 14:

"Je viens de passer quelques jours à Leipzig, où j'ai assisté aux deux concerts de Berlioz le 1er et le 11 de ce mois. Le resultat d'opinion à été en somme très favorable à Berlioz."

And two days later:

"Écrivez-moi de Hanovre, où vous ferez bien de passer une quinzaine de jours. Vous y trouverez Brahms auquel je m'intéresse sincèrement et qui s'est conduit avec tact et bon goût envers moi durant les quelques jours que je viens de passer à Leipzig en l'honneur de Berlioz. Aussi l'ai-je invité plusieurs fois à dîner et me plais à croire que ses 'Neue Bahnen' (New Paths) le rapprocheront davantage de Weimar par la suite. Vous serez content de la Sonate en Ut dont j'ai parcouru les épreuves à Leipzig et qu'il m'avait déjà montré ici. C'est précisément celui de ses ouvrages qui m'avait donné la meilleure idée de son talent de composition. Mille et mille tendres amitiés à Joachim, auquel j'ai fait demander sa partition de l'ouverture de Hamlet par Brahms et par Cossmann. Rappelez-lui que je désire beaucoup la faire exécuter à la prochaine représentation et la maintenir pour les représentations subséquentes."[*]

Brahms allowed himself to be persuaded, in spite of some inward trepidation, to make his first public appearance in Leipzig at one of the David Quartet Concerts, which took place regularly in the small hall of the Gewandhaus. The

---

[*] "Liszt's Briefe." Edited by La Mara.

programme of the occasion consisted of Mendelssohn's D major Quartet, Brahms' C major Sonata and E flat minor Scherzo, and Mozart's G minor Quintet. The reception of the new works by the audience was not discouraging, in spite of the absence from them of the qualities that go to the making of an immediate popular success, and most of the critics treated the composer sympathetically. Some of them, not content with writing about his music, discussed his appearance, and one described his "Raphael head."

"In the second Quartet concert, which took place on December 17," says "Hoplit" [Dr. Richard Pohl, a writer in the interests of the Weimar school, who was on the staff of the *Neue Zeitschrift*], "Johannes Brahms presented himself to the public with his Sonata in C major and his Scherzo. Schumann's article caused much division amongst the uninitiated, but all doubt has been dispelled by Brahms' public appearance, and we concur with all our heart, and with the warmest satisfaction, in Schumann's opinion of the unassuming and richly-endowed young artist. There is something forcible, something transporting, in the works which Brahms performed the other evening. A ripeness rare in one so young, a creative power springing spontaneously from a rich artist-mind, are revealed in them. We find ourselves in the presence of one of those highly-gifted natures, an artist by the grace of God. Some roughnesses and angularities in the outward, very independent form of Brahms' compositions may be overlooked for the sake of the imposing beauty of their artistic aim. His modulations are often of striking effect; they are frequently surprising, but always fine and artistically justifiable. Brahms' spirit is in affinity with the genius of Schumann. He will, advancing steadfastly and safely along his 'new paths,' some day become what Schumann has predicted of him, an epoch-making figure in the history of art."

Stress was laid by the orthodox *Signale* on the originality and freshness of the composer's invention, on the significance of his thematic material, and on his eminent gift for presenting his ideas in varied and interesting forms. His facility in unexpected modulations was noted, but, by this critic, not always approved. With regard to the performance, "much appeared more difficult to the executant than to the creator, for the sonata is very hard to play, and Brahms is a better composer than virtuoso."

Brahms quitted Leipzig on the 20th in the company of Grimm, who had business to transact at Hanover. The intimacy that had sprung up between the two young men was to endure as a life-long friendship, and a treasured memorial of this period of its commencement is in the possession of Fräulein Marie Grimm—Brahms' manuscript of the set of songs, Op. 6, as arranged for publication with the inscription on the title-page: "To my dear Julius in remembrance of Kreisler, jun., 8 Dec., 1853."

Plans made by Johannes to spend a day or two in Hanover fell through, and towards evening on the day of his departure from Leipzig he was in his parents' arms.

It is not difficult to imagine something of the mother's feelings as she welcomed back the long-absent Hannes, who had always been as the apple of her eye, or to picture the simple preparations, the sweeping and scouring, the polishing and decorating, with which she and Elise anticipated his arrival; but who shall measure the father's joy on the return of his young conquering hero? The swiftly-progressing successes of Johannes' journey had been most literally Jakob's own personal triumphs, vindicating emphatically every one of the stages of his career; the obstinate disobedience of his boyhood, the pertinacious struggle of his youth, the reckless adventure of his marriage. What wonder that, as time went on, Johannes became to him as a sacred being in whose presence he felt awed and unable to speak or act naturally, but of whom, when alone with a sympathetic listener, he would talk unweariedly by the hour, tears of joy running down his cheeks.

As to Johannes himself, the feelings he had not been able to describe in his letter to Schumann were probably strong enough within his heart to touch the joy of the first home embraces with a gravity that did not immediately admit of speech. The first emotions over, however, an exuberant mirthfulness asserted itself in the bearing of the happy young fellow. He established at this time a custom from which he never afterwards departed. The first visit paid by him after his arrival was to Marxsen. One to the Cossels soon followed, and, on this occasion of his return from a first real absence, he went the round of several Lokals, where he had been accustomed to work regularly, and in his lightness of heart flourished on some of the instruments that had been the sign of his bondage, in very joy at his emancipation.

The radiance of this year's Christmastide in the little home where the young genius dwelt for a few days, the simple, unspoiled child of loving and beloved parents, might have been taken for granted. We possess an assurance of it, however, in some words written by Johannes, at the end of the year, to Schumann:

"HONOURED FRIEND,

"Herewith I venture to send you your first foster-children (which are indebted to you for their world citizenship), very much concerned as to whether they may rejoice in your unaltered indulgence and affection. To me, they look in their new form much too precise and timid, almost philistine indeed. I cannot accustom myself to seeing the innocent sons of Nature in such decorous clothing.

"I am looking forward immensely to seeing you in Hanover and being able to tell you that my parents and I owe the most blissful time of our lives to your and Joachim's too-great affection. I was overjoyed to see my parents and teacher again, and have passed a glorious time in their midst.

"I beg you to express the most cordial greetings to Frau Schumann and your children of

"Your

"JOHANNES BRAHMS.

"HAMBURG, in *December*, 1853."

As we have said in a previous chapter, the violin and pianoforte sonata that Johannes had thought of publishing as Op. 5 was not given to the world. The manuscript was mysteriously lost. How or by whose agency has never been made clear. The known circumstances of the case lead to the conclusion that it was borrowed by Liszt during his Leipzig visit, and not returned. In a letter addressed six months later to Klindworth, who was giving concerts with Reményi in England, the Weimar master writes:

"Reményi does not answer me about the manuscript of Brahms' violin sonata. Apparently he has taken it with him, for I have, to my vexation, hunted three times through the whole of my music without being able to find it. Do not forget to write to me about it in your next letter, as Brahms wants the sonata for publication."

There is a ring of vexation in these words which suggests that Liszt felt responsible for the work. No trace of it was discovered, however, until 1872, nineteen years after its disappearance, when, says Dietrich, "whilst I was staying in Bonn to conduct my D minor Symphony, Wasielewski showed me a very beautifully copied violin part, and asked me if I knew the handwriting. I immediately recognised it as that of Brahms' first period. We regretted very much that the pianoforte part was not to be found. It will have been the violin part of the lost sonata."

The works actually published, therefore, before and after the New Year were—by Breitkopf and Härtel, the Sonatas in C, Op. 1, and in F sharp minor, Op. 2, dedicated respectively to Joachim and Frau Schumann; the set of Songs, Op. 3, dedicated to Bettina von Arnim, whose acquaintance made by Brahms in Düsseldorf had been cultivated by him during his visits to Hanover; and the Scherzo, Op. 4, dedicated to Wenzel; and by Bartholf Senff, the Sonata in F minor, Op. 5, dedicated to the Countess Ida von Hohenthal, a lady to whom Brahms was presented by Grimm; and the set of Songs dedicated to Louise and Minna Japha, Op. 6. Schumann presented a copy of the songs, Op. 6, to the Japhas immediately on their publication, on which he wrote: "Den Fräulein Japha, zum Andenken an das Weihnachtsfest, 1853, als Vorbote des eigentlichen Gebers. R. Schumann."

In the two sets of songs, Op. 3 and 6, and in the third, Op. 7, dedicated to Dietrich and published but little later, may already be perceived the composer whose lyrics were destined to take their place in the heart of the great German people as a unique portion of a peculiar national treasure. Deeply original, absolutely sincere, of an imagination that is angelic in its purity, feminine in its tenderness, and virile in its reticent strength, Brahms' songs admit us to communion with a rarely ideal nature, and the intuitive power of perfect expression which marks some of his early lyrics anticipates the experience of his later years. The beautiful "O versenk dein Leid" will, no doubt, always be treasured as the most exquisite example, in its domain, of this early period of his fancy, but each of the three first song collections contains one or more tone-poems to which the music-lover returns with delight. Amongst them may be mentioned "Der Frühling" (Op. 6, No. 2) and "Treue Liebe" and "Heimkehr" (Op. 7, Nos. 1 and 6). The last-named little gem is the earliest written of the published songs; unfortunately, it has only one verse.

The energy of imagination dwelling within Brahms' songs is often the more striking from its concentration within the short form preferred by the composer in the majority of instances. In it, as time went on, he gave vivid expression to thoughts wistful or bright, playful or sombre, naïve or deeply pondered; and whilst his lyrics are especially characterised by the clear shaping of the song-melody, and the distinctness of the harmonic foundations upon which it rests, many of them derive an added distinction from a quiet significance in the accompaniment, which, whilst helping the musical representation of a poetic idea, never embarrasses the voice. In spite of their apparent simplicity, the accompaniments are, however, frequently difficult both to read and to perform.

It is to be said, generally, of Brahms' songs that they do not betray the marked influence of either of the two great lyrical composers who preceded him. They have no affinity with those of Schumann, and if many of them share the fresh naturalness of Schubert's inspirations, this is rather to be traced to a partiality for the folk-song, in which both composers found an inexhaustible stimulus to their fancy. On the other hand, in Brahms' songs we frequently meet the musician who has penetrated so deeply into the art of Bach that it has germinated afresh in his imagination, and placed him in possession of an idiom capable of serving him in the expression of his complex individuality. Each song bears the distinctive stamp of the composer's genius, though hardly two resemble each other, and it would be difficult to point to one that could be mistaken for the work of another musician.

The young Kreisler was in the habit of presenting his manuscripts, and especially those of his songs, to intimate friends. Most of these gifts bear his boyish, affectionate inscriptions, some only the date and place of composition. "Göttingen, July, 1853," is written at the end of an autograph copy of "Ich muss hinaus" presented at Düsseldorf to the Japhas. "Weit über das Feld" has a friendly inscription in his hand to the sisters. His manuscripts—probably the originals—of some of the songs from Op. 3, notably "O versenk" and "In der Fremde," the latter dated 1852, were given "To my dear Julius in kind remembrance" (J. O. Grimm). Touching pictures arise in the mind as one looks at these pages, some of them discoloured by time, of the young idealist with his girlish face and long fair hair sitting at his night toil, his soul whole and in his possession, his thoughts straining towards the early morning hours, the only ones of the twenty-four which he was certain of being able to devote to the loveliest inspirations of his muse. In the eager affection of the inscriptions is to be read his bounding joy in his new freedom; in the devoted remembrance with which his gifts have been treasured may be perceived one of the qualities of his personality which he, perhaps, but little understood—the power of attracting the abiding love of loyal friends.

It is now time to sum up the real significance in the life of Brahms of the remarkable first concert-journey, the account of which has so long occupied our attention, and this may be done in a very few words. The journey was the transformation scene of his life. The obscure musician who, having been guarded from the dangers of prodigy fame, had started from Hamburg in April without prestige, without recommendations, without knowledge of the world, its manners or its artifices, had passed from the two or three provincial platforms on which he had appeared as Reményi's accompanist, to present himself as pianist and composer in the Leipzig Gewandhaus, and to return to his home in December the accepted associate of the great musicians of the day; recognised by Weimar, appreciated by Leipzig; encouraged by Berlioz and Liszt, claimed by Schumann and Joachim. Before he had well begun to climb the steep hill of reputation he had found himself transported to its summit. Starting hardly as an aspirant to fame, he had come back the proclaimed heir to a prophet's mantle. His life's horizon had been indefinitely widened, his whole existence changed. Back again amid the familiar scenes of Hamburg, the events of the past nine months must have seemed to him as the visions of an enchanted dream.

To the wise and faithful friend in Altona the occurrences which had startled the musical world had seemed in no wise astonishing.

"There was probably," wrote Marxsen later to La Mara, "but one man who was not surprised—myself. I knew what Brahms had accomplished, how comprehensive were his acquirements, what exalted talent had been bestowed on him, and how finely its blossom was unfolding. Schumann's recognition and admiration were, all the same, a great, great joy to me; they gave me the rare satisfaction of knowing that the teacher had perceived the right way to protect the individuality of the talent, and to form it gradually to self-dependence."

These last words seem to indicate that here is a fitting opportunity for the brief consideration of a question which has not seldom been raised, and has received various answers, often biassed by prepossession. What was Marxsen's share in the art of Brahms? A Brahms would have learned what he did learn, if not from Marxsen then from someone else, has been the opinion of some people to whose judgment respect is due. Such influence as Marxsen had on Brahms' development was merely negative, is the reply of others; and it has been affirmed, on the authority of Herr Oberschulrath Wendt, that Brahms declared on one occasion that he had learned nothing from his master.*

Without stopping to discuss whether it has been just to the memory either of Brahms or of Marxsen to give the permanence and emphasis of print to whatever depreciatory words Brahms may have let fall in an unguarded moment to an intimate friend, it may safely be asserted that if our composer fortunately became aware, at an early age, of what had been the weak points of his master's teaching, he preserved, when at the height of his mastership, a clear recognition and grateful appreciation of the strong ones.

Marxsen has himself indicated, in the last sentence of the above quotation from his letter, the two main purposes of his teaching, both of which were attained by him in the case of Brahms with absolute success. To have "protected the individuality" of an endowment so powerfully original as that of our composer might, perhaps, be regarded as an easy achievement if taken alone; though even here it should be remembered that Marxsen made himself responsible, when the affectionate and impressionable Hannes was at a tender age, for his musical education, and must, therefore, have been instrumental in directing his creative energy to that study of the highest art by means of which it developed to such good purpose. To have trained his talent to the

---

* Kalbeck's "Johannes Brahms," p. 34.

"self-dependence" it had attained by the time the young composer was twenty, however, implies in the teacher a distinctness of aim, a knowledge of method, an insight and originality, an active and potent influence, which few will fail to attribute to Marxsen who have a real acquaintance with the large works of Brahms' earliest period, written at the time that his formal pupilage was drawing or, in the case of one work, had just drawn, to its close.

Limitation of space prevents the possibility of giving here a detailed description of Marxsen's methods of instruction, but, as some account of their excellencies and shortcomings seems to be called for, it may be said that as a teacher of free composition, and especially of the art of building up the forms which may be studied in the works of Haydn, Mozart, and Beethoven, he was great—the more so that he did not educate his pupils merely by setting them to imitate the outward shape of classical models. He began by teaching them to form a texture, by training them radically in the art of developing a theme. Taking a phrase or a figure from one or other of the great masters, he would desire the pupil to exhibit the same idea in every imaginable variety of form, and would make him persevere in this exercise until he had gained facility in perceiving the possibilities lying in a given subject, and ingenuity in presenting them. Pursuing the same method with material of the pupil's own invention, he aimed at bringing him to feel, as by intuition, whether a musical subject was or was not suitable for whatever immediate purpose might be in view. The next step was that the idea should be pursued not arbitrarily, but logically, to its conclusion—a conclusion that was not, however, allowed to be a hard-and-fast termination. Marxsen's pupils were taught to aim at making their movements resemble an organic growth, in which each part owed its existence to something that had gone before. "Unity clothed in variety" might have been his motto.

The strength and freedom of craftsmanship, the immense resource imparted by such training, and the assistance lent by its earlier stages to the later study of construction, hardly need pointing out, nor is it necessary to dwell upon particular instances of its efficacy in the case of Brahms. Every page of his instrumental music teems with illustrations of the fruitfulness of his youthful studies; their result lives in the very core of his technique, and to them may in great part be traced, not only his mastery of form, but the elasticity which from the first marks his essential adherence to the models of classical tradition.

The severe course of apprenticeship in the art of free contrapuntal writing to which Marxsen subjected his pupil, which furthered, and was itself helped, by his training, in thematic development, is abundantly evident in the movements of the three pianoforte sonatas, and the estimation of the precise value especially of the first two of these works is facilitated by some knowledge of the methods from which they resulted. That Brahms, when at the summit of his mastership, expressed his exact sense of his indebtedness to his teacher, to whom he constantly testified his gratitude and affection both by word and action, is in the knowledge of the present writer. Gradually in the course of his career he had, he said, made the acquaintance of nearly all the foremost musicians of Germany, and he believed that in the teaching of the logical development of a theme, and in the teaching of form, especially what is called "sonata form," Marxsen, even if he could be equalled could not be excelled.

Eminent as he was, however, as an instructor in the art of free imitative composition, in that of pure part-writing Marxsen was no trustworthy guide. That he had gone through a course of training in strict counterpoint, canon and fugue—the surest foundation for the attainment of facility in part-writing—in his early days under Clasing, and that he carried his pupils through the same branches of study, goes without saying, but he had retained neither the exact knowledge, nor the interest, necessary to enable him to impart to his pupils purity and ease in the strict style of writing, or to train them to the effective application of the contrapuntal skill they might have acquired, in composition in pure parts for voices or instruments.

It would be a nice question to determine, however, whether the very fact of Marxsen's deficiencies did not result in a balance of gain to Brahms. While his powers of imagination obtained from what his master did do, encouragement and strength and facility in concentrating themselves into shape, they were exempt by the absence of that which he did not do from the danger of being dwarfed or intimidated. Marxsen helped Johannes to the putting forth of his strength in confidence and joy, and if the young musician ever felt it irksome to have to go back to the confining and polishing processes, he knew that the conquests won by him during the time of his pupilage ensured him final victory in the fresh course of serious study to which he soon voluntarily submitted himself.

Marxsen's indifference to the study of part-writing is strangely illustrated by the absence of his name from the list of subscribers to the great Leipzig edition of Bach's works; an absence which can hardly be accounted for, in view of his enthusiasm for the instrumental works of the mighty master, otherwise than by the supposition that his vehement intolerance of religious creeds had impaired his interest in the branch of musical art which originated and reached its highest development in the service of the churches. The majority of the works made generally known by the publications of the Bach Society were written for use in the two churches for the musical portion of whose services Bach was for many years responsible. This hypothesis is equally plausible in its application to the church composers and learned contrapuntists of the early Italian and German schools.

An interesting article on Marxsen is to be found in a little book called "Künstler Charakteristiken aus dem Concert-Saal," by his friend, Professor Josef Sittard, and in an address given by this author at a Brahms memorial concert in Hamburg immediately after the master's death, the following sympathetic allusion was made to the beloved teacher:

"Brahms had the rare good fortune of being trained under a teacher whose like does not fall to the lot of many young musicians. Pledged to no special artistic creed, sworn to no particular tendency or party, Marxsen had interest to bestow upon every important development of musical art. He never gave instruction on an inflexible scheme, but allowed himself to be guided by the separate requirements of each case. He was careful not to interfere with the individuality of young talent, not to meddle with the distinctive peculiarities of his pupil's creative ability; he only guided them within artistic confines. Brahms regarded his teacher with touching gratitude, and when at the height of his creative power still continued to send his compositions, before their publication, for Marxsen's critical inspection. Nothing is more indicative of the intimate relation between the two men than the letters (from Brahms to Marxsen) that I was permitted to see years ago."

Unfortunately for the musical world, only one or two scraps of this correspondence remain. On the death of Marxsen in 1887, Brahms' letters to his teacher were returned to him at his request, and were destroyed.

CHAPTER VI.

1854-1855.

Brahms at Hanover—Hans von Bülow—Robert and Clara Schumann in Hanover—Schumann's illness—Brahms in Düsseldorf—Variations on Schumann's theme in F sharp minor—B major Trio—First public performance in New York—First attempt at symphony.

WITH the opening of the year 1854, Brahms may be said to have entered upon the first chapter of his new life. The transition stage of his career had been defined with unusual sharpness of outline. The eventful journey had been as a bridge by which he had passed from youth to manhood. Behind it were the dark years of lonely effort with issue still untried, the gathering up of strength and treasure but dimly recognised by the worker, labouring under a thick haze of obscurity; in front lay, straight and clear, the pathway of endeavour towards a fixed goal, cheered by companionship and illumined by the consciousness of a measure of success already won. Having tranquillised his mind and shaken off the effects of months of excitement by nearly a fortnight's intercourse with his family and friends at Hamburg, Johannes was impatient to get quietly to work again, all the more since new and forcible motives—the sense of his responsibility to Schumann, and the desire to become as far as possible worthy of his encomiums—added their influence to the energy of his nature, and helped to spur him on to the resolve to outdo even his utmost.

Bringing his stay in Hamburg to a close with the opening of the New Year, he left on January 3 or 4 for Hanover, where he found a new introduction awaiting his arrival. Hans von Bülow, who had passed Christmas in Joachim's "dear society," writes on the 6th to his mother:

"I have become tolerably well acquainted with Robert Schumann's young prophet Brahms. He arrived two days ago, and is always with us. A very lovable, frank nature, and a talent that really has something God-given about it."*

Bülow took an early opportunity of carrying out Liszt's desire, hinted at in the letter of December 16. He played the first movement of the C major Sonata on March 1 at Frau Peroni-Glasbrenner's concert in Hamburg, and was thus the first artist—always excepting the composer himself—to perform a work of Brahms in public. That his attitude towards our composer did not, during the succeeding twenty years, correspond with this promising beginning, as will be seen hereafter, may be chiefly attributed to the disappointment with which the disciples of the New-German school gradually realised that their artistic aims were at variance with the mature convictions of Joachim, whom they reckoned for a while as one of themselves, and of Brahms, whose allegiance they had hoped to secure.

Johannes, established in a lodging of his own at Hanover, began the routine of work, diversified by intimate association with a few chosen friends, which he preferred to the end of his life, and was soon absorbed in the composition of his B major Pianoforte Trio. The intimacy between Joachim and himself was now widened to a triple alliance by the addition of Grimm, now living in Hanover, and lively discussions were carried on in Joachim's rooms late into the night by the three friends. The young violinist had not been a smoker up to this time, but his companions used to envelop him and themselves in such thick clouds of tobacco, that one night, unable any longer to endure his

---

* Bülow's "Briefe und Schriften." Edited by Marie von Bülow.

sufferings passively, he suddenly declared his surrender, and began to puff away with the others, to Brahms' and Grimm's great delight.

Schumann had accepted an invitation from Hille, the founder and conductor of the "New Singakademie" at Hanover, to be present at a performance of his "Paradise and the Peri" on January 28, and, to the joy of the young musicians, wrote to Joachim to suggest that his visit, which was to be made in the company of his wife, should be the occasion of several public appearances. He continues :

"Now where is Johannes? Is he with you? If so, greet him. Is he flying high—or only amongst flowers? Is he setting drums and trumpets to work yet? He must call to mind the beginnings of the Beethoven symphonies; he must try to do something of the same kind. The beginning is the main point; when one has begun, the end seems to come of itself. . . .

"I hope also to see, or better still to hear, something new of yours soon. You, too, should remember the above-named symphony beginnings, but not before Henry and Demetrius.*

"I always get into a good humour when I write to you. You are a kind of physician for me.

"Adieu.
"Your R. SCHU."

Some idea of the happy week passed by the three friends in the constant society of their "master" may be gathered from Moser's charming description in his Life of Joachim. Schumann could not see enough of his beloved young favourites, Joachim and Brahms, and readily extended his cordiality to their companion Grimm. The third subscription concert was a veritable Schumann festival. Joachim conducted the master's fourth symphony, "evidently with great delight and love," says the *Hanover Courier*, as well as Beethoven's Pianoforte Concerto in E flat, played by Frau Schumann, and performed Schumann's lately-written Violin Fantasia dedicated to him and first played at Düs-

---
* Two overtures on which Joachim was working.

seldorf. There were plenty of opportunities for private meetings in Joachim's rooms, in the railway restaurant, and elsewhere, that were unshadowed by any presentiment of an impending catastrophe; for Schumann was unusually bright and communicative, and took pleasure in amusing his young friends with anecdotes of his own early experiences. The hours thus passed were tenderly remembered in after-years by those who had been gladdened by the setting radiance of a light soon to be extinguished.

"What a high festival we have had through the Schumanns' visit," writes Brahms, a few days after their departure, to Dietrich in Düsseldorf. "Everything has seemed alive since. Greet the great ones from me many times."*

A week after their return Schumann wrote:

"*February* 6, 1854.

"DEAR JOACHIM,

"We have been at home eight days, and have not yet sent a word to you and your companions. I have, however, frequently written to you with invisible ink. . . . We have often thought of the past days; may others like them come quickly! The kind royal family, the excellent orchestra, and the two young dæmons moving amid the scenes—we shall not soon forget it.

"The cigars are very much to my liking. It seems they were a handshake from Brahms, and, as usual, a very substantial and agreeable one.

"Write to me soon—in words and in tones!

"R. SCHU."

It is sad to realise that in less than a fortnight after sending this letter, so free from signs of depression, so bright and healthy in tone, Schumann had written down his last musical thought, the now well-known Theme in E flat; and that before the close of the month he was overtaken by the crisis of his terrible malady. Alarming symptoms declared

---

* This and all other extracts from Dietrich are taken from his well-known "Recollections of Brahms."

themselves in the night of February 10-11. The master was distressed by illusions of hearing, one note seeming to sound in his ear from the impression of which he was unable to free himself and which only gave place a day or two later to the sensation of entire movements played as though by a full orchestra. Early in the night of February 17-18 he rose to write down the theme in E flat which had, he said, been sung to him by angels, and during the following week his condition changed rapidly for the worse. He continued to occupy himself at his writing table during intervals of comparative relief from suffering, and was engaged on the 27th with the composition of variations on his theme when a moment's chance occurred that enabled him to escape the watchfulness of his devoted wife. Seizing it, he managed to leave his house unobserved, and, a few moments afterwards, had thrown himself into the Rhine. He was rescued by some sailors belonging to a nearby steamboat, and conveyed to his home in a carriage. But his state continued so distressing that Frau Schumann, herself needing care at the time, was not allowed by the doctors to see him, and he was taken on March 4, in accordance with his own desire, to the private establishment of Dr. Richarz at Endenich, near Bonn.

It would be difficult to describe in exaggerated terms the consternation with which a great part of the musical world, and especially the friends of Schumann's immediate circle, became aware of these overwhelming occurrences. Sorrow for the great master, love for the indulgent friend, alarmed sympathy for the stricken wife, kept the younger of his disciples in a state of restless agitation, which seems to have found its principal relief in the writing of letters of excited inquiry to Dietrich, the only one of their number on the scene of the catastrophe.

"Never in my life has anything so moved and deeply shaken me," wrote Theodor Kirchner, "as the dreadful occurrence with our honoured, beloved Schumann. . . . We should all be terribly lonely without him, and as regards myself, all pleasure in my own endeavours would be gone."

"Pray send me an exact description of the whole catastrophe *as quickly as possible,*" so ran Naumann's letter, "especially if there is any hope of Schumann's complete restoration, how his unhappy wife has borne this cruel stroke of fate, and how you are yourself. I repeat my request for *immediate* news."

To the friends in Hanover, who had so lately seen Schumann in apparent enjoyment of unwonted health both of body and mind, the tidings, of which they first became informed through a paragraph in the *Cologne Gazette*, seemed too sudden and tragic to be credible.

"DEAR DIETRICH—" Joachim dashed off—

"If you have any feeling of friendship for Brahms and me, relieve our anxiety, and write word instantly whether Schumann is really as ill as the paper says, and let us know at once of any change in his condition. It is too grievous to be in uncertainty about the life of someone to whom we are bound with our best powers. I can scarcely wait for the hour that will bring me tidings of him. I am quite beside myself with dread.

"Write soon.

"Your J. JOACHIM."

It was impossible, however, to wait for an answer, and no letter could have appeased the desire of the affectionate young musicians to be on the spot; so Brahms, having no fixed duties to detain him, started immediately for Düsseldorf, and Joachim hoped to follow, if only for a couple of days. On March 3 Johannes sent his report:

"DEAREST JOSEPH,

"Do come on Saturday; it comforts Frau Schumann to see certain dear faces.

"Schumann's condition seems to be improved. The physicians have hope, but no one is allowed to see him.

"I have already been with Frau Schumann. She wept very much, but was very glad to see me and to be able to expect you.

"We expect you on Sunday morning, and Grimm on Wednesday.

"Your

"JOHANNES."*

"To my great relief," wrote Dietrich a fortnight later to Naumann, "Brahms came at once after hearing the dreadful news. Grimm is also here. Joachim was here for two days, and is coming again in a few weeks."

At the end of the letter he adds:

"Brahms has written a quite wonderful trio, and is a man to be taken in every respect as a pattern. With all his depth, he is healthy, fresh, and lively, entirely untouched by modern morbidness."

It now became the cherished duty of the young men to do what in them lay to support and comfort the sorely-tried wife in her desolation. Nothing, perhaps, could have helped and soothed her so much as the feeling that the tie which primarily bound them to her was that of their devotion to her husband, the knowledge that they mourned with her in a common grief, and that their sympathy was touched by their personal sense of what she had lost. Never, indeed, was more loyal sympathy offered for the consolation of sorrow, and it had its reward. After the first terrible days had been lived through, a calm and self-possession returned to the illustrious lady, which heightened, if possible, the young artists' admiration of her. The news from Endenich improved towards the end of the month, and on April 1 even became reassuring. The patient was now passing his time walking, or quietly sleeping, undisturbed by fits of anxiety or delusions of hearing; was gentle towards his attendant, had conversed a little with him, and had even made a joke appropriate to the day. Frau Schumann summoned up courage to look with hope to the future, and allowed herself to be persuaded to resume some of her ordinary avocations. The short remainder of the musical

---

* From the original letter, presented by Dr. Joachim to the author.

season was, indeed, passed in necessary retirement; but the great pianist found solace in quietly studying her husband's compositions anew with Dietrich, Brahms, Grimm, and others of the circle, playing his great orchestral and choral works with them on the pianoforte, and listening in turn to their performances. Dietrich writes in March:

"Yesterday and the day before she went through the whole of Schumann's 'Faust' music with us. We are with her every day, and it is impossible for me to think of leaving at present."

On June 11 Frau Schumann's seventh child was born. His name, chosen in memory of Mendelssohn, was registered as Felix, and Brahms was to stand sponsor, but it was decided that the christening ceremony should be delayed for the present. Perhaps before long the father would be able to take part in it with his loved ones. A touching memorial of the efforts made by the young Brahms to divert the mind of the longing wife from its burden of sorrow exists in his Variations for Pianoforte, Op. 9, on a Theme of Robert Schumann, which were written during Frau Schumann's convalescence; each new variation being brought to her as it was completed. Schumann's theme ("Album-blatt," Op. 99, No. 1), which refers to its composer's early work,

Op. 5 (Variations on a Theme by Clara Wieck), had been chosen by Frau Clara as the subject of variations written by herself for Robert's forty-third birthday, and an entry in her diary records her appreciation of the affection which now inspired Johannes with the idea of using it again.

"He tried to bring solace to my heart. He composed variations on the beautiful, intimate theme, which made such a deep impression upon me a year ago when I composed variations for my beloved Robert, and touched me deeply by his tender thoughtfulness."

Grimm, who remained at Düsseldorf during these months in close companionship with Johannes, christened his friend's work "Trost-Einsamkeit," and remembered it as such ever afterwards. It tells plainly enough the story of the young composer's thoughts. It is full of references to Schumann and his wife—notably in the ninth variation, which contains note for note reminiscences of Schumann's Album-Blatt, Op. 99, No. 2, and in the tenth, in which the first four bar of Clara Wieck's original theme

 etc.

are introduced by diminution into the middle voice:

The work is astounding in its evidence of the mastery already achieved by the young composer over the technique of variation form, in which he uses the complicated resources of contrapuntal science with absolute playfulness. For one illustration of this the reader may again be referred to the tenth variation, in which the original bass of Schumann's theme is used as the melody of the upper part and its inversion as the bass part, whilst the original melody (quoted on p. 166) is imitated by diminution in the middle part.

 etc.

We must resist the temptation to linger over the many interesting details of this noble work, as the aim of our pages is not a technical one; but we may note in passing that, of the sixteen variations which it contains, five are written in keys varying from that of the theme, a circumstance which again brings it into a certain association with Schumann.* Brahms, in his five other independent sets of variations for pianoforte, nearly follows the practice of the earlier masters, who confined themselves to the major and minor modes of one key.

Johannes had meanwhile, according to custom, sent the completed manuscript of his trio to Marxsen, and had speedily received it back again with his master's critical remarks. These he acknowledged on June 28 in a letter from which the following brief extracts are taken, sending Marxsen, at the same time, the new variations and a collection of short pieces written at odds and ends of time, which he proposed to call "Leaves from the Journal of a Musician, published by the Young Kreisler."

"Let me thank you very much for having vouchsafed such a long letter, such a detailed examination to my trio. I will write about the proposed little alterations when I send you the printed copy. I have allowed the trio to lie in order to accustom myself to them."

Asking Marxsen if he considers the pianoforte pieces worth publishing, he adds as to the proposed title: "What do you think of it? Doesn't it please you? I must confess I should be sorry to strike it out."† It must be presumed that Marxsen's opinion was unfavourable, for the short pieces did not see the light. We shall, however, meet with one or two of them in a few concert-programmes before long, and one will be found to have a particular interest for English readers.

The B major Trio, published in 1854 by Breitkopf and

---

* *Cf.* Schumann's great variations: the "Etudes Symphoniques."
† Sittard's "Künstler-Charakteristiken."

Härtel as Op. 8, which remained for many years but little known, has, with its beautiful youthful qualities, long since become dear to those who have yielded their hearts to the spell of Brahms' music. The composer's fertile fancy has betrayed him, in the first allegro, into some episodical writing which somewhat clouds the distinctness of outline, and impedes the listener in his appreciation of the distinguished beauties of the movement, and there are places in the finale where a certain disappointment succeeds to the conviction inspired by the impetuous opening subject; but in wealth of material, in the rare beauty of its principal themes, and in noble sincerity of expression, the trio occupies a distinguished place even amongst the examples of Brahms' maturity. The scherzo with its trio are already masterly both in conception and treatment, and in the adagio we have promise of the deeply impressive slow movements which were moulded in ever-increasing perfection of structure by the composer's ripening genius. That Brahms retained an affection for this child of his young imagination is shown by his having published a revised edition of the work so late in his career as the year 1891. We must confess our preference for the original version, which is consistently representative of the composer as he was when he wrote it. The later one, though in some respects more suitable for concert performance, does not appear to us to have solved the difficulty of successfully applying to a work of art the process of grafting, upon the fresh, lovable immaturity of twenty-one, the practised but less mobile experience of fifty-seven.

The trio was performed for the first time in public, to the lasting musical distinction of America, on November 27, 1855, at William Mason's concert of chamber music in Dodsworth's Hall, New York, by the concert-giver, Theodor Thomas, and Carl Bergmann, to whom, therefore, belongs the honour of having inaugurated the public performances of Brahms' great series of works of this class. It was played, for the second time, at Breslau on December 18 of the same year. Many years elapsed before it was heard in England.

As soon as she was able to travel, Frau Schumann resolved to seek rest and change of scene by visiting her mother in Berlin, whither Joachim also proceeded from Hanover on a visit to some of his own particular friends. Dietrich had quitted Düsseldorf some months previously to follow prospects of success in Leipzig; Grimm and Brahms remained behind to take charge of any urgent tidings from Endenich; and to Johannes was especially entrusted the congenial task of putting Schumann's books and music in order. This was soon accomplished to his satisfaction as he writes to Dietrich:

"And now I sit there the whole day and study. I have seldom felt so happy as now, rummaging in this library."

On July 19, the very day of Frau Schumann's departure, the happy news arrived that a marked improvement had taken place in her husband's health. He had spoken of feeling better, expressed a desire to visit his friend Wasielewski at Bonn; above all, had picked flowers and evidently wished them to be sent to his wife, whom he had not mentioned during his illness. News and flowers were instantly despatched to Berlin and were received with almost overwhelming feelings of hope and longing.

"I cannot describe my agitation," Frau Schumann writes to Dietrich, after informing him of the tidings, "but I never knew how difficult it is to bear a great joy! .... It often seems to me as though I must lose my reason. It is too much, all that I have gone through already and that is yet before me!"

Her agitation of mind made it impossible for her to stay out the intended visit, and leaving her little daughter Julie, who had accompanied her, behind under the grandmother's care, she returned to her home four days after leaving it.

"Ah! How rejoiced I was when I entered the dear room again," she writes, "and saw his writing-table, books, and other possessions. I felt as though I had been long absent, and as though I now atoned for a wrong done to him, the dear one, who was thinking of me again and imagined me to be here whilst I was in Berlin."*

The later movements of the party are chronicled in a letter written by Johannes to the Amstvogt Blume, of Winsen:

"ULM, *August* 16, 1854.

"HONOURED SIR,

"You certainly think that your dear letter did not give me the least pleasure, as I have left it so long unanswered? Ah, the time lately has been so full of excitement that I was obliged to put it off from day to day. Frau Schumann went with a friend on the 10th of this month to Ostend for the benefit of her health. I, after much persuasion, resolved to make a journey through Swabia during her absence. I did not know how greatly I was attached to the Schumanns, how I lived in them; everything seemed barren and empty to me, every day I wished to turn back, and was obliged to travel by rail in order to get quickly to a distance and forget about turning back. It was of no use; I have come as far as Ulm, partly on foot, partly by rail; I am going to return quickly, and would rather wait for Frau Schumann in Düsseldorf than wander about in the dark. When one has found such divine people as Robert and Clara Schumann, one should stick to them and not leave them, but raise and inspire one's self by them. The dear Schumann continues to improve, as you have read in my letter to my parents. There has been a great deal of gossip about his condition. I consider the best description of him is to be found in some of the works of E. T. A. Hoffmann (Rath Krespel, Serapion, and especially the splendid Kreisler, etc.). He has only stripped off his body too soon.—If you would give me pleasure, let me find a letter from you in Ddf.—is that quite too bold? I will write to you again, and more rationally, from there. I am writing this letter in the waiting-room of the railway-station, which accounts for its having become, probably, very confused.—A thousand

---

* Litzmann II, 322.

hearty greetings to dear Uncle Giesemann, I will write to him also from Ddf.; heartiest greetings also to Frau Blume and your daughter. Remember with affection

"Your JOHANNES BRAHMS."*

Stopping at Bonn on his return journey to inquire after the patient at Endenich, Brahms obtained permission to look at Schumann, himself unseen, and from his position behind an open window was able, after he had sufficiently controlled his first agitation, to assure himself that the master looked well and wore the kind, tranquil mien natural to him; and on his arrival at Düsseldorf, whom should he find there but Grimm, who, having missed the object of a journey on which he, too, had set out, had likewise been to Endenich, seen Schumann, and gained an impression of his appearance and manner similar to that which had reassured Johannes!†

Grimm left Düsseldorf in October, for Hanover, and remained there till the following year, when he settled in Göttingen as a pianoforte teacher and the conductor of a choral society. Johannes also went north on a visit to his parents, but for a few weeks only. The Schumanns' house had become a second home to him, and his place in the affections of its master and mistress that of a beloved elder son. Almost every particular that had marked the course of his year's acquaintance with them had been of a kind to stir his true, loving, high-strung nature to its depths. Schumann's noble character, his quick affection for the young stranger and unconditional acceptance of his art, the ideal relation which united the great composer with his wife, the distinguished qualities of the gifted woman who found her greatest happiness in consecrating her genius to the service of her romantic love, the terrible blow which had separated the two lives so closely linked, the sadness of the present,

---

* See footnote on p. 120.

† Compare Grimm's letter to Brahms, written also on August 16, Brahms' "Briefwechsel," IV, No. 2.

the uncertainty of the future—each and all of these things had aroused in the heart of Johannes a tumult of feeling, a poignancy of affection, that allowed him no rest when he was out of immediate touch with the two people who were its object. He could study to his heart's content in Schumann's library, where books and music were unreservedly at his disposal; could be of use to Frau Schumann, who truly valued his sympathy and returned his affection; he was in constant communication with Joachim, and could have as much pleasant society as he cared for. In short, he felt that for the present his place was at Düsseldorf, and at Düsseldorf he remained.

It was in the spring of 1854 that he made the acquaintance of Julius Allgeyer, who, four years his senior, was at the time a student of copper-plate engraving in Düsseldorf under Josef Keller.

"Brahms," says Allgeyer in a letter of this date, "has Schiller's striking profile; his compositions sound different from everything else known to me. He has the bad manners of a frolicsome child and the understanding of a man."

There was much in the circumstances and characters of the two young men to foster an intimacy between them. Allgeyer's youth had, like that of Johannes, been passed in struggle, and he resembled Brahms in his restless hunger after general culture, which he endeavoured to satisfy by constant and varied reading. The composition of Brahms' Ballades for pianoforte, Op. 10, which belongs to this time, has a direct association with Allgeyer, to whom the young musician was indebted for his acquaintance with Herder's "Stimmen der Völker," the volume containing a translation of the Scotch ballad "Edward" that inspired the first of the pieces in question. Brahms' memory for such details is well illustrated by his dedication to Allgeyer of the Lieder und Romanzen, for two voices, with pianoforte accompaniment, Op. 75, published in 1878, the first number of which is a setting of "Edward." Another avowed instance of his partiality for Herder's collection is to be found in a still later work, No. 1 of the three Intermezzi for pianoforte, Op. 117, and it may be surmised that the book contains the secret key to the composer's thoughts during the writing of more than one other of the short pieces for pianoforte designated by the general name of "Intermezzo" or "Capriccio."

Brahms and Allgeyer remained intimate, though with intervals of some estrangement—if this be not too strong a term to express a temporary cessation of intercourse without alleged cause—until Brahms' death; and Allgeyer, who was introduced by Johannes to Frau Schumann, came to be regarded by her as belonging to the circle of her valued friends.*

Schumann's desire that his young protégé should apply his powerful ideal gifts and his skill in the handling of form to the composition of an orchestral work had not been disregarded by Brahms. He had tried his hand at an overture early in the year, and had worked through the spring and summer at a symphony, making his first attempts at instrumentation with the help of Grimm. It could not be otherwise than that the rapid succession of extraordinary events and vivid emotions which had agitated his spirit should prove a strong stimulus to his imagination; and it is not surprising to find that they moved him to the composition of a series of movements, two of which remain amongst the most powerful produced by him, one having been accepted by thousands of mourners all the world over as the most fitting musical expression known to them in the presence of profound grief. The symphony, as such, was never completed, but the work became known in the composer's intimate circle as a sonata for two pianofortes, of which the first two movements are now familiar to the world as the first and second of the Pianoforte Concerto in D minor, and the third is immortalised in the "Behold all Flesh,"

---

* Professor Carl Neumann's introduction to the second edition (1904) of Allgeyer's "Life of Anselm Feuerbach."

the wonderful march movement in three-four time of the German Requiem. Brahms frequently played the sonata at this period with Frau Schumann, or with Grimm, who did not hesitate to urge upon his friend his opinion as to the inadequacy of the form for the expression of the great ideas of the work.

The two sets of Variations composed respectively by Frau Clara and Johannes on Schumann's theme were published simultaneously, by Brahms' desire, in the autumn, with his Songs, Op. 7, dedicated to Dietrich, and the B major Trio; the variations by Johannes appearing as his Op. 9. The song "Mondnacht" also appeared this year, without opus number, in a book of "Album-Blätter" published at Göttingen.

The improvement in Schumann's condition went on so steadily that on September 13, the thirty-fifth anniversary of his wife's birthday, he was permitted to receive a letter from her. His answer, sent the next day, contains no allusion to Brahms, but brings Schumann's tenderness in his home relationships so vividly before the mind that a short extract from it will, we think, be welcomed by the reader.

"ENDENICH, *Sept.* 14, 1854.

"How I rejoiced, beloved Clara, to see your handwriting. High thanks for having written to me on such a day, and that you and the dear children still remember me. Greet and kiss the little ones! Oh, if I could see you and speak to you again, but the way is too far. So much I should like to know; how your life is going on; where you are living and if you still play as gloriously as formerly; if Marie and Elise continue to make progress, if they still sing also—if you still have the Klems pianoforte [a present from Schumann to his wife], where my collection of scores is (the printed ones) and what has become of the manuscripts (such as the Requiem, the Sänger's Fluch); where our album is, containing autographs of Goethe, Jean Paul, Mozart, Beethoven, Weber, and many letters addressed to you and me."

On the 18th he writes:

"What joyful news you have again sent me . . . that

Brahms, to whom you will give my kind and admiring greetings, has come to live in Düsseldorf; what friendship! If you would like to know whose is my favourite name, you will no doubt guess his, the unforgettable one! . . . If you write to Joachim, greet him. What have Brahms and Joachim been composing? Is the overture to Hamlet published? Has he finished anything else? You write that you are giving your lessons in the pianoforte-room. Who are the present pupils? Who the best? Are you not doing too much, dear Clara?"

He goes on to recall the happiness of the journeys made in his wife's company, begs that their double portrait may be sent him, would like some money, in order to be able to give to the poor people whom he meets in his walks, wants a list of his children's birthdays.

A week later, September 26, he says:

"What you write about . . . has given me the greatest pleasure. So also about Brahms and Joachim and their compositions. I am surprised that Brahms is working at counterpoint which does not seem like him. I should like to make acquaintance with Joachim's three pieces for pianoforte and viola. I can remember de Laurens' portrait of Brahms, but not the one of me. Thank you for the children's birthday dates. Who are to be sponsors for the little one, and in what church is he to be baptised? . . ."

In October he acknowledges the arrival of Brahms' variations, sent him by his wife:

"DEAREST CLARA,

"What pleasure you have again given me! Your letter and Julie's, Brahms' variations on the theme which you have varied, the three volumes of Arnim Brentano's Wunderhorn. . . . I remember Herr Grimm very well, we used to be together with Brahms and Joachim at the railway-station [in Hanover]; greet him and above all Fräulein Leser. I shall write to Brahms myself . . ."

That this renewal of intercourse with her husband cheered and encouraged Frau Schumann for the performance of her arduous public duties during the autumn season will be

readily believed. Under the necessity of a heavily increased weight of responsibility to her young children, she had bound herself to the fulfilment of a long list of concert engagements, which scarcely allowed her an interval of rest. Happily, the reports from Endenich continued favourable. Joachim, writing to Liszt on November 16, says:

"What a happiness it is that Schumann's condition is distinctly improved. I had a letter from him from Endenich lately. He relates some of our common experiences quite clearly, expressing himself in a kind, gentle way as though he had just awakened from a dream. Everything seems new to him, and he would like to participate in what is going on, asks about compositions, about friends; one may certainly hope for the best."

On November 27, having had time to study Brahms' variations, Schumann writes, in the course of a letter to his wife:

"The variations by Johannes delighted me at first sight and do so still more on deeper acquaintance. I shall myself write also to Brahms; does his portrait by de Laurens still hang in my study? He is the most attractive and gifted young fellow. I recall with delight the splendid impression he made that first time with his C major Sonata, and afterwards with the F sharp minor Sonata and the Scherzo in E flat minor. Oh, if I could only hear him again! I should like his ballades also."

To Brahms, enclosed in the above:

"Could I but come to you myself, to see you again and to hear your splendid variations or [to hear them] from my Clara of whose wonderful interpretation Joachim has written to me. How incomparably the whole is rounded off, how one recognises you in the rich brightness of the imagination and again in the profound art, united as I have not yet known them. The theme emerging here and there, but very secretly, then so vehement and tender. The theme then quite vanishing, and at the end, after the fourteenth [variation], so ingeniously written in canon in the second; how splendid is the fifteenth in G flat major, and the last. And I have to thank you, dear Johannes, for all your kindness and goodness to my Clara; she always writes to me about it. She sent me yesterday to my pleasure, as you perhaps know, volumes of my compositions and Jean Paul's Flegeljahre. Now I hope soon to see your handwriting, however great a treasure it is to me, in another form also. The winter is fairly mild. You know the Bonn neighbourhood. I enjoy Beethoven's statue and the beautiful view of the Siebengebirge. We saw each other last in Hanover. Only write soon to

"Your affectionate and appreciative
"R. SCHUMANN."

Brahms' answer speaks for itself:

"HAMBURG, *December* 2, 1854.

"MOST BELOVED FRIEND,

"How can I describe to you my pleasure at your dear letter! You have already so often made me happy when you have remembered me so affectionately in the letters to your wife, and now I have a letter belonging entirely to myself. It is the first I have had from you; I value it beyond measure. Unfortunately I received it in Hamburg, where I had come to visit my parents; I would much rather have received it from the hand of your wife.

"I expect to return to Düsseldorf in a few days; I long to be there.

"The overmuch praise which you bestow on my variations fills me with happiness. I have been studying your works industriously since the spring; how much I should like to hear your praise of them also! I have passed this year since spring-time at Düsseldorf; I shall never forget it, I have learned all the time to love you and your glorious wife more and more.

"I have never yet looked forward so cheerfully and confidently, never believed so firmly in a splendid future as now. How I wish it were near, and nearer still the happy time when you will be quite restored to us.

"I cannot then leave you any more; I shall try to earn more and more of your dear friendship.

"Good-bye, and think of me with affection.

"Your warmly venerating JOHANNES BRAHMS.

"My parents and your friends here think of you with the greatest veneration and love. The parents, Herr Marxsen, Otten, and Avé, particularly beg me to give you their most cordial greetings."*

On the 15th of the month Schumann wrote again to Johannes:

"ENDENICH, *December,* 1854.

"DEAR FRIEND,

"If I could but come to you at Christmas! Meanwhile I have received your portrait from my dear wife, your familiar portrait, and I know the place in my room quite well, quite well—under the mirror. I am still refreshing myself with your variations; I should like to hear several of them from you and my Clara; I am not completely master of them; especially the second, the fourth not up to time and the fifth not; but the eighth (and the slower ones) and the ninth—A reminiscence of which Clara wrote to me is probably on p. 14; what is it from? a song?† —and the twelfth—— Oh, if I could only hear you!"

The andante and scherzo from Brahms' F minor Sonata, Op. 5, were included by Frau Schumann in several of her concert programmes of the season, and the B major Trio was introduced by her in private circles to the music lovers of Breslau and Berlin. The sonata-movements, though received with indifference by the general public, were, on the whole, encouragingly noticed by the press. The *Vossische Zeitung* of Berlin dismissed them as wanting in clearness and simplicity, but the *National Zeitung* of the same city perceived in them evidence of an "hervorragenden Produktions-Vermögen," and a Frankfurt critic wrote:

"Frau Schumann deserves the highest acknowledgment for introducing Brahms' compositions to the public with her master-hand, and thus preparing the way for their acceptance."

The interest awakened by the performance of the B major Trio before some of the leading musicians of Breslau, led to

---

* See footnote on p. 136.

† The introduction by diminution of Clara Wieck's theme mentioned on page 167.

the inclusion of the work in the programme of the concert given by Messrs. Mächtig and Seyfrise later in the year, which has been already noted.*

During ten days of her northern tour, Frau Schumann made her headquarters in Hamburg, and Johannes, arranging his visit home in correspondence with her movements, was made happy by seeing the cordiality of the relations established between his great artist-friend and the members of his family circle: "Homely but respectable people," records Frau Schumann's diary, "where I honestly feel so well in this unpretending simplicity."

The last public event of the journey was a soirée given by Frau Clara and Joachim on December 21 in Leipzig. On the 23rd, after a quiet day in Hanover, the traveller returned to Düsseldorf, accompanied by Brahms and Joachim, to spend Christmas in the midst of her children.

Moved by his own restless solicitude concerning Schumann's state, as well as by the affectionate desire to relieve the anxiety that had racked Frau Clara's mind during more than two months of unceasing activity, Joachim went off to Bonn on the morning of the 24th to get news at first hand of the invalid. To his joy he was admitted to the first interview with a personal friend that had been allowed to the master since his residence at Endenich. The impression he derived was to some extent reassuring and there was comfort for the little party in the mere fact that one of their number had seen and conversed with Schumann. A touching picture of the gathering in Düsseldorf of those who stood first in the affections of the great composer is given in Brahms' next letter to him:

"MOST HONOURED FRIEND,

"I should like to write a great deal about the Christmas evening, which was made so happy to us by Joachim's news; how he told us about you the whole evening and your wife wept so quietly. We were filled with joyful hope that we may soon be able to see you again.

---

* See *ante*, p. 169.

"You always turn the days which would otherwise be days of mourning for us, into high festivals. On her birthday your wife was allowed to write to you the first letter. At Christmas a friend first talked with you, the only one to whom we should not grudge this happiness, but only desire for ourselves to be allowed to succeed him soon.

"On the first day of the festival your wife gave her presents. She will now be writing to tell you about it; how well Marie played your A minor Sonata with Joachim, and Elise the Kinderscenen, and how she delighted me with Jean Paul's complete works. I had not hoped to be able to call them my own for many years. Joachim got the scores of your symphonies, which your wife had already given me.

"I returned here the evening before Christmas; how long the separation from your wife seemed to me! I had so accustomed myself to her inspiring society, I had lived near her so delightfully all the summer and learned to admire and love her so much, that everything seemed flat to me, and I could only long to see her again. What nice things I have brought back with me from Hamburg, however! The score of Gluck's Alcestis (the Italian edition, 1776) from Herr Avé, your first dear letter to me and several from your beloved wife. I must thank you most warmly for a pleasant word in your last letter, for the affectionate 'thou'; your kind wife also makes me happy now by using the nice, intimate word; it is the highest proof to me of her favour; I will try always to deserve it more.

"I had a great deal to write to you, dearest friend, but it would probably only be a repetition of what your wife is writing, therefore I conclude with the warmest handshake and greeting. Your

"JOHANNES.

"DÜSSELDORF, 30 *December*, 1854."

Frau Schumann, having before her the fatigues of a concert-journey in Holland, allowed herself a brief rest during the first half of January, and was cheered by the most encouraging letters from her husband. He wrote on the 6th:

" . . . I wish also to thank you most particularly, my Clara, for the artist letters and Johannes for the sonata and ballades.* I know them now. The sonata—I remember to have heard it once from him—so profoundly grasped; living, deep, and warm throughout, and so closely woven together. And the ballades—the first wonderful, quite new; only I do not understand the *doppio movimento* either in this or the second, is it not too fast?† The close beautiful —original! The second how different, how diversified, how suggestive to the imagination; magical tones are in it. The bass F sharp at the end seems to lead to the third ballade. What shall we call this? Demoniacal—quite splendid, and becoming more and more mysterious after the *pp* in the trio. And the return and close! Has this ballade made a similar impression on you, my Clara? In the fourth ballade how beautifully the strange melody vacillates at the close between minor and major, and remains mournfully in the major. Now on to overtures and symphonies! Do you not like this, my Clara, better than organ? A symphony or opera, which arouses enthusiasm and makes a great sensation, brings everything else more quickly forward. He must. Now greet Johannes warmly and the children, and you, my dearest heart, remember your, as of old, loving

"ROBERT."

Brahms was permitted to follow Joachim, and on January 11 paid the master a visit of several hours' duration, in the course of which he played both to and with him. At its close Schumann walked back to Bonn with his dear young friend, and could not make up his mind to part with him. Johannes tore himself away just in time to catch his train, and wrote a few days afterwards:

"DEAR HONOURED FRIEND,

"I must thank you myself for the great pleasure you give me by the dedication of your splendid concertstück.‡ How I rejoice to see my name thus printed! Especially,

---

* In manuscript: Ballades for Pianoforte, Op. 10.

† The *doppio movimento* marked in the manuscript of the first ballade was changed before publication to *allegro ma non troppo*, no doubt in deference to Schumann's suggestion.

‡ Concert-allegro with Introduction for Pianoforte and Orchestra, Op. 134.

too, that I, like Joachim, have a concerto of my own.*
We have often talked of the two works and which we like
best—we have not been able to decide.

"I think with joy of the short hours that I was allowed
to spend with you, they were so delightful—but passed so
quickly. I cannot tell your wife enough about them; it
makes me doubly glad that you received me with such
friendship and kindness, and that you still think of the
hour with so much affection.

"We shall be able to see you thus more and more frequently and pleasantly till we possess you again.

"I have taken the catalogue (chronological), as you
wished, to your copyist (Fuchs).

"I expect you would like the original of Jenny Lind's
letter. It is probably the handwriting that you want. I
need not write out the contents for you.

"We are sending Bargiel's new work, it will give you
great pleasure, as it does us; Op. 8 is a great advance upon
Op. 9. Both are dedicated to your wife; that is what I
should like to do always. I should like to take turns with
the names Joachim and Clara Schumann till I had courage
to add your name. That, probably, will not soon come
to me.

"Now good-bye, dear man, and think sometimes with
affection of your
                                                "JOHANNES.
"DÜSSELDORF, in January, 1855."

"Do you remember that you encouraged me last winter
to write an overture to "Romeo"? For the rest, I have
been trying my hand at a symphony during the past summer, have even instrumented the first movement and
composed the second and third."

During the entire winter, the devotion to Frau Schumann,
through which Joachim and Brahms were alike eager to
express their veneration for the beloved master in his awful
trial, was shared between them in the most practical way.
Joachim remained her frequent artistic companion after her
return from Holland, and the success achieved by the two

---

* Fantasia for Violin and Orchestra, Op. 131, dedicated to
Joachim.

great musicians on the many occasions of their giving concerts together, during this and the following season, was extraordinary and unvarying. Johannes remained at Düsseldorf to attend to Schumann's little requirements, and to send cheery news of all that was going on at home to the anxious wife and mother. In February he writes to Endenich:

"DEAR HONOURED FRIEND,

"Herewith I send you the things you wished for; a necktie and the *Signale*. I must be responsible for the first; as your wife is in Berlin, I had to decide. I only hope you will like it, and that it is not too high?

"I also send you the *Signale*; some of the numbers are missing, we have not been careful enough about them. From this time forward you shall have them regularly.

"I can now already give you the most positive assurance that Herr Arnold has had your proof of the 'Gesänge der Frühe.' There must be some other reason for his having delayed the publication so long.

"I wonder if the long walk with me did you good? I expect so. With what pleasure I think of the delightful day; I have seldom been so perfectly happy! Your dear wife was very much calmed and pacified by my blissful letter.

"I am entrusted with many greetings to you from all your friends here. I will particularly mention those from your children and Fräulein Bertha.*

"May all go well with you, and may you often think with affection of your

"JOHANNES."

"DÜSSELDORF, *in February*, 1855."

Another letter follows early in March:

---

* Fräulein Bertha Bölling, a young lady who was resident for some years in the Schumanns' house as domestic help to Frau Schumann, to whom she was greatly attached, and in whose confidence she stood high. During the first few days of Schumann's illness, before his removal to Endenich, she was allowed by the doctors to go in and out of the sick-room, and her presence had a tranquillising effect on the patient.

"HONOURED MASTER,

"You will have wondered very much that I wrote of an F sharp minor Sonata which was to be sent you with the other things, and none was there. I quite forgot to put it up this morning. I send it you now with the songs and choruses from 'Maria Stuart.' I think you will like to have them; you have often mentioned them.

"Your wife just writes to me, quite delighted with your letter. She is going to send you some beautiful music-paper. I was certainly quick, but not so particular. Only women do everything quickly and well at the same time.

"With warmest greetings, Your
"JOHANNES BRAHMS.
"DÜSSELDORF, *March*, 1855."

Of the F sharp minor Sonata, Op. 2, Schumann answers:

"Your second sonata, my dear, has brought me much nearer to you. It was quite new to me; I live in your music, so that I can half play it at sight, one movement after the other. I am thankful for this. The beginning, the *pp*, the whole movement—there has never been one like it. Andante and the variations and the scherzo following them, quite different from those in the others; and the finale, the sostenuto, the music at the beginning of the second part, the animato and the close—in short, a laurel-wreath for the from-elsewhere-coming Johannes. And the songs, the first one; I seemed to know the second; but the third—it has (at the beginning) a melody in which there are many good girls, and the splendid close. The fourth quite original. In the fifth such beautiful music—like the poem. The sixth quite different from the others. The rushing, rustling, melody-harmony pleases me."

To Joachim, Schumann writes on March 10:

"Your letter has put me into quite a happy mood. The great gaps in your artistic cultivation, and the so-called violinist's eye and the address; nothing could have amused me more. Then I recalled the Hamlet overture, Henry overture, Lindenrauschen, Abend-glocken, Ballade—books for viola and pianoforte—the remarkable pieces which you played with Clara one evening at the hotel in Hanover;[*]

---

[*] Joachim's compositions.

and as I went on thinking I began this letter . . . Johannes has sent me last year's *Signale*, to my great pleasure, for everything that has happened since February 20 was new to me. There has never been such a musical winter [1853-54] as that and the following; such travelling and flying from town to town, Frau Schroeder-Devrient, Jenny Lind, Clara, Wilhelmine Claus . . ."

Thus the months passed on. Towards the close of the musical season Johannes listened to Beethoven's "Missa Solemnis" in Frau Schumann's company at a concert in Cologne, hearing it for the first time; and three weeks later travelled with her to Hamburg in response to an invitation to both artists from Capellmeister Otten, a well known musician of the city, on the occasion of the performance of Schumann's "Manfred" at Otten's subscription concert of April 21. A day was passed at Hanover on the return journey, and on May 7, Brahms' twenty-second birthday anniversary, Joachim joined his friends at Düsseldorf in fulfilment of a promise to make his headquarters near them this season during the period of his "free time"—free from the fixed duties of his post in Hanover—which, according to his contract, extended till the month of October.

Brahms' birthday presents included the manuscript of a romance for the pianoforte composed for him by Frau Schumann, and from the master the score of his overture to "The Bride of Messina," both with affectionate inscriptions. The following letter of thanks was the last written by him to Endenich:

"BELOVED, HONOURED FRIEND,

"I must send you most heartfelt thanks for having remembered me so affectionately on May 7. How surprised and delighted I was by the beautiful present and the loving words in the book!

"The day was altogether such a delightful one as one does not often experience. Your dear wife understands how to give happiness. You, however, know this better than anyone.

"A portrait of my mother and sister surprised me. In

the afternoon Joachim came, we hope for a very long time.

"I heard the overture to 'The Bride of Messina' the other day in Hamburg, as you know. How much the deeply-earnest work took hold of me, and after 'Manfred'! I was wishing all the time that you were there to hear and see what joy you give by your splendid works.

"I have been longing for some time past to hear especially 'Manfred' or 'Faust.' I hope we shall hear the last, greatest, together some time.

"Only your long silence, which made us uneasy, could have kept me from sending you my thanks sooner; accept now the heartiest thanks for your dear remembrance on May 7, 1855.

"In hearty love and veneration,

"Your JOHANNES."

CHAPTER VII

1855-1856

Lower Rhine Festival—Madame Jenny Lind-Goldschmidt—Edward Hanslick—Brahms as a concert-player—Retirement and study—Frau Schumann in Vienna and London—Julius Stockhausen—Schumann's death.

EXTRAORDINARY interest was lent to this year's Festival of the Lower Rhine, again held at Düsseldorf (May 27-29), by the appearance at each of its three concerts of Madame Jenny Lind-Goldschmidt. According to traditional custom, and, indeed, by the *raison d'être* of these great Whitsuntide gatherings, the programmes of the first two days each included a large work for chorus and orchestra, and on this special occasion the combined singing societies of about a dozen towns furnished over 650 voices, perfected by many weeks' previous practice, for the performance of Haydn's "Creation" and Schumann's "Paradise and the Peri." That the selection of Schumann's beautiful work was due, in the first place, to a desire expressed by Madame Lind-Goldschmidt is, under the circumstances of the time, a specially interesting detail. The direction of the concerts was in the experienced hands of Ferdinand Hiller, and Concertmeister David of Leipzig had been invited to lead the splendid body of strings.

It hardly needs telling that Madame Goldschmidt's performance of the soprano solos in the two works mentioned created the usual extraordinary impression. The name "Jenny Lind" is almost synonymous with triumph.

"The most perfect purity and certainty of intonation," says Otto Jahn, "the most strictly correct interpretation, the distinctness and clearness of accent, the extraordinary virtuosity in everything that belongs to vocal technique—all this would suggest a great singer, and that she unquestionably is; but her peculiar characteristic lies in something beyond such qualities. Her phenomenal power is to be traced to the genius which, without disturbing the composer's intention, makes everything she sings literally her own—the mystery of artistic reproduction in its highest perfection, which is as inexplicable as production itself, and cannot be described by ordinary expressions."*

At the third and so-called "artists' concert," chiefly devoted to solos, Madame Lind was heard in trios from Mozart's "Nozze" and Bellini's "Beatrice di Tenda," and in Mendelssohn's song "Die Sterne schaun in stiller Nacht." The stormy applause, recalls, orchestra flourishes, flowers, and poems, in which the enthusiasm of her audience found expression were duly chronicled by the critics of the day. The instrumental solos of this final programme were in the hands of Otto Goldschmidt and Concertmeister David, who performed respectively Beethoven's G major Pianoforte Concerto and a violin concerto by Julius Rietz, conductor of the Leipzig Gewandhaus.

The festival is remembered as one of the most brilliant on record. The immense audience brought together by the magic of one name was as remarkable for its character as its numbers.

"To give a list of the celebrities is impossible," continues Jahn. "Who could count them? To mention a few of the foremost: critics were there, from Chorley of London to Hanslick of Vienna; pianists, from Stephen Heller of Paris to Stein of Reval; composers, from Gouvy to Verhulst; conductors, from Franz Lachner to Franz Liszt. The music-directors were almost more numerous than the privy councillors in Berlin."

---

* "Gesämmelte Aufsätze über Musik."

"In Jacobi's garden," says Hanslick, "a spot hallowed to me by its association with Goethe, I met Brahms and Joachim one morning. Brahms resembled a young ideal hero of Jean Paul, with his forget-me-not eyes and his long fair hair."

This was Brahms' first meeting with the man who was to be one of his most intimate friends and appreciative critics during more than thirty years of his later career.

At a matinée given by Frau Schumann in honour of a few of the famous musicians assembled at Düsseldorf, Johannes again renewed his acquaintance with Liszt, in whom equal ennui seems to have been produced by the works of Haydn and of Schumann to which he had listened on the two first concert days, and it may be accepted as certain that the meeting did not further a rapprochement between the leader of Weimar and Schumann's ardent young friend. Our musician was introduced the same afternoon to Madame Lind-Goldschmidt, meeting her on speaking terms for the only time in his life. No especial feeling of personal interest was awakened between the two artists. Johannes' large capacity for the sentiment of particular enthusiasm was already absorbed by his devotion to Frau Schumann, and it is not surprising, on the other hand, that his lack of training in social conventionalities, which allowed him on this and other occasions to perpetuate some innocuous but decidedly pointless jokes, should have somewhat offended the taste of the fastidious lady who had had the élite of Europe and America at her feet. Madame Goldschmidt's first personal impression was strengthened by an occurrence shortly to be related, nor did she ever develop any great sympathy for Brahms' music. Special circumstances, however, placed her, in later years, in a certain association with it which has an interest of its own, and particularly to the music-lovers of England. On the occasions of the fine performances of the composer's Schicksalslied (April 29, 1878), and of his German Requiem (March 16, 1880, and April 6, 1881), given in St.

James's Hall, London, by the Bach Choir under the direction of its then conductor, Otto Goldschmidt, the great singer, long since retired from public life, was to be found amongst her husband's forces as leader of the sopranos; and the inspiration has not yet been forgotten which was lent to the choir by the co-operation of one, peculiarly fitted by her exalted temperament to appreciate, at all events, the penetrating earnestness of the master's art.

In spite of the melancholy circumstances that kept them in Düsseldorf—and anxiety about Schumann was again increasing—the early summer of this year was a happy one for Brahms and Joachim, who passed many hours of the day in each other's society. Johannes lodged in a flat above Frau Schumann's dwelling; Joachim lived close by. The mornings were devoted by each to his particular avocations, but these frequently brought them together, and they always made part of Frau Schumann's family party at her mid-day dinner during the few weeks she was able to remain at home. The afternoons and evenings were often spent in long walks and excursions. Joachim had forgotten his loneliness, and Johannes' affection for his dearest Joseph had become one of the mainsprings of his life.

"Johannes and I make a great deal of music together," writes Joachim. "We have played through all Haydn's lively sonatas amongst other things. The other day we played Bach's E major Sonata."*

The second fortnight of June was spent by Frau Schumann at Detmold, capital of the small principality of Lippe-Detmold, which, during the fifties and sixties, possessed a very flourishing and enterprising musical life. The reigning Prince, Leopold III, had inherited from his mother, a Princess of Schwarzburg-Sondershausen, a fine taste for music that was shared by his brothers and sisters, and soon after his accession he established a private orchestra, consisting of thirty-three, soon augmented to forty-

---

* "Briefe von u. an Joseph Joachim."

five members, under the conductorship of the violinist Kiel, a pupil of Spohr. A certain number of court concerts were given every year, the programmes consisting of a symphony, two overtures, and several solos, selected from the works of the best classical and modern composers. The Prince was not without interest in the New-German school, and compositions by Wagner and Berlioz were given from time to time. Now and then there was a performance of the whole or part of some large choral work.

Prince Leopold's mother, the Dowager Princess, resided with her daughters, the Princesses Luise, Friederike, and Pauline, in the old castle not far from the palace, and it had been settled that the talented Princess Friederike should enjoy the advantage of lessons from Frau Schumann during the short interval at the disposal of the artist. The arrangement proved a great success, and not only with regard to the lessons. Frau Schumann delighted a circle of sympathetic listeners by playing at several court soirées, was enthusiastically received at a public concert, and, on the eve of her departure, played one of Beethoven's pianoforte concertos at an orchestral court concert, which was made further memorable by the presence of Joachim and his performance of the same master's concerto for violin.

Soon after the return of the two artists, the little party at Düsseldorf dispersed for a time. Joachim started for a tour in the Tyrol, and Frau Schumann, accompanied by Fräulein Bertha and Johannes, went to Ems, where she had announced a concert for July 15, for which Madame Lind-Goldschmidt had, during the week of the Düsseldorf festival, proffered her services. The date decided upon was somewhat in advance of the one originally selected, and Goldschmidt had been called to Sweden meanwhile on affairs of importance. He interrupted his engagements, however, and travelled to Ems, in order to put his services at Frau Schumann's disposal by superintending the general business of the concert and acting as his wife's accompanist; and it was in this connection that a certain appearance of nonchalance in Brahms' proceedings caused a feeling of irritation in Madame Goldschmidt and himself.

The concert was to take place in a room of the Kurhaus, and, owing to the procrastination of some of the authorities, the arrangements to be made on the spot, including those for receiving and seating the large number of ticket-holders, could not be begun until within an hour or two of the time appointed for the commencement of the music. The result was hurry and confusion indescribable, and many last things had to be done even during the assembling of the audience. The brunt of the difficulties was borne by Goldschmidt, who successfully overcame them, but who was annoyed that Brahms, arriving with Frau Schumann and Fräulein Bertha a couple of days before the date of the concert, left again the next afternoon instead of remaining to make himself useful, and was seen no more in Ems. Starting for Braubach, he wandered about alone until the winding up of the concert business, which resulted in a clear profit of 1,340 thalers, left Frau Schumann at leisure again. There is no question that on this occasion it was his invincible dislike to a fashionable crowd which overcame his judgment, but it is not to be wondered at that his real or apparent indifference was commented on by those to whom it seemed inexplicable. Rejoining Frau Schumann and her companion on their departure from Ems on the morning of the 16th, Johannes passed ten happy days walking along the Rhine from Coblenz to Mainz and visiting Frankfurt and Heidelberg in their society. "They were happy days. I should never have thought I could have been so happy travelling with two ladies," he wrote from Heidelberg to Grimm. By the end of the month the three holiday makers were back in Düsseldorf.

The dreaded business of moving to a new house, with its inevitable uprooting of home associations consecrated alike by experiences of joy and sorrow, awaited Frau Schumann on her return, and was accomplished with a courage that enabled her to go north early in August to rest for some weeks at the seaside. Brahms, who definitely took up his abode in the new dwelling—the first-floor flat (étage) of 135 Poststrasse—remained in Düsseldorf to work hard at his pianoforte playing. Accustomed though he might be to declare that his spirits always rose with the spending of his last shilling, yet the precariousness of his outward circumstances had, in truth, weighed heavily upon his mind during the past year. No sure earnings could be derived from publishing; pupils were not to be easily obtained; and he had resolved to follow the advice of his two best friends and try his luck again as a concert player. He looked forward with dread to the ordeal and shrank from the partings it would involve, but kept to his plan; and in the course of September his intention of making a concert journey was announced in the *Signale*. Meanwhile, the return of Frau Schumann from Düsternbrook, near Kiel, and that of Joachim from the Tyrol, secured him a few more weeks of happiness.

"We passed Sunday (August) 26 very pleasantly," writes Frau Clara; "Joachim had much to tell us about his journey and Johannes and I rejoiced that we were all together again."

Joachim held private quartet evenings in his rooms twice a week throughout September, and the party assembled sometimes at Frau Schumann's house, where Johannes had now and again the opportunity of taking part in the performance of some work for pianoforte and strings. His reappearance in public took place, not in Leipzig as had been intended, but in Danzig, where he gave concerts with Frau Clara and Joachim on November 14 and 16, a change of plan that had at least the desired result of benefiting his pocket. A picture of him on his arrival in the town, given by Anton Door,* forms an amusing and perhaps instructive sequel to the foregoing account of the occurrences at Ems:

---

* *Die Musik,* first May number, 1903.

"I had hardly been a week in Danzig, when I saw great bills in the streets announcing the coming concert of Clara Schumann, Joseph Joachim, and Johannes Brahms. I at once called on Joachim, who received me with cordiality, and we chatted, as old acquaintances, of home and our experiences.

"During the whole time we were together, a slender young man with long, fair hair paced continually to and fro in the background smoking cigarettes, without troubling himself in the least about my presence, or even showing by an inclination of the head that he observed me; in a word, I was as empty air for him. This was my first meeting with Johannes Brahms."

Door became, nevertheless, in later years, a cordial friend and admirer of the composer.

Complete equality amongst the three performers was observed in the arrangement of the programmes. Each played solos, and both pianists performed with the violinist at either concert. Brahms' contributions included Bach's Chromatic Fantasia, which remained one of the *pièces de résistance* of his répertoire throughout his pianistic career, and two manuscript pieces, Saraband and Gavotte, from amongst the "Album-Leaves" which he had contemplated publishing in 1854.

Unfortunately his constitutional nervousness, combined with the discouraging effect of a bad pianoforte, to mar his artistic success.

The critical moment had now arrived when Johannes was obliged to bid farewell to his friends and go his own way. He played for the first time in his life with orchestra—and with success—at the Bremen subscription concert of November 20, contributing to the programme Beethoven's G major Concerto and Schumann's great Fantasia, Op. 17; and on the 24th, the date which he had anticipated with ever-increasing anxiety as it drew nearer, made his first appearance in Hamburg since the wonderful turn that had taken place in his fortunes in 1853, at one of G. D. Otten's annual series of orchestral subscription concerts.

No doubt he was additionally weighted by nervousness—that *bête noire* of executive artists to which, from the rarity of his public appearances, Brahms was peculiarly a prey—by feeling, not only that he was on his trial before his fellow-citizens, but that there were, in the audience, loving friends prepared to triumph on his behalf. He had chosen for performance Beethoven's E flat Concerto and unaccompanied solos by Schumann and Schubert, but although he was apparently satisfied with his reception and reported to his friends that he had "played with great animation," he achieved, if contemporary press accounts are to be trusted, little more than a *succès d'estime*.

"The pianoforte part of the concerto," said the critic of the *Hamburger Nachrichten*, "was played by Brahms with the modesty of a young artist, and was kept throughout in subordination to the whole musical effect of the symphonic concerto. In our opinion, he carried his reserve too far. He might, without detriment to the spirit of the work, have displayed rather more virtuosity. That he possesses it was shown by his playing of a canon by Schumann, and a march by Schubert for four hands, arranged by Brahms for two hands."

It will not have escaped the reader's attention that Brahms introduced no new important composition of his own on either of the occasions now chronicled, and that no mention has been made of any fresh publication from his pen since the autumn of 1854. The reason is not far to seek. Neither the extraordinary praise bestowed on his works by Schumann, Joachim, and their circle, nor the reserve with which they had been received by many musicians whose good faith could not be doubted, nor the acrimonious attacks of a portion, and especially the Rhenish portion, of the musical press, could influence to any appreciable extent the tribunal to which he had thus early in his career accustomed himself to submit his works in the last instance—his own searching self-criticism. He had, as has been seen, carried out Schumann's wish, and had tried his hand on a symphony. The discovery that he had not sufficiently mastered some of the fundamental technical qualifications necessary for the successful fulfilment of such an attempt no doubt prevented his carrying it to a conclusion. It will be remembered, also, that he had withheld the string quartet recommended to Dr. Härtel for publication by Schumann in 1853. By the middle of 1855, he had sufficiently gauged both his strength and his weakness to have made the resolve to apply himself to a fresh course of severe study—study which should widen and strengthen and refine his capacity in every direction, but which should have as its special aim the attainment of greater facility and purity in part-writing in the strict style. From this time, for a period of five or six years, he worked on without view to immediate publication, but only with a set determination to become worthy of Schumann's high hopes. He insisted before long that Joseph should join him in his studies; and an exchange of exercises at fixed intervals, agreed upon between the two young musicians, was kept up for some years. Joachim was inevitably much less regular than Brahms in sending his papers, and Johannes by and by instituted a system of fines, to be paid and spent in books in case of unpunctuality on either side. The chief burden of the new rule certainly fell upon the famous young concertmeister, whose great and increasing popularity brought innumerable concert-journeys in its train. The difference in the character of the two men is pleasantly illustrated by this episode, which shows Johannes insisting on having his own way, and Joachim, from whom no excuse was accepted, good-naturedly yielding, and wishing to do more than he could possibly fulfil. Many interesting memorials of Brahms' studies are in existence in the form of music-books, printed or in manuscript, of which he possessed himself at this period. Amongst them is an original edition of the first part of Emanuel Bach's collection of his father's setting of German chorales (1765), on the cover of which is Brahms' autograph and the date 1855, and at the end of

the book is an alphabetical index in Brahms' writing.*
There is also a very beautifully copied manuscript (not by
Brahms) of Sebastian Bach's "Kunst der Fuge," containing one or two trifling pencil corrections in our musician's
unmistakable hand. On the fly-leaf is written "Joh.
Brahms, Nov. 1855, Hamburg," also in pencil, in large and
bold penmanship, probably in one of the styles taught at
Hoffmann's school.* There are, too, a volume containing
compositions by Orlando di Lasso;† and manuscript copies
of, amongst other works, Palestrina's "Missa Papæ Marcelli," with Brahms' autograph and the date 1856; of
Rovetta's "Salve Regina"; and, in Frau Schumann's
hand, of a "Gloria" of Palestrina.‡ Still more valuable
are the manuscripts of several original Mass movements by
Brahms in four and six parts, presented later on by the
composer to his friend Grimm,§ and these recall Dietrich's
mention of an entire Mass written in canon for voices. This
list shows clearly enough the nature of the young composer's aims. He was determined to become thoroughly
acquainted with the historical development of his art, to
know the why and wherefore, as well as the how and when,
of what he had studied in the works of succeeding masters.
The fascination exercised over his mind by the clear, pure
style of the great early writers, whose learning is often
used with such consummate ease as to be unsuspected by the
untrained hearer, is evident enough in many of the choral
works published by him later on. He exercised himself in
the acquisition of their technique until it had become an instrument in his hand for the production of works which,
like everything else that he gave to the world, bear the
impress of his own individuality.

In the issue of the *Neue Zeitschrift für Musik* of December 14 a long article on Brahms appeared, the closing one

---

* Both in the possession of Mr. Evlyn Howard-Jones.
† In the possession of Professor Julius Spengel.
‡ In the library of the Gesellschaft der Musikfreunde, Vienna.
§ In the possession of Fräulein Marie Grimm.

of a series of three begun in July. Until this date, since the very sympathetic notice written by "Hoplit" after the young musician's début at the Leipzig Gewandhaus, not a word had been printed in this paper about his compositions save the bare announcements of publication, in spite of the fact that nine opus numbers had been given to the world in the interval, five of them being important instrumental works, and three consisting severally of six songs. "Hoplit" had now come forward to take upon himself entire blame for the omission, which, he declared, must not be attributed to any indifference of the editor. Brendel had not only sent him each work as it appeared, but had urged him to write, asking repeatedly, "Why nothing about Brahms?" His own great interest in the young composer, his desire to find himself in complete accord with Schumann's opinion, his incapability of entirely agreeing with it, had, he said, always led him to defer his criticism; and, indeed, the reluctant and hesitating tone of the articles leads to the conviction that they were written in complete good faith.

"That Brahms found many opponents on his first appearance was an unusual distinction; it showed that he possessed a very significant artistic individuality. When, however, enthusiastic friends saw in him the prophet of a new time, and especially when they proclaimed the completely developed, ripe artist, we can only regard it as an amiable excess of enthusiasm."

"Brahms," says the second and most interesting article, "has sometimes been described as the most talented and pronounced of the Schumannites. So far as this is true, we regret it . . . . Schumann cannot be carried further. . . . . His very important individuality quite unquestionably possesses a high value, but only in its originality. Brahms is, however, no imitator of Schumann. He displays, in the whole bent of his nature and creative activity, an inner affinity with him which is more than mere sympathy, and has about it nothing forced or borrowed; but he possesses an element not in Schumann which makes us believe that, if it is only given to him to attain full development, he will find his own paths. The more he succeeds in freeing himself from the characteristic Schumann nature, the more may be looked for from his future . . . .

"Brahms is not free from Schumann's danger; he, also, has the subtle habit of mind, the tendency to the indefinite and misty, which characterise the romanticists. He shares Schumann's strong faith, moreover, in impulses of genius and inspirations of the moment, to be followed without discrimination or resistance. He sometimes introduces passages which have neither presupposition nor consequence, but which are not therefore heaven-bestowed. His work is inconsistent and defective in style. He should have been regarded as an artist not yet mature. When all is said, however, it was an unusually striking phenomenon that such a young composer should exhibit in his first works a freedom in the handling of form, a diversity of harmonic and rhythmic development, and an abundance of ideas, such as are to be found in the works only of those who are called to become one day masters. And yet who will deny that much 'lies in the air' to-day which had formerly to be won by hard fighting, or to be developed entirely from within?"

Dr. Pohl's doubt evidently overcomes him again in the last sentence, and it would be quite unjust to refer his hesitation to the influence of party spirit, or to say that he had no ground for his feeling of uncertainty as to the destiny of our composer's genius. It is difficult now to realise the position of the critic who, in 1855, wished to write without bias of the Brahms of twenty-two; but the good faith of these *Neue Zeitschrift* articles is curiously confirmed by a few forcible words written in 1893 by an intimate friend of the Brahms of past sixty.

"Brahms' first works," says Hanslick,* "had interested me in a high degree—interested, however, rather than satisfied me. A young Hercules at the parting of the ways. Will he turn to the left, to the most extreme romanticism, or to the right, to the path of our classics?"

That Brahms himself had become aware of the problem that faced him is conclusively shown by the future course

---

* "Aus meinem Leben."

of his development; and, with the exception of the Ballades for pianoforte, Op. 10, dedicated to Grimm, mentioned by Schumann in his letter of January, 1855, and produced by Breitkopf and Härtel early in 1856, no work of his composition succeeded the publications of 1854 until after a period of six years.

Johannes again passed Christmas with Frau Schumann, and on January 10 played Beethoven's G major Concerto and unaccompanied solos by Schumann at the Leipzig Gewandhaus concert. The impression generally created by his performance is summed up by a few words in the *Signale* which suggest that he again rather overdid his artistic self-restraint:

"Many artists could certainly have displayed more technical brilliancy, but few have the capacity for bringing out so convincingly the intentions of the composer, or following as Brahms does the flight of Beethoven's genius and disclosing its full splendour."

The critic adds that the young artist, who thinks more of the work he happens to be interpreting than of self-display, has already won many friends in the art world by his compositions.

Paying a flying visit to Hanover on his way back to Hamburg, which is, just now, to be considered as his settled home, Johannes for the first time heard Rubinstein, who had come to play at one of the subscription concerts conducted by Joachim, and who shortly afterwards wrote to Liszt:

" . . . As regards Brahms, I hardly know how to describe the impression he made on me. He is not graceful enough for the drawing-room, not fiery enough for the concert-room, not simple enough for the country, and not general enough for the town. I have but little faith in this kind of nature."

It may be remarked here that Rubinstein never acquired a liking for Brahms' art, and that, to the end of his life, he expressed the opinion that the series of great masters had ceased with Schumann. Rubinstein obtained a powerful following, not only as pianist, but as composer, at Leipzig, and in later years his works were pitted against those of Brahms by the large and influential set of musicians and amateurs of the typical Gewandhaus circle. The generosity of Rubinstein's nature is too well established to leave room for any suspicion of his having been moved by paltry feelings of professional jealousy, and his repeated asseverations that he could find no music in Brahms' works must be accepted as genuine expressions of his sentiments.

Many celebrations took place, during the opening month of 1856, of the centenary of Mozart's birth (January 27, 1756), and Johannes, making his second appearance at Otten's concerts on the 26th, contributed the D minor Concerto to a programme selected from the great master's works. Whilst practising for the occasion at the house of Messrs. Baumgarten and Heins, he made the acquaintance of the critic and journalist E. Krause, between whom and himself a permanent friendship was established. Krause became one of the earliest and ablest supporters of his art.

But two concerts of the season remain to be mentioned— one at Kiel, given by Brahms in association with the composer Grädener, of Hamburg, and the violinist John Böie, when his solos were Beethoven's E flat Sonata, Op. 27, No. 1, and C minor Variations; the other at Altona, where he played Bach's Organ Toccata in F major, Beethoven's "Eroïca" Variations, and, with Böie and Breyther, Schumann's trio movements "Märchen Erzählungen," and Beethoven's Sonata for pianoforte and violin, Op. 96. He passed February and March quietly with his parents, making as much money as he could by teaching. Mention may be made of a pupil in whom he was interested at this time—Fräulein Friedchen Wagner, a cousin of Otten's, and herself a pianoforte-teacher. Brahms' acquaintance with her has an association, to which we shall presently refer, with some of the works published by him in the early sixties.

To this period is to be referred the composition of a pianoforte Quartet in C sharp minor, which was shown to Joachim soon after Brahms' return to Düsseldorf in April. The work is identified by Joachim's discussion of the manuscript and quotation of one of its themes, in a letter of the same month, as an early version of the pianoforte Quartet in C minor published in 1895 as Op. 60.

Frau Schumann, who travelled without break, save for a short interval in December, during the season 1855-56, spent more than two months of the early part of the year in Vienna, where Schumann's works were as yet but little known to the general public. Appearing as the inspired missionary of her husband's art, she succeeded in arousing interest in his compositions, whilst her personal achievements as an executant excited extraordinary enthusiasm. She gave six recitals, and introduced into two of her programmes respectively Brahms' Saraband and Gavotte and the andante and scherzo from his C minor Sonata. The critic of the *Wiener Zeitung* of that date, Carl Debrois van Bruyck, speaks of them as "pieces of special beauty, which confirm the impression of the young composer's exceptional talent" already formed by him from the study of other works, especially of a set of variations [Op. 9] and a book of songs. The successful début of Brahms' name in a concert-programme and a prominent journal of the city to which he was to belong during the second half of his life is an interesting point in his history.

It will be convenient to refer at once to a detailed review of our composer's early works contributed to his journal by van Bruyck on September 25, 1857. At this date, as the reader is aware, Brahms' publications had not increased beyond the ten numbers already mentioned, and consisted of the three sonatas, scherzo, variations, and ballades for pianoforte, the B major Trio, and the first three books of songs. The similarity of the remarks of the Vienna critic with those contained in "Hoplit's" *Neue Zeitschrift* articles, already referred to, is the more striking since van Bruyck did not concern himself with the party conflicts of Germany. He was, however, a very great lover of Schumann's art, and if he had any bias in regard to that of Brahms, it inclined in favour of Schumann's young prophet.

He regards the variations as decidedly pre-eminent amongst the ten works. They convince him that Brahms has

"a genuine and entirely original talent, a finely-endowed artist nature. . . . Some of them are quite magic and ethereal, although the finest of all recalls Schumann, perhaps intentionally; and in others, especially the last, the young composer's tendency to the vague and mystical is rather unpleasantly and dangerously apparent. Next to the variations I should place the songs, which contain tones of penetrating depth and sweetness. . . . Brahms certainly stands within the sacred circle, and has already acquired a very definite power of achievement, though it may not at present be sufficient for his purpose; and it is the duty of serious, unbiassed criticism to protect him against the derision which the more highly gifted men have never escaped, especially when their endowment has been peculiarly individual. As we have said, Brahms' natural power seems to be lofty beyond all question, and the danger and doubt as regards his development lies, we think, in his partly instinctive, partly conscious striving after over-refinement; in his excessive bent to the dæmoniacal, the fantastic. Should he succeed in restraining this inclination, we may await with confidence many riper, more perfect fruits whether in the nearer or farther future."

The derision from which van Bruyck desired to protect Johannes emanated chiefly or entirely at this period from the Rhenish press. As it consisted chiefly of the vulgar commonplaces of the journalist—familiar at all times and in all countries—who has neither knowledge of his subject nor instinct to avoid displaying his ignorance, no example will be given of it in these pages.

Whilst Frau Schumann was achieving a series of unbroken successes in Vienna, her private anxieties pressed upon her with ever-increasing severity. The apparent improvement in Schumann's health had been but transitory. He had steadily lost ground since the spring of 1855, and before the winter had well come to an end the physicians were unable to conceal from themselves that his case was hopeless. The afflicted wife was sustained for the fulfilment of her duties by the best accounts that the situation admitted of, but she was obliged, on her return from Vienna, to relinquish all immediate hope of an interview with her husband, whom she had not seen since the hour before the catastrophe of 1854. Nor could she allow herself the solace of remaining near him. She was now sole bread-winner for the family, and a group of young children depended on her exertions. She had entered into engagements for the London season, and after a very short interval of rest, started on April 7 for England.

For Brahms, bound as he was by the closest ties of affection and gratitude to Schumann and his family, it was impossible, under the melancholy trend of events, to remain quietly at his studies in Hamburg. There was some idea of removing the patient from Endenich; at all events, it would be a satisfaction to obtain the opinion of fresh experts on brain disease; and Johannes undertook to make personal inquiries of certain eminent doctors, and to send his report as soon as possible to England. On April 15 Frau Schumann wrote from London to Dietrich, who had in the summer been appointed Wasielewski's successor as music-director at Bonn:

"DEAR HERR DIETRICH,

"I enclose a long letter from Gisela von Arnim. Will you give it to Johannes on his return? I must again thank you and Professor Jahn very fervently for the sympathy which you show Johannes in his undertaking; it is a comfort to me that he does not stand alone, it would be too hard for him. Of myself I have little satisfactory to relate. In spirit I am always in Germany. I played yesterday at the Philharmonic with a bleeding heart. I had a letter from Johannes in the morning, in which I read hopelessness between the lines as regards my beloved husband, although he had tried in all affection to tell me everything as gently as possible. Whence the power to play came to me I do not know; I could do nothing at home, and yet in the evening things went.

"Think sometimes kindly of your

"CLARA SCHUMANN.

"I really think the enclosed letter is worth consideration. Johannes will certainly show it to you and Professor Jahn. I have just heard something about cold-water treatment for brain disease, which makes me very anxious to try it for my husband. Please tell Johannes I will write about it to-morrow."

All was in vain, however. Schumann was already in an advanced stage of the disease which, technically described under different learned names, according to its many varieties, is known to the layman as softening of the brain. Anyone who has watched the powers of friend or acquaintance gradually succumbing to this most cruel of all maladies is familiar with the general course of the symptoms. Minute particulars need not be described. Enough that Johannes, permitted to see Schumann again after an interval of more than a year, had been unutterably shocked, and had felt that the time had arrived when it was his duty to prepare Frau Schumann for the worst. As gently as possible he allowed her, as she expresses it, to read between the lines that no change of treatment could alter the inevitable. All the doctors were agreed in opinion; none, therefore, was attempted.

The concert so pathetically referred to in the letter quoted above was the Philharmonic concert at the Hanover Square Rooms of April 14, the occasion of Frau Schumann's first appearance in England. Could any incident of fiction be more heart-rending in its pathos than this occurrence of real life—this picture of the sensitive, highly-strung woman, whose nerves were habitually in a state of strained tension, obliged to force herself, for the sake of her children's existence, to step for the first time on to a London concert platform, a sea of unknown faces before her, her kith and kin far away, a few hours after she had accepted the certainty of her passionately loved husband's tragic doom? No wonder she could "do nothing" before the concert. Those who knew her best can understand how it was that, after all, "things went." Her début in England was made with Beethoven's E flat Concerto and Mendelssohn's "Variations Sérieuses," and things went with a brilliant success that was but an augury of events to follow.

Through the remainder of April, and throughout May and June, did this great artist work incessantly, going in desolation of spirit from triumph to triumph; and some of Schumann's shorter compositions which were encored by the public became something more than tolerated, even by the conservative press, for the sake of her perfect playing of them. Her numerous concert-journeys through the British Islands extended as far as Dublin. Amongst the most important of her London appearances were those at the Musical Union (John Ella's) concerts and at her own three recitals. At the second of these, which took place on June 17, she imitated her own precedent at Vienna, and introduced Brahms' name for the first time to an English public. The entire selection belongs so peculiarly to the events and period occupying our attention that it may interest the reader to have the complete programme:

Variations (Eroïca) - - - - *Beethoven*
Two Diversions, Op. 17, from Suite de
    Pièces, Op. 24, No. 1 - - - *Sterndale Bennett.*
Variations on a theme from the "Bunten
    Blättern" - - - - - *Clara Schumann.*
(a) Saraband and Gavotte in the style
    of Bach - - - - - *Johannes Brahms.*
(b) Clavierstück in A major - - *Scarlatti.*
"Carnaval" - - - - - *Schumann.*

The Brahms Gavotte was enthusiastically applauded, but Frau Schumann, having regard to the performance of the "Carnaval" still before her, refused the encore. At the close of the recital, however, she returned to the piano in response to continued demonstrations, and repeated the composition. Her performances were given on a pianoforte by Erard, whose instruments were preferred at that date by all the great pianists of Europe. A magnificent "grand" was presented by the house to Frau Schumann at the close of her London season, and despatched to her residence in Düsseldorf. It continued to be her favourite instrument for private use until 1867, when, reappearing in England after an absence of two years, she used a Broadwood pianoforte. On her departure a Broadwood concert-grand was sent to her house near Baden-Baden by Messrs. John Broadwood and Sons. Some years later, when the author was intimate at Frau Schumann's residence, the Broadwood pianoforte stood in the drawing-room, the Erard in the dining-room. On the former Frau Schumann and Brahms often played duets after afternoon coffee; on the latter Johannes—always "Johannes" to his old friend—played one evening after supper several numbers of the third and fourth books of the Hungarian Dances, not yet published, not yet books, his eyes flashing fire the while.

Brahms gave up all idea of returning to Hamburg for the present. Duty and inclination alike prompted him to remain in Schumann's neighbourhood, and the fact of Dietrich's residence at Bonn gave him additional satisfaction in resolving to pass the summer on the Rhine. It was at this time that he made the personal acquaintance of the poet Claus Groth, who was staying at Bonn to be near Otto Jahn; and the musical festival of the year (May 11-13) marked the beginning of his intimacy with the great singer Julius Stockhausen, who, making his first appearance on the Rhine, was heard in the part of Elijah in Mendelssohn's oratorio, in "Alexander's Feast," in an aria by Boieldieu, and in songs by Schubert, Mendelssohn and Schumann.

Stockhausen had been a pupil of Manuel Garcia in Paris and London, and was well known to the musical public and

JULIUS STOCKHAUSEN.

the private artistic circles of both cities before he became a celebrity in Austria and Germany.

"His delivery of opera and oratorio music," says Sir George Grove*—"his favourite pieces from 'Euryanthe,' 'Jean de Paris,' 'Le Chaperon Rouge,' and 'Le Philtre'; or the part of Elijah, or certain special airs of Bach—was superb in taste, feeling, and execution; but it was the Lieder of Schubert and Schumann that most peculiarly suited him, and these he delivered in a truly remarkable way. The rich beauty of the voice, the nobility of the style, the perfect phrasing, the intimate sympathy, not least, the intelligible way in which the words were given—in itself one of his greatest claims to distinction—all combined to make his singing of songs a wonderful event. Those who have heard him sing Schubert's 'Nachtstück,' 'Wanderer,' 'Memnon,' or the 'Harper's Songs,' or Schumann's 'Frühlingsnacht' or 'Fluthenreicher Ebro,' or the 'Löwenbraut,' will corroborate all that has been said. But perhaps his highest achievement was the part of Dr. Marianus in the third part of Schumann's 'Faust,' in which his delivery of 'Hier ist die Aussicht frei,' with just as much of acting as the concert-room will admit, and no more, was one of the most touching and remarkable things ever witnessed."

Cordial relations were so quickly established between Stockhausen and Brahms that before the close of the month they had given two concerts together—one on the 27th, in the "yellow room of the casino" at Cologne; the other on the 29th, in the hall of the Lesegesellschaft at Bonn. Stockhausen's performances, accompanied in each instance by Brahms, created a furore on both occasions. Brahms' solos —consisting on the 27th of Bach's Chromatic Fantasia and Beethoven's C minor Variations, and on the 29th of Beethoven's E flat Variations, Clara Schumann's Romance, a Schubert Impromptu, and the great Bach Fugue in A minor, to be found in vol. iii of the Leipzig Society's edition— were coldly received. This is not to be wondered at. During the half-century which has elapsed since these con-

---

* Grove's "Dictionary of Music and Musicians."

certs took place musical taste has passed through more than one revolution; it is, however, questionable whether at any time within the interval a pianist, of whatever qualifications, not already accepted into the prime affections of the public, could have successfully courted its favour beside the attraction of a really great singer in full possession of his powers, whose selections included a number of the most fascinating lyrics of Schubert, Mendelssohn and Schumann. One of the Cologne critics, at all events, was satisfied with the pianist. It is rather surprising to read, in the *Niederrheinische Musik Zeitung*, that Herr Johannes Brahms played his two solos on the 27th "with such purity, clearness, musical ripeness, and artistic repose, that his performances gave true pleasure."

Brahms' temperament was not really suited, however, to the career of a virtuoso, nor had the obscure circumstances of his youth fitted him for it. He generally felt too nervously self-conscious when before the public to have a chance of gaining its entire confidence, and was too dependent on his mood to be able to throw himself at all times completely out upon his audience and compel their sympathy. The achievement of striking and lasting success as a performer involves a concentration of the best energies of body and mind upon this career, whilst the attainment of real greatness as a composer means the devotion of a life to the end. No illustration of these truths could be more apt than the contrasted careers of Brahms and Joachim. Whatever Joachim's natural creative faculty may have been, his boundless success as an interpreter was fatal to its development. The divergence of the paths pursued by the two friends resulted not altogether, or perhaps chiefly, from variety of musical endowment, but largely from the radical differences in their characters and circumstances. From early childhood Joachim never appeared on a platform without exciting, not only the admiration, but the personal love of his audience. His successes were their delight. They rejoiced to see him, to applaud him, recall him, shout at him. The scenes familiar to the memory of three generations of London concert-goers were samples of the everyday incidents of his life in all countries and towns where he appeared. Why? It is impossible altogether to explain such phenomena, even by the word "genius." Joachim followed his destiny. His career was unparalleled in the history of musical executive art. It began when he was eight; it closed only a few weeks before his death at the age of seventy-six. All possibility of his achieving greatness as a composer—notwithstanding that he produced one or two important works—was excluded by the time he had reached the age of fourteen.

The mistress of Brahms' absorbing passion, on the other hand, was from first to last his creative art, to which all else remained secondary. He never swerved by a hair's-breadth from his devotion, but accepted poverty, disappointment, loneliness, and failure in the eyes of the world, with all the strong faith that was in him, for the sake of this, his true love. He was never drawn by inclination to his virtuoso career, to which he submitted only as a necessity, discarding it as soon as circumstances allowed. He was seldom able to disclose the infinite possibilities of his playing under circumstances in which he was not at ease; and though he possessed a great technique which he could easily have developed into something phenomenal, and which, as it was, enabled him to excite an audience now and again by sounding and dramatic performances of Bach's organ compositions and other imposing works, yet the more distinctive beauties of his style were too subtle for the appreciation of a mixed body of listeners. His imagination of effects of tone was, to quote Schumann's article, quite original, and this was even more strikingly displayed in later years, when he conducted one or other of his orchestral works. His playing even of such a trifle as Gluck's Gavotte in A, arranged for Frau Schumann in 1871, which the author more than once heard, was full of unsought graces that were the immediate reflection of his delicate spirit. His performance of this little piece, and his conception of many works of the great masters, together with his whole style of playing, differed *in toto* from Frau Schumann's. The two artists admired each other's qualities. Frau Schumann courted Brahms' criticisms, and has, on some occasions, quoted to the author his sayings as to the reading of certain of Beethoven's sonatas, declaring she felt them to be right. Nevertheless, her temperament would never have allowed her to carry out these suggestions in actual public performance, and she was better fitted by temperament than Brahms for the interpretation, to the large public, of the masterpieces of musical art.

The author has been carried by this digression, which is the result of her personal intercourse with these great musicians, to a date many years later than that reached by the narrative. Its insertion here may, however, be of advantage to the reader by preparing him to expect that Brahms' career as a pianist, though not without success, was attended by few brilliant triumphs.

On June 8, the forty-sixth anniversary of Schumann's birthday, Johannes again went to Endenich, accompanied on the walk from Bonn by Jahn, Dietrich, Groth, and Hermann Deiters, another notable acquaintance of this summer. He looked very serious on rejoining his companions, though he said that Schumann had recognised and seemed pleased to see him. The end was, indeed, not far off. The mists that had so long been gathering around the lofty spirit of the master continued to close him into ever-increasing darkness. Bad news attended Frau Schumann's return from England early in July, and on the 23rd of the month she was summoned by a telegraphic despatch to Endenich. The doctors had persevered throughout the sad illness in their refusal to sanction her desire for a meeting with her husband, and even now the longed-for interview was again deferred. Fresh symptoms appeared before her arrival and she was obliged to return to Düsseldorf to live through four more days of agonising suspense. She went again to Bonn on Sunday, July 27, there to await the end and, the same evening, after nearly two and a half years of separation, passed with Johannes into the solemn chamber of death. Schumann was lying quietly with closed eyes as she entered, but opened them presently on the figure kneeling at his bedside, and it became evident after a few moments that he knew his wife. His power of speech was almost gone, but a look of recognition passed over his countenance, a tender word was half distinguishable, and suddenly, with a last accession of strength, he was able to place one of his arms round her. Those faint looks of love, that last embrace, dwelt in Frau Schumann's memory as an ever-present solace during the forty years of her widowhood and, in spite of her many sorrows, the radiance was never dimmed that had been shed over her spirit once and for all by the enchantment of an early, ideal happiness.

Schumann lingered yet a day or two, becoming weaker hour by hour, as his wife and young friend watched at his side. Once at least on Monday it was apparent that he felt the solace of his wife's touch as she tenderly moistened his lips with a few drops of wine. He passed quietly away at four o'clock on Tuesday afternoon, July 29, and Frau Schumann, returning from a short interval of repose at her hotel, accompanied by Brahms and by Joachim, who had taken immediate train to Bonn on receiving a hopeless report, learned that her husband's sufferings were over for ever.

Two days more, and on Thursday, July 31, in the stillness of a balmy summer evening, the mortal remains of the master were laid to rest in the cemetery of Bonn. The funeral was arranged with touching simplicity. A pleasant spot had been chosen by the city, some plantain-trees planted by the grave. The coffin, borne from Endenich by the choristers of the Concordia, was immediately preceded by the three chief mourners—Brahms, who carried a laurel wreath, Joachim and Dietrich. Following the body came the clergyman, Pastor Wiesemann, and the Mayor of Bonn, and at an appointed spot in the city a long string of musicians and music lovers joined the procession, which passed on foot through the streets accompanied by a band of brass instruments playing one and another of the most solemnly beautiful of the old German chorales. At the graveside Brahms stepped forward and placed the wife's wreath upon the coffin, bare of other floral decorations. Frau Schumann herself stood a little apart from the mourners, following the service unobserved. A short address was delivered by Pastor Wiesemann, then came a sacred part-song by the choristers, a chorale, a few simple words spoken by Ferdinand Hiller, the last farewell of friends throwing earth upon the coffin, and all was over.*

On the anguish of the widow looking out despairingly to the future of her lonely life, who yet might not despair because of the little ones clinging to her side, on the steadfast loyalty of the affectionate friends in whose sympathy she had found, and continued to find, support, it is unnecessary to dwell; they are matter of history. Rather let the chapter be closed in silent remembrance of the departed master and of the group of his loved ones who lamented together in the sacred presence of an irreparable grief.

---

* Partly taken from the account written at the time for the *Neue Zeitschrift*, by Ferdinand Hiller.

CHAPTER VIII.

1856-1858.

Joachim and Brahms in Düsseldorf—Grimm in Göttingen—Brahms' visit to Detmold—Carl von Meysenbug—Court Concertmeister Bargheer—Joachim and Liszt—Brahms' return to Detmold—Summer at Göttingen—Pianoforte Concerto in D minor and Orchestral Serenade in D major tried privately in Hanover.

FRAU SCHUMANN returned to Düsseldorf the day after the funeral, accompanied by Brahms and Joachim. There were certain things to be done, the performance of which she desired to entrust to the two young musicians who had been so near the master's heart. Together they set in order the papers left by the deceased composer, wrote necessary letters, and made plans for the immediate future. Joachim writes on August 2 to Liszt:

"Frau Schumann returned here yesterday; the presence of her children and of Brahms, whom Schumann loved like a son, comforts the noble lady, who appears to me, in her deep grief, a lofty example of God-given strength. I shall remain here for some days."

Johannes had taken over some lessons which Frau Schumann had arranged to give, on her return from England, to Fräulein von Meysenbug, daughter of the late Minister and sister of the then Hofmarschall at the Court of Lippe-Detmold, and by so doing had added four people to the list of his friends: his pupil, her mother and sister—all settled for a few weeks in Düsseldorf—and her young nephew Carl, who came from Detmold to visit his relations.

"On the occasion of one of the lessons," says Freiherr von Meysenbug,* "I first saw and heard the almost boyish-looking, shy, and socially awkward young artist, who played to us Schubert's 'Moment Musical' in F minor. His rendering of the piece made an indelible impression on me."

The boy's admiration led later on to a fast alliance between Brahms and Carl. The ladies, on their part, became enthusiastic in their admiration of the young musician, and on the termination of the lessons, which could not long be continued on account of the sad circumstances of the moment, they invited him to stay with them in the spring at Detmold, with a view to his appearance at Court.

It was felt that the all-important necessaries for Frau Schumann were rest and good air. Since the crisis of her husband's malady in February, 1854, followed after a few months by the birth of her youngest son, she had enjoyed but little repose, and since the autumn of 1855 practically none. During November and December of that year she travelled, as we have seen, in Germany, giving concerts with Joachim in Leipzig, Berlin, Danzig, Berlin again, Rostock, and many other towns. At home for Christmas, she gave her first concert in Vienna on January 7, which was followed by five others, the last taking place on March 3. Travelling meanwhile, she combined her engagements in the Austrian capital with performances at Prague and other cities. Returning early in March by way of Leipzig, she was at home about a fortnight, and on April 7 started for England, to remain until the second week of July. We have seen to what she returned, and may well understand that she seemed to Joachim and Brahms "an example of God-given strength." It was now decided that she should go to Switzerland, and that Johannes' sister should accompany her. Elise Brahms was not artistic, and had little education. She had suffered all her life from bad headaches, and the constitutional tendency had been aggravated by her

---

* "Aus Johannes Brahms' Jugendtagen," by. Carl, Hreiherr von Meysenbug (*Neues Wiener Tagblatt*, April 3 and 4, 1902).

employment of plain sewing, carried on at home or in the houses of her clients. She was not pretty, but her single personal attraction being an abundance of light-brown hair which grew to a great length, but she was simple, unselfish and kind; she was the sister of Johannes; and Frau Schumann hoped that a respite from her confined life, in the fine air and scenery, might do her good. The whole party—Frau Schumann with some of her children, Elise, and Johannes—set off together as soon as the necessary arrangements could be made, accompanied on the first part of their journey by Joachim, and proceeded by short stages to Gersau, on the Lake of Lucerne, where they settled down for several weeks. The time was spent in quiet walks and excursions, with some amount of music and a few meetings with close friends, and the return was made in the same leisurely way, with ten days' stay at Heidelberg. The holiday had its effect, and the beginning of October found the three musicians prepared to take up the ordinary duties of life. Frau Schumann began to practise for her concert-season, Joachim was at his post at Hanover, and Johannes about to return to his home in Hamburg, to apply himself to the occupations which had been interrupted by the events of the past six months. He appeared at Otten's concert of the 25th of the month with Beethoven's G major Concerto, and this time with immense success. "The concerto was played with such fire and élan as to excite enthusiastic demonstration." Some special outward circumstance or inner mood probably stirred him on this occasion. His performance was so powerful that it is still vividly remembered, with its effect upon the audience. His appearance on November 22 at a Philharmonic concert chiefly devoted to Schumann's works awakened no enthusiasm. He played the master's Pianoforte Concerto, and the indifference with which his performance was received was the more marked by contrast with the stormy applause that followed Joachim's playing of Schumann's Violin Fantasia and of Bach's Chaconne.

It was, however, a joy to Brahms to have his friend with him for a day or two, and a convenient opportunity was welcomed by both young musicians for the leisurely trial of the quartet by Johannes that had been examined by Joachim in the spring of the year. "Ich möchte nicht wagen von Anderungen zu sprechen bevor ich's nochmals gehört, ordentlich gehört!" Joachim had written in April. No record is to be found of the result of the rehearsal, which took place in the dwelling of Brahms' friend, Grädener, a musician of Hamburg, except such as is furnished by the subsequent history of the quartet. The work, in spite of its great imaginative power, proved somewhat of an *enfant terrible* to the composer. It was tried again in Hanover early in 1857, no doubt with such alterations as had been suggested by the experience of the Hamburg rehearsal. After this date there is no more news of it for many years.*

The season 1856-7 was passed uneventfully by Brahms in the studies and other occupations already described, varied by an occasional journey. He may be said to have had at this time at least three possible homes in addition to that of his parents in Hamburg. He knew himself to be sure of a welcome at any moment, not only in Düsseldorf and Hanover but also in Göttingen, where Grimm, lately married to Fräulein Philippine Ritmüller, daughter of the head of the pianoforte firm of that name, was rapidly making a position for himself as the centre of a circle of energetic music-lovers. Moved partly, perhaps, by this

---

* Compare Brahms' "Briefwechsel," Vol. V, No. 6, 93, 94, 116; and Vol. IV, No. XXX.

In the absence of the specific reason on which it is based, it is impossible to endorse the suggestion of the editor of the Brahms-Joachim "Briefwechsel" that the quartet tried in Hamburg was one of the pair Opp. 25 and 26.

The same remark applies to the editor's footnote on Brahms's letter, No. XXX of the Brahms-Grimm "Briefwechsel."

For further elucidation of this point see footnote to p. 265 of this biography.

friend's enthusiastic affection for the symphony movements of 1854, yet convinced, as we have seen, of his present incapacity for the successful completion of a purely orchestral work in large form, Johannes had conceived the idea of rearranging portions of his composition as a pianoforte concerto. The changes of structure involved in the plan proved, however, to be far from easy of satisfactory accomplishment and occupied much of the composer's time during two years. The movements were repeatedly sent to Hanover for Joachim's inspection, and returned with his suggestions; for his time, sympathy, musicianship, and knowledge of the orchestra, were placed, with unfailing generosity, at Brahms' disposal during all the years of ripening experience that led up to the composer's maturity. The immediate fortunes of the work after it was at length completed will be related in due course.

The invitation of the von Meysenbugs having been duly renewed and accepted, the young musician paid a short visit to Detmold at Whitsuntide. Arriving at the little town one pleasant afternoon, the last stage of his journey having been made by post, he was met by his pupil and her nephew Carl, and brought by them to Frau von Meysenbug's house. The article of the Vienna *Neues Tagblatt* already referred to, by Freiherr von Meysenbug, the "Carl," or "Charles," as he was generally called, of 1857, gives a pleasant account of the visit :

"I can still see the young fellow standing in silent embarrassment in the old Excellency's drawing-room, not quite knowing how to begin a conversation with the ladies, who were still practically strangers to him. Just then—it was about four o'clock—a princely carriage drove through the quiet street, in which were seated the three sisters of the reigning Prince on their way to dine with their brother at the palace. The ladies were accustomed to look up, as they passed, to the windows of my relations, and my aunt, seeing the carriage coming, said, 'I will just nod to the Princess (Friederike) that Herr Brahms is come.' Upon this Brahms broke silence with the words, 'Do they live close by, then, like everyone else?' evidently thinking that the sign was to be given to an opposite window. This set the conversation going till I showed Brahms his room."

The same evening Charles reappeared with his parents and Concertmeister Bargheer, of the Detmold court orchestra, a fine player, pupil of Spohr and Joachim, and already an acquaintance of Brahms. The Hofmarschall wished to hear the new-comer as a preliminary to his appearance at Court, and listened to most convincing performances of a thundering prelude and fugue of Bach and of Beethoven's C sharp minor Sonata, Op. 27. An orchestral court concert was arranged, at which Johannes played his favourite Beethoven Concerto in G major and took part in a performance of Schubert's "Forellen" Quintet with Concertmeister Bargheer, viola-player Schulze, violoncellist Julius Schmidt, all soloists of the court orchestra, and a bassist, member of the same body. His success was unequivocal, and he appeared with Bargheer at an assembly of musicians and their friends held after the concert at the chief confectioner's, in rollicking boyish spirits. Capellmeister Kiel, on the other hand, who looked rather askance at a probable future favourite at Court, assumed airs of even unusual importance. He was at present, he said, setting one of the Psalms as a chorus; he often composed Biblical texts, but was sometimes puzzled by the Scriptural expressions. For instance, "To the chief musician on the Gittith." "Pray, can you inform me what a Gittith was?" solemnly to the young hero of the evening. "Probably a pretty Jewish girl," returned Brahms, with a serious air—an answer which procured him a suspicious look over the spectacles of the old musician, and enraptured Charles, who, supposed by his parents to be in bed, had found means of his own to join the party. The entertainment having been prolonged until dawn, the more ardent spirits of the gathering proposed a walk to a neighbouring height to see the sun rise, and Brahms and Charles strode off together, leading the way. Their enthusiasm survived that of their companions, who gradually dropped off; and overcome by weariness as they reached the beginning of the last steep climb, they turned into the garden of a restaurant hard by, where Charles dropped on to the corner seat of an arbour bench, and Brahms, stretching himself out at full length with his head on his companion's knee, immediately went soundly to sleep.

"Just as I, too, was giving way to fatigue," continues Freiherr von Meysenbug, "a fine brown spaniel came sniffing at Brahms' face, and he suddenly jumped up, roused by the dog's cold nose. Meanwhile the house had awakened, we drank some hastily-prepared coffee, satisfied our healthy young appetites with delicious country black bread and golden-yellow butter, and trotted back to the little town. We both presented rather a questionable appearance in the streets, which were already astir, especially so the small Brahms in dress-coat, crumpled and disarranged white necktie, and crush-hat on one side. Paying a passing visit to the faithless Bargheer, whom we disturbed in his morning slumbers, we next set out for my grandmother's dwelling. There—oh, horror!—we suddenly came upon my aunt setting out for her morning walk. A distant look of righteous indignation travelled up and down the two night-enthusiasts, for Brahms' attire betrayed but too clearly that he had not been back since the previous evening. A stormy atmosphere prevailed during the day in the house of the hospitable ladies, who were not only unused to visits from men, but could never have imagined that the ideal artist would commit himself to such extravagances. I was severely censured by grandmother and aunts as the harebrained youth who had led the honoured guest astray. Brahms left the next day, not having been very warmly pressed to prolong his visit! He had, however, given such satisfaction in high quarters that his return in the autumn for a long stay in Detmold was definitely arranged. He was to give lessons to the Princess, play at Court, and conduct an amateur choral society, which, by invitation of the Prince, held its weekly meetings at the castle, and to which His Serene Highness, together with his brothers and sisters, belonged as regular members."

Brahms, who could now look forward to the autumn without anxiety as to his finances, and who appreciated in anticipation the advantages he would derive as a composer from his position as conductor of a choral society and from constant association with a standing orchestra, met Frau Schumann on her return from England, where she had again passed the London season, in happy mood. Any regret he may have felt at resigning his freedom of action for a few months by a binding engagement was mitigated by the fact that his association with Düsseldorf must in any case shortly be severed. Frau Schumann had made up her mind that she would best serve her own happiness and the interests of her family by settling near her mother in Berlin, and was to take up her residence there in September, in readiness for the concert season and for the more advantageous opportunity of working as a teacher in the Prussian capital, by which she hoped to supplement her income. Born September 13, 1819, the great pianist, now not quite thirty-eight, was in the zenith of her powers, and, with the probability of a long career before her, it is not surprising that she should have resolved to begin a new chapter of life away from the town that was chiefly associated in her mind with painful recollections. The summer vacation was passed by her on the Rhine in the more or less constant society of Brahms, Joachim, and Grimm, and a memorial of a few specially pleasant days at St. Goarshausen is in existence in the shape of a copy, in her handwriting, of Brahms' Variations, Op. 21, No. 2. On the outside page is written:

"Ungarische Variationen von Johannes. Herrn Julius Otto Grimm, zur Erinnerung an die Tage in St. Goarshausen. August, 1857. Clara Schumann."*

It was at this moment that Joachim resolved on a step which contributed not a little to inflame the party feeling animating the younger disciples of the New-German school. That they had felt increasingly aggrieved by the position taken up by him since the crisis of Schumann's illness, by

---

* In the possession of Fräulein Marie Grimm.

his thoroughgoing association of his name and influence with the art of the master and his wife, by his intimacy with Brahms, and by his passive attitude towards Liszt's Symphonic Poems, may be read in letters of the period. Bülow, whose correspondence up to the middle of 1854 contains repeated affectionate references to Joachim, to whom he was immensely attached, wrote to Liszt in reference to the numerous concert journeys of 1855 undertaken with Frau Schumann:

"Joachim and the statue of which he is making himself the pedestal are not coming here till the beginning of next month. I am afraid we shall have difficulty in recognising each other, for we are at work in completely opposite directions."

Perhaps their secret conviction of Joachim's artistic sincerity added to the disappointment of the Weimarites, which undoubtedly increased during the two following years, though his dislike of the Symphonic Poems was only to be guessed by his silence about them. On the publication of the works in 1857, however, with a somewhat pretentious preface, the embarrassment he felt from the consciousness that he would be unable to live up to the desires of his quondam associates, stimulated beyond a doubt by the sympathy of Johannes, who fully shared his sentiments, induced him to pen a letter to Liszt in which he made full confession of his apostasy. The intense pain which the writing of it caused him, attached as he was to everything about Liszt excepting his compositions, may be read in every line of the epistle, which is dated August 27, 1857.

" . . . . But of what use would it be if I were to delay any longer saying plainly what I feel? My passivity towards your works could not but reveal it to you, who are accustomed to be treated with enthusiasm, and who regard me as capable of true, active friendship. I will not, therefore, longer conceal what, as I confess, your manly soul had the right to demand of me sooner. I am entirely without sensibility for your music; it contradicts everything upon which my powers have been nourished since early youth from the spirits of our great ones. If it were conceivable that I could ever be robbed, that I must renounce what I have learned to love and reverence in their works, what I feel as music, your tones would be no help to me in the vast, annihilating desert. How, then, could I associate myself with the object of those who, under the banner of your name and in the belief (I speak of the conscientious among them) that they are bound to make themselves responsible for contemporary justice towards artistic achievement, make it the aim of life to spread the acceptance of your works by every means at their command? . . ."

These lines were written when Joachim was twenty-six. That they were wrung from him by the strength of his artistic convictions is clear, and it is certain that they were entirely characteristic of the writer at the time. It is probable that Brahms, if he had been called upon to compose the letter, would have expressed himself differently; but then, he would not, under similar circumstances, have felt the same amount of pain. An element in his great influence over his friends, and one which he encouraged through life by deliberate training, was to accept the inevitable with philosophy, and to look on the bright side of things; and his natural elasticity of temperament would have enabled him, had circumstances demanded of him the sacrifice of a friendship, to yield it with little outward flinching. It is difficult for the present generation, for whom the artistic party questions of half a century ago have little beyond historic interest, to judge of the position of those for whom they were a burning personal topic; but it is certain that Joachim's letter to Liszt added fuel to a fire which raged violently through the next succeeding years, and which occasioned the issue of a mass of controversial pamphlets and articles almost unreadable at the present day.

Liszt himself accepted the young musician's confession with generous dignity, and never allowed a disrespectful word to be uttered about Joachim in his presence. His first and only reply to the letter of 1857 was not made until nearly thirty years later. Joachim, arriving one year early in the eighties at Budapest to perform his great Variations for violin and orchestra, called on Liszt, who happened to be staying in the same hotel with himself. The two artists had not met for many years, and the pleasure felt by each at the accidental rencontre reminded them of the tie of affection that had formerly united them. It turned out that Liszt had already made himself acquainted with the variations, and he proposed now to attend the rehearsal in order to hear the composer's performance of them, saying: "As you do not like my music, dear Joachim, I feel that I must admire yours in double measure."

By the end of September Brahms found himself once more in Detmold. The terms of his engagement, which extended through the last three months of the year, included free rooms and living, and he was lodged in the hotel Stadt Frankfurt, a comfortable inn, since enlarged and modernised, exactly opposite the castle enclosure— close, therefore, to the scene of his duties. The difficulty of procuring a piano in the little town was got over by the loan of an old "grand" belonging to the Frau Hofmarschall that had been superseded in her drawing-room by one of later construction; and Brahms, relieved at having succeeded in obtaining something that had at least been good in its day, rewarded Charles for his suggestion that the instrument should be sent to the Stadt Frankfurt by promising him right of entrance to all practices and performances that he might hold in his room with Bargheer, Schmidt, and others.

The daily life of our musician during the next three months was one very much after his own heart. His mornings were sacred to work. Bargheer joined him at the Stadt Frankfurt for early dinner, and the afternoons were generally passed in exercise in the crisp autumn air of the Teutoburger forest. There were games with Carl and his younger brother Hermann; trials of strength with Bargheer, in which Brahms was invariably defeated; Sunday excursions with Bargheer, Carl, and others, which occupied the whole day and included an al-fresco luncheon carried from Detmold, to which Brahms was proud to be able sometimes to contribute an excellent bottle of Malvoisier. This he procured by dispensing with the half-bottle of ordinary wine daily provided with his dinner until he had covered the cost of the superior vintage to be shared with his friends. "He was as happy as a king at these times, he loved beautiful nature so much," says Julius Schmidt, who was occasionally one of the party.

His post as conductor of the choral society was at first particularly welcome, not only as giving him experience in a branch of musical activity which he had not practised since he stood, a boy of fifteen, at the head of his little society of teachers at Winsen, but as affording opportunity for the practical application and test of the studies to which he had been devoting special attention. He began his duties as conductor with the practice of short works by early and modern masters, and arranged some of his favourite folk-songs expressly for the use of the society, deriving from each rehearsal fresh insight into the art of writing for voices. There were frequent informal musical soirées at Court, which provided occasion for choral performances in the intervals between the instrumental works that formed the bulk of the programmes. These were played by Brahms, Bargheer, Schulze, Schmidt, and the splendid hornist, August Cordes, whose rich, mellow tone drew from Brahms enthusiastic expressions of admiration. Almost the entire répertoire of classical chamber music seems to have been gone through during this and succeeding seasons; all the duet sonatas and pianoforte trios and quartets, etc., of Bach, Mozart, Beethoven, Schubert, and Schumann, were played in turn. Brahms' Trio was performed several times, and it gave the young musician particular pleasure to execute, not only Beethoven's Horn

Sonata with Cordes, but Mozart's and Beethoven's quintets for pianoforte and wind with the soloists of the orchestra, who were one and all artists. The powers of the flutist are said to have been hardly less remarkable than those of Cordes.

The court violoncellist, Julius Schmidt, who in 1857 was a man in the early prime of life, has described to the author Brahms' appearance, on his coming to Detmold, as so delicate and refined as to be almost girlish; and this impression was strengthened by his voice, which was still of the high quality that has been frequently mentioned. Impatient of the remarks elicited by the peculiarity, he began at this time to practise a series of vocal gymnastics for the purpose of forcing his voice down, and was eventually successful in this aim.

When engaged in the performance of his duties, he was always quiet and serious, and would stand, before the commencement of a choir practice or a court concert, at the extreme end of the long room in which the functions took place, speaking to no one, perhaps looking through a piece of music or a letter. His duties in connection with the orchestral concerts were to play from time to time, and to conduct now and then. In the course of the successive autumns passed by him at Detmold, his performances included several of Mozart's and Beethoven's concertos, which were heard with especial delight; Schumann's Concerto; Mendelssohn's G minor and D minor Concertos; E flat Rondo and B minor Caprice; Chopin's E minor and Moscheles' G minor Concertos; and, with Bargheer and Schmidt, Beethoven's triple Concerto. Occasionally, as time went on, the Princess Friederike played a concerto, and on the occasion of a performance of Beethoven's Choral Fantasia the Frau Hofmarschall von Meysenbug undertook the pianoforte solo, whilst Brahms acted as conductor.

The young musician soon became a favourite at Court, not only on account of his musical genius, but also because of the general culture of his mind. He invariably seemed at home on a topic of real interest, and able to contribute something worth hearing at its discussion. "Whoever wishes to play well must not only practise a great deal, but read a great many books," was one of his favourite sayings, and the excellent public library of Detmold afforded him good opportunity for indulging his literary tastes. On the evenings that were free from duties, some of the musicians often dropped into Brahms' room to play, and the performances generally went on until late into the night.

"And how Brahms loved the great masters! how he played Haydn and Mozart! with what beauty of interpretation and delicate shading of tone! And then his transposing!"

He would play a new composition by one or other of his Detmold friends at sight in a transposed key without a mistake, taking it at any interval suggested, and thinking nothing of the feat. He even liked to play tricks on Court Concertmeister Bargheer, and to lead off Mozart's duet sonatas, which Prince Leopold was fond of hearing in private, in transposed keys, in which Bargheer was obliged, and luckily able, to follow.

"His score playing, too, was marvellous. Bach, Handel, Haydn, Mozart, all seemed to flow naturally under his fingers, and each point to come out, as it were, of itself. Then, he was of such a noble character, such a good, kind nature, and so loved children. . . ."

It must be added, however, that Schmidt, like most of the Detmold musicians, whilst enthusiastically admiring Brahms' gifts as an executant, regarded his compositions with scepticism. The B major Trio was by no means a favourite with himself or his colleagues—Bargheer always excepted—and he thought the 'cello part most ungratefully written for the instrument.

Enough has been said to make it evident that Brahms' sojourn at Detmold was an unmitigated success, and before his departure his re-engagement the following season had come to be regarded as a matter of course. The Christmas festival, passed by him in the midst of the Hofmarschall's family party, was as bright and happy as can be imagined. Johannes became for the evening a child of the house, entering eagerly with the boys into the mystery of the hour preceding the great presentation of Christmas gifts, and ready to laugh heartily at the practical jokes of which he and others were made victims later in the evening. A few words written in an album given to Hermann are still treasured by their owner: "This was written in hearty friendship by your Johannes."

Two signs, contrasted one with the other, but both prophetic of things to come, are to be noted in January newspaper issues of 1858. One, which points to the swelling bitterness of feeling with which the Weimarites contemplated the compact phalanx of friends who may conveniently be termed the Schumann party, is contained in a reference to Rubinstein as composer, penned by Bülow in the *Neue Berliner Musikzeitung* of January 27:

"He [Rubinstein] knows his powers; he has tested his arms, and has therefore attained to a higher stage than the brooding Brahms."

The other is the record, in a paragraph of the *Signale*, of what was probably the début of Brahms' name in Italy. The distinguished pianist Alfred Jaell had included one of his compositions in the programmes of a lately-ended concert-tour through that country.

Leaving Detmold on January 1, Brahms, travelling by way of Hanover, where he enjoyed an hour's conversation at the railway station with Joachim, proceeded direct to Hamburg and was soon engrossed with his studies, compositions, and pupils. The question of the completion of the pianoforte concerto had become urgent. Again and again had the several movements of the work been despatched to Hanover and returned to the composer with Joachim's comments. Yet once more had Johannes, before leaving Detmold, sent back the first movement with a request for his friend's opinion on fresh alterations. This last petition remained unanswered for a week or two, but was at length fulfilled in a most practical manner. Joachim returned the manuscript, marked in pencil with his thorough revision of the instrumentation, which Johannes was to keep or reject at his pleasure, but no further interruption of the copyist's task was to be countenanced. The writing out of the parts of the entire work was to be completed without more delay and the concerto tried on the first opportunity at Hanover or Hamburg.

"I refrain from all further remarks on your concerto only that I may not again delay the copying; but I am burning with impatience for the undisturbed enjoyment, through hearing, of the many beauties of the first order which have delighted me on reading it. Let me know if you like what I have done."*

Joachim's mandate helped matters considerably forward. The composer braced himself to face the inevitable, and actually announced in his next letter to his untiring adviser that the parts would be ready in a few days, and that he had, almost in spite of himself, accepted an engagement to play the concerto at Otten's subscription concert of March 25, and would welcome the opportunity of a preliminary rehearsal at Hanover before that date.

The work, however, was not to be heard immediately. The concert engagement fell through because the publisher Cranz, who owned the only adequate piano of which Hamburg could boast, refused the loan of it for the occasion; and the young composer postponed the rehearsal of his work in Hanover on successive pretexts, probably but various spellings of the word "nervousness." Mortified by the equanimity with which Otten received the news of the pianoforte difficulty, Brahms resolved to absent himself altogether from the concert of March 25 even though Joseph was to

---

* Brahms-Joachim "Briefwechsel," No. 139.

take part in it, and went off to Berlin to greet Frau Schumann in her new home on her return from a concert-tour in Switzerland. No doubt he derived encouragement from her sympathy on the completion of his great work, though her step-brother, Woldemar Bargiel, expressed but moderate appreciation of its merits. Matters were brought to a crisis on March 28 by a telegram from Hanover. Joachim had arranged to conduct a trial performance of the composition in two days' time at the end of a rehearsal for the next Hanover subscription concert. He wished Johannes to join him immediately and hoped Frau Schumann would make it possible to be present on the occasion. Thus it came about that after long anxiety and delay, Brahms' first completed orchestral work was heard privately for the first time on Tuesday, March 30, 1858, at Hanover. Not only was Frau Schumann present, Grimm, too, had come to hear the beloved symphony movements in their new dress, and to dream of future triumphs in which Göttingen might participate; and Johannes, helped by the consciousness of his friends' sympathy, forgot his fears and rose to the demands of the hour.

"I think you must be pleased to hear," Frau Schumann wrote to Bargiel, "that the rehearsal went off splendidly to-day. There was only time to play it through once, but it went almost without a mistake and quite roused the musicians. If you had heard it to-day it would have seemed clear to you. Almost everything sounded so fine; better even than Johannes, himself, had hoped or expected.

"The whole is wonderful, so rich and fervent, and has such unity! Johannes was blissful and played the last movement *prestissimo* from sheer delight. We took a walk afterwards; it was as though heaven had desired to lend special brightness to the day. Johannes enjoyed it in full measure; I wish you could have seen his happiness."*

It was too late in the season to make immediate arrangements for a public performance of the concerto, but Brahms

---

* Litzmann III, 35.

returned to his parents' home with confident hope in his heart. The family moved again this year to a more commodious dwelling at 74, Fuhlentwiethe, still in the old quarter of Hamburg, but with good-sized rooms, which were always kept in beautiful order. The parlour was comfortably though plainly furnished, and decorated with ivy after the custom of the time. It had a large open fireplace with old-fashioned hobs on either side, which occasionally served in the summer as a refuge for cake-eating child-visitors, to the preservation of Fräulein Elise's spotless floor. The room set apart for Johannes, who, now as always, was responsible for a large share of the family expenses, afforded ample space for a sleeping sofa, washing-stand, piano, writing-table, and large bookcase, on the top of which stood a bust of Beethoven. Two or three small prints from good pictures decorated the walls, one of them being a representation of Leonardo da Vinci's "Last Supper." There was sufficient space in the dwelling for the accommodation of one or two boarders—a means of income to which Jakob and his wife had had recourse, as we have seen, in the early part of their married life.

A visit to Frau Schumann in April and May of nearly a month's duration and the enjoyment of her society in Hamburg for a few days in June, afforded Johannes some compensation for the loss of the constant daily companionship at certain seasons of the year that had been brought to a close by the removal of his friend's home from Düsseldorf to Berlin. He applied himself closely to work during the summer and in the general character of the composition on which he was chiefly engaged, we may perhaps perceive a reflection of the satisfaction caused him by some of the incidents of the spring and, not least, by the gratifying issue of his long struggle with the pianoforte concerto.

Inspired by the delight with which he had listened to the "cassation music," the serenades and divertimenti of Mozart, as performed by the Detmold orchestra, Johannes had set about writing something in the same style in the form of an octet, bearing in mind the special qualifications of Prince Leopold's band; and he soon became so engrossed in his work as to be disinclined to yield to the persuasions by which Grimm, in a letter of June 30, sought to persuade him that he was called upon by every consideration of health, work and duty to others, to spend the rest of the summer at Göttingen. Satisfied at length, however, that his friends, content to know him near them, would leave him in undisturbed possession of his working hours, Johannes wrote to Grimm to announce his coming and left Hamburg at the end of July. It was understood at home that his absence would be a long one. He would not, at any rate, return before the beginning of the next year, after the close of his Detmold season, and there was great uncertainty as to what his future plans might be. It was a sad time for Fräulein Friedchen Wagner, who had been his regular pupil during all the months of his stay, and at her last lesson she begged her master for some little souvenir, desiring that it should be of a serious character to correspond with her mood. She was not at home when he called to say goodbye, however, and he left Hamburg apparently without a sign. Too melancholy for some days to feel that she could open her piano, her delight was the greater when at length, resolving to go to work again, she found under the lid of the instrument a manuscript in Brahms' hand, which bore the inscription: "To Fräulein Fr. Wagner, in kind remembrance. July, 1858." It was the organ prelude to the chorale, "O Traurigkeit, O Herzeleid," which was published with a fugue, in 1881, in a supplement of a number of the *Musikalisches Wochenblatt.**

Brahms' stay in Göttingen proved memorable in more than one respect. Frau Schumann, after drinking the waters at Wiesbaden, took up her residence with five of her children in the Grimms' house; Johannes lodged close by; Bargiel, with whom Brahms had become intimate in Berlin,

---

* "Brahms in Hamburg," by Professor Walter Hübbe.

and Bargheer joined the party, and about six weeks were passed in work and play that were almost equally delightful. Brahms was left to himself, by general understanding, during the morning hours, and the serenade advanced so rapidly that he was able to announce the work to his deeply interested friends while their circle was still intact. Immediate arrangements were made for its rehearsal; Johannes, himself, Grimm, Bargiel, Bargheer, all set to copy out the parts; Grimm got together the necessary musicians and the work was tried before an audience of friends, under the composer's direction. This was the first performance in its original form—an octet for string and wind instruments in three movements—of the Serenade in D major published later on as Op. 11.*

Grimm and his wife were inexpressibly touched by the beautiful and rare relation in which Johannes stood to Frau Schumann. "He was to her as a careful friend, a loving and protecting son." She was, indeed, the centre of the party, and the chief thought of all the younger musicians gathered about her. Johannes was a famous playfellow for her little ones, proposing all sorts of romping games for them, in which the elders willingly joined. As for music, they had their own share in that, too. One can imagine them cowering quiet in their hiding-places as they heard the approaching voice of the seeker:

Wil-le, wil-le, will, Der Mann ist kom-men;
Did-dle, did-dle dee, There's some-one com-ing;

the demands of the four-year-old Felix for another ride on somebody's knee, in spite of the answer:

---

* For the information that the Serenade in D major was originally composed as an octet for solo instruments, the author is indebted to some unpublished notes on his acquaintance with Brahms written by Concertmeister Bargheer.

Ull Mann will ri - - - den, wull hat er kein Pferd;
He would go ri - - - ding, but no horse had he;

the efforts of the small Eugénie to keep the dust out of her eyes just a little longer, though

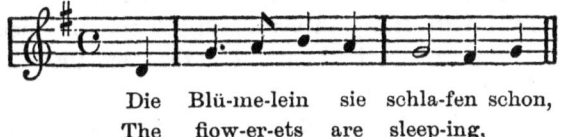

Die   Blü-me-lein   sie   schla-fen schon,
The   flow-er-ets   are   sleep-ing,

These and other songs which were sung by Johannes with and to Frau Schumann's children at Göttingen this summer were published anonymously by Rieter-Biedermann at the end of the year as "Children's Folk-songs, with added accompaniment, dedicated to the children of Robert and Clara Schumann."

About the middle of September the party broke up. The children returned to Berlin; their mother went to visit an old friend at Düsseldorf; others were called away by their respective affairs; and only Johannes, who had his own particular reasons at the moment for thinking Göttingen the most delightful place in the world, remained behind with the Grimms. Nothing could have been more opportune under these circumstances than a note received by Brahms which announced Joachim's return from England and his wish to join his friend, wherever he might be, during the brief remainder of the holiday season. His attendance at Göttingen was commanded forthwith and Brahms, never sure of the value of a new work of his own until he had possessed himself of Joseph's opinion of its merits, lost no time in playing the Serenade movements to his companion, who received them with approval tempered with reserve. There was definite reason for the composer's anxiety on this occasion. His inexperience in the art of instrumentation had again been betrayed by the rehearsal of the Serenade, and

Frau Schumann had declared her belief that no alteration less drastic than its rearrangement for full orchestra would avail for the realisation in performance of the attractive ideas of the composition. Joachim, however, questioned by Johannes, withheld his opinion on this and other points until he should have had opportunity for quiet study of the score, which he took with him to Hanover at the close of the month; and Brahms, who left Göttingen in his friend's company to return to the duties of his post in Detmold, destroyed the parts in the conviction that, as then written, they would be of no further use to him.

With the approach of autumn, the desirability became pressing of arranging for a public performance of the pianoforte concerto, and in the course of October the following paragraph, for which the enthusiasm of Frau Schumann may have been indirectly responsible, appeared in the *Signale*.

"We hear that since the arrival of J. Brahms in Detmold a few weeks ago there has been an animated musical life there, of which the young artist is the centre. Brahms will remain in Detmold until the end of the year, and it is hoped that some of his compositions may be brought to a hearing. He has completed amongst other things, a pianoforte concerto, the great beauties of which have been reported to us."

The same journal notices concerts given by Frau Schumann in Düsseldorf and elsewhere, at which she played arrangements by Brahms for two hands on the pianoforte, of a selection of Hungarian Dances, "that called forth a veritable storm of applause." This unanswerable statement should effectually dispose of the fable which has obtained considerable credence amongst the musical laity, that the "Hungarian Dance" arrangements were the outcome of impressions derived during Brahms' residence in Vienna. As has been shown in an earlier chapter, he owed his first acquaintance with the melodies to the playing of Reményi.

The hope expressed in the *Signale*, that the new works might be performed at Detmold, was only partially fulfilled. As we have seen, Brahms was not seriously accepted as a composer by the musicians there—one of them only excepted—and Capellmeister Kiel regarded his compositions with peculiar jealousy and mistrust. So far as can be ascertained, the D minor Concerto was not even tried at Detmold. The ultimate result of the successful rehearsal at Hanover in March was, however, that Joachim, in spite of some official opposition, carried through his wish that it should be put down for a first performance at one of the Hanover subscription court concerts, choosing for date January 22, 1859, when Johannes would be free from duties; and that through the influence of Court Concertmeister David arrangements were made for its second performance a few days later at Leipzig Gewandhaus concert of January 27.

As to the serenade, Joachim found himself completely in accord with Frau Schumann's high opinion of its musical value, but was still unwilling to judge prematurely on the question of the scoring:

"The last movement is, in its way, as happy as the first," he wrote, "and the trio charming also, only sometimes unfortunately instrumented, especially too difficult for the violins. You played the last movement so carelessly in Göttingen that I could form no opinion about it; here everything is clear to me.... Whether you should really set the serenade for orchestra or leave it as it is with the addition, perhaps, of a horn or an oboe, I cannot decide without hearing it."*

Meanwhile Brahms was making progress with still newer compositions. Until a comparatively late period of his career, his method of working in some respects resembled that of Beethoven. We have seen that he was in the habit, as a boy, of putting his thoughts down as they occurred to him. Later on he was accustomed to keep several large compositions on hand at once, allowing his ideas to expand

---

* Brahms-Joachim "Briefwechsel," No. 155.

gradually; and he sometimes had a work by him for years before completing it in its final shape. The cases of the D minor Concerto, the C minor pianoforte Quartet, and the C minor Symphony, are well established instances in point, though Brahms took care that the process by which his works were developed should not, after his death, become public property, by destroying the vast majority of his sketches.*

Very soon after his departure from Göttingen he sent Grimm, with an urgent request for opinion and criticism, a packet of new MSS., one of which proved to be the completed first movement of a second serenade in A major, scored for small orchestra. The succeeding movements were not yet ready for inspection.

"How does it sound? Shall I go on with it?" he asks.

"The movement is wonderful," replied Grimm, "and as warm as the beautiful summer months of the year. . . . I found no difficulty in reading the score, for after the first few bars I noticed that I was already acquainted with what follows. You must have played the movement incognito to me some time in the summer, though I do not remember where or when."†

The many important claims on the composer's time which were to be fulfilled during the next few months prevented the immediate completion of the second serenade, the history of which will be resumed in a later chapter.

Carl von Meysenbug was not long able this season to enjoy the evening music which was more than ever an institution at the Stadt, Frankfurt. He departed before the end of October to enter upon the life of a university student at Göttingen, where he soon found himself at home with the congenial friends of Grimm's circle.

---

* The few sketches which Brahms allowed to survive him are preserved in the library of the Gesellschaft der Musikfreunde in Vienna.

† Br.: Grimm "Briefwechsel," No. XLIV.

N.B.—The footnote to the preceding letter is an obvious editorial *lapsus*.

"You will see," Johannes said to him as they parted, "how surprised you will be after your admiration of the stiff court ladies here when you become acquainted with the pretty, fresh, lively daughters of the professors."

These words were significant. The age of twenty-five is suitable to romance, and Brahms was at this time in love. That he had passed through the earliest years of manhood without any serious *affaire de cœur* is to be explained by the circumstances in which he had been placed. The prosecution of a noble ambition which involved unremitting application to work occupied one half of his energies, whilst his affections had been absorbed by family ties, by a dear companionship, and by his love for two people to whom he looked up with unbounded reverence. A calmer period had succeeded the exciting course of past events, and he now had leisure to think of himself. His intercourse with the charming young people who frequented the Grimms' house, and the contemplation of his friend's great happiness in his wedded life, had awakened in him a feeling of loneliness, and he thought much of Fräulein Agathe, daughter of Professor von Siebold, of Göttingen University, and Frau Philippine's most intimate friend. Agathe was handsome, lively, cultivated and gifted with a fine voice; and she sang Brahms' songs with especial sympathy, particularly when he played the accompaniments. A memorial of the friendship that sprang up between the pair during the two summer months of their acquaintance is preserved in the correspondence that passed between Detmold and Göttingen in the autumn of the year, which points clearly to the conclusion that the Grimms encouraged the intimacy in the natural hope that it might lead to a nearer relationship. After his return to Detmold Johannes constantly exchanged letters with Agathe, whom he addressed by her christian name, through these mutual friends; composed songs for her which she copied and sang, and constantly spoke in affectionate terms of his "Kleeblatt" in which poetic figure Agathe was associated with Grimm and his wife. Amongst the manuscripts sent in the autumn of 1858 for Grimm's inspection, was a "Brautgesang" (Bridal Song), set for soprano solo and women's chorus, to a poem by Uhland, and Brahms replied to Grimm's critical suggestions on the work:

"So a poor composer sits sadly alone in his room and makes himself dizzy with matters which do not concern him, and so a critic sits down between two beautiful ladies and—I would rather not complete the picture."

The friendship was pursued with ardour during a week's visit to Göttingen, for which Brahms found time on his departure from Detmold at the opening of the New Year, but the very confident rumour that prevailed amongst their acquaintances of the impending, or even accomplished, betrothal of Brahms and Agathe proved a tale without an ending. As the binding words remained unspoken, Grimm thought it right to interpose and, after reminding Brahms of his precarious position in the world, told him that he was in duty bound to make himself clear of his intentions one way or the other, and to shape his course accordingly. It can surprise no one who has grasped the key to the young composer's character and aims that his decision, which caused a temporary rupture of his friendly relations with the Grimms, should have led him away from marriage. Now and afterwards he liked the society of charming girls and perhaps thought it no harm to enjoy the pleasure of a special friendship without going beyond the consideration of the hour; but it may safely be assumed that he would not, at the outset of his career, have risked the sacrifice of his artistic aims by accepting binding responsibilities, even had his worldly prospects been much more certain than they were. He resolutely put away the visions of happiness with which he had dallied for a time and turned cheerfully to confront the future in undivided allegiance to the art that was to maintain supreme sway over his affections till the end of his life. That the remembrance of Agathe, who married happily in the course of time, remained treasured in

BRAHMS AND JOACHIM.

some corner of his heart as the years rolled onward, will seem certain to those who have had opportunity to appreciate the tenacity of his memory for old friendships. Several of the songs published later on by Brahms were the immediate result of his intimacy with Agathe; notably "Die Liebende schreibt" (Op. 47, No. 5); "Schmeiden u. Meiden" (Op. 19, No. 2); "In der Ferne" (Op. 19, No. 3); whilst in the last verse—in B major—of the exquisite "Ewige Liebe" (Op. 43, No. 1) is to be found a survival, crystallised and transfigured, of one of the melodies of the "Brautgesang." This work, if any conclusion may be drawn from the composer's own remarks and those of his friends to whom it was shown, was not one of Brahms' happiest efforts, and it remained unpublished.

CHAPTER IX.

1859.

First public performances of the Pianoforte Concerto in Hanover, Leipzig, and Hamburg—Brahms, Joachim and Stockhausen appear together in Hamburg—First public performance of the Serenade in D major—Ladies' Choir—Fräulein Friedchen Wagner—Compositions for women's chorus.

IT is not difficult to realise something of the mingled feelings of hope and anxiety that must have filled the mind of Johannes on his arrival in Hanover on January 8, 1859. If the first chapter of his career had closed in triumphant fashion with the extraordinary series of events that followed his first little concert-journey, the second chapter can only be regarded as an intermezzo which was spent in quiet preparation for what was to succeed it. The prelude of his artistic life had been successfully completed in 1853; the main action was to begin with the performances in Hanover and Leipzig in the opening month of 1859. Brahms was almost extravagantly self-critical, but he must have felt encouraged when he recalled the substantial success of his début as a composer at Leipzig immediately after the appearance of Schumann's famous article; and the joy of the trial performance of his concerto at Hanover less than a year ago was still bright within his heart. Such recollections, combined with the enthusiasm of his best friends, may well have raised his hopes high.

The concerto was heard at Hanover on January 22 in the

presence of the entire court circle and under the most favourable artistic conditions. Joachim conducted the orchestra, Johannes played the solo, and it would be hard to say which of the two young musicians was the more interested in the occasion, but though the composer was honoured with a recall, the actual result of the performance was that the public was wearied and the musicians puzzled.

"The work had no great success with the public," reported the Hanover correspondent of the *Signale* ten days later, "but"—and we seem to read the promptings of a Joachim in the following words—"it aroused the decided respect and sympathy of the best musicians for the gifted artist."

"The work, with all its serious striving, its rejection of triviality, its skilled instrumentation, seemed difficult to understand, even dry, and in parts eminently fatiguing," said another critic;* "nevertheless Brahms gave the impression of being a really sterling musician, and it was conceded without reservation that he is not merely a virtuoso, but a great artist of pianoforte-playing."

Johannes had to leave almost immediately for Leipzig, and he started from Hanover without knowing more about the impression produced there by his concerto than could be gathered from the politeness of the audience and the enthusiasm of his friend, but that his frame of mind was not despondent may be inferred from a paragraph which appeared in the *Signale* immediately after his arrival.

"Herr Johannes Brahms is here, and will play his Concerto at the Gewandhaus concert of the 27th. He thinks of remaining the rest of the winter at Leipzig."

It is necessary to remind the reader what kind of audience it was for whose acceptance our young composer was now about to submit his work. Leipzig still occupied the position of musical capital of Europe to which it had been raised

---

* Dr. Georg Fischer's "Opern und Concerte im Hoftheater zu Hannover bis 1866."

by the genius of Mendelssohn. By the most influential of its artistic circles, the premature death of this fascinating master (1809-1847) was still deplored as an almost recent event. Most of his old friends were living, and, in virtue of their former personal association with him, looked upon themselves as competent judges of all later aspirants to fame. It is a matter of daily experience that the uninformed satellites of a man of genius are arrogant in proportion to their ignorance, and that even professional adepts of sincerity are apt to allow their horizon to be limited by their hero-worship. Musicians and amateurs, alike, of the Gewandhaus circle associated the idea of a concerto with the clear melody of Mozart and Beethoven, still, perhaps, regarding Beethoven as a little difficult to follow, with the attractive sparkle of Mendelssohn and with the opportunity for a display of the soloist's virtuosity afforded more or less by the works of all three masters. If asked to listen to a novelty, they expected that it should not be too unlike what they had heard before to be difficult to follow. Bernsdorf, newly appointed to succeed Brahms' friendly critic, Louis Köhler, on the staff of the conservative *Signale*, was himself a conservative of the most obstinate type, who was honestly convinced that the series of great masters had closed with Mendelssohn.

On the other hand, the New-Germans had by this time made considerable conquests in Leipzig, where they had established an important party organisation, and had, as we have seen in an earlier chapter, even been admitted on trial to the platform of the Gewandhaus. The *Neue Zeitschrift* was their organ, but they had supporters also amongst the journalists of the daily press, Ferdinand Gleich, of the *Leipziger Tagblatt*, being one of the principal. They were on the look-out for champions who would rally to their cause, and welcomed the unusual as such, though reserving their heartiest approval for the piquant, sounding, sensational, or even revolutionary.

To these two bodies of extremists our Johannes, with his

inexperience, his ideal aims, his genius, and his dislike of the sensational, was now to appeal. Had he been compelled at the moment to declare for either party, he certainly would not have chosen the side of revolution. But he was gifted with an imagination at once profound, original, and romantic. This sealed his fate with the men who considered themselves the modern representatives of classic art. The day after the concert he wrote to Joachim to announce —"a brilliant and decided failure."

"In the first place," he says, "it really went very well; I played much better than in Hanover, and the orchestra capitally. The first rehearsal aroused no feeling whatever, either in the musicians or hearers. No hearers came, however, to the second, and not a muscle moved on the countenance of either of the musicians. In the evening Cherubini's Elisa overture was given, and then an Ave Maria of his uninterestingly sung, so I hoped Pfund's (the drummer's) roll would come at the right time.* The first movement and the second were heard without a sign. At the end three hands attempted to fall slowly one upon the other, upon which a quite audible hissing from all sides forbade such demonstrations. There is nothing else to write about the event, for no one has yet said a syllable to me about the work, David excepted, who was very kind. . . .

"This failure has made no impression at all upon me, and the slight feeling of disappointment and flatness disappeared when I heard Haydn's C minor Symphony and the Ruins of Athens. In spite of all this, the concerto will please some day when I have improved its construction, and a second shall sound different.

"I believe it is the best thing that could happen to me; it makes one pull one's thoughts together and raises one's spirit. . . . But the hissing was surely too much? . . .

"The faces here looked dreadfully insipid when I came from Hanover, and was accustomed to seeing yours. Monday (January 31) I am going to Hamburg. There is interesting church music here on Sunday, and in the evening Faust at Frau Frege's."†

---

* The concerto opens with a long-continued roll of drums.
† Brahms-Joachim "Briefwechsel," p. 167.

The grimness of the young composer's disappointment may be read between these Spartan lines. But perhaps he has exaggerated his failure. Let us see what Bernsdorf has to say.

"It is sad but true; new works do not succeed in Leipzig. Again at the fourteenth Gewandhaus concert was a composition borne to the grave. This work, however, cannot give pleasure. Save its serious intention, it has nothing to offer but waste, barren dreariness truly disconsolate. Its invention is neither attractive nor agreeable. . . . And for more than three-quarters of an hour must one endure this rooting and rummaging, this dragging and drawing, this tearing and patching of phrases and flourishes! Not only must one take in this fermenting mass; one must also swallow a dessert of the shrillest dissonances and most unpleasant sounds. With deliberate intention, Herr Brahms has made the pianoforte part of his concerto as uninteresting as possible; it contains no effective treatment of the instrument, no new and ingenious passages, and wherever something appears which gives promise of effect, it is immediately crushed and suffocated by a thick crust of orchestral accompaniment. It must be observed, finally, that Herr Brahms' pianoforte technique does not satisfy the demands we have a right to make of a concert-player of the present day."

Nothing could be more representative than these lines, of the conscientious bigotry which almost always opposes what is really original, though it is expressed by Bernsdorf with exceptional coarseness. The narrowly orthodox antagonists of Brahms' art resembled those who had levelled their shafts against Beethoven and Schumann each in their day. The young composer fared differently at the hands of the progressists. The *Neue Zeitschrift* wrote:

"The appearance of Johannes Brahms with a new concerto was bound to attract our especial attention. In the first place, on account of the hopes entertained of an artist who had been introduced in a most exceptional manner, even before his first appearance, by the enthusiastic words of a revered master; and secondly, from the rarity of his subsequent public announcements and the retirement in which he has lived.

"Notwithstanding its undeniable want of outward effect, we regard the poetic contents of the concerto as an unmistakable sign of significant and original creative power; and, in face of the belittling criticisms of a certain portion of the public and press, we consider it our duty to insist on the admirable sides of the work, and to protest against the not very estimable manner in which judgment has been passed upon it."

Ferdinand Gleich writes:

"Who would or could ignore in this new work the tokens of an eminent creative endowment! We least of all who regard it as our duty to encourage young talent. Many doubts, however, suggested themselves as we listened to this concert-piece in large form. This work again suggests a condition of indefiniteness and fermentation, a wrestling for a method of expression commensurate with the ideas of the composer, which has indeed broken through the form of tradition, but has not yet constructed another sufficiently definite and rounded to satisfy the demands of the æsthetics of art. . . . The first movement, especially, gives us the impression of monstrosity; this was less the case with the two others, although even there we were not able, in spite of the beauties they contain, to feel real artistic enjoyment. Brahms places the orchestra, as far as is possible in a concert-piece, by the side of the obbligato instrument, and by so doing establishes himself as an artist who understands the requirements of the new era. The treatment of the orchestra shows a blooming fancy and the most vivid feeling for new and beautiful tone effects, although the composer has not yet sufficient command over his means to do justice to his intentions. The work was received calmly, not to say coldly, by the public; we, however, must acknowledge the eminent talent of the composer, of whom, though he is still too much absorbed in his *Sturm und Drang* period, it is not difficult to predict the accomplishment of something great."

Whether or not these two reviews were penned with a deliberate purpose—and a desire on the part of the supporters of the New-German school to identify Brahms with their cause can hardly be regarded as either remarkable or dishonourable—no trace is to be found in either of the insincerity attributed by Kalbeck, in his Life of Brahms, to the journalistic partisans of the Weimarites, and especially to Brendel, editor of the *Zeitschrift* and friend of Liszt. Their honesty of purpose, as well as their liberality of view, has been vindicated by the fate which for many years attended the published concerto, and again we may place the remarks of Hanslick, the avowed champion of classical art and the enthusiastic admirer of the mature Brahms, beside those published in the *Zeitschrift* of the fifties. Writing in 1888, he says:*

"Brahms began, like Schumann, in *Sturm und Drang*, but he was much more daring and wild, more emancipated in respect to form and modulation. The fermentation period of his genius, which is generally supposed to have closed with his Op. 10 (Ballades for pianoforte), should, perhaps, be extended . . . does it not include the D minor Concerto, with its wild genius?"

It has, indeed, taken nearly half a century to establish the concerto in a secure position of public acceptance, and the day, though now probably not far distant, has not even yet arrived when it can be said to rank as a prime favourite amongst compositions of its class with the large body of music-lovers.

Conceived as part of a symphony, the first movement of the work is symphonic in character, though, as Spitta has pointed out, not in form. The desire attributed to the composer by Ferdinand Gleich and by many others since, to create a new form, to compose a symphonic work with a pianoforte obbligato, did not exist. Brahms simply wished to use what he had already written, and did not feel that the time had come when he could successfully complete a symphony. He rewrote his first two movements, therefore, as we have noted, making room in them for a pianoforte

---

* "Musikalisches und Literarisches": "Neuer Brahms Katalog."

solo, put away the third movement, and composed a new finale. How successfully he accomplished his task is to-day apparent to accustomed ears, for which the first movement, though it contains slight deviations from traditional concerto form, has no moment of obscurity. The imagination of this portion of the work is colossal. It has something Miltonic in its character, and seems to suggest to the mind issues more tremendous and universal than the tragedy of Schumann's fate, with which it must be associated. No one will assert that it contains what are termed "brilliant pianoforte passages," the very existence of which is unthinkable in a movement of such exalted poetic grandeur; but that its performance brings due reward to capable interpreters has been proved by the enthusiasm of many a latter-day audience. After all that has been said, the reader will have no difficulty in understanding the fervent intensity of mood which impelled the composition of the slow movement, or in realising something of the emotions which suggested the motto, *Benedictus qui venit in nomine Domini*, written above it in the original manuscript which was presented to Joachim by Brahms. In the finale, the difficult task of creating something which should relieve the tension of feeling induced by the preceding movements, without impairing the unity of the concerto as a whole, has been well achieved. If it is somewhat more sombre in colour than the usually accepted finale in rondo form, it is abundant in vigour and impulse, whilst, on the other hand, though written with a view to the concert-room, it never descends towards the trivialities of mere outward glitter.

Much more might be said in explanation of the dubious position so long occupied in the world of art by this great work of genius. We must not, however, linger too long over such interesting matters. It is enough to say that the purpose expressed by Brahms in his letter to Joachim, of "pulling his thoughts together," was literally carried out, and that his development proceeded in the direction it had already taken, which was the very opposite of that pursued by the adherents of the New-German school. It consisted in the still closer concentration of his powers within the forms of tradition, and the rapidity with which he attained to complete and free mastery over musical structure is marked by the production—soon to be recorded—of the first of the great series of *chefs-d'œuvre* of chamber music which have set his name, in this particular domain of art, as high as that of Beethoven himself.

Unrecognised by the public and misunderstood by the academics of Leipzig, whose sympathies he seems particularly, though for many years vainly, to have desired to gain, our young musician had now no choice but to return to his home and pupils at Hamburg. If, however, he himself felt at all despondent at the failure of his hopes, his friends were determined about the future of his work. Prompted and backed up by Joachim, Avé Lallement, who was a member of the Philharmonic committee, persuaded the directors to engage composer and concerto for their concert of March 24. Joachim had written to Avé:

"DEAR FRIEND,

"Nearer acquaintance with Brahms' concerto inspires me with increasing love and respect. The most intelligent people amongst the public and the orchestra (of Leipzig) with whom I have spoken express a high opinion of Brahms as a musician, and even those who do not like the concerto are at one as to his eminent playing. I have never expected anything else than that prejudice on the one hand, and, on the other, astonishment at an individuality which surrenders itself so unreservedly to the ideal as that of our friend, should present some impediment to the brilliancy of his success. A few places in the composition which, though good in themselves, are too much spun out may also here and there disturb one's enjoyment. Nevertheless, one may say that the concerto has had a success honourable alike to artists and public; the same in Hanover. Now let fault-finders and malicious detractors gossip as they please—I don't mind; we have done right. . . . Now do as you like in Hamburg, but if you give the concerto at the Philharmonic I will come and conduct. That has long been settled."*

Nor was this all. While staying in January with Joachim, who was anxious to hear the effect of the D major Serenade in its original scoring, Johannes had recopied the parts of one movement of the work, which was tried at Hanover on January 23, the day after the important subscription concert. The ineffectiveness of the instrumentation, and especially the want of balance between strings and wind, could not be ignored by the two friends; but Joachim formed the opinion that with certain alterations in the distribution of the passages, the work might prove satisfactory in its original form, not indeed for solo instruments, but for what may best be described as a small orchestra. Brahms' first business on his return to Hamburg was to improve the parts of the work, the dimensions of which he had enlarged in the autumn by the addition of three short movements; and, on the conclusion of the negotiations with the Philharmonic committee for the performance of the D minor Concerto, it was decided between the composer and his friends that a soirée should be arranged which should be signalised by the introduction to the music lovers of Hamburg of the D major Serenade.

The Philharmonic concert of March 24 was made a musical event of unusual importance by the engagement of Joachim and of Stockhausen—his first appearance in Hamburg—and public interest was only increased by the advertisement of a musical soirée in the joint names of Brahms, Joachim and Stockhausen, for the 28th. That Johannes had taken heart again after his disappointments, and was looking forward with pleasure to the visits of his friends, is evident from a letter written by him a few days beforehand to the lady in waiting on the Princess Friederike of Lippe-Detmold.

---

* Moser's "Life of Joachim."

"Very esteemed, gracious Fräulein,

"In the first place I beg you to express my most humble thanks to Her Serene Highness the Princess Friederike for the despatch of the new Bach work.

"How often this present will remind me in the most agreeable manner of Her Highness's kindness. You know how I love the divine master, and may imagine that his tones (so dreaded by you) are often heard here.

"I am glad that Her Serene Highness continues to work so industriously at her music, and only wish I could help her in some way.

"In the trio mentioned by you* the most simple way is that the left hand (which ceases playing) should help the poor right. For what embarrassment the mischievous arrogance of the composer is responsible!

"The day after to-morrow I play my pianoforte concerto here, and a few days later introduce other works at a concert of my own. Joachim and Stockhausen, who are coming for it, will make the days into real musical festivals.

"In spite of the great diversity of opinions expressed about my works, I have reason to be quite satisfied with my first attempts for orchestra, and I confidently hope that they will find friendly hearers in Detmold also.

"And I may venture to hope, above all, for later ripening and better swelling fruits . . . ."†

The Philharmonic committee had no reason to regret their arrangements. The attraction of the two great names filled their concert-room to suffocation. Every seat and every

---

* Brahms's Trio in B major.

† First published in Reimann's "Johannes Brahms." One of the Princess Friederike's Christmas presents to Brahms whilst he was her teacher consisted of the five volumes (1851-1855 inclusive) of the Leipzig Society's edition of Bach's works issued before he became a subscriber, and it would appear from the opening of the above-quoted letter that she made herself responsible for his subscription during the consecutive seasons of his visits to Detmold. It is interesting to read the traces of his movements furnished by the subscription list placed at the commencement of each volume. In 1856 his name appears as belonging to Düsseldorf; 1857-1864 inclusive, to Hamburg; and from 1865 onwards, to Vienna.

standing-place was occupied, and crowds were turned from the doors. Those who have witnessed similar scenes during —how many decades! can picture the excited expectancy that followed the performance of a Cherubini overture, the thunder of welcome at the first glimpse of Joachim, the never-ending applause and recalls at the conclusion of his first solo, Spohr's "Gesang-Scena," the sensation of Stockhausen's first appearance, the magnificent success of his performance of a great aria from his oratorio répertoire. Then a lull, the disappearance of Capellmeister Grund, the opening of the piano, the reappearance of Joachim, this time to take his stand at the conductor's desk, and the entrance of the slight, blonde young Hamburger, pale and nervous, but calm and self-controlled, almost happy in the support of his two friends.

On such an evening of enthusiasm, what public could have refused its tribute to the young fellow-citizen who came before them as a composer practically for the first time, with two heroes at his side to champion his cause? Johannes was really successful. "The concerto created an impression, and excited applause far beyond that of a mere *succès d'estime*," and the critic of the *Nachrichten* records the fact with the more satisfaction from its contrast with the result of the performance at the Leipzig Gewandhaus.

It would appear from the wording of the letter to Detmold quoted on a foregoing page that the concert of the 28th, advertised in the three names, was especially Brahms' undertaking. Ten years had elapsed since his performance of the Variations on a favourite waltz had passed unrecorded save in Marxsen's paper. Since that time he had given no concert in Hamburg, and the change in his prospects is well measured by the different circumstances of the occasions of 1849 and 1859. True that at the age of twenty-six he had achieved no popular success, that his concerto had effectually alienated from him the sympathies of the Leipzigers, and that the Weimarites, whilst encouraging his efforts, partially misunderstood his aims. Thorough-going belief in his art and its promise was more firmly established than ever as a leading principle of the inner Schumann circle, and this was itself gradually spreading. We give the full programme of March 28, as advertised in the *Hamburger Nachrichten*, which is interesting for many reasons:

1. Bach: Sonata for Clavier and Violin.
2. Handel: Aria from "The Messiah."
3. Tartini: "Trillo del Diavolo."
4. Schubert: Song, "Der Erlkönig."
5. Brahms: Serenade for String and Wind Instruments.
6. Boieldieu: Cavatina, "Fête du Village Voisin."
7. Schubert: Rondeau Brilliant for Pianoforte and Violin.
8. Schubert, Schumann, etc.: Songs (including "Der Nussbaum," "Mondnacht," "Widmung").

There was good reason to be delighted with the material result of the undertaking. The large Wörmer hall was thronged. Brahms' artistic success was also assured in regard to his playing of the duet sonata and rondo with Joachim, and many of the musicians present appreciated his wonderful accompaniment of Stockhausen's songs. He was himself, moreover, satisfied with the reception of the Serenade that was conducted by Joachim.

"It really seemed to reach the audience yesterday. The applause continued until I showed myself on the platform. You would scarcely have known the Hamburgers,"

he wrote to Frau Schumann, whose engagements prevented her from going to Hamburg for the eventful week. Nevertheless, the press notices did not adventure beyond the safe limits of patronising encouragement, and the *Nachrichten* expressed the general professional sentiment of the time in the concluding sentence of its review:

"If Brahms will learn to say what is in his heart plainly and straightforwardly, and not go out of his way to cut strange capers, the public will endorse Schumann's hopes, and the laity be able to understand what it is that professional musicians prize so highly in his works."

Such contemporary criticism might well pass unnoticed if it were not that, in spite of the wealth of beautiful material and the fine workmanship contained in the serenade, only one or two of its movements are occasionally heard in the concert-rooms of the present day, whilst the composer's later and more difficult orchestral works grow every year in the favour of the public. The circumstance is to be chiefly explained by considerations similar to those we have already applied to the first concerto. When Brahms wrote the work he had not quite passed from his apprenticeship. Though within sight of mastery, he had not achieved it. The Serenade in D is a serenade in the character of its ideas, but not entirely so in the structure of its movements. The instrumental "serenata" (fair weather), a form which flourished vigorously during the latter half of the eighteenth century, and was exhibited in its greatest perfection by Mozart, was especially cultivated in an age when music was dependent on the patron—the prince or nobleman who kept his private band, and who delighted himself and his friends by open-air performances in his park on fine summer nights. It consisted of a longer or shorter series of movements—a march, an allegro, rondo, one or two andantes, a couple of minuets, none of them developed to any great length, and was composed for more or fewer solo instruments according to circumstances. Brahms, fascinated by the performances of the Detmold wind players, probably began his work with the intention of composing a serenade *pur et simple*; but his interest in the art of thematic development outran his discretion, and, by over-elaborating one of its movements, he injured the balance of his composition and introduced into it a character of complexity foreign to the nature of its form. The Serenade in D consists of an allegro molto, scherzo, adagio non troppo, minuets 1 and 2, scherzo, rondo. Some of the six movements, irresistible from their grace, daintiness, or romance, delight the public when performed as separate numbers, but the length of the opening movement and the somewhat mechanical development of its middle section may perhaps prove in the future, as they have done in the past, obstacles to the frequent performance of the entire work. Traces of the young musician's studies are to be found in the well-known reminiscences of Beethoven and Haydn in the second scherzo.

The few years immediately succeeding Brahms' second return from Detmold must be regarded as forming another turning-point in his career. They witnessed the close of his *Sturm und Drang* period and his complete transformation into a master. They are remarkable not only on account of the appearance of a number of short choral works which, perfect in themselves, lead directly to the splendid achievements of later years in the same domain, to the German Requiem, the Schicksalslied, the Triumphlied, but they form a period of actual magnificent fruition. To them is to be referred the inauguration of those chamber-music works of Brahms which stand in the forefront of the finest compositions of their kind, and the appearance of a classic for pianoforte unsurpassed by any other of its form, the Variations and Fugue on a theme by Handel. This portion of our composer's life belongs especially to his native city, though it is certain that the difficult conditions of his home life supplied some counterweight to the influences of patriotic sentiment and family affection which made him desire to settle in Hamburg permanently. That he was not at once accepted as a great composer by his fellow-citizens should not be a matter of surprise. It has too often been forgotten by Brahms' partisans that his development as a creator was not precocious. The list of Mendelssohn's compositions when he was a boy of sixteen is bewildering in its length and variety; at the same age the most important of Johannes' achievements was presumably the set of Variations on a favourite waltz. Schubert's career was cut short in his thirty-second year; Mozart died at thirty-five. Brahms at the age of twenty-six had not completed any large work which can be regarded as entirely representative of his mature powers, and had introduced but few compositions either to the public or his friends. There were, however, those among the musicians of Hamburg who, belonging to the increasing circle of his personal acquaintances, believed in his creative genius with the enthusiasm of absolute conviction, and as a pianist, though not regarded as a phenomenal performer, he was generally accepted as an artist of first rank.

Brahms' regard for his pupil, Fräulein Friedchen Wagner, had led to his becoming intimate at her father's house, and here he frequently had opportunity of hearing some of the compositions and arrangements for voices which engaged much of his attention. Fräulein Friedchen, her sister Thusnelda, and the charming Fräulein Bertha Porubszky, from Vienna, who arrived in Hamburg to stay for a year with her aunt, Frau Auguste Brandt, were delighted to practise short works in two and three parts under his direction. Probably he hoped gradually to obtain a larger number of recruits for his purpose. Before long, however, accident led to his becoming the conductor of a quite considerable ladies' choir.

On May 19 the wedding of Pastor Sengelmann and Fräulein Jenny von Ahsen took place at St. Michael's Church. There was a large gathering of friends to witness the ceremony. Grädener, already mentioned as a friend of Brahms, who was an accomplished composer and the director of a singing school, conducted his pupils in the performance of a motet for female voices which he had written for the occasion, and Johannes, a very old acquaintance of the bride, accompanied on the organ. Pleased with the effect of Grädener's composition, Brahms expressed a wish to hear his own "Ave Maria" for female voices with accompaniment for organ, composed during his second visit to Detmold, under similar conditions of performance, and with the assistance of Fräulein Friedchen, who exerted herself to procure the requisite number of voices, a rehearsal was arranged. On Monday, June 6, twenty-eight ladies assembled at the Wagners' house, and tried, not only the "Ave Maria," afterwards published as Op. 12, but the "O bone Jesu" and "Adoramus," now known as Op. 37, Nos. 1 and 2. Brahms was seized with a fit of nervousness whilst conducting, and Grädener, who was present amongst a few listeners, stepped forward to the rescue; but a second rehearsal on the following day went well, and the third trial in church with organ accompaniment was in every respect highly successful. The practices had been so enjoyable that, with the concurrence of Grädener, it was arranged that the ladies, most of whom were pupils of the singing school, should assemble every Monday morning to practise with Brahms; and the society thus founded, which soon increased to forty members, became a source of delight to all who were associated with it. The meetings were held during the first season at the Wagners' house in the Pastorenstrasse; later on they took place at several members' houses in turn. Each young lady used to sing from a small oblong manuscript book, into which she copied her parts, and several of these volumes are still in existence. After the business of the morning was over, the conductor usually played to his young disciples and admirers, who soon learned to look upon his performances as not the least memorable part of the weekly programme. Writing in the course of the summer to Fräulein von Meysenbug, Brahms says:

" . . . I am here, and shall probably remain until I go to Detmold. Some very pleasant pupils detain me, and, strangely enough, a ladies' society that sings under my direction; till now only what I compose for it. The clear silver tones please me exceedingly, and in the church with the organ the ladies' voices sound quite charming."[*]

The season closed on September 19 with a performance at St. Peter's Church before an invited audience. Some of the "Marienlieder" (afterwards Op. 22) and the 13th Psalm (Op. 27) were included in the programme. The mem-

---

[*] "Aus Johannes Brahms' Jugendtagen," by Hermann Freiherr von Meysenbug (*Neues Wiener Tagblatt*, May, 1901).

bers of the choir appeared attired in black to denote their grief at the approaching departure of their conductor, and sent him, afterwards, a silver inkstand buried beneath flowers as a mark of their appreciation of his labours. This Brahms acknowledged from Detmold in the following official letter to Fräulein Friedchen, his energetic helper in the founding of the choir:

"Detmold, *end of Sept.*, 1859.

"Esteemed Fräulein,

"Nothing more agreeable than to be so pleasantly obliged to write a letter as I am now.

"I think constantly of the glad surprise with which I perceived the inkstand, the remembrance from the ladies' choir, under its charming covering of flowers.

"I have done so little to deserve it that I should be ashamed were it not that I hope to write much more for you; and I shall certainly hear finer tones sounding around me as I look at the valued and beautiful present on my writing-table. Pray express to all whom you can reach my hearty greeting and thanks.

"I have seldom had a more agreeable pleasure, and our meetings will remain one of my most welcome and favourite recollections.

"But not, I hope, till later years!

"With best greetings to you and yours,
"Your
"heartily sincere
Johs. Brahms."*

That the composer did not forget his maidens during his season at Detmold appears from another letter to Fräulein Wagner written a couple of months later:

"*Dec.*, 1859.

"Esteemed Fräulein,

"Here are some new songs for your little singing republic. I hope they may assist in keeping it together. If I can help towards this end pray command me.

"Kindest greetings to you and yours.

"Most sincerely,
"Johs. Brahms."*

---

* First published, with an account of the Ladies' Choir, in Hübbe's "Brahms in Hamburg."

Acquaintance with the charming circumstances which stimulated Brahms to the writing of most of his published choruses for women's voices gives an additional interest to the study of these beautiful compositions, which undoubtedly take their place amongst the most fascinating works of their class. Those with sacred texts, all evident fruits of the composer's studies in the strict style of part-writing, show, nevertheless, considerable variety of character. The "Ave Maria," with accompaniment for orchestra or organ, Op. 12, first sung by, though not composed for, the ladies' choir, is animated by a gentle, child-like, devotional spirit appropriate to a prayer addressed by a group of tender girls to the Virgin Mother of Christ. The 13th Psalm, with accompaniment for organ or pianoforte, Op. 27, composed expressly for the choir and tried for the first time on August 29, 1859, strikes at once a more solemn note, with its three opening cries to the Lord; and the mourning plaint of the writer is reproduced in tones whose fervent pleading is not impaired by the clear simplicity of style in which the music is conceived. The Three Sacred Choruses, without accompaniment, Op. 37, are alike beautiful, whilst varying in character. The "Adoramus" and "Regina Cœli" (Nos. 2 and 3), written throughout in canon, are fine examples of learned facility; and the last-named, the bright "Regina Cœli," for soprano and alto soli and four-part women's chorus, is an entirely captivating composition.

The secular pieces—the Songs with accompaniment for horns and harp, Op. 17, and the Songs and Romances to be sung *a capella*, Op. 44—most of them composed at Hamburg in the summer of 1859, though fairly well known, should be heard oftener than they are. The dainty charm of such little works as the "Minnelied" and the "Barcarole," to name only two of the most effective from Op. 44, gives welcome refreshment in a miscellaneous choral concert, and never fails to captivate an audience.

In our rapid survey of some of the works which are to be

associated with Brahms' Ladies' Choir, we have only taken account of those that were actually published in the form required by the nature of the society. Many settings and arrangements are to be found, in the little oblong manuscript books, of songs which have become known to the world amongst the composer's settings for a single voice or for mixed choir. The canons Nos. 1, 2, 8, 10, 11, 12, of Op. 113 were sung at the society's meetings. The "Regina Cœli," on the other hand, was not included in the ladies' répertoire.*

---

* Hübbe.

CHAPTER X.

1859-1861.

Third season at Detmold—"Ave Maria" and "Begräbnissgesang" performed in Hamburg and Göttingen—Second Serenade, first performed in Hamburg—Lower Rhine Festival—Summer at Bonn—Music at Herr Kyllmann's—Variations on an original theme first performed in Leipzig by Frau Schumann—"Marienlieder"—First public performance of Sextet in B flat in Hanover.

BRAHMS found himself more than ever in request amongst the general circle of Detmold society during the autumn of 1859. He had become the fashion. It was the thing to have lessons from him, and his presence gave distinction to a gathering. The very circumstance of his popularity, however, caused some friction between himself and his acquaintances. He disliked to waste his time, as he considered it, in mere society, and, when occasionally induced to attend a party against his will, gave his hosts cause to regret their pertinacity. If not silent the whole evening, he would amuse himself by exercising his talent for caustic speech. Carl von Meysenbug, when at home, jealous for his friend's credit, often called Johannes privately to account for his perversity, but was always silenced by the unanswerable reply, "Bah! that is all humbug!" (Pimpkram).

The young musician's relations with the princely family remained undisturbed, and his musical gifts were, on the whole, fairly appreciated by the entire court circle, though he was not regarded personally with unanimous favour by those who did not know him well. Carl's mother, the Frau Hofmarschall, took a few lessons from him to please her friends at the castle, and once accepted his offer to play duets with her; but no subsequent invitation could induce her to repeat this performance. "The good fellow should not have behaved as he did that once; I cannot put up with it," she wrote to Carl. Something in Brahms' manner—independence, artistic self-consciousness, or whatever else it may be called—repelled her; and, in view of the fact that she was not the first person whom he had offended in a similar way, since the time when he had visited as a youth at the Japhas' house in Hamburg, it may fairly be assumed that Her Excellency had justifiable grounds for the reserved attitude she maintained towards him.

It is, indeed, certain that Brahms, during his third season at Detmold, began to grow impatient of his position there. His lessons to the Princess, who was really musical and made rapid progress, continued to give him genuine pleasure, but he chafed at the constant demands on his time arising from his fixed duties, and the rigid etiquette observed at the Court of a very small capital gave him a distaste for his work as conductor of the choral society. The circle of Serene Highnesses, Excellencies, and their friends, did not furnish sufficient voices for the adequate rendering of two or three oratorios and cantatas by Handel and Bach which he selected for practice during his second and third seasons; and, with Prince Leopold's permission, he supplemented them by persuading some of the townspeople to become members. His sense of the ridiculous was strongly excited by the rules of conduct prescribed for these not very willing assistants, who were not even permitted to make an obeisance to the Serenities, and scarcely ventured to lift their eyes from the music whilst in their august presence. There were some good performances of great works, however, and Bach's cantata "Ich hatte viel Bekümmerniss" was given four times; but the difficulty of procuring tenors continued serious, and the entire circumstances of the meetings made Brahms feel increasing desire to be relieved from the necessity of attending them.

Of his own choral compositions, besides the "Ave Maria," the "Begräbnissgesang," for mixed chorus and wind, published later on as Op. 13, was practised during the season. It is strange that this fine work, composed at Detmold during the autumn of 1858 to a sixteenth century text by Michael Weisse, the editor of the first German church hymn book, is not better known. Intended as a song for the graveside, it would be out of place in an ordinary miscellaneous programme, but is well adapted for performance at a Good Friday concert, or as a church anthem in Passion Week. Like all Brahms' sacred compositions of the time it gives evidence of the strong impression he had derived from his exhaustive study of the mediæval church composers; and the music, austere in its simplicity, is characterised by uncompromising fidelity to the almost grimly severe spirit of the words. It was heard, together with the "Ave Maria," for the first time in public, at Grädener's Academy concert of December 2, and Brahms, who obtained leave to go to Hamburg for the occasion, appeared the same evening with Schumann's pianoforte concerto. A day's visit to Hanover on his way back brought about the renewal of his relations with Grimm whom Joachim had invited to meet him, and Grimm soon afterwards obtained the manuscripts of the two choral works for practice by his society, of which Carl von Meysenbug was an enthusiastic member.

"As Grimm was distributing the parts of the 'Ave Maria' and the 'Begräbnissgesang' at one of the practices," says the Freiherr von Meysenbug, "my neighbour, a glib University student with the experience of several terms behind him, said to me in a surprised tone: 'Brahms! who is that?' 'Oh, some old ecclesiastic of Palestrina's time,' I replied—a piece of information which he accepted and passed on."

The compositions were given under Grimm's direction at the society's concert of January 19, 1860. There is little doubt that Philipp Spitta, author of the exhaustive biography of Sebastian Bach, whose essay "Zur Musik" should be read by all earnest students of Brahms' music, took part in the performance of the "Begräbnissgesang." His friendship with the composer dates from this period when he was a student of the Göttingen University and one of the intimates of Grimm's circle.

The Serenade in D major was heard for the second and last time as set for "strings and wind" at one of the Detmold court concerts of the season 1859. The composer soon afterwards rejected this form as a mere "Zwittergestalt." Adopting Frau Schumann's original suggestion, he re-arranged the work for large orchestra and was rewarded for his effort by Joachim's very warm congratulations on the success of his instrumentation.

The tradition once current that an early version of the Pianoforte Quartet in G minor was tried in Detmold has been practically destroyed by the publication of the several volumes of Brahms' correspondence.*

It will be convenient to add here that the invitation to revisit Detmold on the same terms as before was finally refused by Brahms in a letter to the Hofmarschall dated from Hamburg, August, 1860:

---

* The evidence of Litzmann's "Clara Schumann," Vol. VIII, and of the Brahms "Briefwechsel," IV and V (Grimm and Joachim) shows that Brahms, during many years of his career, invariably submitted a new movement, or series of movements, on completion, first for the opinion of Frau Schumann or Grimm, and then for that of Joachim. It has already been explained (p. 203) that the quartet composed in 1856 is identified by one of Joachim's letters as an early version of the work in C minor published twenty years later. No published letter, however, suggests the existence of a second quartet, or part of one, until in July and September, 1861, respectively, Frau Schumann and Joachim write about movements, evidently new to them, with which we are familiar as belonging to the Quartets, Opp. 25 and 26. The inference is that though one or more movements of these works may have been sketched at the time of Brahms's connection with Detmold, no portion of either had advanced sufficiently to be shown, much less rehearsed, during that period. In the author's opinion the whole internal evidence of the two works is indicative of the place which they actually occupy in the catalogue of Brahms' compositions of chamber music.

"After renewed consideration, I must beg to express to His Serene Highness the Prince my regret that I shall not be able to visit Detmold in the winter. I have to add to the causes of this decision which I have already had the honour to communicate, that I shall be much occupied this autumn with the publication of my works, with revising the proofs of some, and preparing others for the engraver. On this account alone, therefore, I must decide to stay here during the winter. I particularly desire to express my regret to the Princess Friederike that I shall be unable to enjoy her progress in playing and her great sympathy for music. . . ."*

The post of conductor to the court orchestra, which became vacant on Kiel's retirement with a pension in 1864, and which might probably under other circumstances have been offered for the acceptance or refusal of Brahms, passed to Bargheer, who retained it until 1876, when Prince Leopold's death put an end to the musical activity of Detmold.

Brahms was able to give his friends a good account of himself at the end of the year. Before leaving Detmold he sent Joachim the completed second Serenade in A major, the first movement of which had aroused Grimm's enthusiasm in the autumn of 1858, scored for small orchestra (wind, violas, 'celli and basses); and despatched part of a sextet for strings in B flat to Göttingen. Grimm again failed signally in the task of fault finding so frequently urged upon him by Johannes, and could only write of the two new movements in terms of wonder and delight. The serenade was tried privately in Hanover.

"I have tried my second serenade in Hanover," wrote Johannes on January 17, 1860, to Frau Schumann, "Joachim thought it was satisfactory and sounded well. What have I not in him?"

The work was performed for the first time in public under the composer's direction at the Hamburg Philharmonic concert of February 10. On the same occasion Joachim transported the audience by his performances of Beethoven's

---

* "Aus Brahms' Jugendtagen." See footnote on p. 216.

Concerto and Tartini's "Trillo del Diavolo," and Johannes had a great success as pianist with Schumann's Concerto.

The second serenade was considered easier to understand than its elder sister, and was received with comparative favour, though not with enthusiasm. To the ears of the present generation the work appears limpidly clear, and it is difficult to realise that it was ever accounted otherwise. In it was have a *chef-d'œuvre* which displays our musician passed finally from his transition stage and standing out clearly as a master in definite possession both of aim and method. Unmistakably he has taken his footing on the basis of tradition, and creates with the freedom of self-control within the forms consecrated by the works of Haydn, Mozart, and Beethoven, no longer betrayed by immaturity into anything that could be misconstrued as the intentional discursiveness of rhapsody. The work is impregnated with a breath as fragrant as the spirit of Schubert's muse, and, though perhaps not fully representative of the very powerful individuality now associated with the name of Brahms, bears the distinct impress of his mind, and could have been written by no other composer. Each of the five movements is a gem of the first water. Each has a character of its own, which yet combines with every other to make the serenade a perfect example of a developed form of garden music, night music. Graceful romance, tender playfulness, lively frolic, just the stirring of the deeper emotions, all the gentler phases of poetic sentiment, are suggested in turn by its lovely melodies.

Why is this masterpiece so seldom heard?

Appropriately called a serenade from the character of its

ideas, and even from the structure of its movements, which, whilst fully developed, are all quite clear, balanced and symmetrical each in itself and as part of a whole, and indicate the composer's perfect fulfilment of his intention, the length of the work again approaches that of a symphony. It must be borne in mind that to a general audience the name "serenade" as applied to instrumental music does not now suggest any particular class of composition, the times and customs which produced this form having long since passed away; whilst it is customary to associate with the word "symphony" a suggestion of the more strenuous emotions of human existence. Thus, the ordinary concert-goer who listens to Brahms' work is puzzled as to what he ought to expect, and his uncertainty interferes with his enjoyment.

Another drawback, under modern concert conditions, to the general appreciation of the beautiful Serenade in A major is the absence of violins from the score. It hardly needs pointing out that the, so to say, muted tone of the combination of instruments employed by the composer would be ideal in the surroundings proper to the performance of the "serenade" as originally so called—palpitating summer heat, deep-blue, starlit sky, flitting to and fro of gallant and graceful forms—but in the prosaic atmosphere of a modern concert-room the bright tone of the violins cannot, perhaps, be safely dispensed with throughout the length of so long a work. It consists of an allegro moderato, scherzo, quasi minuetto with trio, rondo. It may still be hoped, however, that the serenade may be revived, and take its place in the répertoire of our concert societies.

We have lingered so long over the two serenades that a bare mention must suffice of the performance of the first in D major—the first performance in the second and final re-arrangement of the score—by command of King George at the Hanover subscription concert of March 3 under Joachim's direction, nor need we dwell upon the fact that it was received with indifference by audience and critics. It is time to glance again at the party conflicts of the day, and especially to note the activity of the disciples of Weimar, whose partisanship, as the reader may remember, had been stimulated to violence by the candid admissions of Joachim's letter to Liszt quoted on p. 223.

"The Weimarites continue their uproar," reported Johannes in the summer of 1859 to Joachim in England, "my fingers often itch to do battle, to begin to write anti-Liszt. But I! . . . It would be glorious, however, if you were to remain in Germany in the summer, to compose wonderfully and to strike these people dead with a few flying shots, whilst I sat near you and helped write music . . ."*

To put the matter, so far as our narrative is concerned with it, as shortly as possible, Brahms, who had been longing to enter the fray as an active combatant, now induced Joachim to join him in drawing up a manifesto for signature by musicians of their way of thinking, and subsequent publication. An obstacle to the fulfilment of the plan presented itself in the impossibility of obtaining unanimity of opinion as to the suitable wording of the document, and part of the difficulty seems to have arisen from Brahms' desire to differentiate between the works of Berlioz and Wagner on the one hand, and Liszt's "productions" on the other. Before these preliminaries had been satisfactorily arranged, however, accident settled the matter. By a mischance that has never been explained, a version of the manifesto which was presumably going round for signature, found its way, with only four names attached, into the *Echo*, a journal of Berlin. It ran as follows:

"The undersigned have long followed with regret the proceedings of a certain party whose organ is Brendel's *Zeitschrift für Musik*. The said *Zeitschrift* unceasingly promulgates the theory that the most prominent striving musicians are in accord with the aims represented in its

---

* Brahms-Joachim, No. 178.

pages, that they recognise in the compositions of the leaders of the new school works of artistic value, and that the contention for and against the so-called Music of the Future has been finally fought out, especially in North Germany, and decided in its favour. The undersigned regard it as their duty to protest against such a distortion of fact, and declare, at least for their own part, that they do not acknowledge the principles avowed by the *Zeitschrift*, and that they can only lament and condemn the productions of the leaders and pupils of the so-called New-German school, which on the one hand apply those principles practically, and on the other necessitate the constant setting up of new and unheard-of theories which are contrary to the very nature of music.

"JOHANNES BRAHMS.
"JULIUS OTTO GRIMM.
"JOSEPH JOACHIM.
"BERNARD SCHOLZ."

A few days later the answer appeared in the *Zeitschrift* of May 4, in the shape of a parody written, not in a very formidable style of wit, by C. F. Weitzmann:

"DREAD MR. EDITOR,

"All is *out!* — — I learn that a political coup has been carried *out*, the entire new world rooted *out* stump and branch, and Weimar and Leipzig, especially, struck *out* of the musical map of the world. To compass this end, a widely *out*reaching letter was thought *out* and sent *out* to the chosen-*out* faithful of all lands, in which strongly *out*spoken protest was made against the increasing epidemic of the Music of the Future. Amongst the select of the *out*worthies [paragons] are to be reckoned several *out*siders, whose names, however, the modern historian of art has not been able to find *out*. Nevertheless, should the avalanche of signatures widen *out* sufficiently, the storm will break *out* suddenly. Although the strictest secrecy has been enjoined upon the chosen-*out* by the hatchers-*out* of this musico-tragic *out*-and-*out*er, I have succeeded in obtaining sight of the original, and I am glad, dread Mr. Editor, to be able to communicate to you, in what follows, the contents of this aptly conceived state paper—I remain, yours most truly,

"CROSSING-SWEEPER."

"PUBLIC PROTEST.

"The undersigned desire to play first fiddle for once, and therefore protest against everything which stands in the way of their coming aloft, including, especially, the increasing influence of the musical tendency described by Dr. Brendel as the New-German school, and in short against the whole spirit of the new music. After the annihilation of these, to them very unpleasant things, they offer to all who are of their own mind the immediate prospect of a brotherly association for the advancement of monotonous and tiresome music.

"(Signed) J. FIDDLER. HANS NEWPATH. SLIPPERMAN.
"PACKE. DICK TOM AND HARRY.

"Office of the Music of the Future."

Bülow, writing from Berlin to Louis Köhler, says:

"The manifesto of the Hanoverians has not made the least sensation here. They have not even sufficient wit mixed with their malice to have done the thing in good style, and to have launched it at a well-chosen time, such as the beginning or end of the season."

It must be said here that Brendel was sincere in his views, whether or not they commend themselves to us, and that he had an exceptional power of appreciating the ideas put forth by the leaders of the new school. Equally certain is it that the antipathy felt by Joachim and Brahms for Liszt's compositions proceeded from no feeling of malice or personal animosity, but from the most sincere conviction. Joachim's confession to Liszt had been wrung from him by the necessity of escape from a false position. The extraordinary importance attached by the musical parties of the day to his alliance is well illustrated by Wagner's bitter words:

"With the defection of a hitherto warm friend, a great violinist, the violent agitation broke out against the generous Franz Liszt that prepared for him, at length, the disappointment and embitterment which caused him to abandon his endeavours to establish Weimar as a town devoted to the furtherance of music."*

---

* Reprint of Wagner's pamphlet, "Das Judenthum in der Musik."

The baselessness, and even folly, of such a statement is self-evident.

With regard to Brahms particularly, though such works as Liszt's Symphonic Poems and Dante Symphony were abominations to him, he always cherished a profound respect for the powers of Wagner though the artistic principles by which they were guided were not those of his own musical faith. His allegiance, like that of Joachim, was wholly given to the masters of classical art, to whom he had paid homage from childhood, and it was one of the ironies of fate that he should have been widely supposed, during many years, to belong to the New-German party, and that he was handled more tenderly by the *Zeitschrift* than the *Signale*. By Brendel himself, indeed, who from the year 1859 onwards worked earnestly to effect a reconciliation between the contending musical parties, Schumann's young hero was treated fairly, and even generously, and a steady Brahms propaganda was practised in years to come by the fraternity of the Allgemeiner Deutscher Musikverein, a society founded by Brendel in 1861 for the furtherance of his pacific aim.

Our composer, who had been betrayed into polemic partly by loyalty to his convictions and partly by his exuberant vitality, was not by temperament a party man any more than his friend, and was to be removed before very long from the immediate scene of party strife. For the future he took the wiser course of holding himself aloof from the contentions of the day, issuing no other manifestoes than such as were constituted by his works, and never allowing himself to be tempted into answering the many printed attacks that were levelled at him. Henceforth he lived his life, and wrote his works, and followed his faith, leaving the question of the false or the true to the decision of time. Who shall yet say what will be the final judgment of this supreme arbiter of all such matters?

Johannes was again settled in his parents' home during the spring of 1860, but his thoughts were busy with many plans for the future. He longed to extend his travels, and the desire to see Vienna was stirring forcibly within him. He played his Concerto and some numbers of Schumann's Kreisleriana at Otten's concert of April 20; but the concerto was very badly accompanied, and once more proved a complete failure. The critic of the *Nachrichten* confesses his inability to understand the work, "which is recognised so warmly by the musicians of the newest tendency," and elects to say nothing about it.

The young musician's greatest pleasure was derived from his singing society of girls, who resumed with ardour their practices under his direction. He placed it this season on a more formal footing by drawing up a set of rules, signature to which was made a condition of membership. The document, headed "Avertimento," is playfully worded in a bygone style of formality, and after a short prelude, in which is set forth, amongst other things, that the practices are to be held only during spring and summer, five laws are laid down, the first two of which enjoin punctual attendance.

"Pro primo, it is to be remarked that the members of the Ladies' Choir must be *there*.

"By which is to be understood that they must oblige themselves to be *there*.

"Pro secundo, it is to be observed that the members of the Ladies' Choir must be there.

"By which is meant, they must be there precisely at the appointed time. . . ."

Absentees and late-comers were to be fined in various amounts, according to various degrees of delinquency, and the money collected given to "begging people," "and it is to be desired that it may surfeit no one."

The fourth rule relates to the careful preservation of the music entrusted to the care of the "virtuous and honourable ladies," which was not to be used outside the society, and the fifth, to the admission of listeners under conditions. The whole concludes :

"I remain in deepest devotion and veneration of the Ladies' Choir their most assiduous ready-writer and steady time-beater

"JOHANNES KREISLER JUN.
(*alias* BRAHMS).

"Given on Monday,
"The 30th of the month of April,
A.D. 1860."

Amongst the signatures is that of Frau Schumann who, with her eldest daughter Marie, passed a few weeks of the spring in Hamburg and regularly attended the Monday choir practices during her stay. We shall have occasion to mention the name of the great artist more than once again in interesting connection with the sisterhood of singers, who were not a little proud of the right given them, by her signature, to claim her as an honorary colleague.*

Notwithstanding the stringent rules as to punctuality of attendance inserted in this formal document, the meetings were seriously interrupted during the season, and by the absence of no less a person than the director himself. Johannes could in no case, especially in his present restless mood, have remained away from the Rhine Festival of the year (Düsseldorf, May 27-29). Schumann's B flat Symphony was to be performed, Hiller to conduct, Joachim to play the Hungarian Concerto and a Beethoven Romance, and Stockhausen to sing selections by Boieldieu, Schubert, Schumann, and Hiller. Frau Schumann was to attend the concerts, and expected to meet many intimate friends at Düsseldorf, amongst them being Dietrich and his bride, a lady long known to the circle as Clara Sohn, daughter of the painter and professor at the Art Academy. Brahms

---

* The rules, first published by Professor Walter Hübbe in his "Brahms in Hamburg," are given entire in Appendix No. II.

therefore accompanied Frau Schumann and her daughter when they left Hamburg for Düsseldorf on May 24, and the occasion of the festival proved no less enjoyable than those similar ones which have been referred to in our pages. A new feature at one or more of the private reunions that took place in the intervals of the concerts was the singing of quartets, under Brahms' direction, by four members of the Ladies' Choir who had come to the Festival: the sisters Fräulein Betty and Fräulein Marie Völckers, Fräulein Laura Garbe, and—Frau Schumann herself. She, indeed, it was who proposed to her hostess, Fräulein Leser, that the Dietrichs, Joachim, Stockhausen, and a few others, should be invited to listen to what proved a delightful performance.

Under the circumstances, it cannot be regarded as surprising that Brahms did not immediately return to Hamburg after the festival, but made one of a party that proceeded to Bonn, where he remained with his companions till towards the middle of August.

"The spring had set in gloriously," says Dietrich, who, as the reader will remember, had been settled for some years in the city. "There is something enchanting in such a spring on the Rhine. The pink blossoming woods of fruit-trees, the numerous whitethorn hedges on the banks of the river, the voices of nightingales in the light, warm nights, the fine outlines of the Siebengebirge in the distance; what excursions we were induced to make! It was a happy, sunny time rich also in artistic enjoyment.

"For Brahms, after six years' long silence, had brought with him a number of splendid compositions. There were the two serenades, the Ave Maria, the Begräbnissgesang, Songs and Romances, and the Concerto in D minor.

"He had employed his retirement in the most earnest studies; he had composed, amongst other things, a Mass in canon form, which, however, has not been printed.

"We met frequently at the Kyllmanns' hospitable and artistic house for performances of chamber music and the enjoyment of Stockhausen's splendid singing.

"The artists came also often and gladly to our young home, and before we parted they were present with us at the baptism of our first child. Brahms, Joachim, and Heinrich von Sahr were the sponsors."*

Herr Kyllmann's house in Coblenzstrasse, with its beautiful garden situated on the Rhine bank and commanding a view of the Siebengebirge, was the scene of many noteworthy reunions that gave equal pleasure to the famous guests and the art-loving, art-appreciating family, who were proud to entertain them. One party which took place early in June, during the week that Frau Schumann was able to remain amongst her friends, must be recorded in detail, for the musical performances included a string quartet played by Joachim, David, Otto von Königslow (for many years concertmeister of the Gürzenich subscription concerts, Cologne), and the excellent 'cellist Christian Reimers; Schumann's Quintet, by the same artists, with Frau Schumann as pianist; and songs sung by Stockhausen to Frau Schumann's accompaniment—amongst them Schumann's "Mondnacht" and "Frühlingsnacht." Otto Jahn, who was present to enjoy the music, brought with him his friend Dr. Becker, just arrived from England on his resignation of his post of private secretary to the Prince Consort, and Brahms must be counted with them amongst the listeners. He retired to the sofa of an inner drawing-room, and was not to be induced to perform, though Frau Schumann herself came to request him to do so, and Joachim followed with his persuasive "Oh, Johannes, do play!" Johannes, as is abundantly evident, was no diplomatist. He often felt it easier to know himself misunderstood than to overcome his nervous shrinking from the ordeal of sitting down to play before a mixed party of listeners.

The nearly two months passed at Bonn, during which

---

* This pleasant description is given entire, as containing a substantially accurate account of Brahms' artistic progress, though Dietrich, writing after the lapse of many years, has overlooked the fact that the works referred to had already been performed in public from the manuscripts.

Johannes and Joachim lodged respectively at 29 and 27, Meckenheimerstrasse, proved of importance in Brahms' career. It was at this time that he made the acquaintance of Herr Fritz Simrock, a young man about his own age, junior partner in the well-known publishing house of N. Simrock at Bonn, and destined, as the later head of the firm after the removal to Berlin, to usher into the world the great majority of the composer's works. Between Fritz Simrock and Brahms a cordial understanding gradually established itself; the publisher's dealings with the musician were from the first considerate and generous, and when Brahms' fortunes became flourishing, it was Simrock who was his confidant and adviser in business matters. As an earnest of the future, the Serenade in A, Op. 16, was published by the firm before the close of the year, the Serenade in D, Op. 11, being issued in the autumn by Breitkopf and Härtel. The Pianoforte Concerto, refused by this firm, was accepted by Rieter-Biedermann, together with the "Ave Maria," Begräbnissgesang, and the Lieder und Romanzen (Op. 14), all of which were published the following year.*

"I am very glad to see Johannes' things for orchestra in print before me at last," wrote Joachim to Avé Lallement. "Now the *Signale* and other superficial papers may abuse them as they please. We have done right. They will continue to smile on with their beautiful motifs long after the clumsy fault-finders have been silenced."

The meetings of the ladies' choral society were recommenced on Brahms' return to Hamburg in July. Fräulein Porubszky, with whom he had been on terms of lively friendship during her year of membership, which had seen him a frequent visitor at her aunt's house in the Bockmannstrasse, had now returned to Vienna, where the reader will presently renew her acquaintance as Frau Faber. The

---

* A revised edition of the second serenade was published by Simrock in 1875.

members of the choir were, however, one and all thorough-going admirers of their conductor, and amongst the houses open for the holding of the practices, two at which he became intimate, must be particularly mentioned—those of Herr Völckers and his two daughters at Hamm, and of the Hallier family at Eppendorf, both at that time country suburbs of Hamburg.

The large Eppendorf garden was the scene of many a pleasant gathering of the singers; now and again they performed there before an invited audience of friends. Hübbe tells of an open-air evening party, with an illumination, vocal contributions by the choir, which were conducted by the director from the branch of a tree, and fireworks in the intervals. The Halliers lived in town during the winter, and Brahms often dropped in to their informal Wednesday evenings, which were attended by the artists and art-lovers of Hamburg. He was good-natured about playing in this familiar, sociable circle, and would perform one thing after another, unless particularly interested in conversation, when no entreaty could get him to the piano. As his Detmold friends had found out, he formed definite opinions on most current topics of interest, and did not hesitate to avow them, or to confess the unorthodoxy of his religious views. He went constantly also to Avé Lallement's house, where a few men used to meet regularly to read Shakespeare and other authors, and found time to attend lectures on art history and to study Latin under Dr. Emil Hallier, and history under Professor Ægidi of the Academic Gymnasium.

The autumn of this year was signalised by the appearance of the String Sextet in B flat, the first of Brahms' important compositions to attain general popularity. Completed in September, it was at once approved by Joachim, who introduced it to the music lovers of Hanover at his quartet concert of October 20; and it was partly owing to his enthusiastic appreciation that the composition was so quickly and widely received into public favour.

It would be beside the mark to discuss, in a narrative

which has no technical aim, the musical characteristics of a work that has become so entirely familiar as this one, which has long since taken its place among the few classics that attract an audience on their own merits, apart from the consideration of whether a public favourite is to lead their performance. It may, however, be remarked that the String Sextet in B flat is a work to which neither "if" nor "but" can be attached. Both in beauty and variety of idea and in spontaneous clearness of development, it is without flaw, and these qualities combine with the fineness of its proportions, perfectly conceived and perfectly wrought out, to place it with few rivals amongst the greatest examples of chamber music. Fresh, happy, and ingenuous, the mastery it displays over the art which conceals art may be compared with that of Mozart himself. With it opens the great series of works of its class which reveals the powerful individuality of Brahms in all its moods, and includes the first and second Pianoforte Quartets, the Pianoforte Quintet, the second String Sextet, and the Horn Trio—works which, in the author's opinion, were not surpassed even during later periods of the composer's magnificent activity in this domain.

Frau Schumann, Joachim, and Johannes met in November at Leipzig, the two last-named artists to assist actively on the 26th of the month at the annual Pension-Fund concert of the Gewandhaus, which was given under the direction of Carl Reinecke, the lately appointed successor to Julius Rietz. Both Johannes and Joachim appeared as composers —Brahms conducted the second public performance of the second serenade; Joachim played his Hungarian concerto which, completed in the autumn of 1859, had been heard for the first time at one of the Hanover subscription concerts in the spring of the year.

"The serenade is a wonderfully poetic piece," wrote Frau Clara, who heard the work for the first and second times at the rehearsal and concert. "I could have embraced Johannes for producing such a work. But how my heart bled at its cold reception . . . and Joachim's Hungarian concerto created a furore. . . . This gave me the warmest pleasure, but I suffered under the feelings of joy and regret for my two dearest friends. I was relieved to some extent on the morning of the 27th, when Johannes' sextet was very beautifully played in the conservatoire by Joachim and made a decided impression.

"In the afternoon Johannes and I played (I insisted on his doing it, under the pretext that Livia (Frege) had not heard it) the serenade to Schleinitz. I knew that it must please on the piano and this was so. Schleinitz said he had no idea there was so much warmth in the piece, the orchestra had played it so miserably.

"By Schleinitz's special desire Johannes and I played the second serenade in the conservatoire, as the pupils had only heard it once at the rehearsal. It again made the best impression on everyone. Rudorff was quite enchanted with it, which pleased me particularly as I have had such difficulty in getting him to appreciate Johannes' things."*

But scant interest was manifested by the critics of the Leipzig press in the two new works. The daily papers left the concert of the 25th unnoticed; the *Zeitschrift* dismissed it with a few dubious sentences—perhaps not ungenerous treatment under the circumstances—and the *Signale*, candid as ever, declared the serenade to be a terribly monotonous work which showed the composer's poverty of invention, together with his despairing attempts to appear learned. Joachim's concerto was pronounced decidedly richer in invention than his friend's work, but rather monotonous also, and certainly very much too long.

Frau Schumann, nothing dismayed by these discouragements, introduced at her concert of December 8, given in the small hall of the Gewandhaus, Brahms' very beautiful Variations on an original theme, which, though hardly suitable for general concert performance, should be much better known than they are. They show the composer in one of his Bach-Beethoven-Brahms moods, by which is here

---

* Litzmann III, p. 89.

meant his learned and profoundly serious vein touched with exquisite tenderness. The theme, in three-four time, has about it, nevertheless, something of the pace of a grave march, and the opening variations are tender reflections on a solemn idea. In the eighth and ninth we have the imposing tramp of pomp, whilst the eleventh and last breathes forth tones of mysterious spirituality which subdue the mind of the listener as to some passing divine influence.

These Variations composed in 1856, the earlier set on a Hungarian melody (Op. 21, Nos. 1 and 2), and the three Duets for Soprano and Contralto, Op. 20, were published by Simrock in 1861.

The fact that Brahms' sextet was placed in the programme of the Hafner-Lee concert announced for January 4 affords evidence that the composer was gradually penetrating with his works to the heart of musical life in his native city, though he may not have enjoyed the particular favour of its public. The Quartet-Entertainments of these artists were among the regularly recurring artistic events of Hamburg, and enjoyed unfailing support. Hafner, a Viennese by birth and a Schubert enthusiast, had found a second home in the northern city, and was accounted its first violinist; and in the 'cellist Lee he had a sympathetic colleague. He was not, however, destined to lead the sextet. His sudden illness caused the postponement of the concert, and his death followed. The work was played in Hamburg from the manuscript by his successor in the enterprise, John Böie, with Honroth, Breyther, Kayser, Wiemann and Lee, and with immediate success. The impression made was so great that the work was repeated three times within the following few weeks by the same concert party.

CHAPTER XI.

1861-1862.

Concert season in Hamburg—Frau Denninghoff-Giesemann—Brahms at Hamm—Herr Völckers and his daughters—Dietrich's visit to Brahms—Music at the Halliers' and Wagners'—First public performance of the G minor Quartet—Brahms at Oldenburg—Second Serenade performed in New York—The first and second Pianoforte Quartets—"Magelone Romances"—First public performances of the Handel Variations and Fugue in Hamburg and Leipzig by Frau Schumann—Brahms' departure for Vienna.

FRAU SCHUMANN, Joachim and Stockhausen visited Hamburg repeatedly during the year 1861, and all made much of Johannes. Both Joachim and Brahms assisted at Frau Schumann's concert of January 15. Brahms took part in the performance of Schumann's beautiful Andante and Variations for two pianofortes, and conducted the Ladies' Choir, to the great delight of the members, in their singing of several of his part-songs. The first part of the programme included "Es tönt ein voller Harfenklang," "Komm herbei Tod," and "Der Gärtner," from the set with horns and harp accompaniment, Op. 17; the second part the "Minnelied" and "Der Bräutigam" (from Op. 44) and "Song from Fingal" (from Op. 17)—all performed from manuscript. The three artists were heard again the next evening at a soirée in Altona when the part-songs were repeated. On the 22nd of the month Frau Schumann and Brahms appeared together at a concert in the Logensaal

Valentinskamp, with Bach's C major Concerto and Mozart's Sonata, both for two pianofortes.

Frau Schumann and her daughter Marie were, during this somewhat prolonged visit, the guests of the Halliers, who understood the necessities involved by the strain of the great artist's arduous life, and allowed her perfect freedom of action. Johannes visited his old friend every day, dining privately with her and her daughter at an hour that suited their convenience; and on a few free evenings there was glorious music in the Halliers' drawing-room before a few intimate acquaintances.

On March 8 Brahms played Beethoven's triple Concerto with David and Davidoff at the Philharmonic concert, and a few weeks later the Begräbnissgesang was performed under his direction at a Hafner memorial concert arranged by Grädener, and made a profound impression.

"The composer has realised the solemn spirit of mourning with extraordinary insight. As part of a funeral ceremony, the effect of the work would be quite overpowering," wrote one of the critics.

Joachim and Stockhausen came in April for the Philharmonic concert of the 16th, and the brilliant season closed with Stockhausen's and Brahms' soirées on the 19th, 27th and 30th of the month. At the first two concerts, at Hamburg and Altona respectively, the entire series of Schubert's "Schöne Müllerin" was given; and at the last— who can imagine a more enthralling feast of sound than the performance of Beethoven's melting love-songs, "To the Distant Beloved," the very thought of which brings tears to the eyes, sung by Stockhausen to the accompaniment of Brahms, followed by our composer's lovely second Serenade, and this by Schumann's "Poet's Love-Songs." Happy Hamburgers, happy Stockhausen, happy Brahms, to have shared such delights together! Will their like ever come again? Strangely enough, they lead in the course of our story, as by natural transition, to the record of a visit paid to Brahms in the second week of July by a very early friend of his and of the reader. Lischen Giesemann had not met her old playmate since she had bidden him God-speed at the commencement of his concert-journey with Reményi early in 1853. During the years immediately following what proved to be his final departure from Winsen, she had occasionally visited her dear "aunt" Brahms, but, never finding Johannes at home, had been obliged to content herself by rejoicing with his mother over the letters he constantly sent to his parents from Düsseldorf, Hanover, etc. She was now a happy newly married wife, but the memory of the old child-life remained like the warmth of sunshine in her heart, and having ascertained that her now celebrated hero was living at home again, she determined to go with her husband to see him. As ill-luck would have it, Johannes had gone out for the day when Herr and Frau Denninghoff made their call in the Fuhlentwiethe, but his mother, overjoyed to see her young friend again after a long separation, offered such consolation as was in her power by showing her his room. How many remembrances crowded upon Lischen's mind as she entered it! The practices with Reményi, the teacher's choral society, the dances at Hoopte, the story of the beautiful Magelone and her knight Peter. Lischen found herself standing near the piano—and what did she see there? Some manuscript songs, apparently newly composed, stood on the music desk, which bore the name of the beautiful Magelone herself in Brahms' handwriting! It almost seemed like a waking dream to the young wife, and the manuscript appeared to her as a link by which the past would be carried into the future. Nor was she mistaken. Brahms'. "Magelone Romances" have become world-famous, and wherever they are heard the delight which stirred the heart of the youthful Johannes as he and Lischen sat together in the pleasant Winsen fields eagerly devouring the old story from Aaron Löwenherz's purloined volume lives also. Lischen was not again to meet her old friend, but she never forgot either him or his music, and he, too, kept a faithful memory for the old pleasant time. Writing to her twenty years later, when at the height of his fame, he said:

"The remembrance of your parents' house is one of the dearest that I possess; all the kindness and love that were shown me, all the youthful pleasure and happiness that I enjoyed there, live secure in my heart with the image of your good father and the glad grateful memory of you all."

Lischen's daughter inherited her mother's voice, and was endowed with fine musical gifts; and when Agnes came to the right age, Frau Denninghoff sent her to be trained as a singer at the Royal Music School of Berlin, of which, as everyone knows, Joachim was director from the time of its foundation. Joachim invited Agnes to his house one evening to meet Brahms, who, coming forward to greet her, said it was as though her mother were again standing before him. He sent her a selection of his songs, and in due time she became a successful singer, appearing in public under a pseudonym, and the wife of a distinguished musician.

Lischen saw only the first four numbers of the "Magelone" song-cycle, which had, by a strange coincidence, just been completed at the time of her visit; the fifth and sixth were not composed until May, 1862.* These six songs were published by Rieter-Biedermann in 1865, with the title "Romanzen aus L. Tieck's Magelone," and a dedication to Stockhausen; and there can be no doubt that the immediate incitement to their composition is to be traced to our composer's association with this great singer in the performance of the song-cycles of Beethoven, Schubert and Schumann. The remaining nine songs of Brahms' series were not published until 1868, and the exact date of their composition has not been ascertained.

"I am living most delightfully in the country, half an hour from town," wrote Brahms, pressing Dietrich to pay

---

* Max Kalbeck, p. 438.

him a visit; "you would be surprised to find how pleasantly one can live here. Perhaps I can take you in, and at any rate my room at my parents' in Hamburg is quite at your service. In short, I hope you will be comfortable."

He was established for the summer at Hamm in the pleasant country house of Frau Dr. Rösing, aunt of the two girls, the Fräulein Betty and Marie Völckers, already mentioned as members of the choir. Here a large airy room with a balcony, on the first floor, had been allotted him, that had been the billiard room of the house when it was inhabited by Herr Völckers and his family. This gentleman now lived next door with his two daughters in a charming old fashioned habitation built, cottage-wise, with a thatched roof and but two floors, and possessing a spacious apartment on the ground floor that had been frequently used for the choir practices. Both houses had pleasant gardens separated only by a green hedge, and close by, the spreading branches of fine old trees provided shelter for the many nightingales that built their nests in the quiet spot. Brahms' room was cheerful for a considerable part of the day, with the sunlight that shone through the outside greenery and the tinted panes of the open windows, and in it he could enjoy his favourite early morning hours of work with the added relish of feeling that they were but the prelude to days of quiet refreshment. He was intimate with all the branches of his hostess's family, from Herr Völckers, who had been a good public singer of his day, down to his gifted little granddaughter Minna (now Mrs. Edward Stone), one of the young composer's very favourite and most devoted pianoforte pupils; and that he passed a considerable portion of his time this summer in the society of the two girls next door —Betty and Marie Völckers—will astonish none of our readers. He went in and out their house as he liked, and frequently joined them as they sat in their garden with work or books, or chatting with their friends, Fräulein Reuter and Fräulein Laura Garbe, whom they often invited. Johannes would stroll in with his cigar or cigarette, and take a seat near the group, silent or talkative according to his inclination. By and by he would sing a note or two of a well known melody, begin to beat time, and the garden would be glad with the sound of four fresh young voices swelling and dying together in the charming harmonies of a favourite part-song. He often spent the evening with the young ladies and their father, gladly accepting their informal hospitality, and would play to them after supper until late into the night, sometimes performing duets with Fräulein Marie, who was his pupil on the pianoforte.

"I may say with pride that he was happy in our little house," said Frau Professor Böie (Fräulein Marie Völckers) to the author; "his playing was a great delight to our old father. His behaviour to old people was touchingly thoughtful and kind."

Dietrich, who had lately accepted the post of court capellmeister to the Grand Duke of Oldenburg, and was now quite a near neighbour, paid his promised visit to Hamburg in September.

"I occupied his very interesting room [at Hamburg], and was astonished at his comprehensive library, which he had gradually collected since early youth; it contained some remarkable old works.

"After breakfast in the morning I used to sit cosily with his dear old mother, who united true heart-culture with her plainness and simplicity; her Johannes was the inexhaustible subject of our lively conversations. The father generally left home early to follow his calling of bassist and music-teacher. I used to remain a little while with the dear people, and spent the rest of the day with Brahms in his charming country quarters, where we occupied ourselves with the detailed examination of his newest works."

The ladies' choir, which had served its purpose in the composer's course of self training, had been given up in the spring. Since that time Brahms had been devoting much of his energy to the completion of the two great works that were to follow the B flat Sextet in the domain of chamber music, and he no doubt made Dietrich acquainted with the pianoforte quartets in G minor and A major, several movements of which had been sent to Frau Schumann in July. The Handel variations, the manuscript of which bears the date "September 61," must also be associated with the composer's first summer in Hamm, and possibly Brahms may have played his friend portions of a string quintet in F minor which was about to pass from its embryonic stage of growth. He does not seem to have confessed, however, that he was listening again to the stirrings of an earlier ambition, and Dietrich was probably as yet unaware that Brahms, separated by six years of strenuous endeavour and rapid result from the period of an earlier attempt, was once more beginning to test his strength for the arduous flight that should lead to the successful accomplishment of a symphony.

The pianoforte quartets (Opp. 25 and 26) were sent at the end of September—the G minor in its completed form; the A major without the final movement—to Joachim, who took rather serious exception to certain features of the first movement of Op. 25. That the composer left the movement essentially unaltered, however, will be evident to the student who may compare the critical observations in question with the published score of the work. Of the last movement of the same quartet, the brilliant "Rondo alla Zingarese," written in friendly emulation of the finale of Joachim's Hungarian Concerto, the famous violinist declared in generous triumph: "In the last movement you have outstripped me on my own territory by a considerable track." It is not the business of our pages either to endorse or contradict this statement, but it may be permissible to remind the reader, that the increasing perfection of Brahms' instrumental works of the period was in no small degree furthered by the invaluable experience and self-forgetting sympathy of his friend.*

---

* Compare Brahms-Joachim "Briefwechsel," No. 231.

It is difficult to determine by comparison of Joachim's letter with the published score of the Quartet in G minor precisely how far the

SILHOUETTE BY DR. BÖHLER.
Photograph by R. Lechner (Wilh. Müller), Vienna.

Several indications suggest that Brahms' thoughts were still turned longingly in the direction of Vienna; not as a permanent place of residence—at no time in his life, probably, did he so seriously contemplate settling in Hamburg as at the present—but he wished to see the city that had been the home of Haydn, Mozart, Beethoven and Schubert;

composer's own judgment ratified his friend's critical observations since some of the references in the letter to the pagination of the MS. are obscure. It is, however, clear that Brahms made no change in the outlines of the movement, and the study of its design shows that the existing proportion of the parts, in which both Frau Schumann and Joachim felt a want of symmetry is, in fact, essential to the fundamental plan of the work.

The movement is not to be regarded as an example of sonata form arranged with undeviating conformity to the lines of tradition, but as one amongst others of Brahms' compositions in which is exhibited a special characteristic of his art—freedom in the use of classical form. The first subject, derived from a motif of four diatonic notes arrests the attention of the listener by its strong, broad simplicity, and is well adapted for the purposes of the development section with a view to which it was no doubt constructed. The second subjects, primary and derived, in the minor and major modes of the dominant key D, are flowing and melodious. It was to the prolongation of this second part of the statement, and to what they felt as the resultant undue prominence of its key—features which would undoubtedly be objectionable in a movement constructed in strict sonata form—that the composer's friendly critics demurred. In the movement under consideration however, the prolongation is both required and compensated by the treatment of the development section. This opens with a full repetition, without ornamental variation, of the first subject of ten bars' length in its original key, a peculiarity which in itself shows the movement to have been deliberately designed in free form; and the first subject supplies, together with the bridge passage, nearly the whole material treated in the section. Want of space prevents any detailed allusion here to the many interesting features of the repetition section and of the imposing coda, both so constructed as to sustain the balance of the movement, which, as the author ventures to think, is a worthy opening to the whole glorious work. It may be pointed out, in conclusion, that the interest attaching to the immortal pair of quartets is, from the musician's point of view, considerably enhanced by the fact that in the two opening movements are presented fine examples of musical design in the one case in free, in the other case in strict, sonata form. A note in Frau and the enthusiastic sympathy accorded to Frau Schumann on each of her visits to the Austrian capital confirmed him in a desire to try his luck with its music-loving public. He knew his way had been prepared for him, and a good opportunity seemed likely to occur for his appearance there. Joachim, who had enjoyed his customary unequivocal success during an Austrian concert tour on which he had been engaged early in the year, was meditating another journey to Vienna and would gladly have arranged it with Johannes as a companion. Matters went no further, however, than they had done previously. As in a former year, paragraphs appeared in the *Signale* announcing that Brahms was about to visit Vienna, but in the end he remained at home—partly, no doubt, from motives of policy.

It was generally understood that Wilhelm Grund, who had for many years conducted the Philharmonic concerts and the Singakademie connected with them, must soon retire. He had done good work in his day, but his day was over. Musical conditions had changed; he was too old to alter with them, and the Philharmonic performances had long ceased to satisfy modern requirements. It was hoped by Brahms' friends that the young genius of Hamburg would succeed to the post, and Johannes himself may have thought it wise to remain on the spot with such an important issue imminent. The disappointment he felt at giving up the desired journey was partially consoled by the knowledge

---

Schumann's diary, entered soon after Johannes had received the quartets back from Hanover and five days before the first public performance of Op. 25, may probably be accepted as Brahms' own comment on the question:

"Hamburg. 11th November.

"Interesting talk with Johannes on form. How it is the older masters who are perfect in their use of form, whilst modern compositions are confined within the most rigid small forms. He, himself, emulates the older masters and especially admires Clementi's large, free employment of form." Litzmann III, p. 111.

that Frau Schumann, with her daughter Julie, would be much in Hamburg during the autumn months.

He began his concert season on October 19 at Altona, and appeared at one of the Böie-Lee concerts later in the month, playing the Schumann Variations for two pianofortes with Frau Clara. On the 30th there was a music-party at the Halliers', which is charmingly described in a letter written a few days afterwards by Fräulein Julie Hallier:

"The guests were late in coming; it was half-past eight when they had all arrived; and who comes with Frau Schumann?—Our dear friend from Hanover, with his beaming face and delightful friendliness; the glorious Joachim. Everyone was taken by surprise, Frau Schumann and Brahms in the morning, we in the evening. Avé: 'My boy! where have you come from?' After the first excitement was over, Edward showed his Italian photographs. Brahms literally devoured them; he was very nice the whole evening, especially with Edward. He teased me about my punch, which I altered three times, he following it with anxious looks as the bowl disappeared through the door. Frau Schumann and Brahms played beautifully beyond imagination; three rondos by Schubert and two marches. The violin of course had not come; Joachim only arrived yesterday and is already gone again. At first Avé turned over, but he did it badly, so Brahms called Joachim. Avé: 'My dreadful cold; I cannot see properly.' He now stood behind and began to beat time. During the music the table was laid in the small room. It was rather narrow, but comfortable. All went well. We separated at half-past eleven."

A few days afterwards there was a similar gathering at the Wagners', when Frau Schumann performed with Brahms his duet arrangement of the second serenade.

"The best of all was a set of variations by Brahms on a theme by Handel," continues the letter—"another magnificent work! splendidly long—the stream of ideas flowing inexhaustibly! And the work was splendidly played, too, by himself. It seemed like a miracle; one could not take one's eyes from him. The composition is so difficult that none but great artists could attempt it."*

These words give some measure of the progress effected during the last half-century in the technique of pianoforte-playing, partly, indeed, through the demands made upon pianists by the compositions of Brahms himself. Lovers of his art who have learnt his particular technique, which demands of the player certain qualities of endurance and grip, do not find the performance of his works unduly fatiguing. The twenty-five variations, with the fugue that succeeds them, are now in the fingers of most good players, and would undoubtedly be often heard in the concert-room if it were not for the great length of the work. They show a melodious fertility and power of invention which is practically inexhaustible. Each variation or pair of variations presents some fresh idea, some striking change of fancy, figuration, rhythm, mood, to hold the listener's attention, whilst the entire long work is essentially based upon the simple harmonic progression of Handel's theme (to be found in the second collection of Harpsichord Pieces). The changes of key in Brahms' variations are restricted to the tonic minor (Nos. 5, 6, 13) and the relative minor (No. 21). The finale, the great free fugue which invariably "brings down" a house, is, with its grand and brilliant climax, to which extraordinary effect is imparted by an original employment of the dominant pedal point, a unique example of its kind.

If there ever were a young composer who had reason to be made happy from the outset of his career by the appreciation of the most eminent of his colleagues—appreciation sweeter than any other to the soul of the true artist—Brahms was he. At each of Frau Schumann's three appearances in Hamburg during this autumn, she performed a great work of his composition, two being introduced for the first time to the public. At her first concert, on November 16, she performed

---

* First published in Hübbe's "Brahms in Hamburg," pp. 42-4.

1862]   THE HANDEL VARIATIONS.   293

the G minor Pianoforte Quartet with Böie, Breyther and Lee for the first time in public, and on the same evening several of the composer's part-songs were sung under his direction by the former members of the Ladies' Choir; on the 3rd of the month she appeared as the champion of the unpopular concerto, playing it with especial pleasure, in association with Brahms as conductor, at the Philharmonic concert of that date; and on the 7th of the same month she brought forward the Handel Variations and Fugue at her second concert. These she repeated a week later at the Gewandhaus soirée of the 14th in Leipzig.

Not even the magnetic personality of Frau Schumann availed to awaken any show of enthusiasm for the concerto. The new works were more favourably received both in Hamburg and Leipzig, and the *Signale* itself bestowed a mild word or two upon some of the variations. It is easy, however, to read between the lines of the press notices that such encouragement as was awarded to the composer was mainly due to the personality of the performer. The B flat Sextet was given with fair success at the Gewandhaus Quartet concert of January 4 by David, Engelbert, Röntgen, Hermann, Hunger, Davidoff and Krummholtz.

Brahms passed the first two months of the new year in Joachim's society, making his headquarters at Hanover, and undertaking frequent short journeys with his friend. The two artists appeared together on January 20 at one of the Münster subscription concerts, of which Grimm, who had been called to Münster in 1860, was now the conductor; and on February 14 they gave a concert in Celle, a locality which the reader will remember as the scene of Johannes' transposition feat during the Reményi *tournée* of 1853. The A major Pianoforte Quartet was now finished, and was, with its companion in G minor, much appreciated in the private circles of Hanover, where both works were frequently played by Brahms with Joachim and his colleagues.

Brahms, answering an invitation from Dietrich received on the eve of his departure, says:

"Hanover, 1862.

"Dear Friend,

"I have been here for some time, and have your letter forwarded from Hamburg. I go back to-morrow, and write a few words in haste.

"I should much like to visit you and to make the acquaintance of those whom I know pleasantly by name, otherwise I would say no. I will come and see how long I can afford to be idle.

"What shall I play? Beethoven or Mozart? C minor, A major, or G major? Advise!

"And for the second—Schumann, Bach, or may I venture upon some new variations of my own?

"You, of course, will conduct my serenade. We have been playing my quartets a great deal here; I shall bring them with me and shall be glad if you and others approve of them.

"*A propos!* I must have an honorarium of 15 Louis-d'ors [about £14], with the stipulation that if I should play at Court I receive extra remuneration. I much need the money; pro sec. my time is valuable to me, and I do not willingly take concert engagements; if, however, this must be, then the other must also."*

Dietrich had already had the pleasure of welcoming Frau Schumann and Joachim to Oldenburg during this his first season of activity there, and had worked well to prepare the way for Brahms, so that the evening of March 14, the date fixed for the composer's personal introduction to the concert-going public, was awaited with keen interest. Arriving at Dietrich's house a few days previously, Brahms found himself surrounded by new friends, and had won the favour of the musical élite of the town before his public appearance, by playing several of his works in private circles. The members of the orchestra, who assembled *en masse* on the evening of the 13th, were excited to enthusiasm by his performance of the new Handel Variations and Fugue, and

---

* Dietrich.

every condition that could ensure a sympathetic reception for the hero of the 14th was fulfilled.

The concert opened with the D major Serenade (Op. 11), conducted by Dietrich, who had the delight of finding that he had secured an adequate reception for his friend's orchestral work.

"The whole made the most satisfactory impression, and carried the hearers away more and more, especially from the fourth movement onwards, and at the close the applause reached a pitch of enthusiasm not hitherto experienced here. The members of the orchestra, who had been studying the serenade for some time, showed their concurrence in the general approval by a lively flourish." *(Oldenburger Zeitung.)*

No less satisfactory was the verdict of the audience on the performances of Beethoven's G major Concerto and Bach's Chromatic Fantasia, with which our composer came forward as pianist. His success was repeated at the chamber music concert of the 19th, when the sextet was performed by Court Concertmeister Engel and his colleagues. Both in public and private Brahms left endearing memories behind him.

"He was the most agreeable guest," says Dietrich, "always pleased, always good-humoured and satisfied, like a child with the children.

"He took the greatest pleasure in our happiness. He thought our modest lot enviable, and had his position then allowed him to establish a home of his own, perhaps this might have been the right moment, for he was attracted by a young girl who was often with us. One evening, when she and other guests had left, he said with quiet decision: 'She pleases me; I should like to marry her; such a girl would make me, too, happy.' He met many people at our house, and in small and large circles outside it, and everyone liked his earnest nature and his short and often humorous remarks."

It is pleasant to have to record here that a few weeks before the events now described, New York, distinguished, as we have seen, by Mason's timely performance of the

B major Trio in 1855, led the way a second time in connection with Brahms' career. In February, 1862, the first performance after publication of the second serenade took place there at a Philharmonic concert, and the occasion is doubly memorable as marking the earliest introduction of an orchestral work of Brahms to a public audience outside the cities of Hamburg, Hanover and Leipzig. This early appreciation of the composer's genius in America has proved to have been neither accidental nor transitory. It grew steadily year by year with the general growth of interest in musical art, and his works, great and small, were welcomed as they appeared, and performed—often, it must be said, from pirated editions in the earlier days—with ever-increasing success. It has been impossible to ascertain the exact dates of first American performances. New York, the earliest centre in the United States for the cultivation of Brahms' music, was emulated later on, especially by Boston; and the famous Symphony Orchestra of this city has, since its foundation in 1881, performed each of the four symphonies, in Boston and in the course of numerous concert tours, at an average of forty concerts; whilst the two overtures, the concertos, and other large works, have been given with corresponding frequency.

The chamber music has been a special feature in the programmes of several concert-parties resident in various parts of the United States. Of these, special mention should be made of the Kneisel String Quartet of Boston, whose performances, familiar not only to American, but also to some of the circles of European music-lovers, were warmly appreciated by Brahms himself.

In the spring of 1862, an artistic tour undertaken in France by Frau Schumann laid the foundation of Brahms' reputation in Paris, which, little to be noted during many years, has of late been rapidly increasing. That the great pianist, when introducing her husband's works, which were almost unknown to French audiences, had to confront the inevitable prejudice against what is new, explains the fact that

Brahms' name did not appear in the programmes of her concerts at the Salle Erard. The efforts she made in the cause of his art, however, amongst the inmost musical circle of her acquaintance created an impression that was not entirely fleeting.

The two first Pianoforte Quartets, now finally completed, and performed, as we have seen, during the winter of 1861-62—the earlier one in public, and both frequently in private—add two glorious works of chamber music to the series so brilliantly inaugurated by the Sextet in B flat. In their broadly-flowing themes, their magnificent wealth of original and contrasted melody, their consummate workmanship, their fresh, vigorous vitality, their enchanting romance, one seems to hear the bounding gladness of the artist-spirit which has attained freedom through submission to law, and revels in its emancipation. They are so rich in beauty, so transcendent in power, that the attempt to point out this or that particular detail for admiration results in bewilderment. The romantic intermezzo, the riotously brilliant Hungarian rondo, of the first; the graceful scherzo with its bold trio, of the second, and the adagio, with its atmosphere of mystery, lit up twice by the outbreak of passion that subsides again to the hushed expressiveness of the beginning and end; the opening allegro of either work—all are original, great, beautiful; but so is every portion of every movement of both quartets, and each movement proclaims—from Bach to Brahms. That Brahms' course of development proceeded ever further in the direction of concentration of thought and conciseness of structure cannot affect the value of the splendid achievements of his earlier period of maturity, and of these the two quartets stand amongst the greatest.

The sincerity of Brendel's efforts to conciliate the contending musical parties, and his desire to do justice to each, is strikingly proved by the appearance in his journal, in the course of several months of the year 1862, of a series of articles signed "D. A. S.," by Dr. Schübring, a distinguished musician and critic of the Schumann school. The first few numbers are devoted to sympathetic reviews of the works of Theodor Kirchner, Woldemar Bargiel, and others; and following these are five articles in which the whole of Brahms' published works are examined in detail. The composer's genius, his progress, his moods and his methods, are discussed with the skill of a scientific musician, the impartiality of a sound critic, and the affection of a personal and artistic friend. They are too technical for quotation here, but the last sentence of the concluding number may be given in well-deserved tribute to Brendel, who must have known what he was doing when he arranged for Dr. Schübring's contributions.

"The foregoing words may sound inflated, but stopped horns are of no use when it is desired to arouse the great public, which does not yet seem to comprehend in the least what a colossal genius, one quite of equal birth with Bach, Beethoven, and Schumann, is ripening in the young master of Hamburg."

The mediator's task is seldom a grateful one, and it appears probable that Dr. Brendel was reproached for his large-mindedness by some of the New-German party, with whom he had been so long intimately connected, as a half-apologetic explanation of his reasons for desiring the publication of the "Schumanniana," as the articles were entitled, appeared in a later number of the *Zeitschrift*.

It would be unsatisfactory to omit all mention of the first performance of a "Magelone Romance," though there is but little to record save the fact that Stockhausen sang the opening one, the "Keinen hat es noch gereut," from the manuscript, at the Philharmonic concert of April 4, as one of a group of songs by Brahms. It produced no impression whatever on the Hamburgers, who were only mystified. How many persons in the audience had read Tieck's poems? How many had ever heard anything about the adventures of Magelone and Peter? Without such knowledge, the first and second numbers of the cycle cannot be really appreciated. To those who are aware that the first is the song of a minstrel who incites a valiant young hero to journey to distant lands in quest of adventure, and the second the exultant shout of the joyful aspirant as he rides forth from his parents' home, resolved on doughty deeds, the music becomes living, and seems to breathe forth the very spirit of chivalry. The third, fourth, and some other of the songs, notably the ninth—the ravishing "Ruhe Süssliebchen"—are capable of telling a tale of their own, and give rich delight apart from their place in Tieck's version of the story; but the enjoyment even of these favourite and familiar songs is much heightened by an acquaintance with the incidents of the romance. Tieck's "Beautiful Magelone" is contained in his "Phantasus," a collection of tales published between 1812 and 1816, some of which have been made familiar to English readers by the translations of Hare, Froude and Carlyle. The "Magelone" story of the book is a modernised version of an old romance of chivalry, and, by introducing into it a number of songs, Tieck furnished the opportunity seized upon more than forty years later by Brahms, to which the world is indebted for some of the composer's most perfect inspirations.

To provide in this place the much needed clue to their connection with the events of the tale would cause too serious an interruption to our narrative. The author has therefore added, in Appendix I, an account of the romance and the incidence of Tieck's songs, which it is hoped may interest the reader and increase his love for the compositions.

Brahms continued to make Frau Dr. Rösing's house at Hamm his headquarters, and remained there during most of the spring and summer of 1862. Before going to Oldenburg in March, he had written to Dietrich : "It is delightful here in Hamm, and unless I look out of window at the bare trees I fancy summer is come, the sunlight plays in the room so gaily." Later it was: "It is blooming splendidly, and the trees are blossoming in Hamm, so that it is a joy." He occupied his leisure in similar agreeable pursuits to those of the preceding year, and now in the springtime a double choir of maidens and nightingales might often be heard by the passer-by, carolling together as if in mutual emulation of the others' song. He begged, later on, for photographs of his girls' quartet and of the two houses, and said that he neither remembered nor saw before him a happier time than that he had passed in Hamm. The sisters met their fate in due time. Each married a distinguished violinist, and Concertmeister Otto von Königslow of Cologne and Professor John Böie of Altona were amongst the most active admirers of Brahms' art. The composer remained on terms of intimacy with the entire Völckers family, and never failed, when occasionally staying at Hamburg during the later years of his career, to visit both the Böies and the Stones.

Avé Lallement, who personally, perhaps, would gladly have seen Johannes settled in Hamburg as conductor of the Philharmonic, says, in a letter written in the early spring of the year to Dr. Löwe of Zürich:

"We had the 'Matthew Passion' here under Grund; Brahms also was delighted, in spite of the defective performance. He thinks of going to Vienna in the autumn; then I shall be quite alone, but thank God I have learnt to know the man so well. I have come a good piece forward through him."

Brahms and Dietrich met at the Rhine Festival given this year at Cologne (June 8-10), where they made the artistic and personal acquaintance of Frau Louise Dustmann, court chamber singer, and of the court opera, Vienna, whom Brahms knew well in later years. From Cologne they proceeded to Münster-am-Stein, taking lodgings together near Frau Schumann, who was staying there with her family. From Münster Dietrich wrote to his wife:

"The longer I am with Brahms, the more my affection and esteem for him increase. His nature is equally lovable, cheerful, and deep. He often teases the ladies, certainly, by making jokes with a serious air which are frequently taken in earnest, especially by Frau Schumann. This leads to comical and frequently dangerous arguments, in which I usually act as mediator, for Brahms is fond of strengthening such misunderstandings, in order to have the laugh on his side in the end. This to me attractive humorous trait is, I think, the reason why he is so often misunderstood. He can, however, be very quiet and serious if necessary."

Brahms had heralded his arrival by sending Frau Schumann a packet of new manuscripts, the last completed of which was a symphony movement. When he played this work to his friends in the course of his fortnight's stay at Münster-am-Stein, he introduced to them an early version of the first movement of his C minor Symphony, which was not finally completed until fourteen years later.

Frau Schumann received three movements of the string quintet in F minor (two violoncelli) mentioned earlier in the chapter, in August, and the completed work was sent to Joachim in September.

The Sextet in B flat, the Handel Variations, and the horns and harp Songs for women's chorus, were published this year by Simrock. Two works in the hands of Rieter-Biedermann—the Marienlieder for mixed chorus (Op. 22), composed in the autumn of 1859, and the Variations for Pianoforte Duet, Op. 23, finished in the summer of 1861, appeared early in 1863.*

The Marienlieder, seven in number, to be sung *a capella*, are not sacred compositions. They are settings of old texts founded upon some of the mediaeval legends that grew up around the history of the Virgin, and are delightfully fresh examples of the pure style of part-writing of which Brahms had made himself a master. In spite of the restricted means at the disposal of the composer who elects to forego, for the nonce, all but the few diatonic harmonies alone available in this style, there is a something about these attractive little pieces which allows Brahms' individuality to be distinctly felt. If, as is inevitable, they carry back the mind of the

---

* The Variations are dated 1866 in the published catalogue.

listener to the choral music of the sixteenth century, they recall the style of the early German, rather than of either of the Italian schools. Perhaps the most fascinating of the set is No. 2, entitled "Mary's Church-going." Mary, on her way to church, comes to a deep lake, and, finding a young boatman standing ready, requests him to ferry her over, promising him whatever he may like best in return. The boatman answers that he will do what she asks provided she will become his housewife; but Mary, replying that she will swim across rather than consent to the suggestion, jumps into the water. When she is half way to the other side, the church bells suddenly begin to ring, loudly, softly, all together. Mary, on her safe arrival, kneels on a stone in prayer, and the boatman's heart breaks. The first five verses are composed strophically (each like the other) for two sopranos, contralto and tenor, in E flat minor, and are marked *piano*. The bass enters with the sixth verse, composed in E flat major, and, whilst the whole choir bursts into a jubilant *forte*, keeps up a movement in concert, first with the tenor and then with the soprano, suggestive of bell-ringing. The concluding words return to the setting of the first five verses, and by this means the little composition is rounded into definite shape.

The Variations are amongst the most beautiful of Brahms' many fine achievements in this particular domain, and present for admiration conspicuous qualities of their own arising from the opportunities offered by their composition in duet form. The theme on which they are founded is that supposed by Schumann to have been brought to him in the night by angels a fortnight before his malady reached its crisis. The work is dedicated to Fräulein Julie Schumann, the master's third daughter.

And now, in a few weeks the period of Brahms' career which is to be especially associated with Hamburg, was to close. He would gladly have strengthened his ties with the city to which he was so proud to belong; and at this particular moment he had good reason for hoping that the day was not far distant which would find him settled there in a position that might ultimately secure him an income sufficient for his modest needs. He had been privately approached by his friend, Avé Lallement, of the Philharmonic committee, with reference to the proposed appointment of an assistant director to the society's Singverein, by which it was hoped to pave the way for the retirement of Grund from his post as conductor of the subscription concerts. As we shall see, however, his compatriots would have none of him. Twice in the coming years they passed him by, and when the time at length arrived in which they would willingly have proclaimed the world-famous composer as their own special prophet, his interests and affections had become too deeply rooted within the city that he made his second home to be capable of a second transplantation.

Brahms quitted Hamburg for his first visit to Vienna on September 8. That he expected to return speedily is evident from the lines sent by him to Dietrich on the eve of his departure:

"DEAR FRIEND,

"I am leaving on Monday *for Vienna!* I look forward to it like a child.

"Of course I do not know how long I shall stay; we will leave it open, and I hope we may meet some time during the winter.

"The C minor Symphony is not ready; on the other hand, a string quintet (2 v.celli) in F minor is finished. I should like to send it you and hear what you have to say about it, and yet I prefer to take it with me.

"Herewith my Handel Variations; the Marienlieder are not yet here.

"Greet all the Oldenburg friends.

"Pray do not leave me quite without letters. You might address for the present to Haslinger, or to Wessely and Büsing.

"Heartiest farewell meanwhile, dear Albert, to you and your wife.

"Your JOHANNES."

"Father," said Brahms, looking slyly at his father as he said good-bye, "if things should be going badly with you, music is always the best consolation; go and study my old 'Saul'—you will find comfort there."

He had thickly interlarded the volume with bank-notes.*

It is highly interesting to possess a clear conception of Brahms' achievements as a composer, and, therewith, of his exact title to consideration at this important moment of his career. This will be best obtained by a glance at the list of the chief completed works with which he was to present himself in the city associated with the most hallowed memories of his art. His departure for Vienna is by no means to be regarded as coincident with the close of any one period of his creative activity, though it emphatically marks the end, not only of a chapter, but of the first book of his life.

LIST OF BRAHMS' CHIEF COMPLETED WORKS ON HIS DEPARTURE FOR VIENNA.

	Op.
Pianoforte Solos:	
Three Sonatas	1, 2, 5.
Scherzo	4.
Variations on Schumann's theme in F sharp minor	9.
Ballades	10.
Variations on an original theme	21, No. 1.
Variations on a Hungarian song	21, No. 2.
Variations and Fugue on Handel's theme	24.
Pianoforte Duet:	
Variations on a theme by Schumann	23.
Pianoforte with Orchestra:	
Concerto in D minor	15.
Orchestral: Two Serenades ...	11, 16.

---

* Max Kalbeck, I, p. 477.

	Op.
Chamber Music:	
Sextet in B flat for Strings	18.
Trio in B major for Pianoforte and Strings	8.
Quartet in G minor for Pianoforte and Strings	25.
Quartet in A major for Pianoforte and Strings	26.
Songs:	
Five books (thirty-one songs)	3, 6, 7, 14, 19.
"Magelone Romances" (first six)	33.
Vocal Duets: two books	20, 28.
Three Vocal Quartets	31.
Women's Chorus:	
"Ave Maria"	12.
Part-songs	17, 37.
Mixed Chorus:	
Begräbnissgesang	13.
Marienlieder	22.
The 13th Psalm	27.
Motets	29.
Sacred Song	30.

The newly-finished String Quintet is not included in the list, as the work was not published in this its first form. The Hungarian Dances, as being arrangements, are also omitted.

APPENDICES.

I.

THE MAGELONE ROMANCES.

THE story of the Count Peter of Provence and the beautiful Magelone, Princess of Naples, which is associated with a well known ruin on the south coast of France, is said by Raynouard to have formed the subject of a poem written towards the close of the twelfth century by Bernhard de Trèves, Canon of Magelonne in Languedoc. It was adapted as a prose romance not later than the middle of the fourteenth, and printed in at least five different editions before the end of the fifteenth, century. Of these, rare copies are to be found in some of the famous libraries of England and the Continent. Two editions, copies of which are in the British Museum, were issued by Maître Guillaume Le Roy. With slight differences of spelling they begin :

"Au nom de notre seigneur ihesucrist, cy commēce listoyre du vaillant chevalier pierre filz du cōte de provēce et de la belle maguelonne fille du roy de naples."

The romance is constructed from the familiar elements of mediaeval fiction—chivalry, religion and love—and has been translated at various dates into almost every European language, Italian, Spanish, Portuguese, Russian, Norse, etc. It has been republished in German many times through the centuries since it was first done into that language (probably in 1483), and was included by G. O. Marbach in 1838 in his popular series of tales (Volksbücher). That it was this version of the story that found its way into Frau Löwenherz's library and was read by Johannes and Lischen is proved beyond doubt by its title, which is identical with that noted down by the present writer from the lips of Frau Denninghoff, the "Lischen" of our biography —"Geschichte der schönen Magelone und dem Ritter Peter mit den silbernen Schlüsseln"—and it seems probable that Marbach obtained his tale from an edition published in 1661 at Nürnburg: "Historia der schönen Magelona, eines Königs Tochter von Neaples, und einem Ritter, genannt Peter mit den silbernen Schlüsseln, eines Grafen Sohn aus Provincia." Of the many editions, fifteenth and up to the nineteenth century, to which the author has had access, no other contains in its title any mention of the silver keys.

Marbach's version is a fine one. Whilst he has modernised the old romance in certain respects, he has kept, not only to the main incidents of the tale, but to the quaint old dialogues which naïvely portray the characters of the manly-hearted but rather weak-minded Peter and the high spirited, self-willed, yet tender Magelone.

Tieck's version, published in 1812 in the first volume of the "Phantasus," differs considerably, especially in its particulars of the beginning and end of the romance, from the original details of the story. In making his alterations, the poet seems to have been chiefly concerned to eliminate the religious element from his narrative as far as possible, and to provide opportunity for the introduction of seventeen songs of which Brahms composed fifteen. The tale has suffered considerably in his hands. The general atmosphere of French mediaeval fiction, with its characteristic setting of sunrise and sunset, flowers and birds, and, in parts, the wording of the old romance, have, however, been preserved, and we may be grateful to Tieck for the poems which have placed us in possession of Brahms' beautiful song-cycle.

We propose to give an abridgment of his narrative up to a certain point and to summarise ensuing details, which become prolix and involved in all the versions. We shall insert only the first few lines of each song.

How a Strange Singer came to the Court of Provence.

A long time ago, a Count reigned in Provence whose beautiful and noble son grew up the joy of his parents. He was big and strong and his shining fair hair flowed round his neck and shaded his tender, youthful face. Then he was well proved in arms; no one in or beyond the land managed the lance and sword as he, so that he was admired by great and small, young and old, noble and simple. He was often absent-minded as though meditating on some secret desire, and many experienced people concluded that he must be in love, but none of them would awaken him from his thoughts, for they knew that love is like the vision of a dream, which is apt, if disturbed, to vanish and return to its dwelling in the ether and the golden mists of morning.

His father gave a great tournament to which many knights were invited. It was a wonder to see how the tender youth hove the best and strongest from their saddles. He was lauded by everyone, but no praise made him proud; indeed he sometimes felt ashamed at overcoming such great and worthy knights. Amongst the guests was a singer who had seen many lands; he was no knight, but he surpassed many nobles in insight and experience. He made friends with Peter and praised him uncommonly, but concluded his talk with these words: Sir Knight, if I might advise you, you should not remain here, but should see other places and other men, to improve your ideas and learn to associate the strange with the familiar. He took his lute and sang:

> No one yet hath rued the day
> When on charger mounting
> Youthful-strong he sped away,
> Pain nor peril counting, etc.

The youth listened to the song: when it was at an end, he remained awhile sunk in thought; then said: Yes, now I know what I want; many variegated pictures pass through my mind. No greater joy for a young knight than to ride through valley and over field. Here in the morning sunshine stands a stately castle, there over the meadow sounds the shepherd's shawn; a noble maiden flies by on a white palfrey. Oh, I wish I were already on my good horse. Heated by these new thoughts, he went at once to his mother's chamber where he found his father also. Peter immediately sank on one knee and made his request that his parents would allow him to travel and seek adventures: for, thus he concluded his speech, he who only stays at home keeps a narrow mind during his whole life, but by travel, one learns to associate the strange with the familiar; therefore do not refuse me your consent.

The old Count said: My son, your request appears to me unsuitable, for you are my only heir; if I should die in your absence, what would become of my land? But Peter kept to his request, whereat his mother began to weep and said to him: Dear, only son, you have never tasted trouble, and see only your beautiful hopes before you, but remember that if you depart, a thousand difficulties may confront you; you may be miserable and wish yourself back with us.

Peter remained humbly on his knees and answered: Beloved parents, I cannot help it. My only wish is to travel into the wide world, to experience pleasure and sorrow there and to return a known and honoured man. For this you travelled in your youth, my father, and brought home my mother from a strange land. Let me seek a like fortune, I beg for this with tears.

He took the lute and sang the song which he had heard from the minstrel, and at the end he wept bitterly. The parents were moved, especially the mother; she said: Well, I, for my part, will give you my blessing, dear son, for what you have said is true. The father also rose and blessed him, and Peter was glad from his heart that he had received his parents' consent.

Orders were given to prepare everything for his departure, and his mother sent for him to come to her privately. She gave him three precious rings and said: See, my son, I have kept these three precious rings carefully from my youth. Take them with you and treasure them, and if you find a maiden whom you love, and who is inclined towards you, you may give them to her. He gratefully kissed her hand, and the morning came on which he took leave.

HOW THE KNIGHT PETER DEPARTED FROM HIS PARENTS.

When Peter was ready to mount his horse, his father blessed him again and said: My son, may good fortune ever accompany you so that we may see you back again healthy and strong; think constantly of the precepts I have impressed upon your tender youth; seek good, and avoid evil, company; honour the laws of knighthood and never forget them, for they are the noblest thoughts of the noblest men in their best hours; always be loyal even though you may be deceived, for the touchstone of the brave is that though he may seldom meet honourable men, he remain true to himself. Farewell!

Peter rode away without attendance, for like many young knights, he wished to remain unknown. The sun had risen gloriously, and the fresh dew sparkled on the meadows. Peter was in cheerful spirits and spurred on his good horse so that it sprang boldly forward. An old song rang in his head and he sang it out loud:

> Yes! arrow on bow
> Shall swiftly be laid
> To humble the foe.
> The helpless to aid, etc.

He arrived, after many days' journey, at the famous city of Naples. He had heard much talk on his way of the king and his surpassingly beautiful daughter Magelone, so that he was very anxious to see her face to face. He dismounted at an inn to ask for news, and heard from the host that a distinguished knight, Sir Henry of Carpone, had come and that a splendid tournament was to be held in his honour. He learned also that entrance would be allowed to strangers who appeared equipped according to the laws of tourney. Peter at once resolved to be present to try his dexterity and strength.

PETER SEES THE BEAUTIFUL MAGELONE.

When the day of the tournament arrived, Peter put on his armour and betook himself to the lists. He had had two beautiful silver keys of uncommonly fine workmanship placed upon his helmet, and had caused his shield and the cover of his horse to be likewise ornamented with keys. This he did for the sake of his name and in honour of the Apostle Peter, whom he greatly loved. He had recommended himself to his care and protection from his youth and therefore chose this token, as he wished to remain unknown.

A herald rode forward and with sound of trumpet proclaimed the tournament that was opened to the honour of the beautiful Magelone. She herself sat on an elevated balcony and looked down on the assemblage of knights. Peter looked up but could not see her distinctly as she was too far off. . . . Peter opposed the knight in the lists and soon threw him from his horse, so that everyone marvelled at his strength; he did more, for in a short time he had emptied every saddle so that none remained to tilt against him. Then everyone desired to know the name of the strange knight, and the King of Naples himself sent his herald to learn it, but Peter humbly begged leave to remain unknown until he should have become worthy by his deeds to name himself, and this answer pleased the king.

It was not long before another tournament was held, and the beautiful Magelone secretly hoped that the knight with the silver keys might again be visible, for she loved him, but had as yet confided this to no one, since first love is despondent and holds itself a traitor. She grew red as Peter again entered the lists in his conspicuous armour. She gazed at him steadily, and he was victor in every contest; at length she felt no more surprise, for it seemed to her as though it could not be otherwise. At last the tournament was over. Peter had again won great praise and honour.

The king sent to invite him to his table; he sat opposite the princess and was amazed at her beauty. She constantly looked kindly at him, which caused him the greatest confusion. His talk pleased the king, and his noble and strong appearance astonished the attendants. In the hall he found opportunity to speak alone with the princess, and she invited him to come again often, upon which he took leave; she sent him away at length with another very kind glance.

Peter went through the streets as if intoxicated. He hurried into a beautiful garden and walked up and down with folded arms, now slowly, now quickly, without being able to understand how the hours passed. He heard nothing around him, for music within him drowned the whispering of the trees and the rippling murmur of the fountains. A thousand times he spoke the name Magelone and then was suddenly afraid that he had called it loudly through the garden. Towards evening a sweet music sounded, and now he sat down on the grass behind a bush and wept. It seemed to him as though heaven had for the first time displayed its beauty, and yet this feeling made him unhappy. He saw the grace of the princess floating on the silver waves; she appeared like sunrise in the darkening night, and the stars stood still, trees were quiet, and the winds hushed. Now the last accents of the music sounded, the trees rustled again and the fountains grew louder. Peter roused himself and softly sang the following song:

> Is it gladness that is ringing,
> Is it sorrow, in my heart?
> Now a thousand flow'rs are springing
> And all former joys depart, etc.

He was somewhat comforted and swore to win his love or to die. Late at night he returned to the inn, sat down in his room, and repeated every word the Princess had said to him. Now he thought he had reason to rejoice, then he was again troubled and in doubt. He wished to write to his father, but could only address Magelone, and then he reproached himself for his absence of mind in venturing to write to her whom he did not know. At length he lay down; slumber overcame him, and wonderful visions of love and flight, solitary forests and storms at sea, visited his chamber and covered the bare walls as with beautiful variegated hangings.

How the Knight sent Magelone a Message.

During the night Magelone was as restless as her unknown knight. She went often to the window and looked down thoughtfully into the garden. She listened to the rustling trees, looked at the stars mirrored in the sea, reproached the stranger because he was not standing before her window, then wept because she thought it impossible. When she closed her eyes she saw the tournament and the beloved unknown looking up with longing hope. Now she fed on these fancies, now she scolded herself. Towards morning she fell into a light slumber.

At last she resolved to confess her inclination to her beloved nurse. In a confidential evening hour she said to her: Dear nurse, something has for a long time been weighing upon me which almost crushes my heart; I must, at length, tell it you and you must help me with your motherly counsel, for I do not know any longer how to advise myself. The nurse answered: Confide in me, dear child; it is for this that I am older, and love you as a mother, that I may assist you to good purpose, for youth never knows how to help itself.

When the princess heard these words she became more courageous and confidential and said: Oh, Gertrude, have you observed the unknown knight with the silver keys? But of course you have, for he is the only one worth notice; all the others serve but to glorify him, to circle his head with the sunshine of fame. He is the one man, the most beautiful youth, the bravest hero. Since I saw him my eyes have become useless, for they now see only my thoughts in which he dwells in all his glory. If I only knew that he were of high race I would place all my hopes on him; but he cannot come from an unworthy house, who then could be called noble? Oh, answer, comfort me, dear nurse, and give me counsel.

When the nurse heard these words she was frightened and said: Dear child, I have long expected that you would confide to me who it is that you love of the nobles of this or another kingdom, for the highest of the land and even kings desire you. But why have you placed your inclination upon a stranger of whom no one knows whence he came? I tremble lest the King, your father, should observe your love. The princess became much agitated whilst the nurse was speaking, and when she ceased, vehemently reproached her for calling the knight who was so near her heart a stranger. . . . Oh, go and seek him, Gertrude, and find out his rank and his name. He will not keep them secret if I ask them, for I would keep no secrets from him.

When the morning came the nurse went to church to pray for guidance and perceived the knight also kneeling in devout prayer. When he rose, he approached and greeted her politely, for he had seen her at court. She gave him the princess's message and asked his name and his rank: because it did not become so noble a man to remain hidden.

Peter rejoiced, for he perceived that Magelone loved him. He begged leave to keep his name concealed a little longer, but ended his talk with the nurse by saying: Tell the Princess that I am of noble lineage, and that my ancestors are famed in history books. Meanwhile take this remembrance and let it be a little reward for your welcome message which has brought back hope to me.

He gave the nurse one of his rings and she was glad, because she knew from it that he must be of high descent. He modestly gave her, also, a leaf of parchment, saying he did so in the hope that the princess would read some words that he had written down in the sentiment of his love.

> Love drew near from distant places,
> No attendant in her train,
> Beckon'd me, nor called in vain,
> Held me fast in sweet embraces, etc.

The song touched Magelone deeply; it was like the echo of her own feeling. She persuaded the nurse to give her the ring in exchange for another trinket, and before going to rest at night she hung it by a chain of pearls to her neck. She dreamed of a garden, nightingales, music, love, and of another ring even more precious than the first. In the morning she told her dream to the nurse, who became thoughtful, for she saw that the happiness or unhappiness of the princess was fixed on the unknown knight.

How the Knight sent Magelone a Ring.

The nurse tried to see Peter again and found him in church. He went to her directly and asked after the princess. The nurse told him she had kept the ring and had read his words; she also mentioned Magelone's dream. Peter grew red with joy and said: Ah, dear nurse, tell her all I feel and that I must die of longing if I do not speak to her soon; if, however, I may talk with her face to face, I will reveal to her my rank and my name. All my desire is to win her for my wife. Give her this ring also and pray her to keep it as a little token.

The nurse hastened back to Magelone, who ran to meet her and asked for news. See, cried the princess, this is the ring I dreamed of. A leaf contained this song:

> Does pity so tender
> Tell love's sweet surrender?
> Oh, am I awake?
> The fountains are springing,
> The streams softly singing,
> And all for love's sake.

How the Knight received another Message from the Beautiful Magelone

Peter again met the nurse in church. She asked him to swear to her his honourable intentions, and when he had taken his oath, promised to help him and the princess. She told Peter to prepare to go, to-morrow afternoon, through the secret garden gate to her room to see Magelone there, and ended by saying: I will leave you alone, that you may speak out your hearts to each other.

After telling him the hour at which he was to go through the gate, she left. Peter was distracted with joy, and it seemed to him that the time stood still until the evening hours. He sat up late at night without a light, looking at the clouds and stars, his heart beating violently. At length he slept. All the next morning he was unable to calm himself, so at last he took a lute and sang:

> Oh, how shall I measure
> The joy of our meeting?
> My spirit's wild beating
> Acclaimeth my soul's only treasure.

How Peter visited the Beautiful Magelone

When the nurse brought Peter to her room he trembled and was very frightened, and both he and Magelone were much confused. Magelone could scarcely help rising and going towards him. She controlled herself, however, and remained seated. The nurse left the room and Peter sank on one knee before the princess. Magelone gave him her beautiful hand and told him to rise and sit near her. Peter told the princess that all his life was consecrated to her. He gave her the third ring, which was the most precious of all, and in doing so kissed her hand. . . . Then she took a costly gold chain and hung it round his neck, and said: Herewith I take you as mine. Here she took the frightened knight in her arms and kissed him, and he returned the kiss and pressed her to his heart.

When they were obliged to part, Peter hastened at once to his room. He walked up and down with great strides and at length seized his instrument, kissed the strings and wept. Then he sang with great fervour:

APPENDICES.

Were they thine on which these lips were pressing,
　Thine the frankly-offered, tender kiss?
　Dwells in earthly living so much bliss?
Ha! what light and life were in thy sweet confessing,
All my senses tremble in its blessing! etc.

A Tournament in Honour of the Beautiful Magelone.

The King of Naples much wished his daughter to be soon married to the knight, Henry of Carpone, who had now waited at Naples a long time for this purpose, and he proclaimed another tournament more splendid than any that had gone before it. Many famous knights came from Italy and France, and Peter was victor over all.

When it was over he went to see Magelone; he had now visited her pretty often, and thought he would like to try her, so he said that he should now be obliged to leave her and go and be with his parents. Magelone wept very much, but as Peter persisted she at length gave way, and said: Go, then, I shall die. Peter rejoiced at this and told her he would not leave her.

Magelone, however, became thoughtful, and after she had reflected for a while, said to the knight that her father would soon marry her to Sir Henry of Carpone, and that therefore it would, perhaps, be better for Peter to return to his father and mother and to take her with him. She desired him to have two good horses ready the next night at the garden gate: But let them be swift and strong, for if we were to be overtaken we should all be miserable.

The youth heard the princess with joyful surprise. He said it would be best to take her to his parents, and that the horses should be ready. Magelone did not confide their intention even to the nurse for fear lest she should betray them.

Peter took a walk through the town to bid farewell to the places near which he had so often wandered in his intoxication, and which he regarded as witnesses of his love. When he returned to his room he was moved to see his faithful lute on the table. Touched by his fingers, it had often expressed the feelings of his heart. He took it up again for the last time and sang:

　　　　Dear strings, we are parting
　　　　　This night for evermore,
　　　　'Tis time to be starting
　　　　　For the far-off blissful shore, etc.

How Magelone went away with the Knight.

When the night came it was very cloudy and the moonlight showed scantily through the darkness. Magelone said farewell to her favourite flowers as she went through the garden. She found Peter before the gate with three horses, one a palfrey with a light and easy step; the third was to carry provisions, so that they need not enter the inns.

The nurse missed the princess the next morning, and the king sent out many people to search, but all returned after some days without tidings.

Peter chose to ride towards the forests by the sea because they were quiet and lonely. He and Magelone rode on through the night and Magelone was happy. The forest was dark, but whenever they came to an open space she refreshed herself by gazing at Peter. In the morning there was a white mist and by and by the sun shone out. The horses neighed, the birds awoke and sang as they hopped from branch to branch, the happy larks flew upwards and sang from above into the red glimmering world.

Peter also sang cheerful songs. The two travellers saw in the glowing sky, in the brightness of the fresh forest, a reflection of their love. The sun mounted higher, and towards noon Magelone felt a great weariness. They dismounted, therefore, at a cool, shady place in the forest where there was a mound thickly covered with moss and tender grass. Here Peter sat down and spread out his mantle, and Magelone placed herself upon it, resting her head on the knight. She told Peter how happy she was, and begged him to sing to her, to mingle his voice with the birds, the trees, the brooks, in order that she might sleep a little : But wake me at the right time in order that we may soon arrive at the home of your dear parents. Peter smiled, watched her beautiful eyes close, and sang:

> Rest thee, sweet love, in the shadow
> Of leafy, glimmering night;
> The grass rustles over the meadow,
> Refreshing and cool is the shadow,
> And love holds thee in sight.
>   Sleep, lady mine,
>   Hush'd in woodland shrine,
>   Ever I am thine, etc.

APPENDICES. 317

Peter almost sang himself to sleep also. Then something roused him. He looked round and saw a number of beautiful, tender birds on the mound, and it pleased him that they came so near to Magelone. But a slight noise caused him to turn again, and he was startled to perceive a great black raven perched on the branch of the tree behind him; it seemed to him like a rough, coarse churl amongst noble knights.

He fancied that Magelone breathed with some uneasiness, and unlaced the neck of her dress. There he found a little red silk bag; it was new, and he was curious to know what was in it and turned it out. He was overjoyed to find that it contained his three precious rings, and quickly wrapped them up again and placed them beside him on the grass. But suddenly the raven flew down from the tree and carried away the bag, perhaps taking it for a piece of meat. Peter was frightened. Magelone might awaken and be displeased at losing her rings. He therefore folded his mantle and placed it carefully under her head, and then stood up to look for the raven. It flew away, and Peter followed and threw stones to make it drop the bag, but was unable to hit it. As it flew further and further he went after it, without noticing that he was already some distance from the spot where he had left Magelone sleeping, till presently he came to the sea. There was a pointed crag not far from the shore and the raven perched there, and Peter again threw stones. At last the bird dropped the bag and flew away screaming. Peter saw the bag floating in the sea close by and ran up and down to find something to help him into the water. He found an old weather-beaten boat left behind by fishermen as useless, and jumped into it and tried to steer towards the bag. Suddenly a strong wind blew from the land, the waves rose, and in spite of all Peter could do, the boat was carried past the crag and further and further from the shore. The bag was fast disappearing from sight; now it was only like a red spot in the distance, the land receded. Peter cried and lamented loudly, but without avail. His tones were echoed back mingled with the sound of the waves. He thought of Magelone sleeping in the wood, and wished to drown himself in his despair. Presently the sun shone out, and now he was seized with a terrible thirst which he was unable to quench. At length evening began to fall: Ah, dearest Magelone, he thought, how strangely have we been parted! The moon filled the world with golden twilight; stars appeared in heaven, and the firmament was mirrored in the waving water. All was still and only the waves

splashed, and birds fluttered over him from time to time, filling the
air with strange tones. At last Peter lay down in the boat and sang
loudly:

> Foam on then in furious raging,
> Surround me, tempestuous waves,
> Relentless thy forces engaging,
> For death is the boon that love craves, etc.

The sequel may be summarised. Magelone, on awakening and
finding herself alone, waits vainly for Peter's return, and at length,
as night comes on, climbs a tree to be safe from the wild beasts
which she fancies she hears in the distance. In the morning she
loosens the horses which Peter had tied to a tree and lets them go
their own way, and after a little while finds herself on the road to
Rome, where she makes an exchange of dress with a passing pilgrim.
Making her way first to Rome and thence to Genoa, she takes ship
for Provence, where she thinks she may hear something of Peter.
She is sheltered on her arrival there by a kind woman who talks to
her about the good Count and Countess of Provence and of their
great grief. They have heard nothing of their only son since his
departure two years ago in quest of adventure. Magelone now
knows that some sad mishap has befallen Peter, and that he had
not intended to leave her. She resolves to remain unmarried,
think of Peter, and dedicate her life to the service of God. The
kind woman with whom she is staying tells her of a small island
near "the port of the heathen," where all merchant ships and other
vessels call in passing and where many poor and sick folk are to be
found. Here she resolves to settle. She builds a small church, the
altar of which is raised to the honour of St. Peter, and calls it
the Church of St. Pierre de Maguelonne. The fame of her strict
life and good deeds reaches the ears of the Count and Countess of
Provence, who go to see her, and the countess, not knowing who
she is, relates the history of her troubles. Magelone comforts her
and inspires her with the hope that Peter will return. Some time
afterwards the count's cook finds a small red bag in the belly of a
great fish which he has cut open. He runs with it to the countess,
who finds that it contains her three precious rings. This wonderful
event convinces her that she will see her son again.

Tieck's version of Magelone's adventure is that, after untying the
horses and wandering alone for some days till she comes to Provence,
she finds shelter in a shepherd's hut, where she sings the song No. 11
of Brahms' cycle:

APPENDICES. 319

> Not long enduring,
> Light goes by;
> The morning seeth
> The chaplet dry
> That yesterday blossomed
> In splendour bright,
> But drooped and withered
> In gloom of night, etc.

Peter's adventures are various. Rousing himself from his despair on the morning after his separation from Magelone, he resolves to bear the anguish as well as the joy of life with manly courage. Soon a big pirate ship sails towards him. It is full of Moors and heathen who take him on board, and who, struck with his youth and glorious manhood, determine to carry him as a present to the Sultan of Babylon. The Sultan is pleased with Peter and shows him high favour. He puts him in charge of a beautiful garden and lets him wait on him at table.

So far Tieck is faithful to the old story, only introducing the song (No. 12 of Brahms' work) which Peter sings as he walks in the garden thinking sadly of Magelone:

> Are we, then, for ever parted?
> Was our true love all in vain?
> Why must we live broken-hearted?
> Death were surely lesser pain, etc.

From this point the versions differ. In the mediaeval romance, Peter, who, though beloved by everyone in the Sultan's palace, and especially by the Sultan himself, is very unhappy, at length persuades his master to let him go and see his parents, and after adventures on the way, is recognised by Magelone in one of the beds of her hospital to which he has been brought almost lifeless.

Tieck, who does not localise the Sultan, introduces into the story his beautiful daughter Sulima, who falls violently in love with Peter and has him secretly introduced to her presence by a confidential slave. Peter, greatly surprised and embarrassed, is astonished at her beauty, but his heart holds fast to Magelone. He longs to see his native land again, to be amongst christians and with his parents. He often sees Sulima, who observes his unhappiness and one day offers to fly with him in a ship that is already standing in the harbour with sails filled. She will give him a sign for a certain evening; when he hears a little song he likes in the garden, he is to come and fetch her. Peter, after considering the proposal, decides to accept it. He believes Magelone to be dead, and thinks that he will thus be enabled to return to a christian land and to his parents.

On the appointed night he walks up and down the Sultan's garden by the shore. At length he sleeps, and dreams that Magelone is looking at him threateningly. On awaking, he walks up and down again, reproaching himself, and at last resolves to throw himself into a little boat and cast out to sea alone. It is a lovely summer night, a warm breeze is stirring, and Peter gives himself up to chance and the stars. Then he hears the sign. A zither sounds, and a sweet voice sings:

> Belovèd, where dwelleth
> Thy footstep this night?
> The nightingale telleth
> Its tale of delight, etc.

Peter's heart shrinks within him as he hears the song; it seems to call after him his weakness and vacillation. He rows more swiftly; love urges him backwards, love draws him onward. The music becomes fainter and fainter; now it is quite lost in the distance, and only the murmur of the waves and the stroke of the oar sound through the stillness.

Peter gathers heart when the sound of the song no longer reaches him, and lets the little vessel drift before the wind as he sits down and sings:

> Fresh courage on my spirit breaks
> And fading is my sadness;
> New life within me reawakes
> Old longing and old gladness, etc.

Tieck preserves the further adventures of the romance, but brings the knight to Magelone as she sits spinning outside the door of the shepherd's hut. The song of their reunion is the fifteenth and last of Brahms' cycle:

> Faithful love long time endureth,
> Many an hour it doth survive,
> And from sorrow strength secureth,
> And from doubt doth faith derive.

II.

THE HAMBURG LADIES' CHOIR.*

Avertimento.

Sondern weilen es absolute dem Plaisire fördersam ist, wenn es fein ordentlich dabei einhergeht, als wird denen curieusen Gemüthern, so Mitglieder des sehr nuss- und lieblichen Frauenchors wünschen zu werden und zu bleiben jetzund kund und offenbar gethan, dass sie partoute die Clausuln und Puncti hiefolgenden Geschreibsels unter zu zeichnen haben ehe sie sich obgenannten Tituls erfreuen und an der musikalischen Erlustigung und Divertirung parte nehmen können.

Ich hätte zwaren schon längst damit unter der Bank herfür wischen sollen, alleine aberst dennoch, weilen der Frühling erst lieblich präambuliret und bis der Sommer finiret, gesungen werden dürfte, als möchte es noch an der Zeit sein dieses Opus an das Tageslicht zu stellen.

Pro primo wäre zu remarquiren dass die Mitglieder des Frauenchors da sein müssen.

Als wird verstanden: dass sie sich obligiren sollen, den Stehungen und Singungen der Societät regelmässig beizuwohnen.

So nun Jemand diesen Articul nicht gehörig observiret und, wo Gott für sei, der Fall passirete, dass Jemand wider jedes Decorum so fehlete, dass er während eines Exercitiums ganz fehlete:
soll gestraft werden mit einer Busse von 8 Schillingen H. C. [Hamburger Courant].

Pro secundo ist zu beachten, dass die Mitglieder des Frauenchors da sein müssen.

Als ist zu nehmen, sie sollen praecise zur anberaumten Zeit da sein.

Wer nun hiewieder also sündiget, dass er das ganze Viertheil einer Stunde zu spät der Societät seine schuldige Reverentz und Aufwartung machet, soll um 2 Schillinge H. C. gestrafet werden.

|: Ihrer grossen Meriten um den Frauenchor wegen und in Betracht ihrer vermuthlich höchst mangelhaften und unglücklichen Complexion, soll nun hier für die nicht genug zu favorirende und adorirende Demoiselle Laura Garbe ein Abonnement hergestellt

---

* From "Brahms in Hamburg," by Walter Hübbe. See p. 274 of this narrative.

werden, wesmassen sie nicht jedesmal zu bezahlen braucht, sondern aber ihro am Schluss des Quartals eine moderirte Rechnung praesentiret wird:|

Pro tertio : Das einkommende Geld mag denen Bettelleuten gegeben werden und wird gewünscht dass Niemand davon gesättiget werden möge.

Pro quarto ist zu merken, dass die Musikalien grossentheils der Discretion der Dames anvertrauet sind. Derohalben sollen sie wie fremdes Eigenthum von den ehr- und tugendsamen Jungfrauen und Frauen in rechter Lieb und aller Hübschheit gehalten werden, auch in keinerlei Weise ausserhalb der Societät benüsset werden.

Pro quinto: Was nicht mit singen kann, das sehen wir als ein Neutrum an. Will heissen: Zuhörer werden geduldet indessen aber pro ordinario nicht beachtet, was Gestalt sonsten die rechte Nussbarkeit der Exercitia nicht beschaffet werden möchte.

Obgemeldeter gehörig specifizirter Erlass wird durch gegenwärtiges General-Rescript anjesso jeder männiglich public gemacht und soll in Würden gehalten werden, bis der Frauenchor seine Endschaft erreichet hat.

Solltest du nun nicht nur vor dich ohnverbrüchlich darob halten, sondern auch alles Ernstes daran sein, dass andere auf keinerlei Weise noch Wege darwider thun noch handeln mögen.

An dem beschiehet Unsere Meinung und erwarte dero gewünschte und wohlgewogene Approbation.

Der ich verharre in tiefster Devotion
und Veneration des Frauenchors allzeit dienstbeflissener
schreibfertiger und taktfester

Johannes Kreisler jun.
alias : Brahms.

Geben auf Montag
den 30ten des Monats Aprili.
A. D. 1860.

Professor Hübbe adds:

"It must be said in explanation of the jesting note to section 2 that the Demoiselle Garbe mentioned in it was often prevented from being punctual, and that Brahms was unwilling to begin without her. The exception at first taken by her to the note in question was met most kindly by Frau Schumann, who pointed out that the special mention of her name in the highly important document would be the very means of securing its lasting fame.

APPENDICES.   323

"The 'begging people' of section 3 saw nothing, as I am told, of the money collected by the fines, which was used for other purposes —on one occasion for an excursion to Reinbeck.

"One of the ladies' copies still in existence bears the following signatures: Auguste Brandt, Bertha Porubszky, Laura Garbe, Marie Seebohm, Emilie Lentz, Clara Schumann, Julie Hallier, Marie Hallier, Ch. Avé Lallement, Friedchen Wagner, Thusnelde Wagner, M. Reuter, Betty Völckers, Marie Völckers, Henny Gabain, Marie Böhme, Francisca Meier, Camilla Meier, Susanne Schmaltz, Antonie Mertens (Emma Grädener)."

The metal badge which the members had to wear was no doubt adopted at this time (1860). It had the form of a trefoil clover leaf with a circle in the centre. This displayed a B upon red, and the three surrounding parts of the trefoil, the letters H. F. C. upon blue ground.

THE LIFE OF JOHANNES BRAHMS

VOLUME II

BRAHMS AT THE AGE OF THIRTY.
By permission of Mr. E. Howard-Jones.

THE LIFE
OF
JOHANNES BRAHMS

BY
FLORENCE MAY

Second Edition revised by the Author, with
Additional Matter and Illustrations, and an
Introduction by Ralph Hill

IN TWO VOLUMES. VOL. II

WILLIAM REEVES   83 CHARING CROSS ROAD,
BOOKSELLER LIMITED   — LONDON, W.C.2. —

Printed by The New Temple Press, London, S.W.16, Great Britain.

THE
LIFE OF JOHANNES BRAHMS

CHAPTER XII.

1862-1864.

Vienna—Musical societies—Leading musicians—The Prater—Brahms' appearance at a Hellmesberger Quartet concert—Brahms' first concert in Vienna—Conductorship of the Hamburg Philharmonic —First Serenade at Gesellschaft concert—Brahms' second concert—Richard Wagner—Second Serenade at Vienna Philharmonic concert—Return to Hamburg—Brahms elected conductor of the Vienna Singakademie—Return to Vienna—Singakademie concerts under Brahms.

IT would be interesting, on accompanying Johannes Brahms in imagination on his first visit to Vienna—a visit that was to lead to results scarcely less important to his career than those of the first concert-journey through the provincial towns of Hanover undertaken nine years and a half previously—to describe the gradual change which had taken place in the musical life of the imperial city since the times when it had counted Haydn, Mozart and Beethoven in turn among its inhabitants. It would, however, lead too far from the purpose of this narrative to follow the course by which the art of music, from being a luxury to be enjoyed chiefly by the rich—and in Vienna, perhaps, especially amongst the great capitals of Europe—had been opened to the cultivation of the masses of citizens. Suffice it to say that in the autumn of 1862 the conditions of musical activity in the Austrian capital were essentially the same as we know them in 1905.

The Court Opera, the home of which was the Kärnthnerthor Theater, was conducted by Otto Dessoff, who had been a distinguished pupil of the Leipzig Conservatoire, and had succeeded the celebrated capellmeister, Carl Anton Eckert, on his resignation of the post in 1860. In intimate though not official connection with the opera were the Philharmonic concerts given in the same building. These, started in 1849 by the orchestral musicians of the opera as their own undertaking, had, after a period of varying fortune, entered upon a flourishing phase of existence. They were conducted by Dessoff in virtue of his position as capellmeister of the opera, and though his rather cold style at first prevented his winning Austrian sympathy, he by-and-by succeeded in making good his footing by his musicianship and thoroughness, and by the perfect finish of rendering that was attained by the orchestra under his direction.

The annual orchestral concerts given by the great Gesellschaft der Musikfreunde founded in 1813, took place in the Redoubtensaal, and, though given under the society's own "artistic director" had, during the eight or nine years preceding the appointment of Johann Herbeck to this post 1859), been dependent on the services of the opera orchestra. Herbeck, feeling the inconveniences of such an arrangement, determined to form an orchestra of his own, and, whilst successfully carrying out his project, sought to make amends for the first inevitable lack of complete finish in his performances by cultivating a liberal spirit in the choice of programmes, and introducing from time to time unfamiliar works by the best modern classical composers. From this period the Gesellschaft and the Philharmonic concerts came more or less to represent severally the liberal and the conservative spirit of classical art, though it must be added that Dessoff cherished the wish to educate his audience to wider powers of appreciation, and sometimes included the name of Schumann in the Philharmonic programmes, which, before his advent, had been closed to works of more modern tendency than those of Mendelssohn.

Parallel with these two institutions for the performance of instrumental music were two choral societies, both supplied by amateurs. The Singverein, a branch of the Gesellschaft der Musikfreunde, which in 1862 was, like the orchestra, under Herbeck's direction, occupied itself with every kind of classical choral music in turn, and occasionally giving concerts independently, often joined forces in public performance with the orchestra. The Singakademie, founded in 1858 by a circle of amateurs, made a special point of early church music, and of *a capella* singing, but usually devoted one of its three or four annual concerts to the performance of an oratorio or other great work, when, of course, the services of an orchestra were engaged. Under the direction of its first conductor, F. Stegmayer, the Singakademie gave the first performance in Vienna of portions of Schumann's "Faust" (January 6, 1861) and of Bach's "Matthew Passion" (April 15, 1862).

Occupying a position in Vienna at the very top of his profession, partly in virtue of the musical prestige attaching to his family name, but mainly as the result of his personal gifts and attainments, was the violinist Josef Hellmesberger, director and professor of the conservatoire (itself another branch of the great Gesellschaft der Musikfreunde), concertmeister of the opera, and therefore also of the Philharmonic concerts, late artistic director of the Gesellschaft (1851-1859), leader of the only resident and justly celebrated string quartet party called by his name, and accomplished virtuoso. Hellmesberger's playing lacked broadness of tone, but was distinguished by grace, poetic sentiment and a facile instinct for his composer's intention. He possessed a good knowledge of the orchestra, and was a fair pianist.

Of other musicians resident in the Austrian capital in 1862 are to be mentioned the great contrapuntist Sechter, nearly approaching the end of his career, who, in his position of professor of composition at the conservatoire, had in his time taught several of the younger men next to be referred to; Nottebohm, professor of counterpoint at the conservatoire, known to the world by his writings on music, especially those on Beethoven's sketch-books; Rudolph Bibl, organist of the cathedral, and later, of the imperial chapel; Julius Epstein, professor of the pianoforte at the conservatoire, distinguished pianist and widely reputed teacher, and esteemed, not only on account of his professional standing, but also by reason of his kindness to all persons having any sort of claim on his courtesy.

The composer Carl Goldmark, who has since attained European reputation, had been almost entirely resident in Vienna since his sixteenth year, and now at thirty was rising to fame. Peter Cornelius, composer of the comic opera, "The Barber of Bagdad," and already mentioned in our narrative as a disciple of Weimar, was living at this time in the Austrian capital. Anton Brückner was favourably esteemed by some of the first resident musicians, though he had not yet been called there. Carl Tausig, one of the greatest of pianoforte virtuosi, whose sympathies were much with the New-Germans, settled in Vienna for a few years from 1861, and gave occasional concerts there which were but partially successful.

Of writers and critics, Edward Hanslick, Carl Ferdinand Pohl and Selmar Bagge, all believers in the art of tradition and in its modern development as represented by the name of Schumann, were in the flower of their activity. Bagge's name is interesting in the history of Brahms' career on account of the sympathetic and detailed reviews of the composer's works which appeared from time to time in the *Deutsche Musikzeitung*, a paper founded by him in 1860. It became defunct at the close of 1863, when Bagge left Vienna to take up the editorship of the *Allgemeine Musikzeitung*, which he retained for two years. Very able articles were published in this periodical of Brahms' works as they appeared, some of them written by Bagge himself, and others by Hermann Deiters, a musical scholar and critic of exceptional insight and power of happy expression. Bagge remained just long enough in Vienna to witness the interest aroused by Brahms' first appearances there, to which, very likely, the remembrance of the articles of the *Deutsche Musikzeitung* gave additional stimulus.

Of publishers, the name of C. A. Spina should be gratefully remembered as that of the man to whom the world is indebted for the publication of many great and long neglected works of Schubert. A large number of the master's half-forgotten manuscripts—those of the Octet, the C major Quartet, the B flat and B minor Symphonies amongst them —were found by Spina when he took over the business of his predecessors, the firm of Diabelli, and were gradually placed by him in the possession of the world.

On his arrival in Vienna, Brahms put up at the Hôtel Kronprinz in the Leopoldstadt, moving soon afterwards into a room at 39, Novaragasse, of the same inexpensive quarter, then called the Jägerzeil. Several of his old friends were fortunately at hand. Grädener had given up his position in Hamburg the preceding year to try his fortune in Vienna; Frau Passy-Cornet, whose name calls the concert of 1848 to remembrance, was now a professor of singing at the Vienna Conservatoire; and Fräulein Berta Porubszky, lately engaged to be married to Mr. Arthur Faber, was charmed to introduce the former conductor of the wellremembered Hamburg singing society to her family and fiancé. After their wedding, which took place in the autumn, the Fabers' house was open to Johannes who spent many, and especially Sunday evenings there, and on such occasions he was wont to play one after another of his compositions as he could play them when quietly at ease with a few sympathetic friends for his audience.

From the first he felt at home in Vienna. The good natured, easy-going Austrian people attracted him, and he at once conceived an affection for the Prater, in the immediate vicinity of which his hotel was situated. This great park of the Kaiserstadt contains, indeed, attractions to suit every variety of taste. There is the Hauptallée, with its broad drive and shady walks, its open-air cafés and music of military bands, which play waltzes and various dance movements as they are played in no other city. There is the Würstelprater, the playground of children and other simple folk, where, in the fine weather season, a continual fair goes on with shows and games and entertainments of every kind likely to attract the patronage of the multitude, and where in the Hungarian restaurant, the "Czarda," real gipsy music played by a real gipsy band, may daily be heard. There is the wild portion, bounded on one side by the Danube canal and stretching for some little distance beyond the town, where the solitary walker may fancy himself in a forest far from human habitation. Brahms, on this occasion of his first visit to Vienna, particularly attached himself to the Würstelprater, for which he ever after retained his partiality. The motley life to be seen there amused and interested him. He came to be a frequent listener at the "Czarda," and it is whispered that the spirit of fun has occasionally prompted him, when at the height of his fame, to prevail upon a party of friends to take a turn in his company on the curvetting horses of one or other of the "carrousels" which are amongst the most popular attractions of this part of the grounds.

One of Brahms' first visits was to Julius Epstein. He did not send in his name, and as the professor was engaged with someone else at the moment, was not admitted. A second call was successful. "My name is Johannes Brahms," he said as he entered; and his simple manner at once attracted Epstein, who was well acquainted with his published works. An opportunity was arranged without delay for his introduction to some of the leading musicians of the city.

"Brahms in 1862 played the Quartets in G minor and A major with the members of the Hellmesberger Quartet

(Hellmesberger, Dobyhal and Röver) at my house in the Schulerstrasse, in the first place," writes Professor Epstein to the author. "We were all delighted and carried away. The works were shortly afterwards played in public by Brahms with the same colleagues."

The G minor Quartet was, in fact, included in the list of works announced by Hellmesberger for the ensuing season, and the immediate interest awakened in musical circles by the arrival of the composer is even more strikingly testified by the fact that on October 14, only five weeks after his departure from Hamburg, the name of the orchestral Serenade in D major appeared in the forecast of the Gesellschaft season published in the *Blätter für Theater, Kunst und Musik*.

On Sunday evening, November 16, Brahms made his first appearance before his new public at Hellmesberger's Quartet concert, which took place, as usual, in the Vereinsaal (the concert-room of the Gesellschaft der Musikfreunde) before an audience that crowded every part of the house in anticipation of the debut in Vienna of "Schumann's young prophet." The first and last numbers of the programme of three works were severally Mendelssohn's String Quartet in E flat and Beethoven's in C sharp minor, Op. 131, Brahms' G minor Pianoforte Quartet occupying the place of honour between them. If we were to judge of the result by the press reviews of the day, which were either unfavourable or reserved, it would be impossible to chronicle a success, and yet that the work was essentially successful is established by the fact that the composer received overtures after the concert from more than one Vienna publisher, which, however, he declined. He had certainly made his mark in his own characteristic way even before the 16th. A private circle of admirers began to form round him, and he was persuaded to venture on a concert of his own, which took place in the Vereinsaal on November 29.

On this occasion the Pianoforte Quartet in A major headed the programme, the composer being assisted in its performance by the three members of the Hellmesberger party with whom he had already appeared. The remaining instrumental numbers were pianoforte solos, the concert-giver's Handel Variations and Fugue, Bach's F major Toccata for organ, and Schumann's C major Fantasia, Op. 17.

As regards the general audience, the concert was an unmistakable success. The room was fairly filled, and enough money taken to cover expenses. This, however, by the way. The circumstance most worthy of record is that artist and public found themselves *en rapport*. The performer had the infallible instinct of having with him the sympathy of his hearers, and played his best, giving out what was really in him as he had probably never been able to do before his indifferent or sceptical audiences in Germany. A friendly reception was accorded to the quartet, which was followed with close attention. Enthusiasm could scarcely have been looked for on a first hearing of so original a work. The variations and fugue, however, called forth a storm of applause that was renewed after the performance of Schumann's fantasia, the divine last movement of which was given with ideal insight and noble inspiration. The press notices, though respectful, were disappointing in regard to Brahms the composer.

"The quartet by no means pleased us, and we are glad that the unfavourable impression it created was obliterated by the variations which followed. . . ." Hanslick wrote *(die Presse)*. "Brahms' talent has hitherto been displayed at its best in variation form, which requires, above all, facility in inventing figures, and unity of mood. . . . The unsatisfactory features of his creative style are more apparent in the quartet. In the first place the subjects have not enough significance. The composer chooses themes rather with a view to their capacity for contrapuntal treatment than on account of their intrinsic merit, and those of the quartet sound dry and flat. . . . The quartet and others of the composer's works remind us of Schumann's last period; the early works of his first period; but none of Brahms' yet known compositions can take their place beside those of Schumann's ripe middle period."

As a pianist, Brahms was mentioned in the papers in more decided terms of appreciation. Bagge says:

"We have to bestow high praise not only on the enormous technical acquirement, but also on a performance instinct with musical genius, on a treatment of the instrument as fascinating as it was original."

The playing of Bach's organ toccata is especially mentioned in terms of high admiration; the touch employed for the passages written for the pedals "gave the pianoforte the effect of an organ." The performance of each number was musical through and through, and although "he has not the unfailing certainty nor the outward brilliancy of the virtuoso, he reaches and fascinates his audience by other means."

The delightful natural letter to his parents, published by Reimann, written after the concert, shows the pleasure derived by Brahms from feeling his audience in sympathy with him:

"DEAR PARENTS,
    "I was very happy yesterday, my concert went quite excellently, much better than I had hoped.
    "After the quartet had been sympathetically received, I had great success as a player. Every number was greatly applauded, I think there was real enthusiasm in the room.
    "Now I could very well give concerts, but I do not wish to do so, for it takes up too much time so that I can do nothing else. . . .
    "I played as freely as though I were sitting at home with friends; one is certainly influenced quite differently by the public than by ours.
    "You should have seen the attention and seen and heard the applause. . . . I am very glad I gave the concert. You are probably rid of your guests again now and will be able to find a moment of time to write to me.
    "Tell the contents of this letter to Herr Marxsen and say

also that Bösendorfer* will not be able to send a piano before the New Year as so many are required for concerts. Shall I see about another for him? I await orders. . . .

"I think my serenade will be given next Monday.

"I should have liked to introduce some of my vocal things in my concert yesterday, but it gave me a terrible amount of running about and unpleasantness and that is one of my reasons for wishing to be quiet now.†

"Did you sit together on Wednesday over the egg-punch? Write to me about it and anything else.‡

"The publishers here, especially Spina and Levi, have been pressing me for things since the quartet, but much pleases me better in North Germany and particularly the publishers, and I would rather go without the two or three extra Louis-d'ors that these would perhaps pay.

"Does Avé often go to see you? Has he told you anything particular about Stockhausen?

"How about the photograph of the girls' quartet? Am I not to have it? N.B. Every time I write I forget to ask about Fritz. . . . Is he very industrious? He ought to make up his mind to give Trio concerts in Hamburg next winter. I would help him in every way. . . .

"Write soon and have love
"from your
"JOHANNES.

"Hearty greetings to Herr Marxsen, and do not forget about Bösendorfer."§

The two Pianoforte Quartets were despatched to Simrock, and were published by the firm early in 1863—the first one

---

* Head of the celebrated Vienna firm of pianoforte makers.

† The *Deutsche Musikzeitung* of November 29, the very day of the concert, announces vocal duets and choruses by Brahms as part of the programme. The review of the concert in the same paper concludes: "Frau Passy-Cornet and Herr Fürchtgott assisted the concert-giver, whose programme was altered, by performing songs and ballads."

‡ Egg-punch was a birthday institution in the family. The Wednesday in question was probably the birthday of Brahms' mother.

§ Reimann's "Johannes Brahms." Published in facsimile opposite page 28.

in G minor, being dedicated to Baron Reinhard von Dalwigk, Court Intendant to the Grand Duke of Oldenburg, a really musical amateur and a warm supporter of Brahms; and the second, in A major, to Frau Dr. Elisabeth Rösing of Hamm, in whose house it was written.

The tone of the above extracts tells how lovingly the composer's thoughts turned to his home at the moment he was feeling conscious of a real success; and the question about Stockhausen may be taken as an indication of the clinging wistfulness with which he was bringing himself to resign the hope of being able to settle near his family as conductor of the Philharmonic—a position he would at the time have been proud to accept. The decision of the committee was now a foregone conclusion, though it was not made public till the following year. What it was may be told in the following extract from a letter written to Avé Lallement on January 31, 1863, by Joachim, whose influence with the committee had been energetically exerted in favour of his Johannes:

". . . What can I say further about your plan with Stockhausen? You know how highly I esteem his talent, and he is certainly the best musician among the singers, but how anyone, having to choose the director of a concert institution between him and Johannes, can decide for the former, I, with my limited musical understanding, cannot comprehend! It is precisely as a man upon whom one can rely that I regard Johannes so highly, with his gifts and his will! There is nothing he cannot undertake, and, with his earnestness, overcome! You know that as well as I, and if all of you in the committee and orchestra had met him with confidence and affection (as you, his friend, always do in private) instead of with doubt and airs of protection, it would have removed the asperity from his nature; whereas it must constantly make him more bitter, with his touching, almost childlike patriotism for Hamburg, to see himself put second. I dare not dwell on the thought, it would make me too unhappy, that his narrow compatriots have deprived themselves of the means of making him more contented and gentle, and happier in the exercise of his genius. I should like to give the committee a moral cudgelling (and a bodily one too!) for having left you in the lurch with your plan. The slight to Johannes will not be forgotten in the history of art! But basta!"*

To the advertisement of the Hamburg Philharmonic programme of March 6, 1863, the words were added: "Herr Julius Stockhausen has kindly undertaken to conduct the second and third numbers"; and a fortnight later Stockhausen's appointment as capellmeister to the society for the following season, 1863-4, was announced.

Meanwhile Johannes in Vienna may still, in the beginning of November, 1862, have clung to hope in view of the forthcoming performance of his serenade at the Gesellschaft concert of the 14th under Herbeck. The reception of the work proved, in fact, as favourable as might reasonably have been expected. It was listened to with respect by public and critics, and some of its parts, notably the first minuet, were greeted with manifestations of decided approval.

"The serenade, a fine, interesting and intellectual work, deserved warmer acknowledgment," wrote Speidel in the *Wiener Zeitung*. Hanslick, in the *Presse*, pronounced it one of the most charming of modern orchestral compositions, but took exception to the first subject of the opening movement, as he had objected to that of the A major Quartet, as being workable rather than original or significant.

"The first minuet seems to us the pearl of the work and perhaps the prettiest movement as yet written by Brahms. The instrumental colouring and the grace of the melody give it the characteristic of night music, and it is full of moonlight and the scent of lilac."

A remarkable review—remarkable from its admirable appreciation of Brahms' creative personality—was despatched to Leipzig by the Vienna correspondent of the *Neue Zeitschrift*, who signs himself "S.," and appeared in the Vienna résumé contained in the paper's issue of March 23:

---

* Moser's "Joseph Joachim," page 177.

"As regards Brahms' serenade which has been favourably received, albeit in my opinion too severely criticised, only thus much; it is one of the most charming examples, not only of the class of composition from which it has sprung, but of all that has followed Beethoven up to the comprehensive conquests, as to contents and form, of the rising New Germany.

"It is fresh and rich in themes of which nearly every one is pervaded by a rare grace, and a brightness of tone becoming every day more unusual. The score convincingly exhibits, moreover, one of the most prominent sides of Brahms' musical individuality. I would call this a power of re-fashioning, in the best spirit of the present day, the contrapuntal forms of canon and fugue and of their degenerate and inferior representatives. Brahms succeeds in this, as in the majority of his works, in reconsecrating and carrying on the spiritual treasure inherited from Bach, Beethoven and Schumann, in the light of modernity. This fundamental characteristic is still more striking in a second great work of the composer, for the hearing of which opportunity is promised. I will therefore go on to remark on the orchestral colouring of the serenade, which, without being exaggerated, is, throughout, fresh and significant of youthful power. I should find it very difficult to express a preference for either of the six movements, whilst to speak of either of the several parts of this, in its way, masterly whole as inferior in excellence to others, appears to me utterly impossible. The *vox populi*, however, with which the principal journals here coincide on this occasion, has pronounced in favour of the first minuet and the certainly wonderfully tender slow movement."

Brahms appeared on December 20 at Frau Passy-Cornet's concert in the Vereinsaal, playing Beethoven's E flat Sonata for pianoforte and violin with Hellmesberger, and some Schumann solos (Romance and Novelette), and, in spite of his frequently avowed distaste for public appearances, gave a second concert on January 6, 1863, in order to bring forward some of his songs. On this occasion he played Bach's Chromatic Fantasia, Beethoven's C minor Variations, his own Sonata in F minor, Op. 5, and Schumann's Sonata in the same key, Op. 14, with omission of the scherzo.

"Brahms' playing," wrote the Vienna correspondent of the *Signale*, "is always attractive and convincing. His rendering of Bach's Chromatic Fantasia and of Beethoven's Variations was of the highest interest. . . . After repeated recalls Brahms treated his audience to another piece, a four-hand march by Schubert arranged for two hands. The delightful freshness of this composition gave no little pleasure."

Frau Wilt, one of the first resident singers, performed several of the concert-giver's songs, amongst them being "Treue Liebe" (Op. 7, No. 1), "Parole" (Op. 7, No. 2), and "Liebestreue" ("O versenk," Op. 3, No. 1).

"This new experience was most agreeable and welcome to the whole public. All these songs breathe a fine sensibility, and are full of truth to life and nature."

This second concert, indeed, stamped Brahms' visit to Vienna with the seal of decisive and permanent success—a success not immediately wide or popular, but which marked the beginning of a new epoch in the musical life of the city. Though he could not stoop to the attempt to dazzle his public by phenomenal feats of virtuosity, the grace, tenderness and truth of his musical nature appealed to his southern audience, whilst the significance of his genius dawned on the perception of one or two discerning musicians. In a word, he had found a public which partially understood him; and a performance of the second serenade was announced for one of the Philharmonic concerts.

Before the opening of the New Year, musical attention in Vienna was turned to Richard Wagner, who conducted three concerts devoted to selections from his own compositions, and was received and discussed with the extremes of enthusiasm and disapproval that usually attended his appearances and the early productions of his works.

"I shall probably be called a Wagnerian," wrote Johannes to Joachim, "but it will, of course, be chiefly owing to the spirit of contradiction that cannot but be excited in a sensible man by the frivolous way in which the musicians here talk against him."

Wagner mentions in his autobiography that Brahms, as Tausig's friend, undertook to assist in the work of copying the orchestral parts of the selections chosen for performance at the three Vienna concerts, and implies that Brahms was not infrequently present at the social gatherings that took place during this time, at his temporary residence in the suburb of Penzing. On one of these occasions, as we learn from another source, Brahms played some Bach pieces, and by special request, his own Handel variations, which were cordially received by the host.* But though Brahms spoke to his Vienna friends of the pleasure he had found in Wagner's society, there was no future personal intercourse between the two composers who were too widely separated by disposition, tastes and artistic faith, to grow into friendship. It should, however, never be forgotten that Brahms felt, from first to last, immense respect for Wagner's gifts and achievement.

One of our composer's engrossing occupations during his nearly eight months' stay in Vienna was the study of Schubert's manuscripts, which Spina was delighted to show him, generously allowing him to copy from them for his own pleasure as he felt inclined. Shortly before his return home he sent some of the treasures thus obtained for Dietrich's perusal.

". . . It occurs to me that I can send you my Marienlieder and Variations for four hands which arrived lately, and I enclose with them some extracts from an Easter cantata of Schubert's which I copied from the manuscript. They are not specially selected portions of Lazarus. By no means; I merely wrote the beginning and end of the first part. The music is as fine throughout; Simon's aria—oh, if I could send you the whole, you would be enchanted with such loveliness! . . ."†

---

* See first Kalbeck II, 114-17.

† Extracts copied by Brahms from the original score of Schubert's "Lazarus" are preserved in the library of the Vienna Gesellschaft der Musikfreunde.

He decides to send in the same parcel, for Albert's inspection, the string quintet which he had taken to Vienna to get quite to his liking.

The second Serenade was announced for the Philharmonic concert of March 8 as the opening number of the programme, to be followed by Joachim's Hungarian Concerto, with Laub as solo violinist, and this by a new symphony by M. Kässmeyer—an astonishingly progressive list, which was due to Dessoff's influence and was approvingly remarked upon by Hanslick in his review of the 11th of the month. Meanwhile difficulties presented themselves.* The discontent of the members of the orchestra was apparent during the first rehearsals of Brahms' work; complaints were heard of the great difficulty of performing many of the passages, and at the general rehearsal open mutiny broke out. The first clarinettist suddenly rose, and, in the name of the body of instrumentalists, declared their refusal to perform the composition. Dessoff, white with agitation, instantly replied by laying down his baton and announcing his resignation of the post of conductor; Hellmesberger, as concertmeister, followed suit, and the first flutist, Franz Doppler, a celebrated performer, joined them. This decided matters. The malcontents gave way, the rehearsal proceeded, and the performance on the 8th was so greatly appreciated by the public that R. Hirsch, who made his debut as Brahms' critic in the *Wiener Zeitung* in connection with the occasion, and who for many years systematically (and perhaps conscientiously) decried his works, could find nothing worse to say than that the serenade would find many friends amongst those able to content themselves with modest gifts.

"Brahms should be on his guard against excess of things.

---

* "Brahms Erinnerungen," by Franz Fribberg (*Berliner Tageblatt*, December 18, 1898).

N.B.—Fribberg was a member of the Philharmonic orchestra of Vienna at the period in question.

The exorbitant applause raised by his friends had the effect of procuring him very loud hisses from other parties."

"If either of the younger composers has the right not to be ignored, it is Brahms," wrote Hanslick. "He has shown himself, in each of his lately-performed works, as an independent, original individuality, a finely-organised, true, musical nature, as an artist ripening towards mastership by means of unwearied, conscious endeavour. His A major Serenade is the younger, tender sister of the one in D lately produced by the Gesellschaft and is conceived in the same peaceful, dreamy garden mood. . . . The work had an extremely favourable reception. The hearty applause became proportionately greater at the close as the modest composer made himself ever smaller in his seat in the gallery."

The Hungarian Concerto was pronounced:

"a tone-poem full of mind and spirit, of energy and tenderness. One might almost regret Joachim's achievements as a virtuoso, which must be the only cause that his powers are so seldom concentrated on the composition of a great work."

The attraction felt by Hanslick for Brahms' art increased with his opportunities of becoming acquainted with it. He secured his services as pianist at a lecture on Beethoven—one of a series—given by him in February, when Johannes, whose pianistic repertoire was almost inexhaustible, had performed the great Sonata in C minor, Op. 111.

The music season was now coming to a close, but the many attractions of Vienna—and not least among them its beautiful neighbourhood, with which Brahms' frequent long walks with Nottebohm, Faber, Epstein, and others gradually made him familiar—inclined him to stay on for some weeks longer; and it was not until the spring had well set in that he set out for Hanover *en route* for Hamburg, carrying with him many new possessions as mementoes of his visit, engravings of some of his favourite pictures in the Belvedere Gallery,* and the entire collection of the then published

---

* The collection was acquired by the Imperial Gallery on the Burg Ring.

works of Schubert, presented to him by Spina, being the principal. He had a particular reason for wishing to pass a day or two with his friend. He was to be introduced to Fräulein Amalie Weiss, to whom Joachim had lately become engaged. This lady had entered into a three years' engagement as first contralto on the stage of the Hanover court opera in the spring of 1862, and it was not long before her gifts attracted the enthusiastic interest of the celebrated court concertmeister of the same capital. The two artists were betrothed in February, 1863, and the birthday of the Queen of Hanover, April 14, was celebrated by a festival performance of Gluck's "Orpheus," conducted, by Her Majesty's express desire, by Joachim, in which Fräulein Weiss appeared with brilliant success in the title rôle. Brahms, on his arrival a little later on, was a delighted witness of a repetition of the opera. Frau Amalie Joachim, who retired from the stage on her marriage (June, 1863), gradually acquired a very great reputation as a concert singer, and was a much admired interpreter of Brahms' songs.

Readily acceding to Brahms' wish, Joachim arranged during the short visit for a rehearsal at his rooms of the string quintet in F minor which, completed before the composer's departure from Germany, had twice made the double journey between Vienna and Hanover. The effect of the work, which had been tried privately in Vienna, now for the second time proved insufficiently sonorous for its great material; and Brahms rearranged it as a sonata for two pianofortes and subsequently as a quintet for pianoforte and strings, the form in which, as Op. 43, it has become famous. We shall before long have occasion to make mention of the first public, and of an early private, performance of the sonata version.

Brahms returned to Hamburg on May 5, and, after passing his thirtieth birthday with his family, took a lodging at Blankenese, on the Elbe, where an unexpected meeting with some of the former members of his Ladies' Choir agreeably reminded him of the charming society that had served a not unimportant purpose in the composer's course of self-training. Various plans for work and recreation for the summer and autumn months were under consideration, but were to be set aside. Before the month was out, Brahms received a convincing proof of the impression his visit had made in Vienna by getting a call to return there. The post of conductor to the Singakademie had fallen vacant by the death of Stegmayer, and at the general meeting of the society in the course of May, Brahms was elected successor to the post. There was a severe competition between two sections of the members, a large and influential party, led by Prince Constantin Czartoriski, being strongly in favour of the election of Franz Krenn, an excellent musician of the old school, who belonged to Vienna as a choirmaster of the parish church of St. Michael, and professor of composition at the conservatoire, and who had conducted one of the Singakademie concerts during Stegmayer's illness. It happened, however, that amongst those members of the committee who desired that the practices and performances of the not very prosperous society should be placed under the direction of a young, resolute and energetic musician, were several gentlemen belonging to the circle of enthusiastic admirers of Brahms' art which had sprung into existence almost simultaneously with his first appearance in Vienna, and had increased with each opportunity that had offered itself there for the hearing of his music. Amongst them were Dr. Scholz, a surgeon; Herr Adolf Schultz, a merchant; and Herr Franz Flatz, an insurance official of Vienna; and at their head Dr. Josef Gänsbacher, son of the distinguished musician and church composer, Johann Gänsbacher, the pupil of Vogler and Albrechtsberger, acquaintance of Haydn and Beethoven, friend of Weber and Meyerbeer, and capellmeister of the cathedral from 1823 until his death in 1844.

Dr. Josef Gänsbacher, whose name has become known in the musical world of many countries by its appearance on the title page of Brahms' first sonata for pianoforte and violoncello, was, in 1863, a young doctor of jurisprudence and advocate's draughtsman. Later on he adopted music as a profession, and became a valued teacher of singing, professor at the conservatoire, and violoncellist. He was one of Brahms' earliest and truest friends in Vienna, and became a devotee of his art even before making his personal acquaintance. He had considerable influence with the members of the Singakademie, and representatives of both sections of the committee called on him at his bureau to solicit his help, Prince Czartoriski presenting himself in person in Krenn's favour. Gänsbacher's sympathies, however, were all the other way; and, being selected by his party to make a speech at the general meeting in Brahms' interest, he used such forcible arguments as to bring over several of Krenn's supporters and win the election for his own side by a majority of one. It is characteristic of Brahms that he could not at once make up his mind to reply to the offer of the appointment, though he does not seem to have been seriously doubtful about his final decision.

"You will wonder," he wrote to Hanslick, in a letter which indicates the rapid advance of friendship between the two men, "that most glad and grateful reply did not anticipate your own and many other kind letters received by me. I seem to myself, however, as one who has been praised beyond desert and should like to creep into hiding for a while. I resolved, on receipt of the telegraphic despatch (through Flatz who must always be to the fore) to be content with such a flattering summons and not to tempt the gods further. . . . And since nothing more is in question than whether I have the courage to say 'yes,' it shall be so. Had I refused, my reasons would have been misunderstood by the Academy, and by you Viennese generally. . . ."

Writing to the committee on May 30 to ask for particulars of the position, he says:

"The resolve to give away one's freedom for the first time is exceptional; but anything coming from Vienna is doubly pleasant to a musician, and whatever may call him thither is doubly attractive."*

These occurrences put an end to the various holiday projects which Brahms had been considering. "I cannot make up my mind to deprive my parents of any of our short time together," he wrote in answer to Dietrich's pressing invitation, and remained quietly near and at Hamburg. He began at once to occupy himself with plans for his programmes, and begged Dietrich's advice "as a very experienced and learned court conductor" on matters connected with his new duties. "I feel enormously diffident," he says, "about trying my talent for these things in Vienna."

Allowing himself but a flying visit *en route* to beautiful Lichtenthal, a suburb of Baden-Baden, where Frau Schumann had purchased a house the previous year on giving up her residence in Berlin, Brahms was back again in Vienna by the last week of August, and soon engaged with characteristic earnestness in work connected with his new appointment. His scheme for the weekly practices of the Singakademie season included works by Bach, Beethoven, Mendelssohn, Schumann, and masters of the earlier period whose music was a speciality of the society. The first concert of the season 1863-64, given on November 15 under his direction, presented the following programme:

1. Bach: Cantata, "Ich hatte viel Bekümmerniss."
                        (First time in Vienna.)
2. Beethoven: "Opferlied."
3. H. Isaak (late
    15th cent.): Three German Folk-songs—
                     a. "Innsbruck ich muss dich lassen."

---

* This and the preceding extract are from some letters first published by Hanslick in the *Neue Freie Presse* of July 1, 1897, and republished in *Am Ende des Jahrhunderts* ("Der Modernen Oper," Part VIII): "Johannes Brahms."

     b. "Es ist ein Schnitter heisst der Tod."
     c. "Ich fahr dahin wenn es muss seyn."
4. Schumann: "Requiem für Mignon." (First time in Vienna.)

The principal co-operating artists were Frau Wilt and Frau Ferrari; Herr Danzer, Herr Dalfy and Herr Organist Bibl. No doubt could be felt at the close of the performances of Brahms' gifts as a conductor.

"The concert was not only excellent in itself, but was, with exception of the first performance in Vienna of Bach's 'Matthew Passion,' by far the most noteworthy achievement in the record of the Singakademie, and gave us the opportunity of recognising Brahms' rare talent as a conductor."

Bach's cantata was rendered "with splendid colouring and spiritual insight"; the three delightful Volkslieder "opened all hearts." These were received with such stormy applause that a fourth, not less acceptable, was added. Considerable surprise seems to have been excited, not by the conductor's inspired conception of the works performed, but by the precision and clearness of his beat, which, remarks one critic:

"could hardly have been expected of an artist who has shown himself, in his creations and performances, so essentially a romanticist and dreamer."

These last words sound strange as coming from a writer in Vienna who may be supposed to have gained some knowledge of the serenades, the B flat sextet, and the two pianoforte quartets, and they are quoted, not because of their aptness, but as illustrating a difficulty which the composer's individuality, reflected in his works as in a mirror, caused for many a long year to some of his less competent, even though friendly, critics—the difficulty of knowing how to classify him. From an early period his determination was strong to bring the womanly tenderness and dreamy romance that were in him under the complete control of his energetic will, to give supreme dominance in art, as in life, to understanding rather than to emotion, to possess and be master of his powers; but, during the earlier years of his activity, the subtle poetic charm dwelling within his works made itself felt by many sympathetic listeners who could not immediately follow their closely woven texture, and who were puzzled by his independent treatment—at times almost amounting to a recreation—of traditional form. Hence, he has not seldom been spoken of as purely a romanticist long since his position as the representative descendant of Bach, Mozart and Beethoven was recognised by those most competent to judge.

Meanwhile his art was gradually spreading through Europe. On November 10 the first serenade was given at Zürich under Fichtelberger, the conductor of the subscription concerts. The work deserved a warmer reception than was accorded it, in the opinion of the *Neuer Zürcher Zeitung*, whose critic recognised in Brahms a composer, not only of profound knowledge, but of inborn genius. He did not commit himself to pronouncement as to whether the composer's creative power would be of sufficient force to discover really "new paths," or would prove better qualified for making further developments within the already conquered domain of musical art, but thought the serenade pointed to the latter probability.

The B flat Sextet was performed at a concert given in Hamburg in November by Rosé and Stockhausen, whose friendship with Brahms had not been allowed to suffer by the action of the Philharmonic committee. The composition was given in Vienna at the Hellmesberger concert of December 27, when it awakened extraordinary interest and sympathy. In Austria as in Germany it was the first of the composer's important works to become popular.

"After lunch Wagner presented various parts of the 'Ring' and 'Tristan,' then we heard in the evening his (Brahms') Sextet in B major. We believed ourselves suddenly transported into a pure world of beauty," wrote Hanslick a few years later, "it seemed like a dream; so contrasted was their music, so wholly at variance also was the personal appearance of the two. With rather awkward modesty, Brahms approached the piano. Only with reluctance and timidity did he respond to the stormy call to come forward, and he appeared anxious to get back quickly."*

Christmas Eve was passed with the Fabers, Brahms being, as ever, the most cordial, happy, childlike guest. He continued, during the first years of his subsequent residence in Vienna, to spend the festival with these friends, who took pains to invite his favourite companions to meet him. Nottebohm was always of the party. Amongst his presents one Christmas for the gift-making ceremony at home in Hamburg, was a sewing machine for his sister, who had expressed a wish for such a possession as a help in her employment. After the lapse of a few seasons, however, Brahms for a great many years, habitually declined all invitations for Christmas Eve, only breaking his rule by occasionally spending it with Frau Schumann. Within the last decade of his life he again changed his custom, and passed the evening regularly in the happy home circle of some friends to whom the reader will be introduced in a later chapter.

The second and third concerts of the Singakademie took place on January 6 and March 20, with the subjoined programmes:

Programme of January 6.

1. Mendelssohn: Eight-part Motet.
2. Joh. Eccard (1553-1611): "The Christian's Easter Day Song of Triumph" (double chorus).

---

* Wagner conducted selections from "Tristan" and "Die Meistersinger" at a concert given by Tausig in the afternoon of December 27, 1863, which is noticed in the Vienna letter of the *Neue Zeitung für Musik* of February 3, 1864. The dates of the Hellmesberger Quartet concerts are given throughout this volume on the authority of the collected programmes.

3. Heinrich Schütz (1583-1672): "Saul's Conversion" (triple chorus).
4. Giov. Gabrieli (1557-1613): "Benedictus" (double chorus).
5. Giov. Rovetta (1643-1668): "Salve Regina."
6. Beethoven: "Elegischer Gesang" (chorus with string accompaniment).
7. Three German Folk-songs.
8. J. S. Bach: Motet, "Liebster Gott wann werd'ich sterben."

PROGRAMME OF MARCH 20.

J. S. Bach: Christmas Oratorio. (First performance in Vienna.)
With the assistance of the Imperial and Royal Court-Opera Orchestra.

They do not seem to have been so successful as the first. The public found the programme of January 6 monotonous. Hirsch, in his notice of the concert in the *Wiener Zeitung*, goes so far as to speak of "shipwreck," while Hanslick himself owns that the performance of the earlier numbers had the "character of an improvisation or a practice rather than a concert production." The three German folksongs (the two last harmonised by Brahms) were so warmly received that the conductor's Minnelied, "Der Holdseliger," was given in addition. The success of the Bach cantata was injured by a contretemps. The Bösendorfer piano, sent in the absence of an organ, was too high in pitch and therefore unavailable.

The concert of March 20, at which the Christmas Oratorio was given, seems to have been rather overshadowed by the performance of Bach's "St. John's Passion" by the Gesellschaft forces at a somewhat earlier date.

The satisfaction and confidence extended to the conductor by the Akademie remained undiminished, however, by the falling off in the success of the second and third public performances, and were expressed at the close of the subscription season by the arrangement of an extra concert devoted to Brahms' compositions. The instrumental numbers on this occasion were the B flat Sextet, played by the Hellmesberger party, and a sonata for two pianofortes—in reality the arrangement in this form of the manuscript string quintet with two violoncelli, to which reference has already been made. Tausig, a great admirer of Brahms' genius, who took the Paganini Variations which were written during Brahms' first visit to Vienna, under his especial care later on, was the composer's colleague in the performance, for which, therefore, every advantage was secured; but Brahms had not yet, as it seemed, found the right medium for the expression of his thoughts. The sonata fell flat, making no impression on the audience. There were several vocal numbers, and amongst them was the charming "Wechsellied zum Tanze," No. 1 of the three Quartets for solo voices, Op. 31, which stand in an anticipatory relation to the "Liebeslieder." They show Brahms in his graceful, playful, genial mood. The "Wechsellied" is in dance measure, and has two alternative melodies severally adapted to the character of Goethe's verses—the first in E flat, allotted to the contralto and bass, the "indifferent" pair; the second in A flat, to the soprano and tenor, the "tender" pair. Brahms has delightfully expressed the difference of mood animating the two couples, and, by the simple device of writing the first of the two little duets in imitation, the bass following the contralto at a bar's distance, has suggested a tone of bright enjoyment which contrasts effectively with the romantic spirit of the lovers' song. The four voices combine towards the close of the composition, which comes to an end in the key of the lover's melody.

No. 2 of the same opus—"Neckereien" (Raillery), the text of which is a Moorish folk-song, is full of graceful fun. In this the tenors and basses alternate with the sopranos and contraltos; the youths court the girls, who will rather be transformed into little doves, little fishes, little hares, than have anything to do with them. The suitors, on the other hand, hint that such changes may be of small avail against little guns, little nets, little dogs.

No. 3, also set to a national text, this time Bohemian, is a charming four-part song, with a graceful accompaniment in waltz rhythm, and is developed from the melody used by Brahms in No. 5 of his set of waltzes for pianoforte. These quartets were composed at Detmold.

On May 10 the annual foundation concert of the Singakademie took place—as usual, before a private audience. The programme will be perused with interest by English-speaking readers:

1.	Schumann:	First and second movements from "Requiem für Mignon."
2.	Haydn:	Duet for Soprano and Tenor.
3.	Schumann:	Stücke im Volkston for Violoncello and Pianoforte.
4.	John Bennet (1599):	Madrigal (for chorus).
5.	John Morley (1595):	Dance Song (for chorus).
6.	Schumann:	Two Duets from the "Spanisches Liederspiel."
7.	Brahms:	Two Songs for Soprano.
8.	Schumann:	Fifth and sixth movements from the "Requiem für Mignon."

The fourth and fifth numbers of the programme were no doubt selected by Brahms from a collection of early English madrigals, edited by J. J. Maier of Munich.

Our composer's appointment as conductor of the Singakademie lapsed at the end of the season. By the rules of the society, election took place triennially, and Stegmayer's death had left only a year to run. Brahms' re-election was a matter of course, and was accepted by him, though not without doubt and hesitation; but his resolution failed him later on, and before the end of the summer he sent his resignation to the committee.

In the course of the year, Spina of Vienna (Cranz of Hamburg) published a setting of the 13th Psalm for three-part women's chorus, with accompaniment for organ or pianoforte; and four Duets for Contralto and Baritone, dedicated to Frau Amalie Joachim. Breitkopf and Härtel issued two Motets for five-part mixed Chorus *a capella* (the first set to a verse of a church hymn by Paul Speratus, 1484-1551; the second to words from the 51st Psalm); a Sacred Song by Paul Flemming, 1609-1640 (set for two-part mixed Chorus, and written in double canon); and the three Quartets for solo voices to which we have already referred as Op. 31.

Rieter-Biedermann published a set of nine Songs (Op. 32), No. 9 of which is the exquisite "Wie bist du meine Königin," one of the most fragrant love songs ever composed; and a set of German folk-songs, without opus number, dedicated to the Vienna Singakademie.

An Organ Fugue in A flat minor was published as a supplement to No. 29 of the *Allgemeine Musikzeitung*, edited, as the reader may remember, by Selmar Bagge.

CHAPTER XIII.

1864-1867.

Frau Schumann in Baden-Baden—Circle of friends there—Hermann Levi—Madame Pauline Viardot-Garcia—The Landgräfin of Hesse and the Pianoforte Quintet—Death of Frau Brahms—Concert journey—The Horn Trio—Frau Caroline Schnack—Last visit to Detmold—First Sonata for Pianoforte and Violoncello—The German Requiem—Brahms at Zürich—Billroth—Brahms and Joachim on a concert tour in Switzerland—Hans von Bülow—Reinthaler.

BRAHMS spent several weeks of the summer of 1864 in Hamburg. The domestic troubles that had arisen from his father's early marriage with a delicate woman nearly twenty years his senior had come to a crisis, which Johannes, loving both father and mother with tender devotion, could no longer bear. By his advice they separated and he remained near them through part of June and July to superintend the carrying out of the new arrangements for which he was chiefly responsible. Jakob had long since become fairly prosperous in a small way, holding a recognised position as a double-bass player amongst the orchestral musicians of Hamburg, and had even been appointed a member of the Philharmonic band since Stockhausen's election as the society's conductor. He now found quarters for himself in the Grosser Bleichen; the home in the Fuhlentwiethe was given up. Fritz, who, in spite of his want of energy, was doing well as a teacher, took lodgings in Theaterstrasse, and Frau Brahms and Elise removed to comfortable rooms in the Lange Reihe, Johannes, poor as he was, taking upon himself the sole responsibility of their maintenance. The time was still distant, in spite of the composer's steadily growing fame, when his circumstances were to become prosperous. Had money-making been one of his immediate objects, he could certainly have attained it with little difficulty; but his aims were wholly ideal, and directly included pecuniary profit only so far as this was necessary for his own decent maintenance and for the exercise of ungrudging generosity to his family. His income, derived from the sale of his copyrights and from his public activity as a pianist—for he accepted but few pupils after going to Vienna—sufficed for these ends; he had learned from early youth to find happiness in the realities of life, and to treat as superfluities as many things as possible. The cultivation of happiness he viewed, not only as a part of wisdom, but as a duty. "Let us, so far as we may, retain a fresh, happy interest in life, which we have at any rate to live," was not with him a mere phrase to be offered for the benefit of a friend in trouble, but one of the abiding principles by which he shaped his own daily existence.

It is significant alike of the strength and the tenderness of Brahms' nature, that whilst he refrained from any direct mention of his family perplexities in letters even to his most intimate friends, his thoughts turned, on finding himself deprived of the old home to which he had clung with faithful affection during the years of his developing career, to the visions he had allowed himself to indulge during his happy stay in Göttingen of six summers back—dreams, never to be realised, yet never, perhaps, entirely absent from his mind, of a home of his own blessed with the love of wife and child.

"I much want news of you—and should prefer to receive it from yourself personally," he wrote to Grimm a few days before the dwelling in the Fuhlentwiethe was finally vacated. "If, as I fancy, you are on a visit to the Georgia-Augusta

(Göttingen University) take a pen at once and let me know how things are looking in all the houses to which we used to go so gladly. Tell me also about that house and garden near the gate.

"But do it quickly. I am leaving here in a few days and unhappily it is not the worst of my troubles that I do not know in which direction."

Grimm had no very cheerful answer to give to the inquiry which had evidently been the main purpose of Brahms' letter:

"Things are sadly changed in that house and garden near the gate. The old professor died three years ago. Agathe has been a governess in Ireland since last year. She was not happy in Göttingen at last and wished to be independent. . . . How many difficulties she has had to go through. . . . For the rest she has preserved her strength of character and has not lost her humour—but what a melancholy lot is that of a lonely girl!"*

Joachim's return from one of these lengthy visits to England, so much deplored by his friend, solved Johannes' doubts as to what his immediate movement should be. By the end of the third week in July the depressing business that had detained him in Hamburg was completed; he hastened at once to Hanover, and after passing a few days in the companionship to which, in his frequent need of artistic or personal sympathy, he had never turned in vain, he went on to Baden-Baden. "Johannes surprised us on July 31st," is Frau Schumann's entry in her diary of his arrival. He stayed on for the remainder of the season, residing in a charming villa close to the grounds of the Kurhaus, which was placed at his disposal by Rubinstein, who had taken it for the season, but left in August.

There is every reason to believe that Johannes was working at this time at his second Sextet in G minor and that the sketches of some of the movements formed matter of discus-

---

* Brahms-Grimm "Briefwechsel," Nos. LXIX and LXXI.

sion between himself and Joachim whilst the two friends were together in July. In the light of this probability, the composer's above quoted letter to Grimm gains a new and touching interest, since we have the sanction of Joachim himself for associating the sextet with Brahms' remembrance of Agathe. In a letter written thirty years later than our present date, Joachim expressly connects her name with a motif:

(A g a (t) h e)

which forms the continuation of the beautiful second subject of the first movement;* and the present author may supplement this circumstance by adding that on her once asking Joachim a question about Agathe, he softly hummed the same fragment of melody which was evidently suggested to his mind by the mention of her name. No more choice memorial of the romance of his early manhood could have been created by the composer than the Sextet in G minor. If it is not so immediately attractive to the average music lover as its companion work, this is probably to be ascribed to the more subdued mood that pervades it. In the energy of the constructive power that is exhibited in the fine outlines of its several movements, the symmetry of their parts, and the treatment of their material, the second sextet takes its stand beside the first, while the character of its themes which appeal to the sensitive hearer by their spirit of gentle melancholy, sweetness and courageous resignation, has secured for the composition a distinctive position of its own among the works of Brahms' early period of ripe maturity.

"I like the Sextet quite extraordinarily," Dietrich wrote later, on the publication of the work, "and should be

---

* Brahms-Joachim "Briefwechsel" II, No. 506.

inclined to rank it as a whole above the first, even though the first movement of the latter stands alone and incomparable. The second Sextet has a quite wonderful originality, difficult to describe, but quickly felt by musicians, the charm of which is increased by familiarity with the work."

Frau Schumann's residence at Baden-Baden brought in its train results which are of much interest in the history of Brahms' career. The not-distant capital of the duchy of Baden, Carlsruhe, was to become in the course of the next few years, an important centre for the cultivation of his art. It seems convenient, therefore, to mention at once the names of a few members of a group of friends belonging to Frau Schumann's circle who resided or stayed frequently in the neighbourhood, and with whom Brahms became more or less intimate.

Jakob Rosenhain (born 1813), a composer now forgotten, but esteemed in his day, and recognised both by Schumann and Mendelssohn, lived at Baden-Baden, and was sometimes to be met at Frau Schumann's house. His name heads the programme of Johannes' first public concert of 1848. The painter Anselm Feuerbach (1829-1880), a little known and disappointed man in 1864, whose art has attained great posthumous celebrity, came annually with his mother to pass a few weeks there. The name of Frau Henriette Feuerbach appears on the title page of Brahms' work, "Nänie," which was composed soon after the premature death of her son. With the mention of Feuerbach must be associated that of Julius Allgeyer, introduced to our readers in an early chapter as a student of copperplate engraving at Düsseldorf, and now settled in Carlsruhe as a high-class art photographer. Allgeyer had a genius for friendship. He was extraordinarily attached to Feuerbach, of whose art he made himself the apostle; but though his four years' residence in Rome (1856-1860) in close intercourse with the painter caused an interruption of his personal intimacy with Brahms, the two men remained in occasional correspondence, and held each other in cordial esteem. Now the old friendship was renewed, and it was not long before Brahms came to occupy a place in the engraver's affections second only to that of Feuerbach. The thought that he had known and loved both musician and painter through the period of their dawning fame was, in after years, a source of satisfaction and pride to Allgeyer, whose name has become well known in Germany as that of Feuerbach's biographer.

In the middle of the sixties Carlsruhe, under the encouragement of its reigning Grand Duke Frederick, occupied an exceptionally brilliant position amongst the smaller European centres of dramatic and musical art, to which it had been raised by the talents and devotion of Edward Devrient, the eminent stage director of its court theatre, whose name may be familiar to some English readers as that of one of Mendelssohn's intimate friends. A man of wide general culture, the author of the standard work on its subject—"The History of German Dramatic Art"—playwright, singer, actor, possessed of an intimate knowledge of the best traditions of the German stage in the wide sense that includes opera, which had been derived from thirty years of professional association with the court theatres of Berlin and Dresden, Devrient was an ideal man for his post. His own sympathies remained faithful to the classical school of opera upon which his taste had been formed, but he did not allow his devotion to Gluck and Mozart and his interest in the revival of works of an early period to narrow the sphere of his activity. Taking a broad view of the duties of his position, he recognised the claim to hearing of the New-German school, and several of Wagner's musical dramas had been performed in the Carlsruhe court theatre by his permission, if not on his initiative, before his resignation of his post soon after the celebration of his artistic jubilee in April, 1869.

Not the least of his services to music was his choice of a successor to the post of court capellmeister at Carlsruhe, which fell vacant on the resignation of Joseph Strauss (not of the celebrated Vienna family) early in 1864. By recommending Hermann Levi (1839-1900) for the appointment, famous after the middle of the seventies amongst the famous Wagner conductors, and director of the first performances of "Parsifal" (July-August, 1882), and by the generosity with which he permitted the youthful musician to profit by the fruits of his own ripe experience, he contributed in no small degree towards perfecting the technical education of an artist whose name will be remembered in musical history as amongst those of the great in his chosen branch of activity.

A gifted pupil of the Leipzig Conservatoire, Levi resolved, at an early age, to aim at achieving distinction as a conductor, and on entering the service of the Grand Duke of Baden in his twenty-sixth year, he had already laid the foundation of his future celebrity in successive posts at Saarbrück, Mannheim and Rotterdam. He had a large and enthusiastic nature which caused him to reject the formal and stereotyped in art and to sympathise with what seemed to him genuinely progressive, and becoming early in his career a great admirer of Schumann's music, he passed easily to a recognition of the genius of Brahms, with whom he had a slight acquaintance before settling at Carlsruhe.

The singer Hauser, the violoncellist Lindner, the hornist Segisser, the authoress Fräulein Anna Ettlinger—all resident in Carlsruhe—the learned Oberschulrath Gustav Wendt, called there in 1867, whose rooms were the scene of many distinguished gatherings, are to be included in our list; and of particular interest is the name of the violoncellist Bernhard Cossmann, of Weimar celebrity, who settled at Baden-Baden in 1870. Brahms was a willing and heartily welcome visitor at his house, and took part there in performances of his E minor Violoncello Sonata, and with the hornist Steinbrügger, of the Horn Trio.

A noteworthy and picturesque figure, familiar in the artist circle, was that of Turgeniev, who visited Baden-Baden annually from early in the sixties until the opening of the seventies. In conclusion is to be added the name of Pauline Viardot-Garcia, who settled at Baden in 1863, building a spacious villa in the Lichtenthaler Allée for her summer residence, which contained a gallery of fine paintings, chiefly of the Spanish and Netherland schools. Amongst her possessions was Mozart's autograph score of "Don Giovanni," which she kept enshrined in a valuable casket. Madame Viardot was a musician in a very comprehensive sense of the word. Her triumphs on the operatic stage belong to the history of musico-dramatic art; she had been a pupil of Liszt on the pianoforte, had studied counterpoint and composition, and composed a good deal. Several of her operettas, for which Turgeniev furnished the textbooks, were performed privately by her pupils and children in her miniature theatre in Baden-Baden, where she was accustomed to entertain many of the celebrities of the time. One was given in German translation by Richard Pohl, as "Der letzte Zauberer," on the court stages of Carlsruhe and Weimar. At the request of some of her girl pupils, Brahms composed a short choral serenade for her birthday one summer subsequent to our present date, and conducted its performance by the young ladies, outside her house, at an early hour of the morning. This pleasant incident of the seventies recalls that of the forties, when the youthful Johannes consented to fill the offices of composer and conductor at Winsen on the occasion of Rector Köhler's birthday.

Brahms' sonata for two pianofortes was heard privately in Baden-Baden several times in the course of the summer. Receiving the manuscript from the composer in July, Frau Schumann at once found opportunities of trying the work, first with Rubinstein, and a few days later, with Levi. Later in the season she performed it with Brahms himself before the Princess Anna of Hesse, and the work which, as we have seen, had failed to win public sympathy in a Vienna concert-room, made its mark on this occasion. It appealed strongly to the royal listener, who, at the close of the last movement, warmly expressed to the composer her sense of its beauty. Brahms, gratified and pleased at the Princess's unreserved appreciation, called on her the following day, and begged permission, which was readily granted, to dedicate the work to her; and on its publication the following year in its final form—a quintet for pianoforte and strings—Her Royal Highness's name appeared on the title page. The Princess acknowledged the compliment of the dedication by presenting Brahms with one of her treasures—the autograph score of Mozart's G minor Symphony. It passed after his death, as part of his library, into the possession of the Gesellschaft der Musikfreunde, Vienna.

An interesting reference to the dedication and the time passed into the possession of the Landgraf of Hesse, whose musical talent was recognised and encouraged by Brahms twenty years later, and is contained in a letter of thanks written by the master in 1892 on the dedication to him of a fantasia for pianoforte published that year by the Prince:

"YOUR ROYAL HIGHNESS
"MOST GRACIOUS HERR LANDGRAF!

"Whilst I venture to express to Your Royal Highness my most respectful and hearty thanks for the dedication of the fantasia, very many and very pleasant recollections occur to me.

"The high and agreeable distinction, as which I regard the dedication, reminds me of the similar pleasure I experienced when I was permitted to inscribe my quintet to your highly-honoured mother, the Frau Landgräfin. That was in beautiful Baden-Baden, and it would be too tempting to go on chatting about the unforgettable music-hours and pleasant days; but much else crowds upon the memory: Meiningen, Frankfurt, Vienna, Berlin, etc. I think that by my mere mention of these names Y.R.H. will know what a valued memorial your work and its dedication, by which I am so much honoured, will be to me of many pleasant times.

"With my hearty thanks for the valuable present, I unite the wish that our glorious art may bring to Y.R.H. many more hours as happy as those were of which this fantasia gives such convincing testimony.

"Your Royal Highness's deeply obliged
"JOHANNES BRAHMS.
"VIENNA, Jan., 1892."

On September 12 Frau Joachim's first child was born, and there was no doubt as to what he should be called. Johannes must, of course, be godfather, and give his name to Joachim's boy. Brahms was not present at the christening, but he sent to the parents as his congratulatory gift the manuscript of the little song published long afterwards as No. 2 of Op. 91, the "Geistliches Wiegenlied," or, as it is called in the published translated title, "The Virgin's Cradle Song." The words are imitated by Geibel from a text of Lope de Vega, "Die ihr schwebt um diese Palmen" (Ye who o'er these palms are hov'ring). The music, composed for contralto, viola and pianoforte, is founded upon the melody of an old song,* which, given in Brahms' composition to the viola, serves as the basis for the contrapuntal treatment of the voice and pianoforte parts.

Brahms left Baden-Baden on October 10, and returning to Vienna, passed the next few weeks in quiet pursuit of his ordinary avocations, glad to know himself in complete possession of his time, yet perhaps not without an occasional passing regret at the thought of the pleasure he had derived the previous season, as conductor of the Singakademie, from his association with choir and orchestra. The change he had advised in the family arrangements at Hamburg was not greatly to prolong for his mother the peaceful old age he had desired to secure for her. Frau Brahms had taken her last farewell of her dearly loved son when he quitted Hamburg in the summer. She was suddenly struck down by paralysis on her return from the theatre one evening in the last week of January, and on February 2, 1865, quietly

---

* "Josef lieber, Josef mein,
   hilf mir wieg'n mein Kindlein klein.
   Gott der wird dein Lohner sein
   in Himmelreich der Jungfrau Sohn, Maria."

(Joseph dearest, Joseph mine,
 Help me rock the babe divine.
 Heaven's blessing shall be thine
 In th' kingdom of the Virgin's Son, Mariè.)

breathed her last. Johannes, who had no tidings of her illness until some hours after she had passed away, took train for Hamburg at once on receiving a telegraphic summons from his brother, and immediately on his arrival, turned towards his mother's bedchamber.

He had once before passed through a great sorrow, but in Schumann's case death had come in the guise of a friend. This was another kind of bereavement, and the loss of the dear, simply loving old mother wrung his heart. "Do not go in yet, Hannes," said Elise, trying to prevent him, and, indeed, as he passed on into the room the sudden complete realisation of the mother's tenderness gone from his life broke down his self-command on the instant. He knelt down by the quiet bed and sobbed aloud in uncontrollable grief. When he had somewhat collected himself he presently went out. Solitude, however, often welcome to him, was not what he wanted to-day, nor overmuch sympathy, but affection—and affection of a kind that perhaps may have seemed to him something akin to the assured, unreasoning mother's love. He turned into kind Frau Cossel's and asked her to let him have the company of a child. His twelve-year old god-daughter Johanna was most willingly at his service as a companion, and as soon as she was ready the pair walked away together back to Elise, the little girl somewhat awed by the situation and the changed demeanour of the friend whom she was accustomed to regard as the merriest of her companions, but glad to be in his society on any terms. Leaving his godchild with Elise, Johannes soon went out again, and returned after a while with his father, whom he drew with him into the adjoining room, accidentally leaving the door of communication a little open. The scene of the death chamber was thus made visible to the frightened Johanna from her position in the parlour, and imprinted itself indelibly on her brain. She watched it spell-bound, and was not too young a child to be penetrated and touched by what she saw.

The two men stood together by the bedside for a few

seconds without stirring. Then Johannes, putting his hand on his father's arm, gently guided it towards the motionless figure, and placing the husband's hand over that of the dead wife, kept both covered with his own in a last reconciliation. Kind friends came to the funeral, and true sympathy was at hand, but Johannes shrank in his grief from hearing the expression of condolence. "I have no mother now: I must marry," he said miserably when the service was over. Stockhausen and his wife insisted that he and Elise should dine quietly with them that day, and there is little doubt that Brahms was helped by the affectionate consideration shown on all sides, and was quietly grateful for it. He returned to his work in a few days, but the responsibility for the maintenance of Elise, who, having strongly felt the mother's side of the family difficulties, shrank from the idea of rejoining her father, remained entirely his.*

The first two books of the "Magelone Romances," dedicated to Stockhausen, and the Pianoforte Quintet were published by Rieter-Biedermann early in the year. The version of the quintet as a sonata for two pianofortes was issued by the same house in 1872.

The Quintet in F minor, Op. 34, is unquestionably one of the greatest works of chamber music for pianoforte and strings ever written. Some distinguished writers go so far as to give it the first place amongst the composer's works of its class; and if regard be had to the largeness of its proportions, the stormy grandeur and the deep pathos of its ideas, its extraordinary wealth of thematic material, and the astonishing power with which this is handled, it must be admitted that there is something to be said in support of such a view. To the author it certainly appears impossible to select one of Brahms' works of this period and this class for preference as compared with the others. All are so great

---

* The particulars given above were personally communicated to the author severally by Fräulein Johanna Cossel, Mrs. Edward Stone (Minna Völckers) and Frau Professor Stockhausen.

as, so to say, to defy future competition. They seem as unapproachable and secure on their own lines as the immortal "48" themselves in another category. The imaginative power which surges through the first movement of the quintet recalls the daring of the youthful Johannes, and is guided now by a master hand. This movement dominates the whole work. Its contrasted tones of passionate splendour and scarcely less passionate mystery are reflected in the rich pathos of the "andante un poco adagio," in the weird fitfulness of the scherzo with its heart-gripping trio, and in the doubtful tranquillity of the finale, bursting in the coda into a rushing impetuosity which carries the movement to a triumphant conclusion. Few of Brahms' compositions contain more striking illustrations than this one of his power of fertilising his themes and bringing new, out of previous, material, a power which gives to his works a coherence and solidity hardly equalled save in the compositions of Bach himself, and which has a certain artistic analogy with the secret force that governs all natural organic development.

The summer of this year was again spent near Frau Schumann. Brahms took lodgings—two small rooms well provided with windows—in Frau Becker's house, which was situated a little apart from the village of Lichtenthal in an idyllic spot amongst the hills. His plan of life, essentially the same wherever he fixed his summer residence, was to rise with the dawn, and after making himself an early cup of coffee, to enjoy the fresh delights of early morning by going for a long walk in the surrounding forest. He then returned to work in his rooms until the time arrived for his mid-day dinner, taken either at Frau Schumann's house or in the garden of the "Golden Lion"; for in these days he only dined occasionally, when accompanied by a friend, at the somewhat more expensive "Bear." By four o'clock he was generally in Frau Schumann's balcony for afternoon coffee and to pass an hour with her in music, conversation, or walking. More often than not he returned to supper at half past seven, when his place was laid at table, as a matter of course, at Frau Schumann's right hand.

All the circumstances of his surroundings were favourable to his creative activity, which was unceasing, and the profound emotional experience that had recently moved and enriched his spirit had already caused in him the stirrings of the impulse that was to grow and increasingly dominate him until it had become embodied in a work which, had it been the only child of his genius known to the world, would have sufficed to immortalise his name.

Before Brahms' departure from Lichtenthal a communication from Hamburg added to his feelings of tenderness and regret the shadow of a grave family apprehension.

Having accepted engagements in Switzerland and Germany for the ante-Christmas concert season, he remained on till the end of October in his quarters at Frau Becker's, and here, about a week before the commencement of his *tournée*, he received the news that his father had resolved to marry again, and had become engaged to a widow. The intelligence, such as it was, came direct from Jakob, but it contained no particulars whatever to soften the anxiety it aroused, no mention being made in it even of the name of the intended wife, and it threw the son into a state of the strongest agitation, in which the tender pang for the dear old mother may very possibly not have been the predominating element. Who could the wife-elect be? Would she make Jakob happy? Could the marriage state be happy except under the rarest combination of circumstances? Were there children of the widow's first marriage to be provided for? If so, by whom? Jakob's means could bear no additional burden. And yet, the dear, homely, uncultured father, often enough a butt for the wit of the younger musicians standing by his side in the Philharmonic orchestra; this musician without musical endowment, who loved his music and his instruments, as Johannes sometimes declared, if such affection were to be measured by proof given, better even than he himself loved his art; who had persevered doggedly through long years of privation and struggle in his endeavours to attain to some small place in the world of art, and had won it, his father—and it needs no prophet to realise the pathos of this thought to the loving heart of the great composer—did he not deserve happiness if happiness should follow the step? Johannes was that day capable of but two resolutions on the subject: first, that his father should be made happy if anything he could say or do could help to make him so, and, secondly, that as soon as his engagements should permit, he would go to Hamburg and judge for himself of the wisdom of Jakob's choice.

The first of Brahms' concert undertakings for the autumn was fulfilled on November 3 in the hall of the Museum, Carlsruhe, where he performed his Pianoforte Concerto at the first subscription concert of the season, accompanied by the grand-ducal orchestra under Levi. The work was received, for the first time, with every sign of approval. "The people had the surprising kindness to be quite satisfied, to call for me, praise me, and all the rest of it," he wrote to Dietrich. Two of the vocal quartets, Op. 31, were included in the programme, and Brahms played some unaccompanied Schumann solos in the second part of the concert. On the 6th of the month two new "Magelone Romances" were sung for the first time in public by Hauser, at a concert given in the same hall by Frau Schumann and Joachim.

From Carlsruhe Brahms proceeded to fulfil engagements as pianist and composer in Switzerland. Giving his own concerts in Basle and Zürich, he played a number of great pianoforte works by Bach, Beethoven, Schubert and Schumann, and introduced to his new public his two pianoforte quartets (Op. 25 and 26) and Handel-variations. An attractive feature of the Basle concert was the performance under his direction by some members of the Basle choral society of the part-songs with harp and horn accompaniment, Op. 17. He also took a prominent part in the first

Zürich subscription concert of the season, conducting his D major Serenade, which had been given two years previously under Fichtelberger, and playing Schumann's concerto and Bach's Chromatic Fantasia. At Winterthur he gave a chamber music soirée in association with his friend Theodor Kirchner, and the young violinist, Friedrich Hegar, lately appointed municipal conductor at Zürich. Of this concert Widmann, who saw and heard Brahms for the first time on the occasion, has given some account:

". . . There was," he writes, "a something in his countenance which suggested the certainty of victory, the beaming cheerfulness of a mind happy in the exercise of art. . . ."*

Returning to Germany, Brahms appeared on December 5 at Mannheim; and on the 7th took part in the first public performance of his lately completed Trio for pianoforte, violin and horn at the Carlsruhe "Foyez concert," when he was assisted by Straus and Segisser, members of the grand-ducal orchestra. This inspired work has now long occupied a peculiar place in the affection of genuine lovers of Brahms' music on account of the tone of pure beauty that pervades it —beauty of sound, of mood, and of idea. The noble simplicity of its themes and the spontaneous character which distinguishes their development, hold the attention even of the unfamiliar listener throughout its three movements and the great musicianship of the composer has wrought it to a flawless example of its kind in which no weak spot can be detected by deliberate examination. The adagio has the character of a lament and can hardly be matched as an expression of profound sadness except by a few others of Brahms' and some of Beethoven's slow movements. The work was a favourite with the composer and it is of interest to know from his own lips that its inception was due to an inspiration that came to him in the course of one of his walks

---

* "Johannes Brahms in Erinnerung," p. 17.

near Lichtenthal. A year or two later than our present date, as he was ascending one of his beloved pineclad hills in Dietrich's company, he showed his friend the exact spot where the opening theme of the movement had occurred to him, saying: "I was walking along one morning and as I came to this spot, the sun shone out and the subject immediately came into my head."*

On December 12 Brahms conducted his D major Serenade and played Beethoven's E flat Concerto at the fifth Gürzenich subscription concert of the season at Cologne. He had but little success on this occasion either as pianist or composer. The serenade was criticised as being too lengthy and its themes as too "naïve" for his elaborate treatment of them. A different reception was accorded him at a soirée of chamber music held at the Hotel Disch, when he performed with Hiller his Duet Variations, Op. 23, and with von Königslow and his colleagues the G minor Pianoforte Quartet. Both works were received with acclamation, and the composer achieved a success worthy of his position in the world of art. Before leaving Cologne Brahms played at a meeting of the Musikverein to a private audience of the members, most of them professors and students of the conservatoire. Amongst the pieces chosen by him for performance on this occasion were Bach's great Organ Prelude and Fugue in A minor.

And now the anxious son found opportunity to hurry with beating heart to Hamburg to see his father and to make the acquaintance of his stepmother-elect. To find, also, every probability that Jakob had chosen wisely, and that his contemplated change of life bade fair to ensure a happy and peaceful close to a career that had been full of hardship and uncertainty.

Frau Caroline Schnack, a handsome widow who had already been twice a wife, was just turned forty-one, and

---

* Personally communicated to the author by Herr Hofcapellmeister Dietrich.

therefore more than seventeen years the junior of her proposed third husband. She had an only child, her son Fritz, born of her second marriage, now a lad of about sixteen. Capable and managing, she kept an excellent public dining-room for single men not far from the musicians' "Börse," described in an early chapter of our narrative, and had a regular clientele amongst the members of the Stadt Theater orchestra. Since the time when Johannes had thought it advisable for his parents to separate, Jakob had been one of her daily customers, and her good cooking and substantial capacity had gradually opened for her the way to his affection. Johannes, on his interview with Frau Schnack, was at once favourably impressed by her personality and gave his consent to the engagement, only insisting that full time for consideration on both sides should be allowed before the taking of the irrevocable step of marriage; and after a day or two in Hamburg he set out with a greatly relieved mind for Detmold, where he had arranged through Bargheer to spend the Christmas week and to reappear as composer and pianist on the scenes of his former activity.

The visit passed off most happily. The great composer, to whom, after some disappointment, much success and fame had come since his last sojourn in the little capital six years previously, was merry according to his wont when in the midst of familiar associates. Such changes as had taken place in the circle were for the better. Bargheer was married, Carl von Meysenbug engaged. The reunions of the former bachelor friends were enlivened by the presence of ladies—charming young married women and pretty girls—and Brahms was ready to abandon himself to any amount of fun, his almost extravagant buoyancy of spirits being no doubt assisted by the reaction from his late tension of mind in regard to his father's affairs. These social occasions were but the interludes between more serious pleasures. Every day there was music at the palace, the castle, or one or more of the private musical houses. Brahms conducted his A major Serenade and played Beethoven's E flat

Concerto at an orchestral concert, and took part in a soirée at the palace, where, amongst other things, he performed the Kreutzer Sonata with Bargheer before the well remembered sympathetic court circle. The visit, which was the last paid by him to Detmold, formed a fitting close to his association with Prince Leopold's court, to whose memory, and especially to that of the various members of the princely family, must ever attach the artistic distinction of their early recognition of the composer's genius and their appreciation of his personality.

Changing his original plans, Brahms left Detmold on Christmas Eve and surprised Frau Schumann, who, with some of the members of her family, was on a visit to Düsseldorf, by joining her just as the tree had been lighted up in preparation for the distribution of presents. His next destination was Oldenburg, where he arrived in time to celebrate the New Year's festival of 1866 with the Dietrichs.* He played his own Concerto and an unpublished composition of Schubert at the Oldenburg subscription concert of January 5, and at the chamber music soirée of the 10th contributed some Bach solos to the programme and took part with Dietrich in a performance of Schumann's Variations in B flat for two pianofortes, and with Engel and Westermann in the second public performance of his own Horn Trio, which created a deep impression. It is important to add here that Westermann on this occasion, and Segisser on that of the Carlsruhe concert of December 7, used the natural horn by the particular desire of Brahms, who now and always insisted to the hornists of his acquaintance on the impossibility of securing a poetical interpretation of his works with the ventil horn.

"If the performer is not obliged by the stopped notes to play softly the piano and violin are not obliged to adapt

---

* "I shall be in Detmold from about December 20-28," he writes to Dietrich from Hamburg, "and come to you about New Year. My journey has given me great pleasure. It has been in every respect satisfactory beyond expectation."

themselves to him, and the tone is rough from the beginning."*

The appearances at Oldenburg closed the *tournée*. Gratified as our musician declared himself to be with the results of his journey, which, if it had not brought him a series of triumphs, had at least demonstrated the fact that his works were gradually making their way through the musical circles of Europe, it was not, as we know, part either of his inclination or his aim to prolong his occasional artistic travels. He chafed at the restriction to personal freedom resulting from fixed engagements, and at the disturbance of mind inseparable from hurried journeys from place to place, and this year he had more than ordinary reason for desiring to be settled again to the quiet concentration of thought essential to all art-creation worthy to be so called. After a second and longer stay in Hamburg that confirmed the satisfaction with which he had lately contemplated the idea of his father's approaching marriage, he returned to Carlsruhe to pass the rest of the winter in Allgeyer's house in Langenstrasse, now known as Kaiserstrasse.

The first quarter of the year 1866 witnessed the publication of a long list of works. By Rieter-Biedermann, the two sets of extraordinarily difficult and brilliant Paganini Variations for Pianoforte, which, when in the hands of a competent executant, are found to be full of original and striking effects, even if they be inferior in musical value to the composer's other achievements in this form;† the three Sacred Choruses, Op. 37, for unaccompanied women's voices, and mentioned in our first volume in connection with the Ladies' Choir. By Simrock, the second String Sextet in G major, worthy sister to its companion work, though it has not obtained quite so wide a popularity, and the

---

* From a letter published by Richard Heuberger (*Beilage zur Allg. Musikzeitung*, 1899, No. 260).

† Brahms, by giving to the variations the second title of Studies for the Pianoforte, has sufficiently indicated the intention with which he placed them before the world.

Sonata in E minor, dedicated to Dr. Josef Gänsbacher. The Horn Trio was issued by the same house quite at the end of the year.*

The Sonata in E minor for pianoforte and violoncello, the earliest of Brahms' seven published duet sonatas for pianoforte and another instrument, all of which are characteristic examples of certain sides of his genius, is a valuable number in the comparatively short list of works of its class for the violoncello. The first movement is of graceful, expressive, delicately melodious character, rising at one point of the development section towards passion, but returning immediately to the dainty, dreaming mood by which the composer so often subdues his hearers to the spell of his imagination. The "allegretto quasi menuetto" which follows, is an exquisite example of a species of movement in the making of which Brahms stands unrivalled. It fascinates with irresistible certainty by its ethereal, playful, poetic fancy, to which the touch of seriousness in the trio offers just sufficient, not too pronounced, contrast. The finale is written *con amore* in the form of a free fugue, which, full of spirit and energy throughout its course, rattles to its close in a lively coda. Care should be taken not to exaggerate the pace of this movement in performance. If taken too quickly, the violoncello passages lose their due effect.

On his return to Carlsruhe, Brahms settled down to continue the composition of the German Requiem, with which he had been more or less occupied since the early spring of 1865,† and it was one of Allgeyer's favourite recollections in later years that a portion of the inspired work had been put on paper under his roof.

---

* The year of the publication of the Horn Trio is given erroneously in Simrock's Thematic Catalogue as 1868. It was played immediately before publication by Frau Schumann, David and Gumpert at the Gewandhaus Kammermusik soirée of December 15, 1866, and was reviewed in the *Allgemeine Musikalische Zeitung* of January 2, 1867.

† A version of the first movement was sent to Frau Schumann at the end of April of that year.—Litzmann III, p. 178.

It is well known that Brahms' nearest friends accepted the composition as his memorial of his mother. "We all think he wrote it in her memory, though he has never expressly said so," Frau Schumann told the author some years later. "Never has a nobler monument been raised by filial love," said Joachim, referring to the German Requiem in the course of his address at the Brahms Memorial Festival held at Meiningen in October, 1899; and we may at least say with certainty that the work, which must be regarded as the crowning point of much of the composer's previous activity, is, on the whole, a memorial of the emotions by which he was stirred during the period that immediately succeeded his mother's death, irrespective of the question as to whether or not it was developed from a work partly planned at an earlier period of his career. It is, however, a circumstance of great interest that the strains he had conceived in his grief for the tragedy of Schumann's illness recurred to him as appropriate for the solemn mourning march—one of the most vivid and extraordinary of his inspirations—of the Requiem,* and we cannot be wrong in assuming that the remembrance of his beloved friend was with him as he worked. Perhaps we may venture to think that two of the strongest affections and griefs of Brahms' life, associated with strangely contrasted objects—Schumann, the great genius and master, Johanna, the simple old mother—live together in this exalted music. There is no warrant for the statement of anything more precise as to the composer's intention excepting with regard to the fifth number, the soprano solo with chorus, which was added some time after the completion of the other movements. Of this it may be said definitely, as will presently appear, that whilst Brahms was engaged in writing it the thought of his mother was present in a special sense to his memory.

Jakob's marriage with Frau Schnack took place in March, rather more than a year after the death of his first wife.

---

* See p. 174.

Johannes sent a substantial sum of money as a wedding present, and his great contentment in the anticipation of his father's happiness was a constant and favourite theme in his talks with Allgeyer, always an interested and sympathetic listener.

A photograph of the composer taken by Allgeyer was sent to Jakob a few weeks after the wedding as a permanent souvenir of his son's felicitations on the occasion. It subsequently passed into the possession of Herr Fritz Schnack, "the second Fritz," as Johannes caressingly called his stepbrother.

Frau Caroline's business was now given up and the newly married pair settled into a comfortable flat on the fourth floor of No. 5 Anscharplatz, at the corner of Valentin's Camp, a respectable business quarter of Hamburg, where there was sufficient accommodation to allow Frau Caroline to turn her business talents to account by taking two or three men boarders. A large airy room, "the corner-room," was reserved for Johannes, who was ultimately responsible for the rent of the flat, and to it were transferred his bookcases, books, and other Hamburg belongings, whilst Elise, whose plans had been unsettled since her mother's death, arranged to live near an aunt in another part of the city. Johannes was, indeed, so cheered by the satisfactory accounts he continued to receive from the newly established household, that there were times during the year following the marriage when he was inclined to entertain the idea of settling again under his father's roof. Frau Caroline managed her affairs with careful but judicious thrift, and there was peace and contentment in the home. In his own way, Jakob was as regular in his habits as his son. Every morning he went to the "Börse" to inquire for work, and was generally successful in obtaining small engagements, often to act as substitute in the theatre orchestras. His position as bassist at the Stadt Theater had come to an end in the course of the fifties, owing to changes in the management, but he continued a member of the Philharmonic Orchestra until a year before his death. He was proud and fond of Frau Caroline, always came home as soon as his work was done to enjoy the good plain fare which she had ready for him, and was perfectly happy as he sat in the kitchen with his pipe and a large cup of weak coffee, watching her movements. Once a week he amused himself by walking in the Jews' quarter of the city and inspecting the cheap secondhand wares with which the vendors sought to tempt his custom. His weakness for bargains was sometimes a source of embarrassment to his wife in spite of her firmness in limiting his loose pocket money to the sum of a few pence. Now he would send home to her a quantity of wardrobe hooks, another time many pounds' weight of honey. "Heavens, Brahms, what are we to do with it?" she would despairingly inquire. "Well, but I could not let it stand at the price, Lina!" he would answer. Johannes used to lecture his father on his weakness for spending money, telling him how careful he, himself, was obliged to be, and could be seriously vexed if he found that Jakob had been really extravagant or thoughtless. This, however, occurred but seldom.

The fact that Brahms passed so many consecutive months in Germany at this period of his career is, no doubt, partly to be explained by his sensitiveness in regard to the political circumstances of the time. It has, however, a more than passing interest in the study of his life since it confirms the impression to be derived from his entire correspondence, that, attractive as Austria might be to him as the home of some of the most glorious traditions of his art, neither the disappointment of his hopes in Hamburg nor the gratifying experiences of his early visits to Vienna, had reconciled him to the idea of permanent residence in a foreign land:

"I am rather old-fashioned in most respects and in this amongst others: that I am not cosmopolitan, but cling to my native city as to a mother. Now, here, where I have so much reason for gratification, I feel and always should feel that I am an outsider, and am not at rest. . . .

"And yet one would like to be bound and to win that

which makes life real and one dreads loneliness. Activity in association with others and surrounded by the living intercourse of family happiness—who is so little human as not to feel the longing for this?"*

These words, written by the composer at the time of his first successes in the Austrian capital, may be accepted as the expression of his inmost conviction during a good many years of his later life. The breaking up of the family home in the Fuhlentwiethe, and the death of his mother, far from weakening his attachment to his native country, caused him to cling the more fondly to whatever he could associate with the affections and proved friendships of his childhood and youth; and the abruptness of manner and speech of which his associates sometimes complained, was no doubt accentuated at this period by his bitter consciousness that the maintenance of the ideal artistic standard from which his allegiance never faltered, was not accepted by his fellow countrymen as compatible with the practical necessities of a settled official activity in their midst.

Of the two companions with whom Brahms chiefly spent his leisure hours during his residence in Carlsruhe, it is probable that his old friend, the dependable, quietly sympathetic Allgeyer, was in the long run the more congenial to him. Stimulating as Levi's society might be, his excitability of temperament, which frequently betrayed him into an exaggerated exaltation of speech, was apt to jar upon Brahms' absolutely sincere nature. No further explanation is needed of the occasional interruptions that occurred in the twelve years' intimacy between the two musicians than such as may be found in a letter addressed by Levi to Frau Schumann on April 19, 1866, the day of Brahms' departure from Carlsruhe, however well grounded the estimate it expresses of the great composer's capacities of mind and spirit:

"Brahms left to-day. . . . There is a man! Most children of men are stamped with the impress of their time

---

* Litzmann III, 130.

and its weaknesses. He, alone, is able to detach himself from all human relations, to remain untouched by the mire and misery of life, to which we can only gaze after, but cannot follow him. Are we to blame if we sometimes turn giddy? He is not to be measured by any scale which we are accustomed to apply to our equals. He looks down upon us from a sovereign throne; when we feel that we have approached him he cries to us: Find your affinity in the mind you resemble, not in me: we are, for the moment, repulsed, wounded, annihilated, but find ourselves invariably drawn to him again with magnetic power. So long as such spirits are amongst us the materialism of the time will not obtain the upper hand; let us gather round him, we who belong together. . . ."

Taking advantage of his neighbourhood to Switzerland, Brahms redeemed an old promise by staying for some weeks of April and May with his publisher, Herr Rieter of Winterthur. In June he settled into lodgings near Theodor Kirchner, at this time living at Zürich, in a house on the Zürichberg, later known as Mittelberg Str. 29, which in 1866 commanded a fine view of lake and mountain. Here every facility was abundantly at hand for his enjoyment. Dividing his time, from a very early hour of the morning until noon, between musing in the open air and work in his room, he was usually to be met about twelve o'clock in the museum, which became a place of rendezvous for his friends. After the early dinner, always taken out of doors in fine weather, and a more or less prolonged sitting over newspapers, or in chat with acquaintance, in the open air, he would drop in at a friend's house, generally Kirchner's, pass an hour or two in informal sociability, and often make music with some of the resident musicians. It was at Kirchner's that he became acquainted with the celebrated Swiss writer and poet, Gottfried Keller, and with the distinguished Zürich professor of surgery, Dr. Theodor Billroth, who was some four years our composer's senior, and who, called subsequently to Vienna, became one of Brahms' most familiar friends. Billroth's love for music was second only to his devotion to his own great vocation. He had studied the violin under Eschmann, played at a weekly trio meeting at his house in Plattenstrasse, Zürich, and was sufficiently proficient to take part on the viola with professional musicians in private performances of Beethoven's quartets and Brahms' sextets. He could play the piano well, was a good sight reader, and acted occasionally as musical critic to one of the Zürich papers.

"Brahms arrived here a few days ago," he writes on the 22nd of April to his friend, Professor Lübke of Stuttgart. "This morning he and Kirchner played some of Liszt's symphonic poems on two pianofortes. Horrible music! . . . We purged ourselves with Brahms' new sextet that has just come out. Brahms and Kirchner played it as a duet."*

The composer became intimate, also, at the house of Wagner's great friends, Herr and Frau Wesendonck, and could not hear enough about the composer of the "Meistersinger," of whom the Wesendoncks possessed inexhaustible personal recollections and several valuable souvenirs. Amongst these was the master's autograph score of the "Rheingold," an object that was regarded by Brahms with immense interest and respect.

Traits of habit and character similar to those with which the reader is familiar, and which recall the period of the Detmold visits, are described in Steiner's "Recollections," by Capellmeister Friedrich Hegar,† who was the inseparable associate of Brahms and Kirchner:

" . . . We were no less impressed by his extraordinarily sound health. He could venture upon anything. How often has he passed the night on the sofa of my bachelor's quarters when he was disinclined to climb the Zürichberg in the late hours of evening. Once indeed, when an older friend less hardy than himself claimed my hospitality, he

---

* "Briefe von Theodor Billroth" (sixth enlarged edition).

† "Neujahrsblatt der Allgemeinen Musikgesellschaft in Zürich," 1898.

lay down underneath my grand piano, and declared next morning that he had slept splendidly."

Hegar mentions that Brahms' musical memory and unusually rapid power of apprehension excited the astonished admiration of the Zürich musicians.

"When we played him our compositions for the first time, he would afterwards sit down and repeat long portions note for note from memory, pointing out the weak places."

One or two reminiscences of the summer are to be found in the volume of Billroth's letters from which quotation has already been made. Amongst them is the description of a music party at his house, at which Brahms was present to hear a performance of his lately published Sextet in G major. The consciousness of the composer's presence so unnerved Billroth that he was obliged to ask Eschmann, who was amongst the listeners, to relieve him of his part of second viola.

"I have learnt never to play before a composer," he wrote a few days afterwards, "unless his work has been well rehearsed. As I was quite familiar with the composition, I could imagine the vexation Brahms must have felt, although he put the matter aside in the kindest way. Kirchner, Brahms and Hegar had been up late together the night before and were tired. Everything contributed to make the evening dull."

Of the sextet he says: "I think it wonderfully fine; so clear, so simple, so masterly."

Brahms remained in Switzerland until the middle of August, and arriving on the 17th of this month to stay for a few weeks at his old lodgings in Lichtenthal, surprised Frau Schumann by appearing before her for the first time with a beard. He did not at this period persevere very long in wearing the appendage, which changed his appearance in an unusual degree, but he adopted it a second time, and as it proved, permanently, about fourteen years later.

A record of the impression produced by Brahms' personality upon a fashionable lady to whom he was presented a few days after his arrival is to be found in a letter written on August 23 by Madame de Mouchanoff-Kalergis, a well known patroness of music and literature, and a friend of Wagner and Liszt. Her words derive an added interest by comparison with the expressions used by Rubinstein in 1856, after he had made Brahms' acquaintance in Hanover.*

"Madame Viardot a arrangé un peu de musique pour moi avant hier . . . Brahms passe un mois ici avant de retourner a Vienne. Je l'ai eu à diner. C'est une nature intéressante par sa simplicité originale et sauvage. Dans un autre genre que Wagner le premier compositeur de l'époque. Dès que j'ai un peu de forces j'étudie sa musique et ne me pardonne pas d'avoir été dix ans sans le connaître."†

The composer had worked steadily on at the German Requiem during the months of his residence in Switzerland, and that he now completed it in Lichtenthal—save and excepting only the fifth number—is to be inferred from the inscription on the manuscript score—"Baden-Baden im Sommer, 1866"—now in possession of the Gesellschaft der Musikfreunde at Vienna. Great additional interest is given to this date by a short entry made by Frau Schumann in her diary early in August, which is, without doubt, the earliest written note upon the finished work.

"Johannes has been playing me some magnificent movements out of a Requiem of his own and a string quartet in C

---

* See p. 201.

† Marie of Mouchanoff-Kalergis, née Countess Nesselrode. In "Briefen an ihre Tochter," edited by La Mara.

The acquaintance between Madame de Kalergis and Brahms was probably confined to the two meetings referred to above, as they were not again in Baden-Baden at the same time. The composer's name is twice again mentioned in Madame's letters, but only in reference to his music. On June 1, 1866, she writes: "As a distraction I turn to music, Brahms always consoles me"; and on September 12: "Brahms colours my life, and the beauty of his style soothes my nerves."

minor. The Requiem delighted me even more, however. It is full of tender and again daring thoughts. I cannot feel clear as to how it will sound, but in myself it sounds glorious."

The extract has a double interest, as furnishing a new illustration of Brahms' caution with regard to publication, and especially in the case of works which constituted for him a new artistic departure. The String Quartet in C minor was not published until 1873, seven years from our present date. One more publication of the year—the set of sixteen Waltzes for pianoforte duet, dedicated to Hanslick, and issued in the summer by Rieter Biedermann—remains for mention. Several, at least, of the waltzes date from the Detmold period and were played by Brahms and heard by Carl von Meysenbug at the Hotel Stadt, Frankfurt. They are inimitable in their delicate, caressing grace, and possess a charm that is, perhaps, unequalled by any known examples of their kind.

"Your name came in quite of itself just now as I was writing the title of the duet waltzes which are to appear shortly. I hardly know how it was. I was thinking of Vienna, of the pretty girls with whom you play duets, of you yourself, who like such things, of my good friend, and what not."*

A letter of September 10 from Brahms to Dietrich mentions the Requiem, and evidently answers an inquiry from Albert as to the long delayed Symphony in C minor of which we heard in the summer of 1862.

---

* The publication of the waltzes is erroneously dated 1867 in Simrock's catalogue. Their appearance is chronicled, and they are reviewed at length in the *Allgemeine Musikalische Zeitung* respectively of August 15 and September 12, 1866. They were performed by Frau Schumann and Dietrich immediately after publication at a party given by the Grand Duchess of Oldenburg.

"DEAR DIETRICH!

"Before the summer is over you shall be reminded of me by a short greeting. . . .

"Unfortunately I cannot wait upon you with a symphony, but it would be a joy to have you here for a day, to play you my so-called German Requiem.

"I have been till now living in Switzerland, in Zürich. I shall stay here a little and think of going then to Vienna. . . ."*

About the middle of October Joachim arrived in Lichtenthal, and after a few days' stay, carried Brahms away with him. He had become a man at large through the political events of the year by which the kingdom of Hanover became part of Prussia, having felt it impossible to accept the offer made him to retain his appointment after the deposition of King George, and was able to follow his inclination as to his arrangements for the autumn and winter season. These included tours in Switzerland and France and it had been arranged between the friends that Johannes should combine with him in some of his Swiss concerts.

The journey was very successful, and afforded Brahms quite unexpected evidence of the progress his music was making in Switzerland. This country was, in fact, one of the earliest in which his art met with general appreciation, and much of the credit of its acceptance there must be ascribed to the efforts of Theodor Kirchner, who, as the reader may remember, was one of the most gifted musicians of the Schumann circle, and who seized every opportunity that offered from the beginning of Brahms' career, to spread the understanding of his compositions. Kirchner filled an organist's post at Winterthur for nearly ten years before his removal to Zürich in 1862, and whilst developing the active

---

* The date assigned to this letter in Dietrich's "Recollections" is one amongst several similar mistakes that occur in the volume. They are to be explained by the circumstances that Brahms rarely put dates to his letters, and that those in question were supplied from memory.

musical life of the little town, made his influence felt far beyond its limits.

The tour opened on October 24 in Schaffhausen, and included Zürich, Bern, Winterthur, Basle, and finally Mühlhausen in Alsace. An interesting incident of the visit to Mühlhausen was the renewal of friendly relations, after ten years of estrangement, between Joachim and von Bülow, who was resident during the season 1866-7 at Basle, and gave Trio concerts there with Abel and Kahnt. No communication took place between the former Weimar intimates during the week passed by Brahms and Joachim at Basle, but Bülow's affectionate nature was strongly stirred by seeing his old friend again on the concert platform and hearing his public performances, which he describes as "ideal perfection." The sequel may be told in the words of his letter to Raff, dated Basle, November 22.

"And now, a great piece of news. On Sunday the 10th I travelled to Mühlhausen for the Brahms-Joachim concert, and the relation of friendship between Joachim and me was renewed on French soil after ten years' interruption. This will lead to no results of a positive nature, but a stone has been taken from my heart, and from his also as he has assured your sister-in-law. For my sake Joachim returned to Basle for a few hours and then took the night train to Paris."*

Some years were yet to elapse before Bülow could pretend to any cordiality of feeling towards the art of Brahms. In the same letter we read:

"I respect and admire him, but—at a distance. The Pianoforte Quintet seems to me the most interesting of his large compositions. . . . Kiel is much more sympathetic to me."*

He prevailed upon himself, indeed, to play the Horn Trio at his Basle Trio concert of March 26, 1867, when his

---

* "Briefe u. Schriften von Hans von Bülow." Published by Marie von Bülow.

BRAHMS AND STOCKHAUSEN, 1868.

colleagues were Abel and Hans Richter, who commenced his artist's career as a hornist, and was at this time living in Switzerland in the enjoyment of Wagner's intimacy; and he included Joachim's Variations for viola and pianoforte in the same programme; but as late as 1870 he wrote to Raff:

"What do the Br.'s matter to me? Brahms, Brahmüller, Bruch, etc. Don't mention them again! Who knows whether a Riehl may not turn up in 1950 to beplutarch them as maestrinelli? The only one who interests me is Braff!"

The fact that von Bülow's critical faculty was subject to the disturbing influence of his capacity for warm friendship cannot lessen the admiration inspired by his talents and his generous nature. His severe animadversions on Brahms' works, together with his practical neglect of them up to a period when his opinion as to their merits had become very much a matter of indifference, may be pardoned by the lovers of our master's art, who remember that they were, for the most part, the outcome of his deep personal affection for Liszt, Wagner and Joachim, and of his long continued intimate association with the leaders and prominent disciples of the New-German school.

Brahms returned to Vienna, after about a year and a half of absence, immediately after his friend's departure from Mühlhausen, and spent the winter quietly at work in his room on the fourth storey of No. 6, Poststrasse. The earliest event of any importance to his career that marks the opening months of the year 1867 is the first public performance of the Sextet in G major, which was given at the Hellmesberger concert of February 3. The reader will by this time hardly be surprised to learn that the work was received without enthusiasm.

"The composer was certainly called for and applauded," says Schelle, Hanslick's successor in the *Presse*, and a loyal though unbiassed supporter of Brahms, "but it was with a certain reserve. One felt distinctly that the public was not carried away by the work, but desired to do justice to so admirable an achievement. . . . Brahms may be called a virtuoso in the modern development of the quartet style . . . but only that can reach the heart which proceeds from the heart, and the sextet comes from the hand and the head, whilst the warm pulsations of the heart are to be felt only at intervals."

So Bach's works were once spoken of, so Beethoven's in their day. So, it may almost be said, must be criticised all musical creative achievement that adequately expresses an original individuality. The composer of genius has to go through a long apprenticeship before he acquires a language of his own really capable of conveying his thoughts to the world. By the time he is master of it, he has, by the nature of things, placed himself outside the immediate comprehension of all but a few specially qualified listeners, and must be willing to wait for his reward until some of those to whom he speaks have had time to follow him a certain distance along his appointed path, and opportunity to become familiarised with his manner of utterance. Brahms was content to wait, and he waited almost with equanimity of spirit, never losing faith in the future, though he had something more pronounced to encounter than indifference. Hirsch, of the *Wiener Zeitung*, wrote apropos of the sextet:

"We are always seized with a kind of oppression when the new John in the wilderness, Herr Johannes Brahms, announces himself. This prophet, proclaimed by Robert Schumann in his darkening hours, who, for the rest, has his energetic admirers in Vienna—we mention this in our position, from pure love of truth—makes us quite disconsolate with his impalpable, dizzy tone-vexations that have neither body nor soul and can only be products of the most desperate effort. Such manifest, glaring artificiality is quite peculiar to this gentleman. How many drops of perspiration may adhere to these note-heads?"

On the 25th of this same month of February, the earlier B flat Sextet, by this time almost popular in more than one continental city, and long known in New York through Mason's concerts, was performed for the first time in England at the Monday Popular Concerts, St. James's Hall,

London, by Joachim, Louis Ries, Henry Blagrove, Zerbini, Paque, and Piatti. The director, S. Arthur Chappell, printed a notice in the programme books to the effect that he introduced the work by Joachim's desire. It made no impression, and the composer was not again heard at the Popular Concerts for five years.

If the recognition of Brahms' exact claims as a composer, even by his Austrian public, long remained dubious, his qualities as a pianist seldom failed to evoke unmistakable signs of their warm approval. With the arrival of March he prevailed upon himself this year to announce concerts in Vienna, Graz, Klagenfurth and Pesth, and the success of his performances was unequivocal, in spite of the approach of spring and the unusual warmth of the season.

"At last a pianist who entirely takes hold of one," exclaims Schelle, writing of the first concert of March 17; "one only needs to hear his first few chords to be convinced that Herr Brahms is a player of quite extraordinary stamp. The musical critic of the *Wiener Zeitung* writes that Herr Brahms was cordially received by his 'party.' We may remark that Brahms was received, not by a 'party,' but by the entire very numerous public, with applause such as is seldom heard in Vienna concert-rooms. If, however, the audience of the evening is to be described as the 'party' of the distinguished artist, it must be said that his party consists of the cultivated experts of musical Vienna."

The instrumental numbers of the programme were Beethoven's Fantasia, Op. 77; Bach's G major Fantasia; Brahms' Scherzo; Schumann's Etudes Symphoniques; Brahms' Paganini Variations. The concert giver played as an additional piece his own arrangement for the pianoforte of the fugue from Beethoven's String Quartet, Op. 59, No. 3,

"which," says Schelle, "claims almost more admiration even than his performance, for it is a most faithful reflection of the entire score which we meet unchanged in the effective costume."

At the second concert in Vienna, which took place on April 7, after Brahms' return from the provinces, the programme included Bach's F major Toccata; Beethoven's Sonata, Op. 109; Brahms' Handel Variations and Fugue; Schumann's Fantasia in C, Op. 17; and short pieces by Scarlatti and Schubert. As an additional piece, an arrangement of a movement from Schubert's Octet was conceded. Vocal numbers were included in both programmes.

Brahms himself mentions the concerts in a letter to Dietrich.

"The result was so good in every respect," he writes, "that I must call myself doubly an ass for not having secured it earlier and taken the opportunity to get rid of my Requiem."

He let the work lie for several months longer, however, without coming to any decision about it. On July 30 he again wrote to Dietrich.

". . . In all haste: I start to-morrow with my father on a little tour through Upper Austria. I do not know when I shall be back. Keep the accompanying Requiem until I write to you. Don't let it go out of your hands and write to me very seriously by-and-by what you think of it.

"An *offer* from Bremen would be very acceptable to me.

"It would have to be combined with a concert engagement. In short *Reinthaler* must probably be sufficiently pleased with the thing to do something for it.

"For the rest, I am inclined to let such matters quietly alone, for I do not intend to worry myself about them.

"I am ready for anything from Christmas onwards. Joachim and I probably give concerts here before."

There is a trace of nervous anxiety in this letter which leaves little doubt that Brahms had within him the consciousness that in the German Requiem he had transcended all his previous achievements, and that he was even unusually anxious to ensure a favourable opportunity for the hearing of his new work. Until now it had only been submitted in Frau Schumann's drawing-room to a few enthusiastic friends of the Baden circle, and it is evident that he did not easily bring himself to the resolution of sending it away even for Dietrich's sympathetic inspection, and that, whilst he hoped, he somewhat dreaded to hear the result of a communication with Reinthaler. We must postpone for awhile our account of the fortunes of the manuscript in order to follow our musician on his holiday journey, on which he no doubt started with a mind sufficiently relieved by the mere fact of his decision, to be able to await with composure the next issues of fate.

Herr königlich Musikdirektor Carl Martin Reinthaler (1822-1896), municipal music director of Bremen and organist of the cathedral, was a distinguished musician and the composer of numerous works in very varied forms, vocal and instrumental. His oratorio, "Jepthah," was performed in London in 1856 under John Hullah's direction; several of his operas—"Käthchen von Heilbronn," "Edda," etc.—composed later in his career, were given with success in Bremen, Hanover, and other towns, and his "Bismarck Hymn" won the prize in a competition adjudged at Dortmund. By his talent and earnestness in his position as conductor of the orchestral concerts at Bremen, he did much to raise the standard of musical taste in the city.

CHAPTER XIV.

1867-1868.

Brahms' holiday journey with his father and Gänsbacher—Austrian concert-tour with Joachim—The German Requiem—Performance of the first three choruses in Vienna—Tour with Stockhausen in North Germany and Denmark—Performance of the German Requiem in Bremen Cathedral—First performance of Pianoforte Quintet.

OUR composer's invitation to his father to accompany him on a tour amongst the Austrian Alps had mightily gratified Jakob. The violinist, young Carl Bade, happening to call at the Anscharplatz on the day of his start for Vienna, found him carefully dressed for the journey, and in a high state of elation and delight. Wrapping himself in an air of mysterious mock dignity, he scarcely vouchsafed a word of greeting to his wondering young friend, but, drawing himself up to his full height, gravely adjusted his necktie and paced the room in silence. Then, coming to a standstill, he pursed up his lips and looked at Bade with an expression of sly significance. "Min Hannes het mi inladt; ick reis mit min Hannes" (My Hannes has invited me; I travel with my Hannes), he said in answer to Bade's demands for an explanation. A glimpse of him on his arrival is afforded by the recollection of Dr. Josef Gänsbacher, who was to accompany father and son on their journey, and calling to make last arrangements with Johannes, found Jakob with him. The manuscript of the beautiful song, "Mainacht," was at hand, and at his friend's request Gänsbacher sang it then and there, and added the lovely "Wie bist du meine Königin" for the benefit of the elder Brahms, who expressed himself, as in duty bound, pleased with the songs, and was undoubtedly gratified by the compliment paid him.

The route chosen by the travellers lay through Styria and Carinthia, regions abounding in grand and romantic scenery of mountain, lake and forest; but though Johannes, an inveterate optimist in many ways, talked afterwards of his father's enjoyment of the journey, it is to be feared that Jakob, who had scarcely quitted Hamburg since his arrival there as a youth of nineteen, did not develop any great appreciation of the beauties of nature. He got on fairly well when walking on the even, and actually accomplished the long tramp from Mürzsteg to Wildalpen on foot, though it was a great deal too much for him, but he was too old and heavy to begin an apprenticeship as a mountaineer and remained behind whilst Gänsbacher and Johannes made the ascent of the Hochschwab. Jakob was best able to appreciate those parts of the journey which were made by carriage or train, though he was very silent throughout the tour, perhaps hardly knowing how to express himself. One day, however, when the three travellers were in a boat on the secluded and romantic Gründlsee, he stood up and looked round as if impressed by the beauty of the scene. "Just like the Alster at home in Hamburg," he remarked at length as he reseated himself.

Johannes fell in with some parties of his Austrian friends during the expedition, and was plainly gratified by the consideration shown to his father by one and all. One enthusiastic lady went so far as to bestow a kiss on the old man—an attention which procured him some good natured raillery from his son, and which he discreetly left unmentioned for some time after his return to the Anscharplatz. He went back by way of Heidelberg, stopping to see the castle and other attractions by the desire of Johannes, and a little while after reaching home, received from Vienna a souvenir of the doubtful pleasures of his journey in the shape of some mountain charts of the districts through which he had travelled, with blue lines drawn to mark the summits he had been able to attain by mountain railways or other mechanical means of transit. The maps, carefully preserved by Jakob, remain as a memorial of the composer's loving thought of his father, whom he indulged and spoilt almost like a petted child at this period of his life.

The journey over, Brahms' thoughts reverted to the manuscript which he had confided to Dietrich's care, and as soon as he was back in Vienna he wrote to beg for its return:

"Dear Albert,

"Please send my score back to me as soon as possible and turn the opportunity to good account by enclosing this and that—above all a long letter.

"I had the great pleasure of having my father with me for some weeks. We made a pleasant tour through Styria and Salzburg. Imagine what enjoyment my father's pleasure gave me, he had never seen a mountain.

"Now I think of remaining here quietly; it is unfortunately useless for me to make plans, for only that happens which comes of itself.

"Nevertheless I wish to have the Requiem in my own cupboard again, so send . . ."*

To this note Dietrich returned no answer, and Brahms, becoming impatient, applied for information as to the whereabouts of his work to Joachim, who wrote back that he had not seen the manuscript but believed it was in Reinthaler's keeping. Possibly Brahms may have been a little startled at finding that Dietrich, in his eager friendship, had put such an elastic interpretation upon the mention of the Bremen director quoted in our last chapter as to pass over the injunction not to part with the manuscript; he cannot, however, have been otherwise than gratified at finding, as the result, that the musician of his own selection had been so

---

* Dietrich.

impressed by the work as to wish to produce it at the earliest appropriate opportunity in the cathedral of Bremen.

It is of extreme interest to read in Brahms' published correspondence that Reinthaler suggested the addition to the German Requiem of a movement which should associate the work unmistakably with the cardinal doctrines of ecclesiastical christianity and that Brahms unhesitatingly rejected the proposal.

"You occupy not merely religious, but essentially christian ground in the work. The second number already alludes to the prophecy of the Lord's return, and in the last but one the mystery of the resurrection of the dead is treated in detail. The central point around which everything turns in the consciousness of the Christian is, however, absent. 'If Christ be not risen then is our faith vain,' says St. Paul. All the same you say: 'Blessed are the dead which die in the Lord *henceforth*,' which can only mean: since the accomplishment of Christ's work of redemption . . ."

Brahms answered:

"As regards the text I will confess that I should gladly have left out the 'German' and substituted 'human.' Also that I dispensed with passages such as St. John's Gospel, Ch. 3, verse 16, with all knowledge and intention. On the other hand, I have no doubt included much because I am a musician, because I required it, because I can neither argue away nor strike out a 'henceforth' from my venerable parts."*

The first performance of the Requiem, as originally completed, to be given under Brahms' direction in Bremen Cathedral, was fixed for Good Friday, April 10, 1868. Meanwhile the composer's engagements kept him in Austria. The first three numbers of the new work were to be produced

---

* Brahms' "Briefwechsel" III, pp. 7-9.

N.B.—The editor's note on p. 7 of this volume seems irrelevant. The German Requiem was certainly "enlarged" by the addition of the present fifth movement, but not in the direction suggested by Reinthaler.

under Herbeck at the Gesellschaft concert of December 1, and a tour arranged with Joachim for the ante-Christmas concert season included concerts in Vienna, Budapest and various provincial towns. The journey, which opened at Vienna on November 9, was triumphantly successful. Joachim performed the great solos of his repertoire by Bach, Tartini and Spohr, and shorter pieces by Schumann and Paganini, with all of whom concert goers are now familiar, appearing also on his own account in several great orchestral concerts. Brahms played works by Bach, Schumann, Schubert, and some of his own compositions. Together the concert givers were heard in several of Beethoven's duet Sonatas, Schubert's Fantasia, Op. 159, and Rondo Brilliant, Op. 70, etc.

"When Brahms and Joachim play Beethoven, Bach, Schubert together, the conceptions are like living tone pictures," says Billroth, who, called to Vienna about a year after his first acquaintance with Brahms at Zürich and settled there for good, had the delight of receiving and hearing his two great artist friends at his house several times during the two months of Joachim's stay.

The Gesellschaft concert of December 1 was devoted to the memory of Schubert, and the first three numbers of the German Requiem formed an appropriate first portion of a programme of which the second half consisted of a selection from Schubert's music to "Rosamund," given for the first time in a concert room. The choruses were, of course, sung by the Singverein, and Dr. Pänzer, of the imperial chapel, was responsible for the baritone solo of the Requiem.

The performance of Brahms' movements did not result in a success, though the first two were received with some tokens of approval. At the conclusion of the third an extraordinary scene took place. The now celebrated pedal point,* on which the last section of this number is con-

---

* A pedal point is a sound sustained, according to conditions prescribed by the rules of art, during a succession of varying harmonies of which it need not form an essential part.

structed, produced—partly owing to a mistake of the drummer, who drowned the chorus by playing the famous "D" *forte* throughout—a condition of nervous tension in a portion of the audience, a longing to be relieved from the monotony of the one dominating sound; and when the composer appeared on the platform in answer to the calls of some of his hearers, unmistakable demonstrations of hostility mingled with the plaudits. It may, indeed, be confidently surmised, and cannot appear surprising, that but few even of those who supported him on this occasion had any clear conception either of the meaning or importance of his work. To Hanslick it appeared

"one of the ripest fruits in the domain of sacred music, developed out of the style of Beethoven's late works. . . . The harmonic and contrapuntal art learnt by Brahms in the school of Bach, and inspired by him with the living breath of the present, is almost forgotten in the expression of touching lament, increasing to the annihilating death-shudder."

Of its reception he says:

"It is intelligible that a composition so difficult to understand, and which deals only with ideas of death, is not adapted for popular success and that it does not entirely answer to the demands of a great public. We should have supposed, however, that a presentiment of the greatness and seriousness of the work would have suggested itself even to those who do not like it and would have won their respect. This seems not to have been the case with half a dozen gray-haired fanatics of the old school, who had the rudeness to greet the applauding majority and the composer, as he appeared, with prolonged hissing—a requiem on the decorum and good manners of a Vienna concert-room which astonishes and grieves us."

Schelle, after reviewing the first number sympathetically and the second almost enthusiastically, continues:

"Unfortunately the third is extremely inferior to it [No. 2]; the text demanded a strong increase of effect which the composer has been incapable of giving. The bass solo is not written gratefully for the voice and there is much that is obtrusively bizarre and unedifying in the chorus. . . . The movement was a failure. . . ."

Hirsch did not fail to make use of his opportunity in the *Weiner Zeitung*. He speaks of the "heathenish noise of the kettledrums," and declares "in the interest of truth" that the opposition party in the audience had an "immense majority."

The concert is mentioned by Billroth in a letter dated December 24:

"I like Brahms better every time I meet him. Hanslick says, quite rightly, that he has the same fault as Bach and Beethoven; he has too little of the sensuous in his art both as composer and pianist. I think it is rather an intentional avoidance of everything sensuous as of a fault. His Requiem is so nobly spiritual and so Protestant-Bachish that it was difficult to make it go down here. The hissing and clapping became really violent; it was a party conflict. In the end the applause conquered."

It is characteristic of Brahms that his belief in the future of his work was not diminished by the untoward incidents of this occasion. He looked forward to the result of the coming performance in Bremen with a confidence that was even enhanced by the fact that he had gained experience with respect to the instrumentation of the third chorus.

He sent part of his manuscript to Marxsen with a letter from which the following quotation was first published by Sittard in his "Studien und Charakteristiken":

"I send you some novelties and beg you, if time allows, to write me *one* or *many* words about them. I enclose also something from my Requiem and *on this I earnestly beg you to write to me*. It looks rather curious in places and perhaps, in order to spare my manuscript, you would take some music paper and put down useful remarks. *I should like that very much*. The eternal 'D' in No. 3. If I do not use the organ it does not sound. There is much I should like to ask. I hope you have time and some inclination; then you will perceive at once what there is to ask and what to say."

It is, as Hanslick observed, by no means unintelligible that the first part of the German Requiem was not immediately accepted by the general body of listeners assembled at the Gesellschaft concert of December 1, unprepared as they were for the new and important element underlying its conception. The title chosen by the composer was at the time, and has been occasionally since, demurred to as misleading, on account of the long association of the term Requiem with the ritual of the Roman Church. It should, however, be obvious that by the word "German" a departure is indicated from the practice of previous composers, which places the composition in a category of its own and gives to its message an applicableness beyond the limitations of creed. Brahms arranged his own words, and by the fact of doing so, by his inspired musical treatment of his texts, and his direct avoidance of giving to his work an association with a particular church service or a familiar musical form, requiem or mass, cantata or oratorio, has preserved in it, whether or not consciously, an element of personal fervour that constitutes part of the secret of its spell.

The texts, culled from various books of the Old and New Testaments and the Apocrypha,* have been chosen, with entire absence of so-called doctrinal purpose, as parts of the people's book, of Luther's Bible, the accepted representative to Protestant nations of the highest aspirations of man, and have been so arranged as to present in succession the ascending ideas of sorrow consoled, doubt overcome, death vanquished. That they open and close with the thought of love is not of necessity to be ascribed solely to the artistic requirements of the work, or the exigencies of its sacred theme. Whoever has studied Brahms' life and works with

---

* Matt. v, 4; Ps. cxxvi, 5, 6; 1 Pet. i, 24; James v, 7; 1 Pet. i, 25; Isa. xxxv, 10; Ps. xxxix, 4-7; Wisd. iii, 1; Ps. lxxxiv, 1, 2, 4; John xvi, 22; Ecclus. li, 27; Isa. lxvi, 13; Heb. xiii, 14; 1 Cor. xv, 51-55; Rev. iv, 11; Rev. xiv, 13.

sympathetic insight will be aware that the suggestion of love triumphant runs through both like a continuous silver thread, and it is open to those who choose, to accept this as indicative of a faith dwelling within him, which was none the less fruitful for good because it knew nothing of the dogma of the churches.

The opening chorus of the Requiem furnishes the keynote of its spirit:

"*Blessed are they that mourn, for they shall be comforted. He that goeth forth and weepeth, bearing precious seed, shall doubtless come again with joy, bearing his sheaves with him. They that sow in tears shall reap in joy.*"

What more reassuring prelude could prepare the human soul for encounter with its most dreaded foe than these inspired words, heard in the exquisite setting of consolation by which the composer has illumined their meaning? The tenderness of the benediction, the passion of the anticipation, the recurring mournful calm that dies away in the softest whisper of comfort, place the mind in an attitude of awed suspense which finds its solution in the opening bars of the solemn, mysterious march of the second movement. Here we are surely in the majestic presence of death incarnate, wrapped, however, in a haze of beauty, sorrow, tenderness, compassion, that betoken, not the ruthless enemy of mankind, but a deeply mournful messenger subdued to a divine purpose. "*Behold, all flesh is as grass, and all the glory of man as the flower of grass,*" chant the altos and tenors in unison an octave above the basses, something of unearthliness in their tones, with the alternate repetitions of the march; and the delicate, evanescent harmonies of the answering phrase: "*The grass withereth, the flower fadeth,*" strangely deepen the impression of transitoriness conveyed by the text. Relief is given by a middle episode of somewhat more animated character: "*Be patient therefore, brethren, unto the coming of the Lord. Behold, the husbandman waiteth for the precious fruit of the earth, and hath long patience for it until he receive the early and latter rain. Be ye also patient."* The final ending of the march, which is repeated after the episode, is succeeded by the outburst of a transitional passage—*"God's word endureth for ever"*—leading to the vigorous gladness of the second section of the movement (fugato)—*"And the ransomed of the Lord shall return and come to Zion with songs and everlasting joy upon their heads: they shall obtain joy and gladness, and sorrow and sighing shall flee away"*—whose ringing, jubilant tones are checked only by the passing shade of sorrow, until it subsides into the more tranquilly happy mood in which the chorus terminates.

In the third number the vision alters. To exaltation succeeds abasement. We are shown the despondency, that is almost despair, of the soul prostrate before its Lord: *"Lord, make me to know mine end, and the number of my days what it is, that I may know how frail I am."* The movement opens with a baritone solo, supported by basses, drums and horn, which seems to crave nothing, hope for nothing. Words and melody are, however, immediately repeated in chorus with plain harmonies that somewhat relieve the first impressive gloom. Then there is a change. The final cadence of the solo* becomes, in the chorus, a surprise cadence upon which the baritone re-enters: *"Behold, thou hast made my days as an handbreadth, and mine age is as nothing before thee."* The tension relaxes, and a note of pleading makes itself felt that is strengthened in the choral repetition of the phrase by the movement of the accompanying instruments. Through despondency, through resignation, through questioning, the soul gradually rises to hope: *"Verily man at his best state is altogether vanity. Surely every man walketh in a vain show, surely they are disquieted in vain; he heapeth up riches, and knoweth not who shall gather them. Now, Lord,*

---

* The cadences of music are somewhat analogous to the punctuation of literature. A "final cadence" has the effect of closing a musical period.

what do I wait for?" The pleading becomes importunity, and the crisis is reached with the reiteration of the last words, first in an increasing agitation, and finally in deliberate, hushed tones that seem to challenge the Lord. The effect that follows is, perhaps, unsurpassed in its pure loveliness throughout the domain of sacred music. With the passage: "*My hope is in thee,*" all doubt is resolved in a glow of warmth, reconciliation and trust, and the perfect assurance of faith: "*The souls of the righteous are in God's hand,*" becomes the subject of an accompanied choral fugue, constructed from beginning to end upon a tonic pedal point, which establishes the brief inspiration of the transition passage in a protracted expression of unshakable confidence, and forms, not only the climax of the movement, but the first climax of the entire work. In it the soul attains to an elevation of faith from which it does not again falter. Though sorrow may not yet be finally subdued, doubt is conquered, and the fourth number: "*How amiable are thy dwellings, O Lord of Hosts! My soul longeth, yea, even fainteth for the courts of the Lord: my heart and my flesh crieth out for the living God. Blessed are they that dwell in thy house, they will be still praising thee*"—is a clear, melodious choral song with a flowing accompaniment, harmonised simply, and with an occasional point of imitation, that expresses simple affection and trust, emphasised towards the close of the movement by the employment of increased contrapuntal resource.

The fifth number, added, as we have said, after the work was first finished, and not essential to its conception as a whole, may have been conceded to some need of contrast felt by the composer on hearing the completed six movements consecutively. It consists of a very beautiful soprano solo with chorus, of rather mystic character, to the words: "*And ye now are sorrowful. As one whom his mother comforteth, so will I comfort you.*"

The sixth chorus opens with a dirge: "*For we have no abiding city, but we seek one to come*"—soon to be interrupted by the baritone solo: "*Behold, I show you a mystery: we shall not all sleep, but we shall be changed.*" The words are repeated by the chorus with a heightening agitation of mysterious expectancy, that leaps suddenly at the clarion call to tumultuous exultation: "*In a moment, in the twinkling of an eye, at the trump: for the trumpet shall sound, and the dead shall be raised incorruptible, and we shall be changed.*" The wild agitation is stayed by the quiet message of the solo: "*Then shall be brought to pass the saying that is written,*" and a prolonged half-cadence leads to the re-entry of the chorus in a magnificently sustained inspiration of triumphant joy: "*Death is swallowed up in victory. O death, where is thy sting? O grave, where is thy victory?*" The glorious movement, after mounting from height to height of power and splendour, suddenly, with an unexpected change of time and key, reaches its climax in a brilliant fugue, that seems, with its passion of never-ending praise, to reopen the door of heaven and to transport the soul of the hearer to the dazzling scene of the throne that is filled with the ineffable presence of God: "*Thou art worthy, O Lord, to receive honour and power, for thou hast created all things, and for thy good pleasure they are and were created.*"

The great work has now reached its final climax. The imagination of the modern seer, soaring beyond sorrow, doubt, death, has pierced for a moment through the mystery of things and shown us the unspeakable. But the vision is not yet at an end. As in the writing of the Revelation of St. John, so in the inspired music of the German Requiem. After the lightnings and thunders and all the manifold glory of the throne, the voice of the spirit: "*Blessed are the dead which die in the Lord henceforth; Yea, saith the Spirit, that they may rest from their labours, and their works do follow them.*" Confident, tender, majestic, the message floats through the seventh movement, a veritable requiem, a true song of peace, and, heard at length in the tones of the

28

benediction with which the work opens, sinks into silence with reiteration of blessing.

It would be an attractive task to analyse the technical means that Brahms has employed to give musical expression to the varied ideas, all rooted in the central one of overruling love, which together form the subject of this exalted work. Whilst he has used the resources of classical art with a power and ease that recall the mastery of Bach and Handel, he has given warmth and life to his creation by availing himself of the harmonic development of musical means to which the genius of Schumann gave such strong stimulus. Wisely conservative, he was also modern in the best sense, nor could the German Requiem have attained the position it has won in the hearts of thousands of men and women to whom it has brought comfort in bereavement or solace in times of mental distress, if he had not understood and shared in the spirit, and answered to it in an idiom, proper to his time. This should not be forgotten in the performance of the great work, which is sometimes given with a cold, formal correctness supposed to be appropriate in the case of classical compositions. Brahms was not a pedant, but a poet and idealist, and the full beauty and fascination of his music is disclosed only when it is interpreted with the insight that is born of enthusiasm and imagination.

The Horn Trio was played in Vienna at the Hellmesberger Quartet concert of December 29 by Brahms, Hellmesberger, and Kleinecke. Kleinecke performed on the natural horn, and the beauty of his tone was remarked on by one or two of the critics. The trio was received not unfavourably, but with the reserve that usually attended the early performances of the composer's works in the imperial capital at this period of his career.

The publications of the year were but two in number—the Horn Trio, actually issued in December, 1866, and a book of five songs for men's four-part chorus, both by Rieter-Biedermann.

Joachim's prolonged visit to Austria came to an end in

the second week of the new year with a farewell dinner given in his honour by Brahms, Billroth, Hanslick and other friends, and a fortnight later he removed with his family from Hanover to Berlin. His residence was permanently fixed in the Prussian capital in the course of the following year by his acceptance of the post of director of the Royal High School for Music (executive art), which was about to be founded by King William of Prussia (afterwards the German Emperor William I), as an addition to the state department for art and science.

Joachim actively participated in the planning and practical arrangement of the new institution which soon became famous under his devoted management as one of the leading European centres of musical education. The occasion of the opening in 1902, by the Emperor William II, of the spacious buildings of the Royal Schools for Art and Science in Charlottenburg, found the great veteran musician still actively exercising his beneficent influence as director, conductor and teacher; and must have seemed to him, looking back to the modest beginnings of his own special department in 1869, as one that included the crowning of much of the activity of his life. One of Joachim's last appearances as a soloist took place at a private concert of the Music School given in the presence of the German Emperor and Empress in the early spring of 1907. He continued to fulfil the duties of his post with never-failing enthusiasm until within a few weeks of his death on August 15 of that year.

Brahms quitted Vienna soon after his friend to fulfil a series of concert engagements, most of them arranged with Stockhausen, for the months of February and March, by which he hoped to make his journey to North Germany on the business of the Requiem answer a practical as well as an artistic purpose. He took up his headquarters at his father's house, and it was the last time that he returned from Vienna to Hamburg as to his nominal home. The post of conductor of the Philharmonic had again fallen vacant in 1867 by Stockhausen's resignation, and again, though Brahms did not apply for the appointment, there was a strong conviction amongst his friends that he would accept it if it were offered him. But it was not to be. Admired and loved as he was in Hamburg by an ever-increasing circle of friends, it was by a circle only. He was not popular with the average musician or the general public, and the Philharmonic committee passed him over a second time, electing Julius von Bernuth as Stockhausen's successor. Brahms said little on the subject, but it is fairly certain that the mortification caused him by this repeated slight from the musical officialdom of his native city sufficed to lead him to the determination at which he soon afterwards arrived, to settle permanently in Vienna.

Brahms made several public appearances in Hamburg during the second half of February. He performed, at the Philharmonic concert of the 14th, Beethoven's G major Concerto and Schumann's Etudes Symphoniques, adding to the published version of the latter several variations contained in Schumann's original manuscript. On the same occasion Stockhausen sang Schubert's songs, "Memnon" and "Geheimniss" to orchestral accompaniments arranged by Brahms, at his request, a year or two previously. The composer was able to spare a few days for Bremen, in order to make Reinthaler's personal acquaintance, though his numerous engagements for March obliged him to leave the work of preparation and rehearsal in the experienced hands of his new friend. He played at the Oldenburg subscription concert of March 4th,* and gave concerts with Stockhausen during the same week in Dresden and Berlin, appearing for the first time before the public of either capital. At the second concert in Berlin (March 7) Nos. 3 and 5 of the

---

* This concert erroneously dated April 4 in Dietrich's "Recollections," is reviewed in the *Oldenburger Zeitung* of March 5, 1868. **Brahms** performed Schumann's concerto and his own **Handel Variations** on the occasion.

"Magelone Romances" were included in the programme. On the 11th the two artists gave a soirée in Hamburg, when Stockhausen introduced Brahms' "Mailied" and "Von ewiger Liebe" from the manuscripts, and gave several folk-songs as an encore. At Kiel, where they appeared on the 13th, they made the acquaintance of Löwe, the famous ballad composer, now a man of seventy-two, with whose music Brahms proved to be thoroughly familiar. Their next destination was Copenhagen, where they had arranged to give four concerts. Stockhausen's selection on the first of these occasions included songs by Stradella, Schubert and Boieldieu, all accompanied by Brahms, who performed as his solos a Toccata and Fugue by Sebastian Bach, Andante by Friedemann Bach, two Scarlatti movements, Beethoven's Sonata in E flat, Op. 27, and, of his own compositions, Variations on an original theme and the early Scherzo in E flat minor. Both artists created a furore. Stockhausen "electrified the house"; Brahms was "enormously applauded," especially after the performance of his own compositions. The second concert, given within the next few days, was equally successful. The concert room was crowded, the audience extraordinarily enthusiastic, and the financial result brilliant beyond expectation. Then Brahms committed a *faux pas*, which put an end, so far as he was concerned, to further result of the triumph.

Being asked, at a party given by the Danish composer, Niels Gade, in his and Stockhausen's honour, if he had visited and admired the great Thorwaldsen Museum, of which the citizens of Copenhagen are so justly proud, he replied in the affirmative, and added that the building and its collection were so fine it was to be regretted they were not in Berlin. This unfortunate remark, made in a circle representative of educated Danish society, where the remembrance of the recent Prussian occupation of Schleswig-Holstein was still sore, produced an effect which the speaker had been far from intending. It was regarded as a deliberate insult to the country in which Brahms had been a feted guest, and was resented so strongly as to make the composer's reappearance on a Copenhagen platform impossible. Pursuing the wisest course open, he embarked on the next boat for Kiel, leaving Stockhausen to make such arrangements as he could for the third advertised concert, and to pursue his success further by associating himself with Joachim, who was about to pay a short visit to the Danish capital.

Arriving at Kiel at a very early hour in the morning, Brahms proceeded to the house of Claus Groth, whose guest he had been on his outward journey, and, walking in the garden until the inmates were astir, was presently greeted by his friend from an upper window. "Be quick and come out; I have made a heap of money," he cried in answer, slapping his pocket. Coffee was soon served and a lively talk ensued, but, as no explanation was offered by Brahms of his sudden reappearance, Groth at length began to question him. "What have you been about that you have, so to say, run away? Stockhausen has not returned, and you have had great success?" And thus brought to the point, the delinquent was obliged to relate his indiscretion. "Brahms! how could you have said such a thing in a company of Danes!" cried Groth. "I only meant," replied Brahms, "that it would be better if so fine a work, so many beautiful objects, were in a great centre where many people could see them." "But you might have supposed Danes would not put up with such a remark." "It did not occur to me," answered Brahms. "However," he added, after a moment, "I have earned so much money I shall not want more for a long time; so the matter is indifferent to me."

Brahms arrived in Bremen on the first day of April, to remain until after the 10th as the guest of Reinthaler, with whom he soon became intimate. Appreciation of his works had steadily grown in the artistic circles of Bremen since the musical life of the city had been under the leadership of the distinguished artist whose name will remain associated with the first performance of the then complete German

Requiem; and the Good Friday concert of this year was anticipated with the interest attaching to an event of unusual importance, the more so as many distinguished visitors from far and near were expected to be present as performers or in the audience. To the gratification of the former members of the Ladies' Choir, Brahms expressed a wish that the old favourite society should be represented in the chorus, and four of the most enthusiastic and trusty of his quondam disciples—Fräulein Garbe, Fräulein Reuter, Fräulein Seebohm and Fräulein Marie Völckers—answered to his summons, arriving at Bremen in time to take part in the last general rehearsal. The programme of the sacred concert of the Singverein, the proceeds of which were to be devoted to the Bremen musicians' provident fund, included the German Requiem (baritone solo, Stockhausen), between the first and second parts of which, some of the miscellaneous items were placed; movements by Bach and Tartini, and Schumann's Abendlied for violin (Joachim); "I know that my Redeemer liveth" (Frau Joachim); air for contralto with violin *obbligato* from Bach's "Matthew Passion" (Frau Joachim and Joachim); and the "Hallelujah" chorus. Brahms was to conduct his new work, Reinthaler the remaining selections. All the soloists gave their services.

The doors of St. Peter's Cathedral Church opened punctually at six o'clock on Good Friday evening, and during the next hour the visitors, many of them old acquaintances of the reader, streamed to their places. Frau Reinthaler was of course present. The Dietrichs, with their friend, Fräulein Berninger, came from Oldenburg, the Grimms from Münster. The Hamburg contingent included Minna Völckers, the composer's former pupil and very staunch friend, now grown up into a young lady, and her father, who had invited Jakob Brahms to accompany them as his guest. Max Bruch, Schübring, and young Richard Barth were there. Switzerland was represented by the future publisher of the Requiem, Rieter-Biedermann; England by the enthusiastic John Farmer; and shortly before the time of commencement Frau Schumann walked up the nave on Brahms' arm. She had decided at the last moment to undertake the journey and had arrived in Bremen in time to be present in the cathedral with the Joachims and other friends at the general rehearsal of April 9.

"If you could be one of the listeners on Good Friday it would give me great and inconceivable pleasure. It would be half the performance for me," Johannes had written.

No pains had been spared in the preparation of chorus and orchestra, and their difficult tasks were perfectly achieved.

"The impression made by the wonderful, splendidly performed work was quite overpowering," says Dietrich, "and it immediately became clear to the listeners that the German Requiem would live as one of the most exalted creations of musical art."

The composer, the executants, and their friends, to the number of about a hundred, met for supper in the ancient Rathskeller close to the cathedral, and listened afterwards to a short address by Consul Hirschfeld and to about a dozen other speeches.

"It is with great pleasure and justifiable pride," said Reinthaler, "that I greet this distinguished assemblage of visitors, some of them gathered to perform, and others to hear, the new work of the composer who is staying in our midst. The circumstance that it has been performed for the first time here in Bremen gives me quite peculiar happiness. It is a great and beautiful—one may say, an epoch-making work, which has filled us who have heard it to-day with pride, since it has inspired in us the conviction that German art has not died out, but that it begins to stir again and will thrive as gloriously as of old.

"A gloomy, anxious period has intervened since our last dear master was carried to the grave;[*] it has almost seemed as though the evening of musical art had fallen upon us; but to-day we are reassured. In the German Requiem we

---

[*] Schumann.

believe that we have a sequel worthy of the achievements of the great masters of the past.

"That I have had the good fortune to contribute towards ensuring a not quite unworthy performance of the work gives me lively satisfaction. Everyone concerned, however, has supported me to this end. Each has brought cheerful good-will to his task, and devoted himself to it with active zeal and unmixed enthusiasm, for each felt it to be an elevating one.

"You will all certainly rejoice with me that the creator of the glorious work is present amongst us and will joyfully raise your glasses to the health of the composer, our Brahms."

Brahms' answer was characteristically short and to the purpose:

"If I venture to say a few words to-night, I must premise that the gift of oratory is in no wise at my command. There are, however, amongst those present, many to whom I wish to say a word of thanks, many dear friends who have been kind and good to me, and this is especially the case with my friend Reinthaler, who has given himself with such self-sacrifice to the preparation of my Requiem. I place my collective thanks upon his head therefore, and call for three cheers for his name."

It may surprise and interest English readers to know that their country was toasted on an occasion so peculiarly representative of German music and musicians. After the various artists who had assisted in the performance and one or two of the other distinguished guests had been duly honoured, John Farmer rose to his feet, and delivered himself of his sentiments in such German as he could command.

"I have come from a city," he said, "that is much larger than Bremen, in which there are many fine houses and many rich men. You, however, may be prouder than all the rich men in the big houses, who are, indeed, very unfortunate. They have no such beautiful music as you in Germany. If you were to come to England, and Brahms himself were to come with you, to perform the Requiem, they would not attend the concert, or if they were to attend it they would say: 'Is the fellow crazy?' You can have no idea how fortunate you are in being able to understand all this beautiful music. Oh, I have observed and have perceived that each one has followed it with love and the whole energy of his soul! When I return to England, I shall relate what I have seen, and will hope that we may, before long, become as fortunate as yourselves and may be able to understand and perform German music as you do."

England found its defender in Herr Lehmann, who immediately rose to reply:

"I would venture, nevertheless, to say a word in England's honour. So many artists have met with an encouraging reception or have found a happy home there; there are so many Englishmen who understand and sympathise with German art and German life, that I would beg leave to propose a glass to the honour of art-loving England."

The feeling of satisfaction expressed in Reinthaler's speech that the distinction of the first performance of the German Requiem should have fallen to Bremen was generally shared by the musicians and amateurs of the city.

"Reinthaler has, with laudable judgment, concentrated his best powers upon the arrangement of a concert which has given to Bremen a distinctive artistic reputation," says the critic of the *Bremen Courier*, and the sentiment was expressed practically, as well as verbally, in a communication sent to the composer a few days after his return to Hamburg. The work was repeated on Tuesday, April 28, in the hall of the union, under Reinthaler's direction, when the baritone solo was sung by Franz Krolop.*

It is pleasant to be able to associate with the musical

---

* The editor's footnote on page 16 of the Brahms-Reinthaler correspondence to the effect that the baritone part in the Requiem was sung on April 10, 1868, by Otto Schelper, is incorrect (*vide* the *Bremen Courier* of April 11). Schelper sang the part, however, at the performance of the German Requiem that took place in the Bremen Cathedral on Good Friday, April 7, 1871, under Reinthaler. See page 446 of this biography.

events of 1868—the year which, by virtue of the occurrences
now recorded, marked the beginning of a new period in
Brahms' outward career and established him in the eyes of
the musicians of Europe as the greatest living artist in his
own domain—the name of an early friend whose skilled
appreciation of his genius had cheered and encouraged him
in the dark days of his youth. Frau Dr. Louise Langhans-
Japha played the Quintet in F minor for pianoforte and
strings at her concert in the Salle Erard, Paris, on March
24, and secured for it a very decided success. It is impossible actually to affirm that the work was heard for the first
time in public in its final form on this occasion, but it is
the first public performance of which the author has been
able to find record.

CHAPTER XV.

1868-1869.

Max Bruch's E flat minor Symphony—Brahms at Bonn—Friendship with Hermann Deiters—The added number of the German Requiem—Frau Schumann and Brahms—Brahms settles finally in Vienna—Song publications of 1868—Brahms and Stockhausen give concerts in Vienna and Budapest.

BRAHMS stayed on in the north for some weeks after the Good Friday concert at Bremen, and found time to pay a second, this time a short holiday, visit to the Reinthalers and to make the acquaintance of several of their friends. He passed the month of May at his father's house in Hamburg, devoting himself chiefly to the final preparation of the manuscript of his Requiem for the engraver. It was now that he composed the soprano solo which forms the fifth number of the published work, and Marxsen, who, before the composer's departure from the Anscharplatz, again examined the score, was the first musician to become acquainted with the new movement.* A striking illustration

---

* A well known musician of Hamburg, to whom Marxsen, after studying the score of the German Requiem for the second time, entrusted the responsibility of carrying it back from his house in Altona to Brahms in the Anscharplatz, told the present author positively, when she visited Hamburg in 1902, that the soprano solo was added by Marxsen's suggestion.

of Brahms' habitual reluctance at this period of his career
to accept his own revision of any large work as final,
whatever the care he might have bestowed upon it, is
furnished by the circumstance that although he wrote to
his publisher Rieter-Biedermann that he would forward him
the completed score of the Requiem from Cologne, where
he was about to attend the Rhine Festival, he changed
his mind at the last moment and sent it for the inspection of
Dr. Hermann Deiters of Bonn, his appreciative critic in the
Allgemeine Musikalische Zeitung. No doubt his anxiety
was deepened in the case of this important work by the
fact that he had been unable to submit the manuscript to
Joachim who saw only the fifth number before publication:

"How the others have longed for your inspection," he
writes, on receiving No. 5 back from his friend. "I have
been without your eye and ear for once and can never feel
satisfied unless I have them."*

With the three days' Rhine Festival of 1868 (May 31-
June 2 at Cologne) is to be associated the beginning of a
personal acquaintance between Brahms and his younger
colleague, Max Bruch; which, encouraged by the sympathy
each felt for the other's art, placed them at once on terms
of friendship. A letter written later in the year, by Bruch
to Brahms, which mentions this occasion of their first
meeting, supplies a sufficient answer to the charge of
indifference to the artistic activity of others which has
frequently been brought against the composer of the German
Requiem. The symphony to which the letter refers is Max
Bruch's in E flat minor, Op. 28.

"Simultaneously with these lines, honoured friend, you
will receive the score of my symphony. I have ventured to
dedicate it to you without preliminary question, and hope
you will accept it none the less kindly on that account. . . .
"It would be intelligible and pardonable if you, with

---

* "Briefwechsel," No. 288.

your strong convictions, having pursued your own path so energetically for many years, were to take but slight interest in the works of others. All the more delighted was I, therefore, when you proved to me so clearly at Cöln last Whitsuntide, that the contrary is the case. Your lively sympathy, your sincere, warmly expressed approval of my symphony, gave me quite peculiar pleasure, and even then excited within me the desire to associate your name permanently with the work."*

Later correspondence shows that Bruch knew in 1870 of the existence of sketches of Brahms' C minor Symphony, of which we first heard in the summer of 1862, and that his persuasions were of as little avail as Dietrich's had been to induce the master to consent to what he would himself have regarded as a premature production of his work.†

The Rhine Festival also provided opportunity for the renewal of a slight former acquaintance between Brahms and the composer, Friedrich Gernsheim, at this time professor of counterpoint at the Cologne Conservatoire, which ripened, in the course of the summer, to a relation of permanent cordiality. A special link connecting the two names was formed, a little later on, by Gernsheim's selection for the German Requiem for performance at two concerts given in Cologne under his direction; the first in November, 1870, in memory of those who had fallen in the war; the second in March, 1871, for the benefit of their survivors. The inclusion of his work in the programmes of these occasions greatly touched and gratified Brahms; and Gernsheim, who paid a visit to Vienna in January, 1871, was probably the first of his friends to whom the master played from the manuscript the just completed first chorus of the Triumphlied.

On the termination of the Rhine Festival, Brahms settled down for some weeks in Bonn in order to be near Deiters

---

* Brahms, "Briefwechsel," III, p. 90.

† Brahms, "Briefwechsel," Vol. III, Nos. VI and VIII. Compare also pp. 301, 303 and 382 of this biography.

whom he met daily. Playing the Requiem through to this friend, who had been deeply impressed by the study of the manuscript score, he said of the lately composed fifth number that when writing it he had thought of his mother.* Final work connected with the publication still engaged much of his attention. He was also occupied with the C minor Pianoforte Quartet, the inception of which is, as we have seen, to be associated with a very early period,† and which was not completed until after a further lapse of years. The music to Goethe's "Rinaldo" that had been lying in his desk in an advanced condition since 1863, was finished shortly before he left Bonn. Deiters was fortunate enough to have the opportunity of listening, at his own house or in Brahms' rooms, to the composer's interpretation of some of his published works, and to hear his own opinion of many of his songs, which he estimated very variously. Amongst those of which he thought most highly at this time was the "Von ewiger Liebe," published later in the year as No. 1 of Op. 43.

It was the only year of Brahms' life during which there was intimate personal intercourse between himself and Deiters, but the two men remained in correspondence, and the composer frequently sent copies of his new works as they appeared, with an autograph inscription, to the critic whose early appreciation through a period when their personal acquaintance had been of the slightest had awakened in him a strong feeling of regard and esteem. "I feel under a great debt of obligation to friend Deiters," he says in the course of a letter to Dietrich written in 1867.

The master was in happy summer mood throughout the time of his sojourn on the Rhine. The house, 6 Kessenicherweg, in which he lodged, was surrounded by a pretty garden, and the fondness for dumb pets that always characterised him, though he kept none of his own, was

---

* Communicated to the author in a letter by the late Dr. Deiters.
† See page 218.

gratified by the confidence of some pigeons that used to fly into his room and come to him to be fed. He invited his father to join him a few days before his departure, pleased himself by introducing the old man to Deiters and took him for a fortnight's ramble in the Rhine country. Nor was Jakob allowed to return to Hamburg until he had a second time tested his capacity for enjoying the delights of mountain scenery by accompanying his son on a few weeks' journey in Switzerland; but though Johannes made all possible arrangements to spare his father fatigue, it became evident that he was very homesick. "See, Johannes, here is a little blue flower like that which grows near Hamburg," he said one day, lagging a little behind after he had walked some distance in silence. An incident of the tour which pleased him, perhaps, better than his pedestrian and driving experiences was the trial, at which he was present, of the new movement of the Requiem, which the composer wished to hear before delivering it for publication. This was arranged for at Zürich by Hegar. Frau Suter-Weber undertook the soprano solo, and orchestra and chorus were supplied by resident musicians. Jakob, on this, as indeed on all occasions, fully appreciated the distinction he derived from being his son's companion; but it is certain that he was much relieved when the day came for him to return to his quiet home and the unembarrassing society of his wife. "Nu, Line, krigt mi Johannes nit wieder hin" (Now, Lina, Johannes will not get me again), he said, as he settled himself once more in his own chair; and he kept to his determination, though he compromised matters on one or two subsequent occasions by accepting his son's proposal that he should visit the Harz and other districts in Frau Caroline's company.

Johannes accompanied his father from Switzerland to Hamburg and found time to pay visits both to the Reinthalers and Dietrichs. He derived particular pleasure from the society of some small playfellows who welcomed him to Frau Reinthaler's nursery and struck up a special friendship with the eldest daughter of the house, little Henriette. Hearing the child, hardly out of baby years, practising the treble of a little pianoforte duet, he proposed to take the bass, and amusing himself by striking a wrong note, was promptly rebuked by his colleague. "You have played a wrong note," said Musi, stopping short. "Nun, we must begin again," returned Brahms penitently and recommenced. "You have played another!" cried Musi; nor could the master be pronounced perfect in his part until after two more attempts.

Driving one day to Wilhelmshaven with Dietrich and Reinthaler, Brahms was unusually serious and absent-minded, and mentioned that he had been greatly impressed by Hölderlin's poem, "Hyperion's Schicksalslied," which he had read in the morning. After inspecting the naval harbour and its sights, he withdrew to a distant part of the beach, where he was observed by his friends to be busy with pencil and paper. He was putting down the first sketches of his now celebrated work.

Of the many pleasant social events of the year, a gathering at Dietrich's house in Oldenburg remains for mention. Frau Schumann, her daughter Marie, and Brahms enjoyed their old friends' hospitality during the last week of October, and the visit was signalised by the first performance from the manuscript, before a private audience, of the Hungarian Dances in their arrangement for four hands on the piano.

"Frau Schumann and Brahms played them with an inspiration and fire that transported everyone present," says Dietrich.

Frau Schumann gave an evening concert in the hall of the Casino on the 30th, when her programme included a performance with the composer of Brahms' Waltzes.*

These few days of agreeable and not too fatiguing artistic

---

* *Cf.* Dietrich, p. 54 *et seq.* The dates in the text are given on the authority of Frau Schumann's diary.

exertion were particularly welcome to Frau Schumann in view of the physical and mental strain of the approaching concert season. To Brahms they brought deep satisfaction of heart since they availed for the time being to disperse certain clouds of misunderstanding that had for a long while past disturbed the happiness of his intercourse with his old, honoured friend.

That such a friendship as existed unbroken for forty-three years between Frau Schumann and Brahms should have had its difficult phases, was, indeed, the inevitable condition of its circumstances. The nature of Brahms' affection for the great pianist had been determined once for all in the days when the single hearted enthusiastic musician of scarcely twenty-one, had been appointed, as it were by the caprice of destiny, to help Schumann's wife, an artist of European fame, to live through the desolating events that confronted her maturity. It was an affection in which self had no place. In the one and only love of Frau Clara's life, which remained her inspiration till death; in the strength that enabled her to subordinate love's despair to the sacred claims of her tender motherhood; in the scrupulous pride which carried her independent and victorious through years of arduous effort; in the integrity of nature that allowed her to find solace in the affection of true friends; Johannes watched through the years that changed him from youth to man, the realisation of qualities that represented for him the ideal of womanhood, and to her in whom he saw them thus realised he paid homage with the entire devotion of his being, finding in the right she allowed him to serve her, sufficient reward for such service as he was able to render in his gradually established position as her most trusted confidant, adviser and friend. The influence on the young Brahms of this intimate companionship, during the most impressionable period of his life, with a woman raised above himself by every circumstance of age, experience and position; in whom, with great qualities of heart and mind was united the adornment of a glorious artistic achievement; and whose unqualified recognition of his own gifts was raised to personal championship by her consciousness of the still doubtful issues of her husband's much debated prophecy; became stamped on his very soul. That the intensity of his feeling for Robert and Clara Schumann, who lived undivided in his thoughts, dominated the years of his early manhood, has been sufficiently shown by the course of this narrative. It is but a plain statement of fact to add that, mellowed and defined, it remained side by side with his absorption in art as one of the two main influences of his life.

With the normal developments of the years, however, necessarily came a modification, not, perhaps, of Frau Clara's affection for Brahms, but of the place which he occupied in her existence. Loved by her, as she herself deliberately recorded in an early year of her bereavement, above all other friends:

"There is the most complete accord between us. It is not his youth that attracts me; not, perhaps, my own flattered vanity. No, it is the fresh mind, the gloriously gifted nature, the noble heart, that I love in him. Sometimes he is outwardly rough. . . ."*

She admitted him, as an exceptionally privileged spectator, to the sanctuary of her life. But that it was as a spectator only, was of the very essence of his devotion to her, and, with the growing up of her daughters, it could not be otherwise than that the first place in the mother's counsels should gradually fall to those who had the natural right and the natural capacity to fill it. It is clear that this inevitable readjustment of circumstances, proceeding at first almost imperceptibly from the mere movement of time, must have been sensibly accelerated towards its final settlement by Brahms' long absences in Vienna; and it is no less certain that as he gradually awoke to the fact that some change had happened in his life with which he was powerless

---

* Litzmann II, p. 337.

to deal, that he no longer occupied as of right that place in the closest proximity to Frau Schumann's side to which he had been accustomed, the discovery must have caused him many a bitter inward conflict. The difficulty of the situation was rendered more acute by Frau Schumann's unconsciousness of the existence of that intangible change which perplexed Johannes and by the fact that she was apt to ascribe the clouded silence or perverse behaviour which disturbed the harmony of his visits to her house, but which actually resulted from his pained affection, to deliberate waywardness or even unkindness on his part. Nor was this all. It has to be admitted that some of Brahms' idiosyncrasies, unnoticed or forgiven by his friend at the time when her energies were absorbed in meeting the first shock of her life's catastrophe, had, in calmer years become displeasing to her. Johannes was very far from divining the cumulative effect almost certain to be produced on the kind lady whom he served by his habit, referred to by Dietrich in a letter from which we have already quoted,* of insisting upon some jest spoken with an appearance of gravity and taken seriously. His practice "of strengthening slight misunderstandings in order to have the laugh on his side in the end," was unfortunate in its application to Frau Schumann's somewhat difficult temperament which, with all its magnetism, was marked by a tendency to melancholy and a certain inflexibility of earnestness that sometimes prevented her from appreciating the lighter side of passing incidents. Brahms' humour was not invariably flavoured to her taste and in the long run it no doubt induced in her mind a permanent impression that some amount of reality was hidden beneath the fun. Incomprehensible also to Frau Schumann were some of his social proclivities. While he could curtly repulse the civilities of a polite lady too anxious to make herself agreeable to him, he took genuine pleasure to the end of his life in the

---

* Page 300.

easy friendliness of his relations with the country folk with whom the daily chances of his summer sojournings brought him into contact—the genial hostesses, the ready waiters, the bright peasant fräuleins of the country inns and restaurants that he frequented—and could adapt himself on occasion to the harmless amenities which they found pleasing. Some of these traits have been touched upon in the introductory chapter of this biography, where it has been made clear, as we hope, that they were rooted in no meanness of disposition or thought. Brahms' nature was unspotted by common taint. They sprang on the one hand from a fixed suspicion of the ultimate value of those usages of conventionality in which his own early training had been deficient; and, on the other, from a democratic spirit of bonhomie which was part of the inheritance of his birth. It is intelligible, however, that these peculiarities, once fully realised by her, should have been regretted by Frau Schumann, who, conservative by nature, had been accustomed from early childhood to be made much of in the most exclusive circles of her time.

That it was no mere passing uneasiness which troubled the intercourse of the two artists, is shown by the circumstance that, from the summer of 1866 onwards, Frau Schumann did not, as heretofore during Brahms' visits to Baden-Baden, invite him to be her regular guest at her early family dinner, though he still enjoyed the freedom of her house later in the day; and it was the almost inevitable sequel to this tacit admission on her part that something had gone wrong, that Johannes, determined to recognise no change in their relations, should provide her, however unintentionally, with further cause for dissatisfaction. He was certainly guilty of an act of indiscretion, the gravity of which was hardly attentuated by the good motive of anxiety for her health which prompted it, when he took upon himself early in 1868 to write Frau Schumann a letter of urgent advice to retire from public activity as soon as her circumstances should permit. Such an error of judgment could not but make a painful impression on the beloved and feted artist, and the wound it inflicted was long in healing. Perhaps when Brahms wrote the epistle his mind may have been possessed by a fantasia in which the great pianist was pictured as relieved from the too strenuous exercise of her activity and settled in the neighbourhood of a possible home that should make his own happiness. His imagination was strongly influenced at this period by the attractions of his old friend's third daughter, Julie, now about twenty-three years of age, to whom, as a girl of sixteen, he had dedicated his duet variations on her father's theme; and it is not impossible that his consciousness of the many obstacles standing in the way of his wishes may have been partly responsible for the uncertain behaviour that had frequently excited Frau Schumann's displeasure. His attachment, which was known to his Carlsruhe friends, was steadily discouraged by Fräulein Julie herself, and was scarcely suspected by her mother who was not disposed to draw any serious inferences from Johannes' evident admiration of her generally admired child. Brahms had, however, been touched by an inclination that was something more than a mere passing fancy, and it was not until the progress of events had convinced him of its hopelessness that it took its place among the shadows of the past which returned from time to time to visit his memory.

However all these things may have been, there can be little doubt that, at the time at which our story has now arrived, a disposition, not in future to be eradicated, had established itself in Frau Schumann's mind to draw a distinction between Brahms the musician, and Brahms the man, and the shock with which Johannes, now thirty-five years of age, faced the conviction of the fact, is evident enough in his correspondence. It was a distinction which he repudiated with the whole force of his nature.

"I speak in my music," he writes shortly before his visit to Oldenburg in the autumn of 1868; "only so poor a musician as I would like to believe that he is better than his tones. You speak of my moodiness in Baden. Let us both be frank. I also had to regret that I found it impossible to try, as in former days, to gain sympathy in your house. It always seemed to me that I had something to overcome beforehand."

The particular occasion which gave rise to these expressions passed, but a dissonance had been sounded in the composer's life, which was to vibrate with increasing harshness through the coming years, scarcely to find a final resolution.

"Nothing," he writes a year or two later, a few weeks after Frau Schumann's return to Germany from an artistic visit to Vienna, replying, as it would seem, to some complaint from her, "could alter or weaken my opinion of you, my veneration for you. I have often told myself in mournful jest that you regard me as the police do a person who has been thrice punished. I hope, indeed, that such a dubious opinion is very often unjustified; as is, unfortunately, your higher one of my artistic performances. I shall dispute neither any more, but neither need take from you the feeling and belief that nobody can be more attached to you than I."

It would be idle to consider what might have been the result to Brahms' happiness and to his art had he, at any time within the next few years, found courage to accept the inevitable and to take his own independent path in life. The remembrance of the past, aided by the absolutism that was natural to Frau Schumann in matters of affection, was too strong within him to allow him seriously to contemplate such an upheaval of thought and habit as this would have involved. He remained to the last faithful to the chivalrous attitude towards his old friend, which he has himself described as that of "son or brother,"* and which has been commented on by Hübbe, probably with perfect accuracy, in the following passage of his "Brahms in Hamburg":

---

* Litzmann III, p. 216.

"I cannot refrain from appending a remark to Widmann's important communication on the subject of Brahms' bachelorhood. Though one may accept the answer given by Brahms to Widmann on this point as quite valid, yet I would venture to supplement it by a conjecture.

"Just as there are instances of distinguished men having been deterred from marriage by devotion to their mother, so it has often struck me, may Brahms have found a similar obstacle in his peculiar relation to his so warmly revered, maternal friend, Clara Schumann. Widmann's words on the subject (page 98) have confirmed me in the supposition that this relation was a factor—though possibly unrecognised—in determining Brahms' abstention from marriage."

The rare beauty of the man's nature—"pure as the diamond, tender as snow"—finds expression in many a letter to the revered lady, no less than in the melodies which, as he tells her, occurred to him when he was thinking of her. No doubt as he wrote down words or notes, he recalled tenderly enough the years which had bound his sympathies so firmly to the sorrows, the energies and the victories of her life. Brahms, indeed, never wavered from his devotion to Frau Schumann, though his consciousness of something indefinite standing between them, may frequently have emphasised the nervous excitability to which the serious pursuit of his art renders the creative musician peculiarly liable; and, acting on his outward manner towards her, may have caused him to be too vehement, or too silent, as the case might be.

"I feel your anxieties and sorrows much too deeply to be able to express myself about them in words," he writes with reference to the illness of her youngest son. "My own troubles I am accustomed to bear in silence. For you I feel much more strongly and lovingly. No thought goes from me to you which does not entirely surround you and pay heed to all your cares. But I can only quietly await the result of this new trial. . . . How many messages of sympathy I have for you. . . . Take some comfort from this earnest affection. I love you more than myself and anyone or anything in the world."

"I am only conscious of one offence in regard to my friends; awkwardness of behaviour," we read in one of his late birthday letters to her. "I feel that I may by my manner, by nothing else, have deserved the great pain of your estrangement from me...."*

But though the master preserved the treasure of his affection inviolate, his spirit did not entirely escape the impress of the abiding pain caused him by the later phases of the old friendship. To it may partly be traced the veil of pessimism that gathered round him as he approached middle age; never to mar, but more and more completely to shroud from the world, the inner workings of his nature; a veil that was not to be dispersed even by his frank enjoyment of the full tide of artistic success that surrounded the last period of his career.

"Confidential intercourse with women is difficult," he wrote to Hanslick less than a year before his death, in reference to some matter connected with the publication of his letters from Schumann, "the more earnest and confidential, the more difficult."

Brahms and Stockhausen again united their forces in November, and gave several concerts together. At the first of two soirées in Hamburg, Brahms created a furore with some of the Hungarian Dances in their arrangement as solos. The programme included a performance by Stockhausen and his pupil, Fräulein Girzik, of two of the Duets, Op. 28, the second of which was rapturously encored. Brahms, as usual, accompanied his friend throughout the evening. He was received with acclamation at Bremen on the 30th of the month, when he played the pianoforte part of his A major Quartet at a concert of the excellent resident string quartet party led by Jacobsen, a fine player, and second concert-meister of the Bremen orchestra. On this, as on subsequent visits to Bremen, Brahms stayed, as a matter of course, with the Reinthalers.

---

* See Litzmann III, pp. 222, 284, 331, 558.

Carl Bade, paying one of his frequent morning calls at the Anscharplatz about this time, was startled as he entered the house by the appearance of Jakob, who, coming towards him with finger on lip and laboriously treading on tiptoe, solemnly whispered: "Hush!..." "What is it, Brahms? Who is ill?" returned Bade under his breath, seriously alarmed. "Hush!" repeated Jakob as mysteriously as before; "*he is dor*" (he is there); and, opening the door of the corner room, he pushed in the astonished Carl and shut the door behind him without another word, leaving him alone with his son, who was busy weeding out his library in readiness for the dispatch of some of his Hamburg possessions to Vienna. "See here," said Johannes, after a kind word of greeting, giving Bade time to recover the composure of which Jakob's strange *coup* had for a moment robbed him, by pointing to a volume in his hand, "Kuhnau was a capable musician!"

The relation existing at this time between the elder and younger Brahms, of which mention was made in an early chapter, was well illustrated during the homely "second breakfast" for which the party soon assembled. Sociability was rendered impossible, in spite of the persistent efforts of Johannes, by the father's overwhelming consciousness of his son's presence. The awed feeling which possessed Jakob whenever he found himself face to face with the living embodiment of his own miraculous success in life was not unnatural, and can only inspire respect for the memory of the older man, in whose simple humility, rooted in the strongest and most legitimate pride, may, perhaps, be recognised some of the essential qualities which endeared the great composer to all who were privileged to call him friend.

Brahms returned to Vienna in December, and was, of course, present at several concerts given there before and after Christmas by Frau Schumann, who visited Austria after an interval of some years.

The list of publications belonging to this year is an important one, not only because it includes the German

Requiem (Rieter-Biedermann), but because it is representa-tive of the master in what may be roughly called the second period of his activity as a composer of songs. From beginning to end of his career he poured forth songs in several different forms—the simple strophic, the "through-composed," the latter necessarily varying in structure with each fresh example.* This second period, however, is marked not only by the sure mastery which had long char-acterised Brahms' works in whatever domain he chose for the exercise of his powers; its spirit is generally distinctive, and is that of the poet's ripe manhood. Youth with its uncertainties is behind, age with its gathering shadows not yet in sight; the composer holds the present in firm grasp, and presents us with exquisite dream-pictures of life and nature, the children of an imagination penetrated with a sense of the beauty, the tenderness, the pathos of existence, and content in the exercise of its ideality. Each of the five books published in 1868 (Op. 43 by Rieter-Biedermann, and Op. 46, 47, 48, 49 by Simrock) contains such wealth of beauty that it is difficult to select either for particular mention. Perhaps the palm should be given to Op. 43, of which "Von ewiger Liebe" and "Mainacht" are Nos. 1 and 2; but then, Op. 47 contains "Botschaft," and Op. 46 "Die Schale der Vergessenheit." Stockhausen, who stayed at Neuenahr in the summer of 1868, came over to Bonn several times, and sang the greater number of these songs from the manuscript, accompanied by the composer, to Deiters. Brahms seemed determined not to publish "Die Schale der Vergessenheit," declaring it to be too "deso-late," but Stockhausen's enthusiasm prevailed to alter his decision. Some of the shorter numbers belong, by date of

---

* The strict strophic form is that in which voice-melody and accompaniment are the same in each verse. It admits, however, of several kinds of modification, as by varied accompaniment, slight variation of voice-melody, and so forth. The "through-composed" form introduces new ideas and/or developments of the initial idea, according to the varied moods of the poem.

composition, to an earlier period, as Goethe's "Die Liebende schreibt," already mentioned in association with the autumn of 1858. "Herbstgefühl" (Op. 48, No. 7) was written down on May 6, 1867, the eve of Brahms' thirty-fourth birthday. The widely popular "Wiegenlied," Op. 49, No. 4, was composed for one of Frau Faber's children, and the accompaniment is reminiscent of a folk-song which Brahms heard from Fräulein Bertha Porubszky in the old days of the Hamburg Ladies' Choir. The manuscript bears the inscription: "For Arthur and Bertha Faber for ever happy use. July, 1868"; and at the close "Mit Grazie in infinitum."

Now, as ever, Brahms returned with delight to the fresh naïveté of the folk-song, and numerous examples of his settings of texts obtained from German, Bohemian, Italian sources are to be found in these books, of which "Sonntag," Op. 47, No. 3, and "Am Sonntag Morgen," Op. 49, No. 1, are perhaps the best known. "Gold überwiegt die Liebe" is a touching little lament (No. 4 of Op. 48). The text of "Von ewiger Liebe" is itself a Wendic folk-song, but the composer's treatment has placed it amongst the finest works of German art in song-form. As a rule, however, Brahms set folk-songs as such, and his treatment of them was direct, and, so to say, unstudied. He has set for a single voice popular texts of more than twenty nationalities besides his own, and, as he found them, as they appealed to him, so he composed them, without attempt either to interfere with the frank naturalness of the words, or to give national colour to his music. Such musical references as he occasionally makes in his songs to the origin of his texts are so unobtrusive as to be hardly noticeable, except by a special student of the subject.* "Vergangen ist mir," Op. 48, No. 6, points

---

* Those who wish to study Brahms' treatment of folk-music in detail are referred to Hohenemser's articles, "Brahms und die Volksmusik," in *Die Musik*, Nos. 15 and 18, 1903.

back to the tonal system of the Middle Ages. Like "Sehnsucht," Op. 14, No. 8, it is composed in the Dorian mode.

The enumeration of the great song publications of 1868 is not yet at an end. The issue by Rieter-Biedermann of Books 3, 4, 5, containing in all nine numbers, of the "Magelone Romances," of which the first two books had appeared in 1865, completed a song-cycle which ranks among the few supreme achievements of its class, increasing to the number of four a special group of names which had hitherto included only those of Beethoven, Schubert and Schumann.

The fifteen "Magelone Romances" are extremely various in structure, and can hardly be classified categorically under any of the ordinary song-forms. Spitta expresses his sense of their importance by the word "symphonic." Brahms' own name "Romance" sufficiently indicates their nature, however. Some are of great, others of smaller, dimensions. Some consist of several movements, others of one short movement in three sections, of which the last repeats the first; one is bound into a whole by the melody of a refrain. They give vivid expression to a wide range of feelings: chivalric delight, progressive phases of passionate love, the despair of separation, reawakened hope, the confident bliss of reunion, certainty of the sacred power of love. Remembrance of the ideal performances of Stockhausen, to whom the cycle is dedicated, was indubitably present to Brahms' mind as he composed the songs, which, with the exception of Nos. 11 and 13, should be sung by a man. One may read and reread them, hear them and hear them again, but try in vain to decide on a favourite number. Each one places the listener in an enchanted world of noble beauty and romance, and in wealth and individuality of idea the cycle assuredly does not rank last amongst the few works of its kind.

The Songs and Romances, Op. 44, mentioned in our first volume in connection with the Ladies' Choir were now also published by Rieter-Biedermann;* and Cranz of Hamburg issued the three Songs for six-part chorus *a capella*, Op. 42, all of great charm. Its five-bar rhythm is an interesting feature of the second number, the lovely "Vineta." The text of No. 3, "Darthula's Grabesgesang," is a translation from Ossian, and is contained in Herder's "Stimmen der Völker."

"Brahms is here," writes Billroth from Vienna on January 11, "and is to give concerts with Stockhausen. He is going to bring out a cantata, Rinaldo, in February.... He is enthusiastic about the text because it leaves so much to the composer."

Goethe wrote his cantata expressly that music might be set to it by Capellmeister Winter, a respectable musician of his day, for the Prince Friedrich of Gotha, the possessor of an agreeable tenor voice, and a good amateur vocalist. It is founded on an episode in Tasso's "Jerusalem Delivered," and exhibits the conflict between weakness and strength in the brave knight Rinaldo—a fictitious personage introduced into his poem by Tasso—who is roused from his surrender to the witcheries of Armida by the arrival, at the islet on which he is living with her, of a party of knights, his friends —two only in Tasso's epic, but increased to a chorus by Goethe. The cantata opens at a point where the knights have succeeded in awakening Rinaldo from his dream of happiness, but are unable to nerve him to the resolution of departure. As a final resource, they hold up before him a diamond shield, which reflects his own image in its degeneracy. The shock of what he sees restores him to full consciousness, and he leaves the island in spite of Armida's lamentations, fury and enchantments, and his own regrets, encouraged and supported by his friends. The final chorus with solo depicts the happy return voyage, and the safe arrival of the ship at the shore of the Holy Land.

---

* Dated 1866 in the Thematic Catalogue.

Armida does not appear as a dramatis personæ in Goethe's work, and Brahms' music is accordingly composed for tenor solo, men's chorus and orchestra. The poem is short and concise, containing but one dramatic situation, but its very terseness has been advantageous to the composer, for the text has not fettered his imagination by detail, whilst it has supplied him with sufficient material for powerful and contrasted musical presentation in the enchantments of Armida, the storm raised by her to prevent the ship's departure, the calm, persuasive firmness of the knights, the vacillation of Rinaldo (expressed in the first instance in an impassioned scena), his pleadings with his friends, his final awakening and recovery from the intensity of passion. Of all these points Brahms has availed himself with force and warmth of imagination. Many interesting details of the composition tempt our notice, but we may only stay to direct the reader's attention to the conviction inspired by the choruses of the noble, lovable character of the knights; to the masterly means employed—so simple that only a master would have ventured to restrict himself to them—at the moment when the shield is displayed, which, in their place, convey, without any attempt at tone-painting, but with absolute distinctness, the impression of the friends' gentle determination with the shrinking Rinaldo; to the bright martial movement in which the knights encourage him by reminding him of the flashing lances, the wavy pennons, the whole brilliant battle array, of the crusaders' army from which the allurements of Armida have too long detained him. In the final chorus a favourable wind swells the sails of the ship, which rides joyously over the green waves, breaking them into light foam as she passes, whilst Rinaldo and his companions amuse themselves by watching the dolphins at play in the water, and are filled with a light-hearted happiness that, as land is sighted, bursts into exultant shouting of the names of Godfrey and Solyma (Jerusalem).

The work was performed for the first time from the manuscript, under the composer's direction, on February 28, 1869, at a concert of the Akademischer Gesangverein, Vienna. The title-part was sung with great success by Gustav Walter, three hundred students well prepared by Dr. Eyrich, the society's conductor, were responsible for the choruses, and the orchestral accompaniments were performed by the entire body of instrumentalists of the court opera.

A series of three concerts, given in Vienna in February and March by Brahms and Stockhausen were phenomenally successful. The great baritone had not been heard in the Austrian capital for many years, and all tickets for the first concert were sold immediately after its announcement. Brahms' selection for the series included works by Handel, Bach, Couperin, Gluck, Beethoven, Schubert, Schumann, some of his own Variations—notably those of the B flat Sextet—and Hungarian Dances; and he accompanied his friend in many of the most celebrated songs of his repertoire. The wonderful performance by the two artists of Brahms' songs, "Von ewiger Liebe" and "Mainacht," was one of the choice delights of the first concert. A feature of the second was the performance by Stockhausen and Fräulein Girzik of two of the composer's vocal duets. The enthusiasm excited by the concert-givers in Vienna was equalled in Budapest, whither they proceeded on March 10, in order to give a similar series; and it was, if possible, exceeded on their final reappearance in Vienna.

These concerts are of peculiar interest in Brahms' career, because the last of them closes the period of his activity as a virtuoso. For fourteen years, from the autumn of 1855 to the spring of 1869, circumstances had obliged, and happily permitted, him to earn his livelihood chiefly by the exercise of his powers as an executive artist; but his reputation as a composer had grown uninterruptedly throughout this time, and with the production of the German Requiem it attained a height that gave him future independence of action. Though years were still to pass before his circumstances became easy, they were not again straitened, and from

BRAHMS' DWELLING, 4 CARLSGASSE, VIENNA.
By permission of Mr. E. Howard-Jones.

henceforth he undertook concert-journeys only in the rôle of a composer, to assist at performances of his own works. The occasions on which he appeared additionally as pianist with one of Beethoven's or Schumann's great compositions became less and less frequent, moreover, as, with passing time, he felt increasingly out of regular practice. Brahms was, in later life, fond of illustrating the fact of his long struggle with poverty by referring to the manuscript of the Requiem. "The paper is of all sizes and shapes, because at the time I wrote it I never had money enough to buy a stock." The immediate impression created by the great work was, however, sufficiently widespread and profound to place the composer alone, among the musicians of his day, as the accepted representative of the classical art of Germany, and the prices commanded by his copyrights gradually increased accordingly. No long time elapsed before the German Requiem had made the round of the musical cities of Europe. It was given, for the first time after final completion and publication, at the Leipzig Gewandhaus concert of February 18, 1869, under Reinecke, and was performed in the course of the next few weeks in Basle (twice), Zürich (twice), Carlsruhe (twice), Münster, Cologne, Hamburg, Weimar, and, later in the year, Dessau and Chemnitz (twice), Barmen (four choruses only), Magdeburg, Jena, and again twice in Cologne. The complete work was not heard in Vienna until March 5, 1871, when it was given by the Gesellschaft der Musikfreunde under the composer's direction, with Frau Wilt and Dr. Krauss as soloists, but achieved no striking success. It was performed on July 7 of the same year (1871) for the first time in England, before an invited audience, at the residence of Sir Henry Thompson. Stockhausen conducted the rehearsals and performance, and sang the baritone solo, Fräulein Anna Regan the soprano solo. The chorus was composed of about thirty good musicians, and the accompaniments were played in their arrangement as a pianoforte duet by Lady Thompson and the veteran musician Cipriani Potter, then in his eightieth year.

The first, second, fifth and sixth numbers were performed by the students of the Royal Academy of Music at a "public rehearsal" given under the direction of John Hullah, the then conductor of the academy orchestra, on April 1, 1873, at the Hanover Square Rooms; and the first English public performance of the entire work took place on the following day in St. James's Hall, London, at the Philharmonic concert of April 2, 1873, under W. G. Cusins. The solos were sung on this occasion by Mdlle. Sophie Ferrari and Charles Santley. The work was heard for the first time in Berlin, Munich and St. Petersburg in the spring, and in Utrecht in June of the year 1872; and in Paris in 1874.

Probably it was due to the impression created by the German Requiem that the Serenade in D, Op. 11, was performed for the first time in Berlin in November, 1869, at one of the concerts of the Symphony Orchestra under Capellmeister Stern.

"The reception showed that the public is beginning to understand and value the composer Brahms, one of the few living creative artists who are genuine and sincere," wrote a Berlin critic.

In the earlier part of the same year Louis Brassin played the Handel Variations and Fugue in Munich with very great success. Brassin was one of the first artists to perform the work in public, and that he introduced it to a Munich audience is the more interesting since the musicians of the Bavarian capital had in 1869 shown scant, if any, recognition of our composer's art, which was too progressive for Franz Lachner, and too conservative for von Bülow, the successive leaders, up to that date, of the musical life of the city. The work was played by Bülow in November, 1872, in Vienna and throughout a short tour in Germany, and from that time was heard at his concerts with increasing frequency.

CHAPTER XVI.

1869-1872.

Brahms and Opera—Professor Heinrich Bulthaupt—The Liebeslieder —First performance—The Rhapsody (Goethe's "Harzreise") performed privately at Carlsruhe—First public performance at Jena—Geheimrath Gille—The "Song of Triumph"—Performance of first chorus at Bremen—Bernhard Scholz—The "Song of Destiny"—First performance—Death of Johann Jakob Brahms—First performance of completed "Triumphlied" at Carlsruhe—Summary of Brahms' work as a composer since 1862.

THE theory that found wide acceptance during the lifetime of Brahms, and was discussed at length in a feuilleton of the *Strassburger Post* immediately after his death, that he never had and never could have seriously entertained the idea of composing for the stage, was long ago conclusively refuted by Widmann in his "Recollections." He shows that the master's wishes pointed at more than one period of his career in the direction of dramatic composition, and that he was prevented from following them by the same difficulty which proved insoluble to Mendelssohn—that of finding a libretto to suit his fancy.

"He was always particularly animated when speaking of matters connected with the theatre, as for instance when he once very decidedly demonstrated to me the vaudeville character of the first act of 'Fidelio,' which generally passes for a very good text-book. He possessed a genuine dramatic perception, and it gave him real pleasure to analyse the merits and defects of a dramatic subject."*

The interest of this passage is enhanced by a few words that occur in an article on Brahms by Richard Heuberger : †

"We sat together the whole evening and I remember that Brahms spoke in detail of Mozart's 'Figaro' and laid stress on the unparalleled manner in which Mozart has overcome the enormous difficulties of his text: 'Mozart has composed it, not as a mere ordinary text-book, but as a complete, well-organised comedy.'"

It would certainly have been matter for surprise if Brahms, who was peculiarly sensitive to the influence of really poetic dramatic effect, and whose interest in the drama furnished him with a source of frequent pleasure that did not diminish as he grew older—he rarely missed a première at the Vienna Burg Theater—had passed through life without feeling the inclination to test his powers as a composer for the stage, and this is very far indeed from being the case. Widmann's account of what took place between himself and Brahms on the subject of opera belongs to the late seventies, and we shall revert to it in its place; it points back, however, to an earlier time, which proves, as we might expect, to be that of the composer's intimacy with Devrient and Levi, with whose varied professional activity he manifested the warmest sympathy, and especially to the year 1869, when the publication of the German Requiem had left his mind at leisure for new important effort. Perhaps we may perceive the direction in which his wishes were moving in the fact

---

* " Johannes Brahms in Erinnerung," p. 37.

† " Meine Bekanntschaft mit Brahms," *Die Musik*, No. 5 of 1903.

that "Rinaldo," which contains the nearest approach to dramatic composition to be found in the catalogue of Brahms' works, was completed almost simultaneously with the Requiem; and it is possible that an indication of the obstacle that was to prove insuperable to their fulfilment may be read in Billroth's words quoted in the last chapter: "Brahms is enthusiastic about [the text of] Rinaldo because it leaves so much to the composer." However this may be, it is certain that he was strongly possessed at this period and on into the early seventies with the desire to compose an opera, and that he not only opened his mind unreservedly on the subject to his friends at Carlsruhe, but made repeated efforts in other directions to procure a libretto adapted to his views. Allgeyer furnished him with a completed textbook on Calderon's "The Open Secret." Through Claus Groth he obtained an unused text written for Mendelssohn by the poet Geibel, and amongst others with whom he discussed the subject were Paul Heyse at Munich, Turgeniev at Baden-Baden, who provided him with sketches, and Heinrich Bulthaupt, then a rising young dramatic author and an intimate friend of Reinthaler's.

To Bulthaupt he proposed as a subject Schiller's fragment of a play, "Demetrius," which he esteemed very highly, and in a long conversation with this gentleman at his house in Bremen, he explained with precision his ideas as to the desirable treatment even of the minutiæ of dramatic action, taking as the theme of his exposition the libretto, written by Bulthaupt, of Reinthaler's opera, "Kätchen von Heilbronn." Some of the peculiarities of his views which created for him unnecessary difficulties must be attributed to his inveterately logical habit of mind, which made it repugnant to him to take certain things for granted for the sake of stage exigencies. He went too far in a desire that the minor details of the drama should be visibly developed. Pointing to a scene in "Kätchen von Heilbronn," in the course of which three soldiers go into a drinking cellar, not to reappear, he inquired: "What becomes of them?" "It is assumed that they go away," replied Bulthaupt; "do you mean to say that you wish actually to see them come out again on to the stage?" "I should like to do so," Brahms answered. A moment's reflection would, of course, have shown him that the scene in question was, in fact, realistic, since the soldiers might in actual life have left the cellar by a back door, unseen by those who observed them enter through the front one. The anecdote is, however, illustrative of a mental habit which must have confronted Brahms with countless difficulties so long as he merely contemplated the composition of an opera. The work of composing one, had he ever settled down to it, might probably have solved many of them.

The idea of "Demetrius" fell through. Bulthaupt suggested to Brahms a consideration which, in no way applicable to Schiller's piece, seemed to him of importance in view of its adaptation as an opera. He thought that the necessity of introducing some amount of Russian colouring into the music of a drama having for its subject an episode of Russian history, not only might prove irksome to a composer so strongly imbued as Brahms with the sentiment of German nationality, but would be prejudicial to the tragic breadth of Schiller's play as it stands. Brahms, on thinking over the matter, probably felt the weight of his friend's remarks, for he did not return to his proposal.*

Points of interest in the composer's suggestion of Schiller's "Demetrius" for the subject of a tragic opera are that ambition and not love is the mainspring of its action, and that the feminine interest of the piece is centred neither in maiden nor wife, but in Marfa, the mother of Demetrius, in whom are exhibited powerful emotions arising from unerring maternal instinct and baffled affection. It recalls the period, moreover, when Brahms and Joachim shared each other's daily thoughts on all subjects. Joachim composed an

---

* Personally related to the author by the late Professor Bulthaupt, who read and confirmed her notes of his conversation.

overture to Hermann Grimm's play of "Demetrius" in 1854, and, about the middle of the seventies, the well known "Marfa" scena for contralto and orchestra from Schiller's fragment. A similar association is presented in Brahms' favourite suggestion for the textbook of a serio-comic opera or operetta, of Gozzi's "König Hirsch," the work with which Joachim's "Overture to a Play of Gozzi's" is to be connected. Arrangements by Brahms of both these compositions of his friend, as pianoforte duets, were found in his rooms after his death, and were published with the very few manuscripts that he allowed to survive him.

A few weeks after the termination of his concert engagements with Stockhausen, Brahms left Vienna for Carlsruhe where, on May 12, he conducted a repetition performance of the German Requiem, which had been given at the subscription concert of the 9th under Levi's direction. He settled down in his old Lichtenthal rooms immediately afterwards, and in the work completed during the first six weeks of his stay, we may find suggestion of the dreams which, perhaps encouraged by his consciousness that the preceding year had marked a new and hopeful turning point in his career, had of late been rarely absent from his fancy. Early in July he had finished twenty of the charming compositions with which we are familiar as the "Liebeslieder."

A second work belonging to this season, conceived and brought to completion later in the summer, tells of the mood wrought in the composer by the closing of this chapter of his imaginings. Towards the middle of July the intelligence of Fräulein Julie Schumann's betrothal to the Conte Viktor Radicati di Marmorito was communicated to him by Frau Clara herself: "Apparently he was expecting nothing, he seemed quite startled," she remarks; and a little later, writing to an old friend:

"Johannes was as though metamorphosed from the moment I told him of Julie's engagement; wrapped in the old moodiness. He got over it in about a fortnight; but he scarcely speaks to Julie whereas he had before constantly sought her with words and looks. Levi told me the other day that Johannes is devotedly attached to Julie."

Brahms stayed on in Lichtenthal nevertheless, and is represented with Levi and Allgeyer in a photograph of the time contemplating an objet d'art, a brass plate given to the bride by the three friends jointly. The wedding took place on September 22, and a few days afterwards, Johannes brought Frau Schumann the deeply pathetic Rhapsodie for contralto, men's chorus and orchestra, which he described as "*his* bridal song."

"I can only regard the piece as the expression of his trouble. If he would only speak thus from his heart in words for once!" remarks Frau Schumann.*

The two completed fruits of Brahms' year were published severally in 1869 and 1870, as Opp. 52 and 53. The "Liebeslieder," eighteen in number (first set), waltzes for pianoforte duet and vocal quartet, composed to a number of verses from Daumer's "Polydora," translations or imitations of Russian and Polish folk-songs, are amongst the most popular of the composer's works, and are too familiar to need detailed comment. They show Brahms in his perfection of dainty grace and fresh, playful imagination, a mood in which he stands unrivalled. They were performed for the first time in public at the subscription concert of the Carlsruhe court orchestra of October 6. Frau Schumann, who played Beethoven's G major Concerto on the same occasion, and Levi, were the pianists, and Fräulein Hausmann, Frau Hauser, Herr Kürner and Herr Brouillet, the singers. Published shortly afterwards by Simrock, they were heard in Vienna before the close of the year at the first Singakademie concert of the season; and were performed at Frau Schumann's concert in Vienna of January 5, 1870, by the concert-giver and composer and the singers

---

* Litzmann III, 230, 232.

Frau Dustmann, Fräulein Girzik, Herr Gustav Walter, and Dr. Krauss.*

The Rhapsody was first heard privately at the rehearsal of the Carlsruhe concert of October 6, Levi having arranged a performance for the benefit of Frau Schumann and of Brahms himself. The solo was sung by Frau Boni. The composer, writing to Deiters in September, says:

". . . I should like to make a request to-day. I remember to have seen at your house a volume of songs by Reichhardt (possibly Zelter) which contained a stanza from Goethe's Harzreise. Could you lend me the volume for a little while?

"I need hardly add that I have just composed it and should like to see the work of my forerunner. I call my piece 'Rhapsody,' but believe I am indebted also for the title to my respected predecessor.

"I shall hear it in a few days in Carlsruhe, and should I then decide not to print or perform the somewhat intimate music, I shall nevertheless show it to you."†

It seems probable, from the circumstances of the first public performance of the Rhapsody, that Madame Viardot-Garcia was amongst the small audience on this private

---

* Eight numbers with an additional one, were arranged by Brahms for vocal quartet and orchestra, and were performed at a concert in Berlin on March 19, under the direction of Ernst Rudorff. They were placed in the following order: 1, 2, 4, 5, 11, 8, 9, 6; and the later published No. 9 of Op. 65 was inserted between Nos. 5 and 11. The composer presented the autograph score of this arrangement to Professor Rudorff. ("Briefwechsel," III, p. 155.)

The explanation of the, for many years incomprehensible words, "ad libitum," appended in the title of the Liebeslieder, Op. 52, to that portion of the work which was undoubtedly its *raison d'être*, and forms its dominating factor, the vocal quartet; has been supplied by Kalbeck (II, p. 295), who shows that the expression was conceded by the composer to his publisher's desire to add to the market value of the opus by presenting it alternatively as a set of waltzes for four hands on the pianoforte.

† The entire letter is published by Richard Heuberger in the supplement to the *Allgemeine Musikzeitung*, 1899, No. 260.

occasion. The work was given on March 3, 1870, soon after its publication, at the Academic Concerts, Jena, under the direction of the society's conductor, Dr. Ernst Naumann, when Madame Viardot sang the solo; "Rinaldo," with Dr. Wiedemann as tenor, being included in the programme.

Madame Viardot-Garcia, staying early in 1870 with Liszt, who had returned to Weimar in 1869 after an absence of many years, met at his house his devoted friend Geheimrath Gille, a distinguished musical amateur, who occupied an official post at Jena and employed the greater part of his leisure in the interest of the musical culture of the little university town. Gille had in his youth known Goethe and Hummel, and been on terms of close friendship with Henselt. His intimacy with Liszt dated from the commencement of the great man's residence in Weimar, and he soon became a warm supporter of the New-German party, received Wagner into his house at Jena on his flight from Dresden to Liszt at Weimar, and saw him safely over the German border. His sympathy with the new tendencies did not render him insensible to the value of less revolutionary developments of art. He had great interest and respect to spare for Brahms' music, and encouraged its cultivation by Brendel's society (Allgemeiner Deutscher Musikverein), on the committee of which he was very active.* There can be little doubt that the performance of the Rhapsody at Jena in March was the outcome of a friendly chat between Madame Viardot and himself and of their mutual sympathetic admiration of Brahms' art, which was shared by Dr. Ernst Naumann, an old personal acquaintance of the composer. Since the performance of the German Requiem in 1869 already chronicled, Brahms' music was well represented in the programmes of the Jena societies under Naumann's direction.

The Rhapsody was given on March 19 under Grimm at

---

* "Franz Liszt's Briefe an Carl Gille," with a biographical introduction by Adolph Stern.

Münster, and a little later at Capellmeister Hegar's benefit concert at Zürich. It became a favourite work with Frau Joachim, who sang the solo times innumerable with extraordinary power and sympathy and invariable success.

Brahms' Rhapsody, Op. 53, is composed to a fragment—set also by J. F. Reichhardt (1752-1814)—from Goethe's "Harzreise im Winter," which has for its subject the poet's reflections on a visit paid by him to a young hypochondriac whose melancholy had, as he feared, been confirmed by the influence of his own "Werther's Sorrows." Goethe's efforts to raise the youth from his state of mental depression had no immediate visible result, though he ultimately recovered from his malady, and the three verses selected from the poem for musical composition conclude with a prayer to the Father of love on his behalf. Such a text was eminently suited for musical expression by a composer who, intensely realising the problems of life, shaped his course by faith in the power of love; and the Rhapsody furnishes another striking illustration of the strength of imagination which enabled Brahms so to absorb himself in his text as to be able to present it in musical sound—to capable listeners—with a strength and reality usually associated only with impressions of sight. Let anyone who is familiar with the composition read through Goethe's poem from beginning to end, and note the accession of force with which the verses set to music by Brahms come home to him. He will be reminded of an object illuminated by sunlight that stands near others placed in shadow.

The first of the three sections of the single movement that constitutes the Rhapsody, an impressive orchestral picture upon which the independent recitative of the solo voice enters, may be accepted as the reflection of the poet's intense realisation of the unhappy youth's condition. Its tones convey a penetrating impression of rich warmth and pity lying behind the deepest gloom. The feeling of the second section is no less concentrated, though it is expressed with more calm:

> "Ah! how comfort his sorrows
> Who in balsam found poison?
> Who from the fullness of love
> Hath drunk but the hate of men?
> Once despised, now a despiser,
> Secretly he consumeth
> All his own best worth
> In fruitless self-seeking."

The noble declamatory passages of the voice are supported by an accompaniment that becomes agitated or intensely still in accord with the course of the poet's self-questionings, which reach their only possible and beautiful resolution in the third section:

> "If thy Psalt'ry containeth,
> Father of love, one tone
> That can reach his ear,
> Oh, refresh his heart!
> Open his obscurèd sight
> To the thousand sources
> Near to the thirsty one
> In the desert."

Here, by a fine inspiration, the chorus of men's voices enters for the first time *pianissimo*, supporting the solo voice in fervent supplication.

Words and music are fitly associated throughout the movement, which is a treasure amongst works of art, and it is impossible to say that either of its parts is superior to the others, though the divine outpouring of love and pity in the last section often seems to appeal, especially, to the hearer listening for the first time to the composition. This, however, is really due to its position, which contains and brings to an issue the effect of what precedes it. The work has long since been generally recognised as one of the finest of Brahms' shorter compositions, and continues to be more in demand every year, though it had no great immediate success.

"I send you my Rhapsody," Brahms wrote to Dietrich in February, 1870, a week or two after its publication; "the music-directors are not exactly enthusiastic about the opus, but it may, perhaps, be a satisfaction to you that I do not always go in frivolous $\frac{3}{4}$ time!"

It sprang from the composer's very soul.

"He once told me he loved it so," says Dietrich, "that he placed it under his pillow at night in order to have it near him."

The Studies without opus number, Nos. 1 and 2, after Chopin and Weber, were published in 1869 by Senff; and the first two books of Hungarian Dances by Simrock, in the duet form for pianoforte in which they obtained enormous popularity. It was not until 1872 that they were issued in the arrangement as solos, in which, as we know, they had formed part of Brahms' repertoire during some years of his virtuoso career.* Dunkl, a publisher of Budapest, used to relate in after-years that Brahms, on the occasion of one of his early appearances in that city, called on him and offered a selection of six of the Dances for an absurdly small sum. Dunkl said he would give his answer after hearing them in the evening. They had no success and the publisher refused them, a proceeding which he afterwards found considerable reason to regret.

The stirring events of the year 1870, the series of triumphs won by German arms, and the federation of the various independent states under the headship of Prussia which was to lead to the extraordinary development of German political power and industrial progress that has been witnessed by the present generation, were followed by our composer with a mixture of ardent emotions, in which that of swelling patriotic pride gained the predominance as each day brought news of fresh victories won by the soldiers of

---

* Numbers 1, 3, 10, were published in 1874 as arranged by the composer for orchestra, and were frequently conducted by him about that date.

the Fatherland. His vehement exultation at the results of the war found embodiment in a great "Song of Triumph" for chorus and orchestra, with which he was occupied in 1871, and the first chorus, completed early in the year, and sent at once to Reinthaler, was performed from the manuscript in Bremen Cathedral on Good Friday, April 7, under the composer's direction, at a concert given by the Singakademie in memory of those who had fallen in the war.* There is no need to dilate on the feelings which dominated Brahms during the writing of this extraordinary work. They blaze out of it with an intensity and an endurance of passion that well fit it to occupy its own peculiar place amongst the great events that startled Europe at the opening of the seventies. It commemorates heroic deeds in truly heroic strains. By his choice of a text the composer at once raised the scope of his work to a level above that of an ordinary *Te Deum* for victory in war; and the words selected by him from Revelation xix, which admit, throughout each portion of the composition, of an application to the overpowering occurrences of the time, were precisely those for whose setting he alone of modern composers—we may even say of all composers who have succeeded the two giants of the eighteenth century—was, by his temperament, genius and attainments, pre-eminently fitted.

---

* The full programme was as follows:

A German Requiem (under Reinthaler's direction).

Arie from Handel's "Messiah" and Graun's "Der Tod Jesu."

"Hallelujah, Heil und Preis sei Gott." A Song of Triumph for eight-part chorus and orchestra lately composed by Johannes Brahms (under the composer's direction).

Soprano, Frau Wilt from Vienna, Imperial chamber singer.

Baritone, Herr Schelper, of the Berlin Court Opera.

(The chorus of the Singakademie was augmented for the occasion to about three hundred voices.)

The general (public) rehearsal took place on Thursday evening, April 6.

The Triumphlied consists of three great movements for
double chorus and orchestra, the third of which contains a
few passages for baritone solo.

"*Alleluia; salvation and glory and honour and power
unto the Lord our God: For true and righteous are his
judgments.*"

The solemnly jubilant orchestral prelude, the entry of
the full double chorus with loud and sustained Alleluias,
lead to the principal theme of the first movement, already
suggested in the prelude, and derived—though this is hardly
appreciable by the unpractised ear of a general audience—
from the Prussian national air, which is identical with
England's "God save the King." This theme or some
portion of it almost invariably accompanies the phrase,
"*Salvation, honour*, etc., *unto the Lord*," which, with its
surrounding Alleluias, forms the text of the first portion of
the movement, constructed entirely from diatonic harmonies.
The words "*For righteous and true are his judgments*" are
set to the broad themes of the middle portion, to which some
heightened effect is imparted by very sparing use of the more
familiar chromatic chords. The third section is a varied
repetition of the first with a coda. The movement is sustained at the white heat of jubilation until the beginning
of the close, when a few tranquil bars, in the course of which
the voices die away to rest, and the instruments are subdued
to a *pianissimo* that becomes ever softer, prepare for the
glorious outburst with which the chorus terminates. The
second movement has three varying sections:

"*Praise our God, all ye his servants, and ye that fear him,
great and small.*

"*Alleluia, for the Almighty God hath entered into his
kingdom.*

"*Let us be glad and rejoice and give honour to him.*"

The first section opens with pure melodious beauty and
lofty serenity, and displays in its course numerous points of
imitation, direct and by inversion, which are easily discover-

able by the student. It is succeeded by a blast of trumpets, an outburst of Alleluias, and the announcement of the Lord's reign by the voices of the two choirs which enter successively on a sounding tonic pedal; the basses imitating the basses, then the tenors the tenors, and so on, at half a bar's distance. This proclamation section is appropriately concise and of superb grandeur. We hear in it "as it were the voice of a multitude, and as the voice of many waters, and as the voice of mighty thunderings"; whilst the third section, partly woven, by various kinds of imitation, from the phrases of "Nun danket Alle Gott," which is sounded prominently by the flutes and trumpets, is animated by a singularly naïve spirit of light-hearted happiness and rejoicing.

"And I saw heaven opened, and behold a white horse: and he that sat upon him was called Faithful and True, and in righteousness he doth judge and make war.

"And he treadeth the winepress of the fierceness and wrath of Almighty God.

"And he hath on his vesture and on his thigh a name called a King of Kings and a Lord of Lords. Alleluia. Amen."

Subdued awe; firm, proud confidence in a mighty, beneficent ruler; a flash of fierce remembrance of injury—all are rendered with a power, a vividness, a picturesque strength, that are not transcended, even if they are equalled, by anything ever composed in the domain of choral music for the church or the concert-room; and the greatness and glory of "a King of Kings and a Lord of Lords" are celebrated in the long final portion of this gorgeous third movement with dazzling brilliancy of effect, sustained and augmented up to the very end.

The first chorus, performed before the audience of two thousand people assembled in Bremen Cathedral on the evening of Good Friday, 1871, reached its effect to a very considerable extent.

"It has a broad and, as it were, popular character, is conceived simply and wrought with sincerity," writes the correspondent of the *Allgemeine Deutsche Musikzeitung*.

The *Bremen Courier* says:

"One again recognises the titanic capacity of the composer. The work is a vocal joy-symphony, of imposing power and exalted feeling. Praise is due to all concerned in the performance for they have facilitated the understanding of the composer to a large portion of the audience."

The Dietrichs came from Oldenburg to hear the new work. Circumstances prevented the attendance of Frau Schumann and Joachim. Neither artist had returned from what had at this period become an annual visit of each to England, which, in Frau Schumann's case, generally extended over at least two months, and in Joachim's occupied the six weeks of Lent.

Pending Frau Schumann's return, Brahms remained among his friends in the north, and played his D minor Concerto at the Bremen orchestral subscription concert of April 25 with great success, giving pieces by Bach, Scarlatti and Schumann in the second part. Frau Schumann was back in Lichtenthal early in May, and Brahms settled into his usual lodgings there a few days before her arrival. The present writer had the happiness of immediately following her, and the reader interested to learn particulars of the summer life of quiet work and simple pleasures that followed is referred to the Recollections placed at the beginning of our first volume. The details there given are too slight and too personal to be appropriate in the body of the present narrative, though they may be found to have a value of their own for those interested in whatever throws additional light on the true, lovable nature of Brahms.

It may be added here, with reference to questions that have been placed before the author since the publication of the first edition of this biography: that Brahms did not attend the Beethoven Festival held in August at Bonn under Hiller's direction; nor did he gratify his frequently expressed desire to witness the Ober Ammergau Passion Play, performances of which were given in the summer of 1871 to replace those that had been postponed on account of the war of 1870. He went to Stuttgart for a couple of days to witness the Einzug der Truppen, and sometimes visited Carlsruhe, but otherwise, except for a very occasional excursion, remained in Lichtenthal the whole season, leading his usual simple, regular life. He only attended the concerts given in the Kurhaus by rarest exception, though he seldom missed the evening performances of the Johann Strauss orchestra given on the terrace. The term of Strauss' engagement happened to coincide with Frau Schumann's absence in Switzerland, and came to an end the day of her return. Brahms so much regretted that she should not have heard the delightful music, that the genial conductor, by his request, arranged a private performance the next day for her especial benefit.

It was about this time that our composer's art began to make perceptible progress in London. No immediate result was perceptible from the performance of the B flat Sextet led by Joachim at a Monday Popular Concert of 1867, but from the beginning of the seventies we find Brahms' name appearing with some regularity in the programmes of London concerts, whilst the efforts of certain professors and teachers—notably of Cipriani Potter, George and Natalie Macfarren, W. H. Holmes and Adolf Schloesser—steadily fostered the cultivation of his art in private circles. Amongst his earliest English admirers, a special position was occupied by John Farmer, already mentioned in these pages, who filled the post of music master to the Harrow School for twenty-three years (1862-1885) and whose influence, authoritatively exercised in an important educational centre, was sufficiently stimulating to create, during the late sixties, a local interest in Brahms' art that became operative in the course of the seventies in various parts of the United Kingdom. The foundation, in 1872, of the Oxford University Musical Club, an event that was of favourable augury for the widening musical culture characteristic of the time in Britain, had again an appreciable effect in promoting general recognition of the master's true artistic significance. From the date of its establishment Brahms' compositions, both great and small, were prominent in the concert programmes of the club, and the tradition formed by its founder and first president, Mr. C. H. Lloyd, was maintained by his successors. Two years before his death the renowned composer honoured the club by accepting its offer of honorary membership: "It is delightful to meet with such cordial sympathy in student circles," he wrote. In 1873 the appointment of Charles Villiers Stanford to the conductorship of the Cambridge University Musical Society prepared the way for the practice of a very pronounced Brahms' cult at Cambridge and we shall presently have to refer to a musical event which, four years later, associated the Cambridge Society in a special way with the master's art. No opportunity was lost by Frau Schumann, Joachim or Stockhausen for making propaganda for their friend's works in the private artistic circles of London and the provinces. The performance of the Requiem at Sir Henry Thompson's house in the summer of 1871, under Stockhausen, has already been noted. Of minor incidents of the time in this connection, the singing of two duets from Op. 28 by Madame Viardot-Garcia and Stockhausen at a party given by the lady in London on June 10 may be selected for mention.*

---

* The following were, as the author believes, first performances in this country :

Quartet in A major for Pianoforte and Strings: July 6, 1865. Hanover Square Rooms. Concert given by Messrs. Ewer and Co. to the subscribers to their musical library by Miss Agnes Zimmermann, Ludwig Straus, Webbe, Piatti.

Pianoforte Concerto, D minor: March 9, 1872. Crystal Palace (A. Manns), by Miss Baglehole (pupil of the pianist, W. H. Holmes). The concerto was played for the second time in London by Jaell at the Philharmonic concert of June 23, 1873.

Sextet for Strings, G major: November 27, 1872. St. George's

In the same year the call of Bernhard Scholz to Breslau added another to the list of towns, now to increase rapidly, year by year, in which Brahms' art came to be cultivated

---

Hall, Musical Evenings, by Henry Holmes, Folkes, Burnett, Hann, C. Ould, Pezze.
Ballades for Pianoforte, Op. 10, *Nos.* 2 *and* 3: March 17, 1873. St. James's Hall, Monday Popular Concerts (S. Arthur Chappell), by Frau Schumann.
Quartet in G minor for Pianoforte and Strings: May 22, 1873. Oxford University Musical Club. By Walter Parratt, C. Deichmann, F. W. Donkin, A. E. Donkin.
Handel Variations and Fugue for Pianoforte: November 12, 1873. Crystal Palace, by Florence May.
Hungarian Variations for Pianoforte: March 25, 1874. Crystal Palace, by Florence May.
Schumann Variations (Pianoforte Duet): March 30, 1874. St. James's Hall, Monday Popular Concerts, by Miss Agnes Zimmermann and Mr. Franklin Taylor.
Serenade in A major (small Orchestra): June 29, 1874. St. James's Hall, Philharmonic Society. Conductor: W. G. Cusins.
Quartet in C minor for Strings: December 11, 1874. Oxford University Musical Club. C. Deichmann, E. H. Donkin, M. F. Donkin, A. E. Donkin.
Liebeslieder, Op. 52: January 15 and 27, 1877. St. James's Hall, M. and S. Popular Concerts. Pianists: Fräulein Marie Krebs and Miss A. Zimmermann. Singers: Fräulein Sophie Löwe, Fräulein Redeker, William Shakespeare, G. Pyatt.
Neue Liebeslieder, Walzer, Op. 65: May 18, 1877. Cambridge University Musical Society's Concerts. Pianists: C. Villiers Stanford and Raoul C. de Versan. Singers: Fräulein Thekla Friedländer, Fräulein Redeker, Rev. L. Borrisow, Gerard F. Cobb.

N.B.—The *Quartet in G minor* and the *Quintet in F minor,* both for *Pianoforte and Strings,* were played for the first time at the Popular Concerts respectively on January 26, 1874, by Hallé, Madame Norman-Néruda (late Lady Hallé), Ludwig Straus and Piatti; and on February 27, 1875, by Hallé, Joachim, L. Ries and Piatti, but may have been previously given in England elsewhere.

The *Pianoforte Concerto in D minor* was played for the first time in Vienna at one of the Philharmonic Concerts of the season 1870-1, by the composer, and for the second time in March, 1873, by Anton Door.

with particular vigour. Scholz, who had held successive appointments in Hanover and Berlin, had been on terms of familiar acquaintance with the composer from an early period of both their careers. He now found himself in a position, as conductor of the Breslau orchestral subscription concerts, freely to gratify his admiration of the master's art. From this time not only were Brahms' new orchestral works given, with few exceptions as they appeared, at the Breslau subscription concerts, but any existing deficiencies in the Brahms education of the musical public were supplied by performances of the two Serenades and the Pianoforte Concerto. The composer himself played the last-named work at Breslau in 1874 and 1876, when the orchestra was of course conducted by Scholz. No less attention was devoted to the chamber music. At the concerts of the resident string quartet party arranged by Concertmeister Richard Himmelstoss, at which Scholz or Julius Buths often assisted as pianist, the two Sextets, the Quartets and Quintet, and later works in their turn, were frequently heard, and to the successful results of these efforts, to the warm response they elicited from the musical circles of Breslau, we owe the composition of a genial and now favourite work of our master, the Academic Festival Overture, the appearance of which will be noted in its place.

Amongst the friends who visited Lichtenthal during the summer of 1871 were Allgeyer, Levi and Stockhausen, and on September 8 the "Song of Destiny," completed in May, was rehearsed at Carlsruhe.

"Hyperion's Schicksalslied," by Friedrich Hölderlin (1770-1834), sets forth the serene, passionless, unchanging existence of the celestials, surrounded by the clear light of eternity; and its contrast, the ever-shifting, suffering life of humanity, wrapped in the darkness of inscrutable mystery. The poem is entirely fatalistic, containing no comment on what it depicts.

"Ye wander above in light
  On tender soil, blessed immortals!
  Glistening divine breezes
  Touch you gently,
  As the fingers of the artist
  Sacred strings.

"Calm as the sleeping child
  Breathe the celestials;
  Chastely guarded
  In modest bud,
  Their spirits bloom eternally,
  And their blissful eyes
  Gaze in quiet, eternal stillness.

"But to us it is given
  On no spot to rest;
  Suffering men
  Vanish, blindly fall
  From hour to hour,
  As water thrown
  From rock to rock,
  Year-long down into uncertainty."

In Brahms' setting we have yet another fine choral work, characteristic from every point of view, musical, aesthetic, and psychological—one, moreover, which is of quite peculiar interest and value, since it contains an express confession of that creed of love to which the present writer has several times referred as being traceable throughout the composer's life and works. The contrasted pictures of celestial and human existence are set with the vivid force which we have noticed in our brief studies of preceding works, the pathos and tragedy surrounding the lot of mankind being treated with the deep, passionate feeling which is invariably displayed by the composer when he is occupied with this or kindred subjects. Brahms' "Song of Destiny" does not, however, terminate with Hölderlin's, nor could it have done so. Another passion lived stronger within him than that with which he contemplated the phenomena of human suffering, uncertainty, and death; and he has known how to supplement his text with a short, but most exquisitely conceived, orchestral postlude, which, whilst it rounds the work musically into a whole, brings to the despairing soul a message of consolation, hope, faith, courage, such as it is within the peculiar province of music to convey, and which has the more power over the heart since it cannot be translated into articulate words.

That Brahms actually had some such intention in adding the postlude is in the personal knowledge of the present writer. He regarded it as not merely accessory, but as being, in a sense, the most important part of his composition. In rehearsing the work, it was over this portion that he lingered with peculiar care; and when conducting its performance he obtained from the postlude some of his rarest and most exquisite effects of ethereal tenderness.

The work was performed for the first time from the manuscript on October 18, 1871, under the composer's direction, at a concert of the Carlsruhe Philharmonic Society. The overture and garden-scene from Schumann's "Faust" headed, and the conclusion of the second part—both under Levi's direction—closed, the programme, which further included two of Schubert's songs. Fräulein Johanna Schwarz and Stockhausen were the soloists of the occasion.

The impression made by the new work upon the audience of Carlsruhe was profound, and the composer returned to Vienna gratified and pleased by an immediate success which the experiences of his career had by no means led him to regard as a foregone conclusion.

The Schicksalslied was published by Simrock in December, and was performed early in 1872 in Bremen, Breslau, Frankfurt and Vienna.

The only other original publications of 1871, the two books of Songs, Op. 57 and 58, were issued by Rieter-

Biedermann.* All the texts of Op. 57 are original poems or imitations (Nos. 2, 3, 7) by G. F. Daumer, whose texts are amongst the most passionate of those set by Brahms. The composer seems to have imagined a portrait of the poet more or less in correspondence with his verses, and Claus Groth tells an amusing story of the shock sustained by Brahms on taking an opportunity in the spring of 1872 to call on Daumer, who was then living at Würzburg.

"I found him in an out-of-the-way house, in an out-of-the-way street, and was shown to equally retired apartments. There in a quiet room I met my poet. Ah, he was a little dried-up old man! After my sincerely respectful address, the old gentleman replied with an embarrassed word of thanks and I soon perceived that he knew nothing either of me or my compositions, or anything at all of music. And when I pointed to his ardent, passionate verses, he signed me, with a tender wave of the hand, to a little old mother almost more withered than himself, saying, 'Ah, I have only loved the one, my wife!'"

The opening of the year 1872 marks the beginning of a new period, not in the artistic, but in the private life of Brahms. It found him installed in the historic rooms in the third story of No. 4 Carlsgasse, Vienna, which were to remain to the end of his life the nearest approach to an establishment of his own to which he committed himself. He had lodged in Novaragasse, Singerstrasse, Poststrasse 6, Wohlzeile 23, Ungargasse 2, had stayed with his friends the Fabers—had, in fact, since his first visit to Vienna, changed his residence at least with each new season. When he took possession of his rooms in Carlsgasse 4 on December 27, 1871, he had moved for the last time. Here he lived for a little more than a quarter of a century, here he died. He continued as he began, a lodger in furnished apartments,

---

* The author has followed the date given in the published catalogue of the issue of these two books of songs. By their opus numbers they would rather belong to the year 1873 or 1874. Brahms' well known arrangement for pianoforte of Gluck's Gavotte in A was published in 1871 by Senff.

renting his Carlsgasse rooms in the first instance from a Frau Vogl, who, with her husband and family, occupied the rest of the dwelling. Brahms' accommodation consisted in the first instance of two, and later on, of three small rooms communicating one with the other. The middle and largest contained his grand piano and writing table, a small square shaped instrument to which a tradition was attached, and a table and chairs arranged, German fashion, in front of a sofa. Here he received his visitors. In a smaller room were his bookshelves and a high desk for standing to write. There were cupboards for his music, which in time overflowed into the rooms as he required more space for his collections of original manuscripts, engravings, photographs, etc. A few engravings adorned the walls, and his little bust of Beethoven reminded him pleasantly of the old home in the Fuhlentwiethe. Frau Vogl was responsible only for his mending, for the cleaning and dusting of his rooms, and for opening the house-door to visitors. He took his early dinner at a restaurant—the "Kronprinz," the "Goldspinnerin," the "Zur schönen Laterne," and, for about the last fourteen years of his life, at the "Zum rothen Igel," in the Wildpret Markt—and read the newspapers afterwards over a cup of black coffee at one of the coffee houses, in his latter years generally the Café Stadtpark. He supped either at home, with a book for company—when his fare usually consisted of bread and butter and sausage, with a glass of beer or light wine—or again at a restaurant, when, as at dinner, he liked to be joined by his intimates. Needless to say, the private hospitality of friends was abundantly at his command whenever he chose to avail himself of it.

The second performance of the Song of Destiny—the first since publication—took place at the Gesellschaft concert of January 21, under the direction of Anton Rubinstein, who held the post of "artistic director" of the society during the season 1870-71, succeeding Herbeck on his appointment as capellmeister of the imperial opera.

The gratification which must have been felt by the composer at the exceptional impression created by his work on his Austrian public was to be clouded a few days later by news of his father's grave illness. Jakob had been ailing for a year past, and had been obliged to resign his post at the Philharmonic, together with smaller engagements, and accustom himself to the sight of his beloved double-bass standing mute in a corner of his parlour. Johannes, perceiving that advancing years were beginning to tell on his father, had prescribed a change of residence from the fourth story of 5 Anscharplatz to a first floor flat in No. 1 of the same street, but the failure of strength had not been recognised as serious. Jakob did not complain of any particular symptoms, and it was only on the occasion of his fetching the doctor to his stepson Fritz Schnack, who had been brought home ill from St. Petersburg, that he bethought himself to ask advice on his own account, when his alarming condition became immediately apparent to the physician. Johannes, who was immediately sent for, was on the spot without delay, and spent the next fortnight at the bedside of the stricken man, whom he watched with tenderest care and tried to cheer with loving encouragement. But the end was near. Jakob was in the grip of a fatal malady which had ravaged his constitution continuously during the past twelve months, though his sufferings were neither acute nor prolonged. He died on February 11, in his sixty-sixth year, from cancer of the liver, in the presence of his wife and two sons, and an estrangement of some duration between Johannes and the less energetic Fritz—returned from two years' absence in Venezuela—was healed at his death-bed. The son's grief, as may be expected from all that we have related of his clinging family affection, was profound. His consolation was found in endeavours for the protection and comfort of the woman who had brought contentment to the closing years of Jakob's life, and he stayed on with Frau Caroline after the funeral, helping her to make necessary arrangements and to look through his father's little possessions. The old indentures of apprenticeship, the document of citizenship, memorials of Jakob's early struggles and modest personal successes, passed into the composer's keeping. A small portrait in oils, of little value as a picture, but bearing evidence of having been a good likeness of Jakob in his early manhood, was left with the widow. "Mother," said Johannes excitedly the day before his departure from Hamburg, turning suddenly to Frau Caroline after standing for some minutes in silence before the painting, "as long as you live, this of course is yours, but promise that at your death it shall come to me in Vienna!" The promise, readily given, was destined to remain unfulfilled. Frau Caroline, her stepson's senior by more than six years, was to outlive him.

Brahms' care for his father's widow did not cease with his return to his occupations in Vienna. When Fritz Schnack was convalescent, and the year sufficiently advanced for change of air to be desirable, he was sent with his mother to Pinneberg, a pleasant country town of Holstein in great repute with the citizens of Hamburg on account of its health-giving climate. The visit proved so beneficial that Johannes decided to settle his stepbrother there permanently to carry on the business of a watch and clock maker, which he had hitherto followed in St. Petersburg. He established him in a pleasant shop, providing him with all the requisites for a new start, and wished to guarantee a comfortable home for Frau Caroline as mistress of her son's modest household; but the bright, energetic widow did not like the idea of relinquishing her own activity. It was settled, therefore, that she should return to Hamburg and to her business of taking boarders in the first-floor flat in the Anscharplatz, on the condition, rigorously extorted by Johannes, that she was to draw upon him in all cases of need for herself or her son. Brahms was wont to complain to his stepmother in after years that she did not sufficiently fulfil her part of the bargain, to scold her because she did not ask for money, and to propose and insist on holiday journeys for herself and Fritz; and from the day of his father's death to that of his own the kind, capable housewife continued to be the representative to the great tone-poet of the simple, restful tie of family affection to which he clung from beginning to end of his career.

Elise Brahms was supported by her brother until her marriage, some time later than our present date, with a watchmaker named Grund, a widower with a family, and was the recipient of his generosity until her death in 1892. Fritz, "the wrong Brahms," as he was sometimes called, by way of distinguishing him from Johannes, gained a good position in Hamburg as a private teacher of the pianoforte, and was for some years on the staff of visiting teachers at Fräulein Homann's ladies' school at Hamm—an establishment which enjoyed distinguished English as well as German patronage. He had only so far followed in his brother's footsteps as to have been the pupil successively of Cossel and Marxsen, and to have made a few public appearances in Hamburg as pianist in his own Trio concerts. His talents might have carried him farther if he had been more active and ambitious. "Is this your pianoforte-teacher's pace?" demanded Johannes sharply on one of his visits to Hamburg, as he was striding along the street in front of his brother, who could not or would not keep up with him. Fritz was a favourite with his friends; he possessed his share of the family humour, and was never known to brag. "How is your great brother?" an acquaintance asked him one day. "What do you mean?" retorted Fritz, who was tall and thin; "I am bigger than he is!" He died unmarried in Hamburg in 1886, at the age of fifty-one.

Preliminary arrangements were made in good time for the performance of the completed Triumphlied at the Rhine Festival of 1872, held in Düsseldorf; but as the date drew near the committee strangely refused to invite the composer to conduct his work, and Brahms therefore withheld the manuscript. It was performed for the first time on June 5 at a farewell concert arranged by the Grand-Ducal Orchestra and the Philharmonic Society of Carlsruhe jointly, for their departing conductor Hermann Levi, who had been called to the post of court capellmeister at Munich, which he held with brilliant success until failing health compelled his retirement in 1896. Both Frau Schumann and Stockhausen contributed to the programme of the concert, Stockhausen, as a matter of course, singing the short solo of the Triumphlied. The performance seems to have been a fine one, though the chorus at command only numbered one hundred and fifty members. An enthusiastic account of the work sent from Carlsruhe to the *Allgemeine Musikzeitung* by Franz Gehring concludes:

"We Germans may feel proud that such an artist has been inspired by the impression of the most momentous events to which our history can point, to the composition of such a triumph-song. To the year 1870 attaches, not only the renown of our arms, but a new epoch of our musical art.... It is based upon the modern development of long familiar forms and modes of expression. That this development has shown itself to be true and healthy (who had not foreseen it in Brahms' German Requiem!) is the merit of the German master Brahms, the greatest of the present day!"

Comparatively few musicians will be found in these days to deny that Gehring's words were justified by the development of Brahms' own career, though it cannot be concealed that a new epoch such as that to which the reviewer looked forward seems to have closed for the present with the master's death.

Contrary to Brahms' established custom, he accepted a concert engagement in the course of the summer, and appeared with immense success at Baden-Baden Kursaal subscription concert of August 29 as composer, conductor and pianist, with his own A major Serenade and Schumann's Pianoforte Concerto. Amongst the visitors to Lichtenthal in the course of the season were the composer, Bernard Hopffer, the well known conductor, Ernst Frank, Reinthaler and the Simrock family. In the autumn of the year the Countess Julie Radicati di Marmorito was taken from her husband and children after three years of happiness.

With the beginning of autumn, 1872, a period of ten years had elapsed since Brahms' first visit to Vienna, and it will help the reader to obtain a clear view of the development of his career as a composer if we pause for a moment at this point, to consider what had been its special features during the decade in the course of which he had gradually come to regard Vienna as his home. We shall find that it had been entirely logical and continuous, and singularly independent of those influences of his changed environment to which imaginary effects on his art and temperament have not seldom been attributed.

We observe, in the first place, that only one solo has been added to the long list of important works for the pianoforte, accompanied and unaccompanied, which Brahms carried with him to Vienna in 1862, and of this one it must be said that the Paganini studies in two books, immensely brilliant and ingenious though they be, cannot be seriously regarded from the musical standpoint of the Handel or other preceding sets of variations, but must be accepted more or less as diversions of the composer's leisure hours. Several of the variations are little more than transcriptions for the piano of some of those written by Paganini on the same theme for the violin.

In the domain of chamber music, where, so far as it is yet possible to anticipate the verdict of posterity, Brahms' place will be found amongst the greatest composers of all periods, we find that his first series of masterpieces for pianoforte and strings has been brought to a close with the addition of two works—the Horn Trio performed in the autumn of 1865, and the Sonata in E minor for pianoforte and violoncello, whilst by the side of the String Sextet in B flat has been placed another in G major, not indeed transcending, but different from, and in every way worthy of, its companion. With the enumeration of these published works must be associated the mention of two others of peculiar interest in our survey because they mark a fresh stage of Brahms' matured development. The two String Quartets in C minor and A minor were kept in the composer's desk for some years before they were finally completed. The significance of their appearance, which we shall have to note in 1873, as landmarks in Brahms' career, is best illustrated by the remembrance that twenty years had elapsed since the fastidious self-criticism of the young musician of twenty had caused the withdrawal of a string quartet from the list of works proposed by Schumann for the consideration of the publishers.

Brahms' fertility as a song writer for a single voice was constant, though it matured and varied in its manifestations with the onward progress of his life. We have already referred to some of the phases of its long middle period. The decade we are considering witnessed the publication of eight books of miscellaneous songs and three books of the Magelone Romances.

In the Liebeslieder, waltzes for pianoforte duet and vocal quartet, we have the riper artistic fruition of the mood which produced the vocal quartets, Op. 31, "Alternative Dance Song," "Raillery," and "The Walk to the Beloved," composed at Detmold; and to the same early period the Waltzes for pianoforte duet dedicated to Hanslick primarily belong.

The splendid achievement, however, which pre-eminently distinguishes this portion of Brahms' career is to be found in another domain: that in which we may now, in 1872, contemplate the literal fulfilment of Schumann's much discussed prophecy; that in which "the masses of chorus and orchestra *have* lent him their powers." The composer has most truly "sunk his magic staff and revealed to us wondrous glimpses of the spirit world." The period which produced the German Requiem, the Song of Destiny, and the Song of Triumph (1866-1871) could hardly be surpassed in the brilliancy of its own special branch of achievement, and with the completion of the last of these works the growth of Brahms' powers upon this particular line of development had reached its summit. The choral works in which the master hand of the great composer was to be again revealed, whilst they afford additional opportunities of enjoyment to the lovers of his art, could not, from the nature of those that had preceded them, increase the lustre of his fame.

Of works for orchestra alone the two Serenades published in 1860 are still the only examples. As we have seen,[*] Brahms, in the summer of 1862, showed Dietrich the first movement of the C minor Symphony, "which appeared, greatly altered, much later on,"[†] but since then the composer's invariable answer to his friend's inquiries had been that the time for a symphony had not yet arrived. The ten years we are considering are, in fact, characteristic of the composer as well by their silence as by their song. We cannot doubt that just as his choral works were the ultimate outcome of a long period of retirement and study, of which we have traced the early as well as the late results, so the period of his symphonic achievement was being gradually prepared for by special work as fundamental and unwearied. Of this we shall very soon have to note the perfected first-fruits on the appearance of a short orchestral composition, now amongst the most familiar and valued of the treasures with which Brahms has enriched the musical world.

---

[*] Page 301.
[†] Dietrich, p. 42.

CHAPTER XVII.

1872-1876.

Publication of the "Triumphlied," with a dedication to the German Emperor William I—Brahms conducts the "Gesellschaft concerts"—Schumann Festival at Bonn—Professor and Frau Engelmann — String Quartets — First performances — Anselm Feuerbach in Vienna—Variations for Orchestra—First performances—"Triumphlied" at Cologne, Basle and Zürich—Resignation of appointment as "artistic director" to the Gesellschaft—Third Pianoforte Quartet.

BRAHMS returned to Vienna for the concert season of 1872-73 with a new and absorbing interest before him. He had, though not without some heart searching, accepted the appointment of "artistic director" to the Gesellschaft der Musikfreunde, thereby undertaking the duties of conductor, not only of the society's concerts, but of the bi-weekly practices of its choral society. The usual scheme of the Gesellschaft concert season, extending from about the middle of November to April, comprised four regular, and two extra, concerts with orchestra and chorus, one at least of which was devoted to an oratorio or other great choral work.

"Brahms will now conduct the Gesellschaft concerts," writes Billroth on October 25; "he is preparing Handel's 'Te Deum' and 'Saul,' two Bach cantatas, his 'Triumphlied,' etc. At present he is all enthusiasm over the direction of the choral society, and enraptured with the voices and the musical talent of the choir. Should the results be favourable, he will, I think, persevere; a failure might suffice to discourage him so much as to deprive him of all inclination for the work. . . ."

The season opened on November 10 with the following programme:

1. G. F. Handel: *Te Deum* for the Dettingen celebration of victory, 1743.
2. W. A. Mozart: Aria for Soprano, with obl. accompaniment for pianoforte and orchestra (Frau Wilt).
3. (*a*) J. Eccard: "Ueber's Gebirg Maria geht."
   (*b*) H. Isaak: "Inspruk ich muss dich lassen." Choruses *a capella*.
4. F. Schubert: Symphony in C major (arranged for Orchestra from the Pianoforte Duet, Op. 140, by J. Joachim).

This selection hardly invited an enthusiastic demonstration from a mixed audience, but the performances were well received, and the occasion resulted in a substantial artistic success for Brahms, and in the removal of the doubt which had been entertained, even in some friendly quarters, as to his fitness for his new duties. The inclusion of the so-called symphony by Schubert was mentioned with disapproval by some of the papers, though the masterly instrumentation of Joachim's arrangement—made, we may add, at Schumann's suggestion—was duly acknowledged.

The second concert, the first "extra" of the season, was in every respect brilliant. It included the second performance of the complete Triumphlied, published shortly before by Simrock with Brahms' dedication to His Majesty the Emperor William I. The original title inscribed on the manuscript of the work—"Song of Triumph on the Victory of German Arms"—was shortened on publication to the simple "Song of Triumph." The programme of December 6 was as follows:

1. Handel: Concerto for Organ and Orchestra.
2. Mozart: Offertorium for double Chorus, Orchestra, and Organ.
3. Gluck: Aria from the opera "Alcestis" (Frau Joachim).
4. J. S. Bach: Prelude and Fugue in E flat for Organ.
5. J. Brahms: Song of Triumph for Solo, eight-part Chorus, Orchestra, and Organ (solo, Dr. Krauss).

The performances of the great organ player, S. de Lange, invited from Rotterdam for the occasion, on the society's new instrument, which had been inaugurated at the previous concert by Bibl; the singing of Gluck's aria by Frau Joachim; the rendering of two choral works, both new to the audience, the productions of two masters each representative of his day, with the art history of a century lying between them, combined to make a programme of peculiar and varied interest. The Offertorium, an unpublished work composed by Mozart in his twenty-first year, was written for double chorus and organ, to which the composer afterwards added two violins. Brahms now availed himself for the support of his voices of the entire string band, and the performance of the beautiful and unfamiliar work made a great impression. It was published almost immediately by J. P. Gotthard, of Vienna. The most important event of the concert was, of course, the first performance in Vienna of the performer's Song of Triumph.

"A truly magnificent work, which produced a profound and enduring impression," says Schelle; "the German victories have been the occasion of its composition. . . . Both as regards its form and its treatment of masses, this work bears the stamp of a masterpiece. The performances were excellent. The society's concerts could certainly be in no better hands."

The Triumphlied was given a week later, December 14, in Munich, under Franz Wüllner, and was again reviewed at length in the *Allgemeine Zeitung* of the 25th in a highly interesting article by Franz Pyllemann.

"The orchestra develops truly royal splendour.... What wealth of tone-combination, what intoxicating charm of colouring, strike the ear of the listener! The knowledge shown in the use and application of the most appropriate and noble means of expression, as offered by the various instruments, must be noted with deep admiration. Brahms' mastery in the handling of chorus has long been common knowledge. He makes great demands on his singers, and does not readily restrict the development of an artistic idea on account either of their convenience or their uncertainty. But, how his choral movements sound! In this respect, the master stands nearer to the heroes of choral composition, and especially Handel, than any other modern musician. He has studied their works; he has most intimately fused their, for our time, almost enigmatical technique with the many resources of modern art; so that we might often suppose ourselves to be listening, as regards his thematic work, the polyphonic construction of his parts, to a masterpiece of the eighteenth century, whilst the character of the themes, the quality of the harmonies, the condition of the form, on the whole and in detail, are entirely modern, are quite specifically 'Brahms.'"

The work was given at the Gewandhaus Concerts, Leipzig, on February 27, 1873.

The effect of the second "regular" Gesellschaft concert of the season, on January 5, 1873, was marred by a series of misfortunes. Three works were announced for performance:

1. Hiller: Concert Overture in D major.
2. Schumann: "Des Sängers Fluch."
3. Mendelssohn: "Die Walpurgis Nacht."

Hiller, who happened to be staying in Vienna, had promised to conduct his overture to "Demetrius," the most successful of his four works in this form, but, owing to an accident to the music, it was necessary to substitute another, which proved ineffective. The drummer was attacked by sudden illness on the day of the concert, and the substitute provided proved unequal to the emergency; Hiller was obliged to rap for silence immediately after beginning the performance of his work, and to recommence. A similar mishap attended the course of the "Sängers Fluch," under Brahms' direction, in consequence of a misunderstanding between the solo vocalists and the harpists. Mendelssohn's work alone went without a blemish.

A very great success was obtained at the next concert, on February 28, the second "extra" of the season, with Handel's oratorio "Saul," given for the first time in Vienna. The great work was received with enthusiasm, and the performance pronounced perfect both by public and press.*

This was followed, at the next "regular" concert on March 23, by a varied programme:

1. Bach: Easter Cantata, "Christ lag in Todesbanden."
2. Haydn: Symphony in C major.
3. German Folk-songs for unaccompanied mixed Chorus:
     (a) "In stiller Nacht."
     (b) "Dort in den Waiden steht ein Haus."
4. Schubert: "Ellen's zweiter Gesang" (arranged for Soprano solo, women's Chorus, and Instruments by Brahms).
5. Beethoven: Chorus from "Die Weihe des Hauses," for Soprano solo, Chorus, and Orchestra.

The attitude of the audience during the early part of this concert was somewhat doubtful, the opening cantata being followed with earnestness, but with scanty demonstrations of approval. At the entry of the chorale at the close of the work, however, an electric feeling passed through the packed hall as at the release from strained attention, and the applause which followed was loud and resounding.

"It is hardly possible to bestow enough praise upon the

---

* Brahms sent Reinthaler, in a letter dated October, 1873, a few particulars of the cuts, etc., decided upon by him for this performance. Brahms "Briefwechsel," III, p. 53.

performance of the cantata," says Schelle (the *Presse*); "the choral society and their conductor Brahms acquitted themselves most splendidly of their task, and warm acknowledgment is also due to Herr Organist Bibl."

Similar praise is given to the performance of the other numbers of the programme, special mention being made of the folk-songs, one of which had to be repeated.

"In a word," concludes the critic, "the satisfaction caused us by the beautifully arranged concert must, we think, have been equalled by that felt by Brahms at its success."

Billroth gives an interesting account, in a letter dated March 29, of the energy and success of Brahms' work in this new field of labour.

"Brahms is extremely active as a conductor; he has achieved incomparably fine performances, and receives the fullest recognition from all who take art earnestly. His 'Triumphlied,' given with organ and an immense chorus, produced a marvellous effect here; great masses are required for its performance, it is monumental music. . . .

"At the last concert Brahms ventured upon one of the most difficult of Bach's cantatas, composed to Luther's text, 'Christ lay in bonds of death,' which had never before been performed. The Viennese accepted this with amiability from such a favourite as Brahms. Two unaccompanied folk-songs which came next ('In stiller Nacht' and 'Der schönste Bursch am ganzen Rhein') awakened such a storm of applause, however, that one almost felt afraid the house would fall in. The old King of Hanover was almost beside himself with musical intoxication. One becomes quite drunk with the beautiful quality of sound produced by this choir, whose increase and decrease (*f.* and *p.*) are carried on like those of one voice. . . ."

Sufficient detail has now been given of the Gesellschaft concert season of 1872-73 to show the wisdom of the committee in their choice of a new "artistic director," and it only remains to mention the advertised "last" concert of April 6. Two works were brought to a hearing:

1. Bach: Cantata, "Liebster Gott, wann werd' ich sterben."
2. Cherubini: Requiem in C minor.

The success of the performances may be inferred from the fact that the programme was repeated two days later at an additional concert hastily arranged to fulfil the general demand for an encore.

Brahms was singularly unfortunate this year in his efforts to secure a quiet retreat for the pursuit of his usual summer avocations. Flying, after two days' residence in lodgings in Gratwein, Styria, from the attentions of some "aesthetic ladies" who began to threaten his peace, he took refuge in the "Seerose," an inn in the Bavarian village of Tutzing, on Lake Starnberg, to receive, the very night of his arrival, a formal written invitation to make one, during his stay, of a light hearted fellowship of youthful authors, painters and musicians who held their meetings in the house. No more definite answer was vouchsafed to this overture than such as could be deduced from the torn fragments of the missive found on the floor of his room early the next morning by the housemaid. By hiring the miserable old piano of the establishment, however, and causing it to be placed in his own private quarters, the composer made possible his prolonged sojourn at Tutzing, where he stayed on for the greater part of the summer, paying occasional visits to Levi at Munich, and seeing something also of Allgeyer, who had been invited to settle professionally in the Bavarian capital shortly after Levi's departure from Carlsruhe. Later on Brahms attended the Schumann Festival at Bonn (August 17-19), arranged, for the purpose of assisting a fund for the erection of a memorial to Schumann in the city where the master had passed the two last sad years of his life, and where a Beethoven monument had been unveiled in 1871. There were orchestral concerts on the 17th and 18th, both conducted by Joachim, the director of the festival, excepting in the case of one work (Wasielewski), and a matinée of chamber music on the 19th, the programmes, in which Frau Schumann, Frau Joachim, Stockhausen, and others took part, being entirely selected from Schumann's works.* The festival closed with a social function, an excursion by steamer to Rolandseck. The presence at Bonn of each member of the remarkable quartet of great musicians, whom we have seen closely bound together by ties of artistic and personal friendship through nearly twenty years, was made the more interesting by the addition of Ferdinand Hiller, the intimate ally of all four. Many other old friends were there, of whom Otto and Jenny Goldschmidt, Dietrich, Grimm, Reinthaler and von Meysenbug may be particularly mentioned. Brahms made some new acquaintances also, notably Professor Engelmann and his gifted wife, known in the musical world for a few seasons as the pianist Fräulein Emma Brandes, who retired from a public career on her early marriage.

Brahms was not, by all accounts, in his best mood on the occasion of the festival, and the reason is not far to seek. Joachim, as director, had strongly wished to open the concerts with a performance of the German Requiem, a suggestion that was from first to last steadily opposed by the committee who continued to affirm that Brahms was going to compose a new work for the occasion long after he had declined their proposal that he should do so. On learning the real state of the case from his friend, Joachim, supported by a letter from Frau Schumann, returned to the committee with his original plan which was, however, the more easily defeated since scruples of delicacy withheld Brahms from expressing his own wishes in the matter. It is, at this distance of time, easy to read between the lines of the correspondence, that the master would gladly have acceded to such a definite request to conduct his great work as would have spared him the necessity of expressing an

---

* The dates and programmes of the memorial concerts are given in the *Allgemeine Musikalische Zeitung* of July 27, 1873.

opinion as to the propriety of its inclusion in the concert programmes. The ultimate withdrawal of the Requiem from the festival scheme occasioned him keen disappointment and was the cause of a transient tension of feeling between Joachim and himself.

"The performance on such an occasion of the work of a living composer must necessarily, and under all circumstances, be felt by him as an honour. But it is an honour which very real modesty must prevent him from accepting too freely. . . . At all events modesty frequently causes awkwardness and silence, such as mine to you. But in this case, if you had thought simply about the matter and about me, you would have known how truly and closely such a piece as the Requiem belongs to Schumann. Just as I myself am inwardly conscious that it was partly sung for him."*

Frau Schumann and her daughters returned to Lichtenthal for a few weeks on the conclusion of the festival. Later in the year they settled for the second time in Berlin, and in future only visited Baden-Baden for an occasional change. Brahms sometimes met his old friends there in the summer until the year 1878, when Frau Schumann accepted an appointment at the Conservatoire of Music founded by Dr. Hoch at Frankfurt. She then sold her house at Lichtenthal, and Brahms' subsequent association with the neighbourhood was limited to rare visits of a few days. Frau Schumann continued to live at Frankfurt from this time, though she resigned her duties at the conservatoire some years before her death.

Brahms followed his old friend to Lichtenthal and spent a couple of days near her before the close of August, and his visit was accepted by Frau Clara as "the most welcome conclusion of the festival." He had, whilst staying in Bonn, tried with her the just finished variations on a theme by

---

* Compare with these passages from Brahms' letter to Joachim— No. 310 of the Brahms-Joachim "Briefwechsel." Page 374 of this biography.

Haydn—published a little later for orchestra—in the version of the work as a duet for two pianofortes, and he now played her the finally completed String Quartets in C minor and A minor and the "Regenlied." Frau Schumann had heard the C minor Quartet, as the reader may remember, in the summer of 1866. The composer played both works to Dr. Hermann Deiters when he was staying at Bonn in 1868.*

Claus Groth's poem, "Rain-song," and the shorter one, "Echo," which form the texts of Nos. 3 and 4 of Brahms' Op. 59, were particular favourites of our master. He composed the "Nachklang," of which he chose the title, twice. The published version is the second of the two. Musical readers will remember that melody and accompaniment are used again in the duet Sonata in G major.

The composer heard a private rehearsal of both string quartets on his return to Munich, where he passed the rest of the summer. The two works were played for the first time in public; that in A minor in Berlin at the Joachim Quartet concert of October 18 from the manuscript; that in C minor at the Hellmesberger concert of December 11 in Vienna from the printed copies.

The appearance of these two works as Op. 51, Nos. 1 and 2, forms, as we have said, another and important landmark in the development of Brahms' career. The String Quartet holds a position of peculiar significance in the art of music, and a composer, by selecting this form for the exercise of his powers, exposes them to the most unfailing test to which his calibre as a musician can possibly be submitted. He must possess not only fertility in the production of purely musical concentrated ideas, and ideas capable of development; the power to develop them, which means many things, and the capacity for shaping them into clear structure; but

---

* Dr. Hermann Deiters personally communicated to the author that Brahms played him the two string quartets, which we know as Op. 51, in 1868 at Bonn. Probably they had not at that date, been completed quite in their final form.

he must be able to express them with the most bare and simple musical means, with four strings. From the rapid effects of strong and strongly contrasted sensation producible by the pianoforte, or the varied tone-colour of the orchestra, he is precluded. With his four strings he can interest, delight, touch, but hardly astonish his hearers. The String Quartet is absolute music in its purest form, and but few works in this domain can survive their birth unless they be destined to attain a long life. The means are perfect for the end, but this is difficult of achievement; only the quartet of a master has much chance of being heard after its first few performances. It will be evident to the reader that Brahms was fitted by many essential characteristics of his genius for success in this branch of art, though it cannot cause surprise that one of his great qualities, the power of waiting for results, should have strengthened his fastidiousness in accepting as final the fruits of his studies in a form which had been brought to ideal perfection by Haydn and Beethoven, each in their day. On the great musicianship manifest in Brahms' quartets, on his mastery over his means, his power of completely balancing his four parts, of making each a separate individuality whilst all blend harmoniously as equal constituents of an organic whole, it is only necessary to insist here in so far as these qualities are elements in another feature which pre-eminently marks our master's chamber music for strings: the extraordinary beauty of its structure. Throughout the three quartets and two quintets for strings composed by Brahms there is not only no mere passage writing, but it would be difficult to point to a single note that could be called superfluous. Each seems to have been placed with loving care by the master hand of the great musical architect, the artist builder, as an essential part of the whole large design. When we examine the thoughts themselves and their development we find that we are, as in all Brahms' works, in the presence of a powerful and fascinating individuality. Ideas and treatment are the master's own, not easy at once to understand, but offering almost inexhaustible opportunity for discovery and enjoyment to listeners willing to earn such rewards. The two quartets, Op. 51, are more or less severally representative of contrasted sides of Brahms' individuality. The first, in C minor, is generally characterised by fire and impetuosity, exquisitely relieved by the tender romance of the second movement; No. 2, in A minor, is conceived in a softer vein. The last movement of this work contains a beautiful example of the characteristic Brahms coda; the augmented vigour of the climax is preceded by a period of tranquillity that seems to place the listener in an atmosphere of mystic exaltation, to afford him "glimpses of a spirit world" from which the previous thoughts of the movement flow towards him in transfigured tones. Lovers of the master's music will recall a similar feature in other works. In the opening theme of the first movement, which is suggestive of Joachim's early device F.A.E.—

we may, perhaps, perceive a passing reference to the remembrance of his friend which must certainly have been present to Brahms' mind as he planned these works. Instances of the composer's mastery of the art of modulation, of his boldness and facility in going to, and returning from unexpected and distant keys, may be found in the two quartets as in the majority of his instrumental compositions. They were dedicated by Brahms to "his friend Dr. Theodor Billroth of Vienna," and were published in the autumn by Simrock.

Amongst those who had looked forward with particular expectancy to the opening of the great World Exhibition that was held in Vienna in the autumn of 1873 was the painter Anselm Feuerbach. He had, the previous year, accepted the offer of an appointment as director of the historical class about to be formed in the Imperial Academy of Plastic Arts of that city, but had begged for a year's leave of absence in Rome before entering on his new duties, in order that he might finish two great pictures, "The Battle of the Amazons" and "The Second Symposium," the exhibition of which he conceived likely to establish his fame and to secure him an authoritative position on taking up his residence in Austria. The nearly finished pictures were sent to Vienna in March or April, and Feuerbach followed them in May, 1873, but it turned out that they could not be hung in the Exhibition gallery on account of their great size. The painter determined, therefore, to exhibit them one after the other in the "Künstler-Haus," and, in order to secure the advantage of association in the mind of the public with so favourite a celebrity of Vienna as Brahms had at this time become, he requested the master to sit to him on his return in October in order that his portrait might be exhibited with the other pictures.

Feuerbach was a small man of ultra-refined appearance and manners, and a countenance of rather melancholy expression that had evidently been of striking beauty in his youth. He was accustomed to be made much of by ladies, was extremely sensitive and self-centred, and had confidently persuaded himself that his pictures were to achieve an instant and overwhelming success.

"My pictures are splendid and all but finished," he wrote to his mother on October 2; "why should I feel a moment's anxiety since I have eminent power in my hands; genius and position. . . . The Symposium also is quite exquisite, I may say so now as I have seen the Vatican."*

Brahms, who had, as we have seen, a long-standing acquaintance with Feuerbach and sincerely admired his powers, mounted the many flights of stairs leading to the artist's temporary studio more than once. His attention was particularly called to the "Battle of the Amazons,"

---

* Allgeyer's "Life of Feuerbach."

on which, as it was to be exhibited first, Feuerbach was busy with the finishing touches. He mentioned it several times in a reserved manner to Groth, who was in Vienna for the Exhibition, saying he was anxious to have his opinion of it, and persuaded him to pay a visit to the studio one day to be presented to Feuerbach. Groth, however, on coming away, found that he was unable, as Brahms had been, to express himself warmly about the great painting, and merely agreed with our master in "not understanding" it. Brahms, intimately acquainted with the artist circles of Vienna, evidently could not shake off his apprehension as to the result of the exhibition, and took an opportunity of speaking a word of warning to Feuerbach, advising him to be cautious, and to introduce himself to his new public with a smaller work. The integrity of the composer's ideas of friendship and the misunderstanding of his motives which was its frequent result, as well as the general soundness of his judgment in matters on which he ventured to give advice, are well illustrated by the affair. His words produced an immediate effect very different from that intended by him. The wound they inflicted on the irritable susceptibility of the painter was so painful as to deprive him of the power of concentrating his mind upon the "Amazons" for several subsequent days, and he found it impossible to go on with Brahms' portrait.

"Another evening spoilt by Brahms," he wrote on November 3; and again: "I was not for a second angry with Brahms, but I have put his canvas aside for the present." It was never taken up again.

The pictures were duly exhibited in turn, and it may be said that the final breakdown of Feuerbach's never robust constitution was the ultimate result. Not criticism only or even chiefly, but torrents of contempt, derision, insult were poured upon his work.

"A storm broke over my head by which I could at least reassure myself as to the importance of my pictures. I could not sit down to table without finding jests, raillery, caricature—unfortunately always bad—beside my plate, and the story of my discomfiture was related in the house from roof to cellar. I was told that everyone, from the professor to the porter's boy, was laughing at my bad picture."

"Almost the entire press, independent and mercenary alike, was arrayed against Feuerbach," says Allgeyer.

His pupils, however, offered him the mute sympathy and support of punctual attendance and respectful attention at class, and the Minister remained loyal to him. He retained his appointment till the close of 1876, though ill health prevented him from performing his duties during the last half year. He died at Nürnburg in 1880. His friendship with our master did not terminate with the incident of the pictures.

"Brahms has lent me his fur coat for my journey," he wrote in February, 1875, on the eve of his departure for Rome.

The "Battle of the Amazons" was presented by the artist's mother to the city of Nürnburg in the year 1889, and hangs there in the picture gallery of the Town Hall. Many of the studies for the "Amazons" and the "Symposium" were purchased by King Ludwig II of Bavaria, and presented by him to the Royal Pinakothek at Munich.

Of the many letters of congratulation received by Allgeyer after the appearance of his "Life of Feuerbach" in 1894, one of those most highly prized by him came from Brahms.

Brahms paid one visit to the great Exhibition in the company of Groth and other friends, though the noise and bustle of such a scene were by no means to his taste. He was more anxious that his friend should see and hear what was really characteristic of Vienna. "You must go to the Volksgarten on Friday evening when Johann Strauss will conduct his waltzes. *There* is a master; such a master of the orchestra that one never loses a single tone of whatever instrument!"

Having promised to arrange a meeting between Frau Dustmann of the imperial opera and Groth, Brahms came to the poet's hotel one morning, and entering the room where he was lying in bed with a bad feverish cold, exclaimed delightedly: "Come to me this evening, the Dustmann will sing to you." "But you see I am ill," returned Groth testily. "You will be astonished," continued Brahms, whose boast it was that he had never in his life been really ill, "*there* is a singer, *there* is an artist; *she* will please you!" "Ah, my dear fellow, I really cannot come," pleaded the other, "Johann has just put a cold compress on, I am so miserable!" "She is very seldom free just now; she cannot come another day." "Surely you see how miserable I am. How I should like to come, but I cannot," persisted Groth. Then Brahms turned to go. "You are a Philistine!" he declared angrily as he left the room.*

The ante-Christmas season of 1873, signalised on its immediate opening by the performance of the String Quartet in A minor at Berlin, already referred to, was further rendered distinctive in Brahms' career by the first performance from the manuscript of the Variations for Orchestra on a theme by Haydn, which took place at the Vienna Philharmonic of November 2 under the composer's direction. The masterly and attractive work consists, as most amateurs are aware, of eight variations and a finale on the "Chorale St. Antoni." The composer adheres almost entirely to Haydn's harmonies in the giving out of the theme, the five bar rhythm of which lends a distinctive character to the simple old hymn tune "Wallfahrtslied." The variations are constructed on the principle often observable in Brahms' works in this form; they constitute, as it were, a series of little movements each woven more or less appreciably from the matter of the chorale, but each with a character of its own and complete in itself, while the entire composition is gathered together

---

* From the article in the *Gegenwart* already referred to.

BRAHMS AT THE AGE OF FORTY.

and rounded into a whole by the finale. Brahms' vivid and original imagination of tone effect is very clearly discernible throughout the composition, and is especially illustrated in it by his original and effective employment of the double bassoon.

The variations were received by the crowded audience, and reviewed by the press, with warm welcome and with grateful appreciation of their beauty and perfection, if with some trace of disappointment that he who "held the sceptre" in the domain of music for the chamber and the concert room, and must of all living musicians be preeminently qualified for the composition of a symphony, should be the very man to refrain from writing one. Brahms, however, was well aware of the gigantic difficulty of the task that lay before him in the writing of a symphony that should successfully encounter that ordeal of comparison with the greatest works of its class which had become inevitable by the fact of his acknowledged supremacy in other forms. The ultimate cause of his delay and the pledge of his future victory are alike to be found in the nature of his artistic convictions, which, holding him loyal to the traditions of the past masters of instrumental music, made it impossible to him to seek novelty by compromising with modern methods. Brahms elected to wait until, with the gradual ripening of his powers to full maturity, he should feel, not only that he had something of his own to say in the highest domain of pure music, but that he had mastered the power of expressing it in a manner true to himself. Had he never felt assured on these two points it is certain that no symphony of his would ever have been made public, no matter to what sum of months the hours might amount which he had devoted to the study and practice of writing for the orchestra. Having now given a sign of his whereabouts he again drew a veil over the course of his artistic development, and, appearing before the public during the next three years only on ground which he had already made his own, revealed no more upward stages of his achievement until he at length stood victoriously before the world on its summit.

The variations were performed for the second time on December 10 under Levi in Munich.

The Gesellschaft season opened under Brahms' direction on November 9, with Beethoven's Overture, Op. 115, and Handel's "Alexander's Feast." A varied programme was given at the second concert of December 7:

1. Schubert: Overture to Fierrebras.
2. Schubert: Aria for Tenor (written in 1821 for introduction into Herold's Opera "Zauberglöcken" at the Kärnthnerthor Theater, Vienna; unpublished). Herr Gustav Walter.
3. Volkmann: Concertstück for Pianoforte and Orchestra. Pianoforte, Herr Smetansky.
4. (a) Joh. Rud. Ahle (1662) } Unaccompanied Choruses.
   (b) J. S. Bach
5. Bach: Cantata, "Nun ist das Heil," for double Chorus, Orchestra and Organ.
6. Jac. Gallus: Unaccompanied Chorus, "Ecce Quomodo."
7. Beethoven: Choral Fantasia for Pianoforte (Smetansky), Orchestra and Chorus.

The publications of the year, all issued in the autumn, were, in addition to the string quartets, the version for two pianofortes of the Haydn Variations (Op. 56b), by Simrock, and a set of eight Songs (Op. 59), by Rieter-Biedermann. Of these, four are set to texts by Claus Groth, which include "Rain-songs" and the lovely "Dein blaues Auge hält so still." The Variations for Orchestra were published by Simrock in 1874.

Brahms was at this time quite immersed in his various kinds of work.

"I am so enormously occupied that I see my best friends only very rarely and by accident," he wrote in December to the present author.

It had now become his custom to decline invitations for the Christmas festival, and to spend it, partly at the open air Christmas market, where he made himself happy by purchasing gifts for the poor children whom he found crowding round the tempting wares, and partly at home, where he would look in for half an hour at the family party gathered in front of his landlady's Christmas tree; no doubt contributing his share to the surprises of Christmas Eve.

"I always spend festivals in solitude, quite alone in my room with a few dear ones, and very quietly—for the few are dead or far away."*

His Christmas offering to Frau Schumann this year was his beautiful setting of her son Felix's song, "Meine Liebe ist grün wie der Fliederbusch." He himself received a New Year's present of a special kind—the Maximilian Order for Art and Science conferred on him by King Ludwig II of Bavaria.

The year 1874 was unusually full of movement and varied excitement for our composer. From January onwards he was besieged with invitations, many of which he accepted, to conduct his works at concerts and festivals in North Germany, the Rhine, Switzerland, and was obliged to reply in the negative to Dietrich's request, received in the beginning of spring, that he would include Oldenburg in his arrangements.

"DEAR FRIEND,

"I am more than sorry, but you are too late! I have already promised so much, and shall not be coming to your neighbourhood!

"If you had written earlier I could have arranged with Hanover, Bremen, etc., for, *seriously*, I should be too glad to go to you again. . . ."

The third Gesellschaft concert of the season (1873-74) took place on January 25. That the performances under

---
* Litzmann III, 273.

Brahms would be above criticism had become by this time almost a foregone conclusion, and, beyond recording the great success achieved by Goldmark's "Hymn of Spring," it is only necessary to give the programme of the occasion:

1. Rheinberger: Prelude to the Opera "The Seven Ravens."
2. Goldmark: "Frühlings Hymne" (May musings, from the Swedish of Geijer), for Contralto solo, Chorus and Orchestra. (First performance, under the composer's direction.)
3. Mozart: "Davidde Penitente," Cantata for Soli, Chorus and Orchestra.

A few days later Brahms left Vienna to fulfil a group of engagements in Leipzig, a circumstance which in itself affords some indication of the rapid strides by which his career had lately been advancing towards the full sunshine of success that was to flood the latter portion of his path through life.

The relations between Brahms and the city which owed its brilliant reputation as a musical centre to Mendelssohn's influence had been at no time really sympathetic. The attitude of expectant toleration that had been more or less adopted towards him by both its extreme parties after his first visit in 1853 had resulted on the one hand from Schumann's essay, and on the other, from the confidence felt by the Weimarites and expressed by Liszt that his "new paths" must eventually bring him into close touch with themselves. Gradually, however, it became clear how mistaken was the belief that the young musician would drift towards acceptance of the extreme new tendencies, whilst the originality of his musical thoughts and of his manner of expressing them was abhorrent to the inflexible conservatism that had come to represent the traditions of the Gewandhaus. If, moreover, there be reason to surmise that Mendelssohn himself, with all his genuine personal and artistic friendship for Schumann, viewed certain tendencies of his genius with mistrust, the probability is still greater that neither Rietz, who conducted the Gewandhaus concerts from 1848 to 1860, nor Reinecke, who succeeded him, was in very warm sympathy with that of Brahms, and the predilections of the public followed those of their accredited guides.

Brahms' works were, it is true, generally given at the orchestral or chamber concerts of the Gewandhaus soon after publication, but, excepting the Triumphlied, with its special appeal to the patriotic sentiment of the great German people, they met with but scanty response from an audience little accustomed to the exertion of trying to follow the expression of a new and original artistic individuality. That Reinecke was by no means an ideal conductor of them naturally resulted from the fact that by training, by conviction, and by practice, he was attached to a rigidly formal school of modern musical thought, and it can surprise no one that he should have been unable entirely to realise the deeper and richer utterances of Schumann's young prophet. Brahms' chamber music fared differently in the hands of David, who was almost alone amongst the authorities of the Gewandhaus in his sympathy for the composer's genius. To these considerations it must be added that not only the pianist, but the composer Rubinstein, had, as we indicated in an early chapter, an enthusiastic following amongst the typical Leipzig public who were disposed to resent any claim to recognition that might threaten to rival that of their favourite.

In spite, however, of the fact that Brahms was no party man, in Leipzig, as in almost every other city where his music was heard, it struck a root, imperceptible at first, but growing deeper and stronger and more extended with every year that went by. The attention bestowed on it by Brendel's society has been frequently referred to in these pages; it was cultivated, also, by Riedel's celebrated choir. A more representative illustration, however, of a certain mysterious power inherent in Brahms' works of finding their way sooner or later, and not seldom it is sooner, to the heart, in spite of their intellectuality, their difficulty, their reserve, is furnished by the case of two sisters, daughters of the head of one of the great bookselling houses of Leipzig. The Fräulein Wiegand did not live in a musical "set," nor were they personally acquainted with Brahms or his friends, but not long after their first casual introduction to his music in the middle of the sixties, when they were young girls, the appearance of each of his new works had come to be an event in their lives. "You from Leipzig!" exclaimed Hermann Levi, with whom the sisters had a passing acquaintance in the summer of 1871. It was not until three months before the composer's death that these ladies had any personal communication with him. Then, hearing of his hopeless illness, they resolved to address him for the first and last time, and in January, 1897, they wrote to him telling how they had always loved his music and followed his career. No one who really knew him will doubt the pleasure that the letter gave to the dying master. In answer he sent his photograph with his autograph, "Johannes Brahms," and the inscription: "To the two sisters as a little token of heartfelt thanks for their so kind account."

Of the professional critics of Leipzig, Bernsdorf of the *Signale* remained to the last irreconcilable to Brahms' art; but, on the other hand, Dörffel of the *Leipziger Nachrichten*, watched the appearance of his works with profound interest and reviewed them with extreme sympathy and acumen. There was during the sixties no influential "Brahms" community in musical Leipzig, no active "Brahms" propaganda in the houses of wealthy amateurs. Such occasional admirers as the composer may have had in this circle were to be met in the drawing room of the lady introduced to the reader in an early chapter as Hedwig Salamon, later married to the composer, Franz von Holstein. At the beginning of the seventies, however, a few well known residents were to be found who had a strong bond of union in their common sympathy with Brahms' genius. Of these, in addition to the von Holsteins, may be particularly mentioned Philipp Spitta, now remembered in all parts of the musical world as the author of the standard Bach biography, Alfred Volkland, Edmund Astor, of the firm of Rieter-Biedermann, and later on its head, and the distinguished composer, Heinrich von Herzogenberg, who settled in Leipzig in 1872, four years after his marriage with Elizabeth von Stockhausen, daughter of the sometime Hanoverian minister plenipotentiary (ausserordentlicher Gesandter u. hevollmächtiger minister) at the court of Vienna. This lady, endowed in an extraordinary degree with beauty, goodness, intellectual and artistic gifts, domestic qualities, and any other imaginable graces and perfections, had in her girlhood received a few pianoforte lessons from Brahms during one of his early visits to Vienna. She sympathised warmly with her husband's enthusiastic admiration of Brahms' art and gradually came to be numbered with him among its most ardent devotees. It will be convenient to mention here also that Theodor Kirchner settled in Leipzig in 1875, the year in which Spitta accepted a call to Berlin.

These circumstances taken together with the fact that the German Requiem had been given several times in the famous Saxon town in the course of the previous year, seem to explain the master's visit to Leipzig, where he had made no public appearance since the Gewandhaus concert of November 26, 1860, when he and Joachim had appeared respectively with the A major Serenade and the Hungarian Concerto. Brahms was now to take part in a performance of his G minor Quartet and to play his Handel Variations at the Gewandhaus chamber music concert of February 1; to conduct a performance of "Rinaldo" by the University Choral Society of February 3; and at the Gewandhaus subscription concert of the 5th to conduct the Haydn Variations, three Hungarian Dances and the Rhapsody (solo, Frau Joachim), and to co-operate with Reinecke as accompanist in a performance of the Liebeslieder, Op. 52. His arrival in Leipzig was welcomed on January 30 by a

Brahms concert of the Allgemeiner Musik Verein, the programme of which included the Horn Trio, Schumann Variations, Op. 23, Marienlieder, and several songs and pianoforte solos.

The moment when Brahms stepped on to the Gewandhaus platform, the acknowledged representative, in at least two domains of musical art, of the greatest masters who had preceded him, must have been one of quiet satisfaction to himself if he cast a thought backward to the evening, more than thirteen years ago, when he had last appeared in the same hall, and, not for the first time, unsuccessfully sought the suffrages of the same public. Even now, however, though he was received with the respect due to a musician of his great standing, he was not to taste the enjoyment of feeling that he had aroused the enthusiasm, hardly that he had awakened the sympathy, of his audience. The Gewandhaus public, rarely demonstrative, preserved its special attitude of coldness and reserve towards him, only thawing a little at the subscription concert of the 5th, under the influence of the Liebeslieder and Hungarian Dances. In the circle of his personal friends his visit was celebrated as a festival, but much as he may have appreciated the many social gatherings arranged in his honour, he was probably glad to return to the genial atmosphere of his surroundings in Vienna where, in spite of the survival of a hostile attitude in certain organs of the press, his ground had become practically his own.

Of the agreeable impressions which the master carried with him from Leipzig, one of the most enduring was derived from the renewal of his slight previous personal acquaintance with the Herzogenbergs, and on his next visit to the town three years later he accepted the hospitality of their house during the few days of his stay. The friendship that was cemented at that period between hosts and guest became closer as time went on. Brahms admitted both the Herzogenbergs to a rare degree of artistic intimacy, included them in the small number of friends to whom he was in the habit of showing his manuscripts as they were completed, and awaited with impatience the letters in which Frau Elizabeth—who added to her other gifts that of a facile pen—was in the habit of reporting to him her own and her husband's first impressions of his works. Many passages in the master's letters to these friends afford touching illustration of his constitutional lack of self confidence and his desire for sympathy.

"Only believe quite simply," he writes on one occasion, "that it is really a highly acceptable and *necessary* pleasure, to hear a friendly word of approval about a new piece."

The Haydn Variations were performed in February or March at Breslau (twice), Aachen and Münster, under the respective conductors of the subscription concerts, and on March 13 the composer assisted, but with little success, in the performance of a Brahms programme at an Academy concert, Munich, under Levi, conducting the new work, and playing the solo of the D minor Concerto. In spite of Levi's continued efforts the musical circles of Munich remained indifferent to the master's music. The Haydn Variations were heard for the first time in London at the Philharmonic concert of May 24, 1875, under W. G. Cusins.

The programmes performed at the two "extra" concerts of the Vienna Gesellschaft were: On March 2—

1. Schubert: *Kyrie* and *Credo* from the Mass in B flat.
   (Unpublished; first performance.)
2. Schumann: Music to "Manfred."

On March 31—Handel's "Solomon."

"We can only thank the conductor for bringing this work forward; the performance was ideal," says one of the critics in his notice of the oratorio.

The last concert of the season, on April 19, presented a varied programme:

1. Haydn: Symphony in E flat major.
2. A. Dietrich: Concerto for Violin (Violin, Herr Lauterbach).
3. J. Brahms: Schicksalslied.
4. J. Rietz: Arioso for Violin with organ accompaniment.
5. J. S. Bach: Pastorale for Orchestra from the Christmas Oratorio.
6. Handel: Last Chorus from the first part of "Solomon."

Brahms' leisure was considerably curtailed this summer. Of the numerous engagements fulfilled by him after the close of the Vienna concert season three may be particularly mentioned. He conducted the Triumphlied at the first concert of the Rhine Festival (Cologne, May 24-27), at the jubilee anniversary concert of the Basle Choral Society, and at a concert of the Zürich Music Festival (July), and on each occasion the great song was received with acclamation. With this work we may, perhaps, especially associate the honour of the Prussian Ordre pour le Mérite which was conferred twelve years later on the composer by the Emperor William I. He was elected an honorary member of the Royal Academy of Arts, Berlin, in the course of the summer.

"Brahms is becoming so popular," writes Billroth on June 2, "and is everywhere made so much of, that he could easily become a rich man with his composition if he could take it lightly. Fortunately this is not the case."

The Triumphlied was performed in the German imperial capital on December 17, 1874, under Stockhausen, at a concert of the Sternsche Gesangverein. It was given under Levi at the great Bismarck Festival in Munich, and was heard in London at a concert given in St. James's Hall, December 2, 1880, for the benefit of the Victorial Hospital for Children, Chelsea, by George Henschel, whose personal acquaintance with the master dated from the occasion of the Rhine Festival of 1874.

The magnificent work is now but seldom performed:

partly, no doubt, because it was composed to celebrate a particular series of events in history, partly because of the difficulty of securing the large chorus necessary for its due effect, partly, perhaps, on account of the demands it makes on the attention of the listener. Whatever be the cause, the fact itself is to be deeply regretted. The work has sometimes been criticised as wanting in contrast of mood. Undoubtedly it is, from beginning to end, a song of passionate exultation which scarcely makes pause from the first note to the last, and the listener requires time and repeated hearings to become familiarised with its brilliancy before he can follow it with pleasure; but it is full of varied features of interest to lay hearers, and especially to those who will devote a little time to its study before listening to its performance. To the musician it appeals as a marvel of polyphonic art, though it contains no elaborated features of harmonic or contrapuntal learning that might have been prejudicial to its character as a national strain. It is literally "a sound of many voices saying Alleluia."

The master lodged this summer near Nidelbad, above Rüschlikon on Lake Zürich. Amongst the friends and acquaintances old and new with whom he had intercourse were Bargheer, Hegar, G. Eberhard, Gottfried Keller, Bernhard Hoppfer, Professor and Frau Engelmann from Utrecht, and J. V. Widmann. Brahms made Widmann's acquaintance at this time at the house of Hermann Götz, and seems to have been immediately attracted by him; partly, perhaps, because the younger man had the courage of his opinions, and ventured to oppose him in argument. The acquaintance, cemented during the three days of the Zürich Festival, grew into an intimate and lasting friendship, to which the musical world is indebted for Widmann's well known and delightful "Recollections," already several times referred to in these pages.

Hegar mentions* that the works which occupied Brahms

---

* Steiner's "Johannes Brahms."

during his stay at Rüschlikon were the second set of Liebeslieder, the book of songs, Lieder und Gesänge, Op. 63, and the Vocal Quartets, Op. 64, of which the first number, "Heimath," dates, however, from Christmas, 1862, the first passed by the composer outside Germany. It was at this time, also, that he finally completed the Pianoforte Quartet in C minor. The songs and quartets were published in the autumn by Peters; the four Duets for Soprano and Contralto, Op. 61, and the seven Songs for mixed chorus, *a capella*, Op. 62, were issued about the same time by Simrock. The Neue Liebeslieder and the C minor Quartet for Pianoforte and Strings did not appear till 1875.

From this time onward Brahms' copyrights were acquired, as each new work was completed, by Simrock of Berlin, with only four exceptions—Nänie, Op. 82; six Vocal Quartets, Op. 112; thirteen Canons, Op. 113, which were bought by Peters of Leipzig; and a Prelude and Fugue for Organ, published in 1881 as a supplement to the *Musikalisches Wochenblatt* without opus number. In future, therefore, we shall mention the publication, but not the publisher, of the works. Those compositions which were originally acquired from the composer by Breitkopf and Härtel were resold by this firm to Simrock later on, and appear, therefore, in the complete published catalogue of Brahms' works as Simrock's publications.

The third and, as it turned out, the last season of Brahms' work as artistic director of the Gesellschaft der Musikfreunde opened in due course, and at the two ante-Christmas concerts of the season 1874-75 the following programmes were performed: On November 8—

1. Rubinstein: Overture to the Opera "Dimitri Donskoi."
2. Beethoven: Pianoforte Concerto in E flat. (Pianoforte, Herr Brahms.)

3. Brahms: Songs for mixed Chorus, *a capella*, Op. 62—
   (*a*) Waldesnacht.
   (*b*) "Dein Herzlein mild."
   (*c*) "Von alten Liebesliedern."
4. Berlioz: "Harold in Italy." Symphony in four parts.

On December 6—Beethoven's Missa Solennis in D major.

Neither concert seems to have reached the usual high-water mark of success. Of the first programme the items most heartily appreciated were the three choral part-songs, which, attractive in themselves and sung to perfection, were applauded to the echo. Of doubtful wisdom was the selection of the pianist of the occasion. Brahms, who probably yielded to the persuasion of his committee, and was, perhaps, guided in his choice of a concerto by the circumstance of having played Beethoven in E flat in the spring at Bremen, had, as we have seen, given up regular pianoforte practice for some years, and it was inevitable that his performance should be affected by this fact. Berlioz's symphony, which may have owed its place in the programme to our master's broad view of his duties as the artistic director of an important society, was not performed with any great aplomb or heard with particular favour, though extra time and particular pains had been spent on its rehearsal.

Beethoven's great Mass, given on December 6, was followed with strained attention that was rewarded by a good, though, if Brahms' supporters in the press are to be trusted, not a perfect, performance.

"How different are these days from those of the forties," remarks one of the critics, "when many a music lover would rise and leave the room before the commencement of a work by Beethoven."

The String Quartet in A minor was performed for the first time in Vienna at Hellmesberger's concert of December 3, when the andante and scherzo met with considerable appreciation.

"I have heard the string quartets several times this winter," writes Billroth in January, 1875. "When we played them in Carlsruhe as pianoforte duets, we took all the *tempi* much too fast. Brahms desires very moderate *tempi* throughout, as otherwise, owing to the frequent harmonic changes, the music cannot become clear. . . . Beethoven, Schumann, Wagner, Brahms, in their riper works of the last period, all have a preference for the andante *tempo*.

"If you should infer from all I have said that I am much with Brahms, you would be mightily mistaken. I have only seen him twice during the whole winter. . . . We correspond, however; he is pleased when I write to him about his things."

The composer was plunged in his own special work, and would allow neither private nor public calls to occupy his attention, though he made an exception in favour of Bernhard Scholz's invitation to pay an artistic visit to Breslau at the close of the year, and allowed himself opportunity to enjoy a short visit paid to Vienna in January by Joachim and his wife. His doings during the next few months afford but little material to chronicle, and we have to record only the last four Gesellschaft programmes given under his direction, and to lay special stress upon the extraordinary scene of enthusiasm that followed the performance of the German Requiem on February 28, 1875. The rendering of the work on this occasion was one of those, rarely occurring, which seem to hold the audience spellbound by a magnetic sympathy with the music. It brought with it in some mysterious way the sudden flash of revelation. The whole audience, as it were, knew Brahms that day, and most of what was left to be conquered, that was worth conquering, in the musical opinion of Vienna was finally captured. The phenomenal demonstration, joined in by musicians of all schools, Wagnerians not excepted, that occurred on the termination of the great work, noteworthy from its contrast with that earlier one of 1867 which followed the performance of the first three choruses, was the more striking since Wagner had conducted some excerpts from the "Ring" in the same hall a few days previously, and had been the recipient of a similar ovation.

January 10, 1875:

1. Mendelssohn: Overture to the Opera "Camacho's Marriage."
2. Joachim: Hungarian Concerto. (Violin, Herr Joachim.)
3. Brahms: Rhapsody. (Solo, Frau Joachim.)
4. Schumann: Fantasia for Violin and Orchestra. (Herr Joachim.)
5. J. S. Bach: Whitsuntide Cantata, "O ewiges Feuer," for Soli, Chorus, Orchestra and Organ.

February 28:

1. J. S. Bach: Prelude for Organ in E flat, arranged for Orchestra by Bernhard Scholz.
2. Mozart: Aria from "Davidde penitente."
3. Brahms: A German Requiem.

Good Friday, March 23:

J. S. Bach: Passion Music (St. Matthew).

April 18:

Max Bruch: Odysseus.

At the close of the season Brahms laid down his conductor's baton to make room for the return of Herbeck, whose former services had laid the society under a debt of gratitude, and who, unable to endure the annoyances incidental to his position as capellmeister of the opera, resigned the post. Brahms continued his association with the Gesellschaft as a member of the committee, taking great interest in its councils, and exercising influence on the concert programmes and the appointment of professors to the conservatoire. Each year that went by added to the warmth of the esteem with which he was personally regarded and to the deference shown to his judgment by the members of the society, who were all proud of this link of association with him.

Writing to his stepmother from idyllic summer quarters,

of which he took possession in May, after paying a visit to Dessoff, lately settled in Carlsruhe, and attending the Rhine Festival in Düsseldorf, he says:

"DEAR MOTHER,

"I will let you know in haste, that I am living quite delightfully at Zigelhausen near Heidelberg. Thank you also for the socks you have again knitted for me. . . . I am not leaving Vienna, I have only given up my appointment. You do not know the circumstances, and it would be too prolix to tell you why. I am, however, remaining there—and gladly. Write to me if you want money now, or later when the holidays come off! . . .

"Affectionately Your JOHANNES."

"I must tell you that people are very often surprised at my knitted socks, and that I am taken such good care of!"*

"Brahms has had very interesting programmes. Unfortunately we have lost him and Dessoff (Philharmonic) as conductors. Both have been pushed out, and both pushed out by Herbeck," writes Billroth in the month of June.

Brahms invited Dietrich to visit him at Zigelhausen.

"I saw his new works, but cannot now be quite sure which they were," says Dietrich in his "Recollections."

We may confidently conjecture that amongst them must have been the first symphony, on the completion of which Brahms was at this time concentrating much of his attention. The B flat String Quartet was also in progress, and possibly the composer may have played to Dietrich from the sketches of the second symphony.

It was this year that Brahms consented to become a member for the music section of a commission for the awarding of certain gratuities granted annually by the Austrian Government to poor artists of talent who have produced promising works. Three members appointed by the Minister of Education for each of three sections—poetry, music and

---

* Reimann's "Johannes Brahms," p. 117.

the plastic arts—examine the applications and work sent, and judge between them. The fund was established in 1863, and the original adjudicators in the music section were Hanslick, Herbeck and Esser. Brahms now replaced Esser, and a little later Goldmark succeeded Herbeck. The compositions were sent in the first place to Hanslick, who generally made a selection from them for Brahms' inspection, keeping back such as did not fulfil the required conditions or were hopelessly bad. In the *Neue Freie Presse* of June 29, 1897, Hanslick made public a few of the communications he had received from Brahms on these occasions, the first of which, dated September, 1875, was as follows:

"DEAR FRIEND,

"Parcels such as your last are generally so thorny that some kind preliminary guidance like yours is most welcome and necessary as a help in finding one's way through. This time, however, things are not so bad, and seem to me fairly simple. Dvorák and Reinhold thoroughly deserve your proposal by their performances. In Lachner's case (blind) well-justified sympathy counts for something. M. certainly merits some help meanwhile. I mean he ought to win the money more decidedly next year. N. N. alone appears to me so undeserving of the gratuity that it might be given uselessly in his case. Just look again at his small and great sins. They are the most unmusical in the packet. Alas, if he should progress further! At all events he should desire and use the money for instruction and not for a libretto!"

The Quartet in C minor for pianoforte and strings, published in the autumn, was produced at Hellmesberger's concert of November 18 by Brahms, Hellmesberger, Bachrich and Popper, and was played in Hamburg on January 3, 1876, by Levin, Böie, Schmall and Lee.

This composition must, as the reader is aware,[*] be referred to more than one period of Brahms' activity, and it can hardly be accepted as a representative work of either.

---

[*] See pp. 203, 415 and 492.

Standing about midway, as to date of publication, between his two great series of masterpieces for pianoforte and strings, if it is to be classed amongst either, it must indubitably be reckoned with that of the sixties. Internal no less than external evidence, however, leaves little doubt that it points back to a still earlier date. The master of the seventies has so far succeeded in remodelling the work of early youth as to have given to the world in the quartet an interesting, and, on the whole, a clear, presentment of many noble musical thoughts, but it can hardly be said that he has effected its transformation into a homogeneous or apparently spontaneous work of art. Kalbeck mentions that a memorandum of Brahms assigns the date 1873-74 to the third and fourth movements. This, however, certainly refers only to their final completion. The second movement (the scherzo), which undoubtedly belongs to the period of the pianoforte sonata numbered as Op. 1, is consistently characteristic of the composer at that date. The first and third movements suggest a transition period. The character of the ideas of the opening allegro with its impressive, deeply serious, first subject, and of the andante with its sustained melodious phrases, seems to give promise of the power which, manifested in a different mood, was reached in the earlier published companion works. Of the finale it must be said that its themes are lacking in interest and developed mechanically. It may be surmised that the composer's pruning knife was freely used in the course of his successive revisions of the work, and perhaps not only for the purpose of shortening it, but also for that of thinning out the score. From the circumstance that this is neither so luxuriant in detail nor so thickly instrumented as those of the other two pianoforte quartets, the C minor has, perhaps, the one advantage amongst the three of being the most readily appreciable at first hearing. It must, however, as the author conceives, be rated, as a completed work of art, decidedly below its glorious companions.

The relative popularity attained by the three pianoforte

quartets in England may be fairly estimated by comparing the numbers of their respective performances at the Popular Concerts, London. The A major, introduced in January, 1872, was given ten times up to October, 1900, inclusive. The G minor, first performed in January, 1874, was given twenty-six times up to March, 1900. The C minor, first played in November, 1876, was not heard again until December, 1893.

CHAPTER XVIII.

1876-1878.

Tour in Holland—Third String Quartet—C minor Symphony—First performances—Varying impressions created by the work in Vienna and Leipzig—Brahms and Widmann at Mannheim—Second Symphony—Vienna and Leipzig differ as to its merits.

A JOURNEY to Holland early in 1876 brought unmixed gratification to the master. He conducted the Haydn Variations, and played the D minor Concerto at Utrecht on January 22 before an audience which received him with warm greeting, and gave every possible evidence of appreciation of his works. Immense applause followed each movement of the concerto, and at its close, when enthusiasm was at its height, two youthful ladies advanced to the platform, each bearing a cushion on which a wreath was placed, one decorated with ribbons of the Austrian colours (black and yellow), the other with those of Holland (red, white and blue), which they smilingly presented to the composer. Brahms, not always inclined to receive tributes of the kind with urbanity, entered thoroughly into the happy spirit of this occasion, and showed plainly by his manner of accepting the compliment his pleasure at the charming way in which it had been offered. He was the guest during his several days' stay at Utrecht of Professor and Frau Engelmann, in whose house he at once became at home, dividing his time between walking, talking, playing with the children, making music with his hostess, seeing friends, and was in genial mood throughout the visit. It may be remarked *en passant* that Brahms in a companionable frame of mind was not accustomed to let his friends off easily. His constitution was so robust, his spirit so active, his interests so numerous, that he liked, and expected others to like, to sit up talking with vivacity until the small hours of the morning, and would rise after about five hours' rest as unwearied and energetic as though he had had what would be for most people a normal amount of repose. It was a matter of course wherever he stayed that the means for making a cup of coffee should be left every night at his disposal for the next morning, and he generally returned from an early walk at about the hour when the household was beginning to stir.

After leaving Holland Brahms took part as composer, conductor, pianist and accompanist of his own songs, in concerts at Münster (Westphalia); where he conducted the Triumphlied; Mannheim and Wiesbaden—playing the D minor concerto on each occasion—and at Coblenz, where he undertook the pianoforte solos of Beethoven's Choral Fantasia and Schumann's concerto. He was accompanied on the latter part of his journey by George Henschel, composer, pianist and baritone singer, then but twenty-four years of age, who has published some interesting details of the tour.[*] Writing enthusiastically of the performances at the Münster concert (of February 5) Henschel notes the manifest delight with which Grimm, whilst conducting the concerto, listened to the beauties of the work at the birth of which he had, as the reader may remember, assisted many years previously.

At Mannheim the master stayed with his friend, Ernst Frank, the genialischer conductor of the Mannheim subscription concerts; at Coblenz, with Geheimrath Wegeler, who found opportunity to conduct his illustrious guest, with Henschel and Kapellmeister Maszowski, on a tour of in-

---

[*] "Personal Recollections of Johannes Brahms and Pages from a Journal kept by George Henschel."

spection through the famous wine cellars of his firm and entertained them afterwards at luncheon in the sample room.

"Yes, gentlemen," he observed solemnly as the guests sat in almost reverential silence, inhaling the bouquet of some rare old Rauenthaler that had been reserved for the end of the repast, "what Brahms is among the composers, so is this Rauenthaler among the wines." "Ah, then let's have a bottle of Bach now," cried Brahms.

The Wiesbaden concert made a vivid impression on the Landgraf of Hesse, who heard Brahms for the first time on the occasion and, though but a lad, derived an impression from the D minor Concerto which laid the foundation of his enduring enthusiasm for the master's art. A pleasant supper party, to the success of which Brahms and Henschel contributed a due share of sociability, was given after the concert by the Princess of Hesse-Barchfeld; and the musical events of the journey terminated next day with a matinée arranged by the same distinguished lady, in the course of which Brahms joined the Frankfurt artists, Heermann, Müller, and the viola player of their party in a performance of his C minor pianoforte quartet, and accompanied Henschel's singing of the beautiful "Wie soll ich die Freude," from the Magelone cycle. A souvenir of the Wiesbaden visit presented to him by the princess—a box of ebony ornamented with a silver laurel wreath, on each leaf of which was engraved the title of one of his works—was accepted with evident gratification by the master, who showed some amusement on perceiving that the names of his great Triumphlied and tiny Wiegenlied appeared side by side on the shining chaplet. Brahms and Henschel parted company on February 28 at Frankfurt, taking train respectively for Vienna and Berlin, both pleasantly conscious that the close companionship of their journey had developed the cordial acquaintance previously existing between them into a relation of cordial friendship.

In no country in which a growing appreciation of Brahms' genius had been unaided by that stimulus of public familiarity with his person which had helped forward the acceptance of his works in Germany, Holland and Switzerland, had his music, since the beginning of the seventies, advanced so rapidly in the affection of the cultured music lover as in Great Britain. By the year 1876, the German Requiem, if not as yet fully understood, had at any rate been generally accepted there as a work of profound musical learning and exalted spirituality. Several of the then published compositions of chamber music—the B flat sextet, the G minor pianoforte quartet, the pianoforte quintet and the A major pianoforte quartet, to name them in the order of their attractiveness to the concert goer of the time—were becoming almost popular; and the importance of many of the songs, as ranking among the most beautiful inspirations of the German lyric muse, had been considerably recognised. Significant of this progress of British musical sentiment and opinion was the offer of an honorary doctor's degree received by the master in 1876 from the University of Cambridge, which, as a mark of distinguished foreign appreciation of his art, seems to have caused him lively satisfaction. Accepting it with promptitude, he mentioned his "pleasant adventure" to Hanslick who immediately reported it in the *Neue Freie Presse;* and on May 18, the day set apart in Cambridge from time immemorial for such functions, the name of the German composer was included by resolution of the university senate in the short list of honorary graduates-designate for the year. When writing his acceptance, however, Brahms, though he had been privately informed that his presence in Cambridge would be necessary for the actual bestowal of the honour, had received no official intimation of this circumstance, but had merely been invited to celebrate the act of his investiture by conducting a performance of the German Requiem at a concert of the Cambridge University Musical Society. Probably he anticipated that the statute of the university which prohibits the conferring of its degrees *in absentia* might be suspended in his case, for he does not appear at any time to have contemplated such a violation of his usual routine as a visit to England would have involved. The offer of the degree lapsed automatically a year after it had been recorded in the absence of opportunity for carrying it into effect, though Brahms, as will presently be seen, availed himself meanwhile of a convenient occasion for making suitable acknowledgment of the proffered honour.

A letter from Brahms to Joachim of February, 1876, shows that the composer had, before that date, made his friend acquainted with his third string quartet in B flat and had half promised the manuscript to Joachim for his approaching annual visit to England. He delayed sending it, however, and the work was tried for the first time by Joachim and his Berlin colleagues on May 23 at Frau Schumann's house. It was repeated by the same artists on June 4, before a large circle of invited listeners at a matinée given by the Joachims.

Brahms surprised his friends by his arrival in Berlin in the second week of June, to remain for a few days as Frau Schumann's guest. On the 12th of the month he proceeded to Sassnitz in the Isle of Rugen where he stayed for the rest of the summer. Henschel joined him by appointment early in July and it is pleasant to contemplate the refreshment of mind derived by the master from the young artist's bright and sympathetic personality. During the twelve days of Henschel's stay the two musicians were inseparable companions and playmates from eleven o'clock in the morning, when Brahms could afford to lay aside his work for the day, until late at night. They bathed together in the Baltic, diving—at Brahms' suggestion with wide open eyes—for red pebbles or for small coins which they threw into the sea for the purpose of picking them out again; dined together at Henschel's hotel on the Fahrnberg; passed the hottest hours of the July afternoons in a large hammock hung in some shady spot, discoursing on music, poetry, Wagner, friendship, human nature, took wonderful walks far away into heatherland, lying down now and again to smoke a cigarette and listen to the deep surrounding silence that was broken only by the weird cry of the bull frogs inhabiting the moorland pools; they even made music in the drawing room of Fahrnberg hotel on the last afternoon of Henschel's stay, drawing an uninvited audience to listen to songs of Beethoven, Schubert and Brahms. The next morning was wild and stormy; but the master accompanied his young friend in the diligence on the first few miles of his return journey, and when he got out, Henschel looking after his retreating figure as the carriage rolled onward, carried away as his last impression of Rugen, the remembrance of a picture that was all "moor and cloud and—Brahms."

The B flat Quartet was finally revised for the press and announced to Professor Engelmann, to whom it is dedicated, before the master's departure from Sassnitz. It was played shortly before publication at the Joachim Quartett-Abend, Berlin, of October 30; and for the first time from the printed copies at the Hellmesberger concert of November 30 in Vienna.

The general remarks offered in the preceding chapter on Brahms' chamber music for strings are to be applied to the Quartet in B flat major. Of its particular characteristics we may note the joyousness of the first movement, and the weird fantastic pathos of the third, in which a special relation is maintained between the viola and first violin. In the theme—of distinguished simplicity—and variations, with which the work closes, we have a concise but beautiful example of the composer's facility in this form.

The String Quartet in B flat was the first of the three composed by Brahms to be heard at the Popular Concerts, London. It was played on Monday, February 19, and Saturday, March 3, 1877, by Joachim, Ries, Straus and Piatti. The A minor was performed on Monday, October 31, 1881, by Straus, Ries, Zerbini and Piatti, and the C minor on Monday, December 7, 1885, by Madame Norman-Néruda, Ries, Straus and Franz Néruda. These (Op. 51, Nos. 1 and 2) were not immediately repeated.

Brahms spent the autumn in Baden-Baden, occupied with preparations for the great event of the year in his career—the production of the long looked for symphony. As in the case of the Schicksalslied and the completed Triumphlied, the composer chose to produce his work for the first time at Carlsruhe, preferring, maybe, to test it for his own satisfaction in the comparative privacy of a small audience before submitting it to the searching ordeal of performance in either of the great musical centres of the Continent. The musical life of Carlsruhe had suffered sadly by the departure of Levi in 1872, and it was not until the appointment of Dessoff to the post of court capellmeister, on his resignation of his duties in Vienna in 1875, that the city began to regain some of its former artistic prestige. The performance on November 4, 1876, from the manuscript, of Brahms' first Symphony by the grand ducal orchestra under Dessoff, in the composer's presence, was a musical event that revived the recollections of a brilliant past, and added a new and abiding distinction to the artistic traditions of the small capital.

The work was heard in Mannheim on the 7th, and in Munich on the 15th of the month; on both occasions under the composer's direction. Four other performances from the manuscript quickly followed—in Vienna (Gesellschaft), December 17, in Leipzig, January 18, and Breslau, January 23, 1877, in each case under the composer, and in Cambridge, March 8, 1877, under Joachim's direction.

The Symphony in C minor, whose appearance marks the period of Brahms' achievement in the highest domain of instrumental music, and the last that remained to him for conquest, is in the first place remarkable from the fact that it cannot properly be ranged beside the works in the same form produced by either of the two masters who were, chronologically speaking, his immediate predecessors. By its accomplishment, no less than by its aim, it must be regarded as the immediate successor to the symphonies of Beethoven in the same sense as these were the direct descendants of the symphonies of Mozart and Haydn, and it establishes Brahms' right to be accepted in its own domain as the heir, *par excellence*, of one and all of these masters. This alone were much. Still more important, however, is the fact that our composer has known how to graft upon the symphony form inherited from Beethoven, Mozart and Haydn, the giant stock of Bach's learning and resource, studied and absorbed by him until they had become a part of his own artistic individuality, in such a manner as to revivify it root and branch, and make it a supple instrument in his hand, not for the mechanical imitation of what had been done before him, but for the "highest ideal musical expression of his own time."[*] Few who listen with quickened ears to an adequate performance of the C minor Symphony can be in doubt that whilst in outward form and manner of construction it may be regarded as at once the epitome and the latest result of the past history of classical instrumental art, it is in spirit representative of its own time and even anticipatory of the future; that it not only reflects the soul of the musician, poet and philosopher, but is suggestive of the higher vision of the prophet. It is this fact, for those who accept it as a fact, that constitutes the highest significance of Brahms' first symphony, and lends a real meaning to Bülow's well known apophthegm of "the three B's": Bach, Beethoven and Brahms.

The shrill, clashing dissonances of the first introduction at once place the listener in the atmosphere of stern grandeur, passion, mystery, that surround, not this or that human life, but existence itself, in its apprehension by human intelligence; and the allegro to which it leads seems to the present writer to present as near an analogy as art can show to the processes of nature, built up as it is—first and second subjects and their treatment—from a few notes; from what one of the Vienna critics called "mere twigs of

---

[*] Schumann's essay, "New Paths."

thematic material"; from germs which are produced and reproduced, are transformed and reformed, and developed into a great organic whole instinct with noble, living melody. The solemnly fervent andante sostenuto, the graceful, innocent allegretto with its sufficiently contrasted trio, afford the mind the refreshment of change of tone after the stormy splendour of the first movement; but the note of tragedy is resumed with the first sounds of the wonderful adagio that precedes, and essentially contains, the allegro of the fourth movement. Here, for some twenty-eight bars, the tension of feeling increases till destiny itself seems to be held in suspense; then, with the resolution of a chromatic chord, the horn sounds the unexpected major third of the key in a six-four of the tonic triad, and, continuing its strange, passionate cry, gradually disperses the mists of doubt and apprehension that have held the hearer as in a thrall, and carries him forward to the sublimity of joy that dwells in the final allegro.

"The last movement of your C minor Symphony," wrote Billroth to Brahms in 1890, fourteen years after its first performance, "has again lately excited me fearfully. Of what avail is the perfect, clear beauty of the principal subject in its thematically complete form? The horn returns at length with its romantic, impassioned cry as in the introduction, and all palpitates with longing, rapture and supersensuous exaltation and bliss."

These words were not written by a fantastic dreamer, but by one of the most renowned scientific and practical surgeons and busiest men of his time, and in using them he did not employ a mere rhetorical phrase. The quality of imagination which speaks through Brahms' first symphony is, in certain respects, akin to that of the early Sonata in F minor, though it is expressed in the later work with the help of more than twenty years' additional study and experience. It is that of a seer of visions, and seems to culminate, in the passage to which Billroth alluded, in an ecstasy of wonder and joy. Brahms undoubtedly rose to the full height of his great powers in this first symphony, which remains unsurpassed in workmanship and sustained loftiness of idea, as well as in regard to the range of emotion to which it appeals.

It goes without saying that the supposed merits and demerits of the work became the subject of heated argument between the partisans and antagonists of the composer's art, the particulars of which would scarcely prove interesting to readers of the present day. In giving some account of the first impressions made by the symphony, we shall quote from those notices only which, whilst they are in themselves not without value, appear to have been written in a candid spirit, and do not offensively betray the influence of party bias. The reputation attaching to Hanslick's name, and the moderation of his style, seem to make it necessary to include something from his report, though he was avowedly a staunch admirer of Brahms' music, and had little liking for that of the New-German school. To balance this, we shall give a few sentences from the *Wiener Zeitung*, a journal to which, as the reader may remember, no suspicion can attach of handling our master's works with an excess of cordiality. It is necessary to explain, for the benefit of such readers as are not familiar with Brahms' large works, that the references to Beethoven's ninth symphony occurring in some of the press notices are occasioned by what has sometimes been described as Brahms' intentional allusion, in the principal theme of his finale, to Beethoven's setting of Schiller's "Ode to Joy" in the last movement of the great "ninth." The so-called allusion consists, not so much in a similarity of melody in Brahms' theme to that of Beethoven, as in its being written in the same hymn-form and harmonised as plainly as possible. There is no doubt whatever that everyone who listens to Brahms' first symphony thinks immediately, on the entrance of the final allegro, of Beethoven's ninth. The association passes with the conclusion of the subject; Brahms' movement develops on its own lines, which do not resemble those of Beethoven.

"In this work," says Hanslick (*Neue Freie Presse*), "Brahms' close affinity with Beethoven must become clear to every musician who has not already perceived it. The new symphony displays an energy of will, a logic of musical thought, a greatness of structural power and a mastery of technique such as are possessed by no other living composer. It would be a sorry mistake to attempt to criticise a work so serious and difficult of comprehension immediately after hearing it for the first time. Various listeners may have found the music more or less clear, more or less sympathetic; the one thing that we may speak of as a simple fact, accepted alike by friend and foe, is that no composer has yet approached so nearly to the great works of Beethoven as Brahms in the finale of the C minor Symphony."

". . . Brahms was an important personality, one to be treated most seriously before he wrote the symphony," we read in the *Wiener Zeitung;* "to our thinking his position remains just as it was. The strong moral earnestness, the depth and purity of his conception of the world and of life, and the intellectuality, which have always obtained for him the esteem of the noble-minded and withheld from him the favour of the masses, are to be found again in this work. None the less, however, are the shadows there which but too easily accompany such lights; the want of inspiriting fancy, the absence of sensuous charm, and a sullen asceticism almost amounting to insipidity. His musical language has lost nothing of its mysterious reticence, of its close conciseness, of the elevation that on the whole distinguishes it, nor has it gained in facility, clearness, or comprehensibility. . . . So there is nothing that can be admired without reserve, until with sure step, with strong, proud gait that reminds one of the majesty of Beethoven, the finale strides out. After a bar or two of deeply sorrowful complaint, it braces itself to a turbulent pizzicato of the strings, as a man who would get rid of pain by nerving himself to action. . . . With the entry of the chorale, the hearer experiences a sensation of brightness as at the rising of the sun after a night of sorrow. The last mists disappear as before the breaking light, and the movement closes in strong, healthy gladness. . . . Here the arts of music and poetry mingle indissolubly, and the musical, cannot be separated from the poetic, impression. Here is a truly great artistic achievement, the value of which is but slightly prejudiced by the consideration that the 'joy' theme has an unmistakable resemblance as of son to father to that of the 'ninth' symphony. This movement is worthy of the man who composed the German Requiem."

Dörffel, of the *Leipziger Nachrichten*, wrote:

"The interest of all present was centred on the new symphony, which, on the whole, justified the great expectations with which it had been awaited. Its effect on the audience was the most intense that has been produced by any new symphony within our remembrance. Schumann in his time did not attain such . . . The composition is to be viewed and measured from the standpoint of Beethoven's ninth, and of Schumann's second symphony. The aim of the three works is the same. To reach it, Brahms, well-equipped and daring spirit as he is, goes his own way. He is great in attack as his two predecessors, and has the same wide vision over the domain of spiritual-human existence. . . . As regards uninterrupted energy of creative power, we would give the palm to the first movement. The second, with its fervour and longing, accords with it. To the third we should gladly have listened longer. It supplied a counterpoise of sentiment to what had gone before which had not been maintained long enough when the movement closed. Of the finale we would almost venture to surmise that it gave the composer the most trouble. Here he relinquishes his independence, and flies to Beethoven in order to get new force for his climax. We do not regard the resort to Beethoven as accidental, but believe the composer to have been well aware of it. He came, however, to one over whom he could not prevail.

"A long pause followed the symphony; one, however, that was not long enough in some measure to quiet the exaltation of mind produced by the work. The songs and variations which followed, and which we should have welcomed at another time, were almost tiresome to us. Let the symphony be repeated soon, and, if possible, without other music."*

---

* The variations for orchestra on Haydn's theme and six of Brahms' songs, sung by Henschel, and accompanied by the composer, were included in the programme of the concert.

Louis Ehlert says of the symphony:

"Brahms has a wide-reaching and speculative brain, and is a mixture of the musician of the good old times who heard many voices sounding together within him, whose very cradle cover was embroidered with a contrapuntal pentagram, and of the man of the present day with his variously cultured intellect. . . . What distinguishes his music from that of all his contemporaries is the mysterious apparition within it of another world—its gentle, pathetic tapping at the heart.

"The first movement of the symphony is, perhaps, the most artistically important of the work. . . . An inexorable causality proceeds from bar to bar, stayed by no illusion, and softened only by the distant light of a few solitary stars. At the beginning and end the enigmatical sphinx seems to call to us: 'That which ascends from me, mounting upwards to battle and to life, sinks back again within me. Of all life I, the eternal riddle, am the beginning and the end.'"

It will be evident from what has been said that whatever the impression to be derived from familiar acquaintance with the symphony, immediate enthusiasm could hardly have been anticipated from any large general public—least of all by Brahms himself; but the presence at most of these first performances of devotees specially qualified for apprehending something of the significance of the work generally secured for it more than a mere *succès d'estime*. The listeners of Munich were the least appreciative. Those of Carlsruhe, Mannheim and Breslau were friendly. At Vienna certain favoured friends were privileged to listen to a private performance of the symphony by Brahms and his sympathetic colleague, Ignaz Brüll, in the composer's arrangement as a pianoforte duet, at the pianoforte house of his friend, Herr Hoffabrikant Friedrich Ehrbar, and went to the concert, therefore, with minds partially prepared for what they were to hear. At Leipzig a note of enthusiasm was perceptible at the crowded public rehearsal which preceded the Gewandhaus concert, owing partly to the fact that Brahms' Leipzig adherents had been strongly reinforced by the advent of friends from outside, some of whom added warmth and prestige to the occasion by their mere presence. The feeling for our master's art which, as we have seen, had been slowly growing amongst a number of Leipzig residents who belonged to no musical "set," will have been expressed with added zest and enjoyment when it was found that Frau Schumann and Joachim and Stockhausen had come to hear the symphony, whilst to the support of the von Herzogenbergs, von Holsteins, Theodor Kirchner, and other resident or lately resident friends, was added that of the Grimms from Münster, Dr. Hermann Deiters from Bonn, Professor and Frau Engelmann from Utrecht, Simrock from Berlin, and many other distinguished guests. Enthusiasm is contagious, and already at the rehearsal a success was ensured for the work, though perhaps it was not very warmly helped by the official patrons of the Gewandhaus.

"A regular Brahms party meeting had been organised," says Bernsdorf in the *Signale*, now as ever inveterate in his own party bias, "in which a fairly strong contingent from outside was associated with the resident admirers and champions of the composer. It is therefore a matter of course that the consumption of enthusiasm was enormous, and that the success of the symphony was one exceptional in the annals of the Gewandhaus."

A large party of friends assembled at supper at the Hôtel Hauffe after the concert. Brahms' health was proposed in genial fashion by Stockhausen. "Hab' ich tausendmal geschworen,"* he suddenly sang out, starting to his feet and raising his glass. Needless to say that the toast, which was the more effective from the sense of victory filling the minds of those who had assisted at the evening's triumph, was honoured with the utmost enthusiasm.

That the master was gratified and touched by this the

---

* Goethe's song, "Unüberwindlich," set by Brahms and published in 1877 as No. 5 of Op. 72: "Though a thousand vows I've taken."

first striking success achieved by him in Leipzig since his youthful appearance in December, 1853, at a Gewandhaus concert of chamber music; and that he fully appreciated the agreeable private circumstances of his visit during which he was for the first time the guest of Heinrich and Elisabeth von Herzogenberg, henceforth to be numbered among his intimate friends, is evident in one of his letters of the period.

"Think seriously about Leipzig," he wrote to Frau Schumann soon after his return to Vienna. "If you were to move there, I should most certainly visit the town in winter in the future."

Among the young musicians of Leipzig in whom Brahms began to feel an interest at this time, was Julius Röntgen, son of the Gewandhaus concertmeister and an intimate of the Herzogenberg's house, whose relations with the master gradually became those of cordial friendship.

The seventh manuscript performance of the symphony was given under special circumstances to which we have already referred. The score and parts were sent by the composer to Joachim in London for production of the work at Cambridge in acknowledgment of the university's offer to Brahms of an honorary degree. The programme of the Cambridge University Musical Society's concert of March 8, of which it formed part, was as follows:

PART I.

W. S. Bennett:	Overture, "The Wood Nymph."
Beethoven:	Concerto for Violin and Orchestra. Violin, Dr. Joachim.
Brahms:	A Song of Destiny.
Bach:	Violin Solos, Dr. Joachim.
Joachim:	Elegiac Overture (in memory of H. Kleist).

PART II.

Brahms:	Symphony in C minor.

The symphony and the Elegiac Overture, the latter composed by Joachim in acknowledgment of the honorary degree offered him by the university in 1876 and conferred in the afternoon of March 8 in 1877, were given under his direction; the remainder of the programme was under that of the society's conductor, C. Villiers Stanford.

The concert attracted a great audience, which included prominent musicians from various parts of the United Kingdom. The impression created by the symphony was profound, and, following that of the German Requiem and of the great chamber music compositions and songs which, as we have already noted, had for some years been finding their way to the hearts of music lovers in this country, formed, as Stanford says, "an imperishable keystone to Brahms' fame amongst Britons."* The new work was performed in London a few weeks later at the Philharmonic concert of April 16, under W. G. Cusins.

Probably Brahms' Vienna friends and admirers little dreamed how near they had been at this time to losing their favourite. The position of municipal music director at Düsseldorf was pressed on his acceptance in the autumn of 1876, and he was sufficiently tempted by it to be characteristically unable to decide on a negative answer. He was, indeed, so long in coming to a final resolution, that the Düsseldorf authorities had every reason to feel persuaded that they had secured him for the opening of the year 1877; but at the last moment he wrote: "I cannot make up my mind to it." The idea of binding himself to the performance of fixed duties by the acceptance of an official position, even outside his beloved cities of Hamburg or Vienna was not repugnant to Brahms during the middle period of his career. His published correspondence shows that he was attracted in 1869 and again in 1870, by rumours of impending vacancies, towards Cologne and Sondershausen respectively. His refusal of the Düsseldorf post seems, however, to have settled his mind finally as to the question of leaving Austria, and he barely gave a passing thought to the offer

---

* Article in the *New York Outlook*, July 25, 1903.

of the cantorship of the famous Thomas school of Leipzig that was made to him in 1879. It has, indeed, been surmised that he might have consented at a somewhat later period to associate himself with a high class for composition at the conservatoire of the Vienna "Gesellschaft," if he had been approached by the principal, Josef Hellmesberger, on the subject of forming one.

Certain incidents belonging to the autumn of 1877, related by Widmann in his Brahms' "Recollections," show that at this time, when the master had successfully proved his powers in every form of composition for the concert room, the old desire to try his hand at writing for the stage revived within him. Brahms and Widmann met at Mannheim, and were present at the production, on September 30, of Götz's unfinished opera, "Francesca di Rimini," under Frank. In the course of a long *tête-à-tête*, held on their return to their hotel after the performance, Brahms clearly explained his views on the subject of opera texts, "letting it be seen," says Widmann, "that any resolution he might have formed against composing an opera might give way were he to find himself in possession of a libretto really to his liking."

The convictions professed on this occasion by the composer may be traced to an attitude of mind similar to that to which we referred on recording his conversation with Bulthaupt. Strange as it may appear, they have a fundamental kinship with those which led Wagner to embark on his career as a musico-dramatic reformer, though the methods proposed by Brahms were not only much more drastic than those pursued by Wagner, but ran, as Widmann has observed, directly in the opposite direction from that taken by the development of modern art as represented by this master.

"The composition of music to the entire drama seemed to Brahms unnecessary and even mischievous. Only the culminating points and those parts of the action should be set for which music would be an inherently suitable medium of expression. The librettist would thus gain space and freedom for the dramatic development of his subject, whilst the composer would be at liberty to devote himself solely to the purposes of his art which would be best served if he were able to concentrate his energies on a definite situation such as a jubilant *ensemble*."

From this it would appear that the incongruity essential to the very existence of what is generally understood as opera, as distinct from the early German Singspiel, was so strongly felt by Brahms as to seem to him incompatible with dramatic truth, and to be absolutely prohibitive in his own case of the dramatic exercise of his art. The matter is, however, susceptible of another explanation.

It is clear that Brahms, when contemplating the composition of an opera, was bound by the necessities of his position to seek the attainment of dramatic truth in a direction other than that in which Wagner had led the way with such triumphant result. Every circumstance in the careers of the two men, and not least the representative position achieved by each in his own sphere, precluded the possibility that Brahms should run the risk of appearing to seek to emulate Wagner on his own ground. In spite, however, of words written by him in 1870 at the time the "Meistersinger" was produced in Vienna:

". . . In everything else that I attempt I tread on the heels of predecessors who embarrass me. The thought of Wagner would not prevent me from setting to work at an opera with the greatest alacrity."

It would be difficult to believe that Brahms at no time cast longing thoughts towards the logical, consistent, rich means of artistic effect offered by the Melos. No one can doubt that if he had been in a position, and had chosen, to use it, he would have employed it in his own way and for his own original purposes and effects. The skill with which he might have handled it in opera is to some small extent indicated in the Rhapsody (Goethe's "Harzreise"), where the method of the first two sections is very much that of the Melos, whilst the prayer, affording an opportunity "inherently suitable for musical expression," reverts to the rhythmical melody of musical tradition. That Brahms had a profound respect for Wagner's powers is matter of common knowledge. Though he was never present at a Bayreuth performance, he had heard the music dramas frequently at Munich, had studied Wagner's scores exhaustively, and, in the sense of his intimate acquaintance with them, was accustomed to call himself the "best of all Wagnerians." An anecdote related by Richard Heüberger,* to whom the master gave informal instruction in composition for a time from early in 1878, is highly illustrative in this connection. Heuberger says:

". . . Continuing his corrections, Brahms did not confine himself to remarks on the composition itself, but considered the handwriting also worthy of his notice. He pointed out that I had not placed crotchet under crotchet, and that this impaired the legibility of the manuscript; he advised me to be particular to slur the groups of notes with exactness. . . . 'Look here,' he said, fetching from the next room Wagner's autograph score of 'Tannhäuser,' which he opened at the long B major movement of the second act; 'Wagner has taken pains to place each of the five sharps exactly in its place on *every* line of *every* page, and in spite of all this precision the writing is easy and flowing. If *such* a man can write so neatly, you must do so too.' He turned over the entire movement and pointed reproachfully to almost every sharp. I felt continually smaller, especially as Brahms talked himself into a kind of didactic wrathfulness. I was struck completely dumb, however, when, on my remarking that Wagner must be held chiefly responsible for the confusion prevailing in the heads of us young people, Brahms cried as though he had been stung: '*Nonsense;* the *misunderstood* Wagner has done it. Those understand *nothing* of the real Wagner who are led astray by him. Wagner's is one of the clearest heads that ever existed in the world!'"

That Brahms was aware that the resolution to compose

---

* *Die Musik,* in the article referred to in a previous chapter.

an opera would place him in a net of difficulties that might practically be summed up in the one word "Wagner" is no mere conjecture. Fräulein Anna Ettlinger, an intimate friend of Levi and Allgeyer, who knew Brahms well both at Carlsruhe and Munich, relates in an article on Levi, that Brahms answered a question put to him in Munich in the course of the seventies, as to why he had written no opera by saying: "Beside Wagner it is impossible." It may fairly be concluded that Brahms, in the late seventies, merely "coquetted," as Widmann expresses it, with the idea of composing for the stage, though no doubt with considerable regret.*

It cannot be said that the subjects he proposed to Widmann appear happy, but his suggestions must not be taken too seriously.

"He recommended to me Gozzi's magical farces and fabled comedies, especially 'King Stag' and 'The Ravens.' He was also interested in 'The Open Secret,' and preferred Gozzi's lighter arrangement of the piece to Calderon's more formal original.... After reading 'King Stag' carefully through several times, I was not only seized with a certain hopelessness as to whether I could ever succeed in making a rational, poetical opera text out of this mad farce, but disturbed by the anxiety as to whether, even if it were successfully adapted, it could really interest a modern theatre-going public.... I found myself continually thinking that such an opera, even though Brahms had composed for it the most beautiful, glorious music, as would undoubtedly have been the case, could not be regarded as essentially anything else than a sort of second 'Zauberflöte,' and thus as a retrogression in the development of operatic art."†

---

* Fräulein Ettlinger informs the author that it was she herself who put the question to the master and received his answer. For the article on Levi, see "Biographisches Jahrbuch und Deutscher Nekrolog," 1902.

† Widmann's "Brahms Recollections," p. 38 and following.

Nothing, in short, resulted from the talk between Brahms and Widmann, and the suitable libretto was, as we know, never found. This is, perhaps, little to be regretted. Not, indeed, because the composer lacked the dramatic instinct necessary for the successful composition of opera. No one who has heard him quote a few lines from a classical play can doubt that he possessed this qualification in an eminent degree, and his sensitiveness to dramatic effect was matter for frequent comment by those who accompanied him to the theatre. It is, however, difficult to imagine that Brahms could have been content to compose music to a purely comic text, or, indeed, to one that did not contain elements of deep pathos; whilst a quasi-comic opera, in which allegory lay hidden, must almost certainly have been found, as Widmann perceived, unsuitable to modern taste. On the other hand, Brahms' constitutional shyness and reticence, fostered through long years of varied experience until they became invincible, must, we believe, have proved obstacles to the successful completion of a serious opera in any practicable meaning of the word, even if they had allowed him to attempt one. They are more or less traceable in the libretto difficulty; in his suggestion of "King Stag," which he recommended especially on account of its fun, "accompanied throughout by the most pathetic earnestness"; in other words, because the earnestness is covered by the fun. It is difficult to imagine the man who habitually veiled the tenderness of his nature behind a playful saying or an abrupt manner, who did not allow himself to inquire about the possibilities of passionate feeling that might lie dormant within him, coming out of his reserve to use the strong play of emotion as the immediate and capital medium for his effects. The energy of feeling, the deeply pathetic beauty which vitalise the master's purely instrumental music, are surrounded and protected by an intellectual atmosphere which, on a first hearing of his larger works, sometimes seems to amount to austerity, and to repel rather than attract. His love songs—those of them which are not folk-songs—are for the most part dreamings of an ideal, and not the ideal of a man who could lay his heart bare on the theatre boards. Not wholly fanciful is the association in which Brahms, in a letter to Widmann, jokingly placed his two life renunciations, of the composition of an opera and of marriage. The extracts from favourite authors entered by Johannes during the early fifties in the little manuscript books described by Kalbeck, the passages found in "The young Kreisler's treasure chest, March, 1854," remain significant not only of the young musician of twenty, but also of the master of forty, fifty, sixty years, and the quotation from Friedrich v. Sallet might probably stand as the true history of Brahms' inner life.

"One generally finds the highest degree of what is called *openness* in the most frivolous and thoughtless persons; of that which is called *reserve*, in the deepest, richest and truest minds. And, indeed, I am glad to be communicative, and like a full, free flow of conversation during the clinking of cups; whatever noble thought may have occurred to me should not have been gained for myself, but, if possible, for the world. Nevertheless, there is in the mind a holy of holies. I would not bring that forth which shines brightly there, hidden away in the inmost recess, to glimmer vainly and childishly in the universal light of day. Let it remain there in sacred night. I dare not even tell it in barren words to my friend, however noble, not even to my beloved (if I had one). To what purpose? I might use one single misleading expression, the other might misunderstand one single expression, and my divine image, reflected from a concave mirror, become a distortion, common or trivial, or even deformed and ridiculous. . . . To analyse and describe the sacred within us is a shameless desecration. If the other has a spiritual eye that is worthy to perceive, he may quietly await one of those blissful moments when the curtain of mists breaks and a swift, comprehensive glance into the sanctuary of the temple is allowed to the worthy one, and in such moments is celebrated the high festival of friendship as of love. For myself, I dare reveal nothing of it in words save in poetry. There I may do so, for it happens in some divine way that is incomprehensible to me. . . ."*

We have henceforth, therefore, only to observe the unwearied energy with which Brahms, during the succeeding years, added one work after another to the list of his compositions in each and every branch of serious music for the chamber and the concert room: songs, vocal duets, choral works and instrumental solos accompanied and unaccompanied, concerted music for solo instruments, symphonies. The publications of the year 1877 were the Symphony and the four sets of Songs, Op. 69, 70, 71, 72, twenty-four songs in all, some of the texts of which are by Carl Candidus, Carl Lemke, Gottfried Keller, etc., and others imitations of folk-songs of various nationalities. Dr. Deiters says of them in his "Johannes Brahms":

"As it seems to us, the composer identifies himself here more and more closely with classical form and achieves ever purer refinement of his material. Turn where one will (we mention for instance 'Des Liebsten Schwur' from Op. 69) there can be no hesitation in counting these songs with the best to be found of their kind. Again we are constantly reminded of Franz Schubert, whose wealth of melody is revived, whilst in conciseness of construction, in conscious mastery of form, he is here greatly surpassed."

Heuberger gives a pleasant glimpse of Brahms co-operating in a festival performance arranged for December, 1877, by the Academic Choral Society of Vienna in honour of its distinguished honorary member, Billroth. Invited by Heuberger, Dr. Eyrich's successor as conductor of the society, to take part in the proceedings, the master at once promised to conduct two of his choruses, "Ich schnell mein Horn" and "Lied vom Herrn von Falkenstein," as arranged for the occasion for men's voices by Heuberger, and, on his appearance at the last rehearsal to go through the well prepared compositions, was greeted with a hurri-

---

* Kalbeck's "Johannes Brahms," p. 187 and following.

cane of welcome by the over two hundred students who formed the choir. At the festival performance next day

"Brahms joined in the students' songs as lustily as his rough, broken voice would permit. He had, as he told me, a very good soprano voice as a boy, but had spoilt it by singing too much during its mutation period."

Of another occasion, a party at Billroth's house, when choruses by Brahms and Goldmark were to be performed, Heuberger relates:

"By Brahms' suggestion I directed the preliminary practices which took place at the houses of some of his friends, the Osers and others. The day before the party Brahms and Goldmark came to the last rehearsal. The so-reputed cross-grained Brahms now conducted his 'Marienlieder' and other works without much alteration of the nuances that I had practised. Goldmark, on the contrary, who was as much liked in private life as he was dreaded at rehearsal, studied indefatigably on and on."*

The publication of Brahms' first Symphony in C minor was almost immediately followed by the appearance of a second one in D major, partly written down in the summer of 1877 during the composer's residence at Pörtschach on the Wörthersee, and completed in the autumn at Lichtenthal, where Brahms occupied rooms for a short time at the country inn, "Der Seelach." It was, like the earlier work, played by Brahms and Brüll before an invited circle at Ehrbar's as a pianoforte duet (composer's arrangement) a few days before the date, December 11, first announced for its performance at a Vienna Philharmonic concert. Cause arose at the last moment for the postponement of this event, and the work was given for the first time in public at the succeeding Philharmonic concert of December 30, under Hans Richter's direction. The second performance, conducted by Brahms, took place at the Leipzig Gewandhaus on January 10, 1878.

---

* *Die Musik*, No. 5 of 1903.

The early fortunes of this second symphony were singularly various, and contrasted strangely with those of its predecessor. In Vienna, where the first had been received with reserve, the second achieved an instant, almost popular, success. It was warmly received by the audience, and was discussed by nearly all sections of the press in terms of cordial approval. It was of a "more attractive character," more "understandable" than its predecessor. It was to be preferred, too, inasmuch as the composer had not this time "entered the lists with Beethoven." The third movement was especially praised for its "original melody and rhythms." The work might be appropriately termed the "Vienna Symphony," reflecting as it did "the fresh, healthy life only to be found in beautiful Vienna." In Leipzig, on the other hand, the work was little better than a failure. The impression of the preceding year was felt in the general applause, emphasised by a thrice repeated flourish of trumpets and drums, which greeted the composer's entrance, and the audience maintained an attitude of polite cordiality throughout the performance of the symphony, courteously applauding between the movements and recalling the master at the end; but the enthusiasm of personal friends was not this time able to kindle any corresponding warmth in the bulk of the audience, or even to cover the general consciousness of the fact. The most favourable of the press notices damned the work with faint praise, and Dörffel, whom we quote here and elsewhere because he alone of the professional Leipzig critics of the seventies seems to have been imbued with a sense of Brahms' artistic greatness, showed himself quite angry from disappointment.

"The Viennese," he wrote, "are much more easily satisfied than we. We make quite different demands on Brahms, and require from him music which is something more than 'pretty' and 'very pretty' when he comes before us as a symphonist. Not that we do not wish to hear him in his complaisant moods, not that we disdain to accept from him

pictures of real life, but we desire always to contemplate
his genius, whether he displays it in a manner of his own,
or depends on that of Beethoven. We have not discovered
genius in the new symphony and should hardly have
guessed it to be the work of Brahms had it been performed
anonymously. We should have recognised the great mastery
of form, the extremely skilful handling of the material, the
conspicuous power of construction in short, which it displays, but should not have described it as pre-eminently
distinguished by inventive power. We should have pronounced the work to be one worthy of respect, but not
counting for much in the domain of symphony. Perhaps
we may be mistaken; if so, the error should be pardonable,
arising as it does from the great expectations which our
reverence for the composer induced us to form."

Possibly Dörffel's expectations had been founded too
definitely upon his admiration of the first symphony, which
may have caused him to take for granted that he would
find in the second a reiteration of the exalted moods of its
predecessor. The two works should not, however, be
weighed in the balance one against the other, but should be
considered side by side for the reason that they are not
only different, but, as it were, supplementary. The first
partakes of the nature of an epic in so far as it is conceived
on a grand scale and is dominated throughout three of its
four movements by a passionate intensity of feeling which
is occupied only with the sublimities, whether of pain or
of joy, and which, even after the pain has been conquered,
seems to touch the joy theme itself with the pathos of a
past tragedy. The second symphony is an idyll that is
chiefly animated by the spirit of pure happiness and gently
tender grace. A second symphony quickly following the
first, which had shown any attempt to emulate that great
work on its own ground, must of necessity have been
doomed to result in artistic failure. The second symphony
which the master actually wrote was one which, whilst it
probably satisfied a need of his mind for the refreshment
of change, was the appropriate sequel to its predecessor

both in regard to its calm serenity of mood and to the clear melody of the thematic material in which the mood is so perfectly expressed. Those who are inexorable in their demands for "originality" may, however, be referred to the "adagio non troppo," which, with its melodious phrases and its beautiful tone effects, its varied rhythms and its mysterious intention, offers opportunity for the energetic attention even of the accustomed listener, and is the one movement of the work which can hardly be at once followed with entire pleasure by the less initiated.

Meanwhile the first symphony was quickly making its way through Europe. It was given with enormous success on November 11, 1877, at a concert of the Royal Academy of Arts, Berlin, by the orchestra of the music school under Joachim, and was very inadequately performed on the 16th of the same month at a Hamburg Philharmonic concert under von Bernuth. By the strongly expressed desire of many musicians of the city, the composer was invited to conduct a repetition performance at the Philharmonic concert of January 18, 1878, when the work achieved great success, and still more brilliant results followed its performances in Bremen and Utrecht (January 22 and 26), both directed by Brahms. The first symphony was given in the course of the same month in Münster (J. O. Grimm); Dresden (F. Wüllner); in February in Amsterdam (Brahms); and for the second time in Breslau (Scholz); and made its way in the course of a few seasons to most of the principal musical towns of Europe and America.

The honour of the third, fourth and fifth manuscript performances of the second symphony, in D major, fell to Holland. Brahms conducted his new work in Amsterdam on February 4 and 8, and in the Hague on February 6, and was on each occasion acclaimed by his audience. Writing to the Herzogenbergs after rehearsal at Amsterdam, he says:

"Holland is quite charming and satisfies me every time beyond measure. The musicians and others like No. 2 so much that it is not spoiling my visit."*

Brahms now, at the age of forty-four, was, indeed, in the enjoyment of almost unclouded recognition and success, which could be but little affected by the lack of enthusiasm of this or that audience. His position had become the more firmly established from the circumstance that very few of his works had taken the public by storm. The majority of them had grown almost imperceptibly into general acceptance by sheer force of their intrinsic value, of which but a modicum is to be found on the surface. It is certainly the case that at the outset of his modest entry on a public career he had gained with a single stroke, once and for always, the enthusiastic suffrage of some of the princes of his art; but the voice of Schumann, potent as it was, could be and had been only of avail to procure him a hearing—appreciation was, by the nature of things, beyond its control; and though Frau Schumann and Joachim and Stockhausen untiringly used the influence of their position as best beloved among the foremost favourites of the public to make a way for his music, even they could not immediately secure for it enthusiasm. This it had gradually to gain by the independent means of its indwelling virtue, the insistency of its appeal, not to the outward seeming, but to the very heart of things.

A noteworthy addition was made in the course of the year 1877 to the ranks of Brahms' most staunch and

---

* To the fact that Brahms conducted both his symphonies, Nos. 1 and 2, in the course of his journey, some errors are probably to be ascribed that occur in the editor's notes of Brahms' "Briefwechsel": namely, in Vol. I, p. 42, note 1; and in Vol. III, p. 68, note 3. There was no German performance of the second symphony after that of Leipzig until the work was given on March 6 at Dresden. Here, as at Munich, where it was heard a few days later under Levi, it fell completely flat.

influential supporters in the person of Hans von Bülow. Remark has already been made on the change observable in the early seventies in the attitude of this gifted, witty, whimsical, uncompromising, true-hearted musician towards Brahms' art. The publication of the first symphony completed his conversion, and he soon afterwards began an active propaganda on the master's behalf, to which, carried on as it was with characteristic vehemence and eccentricity, and started at the very moment when the great composer was achieving the highest summit of fame, an entirely fictitious importance has sometimes been ascribed in regard to its effect upon the outward development of Brahms' career. That von Bülow during the last ten or twelve years of his public activity partially devoted his energies to the task of forcing the master's works upon certain more or less indifferent audiences, whom he harangued and lectured concerning their lack of interest, had no bearing on the facts that Brahms' place amongst the immortals had been assured, by practically general consent, with the first few performances of the German Requiem, and that by the beginning of the eighties acceptance of his art had become world-wide. Bülow's new partisanship, destined to bring in its train distinguished friendships that were truly prized and reciprocated by the master, was touching from its sincerity, but is not of essential importance to Brahms' biographer. It is, however, pleasant to be able to add to the extracts already quoted from Bülow's writings three which, dated October and November, 1877, mark the beginning of a new epoch in his own career, and in that of Brahms the commencement of an agreeable and valued personal intimacy. The paragraphs are to be taken merely as illustrations of Bülow's changed sentiments, and not as necessarily expressing the personal views of the present writer.

"Only since my acquaintance with the '*tenth*' symphony, alias the *first* symphony of Johannes Brahms, that is since six weeks, have I become so inaccessible and hard towards

Bruch pieces and the like. I do not call it the '*tenth*' in the sense of its relation to the '*ninth*' . . . ."

"I believe it is not without the intelligence of chance that Bach, Beethoven and Brahms are in alliteration."

"The imagination of Bach seems, in his clavier works, to be dominated by the organ, that of Beethoven by the orchestra, that of Brahms by both."

CHAPTER XIX.

1878-1881.

Hamburg Philharmonic Jubilee Festival—Violin Concerto—First performance by Joachim—Pianoforte Pieces, Op. 76—Sonata for Pianoforte and Violin—First performances—Brahms at Crefeld —Rhapsodies for Pianoforte—Heuberger's studies with Brahms —Second Schumann Festival at Bonn—The two Overtures— Breslau honorary degree.

WITH the rapidly increasing appreciation of Brahms' art observable during the second half of the seventies throughout the entire musical world, the condition of his private circumstances changed rapidly also. At the time he completed the second symphony it was very far removed from that of twelve years back, when he had been obliged, by lack of ready cash, to purchase the music paper required for the manuscript of the Requiem in small instalments. He never deviated from the simple manner of daily life agreeable to him by nature and habit, but we find that in the early spring of 1878 he added to the short list of his personal pleasures one that became to him a source of unfailing delight, that of a journey to Italy. On this his first visit, made in April, in Billroth's company, he stayed in Venice, Florence, Rome and Naples, and returned subjugated once and for all by the witcheries of the south. Neither of his Italian tours was associated with a musical purpose; they were undertaken solely for the refreshment of body and mind by a holiday ramble amidst beauties of nature and art, to which his temperament made him peculiarly sensitive, and amongst a people whose *naturel* was congenial to him.

"I often think of our journey," writes Billroth on May 7; "that you were so charmed with everything doubles my pleasure."

The new symphony was included in one of the programmes of the Rhine Festival, held this year at Düsseldorf under Joachim and Tausch. Amongst Joachim's duties was that of conducting the performance of his friend's work, concerning which we read in a contemporary journal:

"The performance of Brahms' second symphony under Joachim was a feast such as we have seldom heard. The audience was jubilant after each movement, and would not be satisfied till the third was repeated."

And again in a final summary:

"The most brilliant event of the festival was the performance of Brahms' symphony."

The composer again spent the summer at Pörtschach, a spot where, as he writes to Hanslick, "so many melodies fly about one must be careful not to tread on them." In the same letter* he talks playfully to his old friend, who, remaining a bachelor till past fifty, had lately surprised his acquaintances by marrying a lady many years his junior, of his intention to compose a new symphony for the winter,

"that shall sound so gay and charming you will think I have written it expressly for you, or rather for your young wife."

This idea, probably not seriously entertained, was put aside, but the reflection of the composer's happy mood is to be found in several of the pianoforte pieces with which he was busy at this time—notably in No. 2 of Op. 76—and in the last movement of the great violin concerto he was composing for Joachim.

---

* First published with others by Hanslick in the *Neue Freie Presse* of July 1, 1897.

The progress of this important work brought with it the necessity for a consultation between the master and his old friend; and Joachim managed to spare a few days for Pörtschach in the beginning of September, when the concerto in its yet unfinished state, was tried and discussed. Brahms' manuscript of the original version of the opening movement, as submitted to Joachim, with annotations—chiefly referring to violin technique—in the handwriting of the master violinist, is preserved in the Royal Library of Berlin. The concerto as originally sketched, contained four movements, but Brahms unable to satisfy himself with the scherzo, finally decided to reject it altogether.

An event was to take place in the last week of September which no doubt possessed a peculiar interest for Brahms, though it was not of an unmixed character: the celebration of the fiftieth anniversary of the Philharmonic Society of his native city of Hamburg, which had been founded in 1828 by a few music lovers, with W. Grund, a composer and teacher of the city, as its conductor. The festival was to last five days, and to include three great orchestral concerts in the Saagebiel Hall and an excursion up the Elbe to Blankenese. Four symphonies were to be performed: Haydn in G minor, Beethoven's "Eroica," Schumann in C major, Brahms in D major. Frau Schumann was to play Mozart's Pianoforte Concerto in D minor; Joachim to perform with Concertmeister Bargheer, Spohr's Duo Concertante for two violins in B minor. A great assemblage of musicians was expected, and Brahms had been invited, but at the beginning of September no one in Hamburg knew whether or not he intended to be present, and the directors of the festival, finding themselves very near a predicament, resolved to appeal to Hanslick, who had received and accepted an invitation, to procure his answer for them. The letter which Hanslick immediately wrote to Pörtschach elicited from Brahms the following reply:

"Pörtschach, *Sept.*, 1878.

"You have once already publicly preached to me the doctrine of decorum; I do not wish this to occur, from no fault of mine, a second time, and tell you, therefore, that it will be the Hamburgers' concern if I do not appear at their festival. I have no opportunity for showing politeness and gratitude; on the contrary, some rudeness would be in place if I had time and inclination to lose my temper over the matter. I do not wish to disturb yours by detailed communication and will therefore only say that in spite of inquiry, not a word has been said about honorarium or any sort of remuneration. I, poor composer, am appraised at doubtful value and lose all right to sit at the festival table, next to your wife, let us say. I therefore beg this time for indulgence for my anyway impaired reputation as a polite man. As regards the symphony, indeed, I do not beg for indulgence, but I fear that unless its direction be offered to Joachim as I wish, there will be a miserable performance. Now, the dinners are good in Hamburg, the symphony is of a favourable length—you can dream whilst it is going on that you are in Vienna! I am thinking of going to Vienna very soon. . . ."*

This dubious epistle need not be taken too seriously, true though it is that the composer rightly made it a point throughout his career that his work should be paid for, and, so to speak, at full market value. The tone adopted by him on this occasion must be partly referred to the remembrance of the old sore, which, perhaps, never quite healed—to the mortification which had on two occasions cut deep into the heart of the loyal Hamburger when his fellow citizens offered to a stranger the opportunity he would have welcomed to settle in their midst. It is not wonderful that the invitation to attend, and presumably to take part in, the jubilee festival of the society of which, had he so chosen, he ought since many years to have been the artistic chief, should have revived past memories in the mind of the renowned master whose mere presence could

---

* Hanslick, *Neue Freie Presse*, as before.

now invest the occasion with a peculiar significance. All's well that ends well, however. How Brahms settled the matter with the committee must be left to conjecture, but it is certain that he astonished friends and acquaintance by coming to Hamburg with a long flowing beard grown during the summer, which changed the character of his face almost beyond recognition. It was, as we know, his second experiment of the kind, and the beard, which he from this time permanently retained, certainly added to the grandeur of his head, though some of his old friends may occasionally have looked back with regret to the days when the firm, purposeful mouth contributed its share to the expression of his countenance.

Nothing was ultimately wanting that could contribute to the success of the Hamburg celebration. The first concert, on September 25, was devoted to three of the musical giants —Bach, Handel, Beethoven; that of the 26th to Haydn, Mozart, Cherubini, Schumann, and, in memory of the society's first conductor, W. Grund. The morning of the 27th was given up to rehearsal—especially of Brahms' new symphony, under the composer's direction; the afternoon, to the excursion and banquet. Almost everyone had come from everywhere. Besides those who were taking part in the concerts there were Hiller, Gernsheim, Gade, Reinecke, Reinthaler, Grimm, Flotow, Theodor Kirchner, Verhülst (from the Hague), Hanslick, Claus Groth, not to mention Grädener, of early days, and a host of old Hamburg friends. Our master was in genial mood, and chatted gaily with acquaintances old and new during the run down the river, but a sign showed that his thoughts were with the past. Claus Groth, who was placed at the banquet next to Brahms, relates that the proposer of the composer's health referred in his speech to the old proverb of the prophet's unworthiness in his own country, and pointed out its inapplicability in the case of the day's ceremony, "when the society unites with me in praise and love of our Johannes Brahms."

"Brahms turned to me," continues Groth, "and whispered in a deep and serious tone: 'This of my case! Twice was the vacant conductor's post of the Philharmonic Society given to a stranger whilst I was passed over. If it had been offered me at the right time I should have become a methodical citizen, and could have married and become like other men. Now I am a vagabond!'"

That Brahms would under any circumstances have summoned up sufficient courage to commit himself to the irretrievable step of matrimony we may be permitted to doubt. That one obstacle which prevented him was his own fear of the interruption that such a change might cause to his own almost too orderly and methodical habits is fairly certain.

The boat started from Blankenese on its return journey to St. Pauli's landing bridge, Hamburg, at 9.30 p.m., and at the moment of its departure three rockets were sent up from deck and three shots fired from shore, by arrangement with the inhabitants of the numerous villas that line the bank of the Elbe, as a signal for the illumination of houses and gardens, which accordingly gave graceful testimony to the returning musicians of the widespread interest felt in the occasion.*

The third and concluding concert of the festival took place on the evening of Sunday, September 29, with performances of Weber's "Oberon" overture, songs by Schubert, Spohr's Concertante for two violins, Brahms'

---

* Claus Groth, in the Brahms "Recollections" to which we have several times referred, speaks of the festival banquet as having taken place at the Hamburger Hof, Hamburg, and "as I think" after the performance of Brahms' symphony. Groth's articles were written in the year 1897, when he was at an advanced age—he was much Brahms' senior—and his memory has misled him in one or two of his details. As regards those here referred to, the author has, in the above description, followed the accounts given in the *Hamburger Correspondent* of the time, with which that of Hanslick, in his very interesting "Essays on Music and Musicians," is in strict accord.

second Symphony, under his own direction, and Mendelssohn's "Walpurgis Nacht."

"The delight of the public at Brahms' symphony was most enthusiastically expressed," says Hanslick. "Brahms, who was received with orchestra flourish and laurel wreath, himself conducted, and Joachim played first violin in the orchestra. At the close of the symphony the ladies of the chorus and in the first rows of the audience threw their flowers to Brahms, who stood there, in the words of his own cradle-song, 'covered with roses.'"

Ludwig Meinardus, of the *Hamburger Correspondent*, after giving a detailed and most appreciative account of the several movements of the work, continues:

"Brahms himself conducted his symphony, which is sealed with the stamp of immortality, in his native city before an audience of thousands raised to festival pitch, in which mingled a large number of musical authorities from outside. The enthusiasm was increased by this circumstance, and by the simplicity and quiet energy with which Brahms handled the baton. It prepared for him an ovation as he ascended the conductor's desk in the shape of a big laurel wreath, a flourish, and a stormy welcome from those upon and in front of the platform; it broke out after each of the four movements, and increased at the close of the third to a *da capo* demand to which the conductor and composer only at length and with the reluctance of modesty resolved to yield; it was expressed finally, at the close of the work, by persistent recalls and by a rain of flowers which poured from all sides upon the admired and revered composer."

The last few words seem to remind us of the early sixties, and to bring us once more face to face with the Halliers, Völckers, Wagners, Fräulein Laura Garbe, and other former members of the ladies' choir, many of whom were still resident in Hamburg, and, having retained their old affectionate admiration of their young musician without a jot of abatement as they watched his course during the passing years, now brought affection, admiration and sympathetic triumph dressed in graceful guise to throw at the feet of the famous master. Marxsen, prevented by

considerations of health from joining the excursion down
the river, was present at the concert, beaming with joy;
Böie, too, associated with early performances of the B flat
Sextet and the G minor Pianoforte Quartet, was there,
whilst the presence of Christian Otterer, who had played
viola as an old friend at the subscription concert given by
the youthful Hannes at the "Old Raven," carried the
associations of the evening back almost to the year of the
composer's birth. Two names which we should gladly
have included are missing from the list of our old
acquaintances. None would have more heartily rejoiced in
the events of the evening than Friedrich Willibald Cossel,
now some thirteen summers passed away; and what may not
be imagined of Jakob Brahms' exultant pride had six more
years of life been spared him! We may picture the pursed-
up lips, the gratified expression of the eyes, the playful
assumption of dignity towards his own particular chums,
the tears of joy with which he would have answered
Joachim's cordial hand grasp, the shy, gratified whisper to
Carl Bade: "Ik segge nix" (I shall not speak), when some
distinguished musician or charming lady had desired to be
introduced to him as the father of his son. Frau Cossel
was present with her talented daughter Marie (Frau Dr.
Janssen), and the old family ties so treasured by our master
were represented by Elise and Fritz, and by kind Frau
Caroline with her son Fritz Schnack, who entertained an
almost adoring affection for his stepbrother. Frau Caroline
was invariably present at any concert in Hamburg in which
Johannes took part, by the composer's express desire.
Elise begged her brother after the concert for the wreaths
that had been presented to him.

"So you want to brag with them?" said he; "come to
me early to-morrow morning; we will go together and lay
them on father's grave."

It may be added here, for the sake of completeness, that
some time later, on von Bernuth's contemplated resignation, a representative of the Philharmonic Society called on

Groth to ask his opinion as to the probability of Brahms' acceptance of an offer of the conductorship. He pointed out that the then committee could not justly be blamed for the mistakes of their predecessors, which they were anxious to repair as far as might now be possible, and Groth, after discussing the matter in detail, consented to lay it informally before Brahms. We cannot wonder that no answer was received to his communication; it must seem obvious to most minds that the master could neither accept nor decline an offer which had not been made. Had the committee decided to risk the slight mortification of a refusal from Brahms by writing a definite proposal to him, it is certain that he would have replied to it, though it seems unlikely that he would have now uprooted himself from the city where he had formed intimate friendships since one of the principal attractions which Hamburg had possessed for him—the presence of his parents—had ceased to exist.

The publications of the year include, besides the Symphony in D major, a set of "Ballads and Romances" for two voices, dedicated to Julius Allgeyer, the first of which, composed in the summer of 1877, has the Scotch ballad "Edward" for its text.

Of other early performances of the second symphony we may mention those of October 22 in Breslau, under the composer, and of November 23 in Münster, under Grimm. Such a furore was created in Münster that the work was repeated by general desire at the concert of December 21.

At the Vienna Gesellschaft concert of December 8, No. 1 of the two Motets, Op. 74, for unaccompanied chorus was sung, under the direction of Edward Kremser, from the manuscript parts. All four movements, the first and last in four, the second and third in six, parts, made a deep impression, and in spite of the serious character of the work it was followed by long continued applause. The texts have the characteristics usually preferred by Brahms for his sacred compositions, and taken together, are expressive of courageous, trustful resignation in the face of mystery.

The music, exquisitely suited to the words, furnishes another example of deeply serious feeling clothed in the beautiful forms of early contrapuntal art.

Great interest was aroused in the musical circles of many lands by the announcement that Joachim would play a violin concerto by Brahms at the Leipzig Gewandhaus concert of January 1, 1879. Such an event was bound to raise a particular question, connected not only with Brahms' musical career, but with the history of musical art. Many concertos for violin solo with orchestral accompaniment had been produced since the days of Viotti, through those of Mozart and Spohr, down to the publication in 1877 of Max Bruch's second in D minor, and, of the most favoured, few had retained more than an occasional place in concert programmes. Two only had survived the test of time as the pre-eminent masterpieces of their class; those of Beethoven and Mendelssohn. If no work of the kind could be placed exactly with Beethoven's Violin Concerto, yet, even as compared with this supreme achievement, no thought of inferiority could be applied to that of Mendelssohn, which immediately on its production took the place it had ever since held as one of two *chefs-d'œuvre*. The question which now naturally suggested itself was whether Brahms' new work would take its place as a third by the side of its two greatest predecessors. It was the more interesting because, though the composer was not now breaking essentially new ground, yet his one previous concerto had been composed for the pianoforte, and whilst two decades had elapsed since its completion in final form (Detmold, 1858), and first public performances (Hanover and Leipzig, January, 1859), it bore distinct traces of a still earlier period, with which we now know it to have been associated. The experience of a life, therefore, may almost be said to have intervened between the two works.

Turning to our old friend Dörffel, already doubly proved impartial, for his immediate impressions of the Gewandhaus concert of January 1, we find his report very interesting reading.

"No less a task," he says, "confronted Brahms, if his salutation to his friend were to be one suitable to Joachim's eminence, than the production of a work that should reach the two greatest, Beethoven and Mendelssohn. We confess to having awaited the solution with some heart palpitation, though we firmly maintained our standard. But what joy we experienced! Brahms has brought such a third work to the partnership. The originality of the spirit which inspires the whole, the firm organic structure in which it is displayed, the warmth which streams from it, animating the work with joy and light—it cannot be otherwise—the concerto must be the fruit of the composer's latest and, as we believe, happiest experiences.

"The first movement is broad, with sharply defined contrasts through which, however, the serious-soft mood is preserved; the second is short, very thoughtful and fervent; the last, very spirited and attractive. There is, moreover, a quite unusual handling of the instrument, and again, a breath in the orchestra, which make us look forward with delight to the study of the score; we have seldom been so enthralled by the composer's genius. But Joachim played, also, with a love and devotion which brought home to us in every bar the direct or indirect share he has had in the work. As to the reception, the first movement was too new to be distinctly appreciated by the audience, the second made considerable way, the last aroused great enthusiasm."

Bernsdorf was less unsympathetic than usual. He considered the concerto "one of the clearest and most spontaneous of the composer's works." Both Joachim and Brahms, who conducted the orchestra, had to respond to numerous recalls.

The work was presented a few days later by the composer and his friend to the music lovers of Budapest and, on January 14, to those of Vienna and was received with enthusiasm on both occasions:

"Also Joachim played my piece better at each rehearsal, and the Cadenza sounded so beautiful at the actual concert that the public applauded it into the start of the Coda," wrote Brahms to Frau von Herzogenberg.*

Joachim, to whom the concerto is dedicated, brought the manuscript with him to London and performed the work at the Crystal Palace Saturday concert of February 22 (August Manns); at the Philharmonic concerts of March 6 and 20 (W. G. Cusins); at some of his appearances in the English provinces; and, on May 25, in Amsterdam.† The concerto was finally revised in the summer, during the composer's third prolonged stay in Pörtschach, and was heard several times with pianoforte accompaniment in the course of a tour in some of the Hungarian and Balkan provinces undertaken by Brahms and Joachim during the last half of September. Published before the close of the year, it was introduced by Joachim during the season 1879-80 in many of the musical towns of Europe and held a conspicuous place in his repertoire throughout the remainder of his career. The violinists, Adolph Brodsky and, a little later, Frau Roeger-Soldat, were amongst those who associated their names in a special manner with the early life of the work.

If the mood of this great concerto has, as Dr. Deiters remarks, something in common with that of the second symphony, the sentiment is maintained at a loftier height than that of the earlier composition, the limpid grace of which has an immediate fascination for a general audience. The concerto requires time for full appreciation, and though, by general consent of the initiated, it undoubtedly occupies a position on the plane assigned to it by Dörffel, it would be too much to assert that it has as yet entirely conquered the heart of the great public. It is gradually making its way, however, to what will probably become unreserved popularity.

---

* "Briefwechsel," No. LV.

† A repetition performance of the concerto at the Crystal Palace proposed for March 22 did not take place.

To the summer of 1879, the third spent by Brahms in Pörtschach, is to be referred the composition of the sonata for pianoforte and violin in G major, and of the "Zwei Rhapsodien" for pianoforte solo in B minor and G minor. The sonata was tried by Brahms and Joachim immediately after completion during a few days' visit paid by the composer to his friend at Joachim's summer residence in Aigen near Salzburg. The year is of further special interest in our narrative since it included the publication of two books of pianoforte pieces (Op. 76), the several numbers of which are entitled "Intermezzo" or "Capriccio." We have traced the remarkable continuity of Brahms' development as a composer during the first ten years of his connection with Vienna, in its relation to the period which directly preceded his earliest visit to the city. The period dating back from 1862 to 1852 is not so unbroken. Quite another sequel than the actual one might have been anticipated from the fact that of the first ten of the composer's published works six had been pianoforte solos, five of them in other than variation form. We have watched his progress from one stepping stone of excellence to another in this form, from the early beauties of the examples contained in the Sonatas, Op. 1 and Op. 2, through the astonishing technical advance displayed in Op. 9, up to a masterpiece, the Handel Variations and Fugue, Op. 24, and have still had to add one more work to the list, the Paganini Variations, with imposing characteristics of its own; but we have not had to record the appearance of a single unaccompanied pianoforte solo in any other form in the course of the twenty-five years which succeeded the completion of the Ballades, Op. 10, in 1854 (published in 1856). Only now when the narrative has been brought to the point appropriate for the contemplation of these facts is it possible to point out the true significance to our master's career of the four years of study passed in complete retirement by the composer, as distinct from the pianist, Brahms, that followed the close of 1854. On his reappearance in

1859 and 1860 with a number of new works, not only had his technique been reformed and transfigured, but the tendency of his career changed. The fascination exercised over his mind by the pure style of part-writing practised by the best masters of the early Italian schools, and the extent of resource he had acquired by constant assimilation of the treasure of Bach's learning, had given him an irresistible bent towards the composition of works that led up to the Requiem and Triumphlied on the one hand, and the String Quartets and Symphonies on the other; and the same influences would naturally dispose him towards the writing of chamber music for pianoforte and strings rather than for pianoforte alone. It is well known that his innate fastidiousness in regard to his own work was augmented in the case of his first symphony by his never-ceasing consciousness of Beethoven's overwhelming achievements in this domain; and his abstention, after his earliest period, from the publication of a pianoforte sonata may have been partially due to a similar, and perhaps even stronger, feeling that Beethoven's sonatas cannot be succeeded. It is, however, difficult to believe that Brahms would not have persevered and conquered—conquered in the sense of producing something appropriate to his time—in the one case as in the other if he had felt a real impulse to do so, and it may possibly be true that his genius was better suited for the forms in which he worked than for those which he avoided.

The two books of Pianoforte Pieces, which, with the two Motets, Op. 74, dedicated to Philipp Spitta, the Violin Concerto, and the three Pianoforte Studies after Bach without opus number, formed the publications of the year 1879, contain, in all, eight numbers, composed, no doubt, at various dates. One of the finest, the Capriccio in F sharp minor, was given to Frau Schumann in 1871, on the eve of her fifty-second birthday. Some of the pieces, written with simplicity of style and pervaded by a spirit of dreamy content or graceful happiness, have become familiar to music lovers; others present difficulties both to listener and performer which have hindered their popularity. Several contain interesting examples of the composer's facility in the art of rhythmic and contrapuntal device.

The Sonata for pianoforte and violin in G major, a pearl of pure and delicate imagination, was issued in November —though catalogued by a publisher's convention under the following year—and performed for the first time in public by Brahms and Hellmesberger at the quartet concert of November 20, from the printed copies. The vivacity of the first movement is painted in pale moonbeam tints, and must, as one fancies, vanish before the first warm ray of sunshine. There is more substantiality about the gentle melancholy of the adagio, though this movement, again, is haunted by a strain of mystery. The last movement, written in rondo form, has for its first subject that of the beautiful "Rain-Song" already alluded to, and is a very dream of wistful charm. Brahms' very original treatment of the pianoforte arpeggio, which is one of the distinctive features of his style of writing for the instrument, is well illustrated in the first movement of this work, in which the arpeggio is raised from the mere position of a brilliant passage to that of an essential part of the entire conception. A particularly clear light is thrown also upon the composer's relation to Bach by the study of the sonata, the methods of which are inherited from those of the early giant-musician, as exemplified in his sonatas for clavier and violin; and whilst Bach's methods flow as easily within the forms of the Austrian masters as though they had always been an inseparable part of them, the association is animated by the distinctive individuality of our Brahms. Not, however, as it impressed itself upon us in his first great series of works for pianoforte and strings. The spirit of the Sonata in G is essentially that of the master's later period of maturity. In it we feel that he has not only his powers, but his emotions, well in hand, and has reached a period of life when he can afford to look back calmly to the conflicts of the past. This no mere fancy; we find as we proceed in the study of Brahms' art, not that the nature of the man changed as he grew older, but that, whilst the sunshine of complete recognition which brightened his later path through life is felt in the clear spirit of some of his works, the reserve which characterises others is now dictated by the complete self-mastery which it had been one of the efforts of his life to attain, and which lends them a singular and pathetic charm as of consciously half-revealed power and beauty.

The Sonata in G major is the fourth composed by Brahms for pianoforte and violin. The first, belonging to his first period, had, as we know, been mysteriously lost. The second and third were rejected after completion by the composer's relentless self-criticism, and the manuscripts destroyed by his own hand. The work now known among its companions as No. 1, was played with immense success by Brahms and Joachim during a short concert tour they made together in Austria in the beginning of February. In the course of his visit Joachim performed the Violin Concerto for the second time in Vienna at one of three orchestral concerts given by him in the large hall of the "Gesellschaft" with the result that invariably attended the association of the two names so dear to the Austrian public.

The sonata was performed for the first time in England at the Monday Popular concert of February 2 by von Bülow and Madame Norman-Néruda, and at the Wednesday Popular concert, Cambridge, on the 25th of the same month by C. Villiers Stanford and Richard Gompertz. One of the earliest performances in Germany was that by Scholz and Himmelstoss at Breslau on February 24.

Brahms' first appearance at Crefeld on January 20, in the course of a short concert journey on the Rhine, must be particularly recorded for two reasons: in the first place because it introduces us to a group of friends, his pleasant associations with whom are commemorated in the dedication of one of his later works. A considerable amount of music was performed during this first visit, and more on subsequent ones, in the informal, sociable way Brahms liked, at the houses of Herr and Frau Rudolph von der Leyen, with whom he always stayed, and of their relatives, Herr and Frau Alwyn von Beckerath. Herr von Beckerath, a good amateur performer, played viola in the resident string quartet led by Professor Richard Barth, a former pupil of Joachim, an old acquaintance of Brahms, and well known later on as von Bernuth's successor at Hamburg, who was always present with his colleagues at these private gatherings; and the enjoyment of the circle was enhanced during Brahms' later visits to Crefeld by the singing, to the master's accompaniment, of Fräulein Antonia Kufferath. This lady (now Mrs. Edward Speyer) has interesting recollections connected with the Crefeld visits. Amongst them is that of Brahms, who when once a composition was published allowed it to pass from his mind, sometimes almost completely, coming unawares upon a difficult passage in the accompaniment of one of his songs, and having an instant's struggle with it. At the end he turned to Fräulein Kufferath, saying: "That is really difficult to read at sight!"

The musical event which gives particular distinction to the Crefeld concert of 1880, the programme of which included Brahms' second Symphony, "Harzreise" Rhapsody and Triumphlied, was the performance by the composer of the two new solos for the pianoforte, the Rhapsodies in B minor and G minor, generally accepted as the finest of Brahms' shorter works for the instrument. The second one especially, marked "molto passionato ma non troppo allegro," is an inspiration from beginning to end, and though not long, its length is sufficient to balance its grandeur of idea and to give the effect of completeness to its performance. Billroth, to whom Brahms, always needing sympathy, confided the manuscripts on their completion in the early summer of 1879, returned them with the words:

"The second piece has quite fascinated me. In both pieces there is more of the young, heaven-storming Johannes than in the other late works of the mature man."

The Sonata in G, Op. 78, the Rhapsodies, Op. 79, dedicated to Frau Elisabeth von Herzogenberg, and the third and fourth books of Hungarian Dances for Pianoforte Duet, without opus number, were the catalogued publications of 1880.

It may have been noticed by the reader that, in our record of the early performances of Brahms' works during the closing seventies, no mention has been made of Munich. The reason is not far to seek, and is such as might almost have been anticipated. The time arrived when the paths of Brahms and Levi separated, and its occurrence may be definitely dated in November, 1876, when our master visited Munich to conduct his first symphony, and stood there for the last time on a concert platform.

The attraction felt by Levi towards Wagner's art and personality had grown continually stronger since his preparation of the "Meistersinger" for performance at Carlsruhe in 1869 and the establishment of personal relations between himself and Wagner to which it indirectly led; and his enthusiasm received constant encouragement from the preoccupation of his energies with the great music dramas which followed naturally on his appointment in 1872, to the conductorship of the Munich court opera. The impulsive expression of his boundless admiration for Wagner and his works in the course of a few days' visit paid him by Brahms in April, 1875, carried beyond the point which should have been prescribed by tact, led to a temporary cessation of intercourse between the old friends and the tension of feeling thus created between them did not entirely yield to the healing influences of time. Levi's constitutional tendency to hero worship received extraordinary stimulus from the first performance of the "Niebelungen-Ring," at which he was present, in the temporary theatre in Bayreuth in August, 1876; and,

though there was a *rapprochement* between himself and
Brahms when our master visited Munich in the autumn of
the year to conduct his symphony, and stayed in Levi's
house, the old familiar feeling of comradeship was gone not
to return. Brahms seems to have become definitely convinced at this time that future personal relations between
himself and the now distinguished Wagner conductor
would become increasingly embarrassing to both; and
though he remained in occasional cordial correspondence
with Levi for a few years longer, he took the wise and
friendly course of abstaining from further visits to Munich.
Enough, it is hoped, has been related in these pages of
Brahms' appreciation of Wagner's powers to exclude the
suspicion that he was actuated by petty feeling in taking
this line. Levi's want of self-restraint was in one sense an
acknowledgment of the master's artistic generosity; but
compliments of this kind should not be carried to extremes,
and Brahms' courage in adhering to a course certain to
expose him to misunderstanding saved Levi as well as
himself from the danger of the false position which must
inevitably have threatened their future intercourse. The
wreath which Brahms sent to Bayreuth on Wagner's death
in February, 1883, was not the sign of a mere decorous
compliance with custom, but was a heart-felt tribute of
recognition from the one great master to the other.

Brahms' separation from Levi necessarily involved a
coolness between himself and Allgeyer, who was one of the
closest intimates of the Levi circle, but this was only temporary, and was probably merely accepted by Brahms as
one of the incidents of the situation. It was got over during
a visit paid by Allgeyer to Vienna, and Brahms' pleasure
at the renewal of personal relations between himself and
his old friend may be read in the dedication of the "Ballads
and Romances" published in 1878, to which reference has
already been made.

To Brahms' activity on the advisory committee for the
granting of government stipendiums to young artists, com-

bined with the growing feeling of mental leisure which must have come to him at this period of his mature mastership, must be ascribed the willingness shown by him, from the middle of the seventies onward, to concern himself with the musical progress of certain young composers who were courageous enough to ask his opinion and advice, and in whose works he discerned talent. Mention has been made of his prompt and emphatic appreciation of Dvorák. Amongst other musicians of distinction who in their youth enjoyed the advantage of his interest and friendship are Drs. Richard Heuberger, Eusebius Mandycweski (who later held the important position of librarian to the Gesellschaft der Musikfreunde), von Rottenberg, and Jenner. We spoke in the last chapter of some of the incidents of the master's friendship for Heuberger, who says that Brahms' great talent for teaching became continually clearer to him. "With gifted young people who had already passed through the school curriculum, he might have achieved great things." His criticism was so ruthless and searching as to be at first profoundly discouraging, but he could praise warmly, too, and there was no mistaking the pleasure he felt in being able to do so. His remarks to Heuberger, chiefly called forth by points in the manuscripts —often songs—laid before him, and by suggested improvements, usually served to elucidate general principles. The close rhythmical association of music with words, the conditions indispensable to the admission of irregularity of bar rhythm, the construction of melody, are but a few of the important points that were handled in the brief, incisive, pregnant manner which illumined every subject that he touched upon.

"Do you think," said he one day, taking exception to an expression inadvertently used by Heuberger apropos to the construction of his melody, "that any one of my half-dozen passable songs 'occurred' to me? I had to worry myself with them rarely! One must be able—don't take this literally—to *whistle* a song . . . then it is good."

"Those *must* have been eyes, but perhaps not so interesting to other people," he said, pointing to the too drawn-out setting of the words "I saw two eyes last Sunday morn," in one of Heuberger's manuscripts, and he improvised the passage in the closer form which the composer has retained in his published song, "Bitt' ihn o Mutter."

The committee formed in 1871 to consider a scheme for the erection of a monument to Schumann at Bonn had been so successful during the few years following the festival of 1873, in collecting funds for their object, that by the beginning of May, 1880, the memorial, designed and executed by the sculptor Donnhorf, had been placed over Schumann's grave in the Bonn cemetery, and nothing remained to be done save to unveil and deliver it over to the municipal authorities. These ceremonies were to be performed on the 2nd of the month, and to be followed by some festival concerts with programmes of the master's music.

Proceedings opened on April 30 when Frau Schumann, arriving at Bonn with some of her family on a visit to Frau Dunkelberg, geb. Kyllmann, was received at the railway station by Joachim, Brahms and the members of the festival committee. She was greeted the next evening by a serenade sung in her hostess's garden by the members of the Concordia and the Academic Vocal Union, which was followed by performances within doors of the "Lotos Blume" and the "Träumender See." President Wrede then delivered an address, and on its conclusion introduced each member of the societies individually to Frau Schumann. With her permission, Herr Branscheidt sang two of Schumann's songs to the accompaniment of Concertmeister Lorscheidt, and after the great artist had acknowledged these compliments in a few suitable words, the vocalists returned to the garden to sing "Thou in the wood hast wandered," from Schumann's "Pilgrimage of the Rose." With this performance the programme of the evening terminated, and after Frau Schumann had again expressed her warm thanks the visitors withdrew.

The cemetery was crowded early the next day by friends desirous of witnessing the unveiling of the monument. Nearly twenty-four years had gone by since the simple funeral procession had followed Schumann's remains through the streets of Bonn; since a group of young musicians stood together at the open grave, supported by the sympathy of a concourse of friends and music lovers, to take their last farewell of the illustrious dead. Now they were reassembled on the same spot to do honour to the beloved master's memory. Not one was missing. Brahms, Joachim, Dietrich, the three young chief mourners of the first occasion, stood together again as middle-aged men; Hiller the older friend, Grimm and Bargiel, all were there, and Stockhausen, since many years one of the circle. Frau Schumann stood with her daughters at the foot of the monument, her usual pathetic expression deepened by the rush of varied memories, but with controlled demeanour. Amongst those present in an official capacity were the mayor of Bonn, Herr Oberburgermeister Doetsch; the sculptor, Professor Donnhorf, from Dresden; the president of the memorial committee, Professor Schaafhausen, and the members of the two choral societies with President Wrede.

The singing of the fine old chorale, "Was Gott thut das ist wohlgethan" was the prelude to the address in which Geheimrath Schaafhausen gave the monument over to the city of Bonn. Whilst he was speaking the covering fell, and as his final word was uttered, the beautiful tones of a chorus from Schumann's "Peri" were sounded by a band of wind instruments, while many wreaths and other floral tributes were laid upon the grave. An address of thanks was delivered on behalf of the city by Oberburgermeister Doetsch, and the performance of a chorus from Mendelssohn's "Elijah," with the placing of more wreaths, brought the formalities to a close. The whole of the music was conducted by Brahms who, with choir and orchestra, stood invisible behind the monument. The following telegram was handed to the mayor in the course of the proceedings.

"The Society of Music-lovers and the Conservatoire of Vienna congratulate Bonn on the honour of having to-day erected the first memorial to Schumann as previously that to Beethoven."

The programme of the orchestral concert which took place in the evening of May 2, beginning at six o'clock, included Schumann's E flat Symphony and Requiem for Mignon, conducted by Brahms; a poetic "Prologue," composed and recited by Herr Emil Rittershaus of Barmen; the Manfred music conducted by Joachim, with Ernst von Possart, director of the court theatre of Munich, in the chief declamatory part; and as single exception in the list of Schumann's works, Brahms' Violin Concerto, conducted by the composer, and played by Joachim in so perfect and ideal a manner as to be, "not merely interpretative, but absolutely creative." A rain of bouquets followed its conclusion. Three works were given at the chamber music concert of the following morning: Schumann's String Quartet in A minor, led by Joachim; Spanisches Liederspiel; and Quartet for pianoforte and strings, of which Brahms and Joachim played the pianoforte and violin parts respectively.

In the summer of this year, the first passed by Brahms in the pretty town of Ischl in Upper Austria, to the inhabitants of which he was to become a very familiar personality during the last eight years of his life, were composed the only two overtures published by the master. He played them to Frau Schumann at her summer quarters in Berchtesgaden on the occasion of a congratulatory birthday visit which he paid her in September; and they were rehearsed from the manuscript by Joachim's school orchestra early in December. The "Tragic" overture, the grave character of which is indicated by its title, was performed for the first time in public on December 26 at the fourth concert of the Vienna Philharmonic season. Dr. Deiters says of it:

"In this work we see a strong hero battling with an iron and relentless fate; passing hopes of victory cannot alter an impending destiny. We do not care to inquire whether the composer had a special tragedy in his mind, or if so, which one; those who remain musically unconvinced by the unsurpassably powerful theme, would not be assisted by a particular suggestion."

The "Academic Festival Overture" which we know, was the one out of three selected by the composer for preservation. It was composed in acknowledgment of the honorary doctor's degree conferred on Brahms in March, 1879, by the university of Breslau, and was performed for the first time in that city on January 4, 1881, under his direction. The companion work, the Tragic Overture, and the second Symphony were included in the same programme. The lately-made Doctor of Philosophy was received with all the honour and enthusiasm befitting the occasion and his work, and was again stormily applauded on the 6th, when he performed Schumann's Fantasia, Op. 17, his two Rhapsodies, and the pianoforte part of his Horn Trio, at a concert of chamber music.

In the Academic Overture the sociable spirit reappears which had prompted the boy of fourteen to compose an ABC part-song for his seniors, the village schoolmasters in and around Winsen. Now the renowned master of forty-seven seeks to identify himself with the youthful spirits of the university with which he has become associated, by taking, for principal themes of his overture, student melodies loved by him from their association with the early Göttingen years of happy companionship with Joachim, with Grimm, with von Meysenbug and others. Four of these, "Wir hatten gebauet," "Hört ich sing," "Was kommt dort," and the "Gaudeamus," are introduced in the course of the movement, which is written in regular classical form, and the composer lingers with particular affection over the third one, the song that in student circles accompanies the merry "Fox-ride," which in the summer of 1853 carried Brahms so many leagues distant from the earlier stages of his life's journey. The favourite "Gaudeamus igitur," given with the full strength of the orchestra, brings the masterly and effective work to a brilliant conclusion. The two overtures, bearing to each other a relation analogous to that which exists between the first and second symphonies, furnish another instance of the composer's occasional habit of writing at once, or in quick succession, two works of the same form animated by contrasted subjective qualities. The "Academic" has become very familiar to concert-goers, and has, so far, attained to more universal popularity than the impressive "Tragic."

Both works were performed from the manuscript, under the composer's direction, at the Leipzig Gewandhaus concert of January 13, but alike failed to make much impression. If, however, Brahms felt any disappointment at the persevering coldness evinced towards his art in the musical metropolis of North Germany, he must have derived some consolation from the success which attended the performances of the overtures and other works conducted by him in Münster on January 22 and in Crefeld on the 25th, and by the warm welcome which awaited him in each of the Dutch cities—Amsterdam, the Hague, Haarlem—which he visited in the course of the same month. Holland, distinguished musically by its early appreciation of Schumann's art, was now repeating history by its enthusiastic acceptance of that of Brahms. In each town where he appeared he had opportunity to perceive how deeply his music had taken root in the country. Of his many distinguished Dutch friends may be mentioned the composer Verhulst, a man of eminent parts and attractive personality, who had enjoyed the friendship of Mendelssohn and of Schumann. No more whole-hearted sympathy was ever accorded to Brahms and his works than that cherished by this musician of an earlier artistic generation. For the continuity of Dutch sentiment in regard to the master's art, pledge was given this year by the appointment of Julius Röntgen of Leipzig, to an important conductor's post in Amsterdam. Brahms did not this winter fulfil any public engagement at Utrecht, but he stayed there for a day or two as the Engelmanns' guest, and did his share of music-making in private. To one old habit he steadfastly adhered during the visit, though it had little to do with art. Every morning on returning from his early walk he made his way to the nursery, and after a game of romps carried one child or another on his shoulder down to breakfast. To say the truth, this was not an unmixed pleasure to the little ones, who were sometimes frightened at their elevation, for the master's gait was not of the smoothest. His persevering sociability, however, was generally rewarded in the end by the confidence of the little ones in which he felt such satisfaction.

It is interesting to find Liszt and Brahms crossing each other's paths again in the month of February, after a long interval of years that had been big with consequence, and not only to the younger musician; since the triumph of Wagner's art must for ever be associated with the name of its first generous protagonist. The two men were brought together by the occasion of a concert given in Budapest by Hans von Bülow, who, on arriving at the Hôtel Ungaria, found Brahms staying there, probably by preconcerted arrangement.

"Très cher unique," writes Liszt to Bülow on February 13; "I have taken a slight cold, and in order not to spoil the day and evening of to-morrow, must retire early to-night.

"Pray express my affectionate thanks to Brahms, and convey to him the invitation of Madame La Baronne Eötoos to luncheon to-morrow at 1 o'clock without ennui or vexation. Quite the contrary. I shall arrive at the Hôtel Ungaria at a quarter before one in order to conduct you to Her Excellency's house."

It no doubt afforded genuine satisfaction to the warm-hearted von Bülow to place his two friends on a passing footing of sociability. He had already begun, in his new position as musical intendant to the Duke of Saxe-Meiningen, to which he had been appointed in the autumn of 1880, to use the increased influence at his command in the interests of our master's art, and before the close of this his first season of activity in the Thuringian capital, Brahms' first and second symphonies and other works had been performed under Bülow's direction before a highly sympathetic audience at the concerts of the court orchestra.

The two overtures, and "Nänie," to which we have yet to refer in detail, were published in the course of 1881.*

---

* See p. 357 of this volume.

CHAPTER XX.

1881-1885.

Second Pianoforte Concerto—First visit to the ducal castle of Meiningen—" Nänie "—Frau Henriette Feuerbach—Hans von Bülow in Leipzig—Brahms' friends in Vienna—Dr. and Frau Fellinger—Pianoforte Trio in C major—First String Quintet—The " Parzenlied "—Third Symphony.

A HOLIDAY taken with Billroth in Sicily in the early spring was succeeded by Brahms' removal to summer quarters, chosen this year at Pressbaum, near Vienna. Here he was occupied with the composition of Schiller's "Nänie," to which Feuerbach's death had moved him, and of a second concerto for pianoforte and orchestra in B flat. The manuscripts of "Nänie" and of portions of the concerto were soon lent to Billroth, the concerto movement being handed to him with the words: "A few little pianoforte pieces."

"It is always a delight to me," writes Billroth, "when Brahms, after paying me a short visit, during which we have talked of indifferent things, takes a roll out of his paletôt pocket and says casually: 'Look at that and write me what you think of it.'"

The composer was pleasantly disturbed in August from his quietly busy life by a visit from Widmann, who was staying in Vienna, and who thus describes his meeting with the friend he had not met for three years:

"Walking through the garden, I came upon the master sitting reading at an open window on the ground floor of his idyllic dwelling, and at once instinctively felt that he had entered upon a period of his career when there could be no longer any thought of his commencing upon an entirely new domain of his art [opera]. It may sound absurd when I confess that the splendid, already slightly grizzled beard in which I saw him for the first time, and scarcely recognised him, seemed to me a symbol of the great composer's present personality, now entirely self-adequate and perfectly defined and assured within its own limits. I was so completely dumbfoundered, however, by the surprise of seeing this Jupiter head that a question burst from me as to the reason of the alteration. 'One is taken for an actor or a priest if one is clean shaven,' answered Brahms, complacently stroking the flowing beard. He now had a naïve satisfaction in his own appearance, and smilingly mentioned that his photograph with beard had been used in the Velhagen and Clasing school book edition to illustrate the Caucasian type. . . . The opera project was not mentioned. . . ."*

Brahms accepted numerous invitations from Germany, Switzerland and Holland to take part in performances of his new works, and an opportune offer from Bülow enabled him to try the effect of the lately completed concerto privately with the assistance of the Meiningen orchestra in October. He had for some time relaxed his early caution, and was now generally ready to introduce his compositions to the public on their completion, though adhering to his old custom of retaining possession of the manuscript of an important work for his own benefit until after its first performances, when he allowed the business of engraving to proceed without delay.

The new Pianoforte Concerto was played by the composer in Budapest on November 9 (first time); Stuttgart on November 22; Meiningen on the 27th; Zürich, Breslau, Vienna (Philharmonic), respectively December 6, 20, 26; Leipzig, Hamburg (Philharmonic), Berlin (Meiningen

---

* Widmann, p. 43.

orchestra), Kiel, Bremen, Hamburg (Meiningen orchestra), Münster, Utrecht, in January, and Frankfurt in February, 1882. The work was received with immense enthusiasm throughout the tour, excepting at Leipzig, where it achieved only a *succès d'estime.*

During his visit to Meiningen, Brahms was the guest of the reigning Duke George and his consort, the Baroness von Heldburg. Three fine rooms *en suite* on the ground floor of the castle were placed at his disposal, and in the most spacious of them, arranged as a music room, one of the Duke's fine Bechstein pianofortes had been placed. The apartment, having direct access to the castle grounds, afforded the composer easy opportunity to indulge in his favourite recreation of walking.

Bülow had left nothing undone that could contribute éclat to his friend's first public appearance in Meiningen, which he heralded a few days beforehand by giving a performance of the German Requiem at an extra concert of the court orchestra. A public rehearsal held on the 26th served to introduce the new works and their composer to the principal music lovers of the town, and the concert hall was completely filled on the evening of the 27th when the arrival of the Duke of Saxe-Meiningen and the Baroness von Heldburg, accompanied by Cardinal Prince Hohenlohe, gave the signal for the commencement of the performance. The Tragic Overture, the opening number of the Brahms programme, was listened to by an eagerly expectant audience, and the first glimpse of the composer as he advanced to the platform to play the solo of the new Pianoforte Concerto in B flat caused an outburst of welcome which made it impossible for him to take his seat immediately. The excitement grew with each movement and reached its climax at the end; "Brahms and Bülow transported the audience to a state of exaltation." The Haydn Variations closed the first part of the concert; the second part, consisting of the C minor Symphony and the Academic Overture, was conducted by the composer. On its termination the Duke expressed his appreciation by decorating Brahms with the cross of his family order.

The visit to Meiningen marked the beginning of a cordial friendship between the art-loving prince and his consort on one hand and Brahms on the other, which brought many pleasant hours to the great musician. He always stayed at the castle when at Meiningen, where he was the centre of many private musical gatherings. Several times he was a guest at the castle of Altenstein, the Duke's country residence. Here, as at Meiningen, he was allowed perfect freedom of action, could work without fear of disturbance, take solitary walks in the neighbourhood, or saunter in the grounds in company, and was even permitted to retain his very unconventional style of dress during the day. In the evening he recognised the claims of ceremonial custom, and actually seemed to take a kind of pleasure in dressing for dinner and wearing his decorations. He did not abate one jot, however, of his usual independent expression of opinion, and would defend his own point of view with characteristic bluntness and tenacity no matter who might happen to differ from him. An instance of this trait, as well as of his singular political acumen, of interest in the light of later events, occurred at the beginning of the war between China and Japan. Brahms declared his belief, which was not shared by others present, in the ultimate success of Japan, and angrily anticipated the injustice by which the selfish interference of the Western Powers would deprive her of the fruits of victory. The Duke's answer, which reminded him that European interests were involved in the question, left him gruffly unconvinced, but the incident was allowed to pass.

It was not only by his illustrious host that the composer came to be loved. He made himself a favourite with everyone in the Duke's service with whom he came in contact; his visits to Meiningen and Altenstein Castles were regarded by the entire household as a distinction and pleasure, and the harmless jokes and playful sayings in

Mürz Zuschlag, in the Styrian Alps, where Brahms completed his Fourth Symphony in the Summer of 1885.

By permission of Mr. E. Howard-Jones.

which he continued to find a childlike satisfaction to the end of his life are remembered by these friends with affection and regret.

The concert at Zürich on December 6, the programme of which included the first performance of "Nänie," made an extraordinary impression, and was so brilliantly successful financially that, in the words of Steiner,

"the committee could not rest satisfied without giving visible and lasting expression to their feelings of gratitude and veneration towards the author of such glorious achievements."

It took the form of a silver cup, designed for the occasion by Bosshard of Lucerne, and was forwarded to the master on its completion. Brahms wrote his thanks to Hegar in the following words:

"MOST ESTEEMED FRIEND,

"Your goblet has arrived, and the étui containing the musical silver angels glitters like an open altar shrine upon the piano. You cannot think how beautiful and kind it stands there, and with what pleasure I look at it!

"But now, please, use your best words to assure your esteemed fellow members of the great pleasure they have given me and how grateful I am for their kindness. You can easily supply details which I am shy of adding and which, if written, might sound trivial and vain. You, however, are aware that such a friendly token of appreciation and sympathy is a very serious matter. . . .

"Now, with hearty greeting to you and yours,

 "Yours most sincerely,
  "J. BRAHMS."*

In his setting of "Nänie," dedicated to Frau Henriette Feuerbach and performed from the manuscript at this concert, Brahms has conceived the calm fatalistic spirit of classical antiquity represented in Schiller's funeral dirge as perfectly as he has embodied in the music of the German

---

* Steiner's "Johannes Brahms," I, p. 25.

Requiem the passionate intensity of the writers of the Old and New Testaments. A current of tender pathos glides evenly through the lament, which is somewhat strengthened during the passing image of Aphrodite bewailing the loss of her son, but not sufficiently to disturb the smooth onward flow of the passages proceeding continuously from beginning to end of the work. It seems to suggest the ancient Greek idea of death as the final decree of destiny, hardly to be dreaded, not to be questioned or resisted, immutable even in the presence of beauty, just as clearly as the powerful contrasts of the Requiem present the biblical conception of death as an enemy to be opposed and finally destroyed in the victory of an all-conquering love.

Dr. Carl Neumann describes a visit paid by him to Frau Feuerbach when she was seventy-five years of age, at her house in Ansbach. He went through two rooms.

"In the first was a grand piano on which lay Brahms' 'Nänie'; in the second, one might say, dwelt the departed. Tall green plants stood in the window recesses obscuring the light. What the mother had of her son's works hung on the walls. The coloured sketch of a 'Descent of the Cross,' a flower study belonging to the time when the frame of 'Plato's Feast' was painted, a drawing of the standing Iphigenia looking towards the land of Greece—here was her altar. . . .

"We left this room. She sat down to the piano, at first as if to rest; then asked if I knew Brahms' 'Nänie,' which, as an admirer of her son's art, he had dedicated to her. She gave me the music to follow and began to play it by heart. . . .

"Suddenly I looked up. . . . The woman at the piano in the black dress, a black veil on her white hair, seemed changed. The tall figure, bent forward and lost in tones and memories; was it not the tragic muse herself and was she not sounding a song of fate?

"In the spring of 1886 she once again met Brahms and heard 'Nänie' under Joachim."[*]

---

[*] Allgeyer's "Feuerbach": introduction to the second edition.

SECOND PIANOFORTE CONCERTO.

The want of appreciation of the new concerto shown by the audience of the Leipzig Gewandhaus did not escape the notice of Hans von Bülow in his capacity as Brahms' champion, and he carried his band to Leipzig in the middle of March to give a series of three concerts, two of them respectively devoted to Beethoven and Brahms, and the other divided between Mendelssohn and Schumann. The Brahms programme included the C minor Symphony, Haydn Variations and the D minor Concerto played by Bülow, the orchestra accompanying without a conductor. The applause which followed the movements of the symphony as the work proceeded was not hearty enough to satisfy the excitable capellmeister, who at the end of the third movement desired his orchestra to repeat it, and on the conclusion of the work turned round and addressed his audience. He had, he said, arranged the Brahms programme by express command of his Duke, who had desired that the Leipzig public should know how the symphony ought to be performed; and also to obtain satisfaction for the coldness manifested towards the composer on his appearance with the new concerto at the Gewandhaus on January 1. It need hardly be said that eccentric efforts such as this on the part of a musician for many years conspicuously identified with the New-German school could have no result one way or the other in directing the artistic leanings of the city.

Brahms' Pianoforte Concerto in B flat is of quite unusual dimensions, and differs not only from his first in D minor, but from almost every other preceding work of its kind, in containing four movements, the additional one of which, a long "allegro appassionato," succeeds immediately to the first allegro. Probably few hearers of the work would subscribe to the reason for this innovation given by the composer to his friend Billroth.

"When I asked him about it, he said that the opening movement appeared to him too simple; he required something strongly passionate before the equally simple andante."

If anything of the usual meaning of the word "simple" is to be attached to its use here—i.e., something without complication and easy of comprehension—it must be said that the second movement of the concerto, in spite of its passionate character, is very much simpler than the first. Its plan, whilst containing points of originality, is perfectly symmetrical, and stands out in well-balanced proportions clearly evident to the imagination.

The first movement, on the other hand, is extraordinarily difficult to grasp as a whole, partly on account of its great length, but still more from the ambiguity of the rôle assigned to the solo instrument on its entry after the first orchestral "tutti." The principle to be traced in the first movements of the concertos of Mozart and Beethoven, by giving to the solo, on each entry, something of the character of a brilliant improvisation, supported by the band, on the material of a preceding "tutti," insures for it a clearly defined position, and whilst preserving a due balance between the orchestra and the solo instrument, lends contrast to the movement as a whole. Brahms would almost seem, in the instance under consideration, to have deliberately degraded the pianoforte from its legitimate position as dominant factor in its own domain. True, it enters with eight bars' quasi-improvisatory restatement of the principal theme, but it sinks immediately afterwards to occupy the subordinate rôle of the answering voice in a kind of antiphonal duet with the orchestra, which it imitates almost servilely, fragment by fragment, during a lengthy succession of bars. This method of treatment robs the solo, not only of its effect, but almost of its very *raison d'être*, and, by blurring the outline of the movement, is probably chiefly answerable for the sense of fatigue, to which even Billroth confessed, that most people feel after listening to a performance of the entire work. This is not the place for a detailed discussion of the movement, which, with all its grandeur, scarcely realises the great expectations warranted by its magnificent opening. A comparison of it with the first movement of Beethoven's Pianoforte Concerto in E flat will make the foregoing remarks clear, the more so as the ground plan is much the same in the two compositions. The third and fourth movements of Brahms' concerto are as easy to follow as the second. The andante is fervent and melodious, and the finale offers to the ear a dainty feast of sound sparkling from beginning to end with graceful vivacity.

This concerto has, like its predecessor, sometimes been described as a symphony with pianoforte obligato. The comparison is in each case misleading. Both works are essentially based on the modern concerto form as established by Mozart.

The Concerto in B flat, published in 1882, was dedicated by Brahms to "his dear friend and teacher Edward Marxsen." It was performed for the first time in England by Oscar Beringer at the Crystal Palace concert of October 14, 1882. The present author played it in London December 13, 1888, at her matinée at Messrs. Broadwood's, and on February 14, 1891, at her private concert at the Royal Academy of Music, kindly accompanied in the composer's arrangement of the orchestral part for two pianofortes, on the first occasion by Mr. Otto Goldschmidt and Mr. Stephen Kemp, and on the second by Messrs. Stephen Kemp and Septimus Webbe. Frederic Lamond introduced it to the audience of the Philharmonic Society, St. James's Hall, on May 14, 1891. Subsequently the concerto was frequently played in Great Britain by Leonard Borwick. Fräulein Marie Baumeyer of Vienna was the first lady to perform the immensely difficult work. She played it in Graz in 1883, and later, in the composer's presence, at one of her concerts in Vienna.

The other publications of 1882 were a book of Romances and Songs for one or for two voices, and two books of

Songs for one voice. The two Overtures and "Nänie" were issued in 1881.

Brahms paid a fortnight's visit to Hamburg in the spring of 1882, to the joy of his friends there. He had accepted an invitation to conduct his Requiem at the annual Good Friday concert of sacred music at the Stadt Theater, and arrived in time to direct the last rehearsals. The choir of two hundred consisted of the members of the Bach Society and opera chorus combined. The performance, which took place on April 7, partook of the character of a solemn memorial service, and the audience properly abstained from applause, though the sixth number created an impression that would make itself audible. At the close of the concert the composer received a vote of cordial thanks tendered in the name of all present.

The master stayed, for the second time, at Ischl during the summer months. Billroth, who was in the neighbourhood, writes of him in August:

"I should like to enjoy myself in Italy from September 15 till October 1. Brahms wishes to accompany me. . . . He has been very busy lately. Three books of songs have been published. A string quintet and a trio are ready, both of them simpler, shorter, brighter than his earlier things; he strives consciously for shortness and simplicity. He lately sent me the manuscript of a true work of art, the 'Parzenlied' [Song of the Fates] from Goethe's 'Iphigenia.' Very deep but simple."

The journey to Italy duly took place, the proposed party of two being enlarged to one of four by the addition of Ignaz Brüll and Simrock. Original plans had to be modified on account of the exceptionally wet season, and the chief places visited were Vicenza, Padua and Venice.

The personnel of Brahms' intimate friends in Vienna had remained on the whole much what it had become a very few years after his arrival in the Austrian capital. Of its closest circle the Fabers, Billroths and Hanslicks, with whom must be associated Joachim's cousins, the various members of the Wittgenstein family—amongst them Frau

Franz and Frau Dr. Oser—still formed the nucleus. An acquaintance with Herr Victor von Miller zu Aichholz and his wife had meanwhile ripened into warm friendship, and their house became one of those whose hospitality was most frequently and gladly accepted by the master. Amongst the musicians, Carl Ferdinand Pohl, biographer of Haydn, and, since 1866, archivar to the Gesellschaft, was one of his dearest friends. With the leading professors of the conservatoire his relations continued very cordial, and amongst the younger musicians to whom, in addition to his early allies, Goldmark, Gänsbacher and Epstein, he extended his friendly regard, may be mentioned Anton Door and Robert Fuchs. The feeling of warm friendship existing between Brahms and Johann Strauss has been commemorated in several well known anecdotes. The autumn of 1881, however, brought to permanent residence in Vienna a family that before long made notable addition to the master's intimate circle. Special circumstances conduced to the speedy formation of a bond of friendship between Brahms and the newcomers, Dr. and Frau Fellinger. In the first place, they were friends of Frau Schumann and her daughters, and as such had an instant claim on his courtesy, which he acknowledged by calling on them as soon as possible after their arrival. In the second, his interest was awakened by the fact that Frau Dr. Fellinger was the daughter of Frau Professor Lang-Köstlin, the gifted Josephine Lang, whose attractive personality and talent for composition made a strong impression upon Mendelssohn when he was a youth of twenty-one and some six years the lady's senior. The story of Josephine, who at the age of twenty-six married Professor Köstlin of Tübingen, is given in Hiller's "Tonleben," and Mendelssohn's congratulations to her bridegroom-elect may be read in the second volume of the "Letters." The talent for art which had come to her as a family inheritance was transmitted to her daughter, though with a difference. Frau Dr. Fellinger's gifts have associated themselves especially with the plastic arts; in the first place with that of painting, but they have become well known in the musical world also by her busts and statuettes of Brahms, Billroth, and others belonging to their circle. Her photographs of our master are familiar to most music lovers. When it is added that Brahms found he could command in Dr. Fellinger's hospitable house, not only congenial intellectual sympathy, but the unceremonious intercourse with a simple, affectionate family circle in which he had through life found a pre-eminent source of happiness, it will easily be understood that he became a more and more frequent guest there, until during the closing years of his life, it became for him almost a second home.

Two of the master's new works, the Pianoforte Trio in C major, partly composed in the summer of 1881, and the String Quintet in F major, each movement of which is dated "Im Frühling 1882," were played in October at Billroth's house in Vienna before a small circle of friends by Brahms and the Hellmesberger party. These compositions and a new choral work, the "Parzenlied," which together constitute the catalogued publications of 1883, were introduced to the musical world in the course of a few weeks' journey undertaken by the master in the winter of 1882-3. An interesting entry in Frau Schumann's diary says:

"I had invited Koning and Müller to come and try Brahms' new trio with me on Thursday 21st [December]. Who should surprise us as we were playing it—he himself! He came from Strassburg and means to stay with us for Christmas. I played the trio first and he repeated it."

Both works were performed on December 29 at a Museum chamber music concert—the Quintet by the Heermann-Müller party, the Trio by Brahms, Heermann and Müller.

Amongst the early performances of the trio were those on January 17 and 22 respectively in Berlin (Trio Concerts: Barth, de Ahna, Hausmann) and London (Monday Popular Concerts: Hallé, Madame Néruda, Piatti), and at Hellmesberger's in Vienna on March 15.

The trio has not even yet become one of the most generally familiar of the master's compositions, but it is, as the author believes, ultimately destined to a long life among the favourite works of his late period. It contains no trace of the "heaven-storming Johannes," but it breathes, and especially the first movement, with a rich, mellow warmth suggestive of one to whom the experiences of life have brought a solution of their own to its problems which has quieted, if it has not altogether satisfied, the aspirations of youth. The theme of the second movement is probably founded on volkslied, and of its five variations, four are delicately plaintive and tender. The third movement contains one of the few genuine scherzi composed by Brahms, the demoniac tone of which is relieved by the ardent, melodious outburst of its trio. The finale is brimful of fun.

The Quintet in F for strings is, for the most part, bright, concise, and easy to follow. As one of its special features may be mentioned the combination of the usual two middle movements in the second. It was given in Hamburg on the 22nd and in Berlin on the 23rd of January, respectively by Bargheer and Joachim and their colleagues (it should be noted that Hausmann had at this time succeeded Müller as the violoncellist of the Joachim Quartet), at Hellmesberger's on February 15, and at the Monday Popular, London, of March 5.

Brahms conducted the first performance of the Parzenlied in Basle on December 8, 1882. Excellently sung by the members of the Basle Choral Society, the work met with extraordinary success, and was repeated after the New Year by general desire. Similar results followed its performance in other towns, of which Strassburg and Crefeld should be specially mentioned. The programme of the Crefeld concert included the fifth movement of the Requiem. "'What is your *tempo?*" Brahms inquired, on the morning of the rehearsal, of Fräulein Antonia Kufferath, who was to sing the solo. The lady, not taking the question seriously from the composer of the music, waived a reply. "No, I mean it; you have to hold out the long notes. Well, we shall understand each other," he added; "sing only as you feel, and I will follow with the chorus."

These are characteristic words, and valuable in more than one sense. The metronome indications attached to the several movements of the Requiem, were added with Brahms' permission, by Reinthaler; and neither to them, nor to those to be found in Rinaldo and Nänie, did the master attach more than a very limited importance. An absolutely and uniformly "correct" pace for a piece of genuine music does not exist. The pace must vary to some extent according to subtle conditions existent in the performer, and the instinct of a really musical executant or conductor will, as a rule, be a safer guide, within limits, than what can be at best but the mechanical markings even of the composer himself.

The Parzenlied, received with enthusiasm throughout Brahms' tour in Germany and Switzerland, was not equally successful in Vienna, where it was heard for the first time at the Gesellschaft concert of February 18 under Gericke. The austere simplicity of the music, which paces majestically onward with the concentrated, resigned calm of despair, adds extraordinary force to Goethe's poem, but does not appeal to every audience, and the work has never become a prime favourite in the Austrian Kaiserstadt. The song is set for six-part chorus with orchestra, in plainer harmonic masses and with less employment of imitative counterpoint than we usually find in the works of Brahms, who has accommodated his music here, as in "Nänie," to the classical spirit of the text. A singular deviation, however, which occurs in the course of the setting, from the uncompromising severity of the words, furnishes a remarkable illustration of the composer's unconquerable idealism. Comment was made in its place on the beautiful device by which he has sought to relieve the dark mood of Hölderlin's "Song of Destiny"—the addition of an instrumental postlude which breathes forth a message of tender consolation that the poet could hardly have rendered in words. In Schiller's "Nänie" the lament, with all its calm, gives expression to a sentiment of compassionate sorrow that is perfectly reproduced in the master's music. Goethe's Fates, however, in the measured recitation of the gods' relentless cruelty, which the poet supposes them to have chanted on the fall of Tantalus, would have seemed to offer no possible opportunity for even the inarticulate expression of truth. Least of all, it might be imagined, could any concession to the demands of the human heart have been found in the penultimate stanza of their song:

> "The rulers exclude from
> Their favouring glances
> Entire generations,
> And heed not in children
> The once so belovèd
> And still speaking features
> Of distant forefathers."

Our Brahms, however, who, in spite of his increasing weight, his shaggy beard, his frequently rough manners, his unsatisfied affections, his impenetrable reserve, remained at fifty, in his heart of hearts, the very same being whom we have watched as the loving child of seven, the simple-minded boy of fourteen, the broken-hearted man of thirty, sobbing by the death bed of his mother, cannot leave the dread gloom of his subject unrelieved by a single ray. He seems, in his setting of the last strophe but one, to concentrate attention on past kindness of the gods, and thus, perhaps, subtly to suggest a plea for present hope. How far the musician was justified in thus wandering from the obvious intention of his poet must be left to each hearer of the work to determine for himself. If it be the case, as has sometimes been suggested, that the variation was made by the composer in the musical interests of the piece as a work of art, it cannot be held to have fulfilled its purpose; for the striking inconsistency between words and music in the verse in question has a disturbing effect on the mind of the listener. We believe, however, that the true explanation of the master's procedure is more radical, and is to be found in the nature of the man in which that of the musician was grounded.

The Parzenlied was dedicated to "His Highness George, Duke of Saxe-Meiningen," and was included in a Brahms programme performed in Meiningen on April 2 to celebrate the duke's birthday. The complete breakdown of Bülow's health necessitated his temporary retirement from his conductor's duties, which were divided on this occasion between Brahms and Court Capellmeister Franz Mannstädt, appointed to assist Bülow. Returning by a circuitous route to Vienna after a few days at the ducal castle, Brahms paid a short visit to Hamburg to take part in another Brahms programme arranged by the talented young conductor of the Cecilia Society, Julius Spengel. This was the first of several occasions on which the master gave testimony of his appreciation of Dr. Spengel's talents and musicianship by co-operating in the concerts of the society.

Brahms celebrated his fiftieth birthday by entertaining his friends Faber, Billroth and Hanslick at a bachelor supper, and left Vienna two days later to play his B flat Pianoforte Concerto, and conduct his second symphony at the Rhine Festival held this season in Cologne during the second week of May. He was occupied during the summer with the completion of a third symphony, on which he had worked the preceding year, and lived at Wiesbaden in a dwelling that had belonged to the celebrated painter Ludwig Knaus, in whose former studio—Brahms' music room for the nonce—the work was finished. The occasion of a musikfest held at Coblenz in July gave him welcome opportunity of meeting many of his friends.

It was known to the composer that a delicate elderly lady inhabited the first floor of the house, 19 Gersberger Str., of which Frau von Dewitz's flat, where he lodged, formed an upper story. Every night, therefore, on returning to his rooms, he took off his boots before going upstairs, and made the ascent in his socks, so that her rest should not be disturbed. This anecdote is but one amongst several of the same kind that have been related to the author by Brahms' intimate associates. Samples of another variety should not, however, be omitted.

A private performance of the new symphony, this time arranged for two pianofortes, was given as usual at Ehrbar's by Brahms and Brüll, and aroused immense expectations for the future of the work. Amongst the listeners was a musician who, not having hitherto allowed himself to be suspected of a partiality for the master's art, expressed his enthusiastic admiration of the composition. "Have you had any conversation with X?" young Mr. Ehrbar asked Brahms; "he has been telling me how delighted he is with the symphony." "And have you told him that he very often lies when he opens his mouth?" angrily retorted the composer, who could never bring himself to submit to the humiliation of accepting a compliment which he suspected—perhaps unjustly in this case—of being insincere.

A terrible rebuff was administered by him on the evening of a first Gewandhaus performance. It must be owned that Brahms was seldom in his happiest mood when on a visit to Leipzig; he was well aware that his music was not appreciated within the official "ring" there, and suspiciously resented any well-meant efforts made to ignore this fact. "And where are you going to lead us tonight, Herr Doctor?" inquired one of the committee a few minutes before the beginning of the concert, assuming a conciliatory manner as he smoothed on his white kid gloves; "to heaven; or to hell?" "It is the same to me where you go," rejoined Brahms.

The first performance of the Symphony in F major (No. 3) took place in Vienna at the Philharmonic concert of December 2, under Hans Richter, who was, according to

Hanslick, originally responsible for the name "the Brahms Eroica," by which it has occasionally been called. Whether or not the suggestion is happy, a saying of the kind, probably uttered on the impulse of the moment, should not be taken very seriously.

Nothing of the quiescent autumn mood which we have observed in the master's chamber music of this period is to be traced in either of his symphonies, and the third, like its companions, represents him in the zenith of his energies, working happily in the consciousness of his absolute command over the resources of his art. Whether it be judged by its effect as an entire work or studied movement by movement, whether each movement be listened to as a whole or analysed into its component parts, all is found to be without halt of inspiration or flaw in workmanship. Each theme is striking and pregnant, and, though contrasting with what precedes it, seems to belong inevitably to the movement and place in which it occurs, whilst the development of the thematic material is so masterly that to speak of admiring it seems almost ridiculous. The last movement closes with a very beautiful and distinctive Brahms coda. The third symphony is more immediately easy to follow than the first, and of broader atmosphere than the second. It is of an essentially objective character, and belongs absolutely to the domain of pure music.

The supreme and glorious pre-eminence which the great master had by this time attained in contemporary estimation naturally made it an object of competition with concert-givers and directors to announce the earliest performances of his works, and this was especially the case in the rare event of a new symphony which succeeded its immediate predecessor after an interval of six years. Brahms, however, who had his own ideas on this matter as on every other that he thought important, had written almost immediately after completing his third symphony, to offer the second performance to Joachim for a concert in Berlin. This proceeding would hardly have been noteworthy under the circumstances of intimate friendship which, scarcely troubled by a passing shadow, had united the two musicians for twenty-seven years, if it were not that since the close of 1880 there had been a cessation of their former affectionate intercourse. To quote the words of Joachim's biographer:

"Brahms had taken the wife's part in Joachim's matrimonial differences and had expressed his views to his friend both by word of mouth (at the musical festival in Coblenz, July, 1883) and in writing in a way which had taken the deepest and most painful hold of Joachim."*

When, therefore, it became known that Joachim, acting on Brahms' wish, proposed to conduct the symphony at one of the subscription concerts of the Royal Academy of Arts, Berlin, much disappointment and heartburning were felt and expressed, and the matter was not brought to a final decision until the composer repeated in a second letter to his old friend his "urgent wish" to commit the performance to Joachim's care. These occurrences led to the renewal of an occasional interchange of letters between Brahms and Joachim on matters of musical business, though their personal intercourse was not resumed until after a further interval of several years.

The symphony was heard for the second time, therefore, on January 4 under Joachim at Berlin, and was enthusiastically received by all sections of the public and press. It was given again three times during the same month in the German imperial capital under the composer's baton.

Detailed description of the triumphant progress of the new work from town to town is no longer necessary. The composer was overwhelmed with invitations to conduct it from the manuscript, and Bülow, convalescent from his illness, and determined not to be outdone in enthusiasm, placed it twice, as second and fourth numbers, in a Meiningen programme of five works. It was given at Düsseldorf under the composer's direction at the Rhine

---

* Brahms-Joachim "Briefwechsel," edited by Andreas Moser.

Festival of the year, and was performed on publication in all the chief music loving towns of Germany, Great Britain, Holland, Russia, Switzerland and the United States.

In an account of a performance of the symphony at a Hamburg Philharmonic concert under Brahms in December, which followed one under von Bernuth after three weeks' interval, the critic of the *Correspondent* says:

"Brahms' interpretation of his works frequently differs so inconceivably in delicate rhythmic and harmonic accents from anything to which one is accustomed, that the apprehension of his intentions could only be entirely possible to another man possessed of exactly similar sound-susceptibility or inspired by the power of divination."

The author feels a peculiar interest in quoting these lines, which strikingly corroborate the impression formed by her on hearing this and other of Brahms' works played under his own direction.*

---

* Joachim, writing to Brahms after the first Berlin performance of the symphony, mentions that the second subject of the last movement irresistibly suggested to his mind a picture of Leander breasting the storm-swept waves in his efforts to swim across the Hellespont to Hero. "Did you think of it at all?" he asks. ("Briefwechsel," 426.) To the author it appears probable that the image was suggested to Joachim—who, by the way, was not prone to indulge in so-called "poetical" interpretations—not directly by Brahms' music, but by an unconscious association of the theme in question with the opening subject of Schumann's Phantasie-stück, "In der Nacht," with which it has a certain distant similarity, and in which Schumann, after completing his composition, discovered, and taught his friends to find, a musical presentment of the famous legend.

The circumstance is not without value to those who may desire to arrive at a true understanding of Brahms' musical individuality, that a good many years later our master, in the course of some remarks to a friend on the subject of programme music, referred to this suggestion of Joachim's as being illustrative of a tendency in some minds to translate the impressions of sound into mental visual images, and added, with regard to himself, that music seldom suggested any pictorial idea—any programme—to his imagination.

The publications of 1884 were, besides the third Symphony, Two Songs for Contralto with Viola and Pianoforte, the second being the "Virgin's Cradle Song," already mentioned as one of the compositions of 1865; two sets of four-part Songs, the one for accompanied solo voices, the other for mixed chorus *a capella*, and the two books of Songs, Op. 94 and 95.

At this date Brahms had entered into what we may call the third period of his activity as a song writer—one in which he frequently chose texts that speak of loneliness or death. The wonderful beauty of his settings of these subjects penetrates the very soul, and by the mere force of its pathos carries to the hearer the conviction that the composer speaks out of the feeling of his own heart. Stockhausen, trying the song "Mit vierzig Jahren" (Op. 94, No. 1) from the manuscript to the composer's accompaniment, was so affected during its performance that he could not at once proceed to the end. Our remarks are, however, by no means intended to convey the impression that Brahms only or generally chose poems of a melancholy tendency at this time.

WITH FORTY YEARS.

BY FRIEDRICH RÜCKERT (1788-1866).

With forty years we've gained the mountain's summit,
    We stand awhile and look behind;
There we behold the quiet years of childhood
    And there the joy of youth we find.
Look once again, and then, with freshened vigour,
    Take up thy staff and onward wend!
A mountain-ridge extendeth, broad, before thee,
    Not here, but there must thou descend.
No longer, climbing, need'st thou struggle breathless,
    The level path will lead thee on;
And then with thee a little downward tending,
    Before thou know'st, thy journey's done.

With the knowledge we have gained of the master's habit of producing his large works in couples, we are prepared to find him employed this summer on the composition of a fourth symphony. Refreshed by the pleasures of a fourth journey in Italy, he settled down to his work at Mürz Zuschlag in Styria, at the foot of the Semmering. Here he was visited in the course of the season by Frau Reinthaler and her daughter; his old friend Musi, now grown up into a young lady, who, staying for a special purpose in Vienna, enjoyed a day or two in lodgings which he took for them near to his own delightfully situated quarters. He went over to see them also at Vienna, and spent the greater part of a morning showing them his valuable collection of autographs and other treasures. "Yes, these would have been something to give a wife!" was his answer to the ladies' expressions of delight. Amongst his collection of musical autographs were two written on different sides of the same sheet of paper—one of Beethoven, the song "Ich liebe dich"; the other of Schubert, part of a pianoforte composition. These, with Brahms' autograph signature "Joh. Brahms in April 1872," written at the bottom of one of the pages, constitute a unique triplet. The sheet now belongs to the Gesellschaft library, and is framed within glass.

The society of Hanslick, who came with his wife to stay near Mürz Zuschlag for part of the summer, was very acceptable to Brahms. The departure of his friends at the close of the season, in the company of some mutual Vienna acquaintances, incited the composer to an act of courtesy of a kind quite unusual with him, the sequel to which seems to have caused him almost comical annoyance that found expression in a couple of notes sent immediately afterwards to Hanslick.

"DEAREST FRIEND,

"Here I stand with roses and pansies; which means with a basket of fruit, liqueurs and cakes! You must have travelled through by the earlier Sunday extra train? I made a good and unusual impression for politeness at the station! The children are now rejoicing over the cakes...."

and, on finding that, mistaking the time of the train, he had arrived a quarter of an hour late:

"How such a stupid thing can spoil one's day and the thought of it recur to torment one. I hope you do not know this as well as I, who am for ever preparing for myself such vexatious worry. . . ."

Later on, writing about other matters, he adds:

". . . I hope Professor Schmidt's ladies do not describe my promenade with the basket too graphically in Vienna! Otherwise my unspoiled lady friends may cease to be so unassuming."*

The journeys of the winter included visits to Hamburg, Bremen and Oldenburg, in the course of which Hermine Spiess, one of the very favourite younger interpreters of Brahms' songs, sang dainty selections of them to the composer's accompaniment, with overwhelming success. The early death of this gifted artist, soon after her marriage, caused the master, with whom she was a great favourite, deep and sincere grief. Brahms went also to Crefeld, where the "Tafellied," dedicated on publication "To the friends in Crefeld in remembrance of Jan. 28th 1885," was sung on the date in question, with some of the new part-songs *a capella*, and other of the composer's works, at the jubilee of the Crefeld Concert Society. The manuscript score of the "Tafellied" is in the possession of Herr Alwin von Beckerath, to whom it was presented by Brahms with an affectionate inscription.

---

* Published by Hanslick in the *Neue Freie Presse*, July 1, 1897.

CHAPTER XXI.

1885-1888.

Vienna Tonkünstlerverein—Fourth Symphony—Hugo Wolf—Brahms at Thun—Three new works of chamber music—First performances of the second Violoncello Sonata by Brahms and Hausmann—Frau Celestine Truxa—Double Concerto—Marxsen's death—Eugen d'Albert—The Gipsy Songs—Conrat's translations from the Hungarian—Brahms and Jenner—The "Zum Rothen Igel"—Ehrbar's asparagus luncheons—Third Sonata for Pianoforte and Violin.

THE early part of the year 1885 offers for record no event of unusual interest to the reader. The greater portion of it was spent by Brahms in his customary routine in Vienna. He was generally to be seen at the weekly meetings of the Tonkünstlerverein, a musicians' club founded by Epstein, Gänsbacher, and others, of which the master had consented to be named honorary life president. The Monday evening proceedings included a short musical programme, sometimes followed by an informal supper. Brahms did not usually sit in the music room, but would remain in a smaller apartment smoking and chatting sociably with friends of either sex. His arrival always became known at once to the assembled company. "Brahms is here; Brahms is come!" being passed eagerly from mouth to mouth. His old love of open air exercise had not diminished with increasing years, and the Sunday custom of a long walk in the country was still kept up. A few friends used to

FOURTH SYMPHONY.

meet in the morning outside the Café Bauer, opposite the Opera House, and, taking train or tram to the outskirts of the city, would thence proceed on foot, returning in the late afternoon. Brahms, nearly always in a good humour on these occasions, was generally soon ahead of his companions, or leading the way with the foremost, and, as had usually been the case with him through life, was looked upon by his friends as the chief occasion of their meetings, allowed his own way, and admired as a kind of pet oracle. The excursions always commenced for the season on his return to Vienna in the autumn, and were continued with considerable regularity until his departure in the spring. They not infrequently gave opportunity for the employment of the composer's unfailing readiness of repartee, as on the occasion of a meeting in the train, on the return journey, with a learned but unmusical acquaintance of one of the party, between whom and Brahms an animated conversation arose. "Will you not join us one day, Herr Doctor? Next Sunday, perhaps?" asked Brahms. "I!" exclaimed the other. "Saul among the prophets?" "Na, so you give yourself royal airs!" instantly rejoined the master.

The fourth symphony was completed during the summer at Mürz Zuschlag, where Brahms this year had the advantage of Dr. and Frau Fellinger's society, and—indispensable for his complete enjoyment of a home circle—that of their children. Returning one afternoon from a walk, he found that the house in which he lodged had caught fire, and that his friends were busily engaged in bringing his papers, and amongst them the nearly finished manuscript of the new symphony, into the garden. He immediately set to work to help in getting the fire under, whilst Frau Fellinger sat out of doors with either arm outspread on the precious papers piled on each side of her. Luckily, all serious harm was averted, and it was soon possible to restore the manuscripts intact to the composer's apartments.

Brahms paid a neighbourly call, in the course of the summer, on the author Rosegger, who was living in his small country house at Krieglach near Mürz Zuschlag, and tasted the unusual experience of a repulse. Absorbed in work at the moment when his servant announced "a strange gentleman," Rosegger, without glancing at the card placed beside him, desired his visitor to "sit down for a moment." Conscious only of the presence of a bearded stranger with a gray overcoat over his shoulder and a light coloured umbrella in his hand, he vouchsafed but scant answer to the trifling remarks with which his caller tried to pave the way to cordiality, and before long Brahms composedly remarked that he would be on his legs again, and took leave. It was not till some minutes after his departure that it occurred to Rosegger to glance at the card, and he has himself described the feelings of despair with which he read the words "Johannes Brahms" staring at him in all the reality of black on white. Not he alone, but the ladies of his family, were enthusiastic admirers of the composer's genius. He was so overwhelmed by his mistake as to be incapable of taking any steps to remedy it, and firmly declined to yield to the entreaties of his wife and daughter that he would return the visit and explain matters to Brahms. He published an amusing account of the misadventure in the year 1894 in an issue of the *Heimgarten*. Perhaps it may have fallen into the master's hands.

Several references to the Symphony in E minor which occur in letters written by Brahms when it was approaching completion, in the summer of 1885, show him to have been fully aware that to offer so intricate and uncompromisingly serious a work for the acceptance of any general body of listeners would be to make very unusual demands on their intelligence and sympathy; and his evident misgivings as to the future of the great composition cannot but have been strengthened by the unmistakable disappointment of the Vienna friends who, according to established precedent, were invited to Ehrbar's house early in October to hear it played, as arranged for two pianofortes by Brahms and Brüll. It could not be pretended on the occasion of this

FOURTH SYMPHONY.

first private trial that the work as a whole had kindled the enthusiasm, or even reached the understanding, of those who had assembled to welcome it, and it is probable that a second experience equally discouraging might have determined the composer, even at the last moment, to withhold the symphony for an indefinite time from a public hearing. It happened, however, that the honour of the first performance had been secured by Bülow for Meiningen where Brahms was not only assured of the sympathetic co-operation of orchestra and capellmeister, but was able to make his own arrangements with regard to rehearsals. Sending the score and parts of the third and fourth movements to Bülow for preliminary rehearsal and correction, he proceeded to Meiningen on October 11, taking with him the first and second movements and devoted the next fortnight to the business of drilling the instrumentalists into a thorough understanding of the new work. Bülow, as a matter of course, gave active help and sustained enthusiasm to the cause, and the first rehearsal was attended by three sympathetic listeners; the Landgraf of Hesse; Richard Strauss, the now famous composer; and the pianist, Frederic Lamond. Under these favourable circumstances it came to pass that Brahms had satisfied himself, before the last rehearsal, that his work would not entirely fail of its effect, and if he did not succeed in entirely shaking off his nervousness, was able to look forward to the concert day without overwhelming anxiety. He was, however, far from anticipating the brilliant success that attended the first public performance of the symphony, which took place under his own direction at the Meiningen subscription concert of October 25, 1885. The first and second movements were received with prolonged applause; determined, though unsuccessful efforts were made by the audience to obtain a repetition of the third movement; and the close of the work was followed by the emphatic demonstration incident to a great triumph.

This initial good fortune determined the immediate future

of the symphony which was repeated, under Bülow's direction, at the Meiningen concert of November 1, and was conducted by the composer throughout a three weeks' tour on which he started with Bülow and his orchestra immediately afterwards, included the towns of Frankfurt (November 3), Siegen, Dortmund, Essen, Elberfeld, Düsseldorf, Rotterdam, Utrecht, Amsterdam, The Hague, Arnheim, Crefeld and Bonn. A performance at Wiesbaden followed, and the work was heard in Vienna at the Philharmonic concert of January 17, 1886, under Richter; in Berlin at the Academy of Arts concert on February 1 under Joachim, and in Cologne at the Gürzenich concert of February 9 again under Brahms. The Vienna performance was celebrated by a dinner given by Billroth at the Hôtel Sacher, the guests invited to meet the composer being Richter, Goldmark, Hanslick, Faber, Door, Epstein, Ehrbar, Fuchs, Kalbeck and Dömpke. A new and important work by Brahms could hardly fail to obtain a warm reception in Vienna at a period when the composer could look back to thirty years' residence in the imperial city with which his name had become as closely associated as those of Haydn, Mozart, Beethoven and Schubert; but though the symphony was applauded by the public and praised by all but the inveterately hostile section of the press, it did not reach the hearts of the Vienna audience in the same unmistakable manner as its two immediate predecessors, both of which had, as we have seen, made a more striking impression on a first hearing in Austria than the first Symphony in C minor. Strangely enough, the fourth symphony at once obtained some measure of real appreciation in Leipzig, where the first had been far more successful than the second and third. It was performed under the composer at the Gewandhaus concert of February 18. The account given of the occasion by the *Leipziger Nachrichten* is, perhaps, the more satisfactory since our old friend Dörffel, who might possibly have been suspected of partiality, had long since retired from the staff of the journal. Bernhard Vögl, his second successor says:

". . . The reception must, we think, have made amends to Brahms for former ones, which, in Bülow's opinion, were too cool. After each movement the hall resounded with tumultuous and long-continued applause, and, at the conclusion of the work, the composer was repeatedly called forward. . . . The finale is certainly the most original of the movements, and furnishes more complete argument than has before been brought forward for the opinion of those who see in Brahms the modern Sebastian Bach. The movement is not only constructed on the form displayed in Bach's Chaconne for violin, but is filled with Bach's spirit. It is built up with astounding mastery upon the eight notes:

and in such a manner that its contrapuntal learning remains subordinate to its poetic contents. . . . It can be compared with no former work of Brahms and stands alone in the symphonic literature of the present and the past."

A still more triumphant issue attended the production of the symphony under Brahms at a concert of the Hamburg Cecilia Society on April 9. Josef Sittard, who had recently been appointed musical critic to the *Hamburger Correspondent*, wrote:

"To-day we abide by what we have affirmed for years past in musical journals; that Brahms is the greatest instrumental composer since Beethoven. Power, passion, depth of thought, exalted nobility of melody and form, are the qualities which form the artistic sign manual of his creations. The E minor (fourth) Symphony is distinguished from the second and third principally by the rigorous and even grim earnestness which, though in a totally different way, mark the first. More than ever does the composer follow out his ideas to their conclusion, and this unbending logic makes the immediate understanding of the work difficult. But the oftener we have heard it, the more clearly have its great beauties, the depth, energy and power of its thoughts, the clearness of its classic form, revealed themselves to us. In the contrapuntal treatment of its themes, in richness of harmony and in the art of instrumentation, it seems to us superior to the second and third, these, perhaps, have the advantage of greater melodic beauty; a guarantee of popularity. In depth, power and originality of conception, however, the fourth symphony takes its place by the side of the first. . . ."

After an interesting discussion of the several movements, the writer adds: "In a word, the symphony is of monumental significance."

Brahms' fourth symphony, produced when he was over fifty, is, in the opinion of most musicians, unsurpassed by any other achievement of his genius. It has been growing slowly into general knowledge and favour, and will, it may be safely predicted, become still more deeply rooted in its place amongst the composer's most widely valued works. The second movement, in the opinion of the late Philipp Spitta, "does not find its equal in the symphonic world"; and the fourth, written in "Passacaglia" form, is the most astonishing illustration achieved even by Brahms himself of the limitless capability of variation form, in which he is pre-eminent.* The autograph score of the work which was acquired from Simrock in 1906 and presented to Capellmeister Friedrich Hegar on his retirement from professional activity, by the

---

* The scope of these pages does not permit the author to yield to the temptation of presenting an analysis of the means by which Brahms has produced the romantic, mysterious atmosphere which pervades the "andante moderato." They will be found strangely simple and intelligible by those inclined to examine for themselves the harmonic material; in the first place of the introductory bars (which consists of the chromatic major concord on the minor sixth of the key, E major, and a couple of passing notes); and in the second place of the full statement of the opening theme (which includes the chords of the dominant minor ninth and the tonic seventh and minor thirteenth, all chromatic).

principal musicians and music lovers of Zürich, shows that the master changed his mind more than once on the question of the opening of the symphony. His original intention, as exhibited in the manuscript was that with which we are familiar in the published score—to start the first movement at once with the principal subject:

At some time previous to the publication of the symphony, however, he inserted four bars of introductory chords in the small space left vacant on the paper at the end of the first movement; and wrote a memorandum at the bottom of the first page of the manuscript to intimate that these bars were to form the commencement of the work. Chords and writing were afterwards crossed out.

It is with something of a mournful feeling that we find ourselves at the close of our enumeration of the master's four greatest instrumental works. Enough, we may hope, has been said to indicate that any comparison of the symphonies as inferior or superior is impossible, for the reason that each, while perfectly fulfilling its own particular destiny, is quite different from all the others, and such natural preference as may be felt by this or that listener for either must be considered as purely personal. The present writer may, perhaps, be allowed to confess that, with all joy in the dainty second and the magnificent third and fourth—emphatically the fourth—neither appeals to her quite so strongly as the first. There is here a quality of youth in the intensity of the soaring imagination that seems to search the universe, which, presented as it is with the wealth of resource that was at the command of the mature composer, could not by its nature be other than unique. The presence of this very quality may be the reason why the first symphony suffers even more lamentably than its companions from the dull, cold, cautious, "classical" rendering which Brahms' orchestral works receive at the hands of some conductors, who seem unable to realise that a composer who founds his works on certain definite and traditional principles of structure does not thereby change his nature, or in any degree renounce the free exercise of his poetic gifts.

Perhaps the present is as good an opportunity as may occur for passing mention of a newspaper episode of the eighties, which was much talked of for a few years, but which, though it may have caused Brahms annoyance, could not possibly at this period of his career have had any more serious consequence so far as he was concerned.

Hugo Wolf, in 1884 a young aspirant to fame, seeking recognition but finding none, poor, gifted, disappointed, weak in health, highly nervous, without influential friends, accepted an opportunity of increasing his miserably small means of subsistence by becoming the musical critic of the *Salon Blatt*, a weekly society paper of Vienna, and soon made for himself an unenviable notoriety by his persistent attacks upon Brahms' compositions. The affair would not now demand mention in a biography of our master if it were not that the posthumous recognition afforded to Wolf's art gives some interest, though not of an agreeable nature, to this association of his name with that of Brahms. For the benefit of those readers who may wish to study the matter further, it may be added that Wolf's criticisms have been republished since his death. For ourselves, having done what was, perhaps, incumbent on us by referring to the matter, we shall adopt what we believe would have been Brahms' desire, by allowing it, so far as these pages are concerned, to follow others of the kind to oblivion.

The summer of 1886 was the first of the three seasons

passed by Brahms at Thun, of which Widmann has written so charming an account. He rented the entire first floor of a house opposite the spot where the river Aare flows out of the lake, the ground floor being occupied by the owner, who kept a little haberdashery shop. According to his general custom, he dined in fine weather in the garden of some inn, occasionally alone, but oftener in the company of a friend or friends. Every Saturday he went to Bern to remain till Monday or longer with the Widmanns, who, like other friends, found him a most considerate and easily satisfied guest, though his exceptional energy of body and mind often made it exhausting work to keep up with him.

"His week-end visits were," says Widmann, "high festivals and times of rejoicing for me and mine; days of rest they certainly were not, for the constantly active mind of our guest demanded similar wakefulness from all his associates and one had to pull one's self well together to maintain sufficient freshness to satisfy the requirements of his indefatigable vitality. . . . I have never seen anyone who took such fresh, genuine and lasting interest in the surroundings of life as Brahms, whether in objects of nature, art, or even industry. The smallest invention, the improvement of some article for household use, every trace, in short, of practical ingenuity gave him real pleasure. And nothing escaped his observation. . . . He hated bicycles because the flow of his ideas was so often disturbed by the noiseless rushing past, or the sudden signal, of these machines, and also because he thought the trampling movement of the rider ugly. He was, however, glad to live in the age of great inventions and could not sufficiently admire the electric light, Edison's phonographs, etc. He was equally interested in the animal world. I always had to tell him anew about the family customs of the bears in the Bern bear-pits before which we often stood together. Indeed, subjects of conversation seemed inexhaustible during his visits."*

---

* Widmann's "Johannes Brahms in Erinnerungen," p. 58 and following.

Brahms' ordinary costume, the same here as elsewhere, was chosen quite without regard to appearances. Mere lapse of time must occasionally have compelled him to wear a new coat, but it is safe to conclude that his feelings suffered discomposure on the rare occurrence of such a crisis. Neckties and white collars were reserved as special marks of deference to conventionality. During his visits to Thun he used on wet Saturdays to appear at Bern wearing "an old brown-gray plaid fastened over his chest with an immense pin, which completed his strange appearance." Many were the books borrowed from Widmann at the beginning, and brought back at the end, of the week, carried by him in a leather bag slung over his shoulder. Most of them were standard works; he was not devoted to modern literature on the whole, though he read with pleasure new and really good books of history and travel, and was fond of Gottfried Keller's novels and poems. Over engravings and photographs of Italian works of art he would pore for hours, never weary of discussing memories and predilections with his friend.

Visits to the Bern summer theatre, a short mountain tour with Widmann, an introduction to Ernst von Wildenbruch, whose dramas the master liked, and with whom he now found himself in personal sympathy—events such as these served to diversify the summer season of 1886:

"We were with him once in the summer theatre on the Schanzli, when he listened with great enjoyment," writes Widmann's stepdaughter, Frau Professor Vetter. "Marie and I could not always keep our feet still during the performance of the lively waltzes, and he said: 'Wait, I will play waltzes to you some day!' And a week afterwards, when we were assembled on Sunday evening with Hegar of Zürich and Munzinger in the Salon in Union str. (Bundesgasse) and the piano stood open and inviting, I plucked up courage, took Marie by the arm, and reminded him of his promise. He smiled and said: 'We must have something serious for the music directors first, then they will have to go away and I will play dances to you.' And he began, and played quite wonderfully, humming and droning the while, till the piano and the room and even the house vibrated. First he played a solo by Paganini, then a movement from a Schubert string quartet; then a splendid Bach toccata and fugue, so that one could have imagined the organ was booming. Then he asked: 'Would you like another little Bach?' and, when Hegar answered: 'We should prefer a big one,' he played another glorious Bach. After that he tried to send the music directors away, but did not succeed; and he played us delightful Strauss waltzes."

The summer was made musically noteworthy by the composition of a group of chamber works, the Sonatas in A and F major for pianoforte with violin and violoncello respectively, and the Trio in C minor for pianoforte and strings, which were played in Widmann's house soon after completion by the composer and his friends, musik direktor Friedrich Hegar, and Professor Julius Hegar, of Zürich. The Sonatas were performed for the first time in public in Vienna; severally by Brahms and Hellmesberger, at the Quartet concert of December 2, and by Brahms and Hausmann at Hausmann's concert of November 24; the Trio was introduced at Budapest about the same time by Brahms, Hubay and Popper, in each case from the manuscript.

Detailed discussion of these works is superfluous; two of them, at all events, are amongst the best known of Brahms' compositions. The Sonata for pianoforte and violoncello in F is the least familiar of the group, but assuredly not because it is inferior to its companions. It is, indeed, one of the masterpieces of Brahms' later concise style. Each movement has a remarkable individuality of its own, whilst all are unmistakably characteristic of the composer. The first is broad and energetic, the second profoundly touching, the third vehemently passionate—in the Brahms' signification of the word, be it noted, which means that the emotions are reached through the intellectual imagination—the fourth written from beginning to end in a spirit of vivacity and fun. The work was tried in the first instance at Frau Fellinger's house. "Are you expecting Hausmann?" Brahms inquired carelessly of this lady soon after his return in the autumn. Frau Fellinger, suspecting that something lay behind the question, telegraphed to the distinguished violoncellist, who usually stayed at her house when in Vienna, to come as soon as possible, if only for a day. He duly appeared, and the new sonata was played by Brahms and himself on the evening of his arrival. They performed it again the day before the concert above recorded, at a large party at Billroth's.

The last movement of the beautiful Sonata in A for pianoforte and violin is sometimes criticised as being almost too concise. The present writer confesses that she always feels it to be so, and one day confided this sentiment to Joachim, who did not agree with her, but said that the coda was originally considerably longer. "Brahms told me he had cut a good deal away; he aimed always at condensation."

Dr. Widmann allows us to publish an English version of a poem written by him on this work, the original of which is published in the appendix to his "Brahms Recollections." We have desired to place it before our English speaking readers, not only because it coincides remarkably with what we related in our early chapters of the delicate, fanciful tastes of the youthful Hannes, but because it gave pleasure to the Brahms of fifty-three, and even of sixty-three, and thus seems to illustrate the fact on which we have insisted, that if in any case then in our master's, the child was father to the man. Only a year before his death the great composer wrote to Widmann to beg for one or two more copies of the poem, which had been printed for private circulation.

BRAHMS' RESIDENCE NEAR THUN.
Photograph by Moegle, Thun.

THE THUN SONATA.

POEM ON THE SONATA IN A FOR PIANOFORTE AND VIOLIN, OP. 100,
BY JOHANNES BRAHMS,

WRITTEN BY

J. V. WIDMANN.

There where the Aare's waters gently glide
  From out the lake and flow towards the town,
Where pleasant shelter spreading trees provide,
  Amidst the waving grass I laid me down;
And sleeping softly on that summer day,
I saw a wondrous vision as I lay.

Three knights rode up on proudly stepping steeds,
  Tiny as elves, but with the mien of kings,
And spake to me: "We come to search the meads,
  To seek a treasure here, of precious things
Amongst the fairest; wilt thou help us trace
A new-born child, a child of heav'nly race?"

"And who are ye?" I, dreaming, made reply;
  "Knights of the golden meadows," then they said,
"That at the foot of yonder Niesen* lie;
  And in our ancient castles many a maid
Hath listened to the greeting of our strings,
Long mute and passed amid forgotten things.

"But lately tones were heard upon the lake,
  A sound of strings whose like we never knew,
So David played, perhaps, for Saul's dread sake,
  Soothing the monarch curtained from his view;
It reached us as it softly swelled and sank,
And drew us, filled with longing, to this bank.

"Then help us search, for surely from this place,
  This meadow by the river, came the sound;
Help us then here the miracle to trace,
  That we may offer homage when 'tis found.
Sleeps under flow'rs the new-born creature rare?
Or is it floating in the evening air?"

---

* A mountain near Thun.

But ere they ceased, a sudden rapid twirl
  Ruffled the waters, and, before our eyes,
A fairy boat from out the wavelet's whirl
  Floated up stream, guided by dragon-flies;
Within it sat a sweet-limbed, fair-haired may,
Singing as to herself in ecstasy.

"To ride on waters clear and cool is sweet,
  For clear as deep my being's living source;
To open worlds where joy and sorrow meet,
  Each flowing pure and full in mingling course;
Go on, my boat, upstream with happy cheer,
Heaven is reposing on the tranquil mere."

So sang the fairy child and they that heard
  Owned, by their swelling hearts, the music's might,
The knights had only tears, nor spake a word,
  Welling from pain that thrilled them with delight;
But when the skiff had vanished from their eyes,
The eldest, pointing, said in tender wise:

"Thou beauteous wonder of the boat, farewell,
  Sweet melody, revealed to us to-day;
We that with slumb'ring minnesingers dwell,
  Bid thee Godspeed, thou guileless stranger fay;
Our land is newly consecrate in thee
That rang of old with fame of minstrelsy.

"Now we may sleep again amongst our dead,
  The harper's holy spirit is awake,
And as the evening glory, purple-red,
  Shineth upon our Alps and o'er our lake,
And yet on distant mountain sheds its light,
Throughout the earth this song will wing its flight.

"Yet, though subduing many a list'ning throng,
  In stately town, in princely hall it sound,
To this our land it ever will belong,
  For here on flowing river it was found."
Fervent and glad the minnesinger spake;
"Yes!" cried my heart—and then I was awake.

Whilst our master had been living through the spring and summer months in the enchanted world of his imagination, coming out of it only for brief intervals of sojourn in earth's pleasant places amidst the companionship of chosen friends, certain hard, commonplace realities of the workaday world, which had arisen earlier at home in Vienna, were still awaiting a satisfactory solution. The death of the occupier of the third floor flat of No. 4, Carlsgasse, the last remaining member of the family with whom Brahms had lodged for fourteen or fifteen years, had confronted him with the necessity of choosing between several alternatives almost equally disagreeable to him, concerning which it is only necessary to say that he had avoided the annoyance of a removal by taking on the entire dwelling direct from the landlord, and had escaped the disturbance of having to replace the furniture of his rooms by accepting the offer of friends to lend him sufficient for his absolute needs. Arrangements and all necessary changes were made during his absence. To Frau Fellinger Brahms had entrusted the keys of the flat and of his rooms, which under her directions were brought into apple-pie order by the time of his return, the drawers being tidied, and a list of the contents of each neatly drawn up on a piece of cardboard, so that everything should be ready to his hand. The greatest difficulty, however, still remained. Who was to keep the rooms in order and see to the very few of Brahms' daily requirements which he was not in the habit of looking after himself? His coffee, as we know, he always prepared at a very early hour in the morning, and he was kept provided with a regular supply of the finest Mocha by a friend at Marseilles. Dinner, afternoon coffee, and often supper, were taken away from home. The master now declared he would have no one in the flat. To as many visitors as he felt disposed to admit he could himself open the door, whilst the cleaning and tidying of the rooms could be done by the "Hausmeisterin," an old woman occupying a room in the courtyard, and responsible for the cleaning of the general staircase, etc. In vain Frau Fellinger contested the point. Brahms was inflexible, and this kind lady apparently withdrew her opposition to his plan, though remaining quietly on the look out for an opportunity of securing more suitable arrangements. By and by it presented itself. In Frau Celestine Truxa, the widow of a journalist, whose family party consisted of two young sons and an old aunt, Frau Fellinger felt that she saw a most desirable tenant for the Carlsgasse flat, and after a renewed attack on the master, whose arguments, founded on the immaculate purity of his rooms under the old woman's care, she irretrievably damaged by lifting a sofa cushion and laying bare a collection of dust, which she declared would soon develop into something worse, he was so far shaken as to say that if she would make inquiries for him he would consider her views. Frau Fellinger wisely abstained from further discussion, but after a few days Frau Truxa herself, having been duly advised to open the matter to Brahms with diplomatic sang-froid, went in person to apply for the dwelling. After her third ring at the door-bell, the door was opened by the master himself, who started in dismay at seeing a strange lady standing in front of him.

"I have come to see the flat," said Frau Truxa.

"What!" cried Brahms.

"I have heard there is an empty flat here, and have come to look at it," responded Frau Truxa indifferently; "but perhaps it is not to let?"

A moment's pause, and the composer's suspicious expression relaxed.

"Frau Dr. Fellinger mentioned the circumstances to me," she continued, "and I thought the flat might suit me."

By this time Brahms had become sufficiently reassured to show the rooms and to listen, though without remark, to a brief description of Frau Truxa's family and of the circumstances in which she found herself.

"Perhaps, Dr. Brahms, you will consider the matter," she concluded, "and communicate with me if you think further of it. If I hear nothing more from you, I shall consider it at an end."

After about a week, during which Frau Truxa kept her own confidence, her maid came one day to tell her a gentleman had called to see her. Being engaged at the moment, she asked her aunt to ascertain his business, but the old lady returned immediately with a frightened look.

"I don't know what to think!" she exclaimed: "there is a strange-looking man walking about in the next room measuring the furniture with a tape!"

"The things will go in!" exclaimed Brahms as Frau Truxa hurried to receive him.

The upshot was that the master gave up the tenancy of the flat, returning to his old irresponsible position as lodger, whilst Frau Truxa, bringing her household with her, stepped into the position of his former landlady, thereby giving Brahms cause to be grateful for the remainder of his life for Frau Fellinger's wise firmness. He was, says Frau Truxa, perfectly easy to get on with; all he desired was to be let alone. He was extremely orderly and neat in his ways, and expected the things scattered about his room to be dusted and kept tidy, but was vexed if he found the least trifle at all displaced—even if his glasses were turned the wrong way—and, without making direct allusion to the subject, would manage to show that he had noticed it. Observing, after she had been a little time in the flat, that he always rearranged the things returned from the laundress after they had been placed in their drawer, she asked him why he did so. "Only," he said, "because perhaps it is better that those last sent back should be put at the bottom, then they all get worn alike." A glove or other article requiring a little mending would be placed carelessly at the top of a drawer left open as if by accident. The next day he would observe to Frau Truxa, "I found my glove mended last night; I wonder who can have done it!" and on her replying, "I did it, Herr Doctor," would answer, "You? How very kind!"

Frau Truxa came to respect and honour the composer

more and more the longer he lived in her house. She made his peculiarities her study, and after a short time understood his little signs, and was able to supply his requirements as they arose without being expressly asked to do so. It is almost needless to say that he took great interest in her two boys, and once, when she was summoned away from Vienna to the sick bed of her father, begged that the maid-servant might be instructed to give all her attention to the children during their mother's absence, even if his rooms were neglected. "I can take care of myself, but suppose something were to happen to the children whilst the girl was engaged for me!" Every night whilst Frau Truxa was away, the master himself looked in on the boys to assure himself of their being safe in bed. For the old aunt he always had a pleasant passing word.

The Fourth Symphony and two books of songs were published in 1886, and the three new works of chamber music, Op. 99, 100, 101, in 1887. Of the songs we would select for particular mention the wonderfully beautiful setting of Heine's verses:

> "Death is the cool night,
> Life is the sultry day,"

Op. 96, No. 1, and Nos. 1 and 2 of Op. 97.

Brahms' Italian journey in the spring of 1887 was made in the company of Simrock and Kirchner. The following year he travelled in Widmann's society, visiting Verona, Bologna, Rimini, Ancona, Loretto, Rome and Turin. Widmann sees in Brahms' spiritual kinship with the masters of the Italian Renaissance the chief secret of his love for Italy.

"Their buildings, their statues, their pictures were his delight and when one witnessed the absorbed devotion with which he contemplated their works, or heard him admire in the old masters a trait conspicuous in himself, their conscientious perfection of detail . . . even where it could hardly be noticeable to the ordinary observer, one could not help instituting the comparison between himself and them."

Brahms had an interview when on this journey with the now famous Italian composer Martucci, who displayed a thorough familiarity with the works of the German master.

Amongst the friends and acquaintances whom the composer met at Thun during his second and third summers there were the Landgraf of Hesse, Hanslick, Gottfried Keller, Professor Bächthold, Hermine Spiess and her sister, Gustav Wendt, the Hegars, Max Kalbeck, Steiner, Claus Groth, etc. He particularly enjoyed making music informally for his friends with Fräulein Spiess: "Hang Brahms!" he suddenly cried after accompanying her one afternoon at Widmann's house in a number of his songs: "Mainacht," "Sapphische Ode," and others. A Schubert selection followed, and then Widmann, at the request of a lady present, begged for the early "O, versenk." "Pfa! Damnation!" he answered. One day, as he had started for a walk from his lodgings in Thun, he was stopped by a stranger, who asked if he knew where Dr. Brahms lived. "He lives there," replied the master, pointing to the haberdasher's shop. "Do you know if he is at home?" "That I cannot tell you," was the reply. "But go and ask in the shop; you will certainly be able to find out there." The gentleman followed this advice, sent his card up, and received the answer that the Doctor was at home, and would be pleased to see him. To his surprise, on ascending the stairs, he found his newly-formed acquaintance waiting for him at the top.

The rumour revived in the summer of 1887 that Brahms was engaged on an opera. This came about, perhaps, from his intimacy with Widmann. "I am composing the entr'actes," he jestingly replied to the Landgraf's question as to whether the report had any foundation. As a matter of fact, the subject of opera was not mentioned between the composer and his friend at this time.

The works which really occupied Brahms during the summer of 1887 were the double concerto for violin and violoncello, with orchestral accompaniment, and the "Gipsy Songs."

The concerto is to be regarded as, in Frau Schumann's words, "gewissermassen ein Versöhnungswerk." Several letters passed between Brahms and Joachim in July on the subject of the work; a *rendezvous* was arranged for September 21 in Baden-Baden between Frau Schumann, Brahms, Joachim and Hausmann; and, on the evening of that date, the concerto was tried with pianoforte at Frau Schumann's hotel, "Das Deutsche Haus," the composer acting as accompanist. "Brahms and Joachim have spoken to each other for the first time for many years," records Frau Schumann the same evening.

A second trial under the same conditions the next morning was followed, on September 23, by a full private rehearsal which took place, with the assistance of the Baden-Baden municipal orchestra, in the "Louise Quinze" room of the Kurhaus, under Brahms. The solos were of course performed on all three occasions by Joachim and Hausmann. Amongst the listeners in the Kursaal were, besides Frau Schumann and her eldest daughter, Rosenhain, Lachner, the violoncellist Hugo Becker, Gustav Wendt and Robert Kahnt. The work was heard for the first time in public on October 18 at Cologne, Brahms conducting, and Joachim and Hausmann playing the solos as before; and the next performances, carried out under the same unique opportunities for success, were in Wiesbaden, Frankfurt and Basle on November 17, 18 and 20.

"Now," said Brahms, soon after his return to Vienna, to a lady who related the story to the author; "now I know what it is that has been wanting in my life for the past few years. I felt something was missing, but could not tell what. It was the sound of Joachim's violin. How he plays!"

In the autumn of this year one of the few remaining figures linked with the most cherished associations of Brahms' early youth passed away. Marxsen died on November 17, 1887, at the age of eighty-one, having retained to the end almost unimpaired vigour of his mental faculties. The last great pleasure of his life was associated with his beloved art. In spite of great bodily weakness, he managed to be present a week before his death at a concert of the Hamburg Philharmonic Society to hear a performance of the Ninth Symphony. "I am here for the last time," he said, pressing Sittard's hand; and he passed peacefully away fourteen days later.

A few years previously his artistic jubilee had been celebrated in Hamburg, and his dear Johannes had surprised him with the proof-sheets of a set of one hundred Variations composed long ago by Marxsen, not with a view to publication, but as a practical illustration of the inexhaustible possibilities contained in the art of thematic development. Brahms, who happened to see the manuscript in Marxsen's room during one of his subsequent visits to Hamburg, was so strongly interested in it that in the end Marxsen gave it him, with leave to do as he would like with it after his death. The parcel of proof-sheets was accompanied by an affectionate letter, in which Brahms begged forgiveness for having anticipated this permission and yielded to his desire of placing the work within general reach during his master's lifetime; and perhaps no jubilee honour of which the old musician was the recipient filled him with such lively joy as was caused by this tribute. Marxsen's name as a composer is, indeed, now forgotten without chance of revival, but his memory will live gloriously in the way he would have chosen, carried through the years by the hand that wrote the great composer's acknowledgment to his teacher on the title-page of the Concerto in B flat.

A peculiar interest attaches to the visit which Brahms paid to Leipzig at the close of the year in fulfilment of an engagement to conduct his double concerto at the Gewandhaus orchestral concert of January 1, 1888, and to take part in a performance of his C minor Trio at the quartet concert of January 2. Business of a similar kind brought Tchaïkovsky to Leipzig on the last day of December; Grieg, who was a well known and favourite personality in the musical circles of the town, happened to be staying there at the time, and the three composers met at midday dinner on New Year's Day at the house of Adolph Brodsky, already mentioned in these pages in connection with Brahms' violin concerto, who, at this period, filled the double post of concertmeister of the Gewandhaus orchestra and leader of the Gewandhaus string quartet. Neither Brahms nor Grieg, who were slightly known to each other, had any personal acquaintance with Tchaïkovsky. Probably, however, neither was entirely unaware that whilst the Russian composer was accustomed to declare himself a warm admirer of Grieg's art, he entertained a dislike amounting to positive aversion for that of Brahms.

Under the circumstances of the case it is not surprising that Frau Brodsky, who had refrained from telling Tchaïkovsky that he would not be the only guest at her dinner, should have been somewhat startled by his arrival before the appointed hour whilst the rehearsal of Brahms' C minor Trio, which had been arranged for the morning of January 1, was still in progress in her husband's music room. Anxious to prevent the occurrence of a possible contretemps, she hastened to receive the Russian visitor in the entrance hall and, after preparing him for the presence he was to encounter, begged him at a pause in the rehearsal, to go in with her to listen to the music. Ceremonious and reserved by nature, Tchaïkovsky was for the moment too much disconcerted to accept the proposal, but when Brodsky was summoned to support the lady's persuasions, he allowed himself to be led into the studio and was forthwith introduced to his German colleague.

"Shall I not disturb you?" he asked as he took his seat.

"Not in the least; but why listen? This is not at all interesting," was Brahms' gruff rejoinder.

Another awkward moment occurred at the end of the rehearsal. Tchaïkovsky, though attracted, as he afterwards confessed, by Brahms' personality, felt unable to say a friendly word about the trio and the room seemed to be filled with the sense of his disapproval. It was but for an instant, however. The entrance of Grieg and his wife, smiling and unconscious, suddenly cleared the atmosphere. Dinner was immediately announced, and the lingering feeling of uneasiness under which the party sat down to table was suddenly dispelled by the impulsiveness of Frau Grieg who, after occupying the place assigned to her between Brahms and Tchaïkovsky for a few minutes, started up exclaiming: "I cannot sit between these two any longer, it makes me so nervous!"

"I have the courage," said Grieg coming from the other side of the table.

So the three composers sat side by side and the polished, rather stiff Tchaïkovsky allowed himself to be thawed by the genial influences of the occasion of which Brahms' determined sociability was not the least potent. The enjoyment of a prolonged after-dinner sitting over coffee and cigars was enhanced for one at least of the famous guests by the presence of a young nephew of Frau Brodsky's ready to respond to overtures of friendship, and the entertainment closed with a display of conjuring tricks by the host, the explanation of each one of which was exacted, immediately after its performance, by the much interested Brahms.

"How did you like the trio?" Brodsky enquired of Tchaïkovsky after the others had taken their leave.

"Do not be angry with me, my dear friend, I did not admire it," was the reply.*

---

* "Recollections of a Russian Home," by Mrs. Brodsky.

Tchaïkovsky was present to hear the performance of the double concerto at the Gewandhaus concert of the same evening and returned to his hotel with one unfavourable impression the more of the art of Brahms. Brahms attended a rehearsal of Tchaïkovsky's Suite, Op. 43, held by the composer the next day, but said little or nothing as to what he thought of it. Perhaps we may conclude from all we know of the personality and musical temperament of the two composers that there was but little common ground between them from which mutual artistic sympathy could have been developed.

"I have been much with Brahms yesterday and to-day," wrote Tchaïkovsky on January 2. "We are ill at ease together because we do not really like each other, but he takes pains to be pleasant with me."*

Three more performances from the manuscript of the double concerto of interest in our narrative remain to be chronicled—those of the Berlin Philharmonic Society, under Bülow, of February 6, 1888; and of the London Symphony Concerts, under Henschel, on February 15 and 21. The work, published in time for the autumn season, was given in Vienna at the Philharmonic concert of December 23 under Richter. On all these occasions the solos were played, as before, by Joachim and Hausmann.

Bülow, having at this time resigned his post at Meiningen, had entered on a period of activity as conductor in some of the northern cities of Germany, and particularly in Hamburg and Berlin. His future programmes, in which our master's works were well represented, though not with the conspicuous prominence that had been possible at Meiningen, do not fall within the scope of these pages, since, with the mention of the double concerto, the enumeration

---

* The apparent discrepancy between the date of Tchaïkovsky's letter as given in the text and as found in his published correspondence results from the difference of the English and Russian calendars.

of Brahms' orchestral works is complete. Bülow's successor at Meiningen, Court Capellmeister Fritz Steinbach, carried on the traditions and preferences of the little Thuringian capital as he found them, until his removal to Cologne about fifteen years later, and has become especially appreciated as a conductor of the works of Brahms, whose personal friendship and artistic confidence he enjoyed in a high degree.

The name of Eugen d'Albert, whose great gifts and attainments were warmly recognised by Brahms, should not be omitted from our pages, though detailed account of his relations with the master is outside their limits. D'Albert's fine performances of the pianoforte concertos helped to make these works familiar to many continental audiences, and certainly contributed, during the second half of the eighties, to the better understanding of the great composer which gradually came to prevail at Leipzig.

But little needs to be said about the double concerto. This fine work, which may be regarded as in some sort a successor to the double and triple concertos of Mozart and Beethoven, exhibits all the power of construction, the command of resource, the logical unity of idea, characteristic of Brahms' style, whilst its popularity has been hindered by the same cause that has retarded that of the pianoforte concertos; the solo parts do not stand out sufficiently from the orchestral accompaniment to give effective opportunity for the display of virtuosity, in the absence of which no performer, appearing before a great public as the exponent of an unfamiliar work for an accompanied solo instrument, has much chance of sustaining the lively interest of his audience in the composition. Of the three movements of the double concerto, the first is especially interesting to musicians, whilst the second, a beautiful example of Brahms' expressive lyrical muse, appeals equally to less technically prepared listeners. On the copy of the work presented by

Brahms to Joachim the words are inscribed in the composer's handwriting "To him for whom it was written."

Widely contrasted in every respect was the other new work of 1887, introduced to the private circle of Vienna musicians at the last meeting for the season of the Tonkünstlerverein in April, 1888. The eleven four-part " Gipsy Songs," published in the course of the year as Op. 103, were sung from the manuscript by Fräulein Walter, Frau Gomperz-Bettelheim, Gustav Walter and Weiglein of the imperial opera, to the composer's accompaniment. Brahms obtained the texts of this characteristic and attractive work from a collection of twenty-five "Hungarian Folk-songs," translated into German by Hugo Conrat, and published in Budapest, with their original melodies set by Zoltan Nagy for mezzo-soprano or baritone, with the addition of pianoforte accompaniment. Conrat's translations have been done in masterly fashion. Literal as far as possible, slight modifications of the original have been admitted here and there in order to obtain a natural flow of the lines; and to some single-strophe songs, including Nos. 3 and 4 of Brahms' work, a second verse, developing the idea of the first, has been added. The German texts, in which the national Hungarian character is admirably preserved, appealed irresistibly to our master, and are well adapted to the four-part setting with pianoforte accompaniment which had proved so successful in the two books of Liebeslieder Walzer.

One of the earliest public performances of the Gipsy Songs was that of the Monday Popular concert of November 26 by Mr. and Mrs. Henschel, Miss Lena Little and Mr. Shakespeare, with Miss Fanny Davies as pianist. They were repeated at the Saturday Popular of December 1, and again on Saturday and Monday, December 22 and 24. The first public performance in Vienna—by the executants who had already given the work privately—took place at

Walter's concert in the Bösendorfer Hall on January 18, 1889.

The Gipsy Songs had an immediate widespread, and enormous success, and were soon heard in all parts of the musical world. They were sung in Paris in a French translation, and many times in Budapest, where the composer's art had become popular, in Hungarian retranslated from Conrat's version. Great though their popularity has remained, however, it has not equalled that of the Liebeslieder, and of these the demand for the first book has continued to exceed that for the second.

A graphic picture of Brahms as he was in the year 1888 and onwards is to be found in an article by Dr. Jenner.* This gentleman made the master's acquaintance under particularly interesting circumstances. When still a very young man, resident at Kiel, and a favourite of Claus Groth, the manuscripts of some of his songs came under Brahms' notice, and so much engaged his sympathy as to induce him to say he would be happy to receive the composer during his visit to Leipzig on the occasion of the above recorded performance of the new double concerto.

"My friend Julius Spengel joined me in Hamburg and we went together to Berlin," says Dr. Jenner. "There I was present for the first time at a Joachim Quartet evening. Immediately after the concert we travelled with the Quartet to Leipzig, arriving in the middle of the night at the Hôtel Hauffe. Never shall I forget the feeling that came over me as I read in the visitors' list: 'Johannes Brahms from Vienna.' He had already retired. By a strange chance I was shown into the room next his and as I entered it a sound of healthy snoring proclaimed the proximity of the mighty one. Moving about quietly, I went to rest with a strange mixed feeling of awe, pride and anxiety. When I came down the next morning Brahms had already breakfasted. Comfortably smoking, he was reading the papers. . . . He received me with pleasant, simple kindness, intimated that

---

* *Die Musik*, first May number of 1903.

he knew why I had come, and took pains to help me over my first embarrassment and shyness by every now and then putting to me some short, direct question, so that I was soon convinced of his good nature and felt unlimited confidence in him. . . .

"It was past 3 o'clock when we returned that night to the Hôtel Hauffe. How delighted but also astonished I was when Brahms, as he said good-night, announced that he would expect me in his room at 7 o'clock in the morning to speak to me about my compositions. I presented myself punctually at the appointed time and found him at breakfast, fresh, rosy and the picture of equanimity. . . .

"I had brought a trio for pianoforte and strings, a chorus with orchestral accompaniment, unaccompanied choruses for women's voices, and songs; and found that he had made himself acquainted with them down to the smallest detail, and, indeed, later he never looked through work with me which he had not thoroughly examined beforehand. After a few introductory remarks, in which he said that he had formed a generally favourable impression of my compositions, he gave me back the accompanied chorus with the words: 'Pity for the beautiful little poem.' It was Claus Groth's 'Wenn ein müder Leib.' The *a capella* choruses met with the same fate; I received them back with the remark: 'Such things are very difficult to make. . . .'"

For the sequel the reader must be referred to the article itself, which amusingly describes the tranquil and ruthless methods by which the master reduced his young friend to the verge of despair. All ended well, however, and the middle of February saw the arrival in Vienna of Herr Jenner and his introduction to Mandyczewski, under whom he was to go through a course of study in strict counterpoint, whilst his work in free composition was to be carried on under the master's personal supervision. After making Mandyczewski's acquaintance,

"I dined with Brahms at the 'Zum Rothen Igel' and afterwards he went with me to find a lodging, giving preference to the old houses. Whilst we were on this expedition, he took every opportunity of making me acquainted with the sacred places of the city. Before one house it was 'This is the Auge Gottes,' before another 'Look, Figaro was written there.' At length a suitable room was found near his own dwelling. 'The young man likes music,' said Brahms to the landlady, 'will he be able to hear a little pianoforte playing or singing here sometimes!' This she could not offer. 'Never mind, it does not matter.' Then he gave me one of his coffee-machines, plates, cups, forks, knives and spoons, so that I was comfortably settled the first day. The use of his library was at my disposal; his purse also. I could have as much money as I needed from him, but I was never obliged to take any and never did so. . . .

"I think with deep melancholy of the glorious evenings when Rottenberg and I sat alone with him in the low back room of the Igel and the silent Brahms thawed and showed us glimpses of a great and strong soul. But he never spoke on such occasions of his works, very rarely of himself and his life. I have, indeed, often had the good fortune of hearing him speak of himself whilst he was giving me a lesson; it was nearly always with some excitement. I was unfortunately obliged to give up the pleasure of dining with him every day during my second winter, as the Igel was too dear for me. Brahms always declared it was the cheapest house in Vienna and in fact he understood so well how to choose that he always had to pay less than I and yet got a better dinner. He was quite extraordinarily moderate in his daily life; 70-80 kreuzers was the most that he spent for his dinner and this included a glass of Pilsener beer or a quarter of a litre of wine. In the evening he drank but little more. It is only because the contrary has been so often affirmed that I think it my duty to tell the truth in such detail."

The old-fashioned restaurant Zum Rothen Igel, where Brahms was for many years a "Stammgast"—i.e., a daily customer—is situated in a corner of the Wildpret Markt close to the Augustinestrasse. Brahms did not frequent the regular dining-room of the house, but took his dinner in a low, dark vaulted chamber at the back, on the ground floor, ordinarily used by waiters, coachmen and similar guests. Here, at a table near a door leading to a small, gloomy courtyard, many a distinguished guest, the Landgraf of Hesse, Joachim, and many another, has partaken in our master's company of the homely but well-cooked dishes that he preferred. In fact, but few prominent musical visitors to Vienna quitted the imperial city without making the acquaintance, under Brahms' auspices, of the dingy apartment in the Wildpret Markt now called "the Brahms room" and decorated with a photograph of the master. He was very often joined at his midday meal by resident friends and acquaintances, and often supped at the Igel after a concert with a party of musicians. Amongst those most frequently seen with him were his old friends Epstein and Door and a circle of the young men in whom he took an interest; at the date now reached by our narrative, Mandyczewski and Rottenberg were his almost daily companions. If he supped alone at the Igel, he preferred to take his place in a corner behind the house door, which was screened from the taproom by a red curtain and was just large enough to hold a table and bench, occupied in slack hours by the manager. During the short time that the weather permitted, he dined, after his return to Vienna at the beginning of October, in the "garden"—i.e., at one of the two or three tables placed outside the house, and flanked by large pots of evergreens which were carried away when the days became cold.

During the last ten years of his life Brahms allowed himself to accept more invitations than formerly to dine or sup with one and another of the small group of families forming his immediate circle, and when invited out he liked, and even expected, to be asked to a good table and to have good wine put before him. He retained the notion, universal in a former generation, but now out of date, that it was incumbent on a bidden guest, not only to appreciate, but to show appreciation of the hospitality of his host and hostess. "There are people," he used to say, "who are afraid of showing that they like a good dinner." Brahms was certainly not one of these. He was prepared to do ample justice to the recherché cookery and excellent wines with which his friends liked to regale him, but he was at no period of his life either a glutton or a wine-bibber, and, indeed, never varied from the abstemious habits which the early circumstances of his life had made incumbent on him as a young man.

One of the annual Brahms festivities was the asparagus luncheon always given by Ehrbar on, or as near as possible to, May 7, in honour of the master's birthday. About twelve or sixteen people were invited, amongst whom the Hanslicks and Billroth and his daughter were regularly included. The luncheon hour was twelve o'clock, and the menu, which never varied, consisted of oysters, caviare, cold meat, then the *pièce de résistance*, asparagus, which was always provided in the proportion of two bundles to each person. This was followed by cheese and dessert, and there was a free flow of fine champagne.

The summer of 1888, the last one passed by Brahms at Thun, did not reach the end of its course in such unbroken tranquillity as the two previous ones. A heated political discussion with Widmann, in which neither disputant would give way, threatened, about the middle of August, to put a sudden end to the intimacy which had been a source of pleasure and advantage to both friends. Fortunately this catastrophe was averted by the good sense of the two men and the cordial affection existing between them; but possibly the incident may have left its traces on the composer's mood during the last weeks of his visit. Frau Vetter, who lived near her parents at Bern, tells a characteristic story, which we may, perhaps, associate with the late summer, of his vexation on finding himself—as he quite wrongly imagined through her indiscretion—the involuntary recipient of a vocal tribute as he was sitting one evening with the family after a festivity held in her garden.

"He thought the lights pretty but did not seem pleased when the men's choral society assembled on the terrace above our house. When I said they were going to serenade him, he exclaimed: 'Eh? What? I am not the mistress of the house! It is for you, birthday-child.' I persuaded him with great difficulty to go up to the gentlemen, and whenever I tried to get away he grasped me firmly by the hand. Then, at the close of a song, he muttered: 'Very pretty,' and there was silence, for everyone was hoping for a few words of acknowledgment from him. He said aloud to me, however: 'It was for you birthday-child, make a speech to the gentlemen.'"

The young mistress of the house, held fast to the spot by the master's firm handgrasp to do retribution for a misdeed of which she was entirely innocent, kept her presence of mind. Thanking the sixty vocalists for their entertainment, she invited them to drink a glass of beer in her garden. The gentlemen took their leave, after partaking of her hospitality, and Brahms, restored to equanimity, resumed his chat with his friends.

When Brahms and Widmann parted in September, both looked forward to renewing the experience of a journey to Italy together that had brought them a succession of delights in the spring of the year.

The third sonata for piano and violin in D minor was composed, like its immediate predecessor, in Thun where it was finally completed in the summer of 1888. Brahms' usual diffidence as to the artistic value of his latest creative achievement would seem to have been scarcely less pronounced in the case of this strikingly original work than we have perceived it on the completion of the fourth symphony. It found naive expression in a letter which he wrote to Frau von Herzogenberg on receiving her sympathetic remarks about the new composition:

"A thousand thanks, but though the sonata-letter has given me great pleasure, it inspires me with much less confidence than the other. Neither should I have expected anything so kind from you about the Gipsy Songs. However, as I would rather believe you have made a mistake than that you are trying to flatter me, best, but briefest thanks, meanwhile."

It is worthy of remark that in the "andern" letter to which the master approvingly refers, his correspondent had adventured far into the region of critical candour.

The Sonata in D minor contrasts effectively with its gentle-souled sisters, not only by reason of its larger dimensions, but from the almost ruggedly passionate character of its first and last movements. An interesting feature of the first movement, and one very characteristic of Brahms is that the development section is worked throughout its forty-six bars' length on a dominant pedal point that has its counterpart in the tonic pedal of the coda. The deep pathos of the second movement and the delicate sentiment of the third appeal peculiarly to Brahms' lovers. The work was played from the manuscript for the first time in public by Brahms and Joachim at Joachim's Vienna concert of February 13, 1889. It was published in the spring, with Brahms' dedication to "his friend Hans von Bülow," and was performed immediately afterwards in London by Miss Fanny Davies and Ludwig Straus at Miss Davies' concert of May 7. The three sonatas for pianoforte and violin were played one summer's day at Gmünden, by Brahms and Joachim, before the Queen and royal family of Hanover, an incident which carries the memory back to the year 1853, when Johannes, having come safely through the first stages of his concert-journey and taken Joachim's heart by storm, appeared with Reményi for the first time before King George and his circle at Hanover.

The other publications of 1889 were a book of five songs for mixed chorus *a capella*, and three books of five songs each, for a single voice with pianoforte accompaniment. Of these "Wie Melodien," "Auf dem Kirchhofe" and "Verrath" (Nos. 1, 4, 5 of Op. 105), and "Serenade" (No. 1 of Op. 106), are great favourites of the author's. Brahms' songs, however, offer such rich choice of beauty that the selection of one or another, even of the more celebrated, for particular mention must be regarded as little more than the indication of a personal preference.

CHAPTER XXII.

1889-1895.

Hamburg honorary citizenship—Christmas at Dr. Fellinger's—Second String Quintet—Mühlfeld—Clarinet Quintet and Trio—Last journey to Italy—Sixtieth birthday—Pianoforte Pieces—Billroth's death—Brahms' collection of German Folk-songs—Life at Ischl—Clarinet Sonatas—Frau Schumann, Brahms and Joachim together for the last time.

FROM the year 1889 onward Brahms chose for his summer dwelling-place the charming town of Ischl, the central point of the beautiful region of the Salzkammergut, and a favourite watering place of the Viennese. He rented rooms, as on one or two former visits, in a cottage prettily situated on the outskirts of the town near the rushing river Traun, away from the visitors' quarter and convenient for his favourite walks about the picturesque mountains which surround the valley. A strong note of affectionate regret, very characteristic of the composer, is observable in the letter in which he announced to Widmann his arrangements for the open-air season of 1889, but it cannot, however, be doubted that his partiality for the country of his adoption had by this time become too strong to allow him to feel at home for any lengthened period outside Austria. His attachment to his Vienna friends, to whom he may be said to have belonged almost entirely during the closing years of his life, probably determined his particular choice of

Ischl, which was well within the reach of any of them who wished to visit him, whilst several had villas for summer residence in the immediate neighbourhood. Johann Strauss always lived at Ischl during the summer, the Billroths' delightfully situated home at St. Gilgen could be reached by train or the lake boat service in an hour, whilst the house and grounds of Herr and Frau Victor von Miller zu Aichholz at Gmünden, and Goldmark's rooms, also at Gmünden, were not much further off, and so on with other friends.

"I have heard by chance," writes Billroth from St. Gilgen to Brahms at Ischl on June 16, "that Mandyczewski and Rottenberg are with you . . . make up your mind quickly therefore and come over with them to St. Gilgen and invite Brüll or Goldmark also in my name. . . ."

Brahms always dined when at Ischl in the "Keller" of the Hôtel Elisabeth, which was reached by a flight of steps leading downwards from the street, and is thus described by Billroth:

"I passed a couple of pleasant hours with Brahms at Ischl. We dined in a damp, underground room belonging to the Hôtel Elisabeth. The same dishes are served there as in the better class dining-room but at rather cheaper prices; it is very cool in the summer and no toilet is required; everything as if made for Brahms."

The city of Hamburg this year conferred its honorary citizenship on Brahms, a distinction he shared with Bismarck and Moltke. Greatly touched by this recognition, the master let himself go for once, and immediately telegraphed his thanks to the mayor in natural, impulsive fashion that he seems to have regretted when he saw his words in print.

" . . . You will find me here," he wrote to Hanslick from Ischl, "until—I must go to the music festival at Hamburg! I must, for my honorary citizenship, with all that is associated with it, has been too pleasant and gratifying. I dread it, however, for I see that my telegram to the mayor has been printed! It sounds very foolish; 'the best that could have come to me from men'—as though I had been thinking of eternal bliss; whereas all that I had in my mind was that when a melody occurs to me it is more welcome than an order, and that if it lead to my succeeding with a symphony, it gives me more pleasure than all honorary citizenships!..."*

In acknowledgment of the honour bestowed on him, Brahms composed three eight-part choruses *a capella*, which he entitled "Fest und Gedenksprüche" (Festival and Commemoration Sayings) and dedicated to the mayor of Hamburg, Herr Oberbürgermeister Dr. Petersen. Patriotic remembrances and hopes were vividly present to his mind as he composed them, and the work is to be accepted as a second great musical memorial and glorification of the events of 1870-71. The texts are again selected from the Bible: from Deuteronomy, the Psalms and the Gospels of St. Matthew and St. Luke. The choruses were studied by the Cecilia Society, and performed under Spengel on September 9 at the first of three festival concerts arranged by Bülow for the opening of the Hamburg Industrial Exhibition. Sittard calls them "a splendid musical gift," and places them amongst the best and finest of the composer's works.

"The 'Sayings' do not address themselves to a particular nation or creed, but speak to every thoughtful mind, to every human heart susceptible to earnest, ideal influences, and striving after the high and the beautiful. There lives in these movements something of that strong confidence which we find—expressive of another period of thought and of art—in Handel's works, and which acts like a tonic on every faithful mind. Brahms is the only composer of the present day who can sufficiently control his own individuality to be capable of expressing his texts in a musical language universally applicable and intelligible."

---

* *Neue Freie Presse*, June, 1897.

The work was received with immense enthusiasm, and the master was obliged to come forward to acknowledge the long-continued plaudits which followed its conclusion. It was the last time that he stood on a concert platform of his native city.

Spengel, who witnessed with Bülow the presentation of the citizens' document, which took place at Dr. Petersen's house, relates that Brahms gave warm verbal expression to the deep feeling animating the written acknowledgment by which he had supplemented his telegram of thanks. This letter ran as follows:*

"YOUR MAGNIFICENCE
"MOST HONOURABLE HERR BÜRGERMEISTER,
"I feel with my whole heart the need to add a few words to my hasty, short telegram. Kindly permit me again to assure your magnificence that my fellow-citizens have delighted and honoured me beyond measure by the bestowal of the honorary citizenship. As the artist is rejoiced by such a distinguished token of recognition, so also is the man by the glorious feeling of knowing himself so highly esteemed and loved in his native city. A feeling doubly proud when this native city is our beautiful, ancient, noble Hamburg! . . . The precious gift of my citizen's letter . . . becomes more precious and dear to me as I place it by the side of my father's citizen's document (still in Low-German). My father was, indeed, my first thought in connection with the pleasant event, and one wish only remains, that he were here to rejoice with me. . . ."

This was not the only mark of the esteem felt for him in high places by which the master was this year honoured. The news that the Emperor Francis Joseph had conferred upon him the distinguished "Leopold's" order reached him in Ischl, taking him completely by surprise, and was followed by an inundation of letters, cards and telegrams of congratulation, to all of which he replied individually.

---

* Spengel's "Johannes Brahms," p. 8.

"I was so pleased that the Austrians, as such, were glad that I was obliged to reply prettily," he wrote to Hanslick.*

Another of the distinctions bestowed upon Brahms late in his career, which gave him, as a German musician, extraordinary pleasure, was that of his election as foreign member of the Académie Française. He endeavoured to write his letter of acknowledgment in French, but, not being able to satisfy himself, was obliged to be content with expressing his gratification in his own language.

It seems appropriate to record, with the mention of these pleasant incidents, the fact of Brahms' warm admiration of the opera "Carmen," the work of the French composer Bizet.

A visit to Cologne—the last—in February is noteworthy as having furnished opportunity for the first (private) performance from the manuscript of three motets for four and eight part chorus *a capella*. They were sung by the students' choral class of the conservatoire, and on the same occasion Brahms played—also from the manuscript—with two of the professors, the revised edition of his early B major Trio, introduced by him early in the month, with the assistance of Hubay and Popper, to the music lovers of Budapest; and to those of Vienna at the Rosé Quartet concert of February 22. We have already, in the early pages of our narrative, expressed our preference for the original version of this lovely work.

A visit to Italy in the spring with Widmann, which included Parma, Cremona, Brescia and Vicenza, afforded Brahms opportunity of deriving pleasure from the most varied sources. The sight of the cathedral of Cremona by moonlight, upon which he and Widmann came suddenly the night of their arrival, as they turned a street corner, quite overpowered him. He could not gaze long enough at the wonderful scene, and was obliged to return with his

---

* *Neue Freie Presse*, June 29, 1897.

friend to look at it once again before he could persuade himself to go in for the night. He was able, on the other hand, to derive amusement from the trifling incidents of each day's adventures, and was always ready to meet the passing difficulties and embarrassments of the traveller with laudable equanimity and resource. He used, later on, to describe, with some zest, an opera performance which he attended at Brescia. The work, he declared, consisted entirely of final cadences, but was so beautifully sung that he had great pleasure in listening to it.

His appearance and manner, which at this period of his life made an irresistible impression of nobility and, generally, of benevolence on strangers, in spite of his short stature and careless dress, attracted the constant admiration of his casual fellow travellers and of the people of the country with whom he had to do; and amongst other anecdotes related by Widmann is one of a guide at Palermo who had fought under Garibaldi:

"Our refined and amiable guide suddenly stopped short in the midst of his flowing discourse, and, with a look at Brahms, exclaimed involuntarily: 'Ah! mi pare di parlare al mio venerabile generale Garibaldi!' at which his eyes lightened enthusiastically."

Brahms was frequently asked to officiate as godfather to his friends' children, and this summer he acceded to the request of Frau Dr. Marie Janssen, eldest daughter of his first teacher, Cossel, that he would stand sponsor to her little son. A few months later Frau Janssen sent him a photograph of two of her children, which he acknowledged in the following words:

"DEAR AND ESTEEMED LADY,

"I am not able to write a real letter however strongly your kind and welcome packet tempts me to do so. Let me, however, briefly express my thanks and believe that my most cordial thoughts go out to you at Kiel, and again to Hamburg to your unforgettable father, whose memory is amongst those most sacred and dear to me. Only one thing were to be wished as to the charming little packet—that it could have smiled at him.

"In warm remembrance and with best greetings

"Yours sincerely,

"J. BRAHMS."

When the Janssens settled at Kiel, Brahms wrote to ask Groth to call upon them, saying:

" . . . The lady is the daughter of my first pianoforte teacher Cossel of whom I must have told you. And when I began to speak of him I was certainly unable to leave off again. . . ."

At the period we have now reached, Brahms had given up his solitary Christmas evenings. The home of Dr. and Mrs. Fellinger became every year more and more a substitute to him in some sort for that home of his own which he imagined, perhaps, with longing and regret till the last year of his life. Each Christmas Eve of his last eight winters found him amongst the Fellinger family group, rejoicing in the joy of the young people, stimulating their fun, happy in feeling himself truly one in the midst of a family circle whose greatest delight it was to know that their friend of friends liked to be amongst them. Frau Fellinger always contrived some charming practical joke in the matter of the Christmas presents prepared for the master, by which he was annually and unfailingly taken in. One year—the first Christmas he passed at the house—part of her own gift table, labelled with his name, was tastefully arranged with toilet accessories. In front of a burnished mirror two candlesticks stood, holding lighted candles; between these was a pincushion, on to which was pinned a black silk necktie; some parcels with pink paper wrappings, tied with ribbon and labelled "Finest perfume," lay near. The only uncovered articles were packets of writing paper of the kinds most used by Brahms, supplied in sufficient quantities to last some time.

The usual general survey of the gift-laden tables took place, and Brahms evinced much sympathetic interest during the tour of inspection, but presently he walked silently away to the other end of the room, passing his hand over his beard, then sauntered back carelessly, only to retire again and pace about apart, the picture of quiet dismay. "But won't you look at your things, Dr. Brahms?" inquired Frau Fellinger by and by, when her guest had summoned sufficient courage to mingle again with the party and admire the young people's presents, though he carefully avoided glancing at his own. Poor Brahms allowed himself to be led to the table, and stood mute and dazed before it. "Ah! *here* is mine," he cried, suddenly catching sight of the paper; "this is for me!" "But all is for you," returned his hostess kindly but firmly. "But these things are all for you," said the master, pleading; "they are not for me, they are yours." "But why, Dr. Brahms?" insisted the lady; "pray look at your things; do you not like scent?" By little and little the master was persuaded to handle his presents, gingerly enough, it is true. And now ensued the transformation scene. Each dainty trifle turned into some useful article suited to Brahms' needs. The two candlesticks became cream jugs, the pincushion a sugar basin, the packets of perfume proved to be tablets of unscented soap. A bread basket containing bundles of English quills such as Brahms always used for writing music, and a clothes brush, stood in bare, attractive reality before his astonished eyes. Soon nothing remained but the mirror. "But this really does belong to you," he implored, still deceived. "Look behind it," said Frau Fellinger; and the mirror became a nickel coffee tray, chosen because of its smooth, brilliantly polished back, which had well served the Christmas Eve purpose. "Now I really must sit down," said Brahms, drawing a long breath, his kind face shining; and he insisted on carrying away all his things in a cab the same evening.

But though Brahms was persuaded, in the later years of his life, to join the family festivities of these kind friends, he kept up to the last his custom of showing himself at his landlady's Christmas Eve party. Frau Truxa used to light up her tree an hour or two earlier than formerly, so that he should feel quite happy in setting out for Dr. Fellinger's. Of course her two boys were always remembered by the master, and his gifts to them, generally books, were found punctually on the table at the hour appointed for the commencement of the festivity.

The publications of the year 1890 were the "Fest und Gedenksprüche," as Op. 109, and three Motets for four and eight part chorus *a capella*, Op. 110.

The writer of these pages was present at a supper party given in Vienna in January, 1890, after a concert of the Joachim Quartet, at which Brahms with Joachim and his colleagues were the chief guests. "What shall we have next?" said Joachim to Brahms in the course of supper; "a quintet; we have one, a very fine one; we will have another." A second string quintet, with two violas, composed during the summer at Ischl, was the next work produced by Brahms, and was heard for the first time in public from the manuscript in Vienna at the Rosé Quartet concert of November 11 (Rosé, Bachrich, Hummer, Jenek and Siebert).

Brahms' Quintet in G major is, in the opinion of most competent judges, one of the most powerful and fascinating of his works of chamber music for strings. If there is, in one or two of his late compositions for pianoforte and other instruments, something that suggests the feeling that in this domain the elasticity of his imagination was approaching its limits, nothing of the sort can be said of either of the works for strings only, and the Quintet in G is certainly second to none of them in wealth of spontaneous melody, in vigour and variety of inventive power, in all, in short, that is included in the word "vitality." To the present writer it appears quite clear and easy to follow, but that there may be two impressions on this point is proved in a remarkable way by two letters written by Billroth, the first to Brahms himself after the work had been performed for the first time from the manuscript at a party at Billroth's house, the second a few months later to Hanslick.

In the letter to Brahms, dated November 6, the famous surgeon, writing evidently under the influence of the great artistic excitement of the day, tells the master that he cannot rest without sending him word of his delight.

"Lately I have been silent, for I know not what more to say than, wonderfully fine and now clear to me at first hearing, clear as the blue sky! . . . Could one compare the various works of Michael Angelo, Raphael, Beethoven, Mozart when they were at the height of their powers? Only in the sense of a limited personal sympathy. . . . I have often wondered what human happiness is—now I was happy to-day when listening to your music. That is quite clear to me."

The following March, however, Billroth wrote to Hanslick that he found the quintet one of the most difficult of Brahms' works.

"The form, when one has found it out, is simple and clear; but the length of the first bass theme and the rhythmic and harmonic over-rich, I might say overladen, five-part development make enjoyment of the movement [the first] impossible except under great mental strain. One must be fresher and better in health for it than I am at present. . . . But it is easy to talk; we are always wanting something new, something which interests us more than the last; no one can quite satisfy us."*

Billroth heard the work the first time under the most favourable imaginable conditions, when his own powers of receptivity were strongly stimulated. He was depressed

---

* Billroth's Briefe.

and out of health when he wrote the second letter. The majority of music lovers would, we fancy, range themselves on the side of his original impression. The power and loveliness of the first movement, the romance of the second (the wonderful adagio), the plaintive daintiness of the third, the vivacity of the fourth, tinged with Hungarian colouring, all seem to foretell a continued prolongation of the composer's creative force and impulse. That Brahms himself, however, in the beginning of the nineties was conscious of needing rest is well known. Billroth says of him in a letter dated May 28, 1890, after visiting him at Ischl:

"He rejected the idea that he is composing or will ever compose anything. He is deep in Sybel's 'Foundation of the German Empire,' three thick volumes and the fourth to come."

To another friend Brahms said in 1891:

"I have tormented myself to no purpose lately, and till now I never had to do so at all; things always came easily to me."

He professed his intention of giving his creative activity a rest, and employing his time in reading, going excursions, and seeing his friends, but did not at once persevere in the resolution.

In the early part of the year 1891 he paid a visit to Meiningen. His enjoyment was the greater since the Duke, to whom the master had often spoken of Widmann, had invited this gentleman to meet his friend. Several delightful details of the time are related by Widmann. For us, however, the fact of particular interest is that it was now that Brahms' admiration of the performances of the clarinettist Mühlfeld, of the Meiningen orchestra, culminated in the determination to write for his instrument. Mühlfeld had gained particular reputation as a soloist by his performances of Weber, whose concertino for clarinet and orchestra had been introduced by him at Meiningen on

BRAHMS' RESIDENCE AT ISCHL. *By permission of Maria Fellinger.*

December 25, 1886, the hundredth anniversary of the composer's birth. Our master, who since that date had had many opportunities of listening to Mühlfeld's wonderful tone and execution, now asked for a private recital with only himself as audience, in the course of which the clarinettist played to him one piece after another from his repertoire, and discussed his instrument with him. The sequel was the composition by Brahms, during his annual residence at Ischl, of a trio for pianoforte, clarinet and violoncello and a quintet for clarinet and strings. These works were performed from the manuscripts before the ducal circle at Meiningen Castle on November 24 of the same year, the trio by Brahms, Mühlfeld and Hausmann, the quintet by the same musicians, Joachim, and two members of the Meiningen orchestra.

Brahms remained on as the Duke's guest for some little time after the performance, and then followed his friends to Berlin in order to take part in the Joachim Quartet concert of December 12, when his new works were heard for the first time in public. This occasion was, and has remained, unique in the history of the famous party of artists. The Joachim Quartet concerts in Berlin, occupying a position in the forefront of the musical life of the city, took place annually for nearly forty years; but into no other programme than that of December 12, 1891, was any work admitted, not written exclusively for strings. That Brahms was much gratified by the compliment paid him is evident from a letter written by him on December 1 to Hanslick, in which he says:

". . . I shall not be able to tell you about it [a performance of Strauss' opera, 'Ritter Paynim'] for another fortnight. This is because Joachim has sacrificed the virginity of his Quartet to my newest things. Hitherto he has carefully protected the chaste sanctuary but now, in spite of all my protestations, he insists that I invade it with clarinet and piano, with trio and quintet. This will take place on the 12th of December, and with the Meiningen clarinettist.

Tell Mandyczewski (or let him read) that the quintet 'adagio con sordini' was played as long and often as the clarinettist could hold out."*

The visit to Berlin resulted in a phenomenal triumph. A public rehearsal was held on the 10th, when every seat was occupied, and at the conclusion of the quintet, the last number of the programme, the audience indulged in an overwhelming demonstration to composer and executants. They went so far as to demand a repetition of the entire work, and Joachim and his colleagues at length consented to repeat the adagio. A similar scene was enacted at the concert on the 12th. Both new works were favourably noticed by the Berlin press, which waxed enthusiastic over the quintet, and especially the adagio.

The trio was played in Vienna the same month at a Hellmesberger concert; the quintet on January 5, 1892, by the Rosé Quartet party, with the clarinettist Steiner. Both works were heard again in the Austrian capital a fortnight later at a concert given there by the Joachim Quartet party, with the co-operation of Brahms and Mühlfeld. The quintet was introduced to a London audience at the Monday Popular concert of March 28 by Mühlfeld, Joachim, Ries, Straus and Piatti, and repeated at the Saturday concert of April 2, when the trio was also played by Miss Fanny Davies, Mühlfeld and Piatti.

The Clarinet Trio appears to us one of the least convincing of Brahms' works, and this in spite of the fact that it bears its composer's name writ large on every page. No one could fail to recognise his handwriting in either of the four movements, and to true Brahms lovers the handwriting must always be dear; but if one may compare the composer with himself, the inspiration of this work seems to us to halt, the spirit to want flexibility. Far otherwise is it with the beautiful and now favourite quintet, which contains,

---

* *Neue Freie Presse*, July 1, 1897.

as Steiner says, richest fruits of the golden harvest of the poet's activity. Here "the brooks of life are flowing as at high noon," though the tone of gentle, loving regret which pervades the four movements, and holds the heart of the listener in firm grip, suggests the composer's feeling that the evening is not far away from him in which no man may work. A fullness of rich melody, a luscious charm of tone, original effects arising from the treatment of the clarinet, "olympian" ease and mastery, distinguish every movement of this noble and attractive work, which, taking its hearers by storm on its first production, has grown more firmly rooted into the hearts of musicians and laymen with each fresh hearing. In the middle section of the second movement Brahms has written for the clarinet a number of quasi-improvisatory passages embracing the entire extent of its compass, which are supported by the strings, and which when competently performed, are of surprisingly attractive effect. A fancy that suggested itself to one of the Berlin critics, as to the position assigned in this movement to the clarinet, seems to have commended itself to Brahms, who was ever afterwards in the habit of introducing the distinguished artist for whom it was written, to intimate friends, as "Fräulein von Mühlfeld, my Primadonna."

In 1891 were published the String Quintet in G, Op. 111; six Vocal Quartets, the last four being additional Gipsy Songs set to Conrat's texts, Op. 112; and thirteen Canons for women's voices, the appearance of which forms a direct link between the composer's late maturity and early youth.

The Clarinet Trio and Quintet and three books of short Pianoforte Pieces, Op. 116, Nos. 1 and 2, and Op. 117, appeared in 1892.

Brahms departed in good time in the spring of 1893 for what was to be his last holiday in the south, meeting Widmann and two Zürich friends (Friedrich Hegar and Robert Freund) in Milan and proceeding with them to Sicily, whose scenery and general romantic charm had made an indelible impression on his mind when he had travelled in the country with Billroth some fifteen years previously. He had an additional and weighty reason for desiring to leave Vienna in April. The coming 7th of May, his sixtieth birthday, could not fail to be made the occasion, not only of friendly rejoicings, but, if he were at home, of formal congratulatory functions in which he would be asked to take part. To his mind, such a predicament left but one course open to him—flight; and for this he had made arrangement months beforehand. As early as the year 1892 he had refused Hegar's invitation to celebrate his birthday by some festival performances at Zürich in the following terms:

"VIENNA, *September 29th*, 1892.

"DEAR FRIEND,

"I hasten to place this pretty sheet of paper before me and will endeavour approximately to express my gratitude to you and your society for your extremely kind and friendly project for the next 7th May. To-day I will only say that I have for some time been intending to make a proposal to you. My indolence in writing is the only cause that you have been beforehand with me. I wished to ask you and Widmann if you would not like, as I should, to go for a little while to Italy?

"When and where is all one to me; if on the 7th of May we are only safe in the Abruzzi or somewhere else where no one can find us; if we can only devote ourselves to touching (and preferably jovial) meditation. You see my plans and ideas are quite different from yours and my next letter will contain only many thanks for your very kind thought. . . ."*

To Herr Ehrbar's annual invitation to the asparagus luncheon, therefore, which was sent as usual about the middle of April to No. 4, Carlsgasse, and which contained a special request that in this particular year the festivity should be celebrated on May 7 itself, a telegraphic reply was received from Genoa. The master was very sorry that

---

* Published in Steiner's "Johannes Brahms," p. 29.

he would not be able to be present this year, but sent his kindest greetings to all friends who should assemble on the occasion. Instead of postponing the party on account of this disappointment, Herr Ehrbach decided not only to gather the old friends about him as usual, but to hold the festivity at the Hôtel Sacher, and to invite some additional guests to drink the health of the absent composer, bringing up the number to about thirty.

Widmann, who had an accident during the return journey which injured his knee and obliged him to remain for two days at Naples under the surgeon's care, has thus described how Brahms spent May 7:

"And so it happened that Brahms passed his sixtieth birthday in the most quiet seclusion, remaining to watch faithfully by my bed after we had persuaded our two friends to make an excursion to Pompeii. The doctor's performances, which gave me little pain, excited him fearfully, though he tried to conceal this by making jesting remarks, as when he muttered grimly between his teeth: 'If it should come to cutting, I am the right man; I was always Billroth's assistant in such cases.' When we were alone he provided for my comfort like a deaconess and took pains to keep up my spirits by chatting cheerfully, saying for instance: 'You have already tramped about so much in the Swiss Alps and Italy. Even if, at the worst, this should not again be possible, you are much better off than a hundred thousand others who have not had such opportunity.' . . . Every now and then whilst he was sitting with me, congratulatory telegrams arrived from intimate friends who had obtained intelligence from one or other of us as to our whereabouts."

It was rumoured in Vienna, nevertheless, that Brahms was present at Herr Ehrbar's luncheon; that he was seen in the Augustinestrasse in the evening of the 6th; that he astonished his friends by joining them at the Hôtel Sacher at twelve o'clock on the 7th, just as they were about to sit down to table; and that he vanished from the city immediately after the festivity, to come back no more until the usual time of his return in October.

The sixtieth birthday of its honorary president was celebrated by a special meeting and musical performance in the club rooms of the Tonkünstlerverein, and the Gesellschaft had a gold medal cast in the master's honour.

A note to Frau Caroline, written in June from Ischl, headed by a diminutive photograph of himself in walking dress, is suggestive of Brahms' happy mood at this time:

"Here I come, dear mother, and thank you for your dear letter.

"I am delighted that Fritz [Schnack] is making a nice tour which shows that you are both well—let him only make further plans, and travel! . . . I will be careful that you get a cast of the medal. It will interest Fritz as a connoisseur—he must imagine the gold. I am very well and the summer becomes finer every day. In the autumn or winter I really must look in upon you myself and not merely in a portrait.

"Have you a great deal too much money, or may I send some? I should like Fritz to spend plenty in travelling and he can afterwards entertain you and himself again with his sufferings! . . .

"Your JOHANNES."*

Years before this date, Frau Caroline had, at the urgent and oft-repeated wish of Johannes, given up her boarding-house in the Anscharplatz, and retired to enjoy the remainder of her life as mistress of her son's quiet home in Pinneberg. Johannes kept his stepmother supplied with the necessary funds, which were regularly transmitted to her through his publisher, Herr Simrock of Berlin; but he was never tired of urging upon her his readiness to meet intermediate demands as they might arise, and particularly of suggesting holiday journeys for Fritz Schnack as a good way of spending extra money. Frau Caroline and her son, who both worshipped Johannes, frequently incurred his

---

* Published in Reimann's "Johannes Brahms," p. 117.

displeasure on account of the moderation with which they availed themselves of his generosity.

He never went to Hamburg after his stepmother's retirement without reserving a few hours to visit her at Pinneberg, and there, in the modest little dwelling he had provided, felt himself, as it were, in the old family home. He would sit in a corner of the sofa in the room by the side of the shop filled with clocks whose hands pointed to the right time and whose pendulums swung cheerily to and fro, and chat happily with her and Fritz, hearing little items of domestic news, asking after this and the other acquaintance; then would suddenly relapse into silence and reverie, which were unfailingly respected by the two people to whom he was so dear. By and by, after he had arranged his thoughts, he would come out again from his musing to continue the pleasant chitchat where it had been left.

Brahms always expected his stepmother to be present at his public appearances in Hamburg, and continued to stay with her, when visiting the city, until she went to live at Pinneberg. On an occasion of his coming, after her retirement, to conduct a symphony at one of Bülow's Hamburg concerts, he took a room for her next his own at the Hôtel Moser, that they might be as much as possible together during the few days of his stay, and led her on his arm to her seat at rehearsals and concert. Frau Caroline did not, perhaps, entirely fathom the depths and intricacies of her stepson's fourth symphony, but she loved the work, and shared in the joy of it with her whole heart. Fritz, too, came over from Pinneberg, and greeted his stepbrother in the artists' room before the concert began. The master's two final visits to Hamburg seem to have been paid during the last illness of his sister, Elise Grund—who died in June, 1892—and early in the year 1893. Possibly he may have been at Pinneberg after this date.

Brahms gave some of his attention in the season 1892-93 to the editing of a supplementary volume to the complete edition of Schumann's works that had been prepared by Frau Schumann during the late seventies for publication by Breitkopf and Härtel. In the appearance of this deeply interesting book is unquestionably to be read our master's desire to associate his name once more with those of Schumann and his wife; and his naive pleasure in the contents of the volume, for the selection and arrangement of which he was solely responsible, as well as in the fact of this his responsibility, cannot but endear his memory the more to those who read his correspondence on the subject.* The task of preparing the volume, with Frau Schumann's sanction, for the engraver seems to have soothed his sensitiveness in regard to his—lately very strained—personal relations with his old friend; and henceforward his letters to her tell only of his affection, his satisfaction in the occasional visits he was able to pay her, and of the efforts made by him from time to time to cheer the suffering to which her advanced years rendered her increasingly liable. The supplementary volume contains, to quote the words of the preface, written and signed by Brahms:

"a few things found amongst Robert Schumann's papers which, on account of their value, or of some special interest, ought not to be omitted from this collection. . . . The theme with which the volume concludes is, in a quite peculiar sense, Schumann's last musical thought. He wrote it on the 7th of February, 1854, and afterwards added five variations which are withheld here. It speaks to us as a kindly greeting spirit [genius] about to depart and we think with reverence and emotion of the glorious man and artist.

"JOHANNES BRAHMS.

"ISCHL, *July,* 1893."†

---

* Contained in Litzmann's "Clara Schumann," Vol. III.

† The theme is the one alluded to on page 162.

N.B.—On the occasion of Schumann's opera, "Genoveva," being put into rehearsal at the Hanover court theatre in 1874, Brahms, with

In such spirit had Brahms ever cherished the memory of the great musician and generous friend whom he had loved and mourned in his youth. "The memory of Schumann is sacred to me," he wrote in 1873 to Professor Heimsoeth, of Bonn; and to his friend, Geheimrath von Hase, head of the house of Breitkopf and Härtel, he said not long before his own years were accomplished:

"Every man has a few experiences which cause him to feel that his life has been worth living. For myself, I can mention three: that I knew Schumann when I was young; that it was my fortune to live, through the year /70; and that I have been privileged to watch the constantly increasing glorification of Bach during the past years through the means of your edition."*

Of the composer's original work of the season Billroth writes a few months later to a friend:

"Brahms has, so far as I know, composed a dozen pianoforte pieces during the summer. I do not know the cause of this sudden passion. I like him least of all in this style, the G minor Rhapsody excepted. He does not sufficiently diversify his form in these little works. . . . He ought to keep to the great style."

The pieces in question were published in the autumn in two books—Op. 118 and 119. The other publications of the year, issued without opus number, were the two books of Technical Exercises for Pianoforte.

Billroth's expression of feeling about the Pianoforte

Frau Schumann's approval, added a few bars to the close of Siegfried's song in the third act, which are bound up as a supplement with the MS. full score of the work preserved at Hanover. They do not, however, appear in the pianoforte score of the work included in Frau Schumann's complete edition.

* The celebrated monumental edition of Bach's complete works published in sixty volumes, 1851-1896, by Breitkopf and Härtel for the Leipzig Bach-Gesellschaft.

Pieces will probably be endorsed by many even of the most
faithful admirers of Brahms' art, whilst all will certainly
agree as to his one exception. Beautiful as many of the
intermezzi, fantasias, etc., are, it is to be doubted whether
Brahms' short compositions for the pianoforte will ever gain
such universal and unreserved affection as has long since
been accorded to those of Schumann and Chopin. The
manner in which the thoughts are expressed sometimes seems
out of proportion to the moderate length of their development, the height of the structure to be, as it were, too great
in comparison with the superficial area allotted to it. In
several instances at all events, however, this 'impression is
due to the unusualness of the pieces, and passes away as
they become really familiar. It is as yet too soon to form
any definite opinion as to the place they may ultimately
take.

True appreciation of Brahms' small as of his great works
is sometimes slow in coming, even to those who love his
music with deepest affection. When, however, from time
to time, the spirit dwelling within his inspirations reveals
itself unsought as in a sudden flash, the whole heart is apt
to go out with complete acceptance to the reception of its
beauty and truth. Only in one instance (Op. 117, No. 1)
has the master given any clue as to the sources which may
have stirred his fancy during the composition of his thirty
short pieces for the pianoforte from Op. 76 onwards, and
where he has been reticent it would ill become others to
stamp any particular piece with a definite suggestion. It
may, however, be surmised that many of the little compositions are expressions derived from his passion for nature.
The mountain storm swept up by the wind and bursting with
a sudden crash, the approaching and retreating roll of its
thunder, with the ceaseless pattering of rain on the leaves;
the gay flitting of butterflies; the lazy hum of the insect
world on a hot summer day; the long sweep of gray waves
breaking into foam on the shore—all may be found in them.

The music of the spheres, also, too ethereal for the perception of ordinary mortals, has been caught by our master's ear, and, woven into gossamer sound-textures, has been conveyed by him to the appreciation of organisations less delicate than his own. Some of the pieces have certainly grown up around the fancies of a legend or a poem. In these we may hear the weird footsteps of the spirit world, the dread strike of the bell of fate, the catastrophe of human lives. In no case, however, except in the one mentioned, are the several works to be taken as having been associated with this or that in the mind of the composer. The same one may mean different things to different people, and Brahms has carefully guarded against the possibility of being suspected of programme music by giving to the fantasias, rhapsodies, ballades, intermezzi, the vaguest of all possible titles. The book, Op. 117, has become really popular, and is sold in the United Kingdom alone in its thousands. One of the first persons—perhaps the first—to hear books, Op. 116 and 117, was Frau Schumann's pupil, Fräulein Ilona Eibenschütz (later Mrs. Carl Derenberg), to whom Brahms played them on their completion, inviting her especially to hear them.

Asking Brahms to be present in October at a festival meeting of the Imperial and Royal Society of Physicians, Billroth says:

"I should like to see you for once in evening dress [*schön decorirt*]. If, however, you object to this, you will find a place among the younger doctors in the (not high) gallery in walking costume."

It was one of the last semi-public functions in which the famous surgeon took part. His health had for some time been declining, and he died on February 6, 1894, regretted by all ranks of Vienna citizens. The funeral procession was witnessed by crowds of people, especially of the poorer classes.

"We do not wear such open hearts," writes Brahms afterwards to Widmann, "nor show such pure and warm affection as they do here (I mean the people, the gallery). . . . In the whole innumerable concourse no inquisitive or indifferent face was to be seen, but upon each countenance the most touching sympathy and love. This did me much good when passing through the streets and at the cemetery."*

Brahms could not trust himself to remain too close a spectator of the last scene. Whilst the relatives and friends of the departed surgeon remained standing round the open grave, he quietly strolled to a sidewalk and paced up and down, talking with an acquaintance of other matters.

The thought of death had, indeed, a power over the master which probably held him in its clutch at times throughout his life. He could not bring himself to face the enemy with resolute front, especially during his later years, when the iron hand laid claim to one of his friends, but would speak of the matter as little as might be, and no doubt kept it as much as possible at bay in his thoughts. Death had, however, till now been kind to our master, sparing him the agony of many severe partings. We have seen his deep grief at the loss of the parents who had loved him with the entire devotion of their simple, affectionate hearts. By the nature of things, his sense of bereavement on the deaths of brother and sister had been less enduring in its sting. His friend Pohl, librarian of the Gesellschaft, died in 1887, but with this exception the old circle of chums remained as it had been. Joachim, Stockhausen, Grimm, Dietrich, Kirchner, Hanslick, Faber, Billroth, Goldmark, Epstein, Gänsbacher, all had continued with him, whilst in Frau Schumann's presence he was at the age of sixty-one still young, with youthful feelings of veneration in his heart. The death of Billroth dealt him a severe blow. Who shall say that even at this time he had not a presentiment that before very long he was to follow?

---

* Widmann's "Recollections."

If this were so, but little change showed itself in his outward habits. The pedestrian excursions near Vienna took place every second or third Sunday as before, and if Brahms, growing every year heavier, found the ascent of the surrounding heights more fatiguing than in past years, he did not openly allude to the fact, but would invite his companions to pause for a few moments to look at the country, whilst they, at once acceding to his wish, always carefully avoided perceiving that he was short of breath. Hugo Conrat frequently made one of the party of walkers at this period, and the master was often a guest at his house, where it is to be feared that Frau Conrat, in no way behind the rest of his friends, sadly spoiled him. He had become in these years a complete autocrat in the circles in which he moved. His comfort was studied, his desires were anticipated, his witticisms appreciated, his tempers accepted, and his utterances recognised as final. Brahms enjoyed his position, and, it must be confessed, did not hesitate to avail himself of his privileges. On one occasion of a dinner party, being asked to escort one of the principal lady guests to the dining room, he turned sharply round and offered his arm to the young governess. On another —a party at the Conrats' country house—finding on his arrival that the cloth had been laid in the dining room, and not in the veranda, he went up to the hostess, saying: "But it is still fine weather. I always dine out of doors in October." The lady sent word to the kitchen that the dinner was to be put back for twenty minutes, and, begging her visitors to 'walk in the garden meanwhile, gave orders for the alteration of her arrangements. "But what did Brahms say when he found he was causing such trouble?" someone asked Fräulein Conrat afterwards. "Then he was good again," she replied. Such incidents could be multiplied from the experiences of many of Brahms' friends. They serve chiefly to prove that the master's mind lost its pliancy as he grew older, and that he became incapable of adapting himself to circumstances outside his ordinary routine. His friends accepted his whims as a part of himself, and, knowing his sensitiveness to contradiction, did not contradict him. They were aware that the sterling nature had not really changed, and did not trouble themselves to criticise the outer crust of irritability and roughness that sometimes concealed it from the appreciation of less indulgent observers.

"All that you tell me is very nice," said Brahms one day to Conrat's two gifted young daughters, who, paying the master a visit in his rooms, had been encouraged by him to talk about the progress of their studies. "You must know these things, which are very important; but I will show you something to be learnt of still greater consequence"; and he fetched from a drawer an old, worn, folded tablecloth. "Look here," said he, showing the two girls some exquisite darning, "my old mother did this. When you can do such work you may be prouder of it than of all your other studies."

After the completion of the Clarinet Quintet and Trio in 1892, Brahms allowed his mind the refreshment of change of work. The only original compositions belonging to the following year are the two books of "Clavierstücke," Op. 118 and 119, the appearance of which we have already chronicled. He was, however, engaged with his collection of German folksongs, arranged with pianoforte accompaniment, six volumes for one voice, and the seventh for leader and small chorus.

The publication of this valuable work in 1894, almost at the end of the life of the great musician who compiled it, adds yet another and most striking illustration to those on which we have commented, of the general continuity of the lines on which Brahms' career was shaped. As he began, so he ended. The boy of fifteen who arranged folksongs for practice by his village society, the youth of twenty who used them in his first published works, the mature master

who returned to them again and again for inspiration and
delight, all live in the veteran of sixty-one, who, as he busies
himself in preparing the unique collection, every page of
which bears mark of his insight, skill and sympathetic tact,
seems to be looking back over the years of the past with
longing to leave behind him a final sign of his love for his
great nation and all belonging to it. "It is the only one
of my works from which I part with a feeling of tenderness,"
he said on its completion for the press. A child of the
people by birth, Brahms remained, with all his literary and
artistic culture, a child of the people by sympathy. He
loved, and ever had loved, the simple peasant folk of the
country places where he dwelt, as part of the great life of
nature which was his delight. His partiality for them had
in it something which resembled his feeling for children.
He was pleased with their *naïveté*, valued their confidence,
and perhaps, idealist as he was, gave them credit for a
genuineness and simplicity not always theirs. In their
songs, it was this same naturalness that attracted him, and
whether in his original settings of national texts, or in his
arrangements of the people's melodies, nearly always, as
we have seen, left the words as he found them in their
spontaneous directness of expression. Writing to Professor
Bächtold, to whom he sent a copy of his collection, he says:

". . . I think you will find some things new to you, for
if you have been interested in the music of our folk-songs,
Erk and now Böhme will have been your guides? These
have hitherto led the (very Philistine) tone, and my collection stands in direct opposition to them. I could and should
like to gossip more if I knew that you were interested and
especially if we were sitting together comfortably. . . ."*

He had sent the manuscript to Frau Schumann in the
spring, hoping, as he wrote:

---

* Steiner, p. 33.

"to bring a little sunshine into the room.

"You must not take them too seriously and solemnly, but enjoy certain things in them, as for instance, the just-mentioned sunbeam. . . .

"Some things must interest or touch you: e.g.: 'The Schwesterlein,' if you picture to yourself the position of the poor jealous girl. In Gunhilde and the story on page 6, you must think of Peri and what the tear of repentance signifies. The man and the woman lead perilous lives but as they repent and atone, the lilies bend over and the angel prays for the sinner. Na—and so forth.

"I am very anxious that you should not take the stories too seriously. And then many of them are incomplete."[*]

Brahms at one time contemplated changing his rather confined quarters at Ischl, but a feeling of loyalty to the good folks in whose house he had spent several summers, and who regarded themselves as having a prescriptive right to their lodger, asserted its sway over his kind heart. He returned to them as each succeeding spring came round, and the little signs that heralded his approach—the opening of shutters, the cleaning of windows, and other preparations visible from outside—were eagerly looked forward to by the country people near as the first tokens of the approaching season.

Frau Grüber's little house, of which Brahms occupied the first floor, was built on a mountain slope, and a short flight of steps at the side led to a small garden furnished with a grass plot, a garden bench and a summer house. Visitors had to mount the steps, cross the garden, find a second entrance door at the back of the house, go in, and knock at the door of the composer's sitting room. Sometimes he would cross the room, open the door and peep cautiously out; but more often than not he called out: "Come in!" and the visitor stepped at once into his presence. He laid strict injunctions on his landlady, however, that the door

---

[*] Litzmann III, p. 579.

BRAHMS AT DR. FELLINGER'S, JUNE 15, 1896.
Photograph by Maria Fellinger.

of his rooms was to be kept locked and the key in her possession whenever he was out, and that on no account was she to allow anyone even to peep into the room containing his papers and piano. If he once found out that she had disregarded this rule, once would be enough for him; that very day he would pack up and leave her, never to return. It was a most necessary precaution to take, for numerous visitors of either sex who were unknown to him found their way to the house, and would gladly have sought consolation for their disappointment at not seeing him by inspecting some of his belongings.

One or other of his friends frequently called for him about half past eleven, and soon afterwards he would start out and gradually make his way to the Hôtel Kaiserin Elisabeth. Between two and three o'clock he usually made his appearance on the promenade by the side of the river. Stopping at Walter's coffee house, he would seat himself at a table under the trees outside, where a cup of black coffee and the daily papers were at once brought to him. Here he generally remained for at least an hour, and sometimes it was much longer, to be joined by one friend and another till his party numbered a dozen or more. Walter's became, indeed, at this hour of the day, a rendezvous not only for Brahms' personal friends, but for many musical visitors to Ischl who did not know him, but who heard that they could easily get a sight of him there. He was very particular in acknowledging the greetings of his numerous acquaintance as they passed along the promenade, and, owing to his anxiety to be courteous and his near-sightedness combined, he sometimes made a mistake and bowed to people whom he did not know.

"Oh, if you had only been with us this afternoon!" a friend and fellow lodger said to the author one day in the summer of 1894. "Paula and I were walking on the promenade, and we met Brahms, who greeted us so kindly. He waved his hand, and looked round, saying: 'Good day! good day!' Of course I returned his greeting. I wonder if it could have been because he was pleased with my little Paula? He takes so much notice of children." Frau F. was far too much gratified by the incident to accept the author's opinion that it was a case of mistaken identity, as Brahms was not in the habit of consciously bowing to strangers.

Herr Oberschulrath Wendt, of Carlsruhe, when staying at Ischl, was daily to be seen in the master's company, and the two men, both of striking appearance, presented a singular contrast as they paced side by side along the promenade. Wendt, tall, thin and pale, was delicate looking, and walked with a slight stoop. Brahms, rather short, very stout, with a good deal of colour, probably acquired by exposure to the weather, that seemed the more pronounced from its contrast with his white hair and beard, went along with head well thrown back, the very personification of vigour. On leaving Walter's he generally betook himself to a friend's house, most frequently that of Johann Strauss. To his intimacy there the world is indebted for some of the best of his late photographs—those of Krziwanek, of Vienna and Ischl—which were taken one afternoon in the summer of 1895 as he was sitting at ease with his friends.

Brahms knew, and was well known to, all the children of the neighbourhood, and when starting on his country walks would fill his pockets with sweetmeats and little pictures, and amuse himself with the eagerness of the small barefooted folk, who knew his ways and would run after him as he passed, on the look out for booty. "Whoever can jump gets a gulden," he would say; and, displaying beyond reach of the little ones a handful of sweetmeats made in imitation of the Austrian coin, he would increase his speed, and raise his hand higher and higher, drawing after him the flock of running, leaping children, until he allowed one and another to gain a prize.

Two Sonatas for clarinet and pianoforte, the last works of chamber music composed by Brahms, were completed during the summer of 1894, and towards the end of September Mühlfeld arrived at Ischl to try them with the composer. The first private performance took place very soon afterwards, when the two artists played them before the ducal circle of Meiningen at the palace of Berchtesgaden.

A reunion at Frankfurt in November is of pathetic interest. It carries us back to the very early pages of our narrative, and is the last complete one of the kind we shall have to record. For the last time we find Frau Schumann and her husband's and her own two special musician-friends making music together. Brahms arrived at her house on a few days' visit on the 9th of the month, and the same evening, listened to a programme of his works—which included the performance of the violin concerto by Joachim—arranged in his honour for the second Museum subscription concert of the season. On the 10th Mühlfeld came from Meiningen by the composer's request and played the two new sonatas to "the revered Frau Schumann," as Brahms used to call her to his younger friends, who had now completed her seventy-fifth year; and to the few intimates assembled in her house. The next day, Joachim, prince of violinists at sixty-three as at twenty-one, the age at which he entered these pages, appeared at a quartet concert, and on the 12th there was a party at Herr and Frau Sommerhoff's, when Brahms and Mühlfeld again played the two sonatas, and Frau Schumann, Joachim and Mühlfeld, Mozart's beautiful Clarinet Trio, a favourite work of Brahms. The reunion of old friends was completed by the presence of Stockhausen, who, like Frau Schumann, had been resident in Frankfurt since 1878. On the 13th, the third Frankfurt performance of the Clarinet Sonatas by Brahms and Mühlfeld took place at a large music party at Frau Schumann's, and another memorable item of the evening's pleasures was the playing by Frau Schumann and Mühlfeld of Schumann's Fantasiestücke for pianoforte and clarinet. Joachim had left to fulfil other engagements before the evening, and Brahms departed on the 14th.

The master's journeys and performances with Mühlfeld gave him extraordinary pleasure, and the publication of the two sonatas, which in the usual course of things would have taken place in the autumn of 1894, was delayed until the summer of 1895, in order that his possession of the manuscripts might be prolonged. Both works were performed at the Rosé concerts, Vienna, by the composer and his friend—No. 2 in E flat on January 8, 1895, when the Clarinet Quintet was also played; and No. 1 in F minor at an extra concert on January 11, the programme of which included the G major String Quintet. They were introduced by the two artists to the musical world of Leipzig at the Gewandhaus chamber music concert of January 27, when the G major Quintet was again performed. Amongst the towns visited by Brahms and Mühlfeld in the month of February were Frankfurt, Rudesheim and Meiningen, and the master was seen for the last time in public by his Frankfurt friends on the 17th, when he listened to a performance of his D major Symphony, and conducted his Academic Overture at a Museum concert. The two sonatas were performed for the first time after publication at Miss Fanny Davies' concert of June 24 in St. James's Hall, London, by the concert giver and Mühlfeld, engaged expressly to come to England for the occasion. On publication of the works the composer presented both manuscripts to Mühlfeld with an appreciative inscription.

Mention must not be omitted from our pages of Brahms' final appearance on the familiar Gewandhaus platform which took place a few days after the Leipzig performance of the Clarinet Sonatas. He achieved one of the crowning successes of his career on the occasion; a success that derives peculiar biographical interest from the fact that in it was included the work which had long been associated in his mind with Leipzig by the remembrance of one of his most mortifying early experiences.

"Nevertheless, the concerto will please some day when I have improved its construction, and a second shall sound different,"

Johannes wrote to Joachim after the "brilliant failure" of the D minor Concerto at the Gewandhaus concert of January 27, 1859.

Exactly thirty-six years had passed away, and the master, now in his sixty-second year, had conducted performances of both his pianoforte concertos, the solos of which had been played with rare technical skill and sympathetic insight by Eugene d'Albert, at the subscription concert of January 31, 1895. Bernsdorff who, in 1859, had condemned the early concerto "to the grave," had been spared to witness the musical events of 1895, and it became his duty to report—for the last time—in the pages of the *Signale* on the composer and his works.

"Johannes Brahms has been staying in Leipzig for about a week," he wrote, "and has been the recipient of what can only be described as extravagant homage. In the first place he was honoured by a chamber music concert that was entirely devoted to his compositions; then his F minor pianoforte quintet was acclaimed at a concert of the Bohemian String Quartet, and he attained the final summit of triumph at the fifteenth Gewandhaus concert with his Academic Festival Overture and two pianoforte concertos in D minor and B flat, all given under his own direction. On this last occasion the ovations reached the utmost pitch of enthusiasm, the recalls and thunders of applause were endless and were supplemented by the customary orchestra flourish and laurel wreath."

So the day came when the concerto *did* please and when the glorious composer found himself acclaimed without stint or question even by the public of the Gewandhaus concerts.

"Brahms arrived to-day in a very cheerful humour," wrote Frau Schumann in her diary on February 13, "he was evidently in good spirits the whole time. He had been greatly pleased by the enthusiastic reception in Leipzig. Naturally it was a great satisfaction to him. So Robert was right after all!"

From details of private incidents connected with Brahms' last artistic visit to Leipzig, we may choose for record some particulars of a conversation that took place between the master and Geheimrath von Hase on the morning after the Gewandhaus concert, when Brahms and d'Albert called together at the house of Breitkopf and Härtel. They touch on the question of the publication of "complete editions" as to the desirability of which Brahms doubts, even in the case of the greatest masters, find expression more than once in his published correspondence.

"I was called to see Brahms in William Volkmann's room," says Dr. von Hase. "As I entered he received me with the exclamation: 'I must confess a great mistake to you, Herr Doctor.' I immediately answered laughing: 'Yes, I know what you mean. The matter occurred a dozen years ago.' I had at that time (1882) gone to Vienna to prepare for a Schubert edition. Brahms had received me delightfully and had shown his readiness to help in every way. He consented to be a member of the committee, came to the meeting at Nicholas Dumba's house, promised his co-operation. He had, however, tried beforehand to dissuade me from the idea. It was very praiseworthy of us to think of making the edition, but what was necessary had already been published. It would now suffice to have the works inspected by a good musician and one copy of each placed either in the Royal Library of Berlin or the Imperial Library of Vienna, to prevent all possibility of their being lost again. The publication of a complete edition and especially of the great mass of songs could have little value except to a few people. Now after twelve years he declared: 'I was mistaken. One sees Schubert quite differently now, and Mandyczewski's edition of the collected songs especially, gives us quite new insight into the character and progress of his creative activity. One sees how it was prepared and then suddenly flowed on in an irresistible stream. It is a unique great picture.'

"From the time of the preparation of the Mozart to that of the projected Haydn edition," continues Dr. von Hase, "Brahms as editor of the Mozart Requiem and the Schubert Masses, as faithful adviser to the Schumann edition, and as helper for Haydn, proved himself a true friend."

With the publication of the two Clarinet Sonatas, our master's career is all but closed, and closed as we would have it. The more familiar they become, the more firmly will they root themselves, as we believe, in the affection of the lovers of his music. The fresh, bounding imagination of youth is, indeed, not in them, nor would we wish it to be there; but both works are pervaded by a warmth and glow as of sunset radiance, which, reflecting the spirit of the composer as he was when he wrote them, fill the mind of the listener with a sense of the mellow beauty, the rich pathos, the unwavering sincerity of his art. To compare the two sonatas one with the other is unnecessary. We prefer simply to commend them to the study of those of our readers to whom they are not entirely familiar, holding them, as we do, to be amongst the especially lovable examples of the late period of Brahms' art.

CHAPTER XXIII.

1895-1897.

The Meiningen Festival—Visit to Frau Schumann—Festival at Zürich—Brahms in Berlin—The "Four Serious Songs"—Geheimrath Engelmann's visit to Ischl—Frau Schumann's death—Brahms' illness—He goes to Carlsbad—The Joachim Quartet in Vienna—Brahms' last Christmas—Brahms and Joachim together for the last time—The Vienna Philharmonic concert of March 7—Last visits to old friends—Brahms' death.

BUT few events remain for record in the life which we have now followed step by step nearly to the end of its progress. Of these few, several have the pathetic interest of last visits to dear and familiar places made, so far as appears, without presentiment that they were final. The composer was present at a three days' festival held in Meiningen September 27-29, 1895; "the Festival of the three B's," as it has sometimes been called, from the circumstance that the programmes were devoted to works by Bach, Beethoven and Brahms. Those of Brahms selected for performance included the Song of Triumph, the Fourth Symphony, the B flat Pianoforte Concerto, with d'Albert as pianist, the Clarinet Sonatas performed by the same artist with Mühlfeld, some of the Vocal Quartets, amongst them the early favourite "Alternative Dance Song," and others.

The festival was an immense success, and the pleasure which the master derived from the concerts is evident in the following lines written to Steinbach immediately after the last one:

"DEAR FRIEND,

"However tempted I may feel, I dare not break in upon your well-deserved rest; but you shall find my hearty greeting awaiting you on your happy awakening; how hearty and grateful it is there is no need to tell you in detail. You must have perceived each day that you gave me and all who took part in your splendid festival, a quite exceptional pleasure. . . ."*

Brahms was, of course, a guest at the castle, and he remained on for a few days after the last concert. Leaving Meiningen on October 3, he proceeded to Frankfurt on a flying visit to Frau Schumann. Professor Kufferath, of the Brussels Conservatoire, with Mr. and Mrs. Edward Speyer, were, by his particular suggestion, invited to spend the evening at Frau Schumann's house. Professor Kufferath, a pupil of Mendelssohn at Leipzig, and on a very old footing of intimacy at the Schumanns, had been for more than twenty years on terms of cordial friendship with Brahms also, though the two men met but seldom. Frau Schumann's daughters, Marie and Eugénie, and Stockhausen, were the only others present. The hours were spent in pleasant chat as between old friends, and music was represented only by a few of Brahms' folksongs sung by Mrs. Speyer (Fräulein Antonia Kufferath) to the master's accompaniment.

Brahms left the next morning, but before his departure he requested his old friend to play to him. Forty-two years had passed since Schumann had desired him to play for the first time to her, marking both musicians with inevitable outward signs. The traces of suffering and sorrow had deepened of late on Frau Schumann's countenance, but those who were happy enough to listen to her playing at this period, in the privacy of her home, knew that the burden

---

* Reimann, p. 109.

of the years had left the poetry of her genius untouched and Brahms' last remembrance of the great artist will have fitly completed the long chain of personal associations begun when Schumann called his wife to rejoice with him in the daring power and romantic enthusiasm of Johannes' inexperienced youth. When she rose from the piano on that October morning, the final link had been added. Frau Schumann and Brahms were not to meet again on earth.

A four days' festival in October (19-22) to celebrate the inauguration of the new concert hall at Zürich seems to carry us more than one stage nearer the end. It brought Brahms for the last time to Switzerland to conduct his Triumphlied; a fine close—for as such it may almost be regarded—to a noble career.

Let us pause for a moment to picture the robust figure of the composer as he stands before the vast audience completely filling the brilliantly lighted hall, and leads with sure, quiet dignity the "masses of chorus and orchestra" that swell out in proud tones of thankfulness for his country's glory. Listen! for with the sounds of the grand old hymn, "Now thank we all our God," the bells of victory are pealing, and a sensation of happiness spreads through the mass of hearers, a vibration that stirs something of the feeling which roused the great German audience at Cologne to enthusiasm as they listened many years ago to the same jubilant tones. Who so fitted to raise the strain as the patriot citizen of ancient Hamburg, the unique descendant of the mighty Bach, the musician of true, rich, loving spirit, conqueror of life and of himself, our Johannes Brahms? Conqueror, too, of death; for surely we cannot be mistaken in accepting the likeness of the master, that looks down with those of the greatest of his art from the painted ceiling of the new hall, as the symbol of a further life to be his even here on earth, when he has entered the darkness that is soon to cover him from our sight.

Brahms was in overflowing spirits during the entire

festival, enjoying the concerts, the private gatherings, the meetings with old friends, in a mood of harmless gaiety that recalls the Detmold days.

"We have seen Brahms and Joachim together again, both in full vigour; may we not hope for a prolongation of this happy state of things?" writes Steiner a few days after the festival.

Widmann was, of course, there, and stayed with Brahms at Hegar's house. When he bade the master farewell on the day after the concert, the two friends clasped hands in a final grasp.

One of Brahms' late public appearances was on the occasion of the concert given in the Bösendorfer Hall, Vienna, by Signorina Alice Barbi (later the Baroness Wolff Homersee) shortly before her marriage. He pleased himself by acting as accompanist to the distinguished cantatrice, whose programme included a number of his songs. He held the baton for the last time on a Vienna platform when he directed the performance of his Academic Overture by the students of the conservatoire at the festival concert given to celebrate the twenty-fifth anniversary on March 18, 1895, of the opening of the present home of the Gesellschaft der Musikfreunde. He officiated for the last time in public at d'Albert's concert in Berlin of January 10, 1896, conducting his two Pianoforte Concertos and the Academic Overture, and was received with the usual enthusiasm. Stanford speaks of being present at a dinner party given by Joachim during Brahms' brief visit.

"Joachim, in a few well-chosen words, was asking us not to lose the opportunity of drinking the health of the greatest composer—when, before he could say the name, Brahms started to his feet, glass in hand, and calling out: 'Quite right; here's to Mozart's health,' walked round clinking glasses with us all. His old hatred of personal eulogy was never more prettily expressed. . . . The last vision I had of him was as he sat beside the diminutive form of the aged Menzel, drinking in, like a schoolboy, every word the great old artist said with an attitude as full of unaffected reverence as of unconscious dignity."

Of all modern painters, Adolph von Menzel was the most admired by Brahms. He visited him on several occasions, and spoke of him and his works with unfailing enthusiasm.

The master made a détour on his return journey to spend a day in Leipzig, where we hear of him supping, in capital spirits, at a well known restaurant with Grieg, Henschel and Nikisch. Very early Leipzig recollections invested, probably, with something of the tenderness that belongs to the memory of past struggle, were revived within him a few weeks later when he received a call in Vienna from Reinecke, retired a year since from public activity.

"His (Brahms') caustic manner with acquaintances had quite disappeared and intercourse with him had become easier. . . . He eagerly showed me his valuable collection of autographs; a number of Schubert's songs (including some of the most celebrated); Beethoven's sketches; Holderlin letters; six string quartets of Haydn; Mozart's G minor Symphony; and many more."*

That the master had realised a competence some years before his death—more than a competence for one of his extraordinarily simple habits—is generally known. How he regarded it, how he used it, may have been but little suspected outside a small circle. His friend and publisher, the late head of the firm of Simrock, shared his confidence on the subject more than anyone else, for it was often through his agency that Brahms' munificence was applied to its object; the substantial help, perhaps, of a needy musician, or a promising talent. He contributed more than one large donation to the "Franz Liszt Pensionsverein" of Hamburg, a society founded by Liszt in 1840 for the benefit of aged or disabled members of the Stadt Theater orches-

---

* "Gedenkblätter an berühmte Musiker," Reinecke.

tra. Several authentic stories are told by accidental witnesses of some of his particular acts of generosity. One has been related to the author by the Landgraf of Hesse, who was sitting with the master one morning when a caller appeared with a tale of distress which touched his heart. He listened quietly, asked some questions, then went to his writing table, and, handing his visitor the entire sum of money towards which he was asked for a contribution, said quietly:

"Take this from me; I do not need it. I have more money than I want for myself."

This was his usual formula on such occasions:

"I do not need it," to which was sometimes added: "If you should ever have it in your power, you can pay me back."

Brahms' heart was of gold, if ever such existed. He was rough sometimes—often, perhaps—let it be freely granted. The spoiled humours of his last two or three years have already been noted; they do not amount to much. He permitted himself deliberately to repulse strangers or slight acquaintances when he felt so disposed; necessarily, if his time and tranquillity were to be protected. Now and then he was inconsiderate or blunt to his friends. The concentration of mind, the sacrifice of immediate inclination, the devotion of energy, involved in the fulfilment of the career of genius are often but imperfectly realised even by the friends of a famous man. The great poet, the great painter, the great musician, has his brilliant rewards. He has also his bitter disappointments, and one of the hardest of these —which is especially apportioned to the lot of the creative musician—is the discovery that, as in the case of other princes and sovereigns of the world, his path in life must be solitary. Brahms may sometimes have imagined he had reason for his impoliteness; more frequently a gruff manner, an awkward joke, was the result of a constitutional want of presence of mind in trifling matters, which frequently caused him to be misunderstood. His real attitude is expressed in a note published after his death by Hanslick in the *Neue Freie Presse* article from which we have already more than once quoted.* Hanslick had sent him a packet of letters to read, and had inadvertently enclosed in it one from a mutual friend which contained a comparison of Beethoven and Brahms. In it were these words:

"He is often offensively rough to his friends like Beethoven, and is as little able as Beethoven was to free himself entirely from the effects of a neglected education."

Hanslick was very much upset on remembering what he had done, and immediately wrote to Brahms to throw himself on his mercy and beg his silence on the matter. The master immediately answered:

"Dear Friend,

"You need not be in the least uneasy. I scarcely read ——'s letter, but put it back at once into the cover, and only gently shook my head. I am not to say anything to him—ah, dear friend, that happens, unfortunately, quite of itself in my case! That one is taken even by old acquaintances and friends for something quite different from what one is (or, apparently, shows one's self in their eyes) is an old experience with me. I remember how I, startled and confounded, formerly kept silence in such cases; now however, quite calmly and as a matter of course. That will sound harsh or severe to you, good and kind man—yet I hope not to have wandered too far from Goethe's saying, 'Blessed is he who, without hate, shuts himself from the world.'"

Brahms was ready for another journey to Italy in the spring, but Widmann was unable to accompany him, and he passed his sixty-third birthday anniversary in Vienna. When it dawned, the work that was for a short time gener-

---

* July 1, 1897.

ally accepted as his swan-song had been completed. Deiters writes that the immediate occasion of the composition of the "Four Serious Songs" was the death of the artist Max Klinger's father, which occurred earlier in the year. The not unnatural assumption that has sometimes seen in these solemn utterances of the great composer a presentiment of his own fast approaching end may or may not represent a fact. It has not been accepted by those of his friends amongst whom he passed the last few months of his life, and certainly nothing that is known of his individuality lends likelihood to the notion of his going out, as it were, to meet the thought of his death. On the other hand, his repeated assertion that the songs had been composed for his own birthday points to the possibility that his mind may have been under the influence of forebodings of which he was, perhaps, but vaguely conscious. "Yes, Grüber, we are in the front line now," he said to his landlord on hearing of the death of some of the old people in the course of one of his last summers at Ischl.

The "Four Serious Songs" were published in the summer of 1896 with a dedication to Max Klinger, Brahms' personal friend, of whose work, including that inspired by his own compositions, the master became a warm admirer, though he at first disliked the painter's "Brahms Fantasie." They were sung for the first time in public by Stockhausen's pupil, Anton Sistermann, at his concert of November 9, 1896, in the Bösendorfer Saal, Vienna, when the accompaniments were played by the pianist, Ruckauf.

"What breathless stillness and awe in the crammed room! What reverential applause after each number!" writes Hanslick, referring in his notice of the concert, to the solemn character of the "Serious Songs," "and the most remarkable thing of all, the demand for a repetition of the third song, 'O Death,' could not be resisted. Brahms had succeeded in educating his public, or has overawed them."

Three of the songs deal grimly with the thought of death

(Eccles. iii, 19-22, iv, 1-3; Ecclus. xli, 1, 2); the fourth has for its text St. Paul's beautiful glorification of love (I Cor. xiii, 1-3, 12, 13):

"For that which befalleth the sons of men befalleth beasts; as the one dieth, so dieth the other, for all is vanity. . . .
"Though I spake with the tongues of men and of angels, and had not love, I should be as sounding brass or a tinkling bell. . . .
"We see now through a glass, in a dark word, but then face to face. Now I know it partly, but then I shall know it as I am known.
"Now remain faith, hope, love; but the greatest is love."

It is certain that Brahms speaks to us in the songs from the depth of his convictions. Herr Geheimrath Dr. Engelmann arrived one evening in the course of the summer on a day's visit to Ischl. Brahms called at his hotel at six o'clock the next morning, and after breakfast brought his friend back to his rooms, where they spent several hours together. The composer was in delight over some lately-arrived volumes of the complete edition of Schubert's works, then in progress, and could not sufficiently express his joy in their contents. "See here," he said, with his energetic enthusiasm, as he pointed to one place after another with beaming face and lightening eyes—" see here, what a splendid fellow he was! People talk of him as a mere melodist, but look what material he had even in his early works; look what the melodies are, how they grow." By and by, taking up a copy of the "Four Serious Songs," he said: "Have you seen my protest? I wrote these for my birthday."

The explanation of these words is that the master viewed with mistrust, or even dislike, modern efforts to revivify and popularise the services of the Evangelical Church by the introduction of sacred musical works composed for the purpose, of which those of Heinrich von Herzogenberg may be taken as the type. Brahms, who subscribed to no church dogmas, regarded this tendency as artificial, and therefore as weak and unhealthy, and much as he admired Herzogenberg's powers, he regretted that they were dominated during the last ten years of his creative activity by his strong ecclesiastical bias.* Brahms' love of the Bible and his preference for scriptural texts was, as we know, not that of what is conventionally called a "pietist." He spoke in the language of the people's book as a realist who was at the same time an idealist. He has so arranged the texts of his German Requiem that it would be difficult to construe the work as the embodiment of a definite belief, and we know that he expressly refused to limit its significance by stamping it with the sign manual of christian church dogma; and yet, as we have endeavoured to show, it contains the presentiment, the inspiration, of something positive. From Brahms' standpoint the attempt to go behind the mysteries of life and death, to construct the unspeakable, the unthinkable, into verbal formulæ, is not only predoomed to failure, but is almost irreverent. Yet, as we may remember, "he had his faith," and if anything may be judged of it from the story of his life, the spirit of his works, this faith lay in acceptance of the immutability of truth, the sacredness of life, and the sovereignty of love.

Brahms, who had been detained in Vienna longer than usual this year by anxiety about Frau Schumann's health and the desire to remain within reach of direct tidings from Frankfurt, had been settled in his rooms at Ischl but a few days, when he was profoundly shaken by the tidings of his old friend's death. She passed away peacefully at her home in Frankfurt on May 20, in the seventy-seventh year of her age, and was laid to rest by her husband's side at Bonn on Whit Sunday, May 24. The story of her life, triply

---

* See for an account of Herzogenberg's church music, "Heinrich von Herzogenberg und die evangelischen Kirchenmusik," by Friedrich Spitta. Reprint from the *Monatschrift für Gottesdienst und kirchliche Kunst*, 1900, No. 11.

crowned by fame, love and sorrow, remains amongst the cherished possessions of the world.

A great crowd of musicians and friends assembled at the funeral, those of Frankfurt, Bonn and Cologne being strongly represented. The custom of the ceremony had changed with time since Johannes had borne Frau Clara's laurel wreath to Schumann's grave, and on the conclusion of the service, which consisted of the singing of chorales and an address by Dr. Sell, of Bonn University, more than two hundred floral tributes were piled up around the spot. Joachim with Herzogenberg, bound by Italian engagements, had attended a service held in the Schumanns' house at Frankfurt. Woldemar Bargiel and Bernhard Scholz were at the cemetery, and of our own particular musicians, Stockhausen and Brahms. Another last meeting.

On the termination of the service, Brahms, whose agitation had been very unpleasantly heightened during his journey from Ischl by the delay of a train, and his consequent anxiety lest he should be late, went to Honnef to stay till the next day with Herr and Frau Wehermann, the near relatives of his Crefeld friends, the von Beckeraths and von der Leyens, who were at the time on a visit there. Professor Richard Barth and his wife, Dr. Ophüls, and two of the Meiningen musicians, Concertmeister Eldering and Herr Piening, were also of the party. The master was very much excited and overcome on his arrival at Honnef, but the soothing influence of the Rhine country, so closely associated with the recollections of his youth, did him good, and he prolonged his visit to nearly a week. Confiding to Barth the day after his arrival that he had with him something new, which he would like to play very quietly to one or two chosen listeners, his three most intimate friends retired with him to a room secure from interruption, impressed by his manner with the feeling that something unusual was about to ensue. When the little party had taken their places, Brahms, with every sign of the most profound emotion, which communicated itself to his companions, played through the "Four Serious Songs" from the manuscript. "I wrote them for my birthday," he said in the same words which he afterwards used to Dr. Engelmann. He then played some new organ preludes.

He was agreeably interested in Dr. Ophüls' project of arranging a collection of his composed texts. "I have often wished for such a thing, for though I do not care to look closely at my music, it would be quite pleasant to recall it now and then by reading the texts." The collection was completed during the ensuing months, and the manuscript placed in the master's hands.*

Brahms appeared unannounced in Vienna in the middle of June to take part in the family celebration of Dr. and Frau Fellinger's silver wedding day. Returning immediately to Ischl, he spent the next few weeks in his usual fashion, though neither mind nor body really recovered the double shock of Frau Schumann's death and of the anxious journey to Bonn. He occupied himself still with his art, and on June 24 had completed seven organ preludes, which he played to Heuberger on that date at Ischl. "Splendid pieces," says Heuberger's diary; and in another entry, dated July 5: "Brahms' things must have been sent away already, for he has promised to show me *new* compositions."† These were, no doubt, some more preludes. Eleven were found after Brahms' death, the last four being written on a different kind of paper from that used for the first seven.

The "Elf Chorale-Vorspiele" (Eleven Chorale-Preludes) for organ are instrumental movements founded, as their

---

* Preface to the "Vollständige Sammlung der von Johannes Brahms componirten und musikalisch bearbeiteten Dichtungen," by Dr. G. Ophüls.

† "Der musikalische Nachlass von Johannes Brahms," by Ludwig Karpath. *Signale*, March 26, 1902.

name implies, upon some of the grand old church tunes for which Germany is famous. They are worked in florid counterpoint in a style which may be studied, also, in the organ preludes contained in the third volume of the Leipzig Society's edition of Bach's works, and are written with an ease to which no other composer than Brahms has attained in this style since Bach's day. That the great modern master had studied it during the years of his retirement in the fifties, before he was in possession of the society's volumes, seems certain, from the fact that three old books of Bach's Chorale-Preludes once belonging to Brahms are still in existence. One, bearing Brahms' pencil autograph, is in manuscript, possibly that of his father or brother; the others are early published editions.*

The majority of the chorales selected for treatment in 1896 have death for their subject, and are written in the profoundly serious vein to which we are accustomed in the composer's sacred works. The fourth prelude, "Herzlich thut mich erfreuen," is in a somewhat lighter vein than the others, but is, none the less, absolutely and distinctly Brahms. One of the most delicately touching is the eighth, "Es ist ein Ros' entsprungen." "Herzlich thut mir" is the subject of two of the movements, "O Welt ich muss dich lassen" of two, of which one is the eleventh and last.

It is impossible that we can be mistaken in accepting the Chorale-Preludes, together with the "Four Serious Songs" which immediately preceded them, as indicating the bent of the composer's thoughts during his last year of life, and we involuntarily apply to them the words, quoted in the preceding chapter, used by Brahms in reference to Schumann's theme. They speak to us "as the message of a spirit about to depart, and we think with reverence and emotion of the glorious man and artist." Nevertheless, a note written by the composer to Frau Caroline on August

---

* In the possession of Mr. Howard-Jones.

13 contains little sign of his depressed condition. It opens with charming, simple comments on his stepmother's last little budget of home news, urges a tour in Norway and Sweden on Fritz Schnack—"it would give me real pleasure if he would do it, and tell me all about it afterwards"— and ends:

"The summer is not exactly fine, but whoever, like myself, rises early and can go out walking when he will, may be content and there are innumerable beautiful walks here. I hope you will continue so well and write sometimes to
"Your heartily greeting JOHANNES."*

It had not escaped the notice of Brahms' friends, however, that his ruddy complexion had changed to a yellow colour, and some of them were courageous enough to speak to him about his health, and urge him to consult a doctor. At first he showed much annoyance when the subject was broached, and turned it off impatiently with the reply that, as he never used a glass, he did not know how he looked. But the uneasiness felt about his condition increased, and he was at length persuaded to seek medical advice in Vienna. The doctor whom he consulted did not issue an alarmist report, but, pronouncing him to be suffering from jaundice, ordered him to Carlsbad for the "cure." Much against his will, the master, who hated the very idea of waters and cures, and who prided himself on never having been ill in his life, gave up some pleasant Ischl engagements and started on September 2 for Carlsbad. He was met at the station by two friends of Hanslick, Herr Emil Seling and Musikdirektor Janetschek, who took him to the "Stadt Brussels," near the Hirschensprung. Here, during the fine autumn days which succeeded the wet summer, he made himself content, and even wrote cheerful reports to his friends, in which he expressed satisfaction at having been obliged to make the acquaintance of the celebrated water-

---

* First published by Reimann, p. 118.

ing place. He was the object of much considerate and respectful attention, which seemed to cheer him; and Faber came to be near him, accompanied him in his daily walks, and took tender care of him.

The report written to Hanslick by the distinguished Carlsbad physician, Dr. Grünberger, after three weeks' careful observation, was ominous. There was considerable swelling of the liver, with complete blocking of the gall passages, and the inevitable results—jaundice, indigestion, etc. The eminent medical authority could not but regard the condition of his patient as "very serious."

No more definite name was given to the malady on the master's return to Vienna after several weeks' treatment at Carlsbad, and his request that he should be told "nothing unpleasant," was scrupulously observed. He went about as before, dining more frequently, however, with his most intimate friends the Fellingers, Fabers, Millers, Conrats, Strauss' and von Hornbostels, and often accepting the offer from one or another of a seat in a box at the Burg Theater. He frequently called to inquire after Grieg, who arrived in Vienna in the course of November to take part in concerts of his own compositions, and was attacked with sudden illness that confined him for several weeks to his room; and the two composers, after having been for ten years on terms of acquaintance that had never ripened into actual friendship, now developed a sincere personal liking for each other. Brahms attended at least one of the Grieg concerts when they at last took place, and joined the Norwegian master and his wife at supper afterwards, sitting with them until late into the night. Brahms became very testy if asked how he was or if told that he looked better, and answered to every inquiry: "Each day a little worse," but continued in letters to his stepmother and other friends at a distance to keep up the fiction that he was suffering from an ordinary jaundice which only needed patience. Those who loved him, however, looked with dismay at the alteration that was taking place in his appearance. The yellow colour, which had been the first striking symptom of his condition, was changing gradually to a darker hue, the bulky figure shrinking to terrible emaciation; the firm gait was beginning to falter, the head was no longer held erect. A visit to Vienna, early in December, of Joachim and his colleagues of the Quartet gave him touching pleasure; he was with them as much as possible during the day, and generally remained with them, after attending their concerts, until late at night. He continued to take interest in important new compositions, and begged Hausmann to come to his rooms to play him Dvorák's Violoncello Concerto. He accompanied the entire work on the piano, and broke into enthusiastic admiration at the end of each movement, exclaiming after the last one: "Had I known that such a violoncello concerto as that could be written, I could have tried to compose one myself!"

He not only spent Christmas Eve with the Fellingers, but invited himself to dine with them also on December 25, 26 and 27. Frau Fellinger gave him a "sacco," a soft, short coat, as one of her Christmas presents, and it seemed a sort of comfort to him to put it on when he was at the house, where it was kept in readiness for his use, and to sit quietly in the family sitting rooms without need of exerting himself. After dinner on the 27th he raised his glass, saying: "To our meeting in the New Year," but by and by added, pointing downwards: "But I shall soon be there." He dined again on New Year's Day with the same dear friends, whose joy it was to feel that they were privileged to afford him some solace in his weakness and suffering.

The Joachim party returned to Vienna after a tour in the Austrian provinces, and gave two concluding concerts in the Bösendorfer Hall on January 1 and 2, 1897. Ill as he was, Brahms not only attended both concerts, but came on the morning of the 2nd to Joachim's rooms at the Hôtel

Tegethof to listen to the rehearsal of his G major Quintet, which was in the evening's programme. He derived peculiar pleasure from hearing it. "That is not a bad piece," he said, as though half ignoring that it was his own. The scene which took place after the performance of the work in the evening is remembered with emotion by those who took part in it. It was the final one in the friendship of Brahms and Joachim—a friendship as striking and interesting as any contained in the history of art. Its character may be suggested to the reader's imagination in a few words written to the author by the great musician whose love and recognition Brahms enjoyed from beginning to end of his career.

"He had great pleasure that evening in the G major Quintet. It was touching to see him come before the public to acknowledge the enthusiasm aroused by his work. The tears were in his eyes and he was very weak. The people cheered and cheered endlessly."

Thus the master's state gradually changed for the worse. He dined with the Fellingers in the middle of the day on February 7, and seemed excited and restless throughout the meal. When it was at an end, he intimated that he wished to be alone with Dr. and Frau Fellinger, and, retiring with them, began to speak about his affairs. He desired, he said, to make a new will, but dreaded the necessary formalities to such a degree that he knew not how to resolve to go through them. Would it not be possible to arrange his affairs quietly without having to speak about them with strangers? Dr. Fellinger said it could be done, and that by the Austrian law things could be so managed that there need not even be witnesses. The master remained for four hours—from two till six o'clock—with Dr. and Frau Fellinger, discussed his affairs in minute detail, and asked Dr. Fellinger to be his curator. He seemed relieved at the end of the conversation, and stayed on with the family, chatting about other topics. The following morning Dr.

Fellinger took to the composer at his rooms in Carlsgasse the copy of a will which he had drawn out to meet Brahms' expressed desires, and explained to him that he had only to write it out himself, date and sign his name to it, and it would be valid according to Austrian law. Brahms, who was on the point of starting out to his dinner, expressed himself as glad and relieved, and placed the paper in a drawer of his writing table; and Dr. Fellinger, pleased to have cheered him, returned home with the conviction that he would copy it without delay. The master did not return to the subject at any future meeting with his friends, whilst they, believing the matter to have been finally settled, did not again allude to it.

February passed, and Brahms grew continually worse. Every day he spent a good deal of time in looking through and destroying old letters and other papers. "It is so sad," he would say, when one or other intimate friend called and found him thus employed, his stove filled with ashes. He attended the Philharmonic concert on March 7, when Dvorák's Violoncello Concerto, played by Hugo Becker, and his own Fourth Symphony in E minor were in the programme. Going into the concert room he met his old friend Gänsbacher. "Ah," he said, "you have been so often to see me, and I cannot go to you, I am so suffering"; then, rousing himself a little, went on: "You will hear a piece today, a piece by a man!" (Dvorák's concerto).

The fourth symphony had never become a favourite work in Vienna. Received with reserve on its first performance, it had not since gained much more from the general public of the city than the respect sure to be acceded there to an important work by Brahms. Today, however, a storm of applause broke out at the end of the first movement, not to be quieted until the composer, coming to the front of the "artists'" box in which he was seated, showed himself to the audience. The demonstration was renewed after the second and the third movements, and an extraordinary scene followed the conclusion of the work. The applauding shouting house, its gaze riveted on the figure standing in the balcony, so familiar and yet in present aspect so strange, seemed unable to let him go. Tears ran down his cheeks as he stood there shrunken in form, with lined countenance, strained expression, white hair hanging lank; and through the audience there was a feeling as of a stifled sob, for each knew that they were saying farewell. Another outburst of applause and yet another; one more acknowledgment from the master; and Brahms and his Vienna had parted for ever.

Brahms appeared after the concert at a luncheon party given by Excellenz Dumba, a distinguished protector of art in Vienna. About twenty-five gentlemen, chiefly artists and art-lovers, and the ladies of the house were present. Brahms was placed near to several of his intimate friends—Epstein, Conrat, Hanslick, Gänsbacher and Mandyczewski—but he was not able to remain long. Within a few days of this date his Ischl landlady received a postcard from him announcing his intention of going to Ischl earlier than usual, and desiring that his rooms might be got ready. The last opera he heard was his friend Goldmark's "Das Heimchen"; he entered a theatre for the last time on March 13, sitting with Hanslick at the production of Johann Strauss' "Die Göttin der Vernunft," but was obliged to leave at the end of the second act, and, much against his will, suffered a friend to accompany him home in a cab.

From this time he rapidly grew worse. He complained that he could no longer remember what he read, but wished for Busch's "Bismarck," the last book with which he tried to occupy himself. He soon became unable to take a walk even in a friend's care, and Dr. Victor von Miller called every day in his carriage to take him to drive in the Prater, where the fresh air somewhat revived him. His strength of will remained phenomenal to the last. He dragged himself to a rehearsal of the Roeger-Soldat Quartet party held at

Frau Wittgenstein's less than a fortnight before his death, to hear Weber's Clarinet Quintet with Mühlfeld's co-operation. A performance of the work at Meiningen had particularly pleased him, and its inclusion in the Soldat programme was by his suggestion. In the same week he paid his last visit to the Fabers, and, whilst ascending the staircase to their flat, nearly fainted with pain. Herr Faber revived him, and got him on to the drawing room sofa, where he sat exhausted, his head on his breast. He was obliged to leave the family dinner table of some other intimate friends, and, retiring to the next room, sank down in agony. Frau Fellinger was ill at this time, and unable to leave her room. Brahms' last call of inquiry at her house was made on March 19.

The master was very gentle during the last months of his life, and touchingly grateful for every attention shown him. His evenings were of necessity passed in his rooms, for he firmly refused all the entreaties of his friends that he would take up his abode in one or another house, and it was probably about this time that he added a few extracts, with trembling hands, to the "young Kreisler's treasure chest" of 1854.* Every evening at dusk he used to place himself at the piano, and play softly for about half an hour, and when too tired to continue, would sit by the window gazing out on the familiar scene till long after darkness had set in. On March 24 Frau Door, who had always been a favourite with him, called to take him a bunch of violets. She was not admitted, but, observing Dr. von Miller's carriage before the house door, waited near the entrance, hoping to see Brahms pass out. He came down in about half an hour leaning on his friend's arm, and, noticing Frau Door, gave her his hand. "I am very ill" (Mir geht es sehr schlecht), he answered faintly to her inquiry. He did not go out again. The next day Conrat was admitted,

---

* See page 521 of this volume.

and was sitting talking quietly with him, when Brahms, who was on the sofa smoking, suddenly dropped his head. " There must be something in it," he muttered. Conrat gently left the room without disturbing him. On the 26th the physician wrote word to Frau Fellinger that all chance of moving him was over. Brahms did not leave his bed again. His two or three closest friends were constantly at his side, whilst his landlady, Frau Truxa, was his faithful and devoted nurse. He spoke little during the last days, and was too weak to notice much of what was passing in his room, but he managed on the 29th to write a few pencil lines from his bed to Frau Caroline:

"D. M. For the sake of change I am lying down a little and cannot, therefore, write comfortably. Otherwise there is no alteration and as usual, I only need patience.

" Affectionately your JOH."*

A few more weary days and nights, during which the beloved master's life ebbed rapidly away, bring us to the early morning of April 3. He had lost consciousness several times in the night and been restored, and had recognised Faber, who, calling at about six o'clock and performing some slight service for him, caught the whispered words: "Du bist ein guter Mensch" (You are a kind man). It is now nearly nine o'clock, and Brahms has fallen asleep. Early messages of inquiry have been answered, and the doctor, who has been at hand during the night, has departed, promising soon to return. The day has begun with the bright spring promise that the master was wont to greet year after year with joyful welcome; the sun shines, a soft breeze enters through the open window; outside there is a twittering of birds. Near the bed sits the untiring nurse, noticing the signs of the fast approaching end. A movement from the bed claims her assistance. Brahms has

---

* Reimann, p. 118.

opened his eyes, and tries to raise himself. With Frau Truxa's help he attains a sitting posture, and, looking at her, tries to speak. The lips move, but the tongue has lost its power, and he can only utter an inarticulate sound. Great tears roll down his cheeks; a last sigh, a last breath, and he sinks back, supported by gentle hands, on to his pillow, rid of his sufferings, passed quietly to his rest.*

Dr. von Miller, whose house was in the vicinity, was the first of the friends to receive intelligence of the master's decease. He hurried at once to Carlsgasse, and was immediately joined by Dr. Fellinger and Herr Faber. Many others called during the morning, some of whom were admitted to look at the still features, smoothed by the caress of death into an expression of noble serenity. A sketch was taken by the painter Michalek, a mask by Professor Kundemann, a photograph by a private friend. The cause of death was certified, after a medical examination of the remains, as degeneration of the liver. The body, in evening dress, was placed the same afternoon in the coffin, and the room arranged with candelabra containing lighted candles; on a crimson cushion were displayed the various orders of the deceased composer. The next day the arrival began of the flowers, wreaths, crosses and other floral tributes that transformed the room into a temple of beauty.

On the afternoon of the 4th General Secretary Koch, Dr. Fellinger and Herr Faber met in the dwelling, and searched for a will in the presence of a notary, but only found one written in May, 1891, on two sheets of paper, the last of them signed and dated, in the form of a letter to Simrock. This, a legally competent document in Austria in its original form, except for the slight omission of the signature on the first sheet of paper—which, under the indisputable circumstances establishing the authenticity of the will,

---

* See "Am Sterbebett Brahms," by Celestine Truxa, *Neue Freie Presse*, May 7, 1903.

would not have rendered it invalid—had been returned to the master at his own request by Simrock some time subsequent to the death of his sister, Elise Grund, in 1892. It was found, however, to have been marked by Brahms in pencil, some of the clauses lined out, whilst notes in the margin indicated designed alterations. These were in exact correspondence with the wishes expressed by Brahms in February to Dr. and Frau Fellinger, and embodied by Dr. Fellinger in the paper he had delivered into the hands of the composer to be copied by himself and signed. Another search was made the next day, therefore, but it proved fruitless. Only Dr. Fellinger's manuscript was found, and it must be presumed that Brahms had put off the dreaded task from day to day in the hope of feeling more capable of it, until his strength was no longer equal to its fulfilment. Nothing remained, therefore, but to apply to the proper authorities for the nomination of a curator in order that the necessary arrangements might be proceeded with. This was done; Dr. Fellinger was appointed, and on the afternoon of the 5th the sitting room which, with the small inner room leading from it, contained Brahms' library, manuscripts and other possessions, was formally sealed. The coffin was closed the same day.*

As soon as the master's death became known, the offer of an honorary grave was made by the city of Vienna. There was no hesitation in accepting it, but a deliberation was held as to whether the remains should be taken direct to the Central Friedhof or should be cremated at Gotha, according to directions contained in the letter to Simrock, and the ashes only deposited in Vienna. The remembrance of a few words dropped by Brahms himself when speaking of the "sacred spot" which contains the graves of Beethoven and Schubert decided the point. It was felt that he

---

* These particulars, together with those related on page 664 were personally communicated to the author by Frau Dr. Maria Fellinger.

would have chosen to rest in the place selected for him : the particular garden of the Friedhof in which the remains of Beethoven and Schubert lie, and which is sacred also to the memory of Mozart.

"All musical Vienna accompanied the great dead to the grave on the afternoon of April 6 and a stranger not knowing the man's greatness might have measured it by the number of prominent artists mingling in the great assemblage of the funeral procession, by the celebrated men and women who came from afar to show the last honour to Brahms."

Till the hour appointed for the commencement of the ceremony deputations continued to arrive, from various parts of Europe, from the numerous societies of which the composer had been an honorary member, and telegrams and messages to pour in. At one o'clock a deputation from the Hamburg Senate was admitted to the house to lay a magnificent wreath on the coffin side by side with that from the Corporation of Vienna. Wreaths had been sent by the Queen of Hanover, the Duke of Cumberland, the Princess Marie of Hanover, George, Duke of Saxe-Meiningen, the Princess Marie of Saxe-Meiningen, Helene, Baroness von Heldburg, and innumerable private friends known and unknown to Brahms; by the Society of Plastic Arts, Committee of the Opera, Gesellschaft, and other societies of Vienna; by the Philharmonic Society, Society of Music-lovers, Cecilia Society of Hamburg; by the Royal Academy of Arts, Berlin; by the various musical societies of Berlin, Leipzig, Budapest, Cologne, Salzburg, Mannheim, Frankfurt, Jena, Laubach, Lemberg, Graz, St. Petersburg, Brussels, Amsterdam, Cambridge, Basle, Zürich and many other towns. Six cars scarcely sufficed to hold them.

The arrangements of the public funeral with which the city of Vienna honoured the remains of the great composer formed a singular contrast to the simplicity which had marked the daily habits of his life. Details may be read in the journals of the time. We shall confine ourselves to the record of a few of those appropriate to our narrative. The cortège, followed by a long train of mourners, started from Carlsgasse about half past two, and, proceeding to the building of the Gesellschaft der Musikfreunde, halted before the principal entrance, where arrangements had been made for a short ceremony, consisting of an address by Herr Direktor J. R. Fuchs, of the conservatoire, and the singing of Brahms' partsong, "Fahr'wohl," for unaccompanied chorus, under the direction of Richard von Perger, conductor of the Singverein. The procession then passed on to the Evangelical Church in Dorotheenstrasse, where the clergy and choir and several of the city dignitaries were assembled. After the coffin had been carried into the church, the choir sang Mendelssohn's "Es ist bestimmt in Gottes' Rath." The funeral address was delivered by Dr. von Zimmermann, who especially dwelt on the inspiration derived by the deceased composer's art from the pages of the Bible, on his love for children and the childlike spirit, and on his sympathy with distress.

"Wherever he could bring support to the unknown sufferer, the laborious striver, the helpless, the dying, there, in the man who, in his own habits, was frugal to the verge of parsimony, was found the most eager benefactor. The master Johannes Brahms is not dead. His spirit has conquered death and has entered into the light and blessed world of the pure harmonies of peace."

At the entrance to the Friedhof the coffin was surrounded by personal friends of the deceased composer, carrying lighted wind torches, and was accompanied by them to the grave. They were Ignaz Brüll, Anton Dvorák, Arthur Faber, Dr. Fellinger, Robert Fuchs, Georg Henschel, Richard Heuberger, Max Kalbeck, Ludwig Koch, Eusebius Mandyczewski, Dr. von Miller-Aichholz, Richard von Perger. At the graveside von Perger spoke a few words of last farewell:

"This sacred place is now to receive the mortal remains of our great contemporary. He who has so enriched and blessed the whole world, what has he been to us musicians! In the light which streamed from his creative genius, his penetrating art-comprehension, we were able to look up confidently to his incomparable mastership, to his lofty, unbending artistic intelligence. Amid the countless paths and by-paths which to-day intersect the domain of musical art, we were guided by the torch held high and secure by the hand of her first priest. He has met his worthy spiritual brothers, indeed, for the first time to-day in this resting-place, but he was always a simple, sympathetic friend to his living colleagues in art, in spite of the great distance which raised him above them; always a helper of uprising talent, a sure and faithful friend in adversity and suffering. . . . Here thou restest now, thou blessed of heaven, in this vast, awful world-solitude; clouds of light float above thee and that of thee which is immortal floats with them through eternal spaces. Ade Meister Johannes, fahr'wohl, fahr'wohl."

Joachim was in England at the time of Brahms' death, fulfilling long-contracted engagements. Stockhausen, now a man of seventy-three, and not in strong health, was at this period unequal to a hurried and distressing journey from Frankfurt to Vienna.

Memorial performances were given by the Cecilia Verein, Hamburg, on April 5, the day preceding the funeral; by the Vienna Gesellschaft on the 11th; by the Beethoven-Haus Verein, Bonn, in May; by the Royal High School for Music, Berlin, in the summer; by the Leipzig Gewandhaus committee in October; and by innumerable musical societies of Europe and America during the season 1897-98. In nearly all instances the German Requiem formed part of such concerts as were orchestral.

A clause in Brahms' will provided that any of his unpublished works found in his rooms after death should be the property of Simrock. There was one opus only—the eleven Organ Preludes. With them were the arrangements, as pianoforte duets, of Joachim's two overtures referred to in an earlier chapter. All three works were published in 1902, a delay of five years having been caused by difficulties that arose in connection with the will. Apart from detail, these may be generally stated as follows:

Brahms is said to have left, besides his library, which included valuable autograph musical manuscripts, and a very few personal possessions, about £20,000 in investments. In the original will three societies—the Liszt Pensions-Verein of Hamburg, the Czerny Verein and the Gesellschaft der Musikfreunde of Vienna—were named as the inheritors, subject to the payment of a legacy to the composer's landlady, Frau Truxa, and of two life annuities—one to his stepmother, Frau Caroline Brahms, to be continued after her death to her son, Fritz Schnack, for his life; the other to Brahms' sister, Elise Grund. These would practically account for the time being for the income arising from the investments.

In the absence of any legally valid document, about twenty cousins of various degrees of kinship came forward, in answer to advertisements in the newspapers, as claimants to the property. Litigation ensued, and was protracted through several years. The original process and the first appeal were determined in favour of the societies; the second appeal reversed these decisions, and declared the blood relations to be the heirs. To prevent the further expense and delay of another appeal, a compromise was now arrived at by the contending parties, and the general results of the will, the law processes and the compromise have been that the blood relations have been recognised as the heirs to all but the library, which is now in the possession of the Gesellschaft der Musikfreunde; that Frau Truxa's legacy has been paid; and that certain sums accepted by the societies, by which they will ultimately benefit, have been invested, and the income arising from them secured for the payment of the life annuity to Herr Schnack. (Frau Caroline Brahms died in the spring of 1902.)

Projects for the erection of memorials to the master in Hamburg, Vienna and Meiningen, were set on foot soon after his death. The first to be completed was that now standing in the "English Garden" at Meiningen, the unveiling of which was made the occasion of a Memorial Festival in October, 1899. The bust of the master which it displays is the work of Hildebrandt.

The memorial erected at the grave by the heirs, after the final settlement of the property, designed and executed by Fräulein Ilse Conrat, was unveiled on May 7, 1903, the seventieth anniversary of Brahms' birth. It consists of a marble bust and pedestal in front of a marble headstone, on which are allegorical figures in bas-relief.

The marble statue of Brahms erected by subscription on the Karlsplatz, Vienna, in the immediate neighbourhood of the site formerly occupied by the old Carlsgasse dwelling houses in No. 4 in which the composer resided during the last twenty-five years of his life, was designed and executed by Rudolf Weyr and unveiled on May 7, 1908.

The memorial to the master which stands in the foyer of the Musikhalle, Hamburg, raised by subscription and designed and executed by Max Klinger, was unveiled on May 7, 1909.

Memorial tablets have been placed by the respective municipalities on the houses in which Brahms lived in Göttingen (with Joachim), Düsseldorf, Ischl and Thun, and the garden of the house at Mürz Zuschlag has been bought by the town and made into a music garden. A bronze bust of the master by Frau Dr. Fellinger stands in the musicians' pavilion.

A Brahms-Haus has been erected by Dr. von Miller-Aichholz in his private grounds at Gmünden, the rooms of which are constructed to the exact dimensions of those occupied by Brahms in Ischl, and furnished with the Ischl furniture as it used to stand. They contain an interesting collection of musical and other autographs of the master, photographs, programmes and other mementoes.

The "Brahms Society" of Vienna was formed shortly after the composer's death for the purpose of collecting and preserving available mementoes in a special museum.

The "German Brahms Society," established in 1906 has had for its special object the preservation and publication of the master's correspondence and few unpublished original manuscripts. Its later development, constituted in 1908 under the name "Vereinigung der Brahmsfreunde" aims at "the care and cultivation of the memory of Johannes Brahms and of everything relating to his life and work, and especially the arranging of festival Brahms' concerts, and the circulation of the published posthumous works of the deceased musician."

Our task is now completed. If it should prove to have been so far successfully accomplished as to suggest to our readers at all a true conception of the character and individuality of Brahms, to throw some additional light upon the spirit which dictated the composition of his works, our aim will have been achieved. It is as yet perhaps too soon to attempt any surmise as to the exact ultimate place that he will occupy amongst the great ones of his art. Schumann's words, however, spoken more than half a century ago, which proclaimed Johannes as the prophet destined to give ideal musical presentment to the highest spirit of his time, have, even now, been surely proved true. Brahms stands immovable in his position as the presentative of the musical thought of the ages as it has gradually developed through three hundred and fifty years from Palestrina's day to his own; and in his works dwells the high and beautiful spirit—the essential spirit of life—which, whilst it knows no compromise with truth, works out its appointed course in "faith and hope and love, these three; and the greatest of them is love."

CHRONOLOGICAL CATALOGUE OF THE PUBLISHED WORKS OF BRAHMS.

The references are to the pages of this work.

OP.	TITLE OF WORK.	PUBLISHED*	PAGES.
1	Sonata in C major for pianoforte	1853	96, 100, 111, 119, 122, 134, 136-8, 140-1, 147, 150, 160, 177, 304, 498, 542-3.
2	Sonata in F sharp minor for pianoforte	1853	95-6, 119, 123, 136-41, 150, 177, 185, 304, 508, 542.
3	Six Songs for tenor or soprano†	1854	109, 119, 141, 150-2, 305.
4	Scherzo in E flat minor for pianoforte	1854	92, 97, 110-1, 119, 123-4, 134, 136-7, 140-1, 145, 147, 150, 177, 304, 387, 405.
5	Sonata in F minor for pianoforte	1854	120, 128, 138-9, 141, 150, 203, 304, 337.
6	Six Songs for soprano or tenor	1853	141, 150-1, 305.
7	Six Songs for one voice	1854	151, 175, 305.
8	Trio in B major for pianoforte, violin and violoncello	1854	160, 168, 175, 179, 203, 226, 228, 252, 296, 305.
	The same; revised edition	1891	169, 618.
9	Variations on a theme by Schumann for pianoforte	1854	166-8, 175-7, 179, 203, 304, 542.
10	Ballades for pianoforte	1856	173, 182, 201, 248, 304, 452, 542.
11	Serenade in D major for large orchestra	1860	234-5, 237, 251, 254-5, 265, 268, 275, 277, 295, 304, 331, 341, 346-7, 368-9, 434, 453, 464.
12	Ave Maria for women's chorus with accompaniment for orchestra or organ	1861	257-8, 260, 264, 275, 277, 305.
13	Funeral Song for chorus and wind instruments	1861	264-5, 275, 277, 283, 305.

* The dates of publication here printed are those given in Simrock's published Thematic Catalogue of Brahms' works, excepting in the few instances especially indicated in the main narrative.

† Unless otherwise described, all songs for a single voice are composed with pianoforte accompaniment only.

Op.	Title of Work.	Published	Pages.
14	Songs and Romances for one voice	1861	275, 277, 305, 429.
15	Concerto in D minor for pianoforte with accompaniment for orchestra	1861	31, 174, 229, 236-8, 242-54, 273, 275, 277, 304, 449, 451-3, 489, 500-2, 563, 645, 651.
16	Serenade in A major for small orchestra	1860	6, 238, 266-8, 275, 277, 279, 280, 283, 291-2, 296, 304, 334, 337, 340-1, 346, 370, 452-3, 461, 464, 487.
	The same; revised edition	1875	
17	Songs for women's chorus with accompaniment for two horns and a harp	1862	260, 282, 301, 305, 367.
18	Sextet in B flat major for two violins, two violas and two violoncellos	1862	6, 19, 278-81, 287, 293, 295, 297, 301, 305, 346-7, 350, 386, 432, 450, 453, 462, 503, 537.
19	Five Songs for one voice	1862	241, 305.
20	Three Duets for soprano and contralto with pianoforte accompaniment	1861	281, 305.
21	No. 1, Variations on an original theme for pianoforte	1861	280-1, 304, 405.
21	No. 2, Variations on a Hungarian air for pianoforte	1861	222, 281, 304, 452.
22	Marienlieder for mixed chorus *a capella*	1862	258, 301-3, 305, 339, 488, 523.
23	Variations on a theme by Schumann for pianoforte duet	1863*	301-2, 304, 339, 369, 422, 452, 488.
24	Variations and Fugue on a theme by Handel for pianoforte	1862	256, 288, 291-4, 301, 303-4, 332, 339, 367, 388, 404, 452, 487, 542.
25	Quartet in G minor for pianoforte, violin, viola and violoncello	1863	265, 279, 288, 293-4, 297, 305, 330-1, 334, 346, 367, 369, 452-3, 487, 499, 503, 537.
26	Quartet in A major for pianoforte, violin, viola and violoncello	1863	265, 279, 288, 293-4, 297, 305, 330-1, 334, 336, 346, 367, 425, 451, 453, 493, 499, 503.
27	The 13th Psalm for three-part women's chorus with pianoforte accompaniment	1864	259-60, 305, 351.
28	Duets for alto and baritone with accompaniment for pianoforte	1864	305, 352, 425, 451.
29	Two Motets for five-part mixed chorus *a capella*	1864	305, 352.

* Cf. footnote on page 301.

CHRONOLOGICAL CATALOGUE OF WORKS. 679

Op.	Title of Work.	Published	Pages.
30	Sacred Song (by Paul Fleming) for four-part mixed chorus with accompaniment for organ or pianoforte	1864	305, 352.
31	Three Quartets for solo voices with pianoforte	1864	305, 350-2, 367, 463.
32	Songs for one voice	1864	352, 391.
33	Romances from Tieck's "Magelone" for one voice. Nos. 1-6	1865	284-5, 298-9, 305, 364, 405, 429, 463, 502.
	Nos. 7-15	1868	367, 429.
34	Quintet for pianoforte, two violins, viola and violoncello	1865	279, 288. 301. 303, 305, 342, 361, 364-5, 411, 452-3, 503, 645.
34 bis	Sonata for two pianofortes (after the Quintet)	1872	350, 360-1, 364.
35	Variations on a theme by Paganini for pianoforte. (Two sets)	1866	350, 372, 387, 462, 542.
36	Sextet in G major for two violins, two violas and two violoncellos	1866	6, 279, 355-7, 372, 379-80, 385, 451, 453.
37	Three Sacred Choruses for women's voices without accompaniment	1866	258-60, 372.
38	Sonata in E minor for pianoforte and violoncello	1866	343, 359, 373, 462.
39	Waltzes for pianoforte duet	1866*	382, 463.
40	Trio for pianoforte, violin and French horn	1867†	279, 359, 368, 371, 373, 384, 402, 462, 488, 553.
41	Five Songs for four-part men's chorus	1867	402.
42	Three Songs for six-part chorus *a capella*	1868	430.
43	Four Songs for one voice	1868	241, 342, 390-1, 405, 415, 427, 432, 599.
44	Twelve Songs and Romances for women's chorus. Pianoforte accompaniment *ad libitum*	1868‡	260, 282, 349, 429.
45	A German Requiem for soli, chorus and orchestra. Organ *ad libitum*.	1868	6, 175, 190, 198, 254, 373-4, 381-3, 388, 392-402, 407-10, 412-6, 427, 432-4, 436-7, 439, 446, 451, 461, 463, 472-3, 487, 494-5, 503, 511, 515, 528, 530, 543, 559, 562, 566, 569-70, 657, 673.
46	Four Songs for one voice	1868	427.
47	Five Songs for one voice	1868	241, 427-8.

* Compare footnote page 382.
† Compare footnote page 373.
‡ Compare footnote page 430.

Op.	Title of Work.	Published	Pages.
48	Seven Songs for one voice	1868	427-8.
49	Five Songs for one voice	1868	427-8, 502.
50	Rinaldo (cantata by Goethe) for tenor solo, men's chorus and orchestra	1869	430-2, 487, 570.
51	Two Quartets for two violins, viola and violoncello (C minor and A minor)	1873	381-2, 452, 463, 474, 476, 480, 493, 505.
52	Love Songs. Waltzes for pianoforte duet with voices *ad libitum*	1869	439-41, 452, 463, 487-8, 492.
53	Rhapsody (fragment from Goethe's "Harzreise") for contralto solo, men's chorus and orchestra	1870	440-5, 487-8, 495, 517, 546.
54	Song of Destiny for chorus and orchestra	1871	190, 256, 453-5, 457, 463, 490, 506, 514, 571.
55	Song of Triumph for eight-part chorus and orchestra. Organ *ad libitum*	1872	256, 414, 446-9, 460-1, 463, 465-7, 470, 485, 490-1, 501-2, 506, 543, 546, 648, 650.
56A	Variations on a theme by Joseph Haydn for orchestra	Jan. 1874	480-2, 489, 500, 559, 563.
56B	Variations on a theme by Joseph Haydn for two pianofortes	Nov. 1873	482, 487.
57	Songs for one voice	1871	455-6.
58	Songs for one voice	1871	455.
59	Songs for one voice	1873	474, 482.
60	Quartet in C minor for pianoforte, violin, viola and violoncello	1875	203, 238, 415, 482, 492, 497-9, 502.
61	Four Duets for soprano and contralto with pianoforte	1874	492.
62	Seven Songs for mixed chorus *a capella*	1874	492-3.
63	Songs for one voice	1874	492.
64	Quartets for solo voices with pianoforte	1874	492.
65	New Love Songs. Waltzes for four solo voices and pianoforte duet	1875	441, 452, 492.
66	Five Duets for soprano and contralto with pianoforte accompaniment	1875	
67	Quartet in B flat major for two violins, viola and violoncello	1876	496, 504-5.
68	Symphony in C minor for large orchestra. (No. 1)	1877	238, 301, 303, 382, 414, 464, 496, 506-15, 522-3, 525-9, 547, 559, 563.
69	Nine Songs for one voice	1877	522.
70	Four Songs for one voice	1877	522.
71	Five Songs for one voice	1877	522.

CHRONOLOGICAL CATALOGUE OF WORKS. 681

Op.	Title of Work.	Published	Pages.
72	Five Songs for one voice	1877	513, 522.
73	Symphony in D major for large orchestra. (No. 2)	1878	138, 496, 523-7, 531, 536, 538, 546, 553, 644.
74	Two Motets for mixed chorus a capella	1879	538, 543.
75	Ballads and Romances for two voices with pianoforte accompaniment	1878	173, 538, 548.
76	Pianoforte Pieces. (Two books)	1879	531, 542-3, 634.
77	Concerto in D major for violin with accompaniment for orchestra	1879	531-2, 539-41, 543, 552, 602.
78	Sonata in G major for pianoforte and violin	1880	473, 542, 544-5, 547.
79	Two Rhapsodies for pianoforte	1880	542, 546-7, 553, 633.
80	Academic Festival Overture for large orchestra	1881	453, 553-4, 556, 566, 599, 644-5, 651.
81	Tragic Overture for orchestra	1881	552-4, 556, 559, 566.
82	Nänie (by Friedrich Schiller) for chorus and orchestra (harp *ad libitum*)	1881	357, 492, 556-7, 561, 566, 570-1.
83	Concerto for pianoforte in B flat major with accompaniment for orchestra	1882	28-30, 35, 557-9, 563-5, 572, 601, 645, 648, 651.
84	Romances and Songs for one or for two voices with pianoforte accompaniment	1882	565.
85	Six Songs for one voice	1882	566.
86	Six Songs for a deep voice	1882	565-6.
87	Trio in C major for pianoforte, violin and violoncello	1883	123-4, 568-9.
88	Quintet in F major for two violins, two violas and violoncello	1883	568-9.
89	Song of the Fates (by Goethe) for six-part chorus and orchestra	1883	566, 568-72.
90	Symphony in F major for large orchestra. (No. 3)	1884	572-7.
91	Two Songs for contralto with viola and pianoforte	1884	362, 577.
92	Quartets for soprano, contralto, tenor and bass with pianoforte	1884	577.
93A	Songs and Romances for four-part mixed chorus a capella	1884	577, 672.
93B	Tafellied for six-part mixed chorus with pianoforte	1885	579.
94	Five Songs for a deep voice	1884	577, 599.
95	Seven Songs for one voice	1884	577.
96	Four Songs for one voice	1886	598.
97	Six Songs for one voice	1886	598.
98	Symphony in E minor for large orchestra. (No. 4)	1886	578, 581-7, 598, 631, 648, 665.

Op.	Title of Work.	Published	Pages.
99	Sonata in F major for pianoforte and violoncello	1887	591, 598.
100	Sonata in A major for pianoforte and violin	1887	591, 593-4, 598.
101	Trio in C minor for pianoforte, violin and violoncello	1887	591, 598, 602-3.
102	Concerto in A minor for violin and violoncello with accompaniment for orchestra	1888	600, 602, 604-5.
103	Gipsy Songs for four solo voices with pianoforte accompaniment	1888	35, 600, 606-7, 612.
104	Five Songs for mixed chorus *a capella*	1889	613.
105	Five Songs for a deep voice	1889	613.
106	Five Songs for one voice	1889	613.
107	Five Songs for one voice	1889	613.
108	Sonata in D minor for pianoforte and violin	1889	612-3.
109	Fest und Gedenksprüche for double chorus *a capella*	1890	612, 622.
110	Three Motets for four and eight-part chorus *a capella*	1890	618, 622.
111	Quintet in G major for two violins, two violas and violoncello	1891	622-3, 627, 644, 664.
112	Six Quartets for soprano, contralto, tenor and bass with pianoforte	1891	492, 627.
113	Thirteen Canons for women's voices	1891	261, 492, 627.
114	Trio in A minor for pianoforte, clarinet (or viola) and violoncello	1892	625-7, 638.
115	Quintet in B minor for clarinet (or viola), two violins, viola and violoncello	1892	41, 625-7, 638, 644.
116	Fantasias for pianoforte (two books)	1892	627, 635.
117	Three Intermezzi for pianoforte	1892	174, 627, 634-5.
118	Pianoforte Pieces	1893	633, 638.
119	Pianoforte Pieces	1893	633, 638.
120	Two Sonatas for clarinet (or viola) and pianoforte (F minor and E flat major)	1895	643-4, 648.
121	Four Serious Songs for a bass voice	1896	655-6, 659-60.
122	Eleven Chorale-Preludes for Organ (the only posthumous work)	1902	659-60, 673.

CHRONOLOGICAL CATALOGUE OF WORKS. 683

WORKS WITHOUT OPUS NUMBER.

Title of Work.	Published	Pages.
Song, "Mondnacht," for one voice republished	1854 1872	175.
Children's Folksongs with added pianoforte accompaniment	1858	235.
German Folksongs arranged for four-part chorus	1864	352.
Fugue in A flat minor for organ	1864	352.
Studies for pianoforte (Nos. 1 and 2) after Chopin and Weber	1869	69, 445.
Hungarian Dances arranged for Pianoforte Duet, Books 1 and 2	1869	425, 445.
Gavotte by Gluck arranged for pianoforte	1871	211.
Hungarian Dances arranged for pianoforte solo, Books 1 and 2	1872	236, 417, 432, 445.
Hungarian Dances arranged for orchestra, Nos. 1, 3, 10	1874	487-8.
Studies for pianoforte (Nos. 3, 4, 5) after Bach	1879	543.
Hungarian Dances arranged for pianoforte duet, Books 3, 4	1880	208, 547.
Chorale-Prelude and Fugue for organ	1881	233, 492.
Fifty-one Technical Exercises for pianoforte. (Two books)	1893	633.
German Folksongs with pianoforte accompaniment. (Seven books)	1894	82, 638-9.
Arrangements of Joachim's Overtures to "Henry IV" and "Demetrius" as pianoforte duets	1902	439, 673.
Trio in A major for pianoforte, violin and violoncello	1938.	

Published by the German Brahms Society, founded in 1906:
Sonatensatz for violin and pianoforte.
Two Cadenzas to Beethoven's Pianoforte Concerto in G.
Song, "Nachklang," II.

CLASSIFIED CATALOGUE OF WORKS.

INSTRUMENTAL MUSIC.

For Orchestra.
Op. 11. Serenade, D major.
Op. 16. Serenade, A major.
Op. 56A. Variations, Haydn's Theme.
Op. 68. Symphony, C minor.
Op. 73. Symphony, D major.
Op. 90. Symphony, F major.
Op. 98. Symphony, E minor.
Op. 80. Overture, Academic.
Op. 81. Overture, Tragic.
Arrangement: Three Hungarian Dances.

Pianoforte with Orchestra.
Op. 15. Concerto, D minor.
Op. 83. Concerto, B flat major.

Pianoforte Solos.
Op. 1. Sonata, C major.
Op. 2. Sonata, F sharp minor.
Op. 5. Sonata, F minor.
Op. 4. Scherzo, E flat minor.
Op. 10. Ballades.
Op. 9. Variations, Schumann's Theme.
Op. 21, No. 1. Variations, Original Theme.
Op. 21, No. 2. Variations, Hungarian Air.
Op. 24. Variations and Fugue, Handel's Theme.
Op. 35. Variations, Paganini's Theme.
Op. 76. Pianoforte Pieces, two books.
Op. 79. Two Rhapsodies.
Op. 116. Fantasias, two books.
Op. 117. Three Intermezzi.
Op. 118. Pianoforte Pieces.
Op. 119. Pianoforte Pieces.
Technical Exercises, two books.
Arrangement: Hungarian Dances, two books.
Arrangement: Studies 1-5.
Arrangement: Gavotte by Gluck.

Pianoforte Duets.
Op. 23. Variations, Schumann's Theme.
Op. 39. Waltzes.
Op. 52A. Waltzes.
Op. 65. Waltzes.
Arrangement: Hungarian Dances, four books.

Two Pianofortes.
Op. 34 bis. Sonata in F minor (after the Pianoforte Quintet).
Op. 56B. Variations, Haydn's Theme.

Pianoforte and Violin.
Op. 78. Sonata, G major.
Op. 100. Sonata, A major.
Op. 108. Sonata, D minor.
Sonatensatz, C moll, Nachg. Werk.

Pianoforte and Violoncello.
Op. 38. Sonata, E minor.
Op. 99. Sonata, F major.

CLASSIFIED CATALOGUE OF WORKS.

PIANOFORTE AND CLARINET (OR VIOLA).
Op. 120, No. 1. Sonata, F minor.
Op. 120, No. 2. Sonata, E flat major.

TRIOS.
Op. 8. Pianoforte, Violin, Violoncello, B major.
Op. 87. Pianoforte, Violin, Violoncello, C major.
Op. 101. Pianoforte, Violin, Violoncello, C minor.
Op. 40. Pianoforte, Violin, Horn, E flat major.
Op. 114. Pianoforte, Clarinet, Violoncello, A minor.

QUARTETS.
Op. 25. Pianoforte, Violin, Viola, Violoncello, G minor.
Op. 26. Pianoforte, Violin, Viola, Violoncello, A major.
Op. 60. Pianoforte, Violin, Viola, Violoncello, C minor.

QUINTET.
Op. 34. Pianoforte, two Violins, Viola, Violoncello, F minor.

PIANOFORTE WITH VOICES.
Op. 52. Liebeslieder, Waltzer (voices *ad libitum*).
Op. 65. Neue Liebeslieder.

ORGAN.
Op. 122. Eleven Chorale-Preludes.
Chorale-Prelude and Fugue.
Fugue in A flat minor.

STRINGS WITH ORCHESTRA.
Op. 77. Violin Concerto, D major.
Op. 102. Concerto for Violin and Violoncello, A minor.

STRING QUARTETS.
Op. 51, No. 1. C minor.
Op. 51, No. 2. A minor.
Op. 67. B flat major.

STRING QUINTETS.
Op. 88. F major.
Op. 111. G major.
Op. 115. Quintet for Clarinet, two Violins, Viola, Violoncello, B minor.

STRING SEXTETS.
Op. 18. B flat major.
Op. 36. G major.

VOCAL MUSIC.

MIXED CHORUS WITHOUT ACCOMPANIMENT.
Op. 22. Marienlieder.
Op. 29. Two Motets; five-part.
Op. 42. Three Songs (Gesänge); six-part.
Op. 62. Seven Songs (Lieder).
Op. 74. Two Motets; four and six-part.
Op. 93A. Songs (Lieder) and Romances.
Op. 104. Songs (Gesänge).
Op. 109. Fest und Gedenksprüche.

Op. 110. Three Motets; four and eight-part.
German Folksongs (dedicated to the Vienna Singakademie).

WOMEN'S CHORUS WITHOUT ACCOMPANIMENT.
Op. 37. Three Sacred Choruses.
Op. 44. Twelve Songs and Romances.
Op. 113. Thirteen Canons.

Men's Chorus without Accompaniment.

Op. 41. Five Songs (Lieder).

Vocal Music with Orchestral Accompaniment.

Op. 12. Ave Maria: women's Chorus.
Op. 45. A German Requiem: Soli and Chorus.
Op. 50. Rinaldo: Tenor Solo and men's Chorus.
Op. 53. Rhapsody: Contralto Solo and men's Chorus.
Op. 54. Song of Destiny: mixed Chorus.
Op. 55. Triumph-Song: double Chorus.
Op. 82. Nänie: mixed Chorus.
Op. 89. Song of the Fates: mixed Chorus.

Vocal Music variously Accompanied.

Op. 13. Funeral Song: mixed Chorus and Wind.
Op. 17. Songs for women's Chorus with accompaniment for two Horns and a Harp.
Op. 91. Two Songs for Contralto with Viola and Pianoforte.

Choruses with Pianoforte or Organ Accompaniment.

Op. 12. Ave Maria: women's Chorus.
Op. 27. The 13th Psalm: women's Chorus.
Op. 30. Sacred Song: mixed Chorus.

Choruses with Pianoforte Accompaniment.

Op. 93B. Tafellied: mixed Voices. German Folksongs.

Vocal Quartets with Pianoforte Accompaniment.

Op. 31. Three Quartets.
Op. 64. Three Quartets.
Op. 92. Four Quartets.
Op. 112. Six Quartets.
Op. 52. Love Songs (Pianoforte Duet).
Op. 65. New Love Songs (Pianoforte duet).
Op. 103. Gipsy Songs.

Vocal Duets with Pianoforte Accompaniment.

Op. 20. Soprano and Contralto.
Op. 61. Soprano and Contralto.
Op. 66. Soprano and Contralto.
Op. 28. Contralto and Baritone.
Op. 75. Ballads and Romances.
Op. 84. Romances and Songs.

Songs for One Voice with Pianoforte Accompaniment.

Op. 3. 6 Gesänge.
Op. 6. 6 Gesänge.
Op. 7. 6 Gesänge.
Op. 14. 8 Lieder und Romanzen.
Op. 19. 5 Gedichte.
Op. 32. 9 Lieder und Gesänge.
Op. 33. 15 Magelone Romanzen.
Op. 43. 4 Gesänge.
Op. 46. 4 Gesänge.
Op. 47. 5 Lieder.
Op. 48. 7 Lieder.
Op. 49. 5 Lieder.
Op. 57. 8 Lieder und Gesänge.
Op. 58. 8 Lieder und Gesänge.
Op. 59. 8 Lieder und Gesänge.
Op. 63. 9 Lieder und Gesänge.
Op. 69. 9 Gesänge.
Op. 70. 4 Gesänge.
Op. 71. 5 Gesänge.
Op. 72. 5 Gesänge.
Op. 84. 5 Romanzen und Lieder.
Op. 85. 6 Lieder.
Op. 86. 6 Lieder.
Op. 94. 5 Lieder.
Op. 95. 7 Lieder.
Op. 96. 4 Lieder.
Op. 97. 6 Lieder.
Op. 105. 5 Lieder.
Op. 106. 5 Lieder.
Op. 107. 5 Lieder.
Op. 121. 4 Gesänge.
Mondnacht (total 195 Songs).
German Folksongs.
Children's Folksongs.

WORKS EDITED BY BRAHMS.

Chopin : Breitkopf and Härtel's kritisch durgesshene gesammtausgabe.
Bd. II. Mazurkas.
Bd. VIII. Sonaten B moll, Op. 35, and H moll, Op. 58.
Bd. X. Verschiedene Werke, Nos. 7, 8, 10, 12.
Bd. XIII. Nachgelessene Werke, Nos. 3, 4, 5, 9, 14, 32.

Couperin : Clavierwerke (Chrysander's "Denkmäle der Tonkunst," IV).

Handel : Deutsche Handel Gesellschaft Leipzig, founded by Chrysander.
Band XXXII of 1880. Italian Duets.
Nos. Ic and IX-XX, and Italian Trios, I, II, with added pianoforte accompaniment.
N.B.—The duets Ic and IX-XIV (in a different order) and the Trios, appeared in Band XXXII of 1870. (Breitkopf and Härtel.)
The duets. XV-XX, have been republished by Peters as "Six duets with piano accompaniment by J. Brahms."

Mozart : Requiem (Breitkopf and Härtel's complete edition. Serie 24, No. 1).

Schubert : Symphonies (in co-operation with Mandyczewski). (Breitkopf and Härtel's complete edition. Serie 1.)
Three Pianoforte Pieces. Waltzes, etc.
"Ellen's Zweiter Gesang," arranged for soprano solo, women's chorus and wind instruments. (German Brahms-Gesellschaft.)

Schumann : Supplement Band to Clara Schumann's complete edition, Serie 14. (Breitkopf and Härtel.)

Brahms' name appears for the first time in 1878 in the list of the committee of the Leipzig Societ's edition of Bach's works. Breitkopf and Härtel.)

Brahms was a member of the commission appointed by the Königlich Preussische Kultusministerium for the publication of "Denkmälern deutscher Tonkunst," the Probeband of which appeared in 1892. (Breitkopf and Härtel.)

INDEX.

For Index of Works, see Chronological Catalogue, page 677.

A.

Abel, 384-5.
Ægidi, 278.
Ahle, J. R., 482.
Ahna, de, 568.
Ahsen, Jenny von, 257.
Albers, 76.
d'Albert, Eugen, 605, 645-6, 648, 651.
Albrechtsberger, 66, 69, 343.
Allgeyer, Julius, 173-4, 357-8, 372-3, 375, 377, 437, 440, 453, 471, 477, 479, 519, 538, 548, 562.
Angelo, Michael, 623.
d'Arien, 86.
Arnim, Bettina von, 129, 150.
——, Gisela von, 130, 205.
Arnold, 184.
Artôt, 85.
Asmus, Christiana, 49-50.
Astor, Edmund, 487.
Austria, Francis Joseph, Emperor of, 617.

B.

Bach, Carl Philipp Emanuel, 65, 116, 197.
——, Friedemann, 405.
——, Johann Sebastian, 12-3, 15, 17, 37, 65, 67, 69, 86, 88, 116, 152, 157, 198, 209, 211, 217, 226, 228, 252, 254, 263-4, 280, 294, 297-8, 327, 337, 345-7, 349, 386, 394-6, 402, 407, 432, 465, 467, 469-71, 482, 490, 495, 507, 514, 529, 534, 543-4, 585, 633, 648, 650, 660.
Bach, Works of, played by Brahms on the pianoforte, 15, 17, 69, 191, 195, 202, 209, 220, 283, 295, 332-3, 337-9, 367-9, 371, 387-8, 394, 405, 449, 591.
Bachrich, 497, 622.
Bächthold, 599, 639.
Backhaus, 76.
Bade, Carl, 56, 390, 426, 537.
Baden, Frederick, Grand Duke of, 358-9.
Bagge, Selmar, 328-9, 333, 352.
Baglehole, 451.
Balcke, 101.
Barbi, Alice, 651.
Bargheer, Carl, Concertmeister, 220-1, 225-8, 234, 266, 370-1, 491, 532, 569.
Bargiel, Woldemar, 131, 183, 231, 233-4, 298, 551, 658.
Barth, Heinrich, 568.
——, Mrs. R., 658.
——, Richard, 407, 546, 658.
Baumeyer, Marie, 565.
Baumgarten and Heinz, 90, 202.
Bavaria, Ludwig II, King of, 479, 483.
Bechstein, 559.
Becker, Dr., 276.
——, Frau, 365-6.
——, Hugo, 139, 600, 665.
Beckerath, Alwyn von, 546, 579, 658.
Beethoven, Ludwig van, 3, 66, 81, 88, 93, 107, 116, 129, 155, 175, 178, 186, 189, 192, 195,

INDEX. 689

207, 226, 232, 244, 246, 250, 256, 266-7, 274, 280, 285, 289, 294, 298, 325, 328, 337, 341, 343, 345, 347, 349, 386, 394-6, 429, 432-3, 440, 457, 469, 471, 475, 482, 493-4, 505-7, 509-11, 514, 525, 529, 532, 534, 539-40, 543, 552, 563-5, 578, 584-5, 605, 623, 648, 652, 654, 671.
Beethoven, Works played by Brahms, 62, 86-7, 98-9, 101, 195-6, 201-2, 209, 217, 220, 227, 237, 283, 295, 331, 337-8, 341, 367, 369-70, 387-8, 394, 404-5, 492-3, 501.
Begas, 94.
Bellini, 189.
Bennet, John, 351.
Bennett, W. Sterndale, 133, 207, 514.
Bergmann, Carl, 169.
Beringer, Oscar, 565.
Berlioz, Hector, 103, 142, 145-6, 153, 192, 269, 493.
Bernhard de Trèves, 306.
Berninger, 407.
Bernsdorf, Edward, 244, 246, 486, 513, 540, 645.
Bernstorff, Countess, 110.
Bernuth, Julius von, 404, 526, 537, 546, 576.
Bibl, Rudolph, 328, 346, 467, 470.
Billroth, Theodor, 378-80, 394, 396, 403, 430, 437, 465, 470, 476, 490, 494, 496, 508, 522-3, 530-1, 546, 557, 563-4, 566, 568, 572, 584, 592, 611, 615, 623-4, 628, 633, 635-6.
Birgfeld, 62, 81.
Bismarck, Otto von, 43, 490, 615, 666.
Bizet, G., 618.
Blagrove, Henry, 387.
Blume, Amtsvogt, 81-3, 93, 97-8, 100, 120, 171.
——, Frau Amtsvogt, 81-2, 120, 172.
——, Calculator, 100, 120.
——, Frau Calculator, 100, 120.
Bocklet, C. M. von, 66.
Bockmühl, 139.
Böhm, Joseph, 94, 105.
Bohme, 639.
——, Marie, 323.
Böie, John, 202, 281, 290, 293, 300, 497, 537.

Böie, Marie, 127, 287. See also under Völckers.
Boieldieu, F. A., 208, 254, 274, 405.
Bölling, Bertha, 184, 192-3.
Boni, 441.
Bonn, Mayor of, 213.
Borrisow, Rev. L., 452.
Börs, 87.
Borwick, Leonard, 565.
Bösendorfer, 334.
Bosshard, 561.
Boston Symphony Orchestra, 296.
Braff, 385.
Brahms, Caroline, 376, 458-60, 495-6, 537, 630-1, 660-2, 668, 674.
——, Elise, 54, 77, 148, 186, 216-7, 232, 348, 354, 363-4, 375, 460. See also under Grund.
——, Fritz, 56, 73, 84, 334, 353, 363, 458, 460, 537, 660.
——, Johann, 48, 50, 54.
——, Johann Jakob, 50-60, 62-3, 70-3, 89, 135, 137, 141, 148-9, 171, 178-9, 202, 232, 273, 284, 286-7, 304, 333, 342, 353-4, 363-4, 366-7, 369, 372, 374-6, 388, 390-2, 403, 407, 412, 416, 426, 458-9, 537, 617, 660.
——, Johanna Christiana, 53-6, 60, 64, 77-8, 83, 97, 126, 141, 148-9, 171, 178-9, 186, 202, 232, 273, 284, 286-7, 333-4, 342, 353, 362-4, 374-5, 377, 415-6, 571. See also under Nissen.
——, Peter, 47.
——, Peter Hinrich, 49.
Brahmüller, 385.
Brandes, Emma. See Engelmann.
Brandt, Auguste, 257, 323.
Branscheidt, 550.
Brassin, Louis, 434.
Breitkopf and Härtel, 136, 141, 150, 168-9, 201, 277, 352, 492, 632-3, 646.
Brendel, Franz, 104, 133, 143-4, 146, 248, 269, 271-2, 297-8, 442, 485.
Brentano, Arnim, 176.
——, Bettina, 129.
Breyther, F., 202, 281, 293.
Broadwood, 208, 565.
Brodsky, Adolph, 541, 602-3.
——, Frau, 602-3.
Brouillet, 440.

46

INDEX.

Bruch, Max, 385, 407, 413-4, 495, 529, 539.
Brückner, Anton, 328.
Brüll, Ignaz, 512, 523, 566, 573, 582, 615, 672.
Bruyck, Carl Debrois van, 203-4.
Bull, John, 4-5.
Bülow, Hans von, 27-31, 103, 105-6, 114, 129, 133, 139, 146, 160, 223, 229, 271, 384-5, 434, 507, 528, 545, 555-6, 558-9, 563, 572, 575, 583-5, 604-5, 613, 616-7, 631.
——, Marie von, 160, 384.
Bulthaupt, Heinrich, 437-8, 516.
Burnett, 452.
Busch, 666.
Buths, Julius, 453.

C.

Calderon, 437, 519.
Candidus, Carl, 522.
Carlyle, Thomas, 299.
Chamisso, Adalbert von, 91.
Chappell. S. Arthur, 387, 452.
Cherubini, M. Luigi, 245, 253, 471, 534.
Chopin, Frederic, 111, 227, 445, 634.
Chorley, Henry, 189.
Cicero, 91.
Clasing, Johann Heinrich, 65, 156.
Claus, Wilhelmine, 186.
Clementi, Muzio, 10, 12, 22, 60, 290.
Cobb, Gerard F., 452.
Conrat, Frau, 637, 662.
——, Hugo, 606-7, 627, 637-8, 662, 666-8.
——, Ilse, 637-8, 662, 675.
Cordes, August, 226-7.
Cornelius, Peter, 105, 129, 328.
Cornet, Fräulein, 85-7. See also under Passy-Cornet.
——, Madame, 85-7, 93.
Cossel, Frau, 71, 149, 363, 537.
——, Johanna, 363-4.
——, Marie, 537. See also under Janssen.
——, Otto Friedrich Willibald, 59-64, 68, 70-1, 121, 149, 460, 537, 619-20.
Cossmann, Bernhard, 105, 146, 359.
Couperin, François, 432.

Cramer, John, 60-1.
Cranz, August, 88, 230, 351, 430.
Cumberland, Duke of, 671.
Cusins, W. G., 434, 452, 489, 515, 541.
Czartoriski, Prince Constantin, 343-4.
Czerny, Carl, 13, 60, 674.

D.

Dalfy, 346.
Dalwigk, Baron Reinhard von, 335.
Dante, 91, 113.
Danzer, 346.
Daumer, G. F., 440, 456.
David, Ferdinand, 140, 146, 188-9, 237, 245, 276, 283, 293, 373, 485.
Davidoff, C., 283, 293.
Davies, Fanny, 606, 613, 626, 644.
Deichmann, 118-9, 137, 452.
——, Frau, 118-9.
Deiters, Hermann, 212, 329, 413-6, 427, 441, 474, 513, 522, 541, 553, 655.
Demetrius, 161.
Denninghoff, 284.
——, Agnes, 285.
Denninghoff-Giesemann, Frau, 284-5, 306. See also under Giesemann.
Derenberg. See under Eibenschütz.
Dessoff, Otto, 326, 340, 496, 506.
Detmering, 64.
Detmold, Lippe—
  Dowager Princess of, 191-2.
  Friederike, Princess of, 192, 219, 221, 227, 251-2, 263, 266.
  Leopold III, Prince of, 191-2, 219, 221, 228, 233, 263, 266, 371.
  Luise, Princess of, 192, 219, 221.
  Pauline, Princess of, 192, 219, 221.
Devrient, Edward, 358, 436.
Dewitz, Frau von, 573.
Diabelli, Anton, 329.
Dietrich, Albert, 95-6, 124-5, 129-31, 139-40, 150-1, 162-6, 170, 175, 198, 205, 208, 212-3, 274-6, 285, 287-8, 293-5, 299-300, 303, 339, 345, 356, 367,

INDEX.

369, 371, 382-3, 388-9, 392, 404,
407-8, 414-5, 417, 420, 445, 449,
464, 472, 483, 490, 496, 551,
636.
Dietrich, Clara, 274-5, 300, 303,
371, 407, 449.
Dobyhal, 331.
Doetsch, 551.
Döhler, Theodor, 85.
Dömpke, 584.
Donizetti, 86.
Donkin, A. E., 452.
——, E. H., 452.
——, F. W., 452.
——, M. F., 452.
Donnhorf, 550-1.
Door, Anton, 194-5, 452, 567,
584, 610.
——, Frau, 667.
Doppler, Franz, 340.
Dörffel, A., 486, 511, 524-5, 539,
541, 584.
Dumba, 646, 666.
Duncker, 99.
Dunkelberg, Frau, 550.
Dunkl, 445.
Dustmann, Louise, 300, 441, 480.
Dvorák, Anton, 497, 549, 663,
665, 672.

E.

Eberhard, G., 491.
Eccard, J., 348, 466.
Eckert, Carl Anton, 326.
Ehlert, Louis, 512.
Ehrbar, Friedrich, 512, 523, 573,
582, 584, 611, 628-9.
Ehrlich, Heinrich, 110, 127.
Eibenschütz, Ilona, 635.
Eichendorff, J. von, 91, 144.
Eldering, 658.
Ella, John, 207.
Engel, 295, 371.
Engelbert, 293.
Engelmann, Dr., 656, 659.
——, Frau, 472, 491, 500, 513,
555.
——, Professor, 472, 491, 500,
505, 513, 555.
Eötoos, Baroness, 555.
Epstein, Julius, 329-31, 341, 567,
580, 584, 610, 636, 666.
Erard, 208.
Erk, 639.
Ernst, 98.
Eschmann, 379-80.

Esser, 497.
Ettlinger, Anna, 359, 519.
Ewer and Co., 451.
Eyrich, 432, 522.

F.

Faber, Arthur, 329, 341, 348,
428, 456, 566, 572, 584, 636,
662, 667-9, 672.
——, Bertha, 277, 348, 428, 456,
566, 662, 667. See also under
Porubszky.
Falk, Clementina, 14-5.
Farmer, John, 407, 409, 450.
Fellinger, Dr., 567-8, 581, 620,
622, 659, 662-5, 669-70, 672.
——, Frau, 567-8, 581, 592,
595-6, 620-2, 659, 662-4, 667-8,
670, 675.
——, Maria, 670.
Ferrari, Frau, 346.
——, Sophie, 434.
Feuerbach, Anselm, 174, 357-8,
476-9, 557, 562.
——, Frau, 477, 562.
——, Henriette, 357, 561-2.
Fichtelberger, 347, 368.
Fischer, Georg, 243.
Flatz, Franz, 343-4.
Flemming, Paul, 352.
Flotow, 534.
Folkes, 452.
Formes, 83.
Frank, Ernst, 461, 501, 516.
Franz, Frau, 567.
——, Robert, 131.
Fräsch, 87.
Frege, Livia, 245, 280.
Freund, Robert, 627.
Fribberg, Franz, 340.
Friedländer, Thekla, 452.
Froude, J., 299.
Fuchs, 183, 567, 584, 672.
Fürchtgott, 334.

G.

Gabain, Henny, 323.
Gabrieli, Giovanni, 349.
Gade, Niels W., 131, 143, 405,
534.
Gallus, Jac., 482.
Gänsbacher, Johann, 343.
——, Josef, 343-4, 373, 390-1,
567, 580, 636, 665-6.
Garbe, Laura, 275, 286, 321-3,
407, 536.

47*

Garcia, Manuel, 208.
Garibaldi, 619.
Gehring, Franz, 461.
Geibel, Emanuel, 362, 437.
Gericke, W., 570.
Gernsheim, Friedrich, 414, 534.
Giesemann, Adolph, 72-4, 76, 79, 81-3, 92-4, 96, 98, 116, 120, 172, 285.
——, Elise, 73-4, 76-9, 81-4, 93-5, 98, 126, 284-5. See also under Denninghoff.
——, Uncle, 77.
Gille, Geheimrath, 442.
Girzik, Fräulein, 425, 432, 441.
Glade, 86.
Gleich, Ferdinand, 244, 247-8.
Gluck, C. W. von, 6, 181, 211, 342, 358, 432, 456, 467.
Goethe, Wolfgang von, 16, 91, 129, 175, 190, 350, 415, 428, 430, 441-3, 513, 517, 566, 570-1, 654.
Goldmark, Carl, 328, 484, 497, 523, 567, 584, 615, 636, 666.
Goldschmidt, Otto, 90, 189, 191-3, 472, 565.
——, Lind-, Jenny, 183, 186, 188-93, 472.
Goltermann, C. E., 62.
——, Louis, 62.
Gompertz, Richard, 545.
Gomperz-Bettelheim, 606.
Gotha, Friedrich, Prince of, 430.
Gotthard, J. P., 467.
Götz, Hermann, 491, 516.
Götze, 145.
Gouvy, Theodor, 142, 189.
Gozzi, 439, 519.
Grädener, 202, 218, 257-8, 264, 283, 329, 534.
——, Emma, 323.
Graun, 446.
Grieg, Edvard, 602, 653, 662.
——, Nina, 603, 662.
Grimm, Hermann, 439.
——, Julius Otto, 140, 148, 150, 152, 160-1, 165-7, 170, 172, 174-6, 193, 198, 201, 218, 222, 231, 233-5, 238-40, 264-6, 270, 293, 354-6, 407, 439, 442, 472, 501, 513, 526, 534, 538, 551, 553, 636.
——, Marie, 148, 198, 222, 235, 513.
——, Philippine, 218, 234-5, 238, 240, 407, 513.

Groth, Claus, 48-9, 51, 208, 212, 406, 437, 456, 474, 478-80, 482, 534-5, 538, 599, 607-8, 620.
Grove, Sir George, 209.
Grüber, Frau, 640-1, 655.
Grünberger, Dr., 662.
Grund, Elise, 537, 631, 670, 674. See also under Brahms.
——, William, 253, 290, 303, 460, 532, 534.
Gumpert, 373.

H.

Hafner, Carl, 281, 283.
Hallé, Lady. See Norman-Néruda.
——, Sir Charles, 452, 569.
Hallier Family, 278, 283, 291, 536.
——, Julie, 291, 323.
——, Marie, 323.
Hamburg Ladies' Choir, 321-2, 342, 407, 428-9.
Hamlet, 146.
Handel, G. F., 116, 228, 254, 256, 263, 288, 294, 402, 432, 434, 446, 465-9, 482, 489-90, 534, 616.
Handel's "Saul," 304, 469.
Hann, 452.
Hanover, King George of, 110, 268, 383, 470, 613.
——, Marie, Princess of, 671.
——, Queen of, 342, 613, 671.
Hanslick, Edward, 189-90, 200, 248, 328, 332, 336, 340-1, 344-5, 347, 349, 382, 385, 395-7, 403, 425, 463, 497, 503, 509-10, 531-6, 566, 572, 574, 578-9, 584, 599, 611, 615, 618, 623, 625, 636, 654-5, 661-2, 666.
——, Frau, 533, 566, 578, 611.
Hare, 299.
Härtel, Dr., 128-9, 134-6, 140, 197.
Hase, Geheimrath von, 633, 646-7.
Haslinger, 303.
Hauptmann, Moritz, 143.
Hauser, 359, 367.
——, Frau, 440.
Hausmann, Fräulein, 440.
——, Robert, 41, 568-9, 591-2, 600, 604, 625, 663.

INDEX.

Haydn, 66, 72, 93, 155, 188, 190-1, 228, 245, 256, 267, 289, 325, 343, 351, 469, 474-5, 480, 490, 507, 511, 532, 534, 567, 584, 647, 652.
Heermann, 502, 568.
Hegar, Friedrich, 368, 379-80, 416, 443, 491, 561, 586, 591, 599, 627.
——, Julius, 416, 491, 561, 590-1, 599, 628, 651.
Heimsoeth, 633.
Heine, 598.
Heldberg, Helene, Baroness von, 559-60, 671.
Heller, Stephen, 131, 189.
Hellmesberger, Josef, 327, 331-2, 337, 340, 347, 385, 402, 474, 493, 497, 505, 516, 544, 568-9, 591, 626.
Henschel, George, 490, 501-2, 504-5, 511, 604, 606, 652, 672.
——, Lilian, 606.
Henselt, Adolf, 442.
Herbeck, Johann, 326-7, 336, 394, 457, 495-7.
Herder, 173, 430.
Hermann, 293.
Herold, 482.
Herz, Henri, 62, 86.
Herzog, 86.
Herzogenberg, Elizabeth von, 487-9, 513-4, 526, 541, 547, 612.
——, Heinrich von, 487-9, 513-4, 526, 656-8.
Hesse, Alexander Friedrich, Landgraf of, 360-1, 502, 583, 599, 609, 653.
——, Anna, Landgräfin of, 360-1.
Hesse - Barchfeld, Princess of, 502.
Heuberger, Richard, 101, 372, 436, 441, 518, 522-3, 549-50, 659, 672.
Heyse, Paul, 437.
Hildebrandt, 675.
Hille, 161.
Hiller, Ferdinand, 104, 107, 121, 123, 188, 214, 274, 369, 449, 468, 472, 534, 551, 567.
Himmelstoss, 453, 545.
Hirsch, R., 340, 349, 386, 396.
Hirschfeld, 408.
Hoch, 473.
Hoffmann, E. T. A., 91, 95, 119, 126, 144, 171.
——, F. C., 68-9, 76, 198.

Hohenemser, 428.
Hohenlohe, 559.
Hohenthal, Countess Ida von, 150.
Hölderlin, F., 417, 453, 652.
Holmes, Henry, 452.
——, W. H., 450-1.
Holstein, Franz von, 143, 486, 513.
——, Hedwig von, 513. See also under Salamon.
——, Princes of, 48.
Homann, Adela, 460.
Honnef, 85.
Honroth, 281.
Hopffer, Bernard, 461, 491.
Hoplit. See Pohl, R.
Hornbostel, 662.
Howard-Jones, Mr., 199, 660.
Hubay, Eugen, 591, 618.
Hübbe, Walter, 233, 259, 261, 274, 278, 292, 321-2, 423.
Hullah, John, 389, 434.
Hummel, J. N., 442.
Hummer, 622.
Hunger, 293.

I.

Isaak, Heinrich, 345, 466.

J.

Jacobi, 190.
Jacobsen, 425.
Jaell, Alfred, 229, 451.
Jahn, Otto, 189, 205-6, 208, 212, 276.
Janetschek, 661.
Janovitch, 95.
Jansen, Gustav, 128, 135.
Janssen, Marie, 537, 619-20.
Japha, Louise, 70, 90-2, 95, 114, 116, 122-4, 126, 137, 150-2, 263, 411.
——, Minna, 92, 95, 122, 126, 150-2, 263.
Jenek, 622.
Jenner, 549, 607-8.
Joachim, Amalie, 342, 352, 362, 407, 443, 467, 472, 487, 494-5, 504, 575.
——, Johannes, 114.
——, Joseph, 41, 67, 94, 97, 103-10, 114-23, 125, 127-37, 140-1, 143-4, 146, 150, 153, 160-2, 164-5, 170, 173, 176-7, 180-1, 183, 185-7, 190-2, 194-7,

201, 203, 210-1, 213, 215-20, 222-5, 229-31, 235-7, 243, 245, 249-54, 264-6, 268-72, 274-80, 282-3, 285, 288, 290-1, 293-4, 301, 335-6, 338, 340-2, 355-6, 362, 367, 383-5, 387-8, 392, 394, 402-3, 406-8, 413, 438-9, 449-52, 466, 471-4, 476, 487, 494-5, 504-6, 513-4, 526-7, 531-3, 536-7, 539-42, 545, 550-3, 562, 566, 569, 574-6, 584, 592, 600, 604, 606, 609, 613, 622, 625-6, 636, 643-5, 651, 658, 663-4, 673, 675.

K.

Kahnt, 384, 600.
Kalbeck, Max, 51, 89, 91, 154, 248, 285, 304, 339, 441, 498, 521-2, 584, 599, 672.
Karpath, Ludwig, 659.
Kässmeyer, 340.
Kayser, 281.
Keiser, 116.
Keller, Gottfried, 378, 491, 522, 590, 599.
——, Josef, 173.
Kemp, Stephen, 565.
Kiel, Capellmeister, 192, 220, 237, 266.
——, Friedrich, 384.
Kirchner, Theodor, 125, 131, 163, 298, 368, 378-80, 383, 487, 513, 534, 598, 636.
Kleinecke, 402.
Kleist, Heinrich von, 514.
Klems, 175.
Klindworth, Carl, 111-2, 114, 150.
Klinger, Max, 655, 675.
Klopstock, 91, 116.
Knaus, Ludwig, 572.
Kneisel, 296.
Koch, General Secretary, 669.
——, Ludwig, 672.
——, Sophie, 93.
——, Town musician, 93.
Köhler, Dr., 98.
——, Louis, 244, 271.
——, Rector, 76, 80, 98, 360.
Königslow, Otto von, 276, 300, 369.
Koning, 568.
Koppelhöfer, 87.
Köstlin, Josephine Lang, 567.
——, Professor, 567.
Krause, Emil, 202.

Krause, Pianist, 145.
Krauss, Dr., 433, 441, 467.
Krebs, Marie, 452.
Kreisler, Johannes (pseudonym for Johannes Brahms), 95, 171, 322.
——, Joh., jun., 95, 117, 119, 127, 148, 152, 168, 274, 521, 667.
Kremser, Edward, 538.
Krenn, Franz, 343-4.
Kreutzer, 83.
Krolop, Franz, 410.
Krummholtz, 293.
Krziwanek, 642.
Kufferath, Antonia, 546, 570, 649. See also under Speyer.
——, Professor, 649.
Kuhnau, Johann, 426.
Kundemann, 669.
Kürner, 440.
Kyllmann, 275-6.

L.

L——, Fräulein, 44.
Lachner, Franz, 189, 434, 497, 600.
Lallement, Avé, 179, 181, 250, 277-8, 291, 300, 303, 323, 334-5.
Lamond, Frederic, 565, 583.
Lange, S. de, 467.
Langhans-Japha, Louise. See under Japha.
Lasso, Orlando di, 198.
Laub, Ferdinand, 142, 340.
Laurens, de, 127, 176-7.
Lauterbach, 490.
Lee, Louis, 281, 291, 293, 497.
Lehmann, 410.
Leipzig Gewandhaus, 433, 512-4, 523, 539, 563, 573, 584-5, 602, 604, 644-6, 673.
Lemke, Carl, 522.
Lentz, Emilie, 323.
Le Roy, Guillaume, 306.
Leser, 176, 275.
Lessing, C. F., 125.
——, Gotth. Eph., 91, 116.
Levi, Hermann, 359-60, 367, 377, 436, 439-41, 453, 455, 461, 471, 482, 486, 489-90, 506, 519, 527, 547-8.
——, publisher, 334.
Levin, 497.
Leyen, Frau, 546, 658.
——, Rudolph von der, 546, 658.

INDEX.

Lind, Jenny. See under Goldschmidt.
Lindner, 359.
Linke, 66.
Liszt, Franz, 102-3, 105-6, 110-4, 124, 129, 133, 142, 146, 150, 153, 160, 177, 189-90, 201, 215, 223-5, 248, 269, 271-2, 360, 379, 381, 385, 442, 484, 555, 652.
Litolff, Henry, 92.
Littie, Lena, 606.
Litzmann, 123-4, 139, 171, 231, 265, 280, 290, 373, 377, 419, 423, 425, 440, 483, 632, 640.
Lloyd, C. H., 451.
Lohfeldt, Rudolph, 88.
Lorscheidt, 550.
Löwe, 300, 405.
——, Sophie, 452.
Löwenherz, Aaron, 79-80, 284.
——, Frau, 79, 306.
Lübke, 379.
Luther, Martin, 397, 470.

M.

M——, 497.
Macfarren, George, 450.
——, Natalie, 450.
Mächtig and Seyfrise, Messrs., 180.
Maier, J. J., 351.
Mandyczeweski, Eusebius, 549, 608, 610, 615, 626, 646, 666, 672.
Mangold, C. F., 131.
Manns, August, 451, 541.
Mannstädt, 572.
Mara, La, 61, 69-70, 87, 113, 136, 146, 153, 381.
Marbach, G. O., 306-7.
Marks, G. W. (pseudonym Joh. Brahms), 88.
Martucci, 599.
Marxsen, Edward, 59, 61-70, 76, 81-2, 85-7, 91-3, 100, 116, 121, 149, 153-8, 168, 179, 253, 333-4, 396, 412, 460, 536, 565, 601.
Mason, William, 110, 114, 133, 169, 295, 386.
Maszowski, 501.
Mattheson, Johann, 116.
May, E. C., 1, 9, 11, 14, 16, 19-22, 24.
——, Florence, 16, 287, 306, 452, 565, 641.

Meier, Camilla, 323.
——, Francisca, 323.
Meinardus, Ludwig, 536.
Mendelssohn, Felix, 22, 67, 102-6, 115-6, 121, 138, 143, 147, 166, 189, 207-8, 210, 227, 244, 256, 327, 331, 345-6, 357-8, 435, 437, 468-9, 484, 495, 536, 539-40, 551, 554, 563, 567, 649, 672.
Menzel, Adolph von, 651-2.
Mertens, Antonie, 323.
Meyer, 76.
——, C., 87.
Meyerbeer, 343.
Meyer-David, 82.
Meysenbug, Carl von, 215-6, 219-21, 225, 238-9, 262-4, 370, 382, 472.
——, Frau, 215-6, 219-20.
——, Frau Hofmarschall, 225, 227, 229, 262-3.
——, Fräulein von, 215-6, 219, 258.
——, Freiherr Carl von, 216, 219-21, 264.
——, Hermann, 226, 229, 258.
——, Hofmarschall, 215, 220, 229, 265.
Michalek, 669.
Miller, Christian, 71, 92.
——, Victor von zu Aichholz, 567, 615, 666-7, 669, 672, 675.
Mollenhauer, 87.
Moltke, 615.
Morley, John, 351.
Moscheles, Ignaz, 140, 227.
Moser, Andreas, 106, 114, 161, 251, 336, 575.
Mouchanoff-Kalergis, Mme. de, 381.
Mozart, Wolfgang A., 18, 66, 72, 85, 88, 93, 133, 155, 175, 189, 202, 226, 228, 232, 244, 255-6, 267, 279, 289, 294, 325, 347, 358-60, 466-7, 484, 495, 507, 532, 534, 539, 564-5, 584, 605, 623, 647, 651-2, 671.
——, "Marriage of Figaro," 83, 85-6, 189, 436.
——, Works played by Brahms, 62, 202, 226, 228, 283.
Mühlfeld, Fräulein von, 627.
——, Richard, 41, 624-6, 643-4, 648, 667.
Müller, 502, 568-9.
Münzinger, 590.

N.

Nagy, Zoltan, 606.
Naumann, Ernst, 125, 131, 164-5, 442.
Néruda, Franz, 505.
Nesselrode, Countess, 381.
Neumann, Carl, 174, 562.
Niebuhr, 48.
Nikisch, 652.
Nissen, Johanna Christiana. See under Brahms.
Nissen, the sisters, 56, 64.
N. N., 497.
Norman, Ludwig, 131.
——-Néruda, Mme., 452, 505, 545, 569.
Nottebohm, M. G., 328, 341, 348.
Novello, Clara, 107.

O.

Oldenburg, Grand Duke of, 287, 335.
——, Grand Duchess of, 382.
Ophüls, G., 658-9.
Oser, Dr. and Frau, 523, 567.
Ossian, 430.
Otten, G. D., 179, 186, 195, 202, 217, 230, 273.
Otterer, Christian, 62, 71, 537.
Ould, C., 452.

P.

Paganini, Nicolo, 394, 591.
Palestrina, G. P. da, 198, 264.
Panzer, 394.
Paque, W., 387.
Parratt, Walter, 452.
Passy-Cornet, 329, 334, 337. See also under Cornet.
Paul, Jean (F. Richter), 91, 119, 144, 175, 178, 181, 190.
——, Jeanette, 145.
Perger, Richard von, 672.
Peroni-Glasbrenner, 160.
Peters, 492.
Petersen, 616-7.
Pezze, 452.
Pfund, 245.
Piatti, Alfredo, 387, 451-2, 505, 569, 626.
Piening, 658.
Pohl, Carl Ferdinand, 328, 567, 636.
——, Richard (Hoplit), 147, 199-200, 203, 360.

Pope, Alexander, 91.
Popper, David, 497, 591, 618.
Porubszky, Bertha, 257, 277, 323, 329, 428. See also under Faber.
Possart, Ernst von, 552.
Potter, Cipriani, 433, 450.
Prince Consort, 276.
Pruckner, Dionys, 111, 129.
Pyatt, G., 452.
Pyllemann, Franz, 467.

R.

Radicati di Marmorito—
 Count, 439, 462.
 Countess, 462. See also under Julie Schumann.
Raff, Joachim, 103, 105, 111, 113, 142, 384-5.
Rameau, J. P., 39-40.
Raphael, 623.
Raynouard, 306.
Redeker, 452.
Regan, Anna, 433.
Reichhardt, J. F., 441, 443.
Reimann, Heinrich, 252, 333-4, 496, 630, 649, 661, 668.
Reimers, Christian, 118, 276.
Reinecke, Carl, 121, 279, 433, 485, 487, 534, 652.
Reinhold, 497.
Reinthaler, Carl Martin, 388-9, 392-3, 404, 406-10, 412, 416-7, 425, 437, 446, 461, 469, 472, 534.
——, Frau, 407, 412, 416-7, 425, 570, 578.
——, Henriette, 417, 578.
Reménvi, Edward, 94-101, 108-14, 116, 122, 133, 139, 142, 150, 153, 236, 284, 293, 613.
Reuter, 286, 323, 407.
Rheinberger, 484.
Richarz, 163.
Richter, Hans, 385, 523, 573, 584, 604.
Rieckmann, 76, 84.
Riedel, 485.
Riehl, 335.
Ries, Louis, 387, 452, 505, 626.
Rieter-Biedermann, 235, 277, 285, 301, 352, 364, 372, 378, 382, 402, 407, 413, 427, 429, 430, 455, 482, 487.
Rietz, Julius, 140, 189, 279, 485, 490.
Risch, 85.

Ritmüller, Philippine, 218, 239.
  See under Grimm.
Ritter, 116.
Rittershaus, 552.
Roeger-Soldat, Marie, 541, 666-7.
Röntgen, Engelbert, 293.
——, Julius, 514, 555.
Rosa, Carl, 57.
Rosé, Arnold, 347, 622, 626, 644.
Rosegger, 581-2.
——, Fräulein, 582.
Rosenhain, Jakob, 85, 357, 600.
Rösing, Elisabeth, 286, 299, 335.
Rossini, G. A., 85.
Rottenberg, von, 549, 610, 615.
Röver, 331.
Rovetta, Giovanni, 198, 349.
Rubinstein, Anton, 3, 67, 201-2, 229, 355, 360, 381, 457, 485, 492.
Ruckauf, 655.
Rückert, Friedrich, 577.
Rudorff, Ernst, 280, 441.

S.

S., 336.
Sahr, Heinrich von, 139-40, 143, 276.
Salamon, Hedwig, 143, 486, 513.
Sallet, Friedrich von, 521.
Santley, Charles, 434.
Saxe-Meiningen—
  George, Duke of, 556, 559-60, 572, 624-5, 671.
  Marie, Princess of, 671.
Sayn - Wittgenstein, Princess Caroline von, 110, 114.
Scarlatti, D., 5-6, 18, 39, 207, 388, 405, 449.
Schaafhausen, 551.
Schäffer, Julius, 131.
Schelle, 385, 387, 395, 467, 470.
Schelper, 410, 446.
Schiller, Friedrich, 79, 91, 144-5, 173, 437-8, 509, 557, 561, 571.
Schirmer, J. W., 125.
Schleinitz, 143, 280.
Schloenbach, 143-4.
Schloesser, Adolf, 450.
Schmall, 497.
Schmaltz, Susanne, 323.
Schmidt, Julius, 220, 225-8.
——, Professor, 579.
Schnack, Caroline, 369-70, 374-5.
  See also under Brahms.

Schnack, Fritz, 370, 375, 458-60, 537, 630-1, 661, 674.
Scholz, Bernhard, 270, 343, 452-3, 494-5, 545, 658.
——, Dr., 526.
Schröder, 70, 76, 92-3, 98.
Schroeder-Devrient, 186.
Schubert, Franz, 22, 66-7, 87, 152, 208-10, 256, 267, 274, 281, 285, 289, 329, 339, 342, 404-5, 429, 432, 455, 466, 469, 482, 505, 522, 535, 578, 584, 646-7, 652, 656, 670-1.
——, Works played by Brahms, 5, 196, 209, 216, 220, 226, 254, 283, 291, 338, 367, 371, 388, 394, 489, 591, 599.
Schübring, Dr. Julius, 122, 297-8, 407.
Schultz, Adolf, 343.
Schulze, 220, 226.
Schumann, Clara, 1-6, 8-10, 13, 15, 23-4, 67, 95, 105, 107, 121-4, 126, 129-30, 139, 141, 149-50, 161, 163-7, 170-85, 190-5, 198, 201, 203-9, 211-7, 222-3, 231-7, 254, 265-6, 274-6, 279-80, 282-3, 288, 290-4, 296-7, 300-1, 322-3, 345, 348, 355, 357, 360, 365-7, 371, 373-4, 377, 380-2, 388, 408, 417-24, 426, 439-41, 449-52, 461, 472-4, 483, 504, 513-4, 527, 532, 543, 550-2, 567-8, 600, 632-3, 635-6, 639, 643, 646, 649-50, 657-9.
——, Elise, 175, 181, 419, 473, 551, 567.
——, Eugénie, 235, 419, 473, 551, 567, 649.
——, Felix, 166, 234, 424, 483.
——, Julie, 170, 176, 291, 302, 419, 422, 439-40, 473, 551, 567.
——, Marie, 175, 181, 274-5, 283, 417, 419, 473, 551, 567, 649.
——, Robert, 67, 91-2, 95, 102-5, 107, 116-9, 121-4, 126-39, 141-3, 145-53, 159-68, 170-88, 190-1, 196-7, 199-216, 222, 226, 235, 242, 246, 248-9, 254, 272, 274, 276, 285, 294, 296, 298, 302, 327-8, 331-3, 337, 345-6, 351, 357-8, 363, 374, 386, 394, 402, 407-8, 418-9, 425, 429, 432-3, 455, 463, 466, 468, 471-3, 484-5, 494-5, 507, 511, 527, 532, 534, 550-2, 554, 563, 576, 632-4, 643-4, 646-7, 649-50, 657-8, 660.

Schumann, Works played by Brahms, 195-6, 201-2, 217, 227, 264, 267, 273, 282-3, 291, 332, 337, 367-8, 371, 387-8, 394, 404, 449, 461, 489, 501, 552-3.
Schuppanzigh, 66.
Schütz, Heinrich, 349.
Schwarz, Johanna, 455.
Schwarzburg-Sondershausen, Princess, 191.
Schwenke, 65.
Sechter, Simon, 327.
Seebach, Elizabeth von, 144.
Seebohm, Marie, 323, 407.
Segisser, 359, 368, 371.
Seling, Emil, 661.
Sell, Dr., 658.
Senff, 140-1, 150, 445, 456.
Sengelmann, 257.
Seyfried, Ignaz von, 66, 69.
Shakespeare, 278.
——, W., 452, 606.
Siebert, 622.
Siebold, Agathe, 239-41, 355-6.
——, Professor, 239, 355.
Simrock, Fritz, 277, 461, 513, 566, 598, 652, 670.
——, N., 277, 281, 334, 372-3, 382, 427, 440, 445, 455, 461, 466, 476, 482, 492, 513, 586, 630, 669, 673.
Sistermann, Anton, 655.
Sittard, Josef, 157, 168, 396, 585-6, 601, 616.
Smetansky, 482.
Sohn, Carl, 95, 125, 274.
——, Clara. See under Dietrich.
Sommerhoff, 643.
Sophocles, 91.
Speidel, 336.
Spengel, Julius, 198, 572, 607, 616-7.
Speratus, Paul, 352.
Speyer, 649. See also under Antonia Kufferath.
Spiess, Hermine, 579, 599.
Spina, 329, 334, 339, 342, 351.
Spitta, Friedrich, 657.
——, Philipp, 248, 264, 429, 487, 543, 586.
Spohr, L., 192, 220, 253, 394, 532, 535, 539.
Stanford, Sir Charles Villiers, 451-2, 515, 545, 651.
Steche, Lily, 145.
Stegmayer, F.. 327, 343, 351.
Stein, 189.

Steinbach, Fritz, 605, 649.
Steinbrügger, 359.
Steiner, A., 71, 379, 491, 561, 599, 626-8, 639, 651.
Stern, Adolph, 442.
——, Capellmeister, 434.
Stockhausen, Frau, 364.
——, Julius, 208-9, 251-4, 274-6, 282-3, 285, 298, 334-6, 347, 353, 364, 403-7, 425, 427, 429-3 ¹, 432-3, 439, 451, 453, 455, 461, 472, 490, 513, 527, 551, 577, 636, 643, 649, 655, 658, 673.
Stone, Edward, 300.
——, Mrs. Edward, 286, 300, 364. See also Minna Völckers.
Stradella, A., 405.
Straus, Ludwig, 368, 451-2, 505, 613, 626.
Strauss, Johann, 23, 450, 479, 567, 591, 615, 625, 642, 662, 666.
——, Joseph, 358.
——, Richard, 583, 662.
Suter-Weber, 416.
Sybel, 624.

T.

Tartini, 254, 267, 394, 407.
Tasso, Torquato, 91, 430.
Tausch, 531.
Tausig, Carl, 328, 339, 350.
Taylor, Franklin, 452.
Tchaïkovsky, 602-4.
Telemann, G. P., 116.
Thalberg, Sigismund, 81-2, 87, 90.
Thomas, Theodor, 169.
Thompson, Lady, 433.
——, Sir Henry, 433, 451.
Thorwaldsen, 405.
Tieck, Ludwig, 285, 298-9, 307, 318-20.
Truxa, Celestina, 596-8, 622, 668-9, 674.
Turgeniev, 359-60, 437.

U.

Uhland, 240.

V.

Vega, Lope de, 362.
Verhülst, 189, 534, 554.

INDEX.

Versan, Raoul de, 452.
Vesque, Helene von, 143.
Vetter, Frau, 590, 611.
Viardot-Garcia, Pauline, 359-60, 381, 441-2, 451.
Vienna Gesellschaft Concerts, 381, 394, 397, 433, 457, 465-71, 482-3, 489-90, 492-5, 516, 538, 571, 630, 651, 671, 673-4.
—— Singakademie Concerts, 345, 348-51.
Vieuxtemps, Henry, 98, 101.
Vinci, Leonardo da, 232.
Viotti, 539.
Vögl, Bernhard, 585.
——, Frau, 457.
Vogler, 343.
Völckers, Betty, 275, 278, 286, 300, 323, 536.
——, Herr, 278, 286-7, 300, 407.
——, Marie, 275, 278, 286-7, 300, 323, 407, 536. See also under Böie.
——, Minna, 286, 364, 407, 536.
Volkland, Alfred, 487.
Volkmann, William, 482, 646.

W.

Wachtel, Theodor, 86.
Wagner, Friedchen, 202, 233, 257-9, 291, 323, 536.
——, Richard, 103-5, 145, 192, 269, 271-2, 338-9, 347-8, 358-9, 379, 381, 385, 442, 494, 504, 516-9, 547-8, 555.
——, Thusnelda, 257-8, 291, 323, 536.
Wahrendorf, Fritz, 90.
Waiz, 116.
Walter, 641-2.
——, Fräulein, 606.
——, Gustav, 42, 432, 441, 482, 606-7.
Wasielewski, J. W. von, 117-8, 121, 137, 150, 170, 205, 471.
Webbe, 451, 565.
Weber, C. M. von, 69, 175, 343, 445, 535, 624, 667.
Wegeler, Geheimrath, 501-2.
Wehermann, 658.

Wehner, Arnold, 109, 121, 144.
Weiglein, 606.
Weiss, Amalie, 342. See under Joachim.
Weisse, Michael, 264.
Weitzmann, 270.
Wendt, Gustav, 154, 359, 599-600, 642.
Wenzel, Ernst F., 140, 150.
Wesendonck, 379.
Wessely and Büsing, 303.
Westermann, 371.
Weyr, Rudolf, 675.
Widmann, 69, 88, 368, 424, 435-6, 491, 516, 519-21, 557-8, 589-93, 598-9, 611-2, 614, 618-9, 624, 627-9, 636, 651, 654.
Wieck, Clara, 166-7, 179.
——, Friedrich, 140.
——, Marie, 140.
Wiedemann, Dr., 442.
Wiegand, Fräuleins, 486.
Wiemann, 281.
Wierss, 99.
Wiesemann, 213-4.
Wildenbruch, Ernst von, 590.
William I, German Emperor, 403, 466, 490.
—— II, German Emperor, 403.
German Empress, 403.
Wilsing, E. F., 131.
Wilt, 338, 346, 433, 446, 466.
Winter, 430.
Wittgenstein Family, 566, 667.
Wolf, Hugo, 588.
Wolff-Homersee, Baroness, 651. See under Barbi.
Woronzow, Count, 58.
Wrede, President, 550-1.
Wüllner, Franz, 118-9, 467, 526.

Y.

Young, Edward, 91.

Z.

Zelter, 441.
Zerbini, 387, 505.
Zimmermann, Agnes, 451-2.
——, Dr. von, 672.

THE END.

Printed by NEW TEMPLE PRESS, London, S.W.16, Great Britain.

HISTORICAL, DESCRIPTIVE AND ANALYTICAL ACCOUNT OF THE ENTIRE WORKS OF

BRAHMS

BY

EDWIN EVANS
(SENIOR)

The works are treated in the order of their opus number, and **every** single composition is dealt with **exhaustively**. No other work with such a wealth of detail exists in any language. The whole, being adequately indexed, forms a complete reference book for pianist, student and concert-goer, and may be described as **monumental**.

Of the **CHAMBER AND ORCHESTRAL** music, a minute analysis reaching to the rhythmical significance of each bar is given.

The analytical accounts of the **PIANO** works are each subdivided under the headings: Key; Time and Extent; Thematic Material; Melody; Harmony; Rhythm; etc.

The **CHORAL** works are dealt with in the fullest detail, and original English translations have been made to most of the **SONGS**.

Each volume is a self-contained unit and a complete textbook on its particular subject.

WITH 1,500 PAGES AND OVER 1,000 MUSIC EXAMPLES AND TABLES, COMPLETE IN 4 VOLUMES, OCTAVO, CLOTH, OR SOLD SEPARATELY AS FOLLOWS :—

Chamber and Orchestral Works. First Series to Op. 67.

Chamber and Orchestral Works. Second Series. Op. 68 to the end.

Piano and Organ Works. Comprising the complete Solo Works; Works for Piano and Orchestra: also Works for Piano Duet and Organ Works as applicable to Pianoforte Solo.

Vocal Works. With portrait. 599 pages.

Send for 8 page prospectus sent post free.

"This treatise is comparable only to the Kochel catalogue of Mozart. Research and detail could go no further; this book, a labour of love indeed, will be the standard work of reference on Brahms for this century, if not longer."—*The Library Assistant.*

WILLIAM REEVES   83 Charing Cross Road,
Bookseller   Limited.   — London, W.C.2. —

Discographies by Travis & Emery:

Discographies by John Hunt.

1987: From Adam to Webern: the Recordings of von Karajan.
1991: 3 Italian Conductors and 7 Viennese Sopranos: 10 Discographies: Arturo Toscanini, Guido Cantelli, Carlo Maria Giulini, Elisabeth Schwarzkopf, Irmgard Seefried, Elisabeth Gruemmer, Sena Jurinac, Hilde Gueden, Lisa Della Casa, Rita Streich.
1992: Mid-Century Conductors and More Viennese Singers: 10 Discographies: Karl Boehm, Victor De Sabata, Hans Knappertsbusch, Tullio Serafin, Clemens Krauss, Anton Dermota, Leonie Rysanek, Eberhard Waechter, Maria Reining, Erich Kunz.
1993: More 20th Century Conductors: 7 Discographies: Eugen Jochum, Ferenc Fricsay, Carl Schuricht, Felix Weingartner, Josef Krips, Otto Klemperer, Erich Kleiber.
1994: Giants of the Keyboard: 6 Discographies: Wilhelm Kempff, Walter Gieseking, Edwin Fischer, Clara Haskil, Wilhelm Backhaus, Artur Schnabel.
1994: Six Wagnerian Sopranos: 6 Discographies: Frieda Leider, Kirsten Flagstad, Astrid Varnay, Martha Moedl, Birgit Nilsson, Gwyneth Jones.
1995: Musical Knights: 6 Discographies: Henry Wood, Thomas Beecham, Adrian Boult, John Barbirolli, Reginald Goodall, Malcolm Sargent.
1995: A Notable Quartet: 4 Discographies: Gundula Janowitz, Christa Ludwig, Nicolai Gedda, Dietrich Fischer-Dieskau.
1996: The Post-War German Tradition: 5 Discographies: Rudolf Kempe, Josep Keilberth, Wolfgang Sawallisch, Rafael Kubelik, Andre Cluytens.
1996: Teachers and Pupils: 7 Discographies: Elisabeth Schwarzkopf, Maria Ivoguen, Maria Cebotari, Meta Seinemeyer, Ljuba Welitsch, Rita Streich, Erna Berger.
1996: Tenors in a Lyric Tradition: 3 Discographies: Peter Anders, Walther Ludwig, Fritz Wunderlich.
1997: The Lyric Baritone: 5 Discographies: Hans Reinmar, Gerhard Hüsch, Josef Metternich, Hermann Uhde, Eberhard Wächter.
1997: Hungarians in Exile: 3 Discographies: Fritz Reiner, Antal Dorati, George Szell.
1997: The Art of the Diva: 3 Discographies: Claudia Muzio, Maria Callas, Magda Olivero.
1997: Metropolitan Sopranos: 4 Discographies: Rosa Ponselle, Eleanor Steber, Zinka Milanov, Leontyne Price.
1997: Back From The Shadows: 4 Discographies: Willem Mengelberg, Dimitri Mitropoulos, Hermann Abendroth, Eduard Van Beinum.
1997: More Musical Knights: 4 Discographies: Hamilton Harty, Charles Mackerras, Simon Rattle, John Pritchard.
1998: Conductors On The Yellow Label: 8 Discographies: Fritz Lehmann, Ferdinand Leitner, Ferenc Fricsay, Eugen Jochum, Leopold Ludwig, Artur Rother, Franz Konwitschny, Igor Markevitch.

1998: Mezzos and Contraltos: 5 Discographies: Janet Baker, Margarete Klose, Kathleen Ferrier, Giulietta Simionato, Elisabeth Höngen.
1999: The Furtwängler Sound Sixth Edition: Discography and Concert Listing.
1999: The Great Dictators: 3 Discographies: Evgeny Mravinsky, Artur Rodzinski, Sergiu Celibidache.
1999: Sviatoslav Richter: Pianist of the Century: Discography.
2000: Philharmonic Autocrat 1: Discography of: Herbert Von Karajan [Third Edition].
2000: Wiener Philharmoniker 1 - Vienna Philharmonic & Vienna State Opera Orchestras: Disc. Part 1 1905-1954.
2000: Wiener Philharmoniker 2 - Vienna Philharmonic & Vienna State Opera Orchestras: Disc. Part 2 1954-1989.
2001: Gramophone Stalwarts: 3 Separate Discographies: Bruno Walter, Erich Leinsdorf, Georg Solti.
2001: Singers of the Third Reich: 5 Discographies: Helge Roswaenge, Tiana Lemnitz, Franz Völker, Maria Müller, Max Lorenz.
2001: Philharmonic Autocrat 2: Concert Register of Herbert Von Karajan Second Edition.
2002: Sächsische Staatskapelle Dresden: Complete Discography.
2002: Carlo Maria Giulini: Discography and Concert Register.
2002: Pianists For The Connoisseur: 6 Discographies: Arturo Benedetti Michelangeli, Alfred Cortot, Alexis Weissenberg, Clifford Curzon, Solomon, Elly Ney.
2003: Singers on the Yellow Label: 7 Discographies: Maria Stader, Elfriede Trötschel, Annelies Kupper, Wolfgang Windgassen, Ernst Häfliger, Josef Greindl, Kim Borg.
2003: A Gallic Trio: 3 Discographies: Charles Münch, Paul Paray, Pierre Monteux.
2004: Antal Dorati 1906-1988: Discography and Concert Register.
2004: Columbia 33CX Label Discography.
2004: Great Violinists: 3 Discographies: David Oistrakh, Wolfgang Schneiderhan, Arthur Grumiaux.
2006: Leopold Stokowski: Second Edition of the Discography.
2006: Wagner Im Festspielhaus: Discography of the Bayreuth Festival.
2006: Her Master's Voice: Concert Register and Discography of Dame Elisabeth Schwarzkopf [Third Edition].
2007: Hans Knappertsbusch: Kna: Concert Register and Discography of Hans Knappertsbusch, 1888-1965. Second Edition.
2008: Philips Minigroove: Second Extended Version of the European Discography.
2009: American Classics: The Discographies of Leonard Bernstein and Eugene Ormandy.

Discography by Stephen J. Pettitt, edited by John Hunt:
1987: Philharmonia Orchestra: Complete Discography 1945-1987

Available from: Travis & Emery at 17 Cecil Court, London, UK. (+44) 20 7 240 2129. email on sales@travis-and-emery.com .

© Travis & Emery 2009

Music and Books published by Travis & Emery Music Bookshop:

Mellers, Wilfrid: Beethoven and the Voice of God
Mellers, Wilfrid: Caliban Reborn - Renewal in Twentieth Century Music
Mellers, Wilfrid: François Couperin and the French Classical Tradition
Mellers, Wilfrid: Harmonious Meeting
Mellers, Wilfrid: Le Jardin Retrouvé, The Music of Frederic Mompou
Mellers, Wilfrid: Music and Society, England and the European Tradition
Mellers, Wilfrid: Music in a New Found Land: ...... American Music
Mellers, Wilfrid: Romanticism and the Twentieth Century (from 1800)
Mellers, Wilfrid: The Masks of Orpheus: ...... the Story of European Music.
Mellers, Wilfrid: The Sonata Principle (from c. 1750)
Mellers, Wilfrid: Vaughan Williams and the Vision of Albion
Panchianio, Cattuffio: Rutzvanscad Il Giovine.
Pearce, Charles: Sims Reeves, Fifty Years of Music in England.
Pettitt, Stephen: Philharmonia Orchestra: Complete Discography 1945-1987
Playford, John: An Introduction to the Skill of Musick.
Purcell, Henry et al: Harmonia Sacra ... The First Book, (1726)
Purcell, Henry et al: Harmonia Sacra ... Book II (1726)
Quantz, Johann: Versuch einer Anweisung die Flöte traversiere zu spielen.
Rameau, Jean-Philippe: Code de Musique Pratique, ou Méthodes.
Rastall, Richard: The Notation of Western Music.
Rimbault, Edward: The Pianoforte, Its Origins, Progress, and Construction.
Rousseau, Jean Jacques: Dictionnaire de Musique
Rubinstein, Anton : Guide to the proper use of the Pianoforte Pedals.
Sainsbury, John S.: Dictionary of Musicians. Vol. 1. (1825). 2 vols.
Simpson, Christopher: A Compendium of Practical Musick in Five Parts
Spohr, Louis: Autobiography
Spohr, Louis: Grand Violin School
Tans'ur, William: A New Musical Grammar; or The Harmonical Spectator
Terry, Charles Sanford: Four-Part Chorals of J.S. Bach. (German & English)
Terry, Charles Sanford: Joh. Seb. Bach, Cantata Texts, Sacred and Secular.
Terry, Charles Sanford: The Origins of the Family of Bach Musicians.
Tosi, Pierfrancesco: Opinioni de' Cantori Antichi, e Moderni
Van der Straeten, Edmund: History of the Violoncello, The Viol da Gamba ...
Van der Straeten, Edmund: History of the Violin, Its Ancestors... (2 vols.)
Walther, J. G.: Musicalisches Lexikon ober Musicalische Bibliothec (1732)

Travis & Emery Music Bookshop
17 Cecil Court, London, WC2N 4EZ, United Kingdom.
Tel. (+44) 20 7240 2129

© Travis & Emery 2009

Music and Books published by Travis & Emery Music Bookshop:

Anon.: Hymnarium Sarisburense, cum Rubris et Notis Musicus
Agricola, Johann Friedrich from Tosi: Anleitung zur Singkunst. (Faksimile 1757)
Bach, C.P.E.: edited W. Emery: Nekrolog or Obituary Notice of J.S. Bach.
Bateson, Naomi Judith: Alcock of Salisbury
Bathe, William: A Briefe Introduction to the Skill of Song
Bax, Arnold: Symphony #5, Arranged for Piano Four Hands by Walter Emery
Burney, Charles: The Present State of Music in France and Italy
Burney, Charles: The Present State of Music in Germany, The Netherlands ...
Burney, Charles: An Account of the Musical Performances ... Handel
Burney, Karl: Nachricht von Georg Friedrich Handel's Lebensumstanden.
Burns, Robert (jnr): The Caledonian Musical Museum (1810 volume)
Cobbett, W.W.: Cobbett's Cyclopedic Survey of Chamber Music. (2 vols.)
Corrette, Michel: Le Maitre de Clavecin
Crimp, Bryan: Dear Mr. Rosenthal ... Dear Mr. Gaisberg ...
Crimp, Bryan: Solo: The Biography of Solomon
d'Indy, Vincent: Beethoven: Biographie Critique
d'Indy, Vincent: Beethoven: A Critical Biography
d'Indy, Vincent: César Franck (in French)
Fischhof, Joseph: Versuch einer Geschichte des Clavierbaues
Frescobaldi, Girolamo: D'Arie Musicali per Cantarsi. Primo Libro & Secondo Libro.
Geminiani, Francesco: The Art of Playing the Violin.
Handel; Purcell; Boyce; Green et al: Calliope or English Harmony: Volume First.
Hawkins, John: A General History of the Science and Practice of Music (5 vols.)
Herbert-Caesari, Edgar: The Science and Sensations of Vocal Tone
Herbert-Caesari, Edgar: Vocal Truth
Hopkins and Rimboult: The Organ. Its History and Construction.
Hunt, John: some 40 discographies – see list of discographies
Isaacs, Lewis: Hänsel and Gretel. A Guide to Humperdinck's Opera.
Isaacs, Lewis: Königskinder (Royal Children) A Guide to Humperdinck's Opera.
Lacassagne, M. l'Abbé Joseph : Traité Général des élémens du Chant.
Lascelles (née Catley), Anne: The Life of Miss Anne Catley.
Mainwaring, John: Memoirs of the Life of the Late George Frederic Handel
Malcolm, Alexander: A Treaty of Music: Speculative, Practical and Historical
Marx, Adolph Bernhard: Die Kunst des Gesanges, Theoretisch-Practisch
May, Florence: The Life of Brahms
Mellers, Wilfrid: Angels of the Night: Popular Female Singers of Our Time
Mellers, Wilfrid: Bach and the Dance of God

Travis & Emery Music Bookshop
17 Cecil Court, London, WC2N 4EZ, United Kingdom.
Tel. (+44) 20 7240 2129